THE ROUTLEDGE COMPANION TO NAZI GERMANY

The Routledge Companion to Nazi Germany combines a concise narrative overview with chronological, bibliographical and tabular information to cover all major aspects of Nazi Germany. This user-friendly guide provides a comprehensive survey of key topics such as the origins and consolidation of the Nazi regime, the Nazi dictatorship in action, Nazi foreign policy, the Second World War, the Holocaust, opposition to the regime and the legacy of Nazism.

Features include:

- Detailed chronologies
- A discussion of Nazi ideology
- Succinct historiographical overview with detailed information on more than 60 major historians of Nazism
- Biographies of 150 leading figures of Nazi Germany
- A glossary of terms, concepts and acronyms
- Maps and tables
- A concise thematic bibliography of works on the Third Reich.

This indispensable reference guide to the history and historiography of Nazi Germany will appeal to students, teachers and general readers alike.

Roderick Stackelberg is Emeritus Professor of History at Gonzaga University. He is the author of *Hitler's Germany: Origins, Interpretations, Legacies* (1999) and *Idealism Debased: From Völkisch Ideology to National Socialism* (1981), and co-editor of *The Nazi Germany Sourcebook* (2002).

Routledge Companions to History
Series Advisors: Chris Cook and John Stevenson

Routledge Companions to History offer perfect reference guides to key historical events and eras, providing everything that the student or general reader needs to know. These comprehensive guides include essential apparatus for navigating through specific topics in a clear and straightforward manner – including introductory articles, biographies and chronologies – to provide accessible and indispensable surveys crammed with vital information valuable for beginner and expert alike.

THE ROUTLEDGE COMPANION
TO NAZI GERMANY

Roderick Stackelberg

Routledge
Taylor & Francis Group

NEW YORK AND LONDON

First published 2007
by Routledge
270 Madison Ave, New York, NY 10016

Simultaneously published in the UK
by Routledge
2 Park Square, Milton Park, Abingdon, Oxon OX14 4RN

Routledge is an imprint of the Taylor & Francis Group, an informa business

© 2007 Roderick Stackelberg

Typeset in Times by
Keystroke, 28 High Street, Tettenhall, Wolverhampton
Printed and bound in Great Britain by
The Cromwell Press, Trowbridge, Wiltshire

British Library Cataloguing in Publication Data
A catalogue record for this book is available from the British Library

Library of Congress Cataloging in Publication Data
A catalog record for this book has been requested

ISBN10: 0–415–30860–7 (hbk)
ISBN10: 0–415–30861–8 (pbk)

ISBN13: 978–0–415–30860–1 (hbk)
ISBN13: 978–0–415–30861–8 (pbk)

CONTENTS

ILLUSTRATIONS

MAPS

TABLES

PREFACE

Like other volumes in the Routledge Companion series, this book is intended as a reference work for scholars, teachers, students, and general readers. It fits the German definition of *Handbuch*, a comprehensive, but handy, learning and teaching guide to a particular area of scholarship – in this case the history of Nazi Germany. It can be used in various ways: as a readily accessible source of historical, historiographical, biographical, bibliographical, and lexical information; as a guide to major developments in recent historical scholarship; and also, especially in Part II, as a condensed narrative history text of the Third Reich. The challenge in such a work is how to summarize and simplify historical and historiographical information without diluting the inescapable complexities and ambiguities of history. This book makes no claim to completeness. Some readers will inevitably disagree with my choice of events to include in the chronology, which historians to select for detailed discussion, whom to tap for extended biographical coverage, and which books to list in the bibliography. In every case my criterion for inclusion was the following question: what information will be most helpful to readers to better understand the nature, history, and historiography of Nazism?

Except for the section on historiography, I have kept end-note references to a minimum, usually documenting only direct quotes. My English-language sources are acknowledged in the bibliography at the end of this volume, to which I would like to add the very useful general reference work, *Modern Germany: An Encyclopedia of History, People, and Culture, 1871–1990*, 2 vols., edited by Dieter K. Buse and Juergen C. Doerr, New York and London, Garland, 1998. To acknowledge all my German-language sources adequately would require a separate volume. However, I would like to mention several highly useful reference works from which I retrieved a great deal of information: *Enzyklopädie des Nationalsozialismus*, edited by Wolfgang Benz, Hermann Graml, and Hermann Weiss, Munich, Deutscher Taschenbuch Verlag, 1997; Ernst Klee, *Das Personenlexikon zum Dritten Reich: Wer war was vor und nach 1945?*, Frankfurt, S. Fischer, 2003; *Biographisches Lexikon zum Dritten Reich*, edited by Hermann Weiss, Frankfurt, Fischer, 1999; *Lexikon des deutschen Widerstandes*, edited by Wolfgang Benz and Walter H. Pehle, Frankfurt, Fischer, 2001; and *Lexikon des Widerstandes 1933–1945*, edited by Peter Steinbach and Johannes Tuchel, 2nd edition, Munich, Beck, 1998. Space limitations precluded a full discussion of archival resources on Nazi Germany. A useful guide is *Archives in Germany:*

An Introductory Guide to Institutions and Sources, edited by Frank Schumacher with Annette M. Marciel, Reference Guide No. 13, Washington, DC, German Historical Institute, 2001. The best source for up-to-date information on research on the Holocaust are the various publications of the United States Holocaust Memorial Museum Center for Advanced Holocaust Studies in Washington, DC.

I would like to acknowledge the helpful suggestions and criticisms I received from four outside readers for Routledge who evaluated my original proposal. I want to express my thanks also to the efficient interlibrary loan services at Gonzaga University and to the secretarial staff, especially Sandy Hank, for help in preparing the manuscript. My greatest debt, as always, is to my wife Sally Winkle, who took the time from her own work to read and critique the manuscript and who also provided much-appreciated emotional support. Thanks also to my son Emmet, who frequently came to the rescue when his superannuated dad had trouble with the technological intricacies of the information age.

Roderick Stackelberg
Spokane, Washington
5 March 2007

1

INTRODUCTION AND BACKGROUND

Nazi Germany and particularly the **Holocaust**, the signature crime of the twentieth century, present perhaps the greatest challenge to the explanatory powers of historians. Many explanations for Nazism have been offered in the course of the nine decades since the first fascist movement was founded in Italy in 1919. The most important interpretations are discussed in the section on historiography that follows the chronology in Part I. Whether we understand *why* the Nazis rose to power and *why* the Holocaust happened any better at the beginning of the twenty-first century than contemporaries did at the time remains an open question. History is, after all, an ongoing argument conducted from different and ever-changing perspectives very much dependent on the unpredictable course of events, changing public attitudes, and varying personal loyalties. But more than 60 years of intensive research have incontestably given us a clearer understanding of *how* the Nazis rose to power and *how* the Holocaust occurred. This book is intended to provide in readily accessible form the basic factual and conceptual tools and resources to understand how the Nazis established and consolidated their rule in Germany, how they drove the nation to war, how they committed their terrible atrocities, how they were resisted and eventually destroyed, and how their actions have been viewed by posterity. It sets forth basic information on what happened, how it happened, where it happened, when it happened, and who were the major actors in Germany who made it happen. By describing how the Nazi era has been interpreted, I hope this book also provides insight into why these catastrophic events occurred, without, however, presuming to offer definitive explanations to questions that historians have wrestled with for years and that will continue to challenge historians for many years to come.

To make sense of Nazism certain basic conceptual clarifications are indispensable. Although crude binary oppositions rarely do justice to the complexity of events, certain conceptual categories are helpful in recognizing the kind of movement Nazism represented and in distinguishing the fundamental values of historians who have interpreted its nature and meaning. One such binary opposition is the distinction between political movements and values of "left" and "right," shorthand terms that are useful in identifying basic attitudes to the ideal of human equality. "Left" broadly denotes egalitarian attitudes toward human rights, material benefits, and the exercise of political power (hence partisanship for the impoverished, disadvantaged, and excluded people of the world), while "right" broadly denotes preferences for natural or traditional hierarchies of authority or power (whether based on birth, race, gender, ethnicity, talent, intelligence, wealth, or other traits that can be ranked on a comparative scale from superior to inferior). These terms "left" and "right" are most useful (and least confusing) when not overburdened by any other criterion than attitude toward human equality. The left–right conflict in the modern post-Enlightenment era has been most fiercely fought out on the issues of political power and distributive economic justice. The issues on which left and right have been in greatest disagreement are the questions of how widely and evenly political power is to be dispersed and how the material benefits of the world are to be shared among contending claimants.

The nineteenth century can be broadly described as an era of left-wing ascendancy in Europe. In fits and starts throughout the century political and social movements favoring greater equality and democracy seemed everywhere to be making headway in Europe to a greater or lesser degree. Often, to be sure, progress toward liberalization and democracy in Europe came at the expense of colonized people on other continents, even though opposition to imperialism was generally stronger on the left than on the right. To what extent the left–right class conflict in Europe contributed to the outbreak of the deadly internecine war that came to be known as the First World War is a question much debated by historians. Although the First World War was not in any clear-cut sense a war *between* left and right, the left–right conflict raging in different proportions within each of the combatant nations may have contributed to their respective readiness to go to war with each other. Even before the war the political right in most European countries was alert to the egalitarian challenge of the left, and right-wing extremists advocated radical policies (including discriminatory measures against Jews, proverbial outsiders and the perceived agents of divisive social change) to stem the tide of liberalism, socialism, and democracy. This left–right polarization became even more pronounced after the end of the war, particularly in the nations of central Europe. From a right-wing perspective – especially in the defeated nations – the war had been an absolute disaster, resulting in the collapse of monarchical governments, the victory of the democratically inclined Western powers, and the outbreak of the ruinously egalitarian and destructive Bolshevist revolution in Russia.

The outcome of the First World War – its economic and political consequences, its nationalist passions, its revolutionary aftermath – gave rise to the era of **fascism** in Europe, a period of right-wing ascendancy and radicalization. The Fascist Party founded by Benito Mussolini (1883–1945) in 1919 was expressly designed to counter the left-wing revolutionary threat – not by restoring the *status quo ante*, but by mounting a counter-revolution that appropriated much of the dynamic, the symbols, the methods, and the rhetoric of the revolutionary left to appeal to the left's working-class constituency in an age in which the institution of universal suffrage made mass support indispensable to gaining and wielding political power. Hitler modeled his National Socialist Party and its paramilitary formations on Mussolini's example (disastrously so in 1923, when his first effort to gain power by the threat of force, as Mussolini had successfully done in Italy a year earlier, failed in the Munich-based **Hitler Putsch**). Because Hitler's movement turned out to be so much more radical in its **anti-Semitism** and genocidal aims than Mussolini's movement, some historians question the usefulness of subsuming Nazism under the broader rubric of fascism, preferring the even broader rubric of **totalitarianism** instead. But whatever the differences from Mussolini's Fascism, historians agree that Nazism was part of the broad right-wing counter-revolutionary movement that marked the era between the two world wars. It was also, however, a distinctly German version of that wider European movement of fascism.[1]

Because fascist movements were determined to combat the egalitarianism of the left by mobilizing the masses for right-wing goals, fascism is much easier to define by what its adherents opposed than by what they favored. Defining fascism negatively – by what fascists opposed – also makes sense because their ability to attract support from mainstream conservatives was primarily due to the fact that they shared common enemies on the left. Fascists opposed what they viewed as the major leveling trends of the nineteenth century, including Marxist socialism, parliamentary democracy, constitutionalism, and political liberalism – the emancipatory political movements associated with the modern era, all embracing to a greater or lesser degree the idea of progress toward a more just society. Fascism and Nazism were part of a massive backlash against these "subversive" forces of the left, which supposedly undermined traditional hierarchies, values, and institutions (the state, the Church, the aristocratic estates) by their insistent advocacy of equality, justice, tolerance, popular sovereignty, human rights, and sharing the wealth. Fascists were radically anti-establishmentarian as well insofar as they held traditional conservatives responsible for failing effectively to counter the perceived threat to the nation from the left or from foreigners. Many of the social changes that alarmed fascists (democratization, liberalization, commercialization, secularization, labor militancy, urbanization) were actually unavoidable and unplanned consequences of European industrialization, but fascists and their conservative allies unwilling to face this unpleasant reality preferred to blame these social disruptions on left-wing organizers of the rebellious subordinate classes, and particularly on the Jews.[2]

But to properly appreciate both the revolutionary dynamic and insidious nature of fascism and Nazism we have to recognize its positive appeal as well, its putative normality, and its orientation toward a more productive future, at least in the perception of its contemporary followers. Fascists certainly rejected the left-wing forms and expressions of modernity mentioned above, but they fanatically embraced another important product of the modern era – namely, nationalism. The common denominator of fascist movements throughout Europe was commitment to the regeneration and rejuvenation of their own national communities, understood as communities of people related to each other by ethnicity, culture, language, and homeland – in short by "blood and soil." That such a doctrine should have particular appeal in the defeated nations of the First World War, or in those whose national aspirations had been somehow disappointed by events, is not surprising. Italy, for example, had failed to gain the territorial acquisitions it had been promised by England and France during the war. Strong fascist movements developed, especially in nations in which there was either a widespread feeling of victimization as a result of the post-First World War settlement or a sense of threat from forces proclaiming or representing democracy, socialism, internationalism, or pacifism – allegiances that threatened to undermine the power of the nation to regenerate itself in the fascist sense. What rendered this mix of frustrations especially volatile and lethal were economic crises and redistributive pressures from below. The propertied classes who had the greatest stakes in existing property relations within each nation were prepared to support fascism especially when their economic status and hold on power was threatened by the breakdown of the deferential attitudes that traditional political and religious institutions had fostered for centuries. Fascism promised national unity and solidarity while protecting the rights of private property, an end to class conflict and selfish individualism, full popular mobilization for the national interest, an efficient chain of command for decisive national action, and a new youthful vigor and readiness to make personal sacrifices for the national good.

The general characteristics of fascism should not, however, obscure the specificity of Nazism and the unparalleled horrors it unleashed. Historians agree that for various reasons, not least the enormous military and economic power it commanded at the height of its power, Nazi Germany generated the most extreme form of European fascism and system of rule. All fascist movements shared racist attitudes to some extent, a function of the typically fascist proclivity to rank races and peoples according to their supposed innate attributes as well as the typically fascist commitment to the supremacy of the ethnic group native to the homeland. Fascist movements also shared at least a latent anti-Semitism, a function of the perception that Jews represented and promoted precisely the modernizing trends that fascists opposed. The Nazis gave exceptional priority and importance to the pseudo-science of race, an ideology that paved the way to the Holocaust. Bio-politics – the project of solving social problems through biological means, such as **eugenics** – had a tradition in Germany dating back to the pre-war era, but defeat in the First World War gave particular urgency to the project of strengthening the biological fibre of the German race

Why did Nazi Germany develop the most lethal form of fascism, racism, and anti-Semitism, eventually culminating in the genocide of the Holocaust? To this heavily researched but not definitively explained question this book hopes to make a contribution by assembling a variety of useful data. The interpretations that historians have offered to explain fascism in general and Nazism specifically have varied according to such factors as the availability of archival documentation and the state of current research. Interpretations also reflect the changing generational social, cultural, and political concerns that determine research agendas and affect the perspectives of individual historians. Part I of this book provides a basic chronology, a historiographical survey from the 1920s to the present, and capsule intellectual biographies of major historians and their most important contributions to the research on Nazi Germany. Part II offers an exposition of the major narrative and analytical themes of the Nazi era in roughly chronological format. Part III provides mini-biographies of major personages and representative figures in Nazi Germany, both Nazi and anti-Nazi, as well as a glossary of terms, concepts, and acronyms, and a selective bibliography of monographs and historical works grouped according to the themes discussed in Part II. The aim of this book is to give students, teachers, and scholars of Nazi Germany the informational tools, based on the current state of knowledge and thinking, to enable readers to reach their own conclusions on how best to understand and interpret this extraordinary chapter of recent history.

I
NAZI GERMANY IN HISTORICAL PERSPECTIVE

2

CHRONOLOGY

1871

(January) Unification of Germany and founding of the German Empire under Kaiser Wilhelm I and Chancellor Otto von Bismarck

1888

Wilhelm II becomes kaiser

1889

(20 April) Adolf **Hitler** born in Braunau am Inn in Austria

1914

(August) **Hitler** welcomes the start of the First World War in Munich

1916

(August) Field Marshal Paul von **Hindenburg** appointed commander-in-chief of German forces with General Erich **Ludendorff** as his chief of staff

1917

(November) Russian Revolution; **Bolsheviks** under Vladimir Ilyich Lenin seize power

1918

(19 February) Germany signs peace treaty with independent Ukraine
(14 March) Treaty of Brest-Litovsk imposes punitive peace on Russia

(May) Civil war in Russia
(October) German government under Prince Max von Baden sues for peace
(November) Revolution in Germany
(9 November) Abdication of Kaiser Wilhelm II; proclamation of German republic
(11 November) German government emissaries sign armistice at Compiègne ending the First World War

1919

(January) Spartacus uprising crushed in Berlin
(6 February) National Constitutional Assembly convenes in **Weimar**
(23 March) Benito Mussolini organizes new fascist movement in Italy
(May) Soviet government crushed in Bavaria
(28 June) Signing of Treaty of **Versailles**
(1 July) Mussolini issues Fascist manifesto
(31 July) Adoption of Weimar Constitution
(12 September) **Hitler** joins the **German Workers' Party** in Munich

1920

(24 February) **German Workers' Party** adopts "**Twenty-five Point Program**"
(March) **Kapp Putsch** fails in Berlin

1921

(29 July) **Hitler** becomes chairman of renamed National Socialist German Workers' Party (**NSDAP**)

1922

(16 April) Germany recognizes Soviet Russia in Treaty of **Rapallo**, angering the radical right

(24 June) German foreign minister Walter Rathenau assassinated by **Free Corps** members

(August) Fascists clash with communists in Italy

(30 October) Mussolini asked to head Italian government in Italy after threatening a "march on Rome"

1923

(11 January) French army occupies **Ruhr** to collect reparations

(27 January) First Nazi Party Congress in Munich

(June–November) The Great Inflation in Germany

(12 August) Gustav Stresemann becomes German chancellor and ends passive resistance to the French occupation

(20 October) Authoritarian Bavarian government under Gustav von Kahr breaks relations with liberal national government in Berlin

(9 November) **Hitler** and **Ludendorff** launch "**Beer Hall Putsch**" in Munich on the "Day of the Republic"

(15 November) Introduction of new currency ends Great Inflation

1924

(1 April) **Hitler** sentenced to minimum term of five years in prison for high treason with eligibility for parole in six months

(20 December) **Hitler** released from prison

1925

(27 February) **Hitler** reorganizes **NSDAP**

(25 April) **Hindenburg** elected German president

(July) Publication of first volume of *Mein Kampf*

(16 October) Germany recognizes western borders in Treaty of **Locarno**

(9 November) Formation of **NSDAP** protection squad (**SS**)

1926

(January) Hitler rejects any change to "**Twenty-five Point Program**"

(8 September) Germany admitted to **League of Nations**

1927

(10 March) Speaking ban on **Hitler** lifted in Prussia

1928

(20 May) Nazis receive only 2.6 percent of the vote in **Reichstag** elections

(28 June) Hermann Müller (**SPD**) heads coalition government in Germany

1929

(4 October) Start of stock market crash in New York

(22 December) Right-wing supported **Young Plan** referendum on reparations defeated

1930

(23 January) Wilhelm **Frick** becomes first Nazi to hold state office in Germany as interior minister in Thuringia

(30 March) Heinrich **Brüning** becomes chancellor of right-wing coalition government

(30 June) French troops evacuate Rhineland five years ahead of schedule

(16 July) **Brüning** overrules **Reichstag** to impose budget under Article 48 of the **Weimar** Constitution

(14 September) Nazis become second-largest party in the **Reichstag** with 18.3 percent of the vote and 107 seats

1931

(14 July) Financial crisis closes banks in Germany (reopening three weeks later)

(29 August) Austrian government forced to drop plans for customs union with Germany

(October) **Hitler** joins Nationalists (**DNVP**) in giant **Harzburg Front** rally aimed at supplanting **Brüning**'s government with a nationalist regime

1932

(7 January) Chancellor **Brüning** declares Germany will not resume reparations

(27 January) **Hitler** gains enthusiastic reception by industrialists in Düsseldorf

(22 February) **Hitler** announces his candidacy for president

(13 March) **Hitler**, with 11 million votes, prevents **Hindenburg** from getting an absolute majority in the first round of the presidential election

(10 April) **Hindenburg** reelected president in run-off against **Hitler**

(13 April) **Brüning** prohibits paramilitary units from marching in public

(30 May) **Brüning** resigns as chancellor and is replaced by Franz von **Papen**

(16 June) Ban on Nazi storm troopers (**SA**) lifted

(20 July) **Papen** removes SPD prime minister in Prussia and declares martial law

(31 July) Nazis double their strength and become largest party in **Reichstag** with 37.4 percent of the vote and 227 seats

(13 August) **Hitler** refuses post of vice-chancellor in **Papen**'s government

(30 August) Hermann **Göring** elected president of **Reichstag**

(November) Transit strike paralyzes Berlin

(6 November) Nazis lose 35 seats in **Reichstag** election, while Communists continue to gain

(21 November) **Hitler** again refuses to join the government without full power

(2 December) General Kurt von **Schleicher** named German chancellor

1933

(30 January) **Hitler** appointed chancellor with **Papen** as vice-chancellor

(6 February) Nazi government introduces press censorship

(27 February) Fire destroys **Reichstag**

(28 February) **Hitler** suspends basic civil liberties

(5 March) Nazis win 43.9 percent of **Reichstag** vote, enough for a majority with the Nationalists; Communist Party banned

(12 March) By order of **Hindenburg**, the black–red–orange republican flag replaced by the Imperial colors black–white–red and the **swastika**

(20 March) Nazis open first official concentration camp in **Dachau** near Munich

(21 March) "Day of Potsdam"; opening of the new **Reichstag** in the Garrison Church

(24 March) **Reichstag** passes **Enabling Act** giving **Hitler** full dictatorial power

(31 March) Beginning of *Gleichschaltung* of the states

(1 April) Nazis organize one-day boycott of Jewish businesses

(7 April) Removal of Jews, Communists, Social Democrats, and liberal political opponents from the Civil Service

(25 April) "Law against the Overcrowding of German Schools" limits number of Jewish students in German schools

(2 May) Dissolution of labor unions and formation of German Labor Front (**DAF**)

(10 May) Public burning of "un-German" books in Berlin and other university cities

(21 June) Nationalist Party (**DNVP**) votes to dissolve

(22 June) Social Democratic Party (**SPD**) banned

(14 July) Nazis become only legal party in Germany; Nazis pass **sterilization law** to prevent "genetically diseased offspring"

(20 July) **Concordat** between German **Reich** and the Vatican
(25 August) **Haavara Agreement** (transfer) between Reich Ministry of Economics and Zionist organization facilitates emigration of Jews from Germany to Palestine
(22 September) Creation of German Chamber of Culture
(29 September) **Hereditary Farm Law**
(14 October) Germany leaves **League of Nations** and disarmament conference
(12 November) 93 percent approval for leaving the League in nationwide plebiscite; Nazi **Reichstag** elected without opposition

1934

(10 January) Marinus van der Lubbe executed for setting **Reichstag** on fire
(26 January) Germany signs non-aggression pact with Poland
(13 June) Germany cancels mutual aid treaty with Soviet Russia
(17 June) **Papen**'s Marburg speech
(30 June) "**Night of the Long Knives**"; approximately 120 persons killed in purge of Ernst **Röhm** and the SA
(3 July) Franz von **Papen** resigns as vice-chancellor
(9 July) Heinrich **Himmler** placed in charge of Prussian police
(25 July) Austrian Nazis fail in attempt to gain power; Chancellor Dollfuss assassinated
(2 August) Death of President **Hindenburg**; **Hitler** takes over presidency while retaining office of chancellor
(5 September) At annual party rally in Nuremberg, **Hitler** announces that there will be no more revolution in Germany for a thousand years
(9 October) Assassination of King Alexander of Yugoslavia and French foreign minister Louis Barthou by Croatian fascists

1935

(13 January) 90.8 percent vote in favor of reunion with Germany in **Saar** plebiscite; the Saar to be returned to Germany on 1 March
(16 March) **Hitler** announces introduction of universal military training in defiance of **Versailles Treaty**
(31 March) Britain and Soviet Union agree to work for collective security in **League of Nations**
(11 April) **Stresa** conference (Italy, Britain, France)
(17 April) **League of Nations** condemns German rearmament
(18 June) Anglo-German Naval Treaty
(31 August) President Franklin Roosevelt signs neutrality act prohibiting arms shipments to countries at war
(15 September) **Nuremberg racial laws** deprive Jews of rights
(28 October) Mussolini's armies invade Ethiopia
(18 November) **League of Nations** imposes economic sanctions on Italy but rejects oil embargo

1936

(6 February) Winter Olympics opened in Garmisch-Partenkirchen
(7 March) Nazis enter **Rhineland** in violation of **Versailles** and **Locarno** treaties
(29 March) 99 percent vote in favor of **Rhineland** occupation in plebiscite
(9 May) Italy formally annexes **Ethiopia**
(8 June) **Popular Front** government under Léon Blum takes power in France
(17 June) Heinrich **Himmler** named head of **Reich** police
(11 July) **Hitler** and Austrian chancellor Schuschnigg sign "July Agreement" to respect Austrian independence
(19 July) Right-wing forces under Francisco Franco start rebellion against

Popular Front government of Spanish Republic

(25 July) Germany formally recognizes **Ethiopian** conquest

(1 August) **Hitler** opens Olympic summer games in Berlin; France declares non-intervention in Spain

(11 August) **Ribbentrop** named German ambassador to England

(13 September) Founding of *Lebensborn* agency for aid to single mothers

(18 October) **Göring** named to head **Four-Year Plan**

(1 November) Creation of "**Axis**" through Italo-German treaty

(14 November) Corollaries to **Reich Citizenship Law** define categories of *Mischlinge*

(18 November) Germany and Italy recognize Franco government

(25 November) German–Japanese **Anti-Comintern Pact**

(1 December) Membership in **Hitler Youth** made compulsory

1937

(30 January) **Enabling Act** extended for another four years

(14 March) Papal encyclical on "The Church in Germany" condemns racism

(27 April) German warplanes kill hundreds of civilians at **Guernica**, Spain

(28 May) Neville Chamberlain becomes prime minister in England

(1 July) Martin **Niemöller** arrested

(15 July) Opening of the **concentration camp** at **Buchenwald**

(July) Japan renews offensive in China

(20 October) British restrict Jewish emigration to Palestine

(5 November) **Hitler** outlines his plans for expansion in "**Hossbach Memorandum**"

(6 November) Italy accedes to **Anti-Comintern Pact**

(19 November) Lord Halifax visits Germany to seek British–German agreement

1938

(4 February) **Hitler** assumes direct control of armed forces through creation of new High Command (**OKW**)

(12 February) Schuschnigg forced to agree to legalize Nazi Party in Austria

(9 March) Schuschnigg calls for **plebiscite** in Austria

(12 March) German troops enter Austria

(10 April) Daladier forms anti-communist cabinet in France; more than 99 percent of voters in Germany and Austria approve the Austrian *Anschluss*

(May) **Hitler** informs his generals of his "unalterable decision to smash Czechoslovakia by military action in the near future"

(6 June) Jews in Germany forbidden to buy or sell real estate

(1 July) Italy introduces **anti-Semitic** laws

(6–15 July) International conference at Evian in France fails to find a solution to the Jewish refugee problem aggravated by the *Anschluss* of Austria

(17 August) Jewish women and men without identifiably Jewish names ordered to add "Sarah" and "Israel," respectively, for easier identification

(18 August) Resignation of army chief of staff Ludwig **Beck**

(20 August) Central Office for Jewish Emigration set up under Adolf **Eichmann** in Vienna

(29 September) **Munich Agreement** transfers **Sudetenland** from Czechoslovakia to Germany

(1 October) German troops march into **Sudetenland**

(5 October) German Jewish passports stamped with "J" at request of Swiss government

(19 October) Unemployed Jews obligated to do forced labor

(28 October) Germans expel Polish Jews living in Germany after Poland revokes citizenship of all Jews living outside Poland for more than five years; 17,000 Jews caught in no man's land before being granted admission to Poland

(7 November) Herschel Grynszpan, son of Polish Jewish parents expelled from Germany, assassinates German diplomat Ernst vom Rath in Paris

(9 November) **Reichskristallnacht** pogrom against German Jews

(12 November) **Göring** convenes conference to plan compulsory "**Aryanization**" of Jewish businesses

(16 November) Jewish children prohibited from attending German schools

1939

(24 January) **Heydrich** authorized by **Göring** to develop comprehensive plan for Jewish emigration

(30 January) **Hitler** threatens annihilation of European Jews in speech to **Reichstag**

(27 February) Britain recognizes Franco's regime in Spain

(2 March) Cardinal Pacelli elected Pope Pius XII

(15 March) Nazis occupy Prague in violation of **Munich Agreement** and establish **Protectorate of Bohemia and Moravia**

(22 March) Lithuania returns port of Memel to Germany

(28 March) Franco enters Madrid as Spanish Civil War ends

(1 April) Prime Minister Neville Chamberlain pledges to support Poland militarily against threats to her sovereignty; Germany renounces Anglo-German **Naval** Treaty and Non-Aggression Treaty with Poland

(3 April) **Hitler** orders preparation of plans for military attack on Poland

(30 April) Soviet Union proposes military alliance with France and Britain

(3 May) Vyacheslav Molotov named Soviet foreign minister

(17 May) British "White Paper" limits Jewish immigration in Palestine

(22 May) Italy and Germany sign **Pact of Steel**

(23 May) **Hitler** informs his leading generals of his decision "to attack Poland at the first suitable opportunity"

(1 August) Opening of Central Office for Jewish Emigration in Prague

(2 August) Albert Einstein writes to President Roosevelt suggesting feasibility of atomic bomb

(16 August) Germany demands **Danzig** (Gdansk) from Poland

(22 August) France and Britain reaffirm pledge of aid to Poland

(23 August) **Nazi–Soviet Non-Aggression Treaty** signed, with secret protocol dividing Poland and Eastern Europe into spheres of influence

(1 September) Germans invade Poland; Italy declares neutrality; **Hitler** authorizes secret **euthanasia** program (**Aktion T-4**)

(3 September) Britain and France declare war on Germany

(5 September) The US declares neutrality and continues embargo of arms to warring nations

(9 September) German forces reach Warsaw

(16 September) Soviet forces invade Poland

(21 September) **Heydrich** issues guidelines for **SS** *Einsatzgruppen* in Poland

(27 September) Warsaw surrenders

(1 October) SS Main Office for Reich Security (**RSHA**) established in Berlin under Reinhard **Heydrich**

(6 October) Britain and France reject **Hitler**'s offer of peace in return for acceptance of conquest of Poland

(7 October) Office of "**Reich Commissar for the Strengthening of German Ethnicity**" established under **Himmler**

(26 October) Annexation of western Polish provinces (**Wartheland**); Hans **Frank** named to head occupied Poland (**General-gouvernement**)

(4 November) US embargo on arms sales to Britain and France lifted

(8 November) **Hitler** escapes attempt on his life by Johann Elser in Munich

(23 November) All Jews in Nazi-occupied Poland required to wear **yellow Star** of David

(28 November) **Jewish Councils** (*Judenräte*) created on German orders in ghettos of Nazi-occupied Poland

(30 November) Soviet Union invades Finland to start "**Winter War**"

(1 December) Deportations begin of Jews and Poles from annexed "incorporated territories" to the **Generalgouvernement**

(12 December) Jewish males between 14 and 60 in **Generalgouvernement** required to do forced labor in camps set up for that purpose

(14 December) Soviet Union expelled from **League of Nations**

(19 December) Conference in **RSHA** on plans to create a Jewish reservation in Poland

1940

(21 February) Construction of **concentration camp** at **Auschwitz**

(13 March) Finland signs peace treaty with Soviet Union, ending "**Winter War**"

(23 March) **Göring** prohibits further deportations into the **Generalgouvernement**

(9 April) Germans occupy Denmark and invade Norway

(1 May) **Lodz** Ghetto sealed off with barbed wire

(7 May) Resumption of "resettlement" of Jews and Poles from the "incorporated territories" into the **Generalgouvernement**

(10 May) Germans launch **Blitzkrieg** against France and Benelux countries;

Winston Churchill replaces Chamberlain as prime minister

(14 May) Holland surrenders

(28 May) Belgium surrenders

(4 June) Allied expeditionary force evacuated from **Dunkirk**

(10 June) Italy declares war on Britain and France; President Roosevelt promises aid to Britain and France

(14 June) Germans occupy Paris

(22 June) French sign armistice in Compiègne

(24 June) **Heydrich** calls for a "territorial solution" to the Jewish problem

(July) German Foreign Ministry (in consultation with **RSHA**, the Office of the **Four-Year Plan**, and the Propaganda Ministry) proposes plan to deport Jews to **Madagascar** after peace with Britain

(3 July) British naval squadron destroys French fleet in Algeria, leading to a break of diplomatic relations with **Vichy** France

(10 July) Authoritarian government under Marshal Henri Pétain formally established at **Vichy** in unoccupied France

(16 July) **Hitler** issues orders for the preparation of "**Operation Sea Lion**," the invasion of Britain

(22 July) British reject **Hitler**'s peace proposal

(31 July) **Hitler** announces plans for an invasion of the Soviet Union to his generals

(26 August) First British air raid on Berlin; **Hitler** launches **Blitz** on British cities

(17 September) Standoff in **Battle of Britain** forces postponement of plans to invade Britain; **Madagascar Plan** tabled in favor of an "eastern territorial solution"

(27 September) Signing of Italo-German-Japanese **Tripartite Pact**

(2 October) Hans **Frank** protests in Berlin against further deportation of Jews into the **Generalgouvernement**

(3 October) **Vichy** France passes **anti-Semitic** legislation

15

(23–24 October) **Hitler** unsuccessful in persuading **Vichy** France and Franco's Spain from joining war against Britain.

(28 October) Italians invade Greece

(12 November) Soviet foreign minister Molotov confers with **Hitler** in Berlin

(15 November) **Warsaw Ghetto** walled off from rest of the city

(18 December) **Hitler** authorizes plans for "Operation **Barbarossa**," the invasion of the USSR

(29 December) Roosevelt describes the US as "the arsenal of democracy"

1941

(9 January) Plans for "Operation **Felix**," the seizure of Gibraltar, abandoned

(1 March) **Himmler** begins plans for expansion of **Auschwitz** complex to hold 130,000 inmates

(March) Deportations into **General-gouvernement** halted because of worsening food situation

(7 March) Jews in Germany now subject to forced labor

(11 March) Roosevelt signs Lend-Lease Act

(27 March) Military revolt overthrows pro-German government in Yugoslavia

(4 April) Beginning of "**Aktion 14 f 13**" for the killing of **concentration camp** inmates, mainly Jewish, incapable of work

(6 April) Germans invade Yugoslavia and Greece

(10 April) US occupies Danish colony of Greenland

(13 April) Soviet Union signs non-aggression pact with Japan

(17 April) German forces occupy Belgrade; establish separate fascist state of Croatia

(27 April) Greece surrenders; Germans occupy Athens

(May) Formation of SS *Einsatzgruppen* for war against Soviet Union with assignment to kill all Jews in Communist Party or government positions

(10 May) **Hitler**'s deputy Rudolf **Hess** flies to Scotland in hopes of negotiating peace with Britain in anticipation of the invasion of the USSR

(6 June) **OKW** issues the "**Commissar Order**," calling for execution of captured political commissars

(21 June) **Himmler** orders his staff to draw up a "**general plan for the east**" (Generalplan Ost)

(22 June) German troops invade the Soviet Union; *Einsatzgruppen* begin roundup and execution of Jews and Communists

(28 June) **Wehrmacht** and **SS** agree on selection and execution of Soviet POWs

(7 July) US forces land in Iceland to prevent German occupation

(15 July) Generalplan Ost submitted by Konrad **Meyer**, calling for the "evacuation" of 31 million persons

(17 July) New Ministry for the Occupied Eastern Territories established under Alfred **Rosenberg**

(31 July) **Heydrich** authorized to draw up plan for "**final solution**" of **Jewish Question** in Europe

(August) **Eichmann** visits **Auschwitz** and informs Commandant **Höss** of the planned "**final solution**" of the **Jewish Question**

(14 August) Churchill and Roosevelt sign **Atlantic Charter**

(16 August) **Himmler** is witness to *Einsatzgruppen* executions in Minsk; first reported killings of Jewish women and children

(23 August) **Hitler** calls official halt to **euthanasia** program after church protests

(27 August) German troops take Smolensk, 200 miles from Moscow

(1 September) All Jews in Germany over the age of six compelled to wear **yellow Star** of David for identification

(2–5 September) **Cyclon B** tested for the first time on Soviet POWs at **Auschwitz**

(4 September) Leningrad surrounded

(19 September) Kiev falls to German troops

(29 September) Massacre of Jews at **Babi-Yar** on outskirts of Kiev

(14 October) Deportation of German Jews to the east (first trainloads to Minsk, Riga, and Kovno) begins

(16 October) Odessa falls to German troops

(23 October) Emigration of Jews prohibited from Nazi-occupied Europe

(30 October) US destroyer *Reuben James* sunk by German submarine

(November) **Euthanasia** personnel arrive in Poland to prepare for "**final solution**"

(9 November) **Heydrich** issues invitations to various ministries for conference on "**final solution**," originally planned for 9 December, but postponed to 20 January

(24 November) "Model" ghetto for elderly Jews created at **Theresienstadt**

(26 November) Completion of construction of barracks at **Auschwitz-Birkenau**

(5 December) Soviets launch counterattack at Moscow

(7 December) Japanese attack on Pearl Harbor

(8 December) US declares war on Japan; gassing of Jews in mobile gas vans at **Chelmno** begins

(11 December) Germany and Italy declare war on the US

(12 December) **Hitler** announces coming "**final solution**" to **Gauleiter** conference in Berlin

(16 December) Hans **Frank** announces planned murder of the Jews to his staff

(19 December) Field Marshal Walther von **Brauchitsch** dismissed as commander of the army; **Hitler** assumes operational command of the army

1942

(20 January) **Wannsee Conference** to coordinate "**Final Solution** of **Jewish Question**"

(21 January) General **Rommel** launches North African offensive to drive British out of Libya

(9 February) Albert **Speer** takes control of German war production

(13 February) "**Operation Sea Lion**" postponed indefinitely

(15 February) First transports of Jews arrive at **Auschwitz**

(16 March) First transports of Polish Jews to **Belzec** death camp under "**Aktion Reinhard**"

(4 June) Reinhard **Heydrich** killed by Czech partisans near Prague

(7 June) US naval victory over Japanese fleet at Midway Island in the Pacific

(10 June) Czech village of **Lidice** liquidated in revenge for assassination of **Heydrich**

(21 June) Tobruk falls to German forces

(1 July) Soviet Black Sea naval base at Sevastopol falls to Germans

(22 July) Beginning of deportation of Jews from **Warsaw Ghetto** to **Treblinka**

(31 August) Communist resistance network "**Red Orchestra**" broken up by **Gestapo**

(17 September) German troops reach Stalingrad

(31 October) British counter-offensive forces **Rommel**'s **Africa Corps** to retreat at **El Alamein** in Egypt

(8 November) Anglo-American landing in North Africa

(11 November) Germans occupy **Vichy** France

(12 November) Allies recapture Tobruk

(16 November) Beginning of deportation of German gypsies to **Auschwitz**

(17 November) Allied Declaration denouncing murder of European Jews and announcing that those responsible will be punished

(19 November) Soviets launch counter-offensive that eventually encircles German Sixth Army in Stalingrad

1943

(15 January) Roosevelt and Churchill announce policy of "unconditional surrender" at **Casablanca Conference**
(18 January) Soviet forces break the siege of Leningrad
(31 January) Surrender of the German Sixth Army at Stalingrad
(18 February) **"White Rose"** student resistance leaders arrested; **Goebbels** announces **"total war"** at mass rally in Berlin
(10 March) **Rommel** recalled from Tunisia
(14 March) **Kracow** Ghetto is liquidated
(19 April) Start of **Warsaw Ghetto uprising**
(12 May) Surrender of **Africa Corps** at Tunis
(16 May) **Warsaw Ghetto uprising** suppressed and ghetto destroyed
(24 May) Admiral **Dönitz** recalls German submarines in Atlantic due to heavy losses
(June) On **Himmler**'s orders bodies are exhumed from death camps in order to obliterate evidence of **Holocaust**
(19 June) **Goebbels** announces that Berlin is free of Jews
(5 July) Germans launch "Operation Citadel" at **Kursk** in central Russia
(10 July) Allies land in Sicily
(13 July) German defeat in the Battle of **Kursk**
(25 July) Mussolini deposed by Fascist Grand Council
(28 July) Allies launch "Operation Gomorrha," the firebombing of Hamburg
(2 August) Crushing of prisoner revolt at **Treblinka**
(24 August) **Himmler** named Reich interior minister
(3 September) Allies invade Italian mainland; Italy signs armistice with Allies
(12 September) German task force under **Skorzeny** frees Mussolini from Italian captivity

(15 September) Mussolini established as head of Republic of Salò
(25 September) Soviets retake Smolensk
(13 October) Italy declares war on Germany
(14 October) Partial success of revolt at **Sobibór**
(16 October) Deportation of Italian Jews begins after Germans occupy northern Italy
(6 November) Soviets retake Kiev
(28 November) Conference of Roosevelt, Stalin, and Churchill at **Teheran**

1944

(4 January) Soviet troops reach former Polish–Soviet border
(22 January) Roosevelt establishes War Refugee Board to assist relief and rescue of Jews
(19 March) German troops occupy Hungary; beginning of roundup of Hungarian Jews under personal direction of Adolf **Eichmann**
(10 April) Soviet forces retake Odessa
(9 May) Soviet forces retake Sevastopol
(15 May) Deportation of Hungarian Jews to **Auschwitz** begins
(4 June) Allied forces enter Rome
(6 June) **D-Day**: Allied invasion of Normandy
(16 June) Hungarian government halts deportation of Jews
(22 June) Opening of Soviet summer offensive
(20 July) German military revolt fails
(23 July) Red Army liberates **Lublin-Majdanek** death camp
(1 August) Start of uprising of Polish Home Army (**Warsaw Uprising**)
(15 August) Allied landing in southern France
(18 August) Red Army reaches German borders in East Prussia
(25 August) Liberation of Paris; Romania declares war on Germany
(3 September) Brussels liberated by Allied troops

(8 September) Bulgaria declares war on Germany

(12 September) Anglo-American forces reach German borders in west

(3 October) Surrender of Polish Home Army in Warsaw

(15 October) Fascist **Arrow Cross** government installed in Hungary by the Nazis

(18 October) Allies recognize Tito as head of Yugoslav state

(20 October) German city of Aachen falls to Allies

(3 November) British forces join in fight against Communist National Liberation Army in Greek civil war

(7 November) Roosevelt elected to fourth term as president

(November) End of gassing operations at **Auschwitz**; demolition of crematoria

(16 December) German counterattack in the "**Battle of the Bulge**" in the Ardennes

1945

(15 January) Last German offensive in west fails; Allies resume forward march

(17 January) Red Army enters Warsaw

(27 January) Liberation of **Auschwitz** by Red Army troops

(4–11 February) Big three (Roosevelt, Stalin, Churchill) meet at **Yalta** in the Crimea and decide on temporary division of Germany into occupation zones after the war

(13 February) Red Army takes Budapest

(14 February) Allied planes devastate **Dresden**

(6 March) Allied forces take Cologne

(8 March) American troops cross Rhine River at Remagen

(19 March) **Hitler** orders scorched earth policy

(30 March) Soviet forces take **Danzig**

(11 April) **Buchenwald** liberated by Allied troops

(12 April) President Roosevelt dies and is succeeded by Harry S. Truman

(13 April) Soviet forces take Vienna

(15 April) **Bergen-Belsen** liberated by British troops

(16 April) Red Army launches its final assault on Berlin

(25 April) American and Soviet troops meet at Torgau on the Elbe River; United Nations conference opens in San Francisco

(27 April) **Sachsenhausen** liberated by Red Army

(28 April) Mussolini killed by partisans in Milan; **Dachau** liberated by American troops

(30 April) **Hitler** commits suicide in his bunker in Berlin; Admiral **Dönitz** appointed to succeed him

(1 May) **Goebbels** commits suicide in Berlin

(2 May) Soviet forces complete capture of Berlin

(8 May) Germany surrenders unconditionally

(23 May) **Dönitz** and other government leaders arrested; **Himmler** commits suicide

(July–August) **Potsdam Conference** confirms formation of Allied Control Council to govern Germany from Berlin

(6 August) Atomic bomb destroys Hiroshima

(2 September) Japan signs unconditional surrender, ending the Second World War

(20 November) Beginning of **Nuremberg** War Crimes trials

1946

(16 October) Execution of Nazi war criminals at **Nuremberg**

1947

(1 January) American and British zones of occupation combined into "Bizonia"

(5 June) Secretary of State George Marshall announces European Recovery Program

1948

(21 March) Soviets walk out of Allied Control Council in protest against failure to create central German government
(25 June) Soviets blockade Western land access to Berlin to protest introduction of new Western currency and creation of separate West German state; Allies mount airlift to supply Western sectors

1949

(12 May) End of Berlin blockade
(23 May) Establishment of **Federal Republic of Germany (FRG)**
(15 September) Konrad Adenauer becomes first chancellor of **FRG**
(12 October) Establishment of **German Democratic Republic (GDR)**, with Walter Ulbricht as head of the Socialist Unity Party (SED)

1951

(10 April) West German parliament passes bill for rehabilitation and re-employment of civil servants removed from employment in the course of **denazification**

1952

(10 September) The **FRG** and Israel sign agreement providing restitution payments to Jewish people

1953

(5 March) Death of Stalin

1955

(5 May) Paris Agreements give **FRG** full sovereignty with authority to rearm, without nuclear, biological, or chemical weapons; **FRG** joins NATO
(14 May) Soviet Union forms Warsaw Pact in response to German rearmament and membership in NATO

(15 May) Austrian State Treaty ends occupation
(September) Adenauer visits Moscow to open diplomatic relations between the **FRG** and USSR and to secure the return of remaining German POWs

1956

(17 August) Communist Party outlawed in **FRG**

1960

(23 May) Adolf **Eichmann** seized in Argentina and brought to Israel for trial

1961

(11 April) Beginning of **Eichmann** trial in Jerusalem
(13 August) Construction of Berlin Wall separating East and West Berlin

1962

(31 May) Execution of **Eichmann**

1965

(21 April) West German parliament extends 20-year statute of limitation on prosecution of murder
(2 May) Full diplomatic relations established between **FRG** and Israel

1967

(2 June) The killing of a student by a policeman at a demonstration against the Shah of Iran in Berlin precipitates militant student protests

1969

(11 June) Further extension of statute of limitation on Nazi war crimes
(21 October) Willy Brandt (SPD) is elected chancellor

1970

(7 December) Brandt signs treaty of reconciliation with Poland and kneels at memorial to the victims of the **Warsaw Ghetto uprising**

1971

(3 May) Walter Ulbricht replaced by Erich Honecker as first secretary of the SED
(3 September) Four-Power Accord recognizes special status of West Berlin

1972

(17 May) The West German parliament ratifies treaty recognizing the **GDR** as a separate state within the German nation

1977

(18 October) Leaders of the terrorist Red Army Fraction (RAF) commit suicide in prison

1979

(3 July) West German parliament votes to lift statute of limitation on Nazi war crimes

1982

(1 October) Chancellor Helmut Schmidt (**SPD**) replaced by Helmut Kohl of the conservative Christian Democratic Union (CDU)

1984

(6 June) Neither **FRG** nor **GDR** invited to participate in ceremonies commemorating the 40th anniversary of **D-Day** landings

1985

(5 May) US president Ronald Reagan joins Chancellor Kohl for a controversial ceremony at the military cemetery in Bitburg as an act of conciliation on the 40th anniversary of the end of the Second World War
(8 May) West German president Richard von Weizsäcker reaffirms German responsibility for remembering the crimes of Nazism

1986–1987

Historian Ernst **Nolte**'s revisionism precipitates bitter historians' dispute (*Historikerstreit*) on the place of National Socialism in German history

1989

(9 November) Opening of the Berlin Wall

1990

(18 March) Elections in the **GDR** bring the CDU to power
(18 May) The **FRG** and **GDR** sign a treaty to unite Germany under the West German constitution
(12 September) Four victor powers and two German states sign a treaty in Moscow conferring full sovereignty on a united Germany and renouncing all German territorial claims arising from the Second World War
(3 October) Reunification of Germany with its capital in Berlin

3

HISTORIOGRAPHY

The debate about how best to understand and interpret Nazism and its causes began with the rise of the Nazi Party and the triumph of **fascism** in Italy in the early 1920s and has hardly abated since then. Historical interpretations are ultimately crucially dependent on the vantage point from which history is written. Nazism is today remembered above all as a cultural and political movement of unique destructiveness. After its failure and collapse in universal disgrace in the Second World War, and after revelations of the atrocities of the **Holocaust**, there is no dispute about the perniciousness of Nazism. This almost universal perception has led to the vigorous and well-justified condemnation of Nazism, but it has not diminished differences of opinion about its nature, significance, or causation. Because neutrality toward Nazism is hardly possible, interpretation of its origins, meaning, and causes has become a battleground between competing political orientations, whether of the egalitarian left, the liberal center, or the conservative right.

Ideological assumptions are ultimately the most important determinants of where the explanatory emphases of histories of National Socialism lie. It must be borne in mind that interpretations of Nazism are often used in polemical fashion to discredit opposing political movements and values by attributing to them some of the evil features of Nazism. Because its ideology, ascent to power, and system of rule had so many contrasting – indeed contradictory – features, diverse movements can interpret Nazism in ways primarily designed to reinforce their own value system and policy priorities and to refute those of political opponents.

PRE-WAR CONSERVATIVE INTERPRETATIONS: THE "RISE OF THE MASSES"

Before the war, however, neither fascism nor Nazism were universally perceived as evil or even objectionable. Conservatives in Germany, Britain, and France were particularly reluctant to recognize or acknowledge the extremism of the Nazi movement, or, if they did, to condemn it. Many conservatives, not just in Germany, welcomed **Hitler**'s accession to power as a salutary setback to international communism. One such conservative, the Christian monarchist Hermann **Rauschning**, had joined the Nazi Party in 1931, but turned against the Nazis when it became evident that they would not bring about a conservative restoration. His analysis of Nazism, *The Revolution of Nihilism*, published in 1938, provided the model for many disenchanted conservatives who had hoped that Nazism would strengthen religion, the family, law and order, and traditional institutions. Predisposed to favor authority, hierarchy, and the traditional order, disillusioned conservatives generally associated Nazism with the democratic instinct run wild, the rebellion of plebeian types dissatisfied with their subordinate place in society. Rauschning dismissed Nazi ideology (key elements of which conservatives shared) as purely opportunistic. For Rauschning Nazism was a revolution without a doctrine or Weltanschauung, a movement powered solely by the desire to exercise dominance.

In Rauschning's view the Nazis only gave lip-service to conservative ideals to hoodwink the people. For Rauschning Nazism was a product of the modernity he despised, a symptom of the decline of traditional Western moral and religious values and the "rise of the masses." According to Rauschning even Nazi **anti-Semitism** (which Rauschning himself promoted in legislation proposed as president of the Danzig city senate in the mid-1930s) was only opportunistic, not a principled conviction (as presumably was the case with true conservatives). Cultural pessimists like Rauschning could not concede to Nazism any coherent ideology without implicating their own hostility to democracy (at least of the **Weimar** variety) and to the left. Hence they preferred to view Nazism as a cynical and total break with the past, a movement of criminals pursuing power solely for its own sake and for their own gain.

In some respects Rauschning anticipated **totalitarianism** theory, the hallmark of which was to stress the structural resemblances between Nazism and communism. The use by Nazis and Bolsheviks of similarly radical methods, including violence, propaganda, and mass mobilization, made doctrinal differences seem largely irrelevant. This has been a perspective particularly favored by liberals of the center (or center-right) of the political spectrum for whom the repression of individual rights and representative government is the defining characteristic of totalitarian systems. To liberals who valued individual freedom above all else it often made little difference whether such repression occurred in the cause of human equality, as under communism, or in the cause of racial supremacy, as under Nazism. The target populations may have differed, but the effect on victims was the same. The more oriented toward the right such a liberal perspective was, the more likely it was to stress resemblances between Nazism and communism or to locate Nazism on the left of the political spectrum. Rauschning, for instance, called the opportunistic new Nazi elite (in a reference to Catiline, the ancient Roman conspirator against Cicero) "Catilinarians of the Left."[1] Rauschning's analysis was unhistorical, treating Nazism as an unchanging essence while ignoring its evolution and slighting the historical context in which it arose (as later cold war-inspired interpretations were to do as well). *The Revolution of Nihilism* described the unscrupulous nature of Nazism well enough, but it is not very useful in explaining how it arose and why it gained power.

NAZISM AS A PECULIARLY GERMAN IDEOLOGY

Very different from Rauschning's ahistorical analysis was the approach of the French scholar of German literature, Edmond **Vermeil**, whose *Doctrinaire de la révolution allemande* was published in 1938 and reflected the animosities of the First World War. If Rauschning saw Nazism as a totally novel phenomenon without any precedents in German history, Vermeil was excessively fixated on alleged continuities in German history. For Vermeil Nazism was ultimately rooted in the characteristically German tradition of what he called "organized romanticism," the schizoid German penchant for contradictory ideals, whether of mysticism and technology, imperialism and subservience to authority, elitism and populism, order and disorder. According to Vermeil, the tension between these contradictory deep-historical strands could only be resolved through characteristically German aggressiveness.[2] Vermeil's was probably the best and least rigid of a number of works that sought to trace the roots of Nazism deep in the German past and in the German national character. It became a model of sorts for many subsequent works, most of them polemics written in the heat of the Second World War, patterned on the "from Luther to Hitler" theme.[3]

Some of these works can be subsumed under what at the time was called "Vansittartism" (after the anti-German British Foreign Office official Robert Vansittart [1881–1957]), the notion that Germans were incorrigibly aggressive and shared a collective guilt for their inherited militarism and the rise of Nazism. "Vansittartists" rejected the idea that Nazism was imposed on an innocent, terrorized German society against the will of the people, but argued instead that it fulfilled long-cherished German aspirations.[4] What made all such generalizations problematical, however, was not only their tendency to take abstract ideas out of their social and political contexts but also their implicit acceptance and inversion of the Nazi postulate of German exceptionalism (with values reversed). In many respects these "from Luther to Hitler" narratives unreflectively echoed the Nazis' own dubious claims of embodying Germany's great cultural and philosophical traditions. While the Nazis celebrated German culture as proof of German racial superiority, "Vansittartists" denounced it as the source of Germany's recurrent criminality. Later critics of an alleged German *Sonderweg* would point out that German political culture was not as different from Western models as the adherents of German exceptionalism claimed. On the other hand there is little doubt that the Nazis' cynical evocation of specifically German intellectual and cultural traditions contributed to their popularity and success.

MARXIST INTERPRETATIONS: THE OFFICIAL PARTY LINE

From the early 1920s Marxist interpretations of fascism and Nazism have provided the major stimulus for scholarly inquiry and debate. There is no doubt that both before and after the war the most incisive and thorough – but also the most controversial – analyses of fascism were put forward by theorists who, for all their differences, identified themselves as part of the Marxist tradition. One reason Marxists dominated the discussion before 1945 is that for Marxists an accurate analysis of Nazism was not just an academic exercise but a necessary precondition for effective action to counter the Nazi threat. The goal of committed Marxists, after all, is not just to interpret the world but also to change it. As the primary targets of Nazi aggression and repression, Marxists developed far greater sensitivity to the extraordinary dangers of Nazism than did conservatives or even liberals, who often shared at least some of the Nazi premises, whether it was nationalism, the enforcement of law and order, the promotion of conventional moral norms, or the defense of private property rights.

Marxist historians sought the causes of fascism (as of every major historical event) in economic developments, in changes in methods of production and exchange, and in the struggle between the classes to which economic relations under capitalism gave rise. The basic Marxist assumption that fascism was an extreme consequence of capitalism, and that the study of fascism therefore can't be isolated from the study of the capitalist economy in which it arose, was tersely expressed by the founder of the Frankfurt School of Social Research, Max Horkheimer (1895–1973), in 1939: "Anyone who doesn't want to speak about capitalism should also keep quiet about fascism."[5]

Yet theorists of the communist parties in Europe, disappointed by the failure of revolution in the wake of the First World War and constrained by the Stalinist axiom that whatever served the Soviet national interest was best for the communist cause, often came to simplistic and misleading conclusions about fascism that hampered effective opposition to Nazism in Germany. Embittered by the suppression of communist revolutions by liberal and Social Democratic governments in post-First World War Germany, members of the German Communist Party (**KPD**) denounced Social Democrats (**SPD**) as merely lackeys of the bourgeoisie and the pacemakers of fascism, condemning them as "social fascists." By recruiting workers for reformist policies, the SPD allegedly provided the mass base for bourgeois capitalist interests.

In the late 1920s, before the advent of the Nazi state, communists loyal to the Soviet Union tended to view liberal democratic systems such as Weimar Germany as little better than the seedbeds of fascism. The **Comintern** dubiously defined fascism as simply a more extreme form of bourgeois dominance than liberal democracy. Communists attributed to liberal and social democratic parliamentary parties the same function as fascism; namely, to serve the interests of capital. According to official Communist doctrine, capitalists resorted to fascism when they could no longer rely on parliamentary coalitions to serve their needs. By lumping all anti-communist formations together on the assumption that they were merely agents of capital, such a perspective trivialized fascism and made a united opposition to Nazism impossible. Indeed, based on this fallacious analysis, the KPD supported the Nazis' efforts to bring down the SPD minority government in Prussia in 1931.

This misjudgement of the role of the SPD as facilitators of fascism was not revised until after Hitler's accession to power. The revised Comintern definition of fascism, first put forth in 1933 and officially adopted in 1935, still identified capitalism as the source of fascism. But by calling fascism in power "the open terroristic dictatorship of the most reactionary, the most chauvinistic, the most imperialistic elements of finance capital," the new definition did draw a sufficiently sharp distinction between fascist and liberal capitalist parties to leave Communists free to form the anti-fascist coalitions with Social Democrats and liberals that they had previously scorned.[6] It did, however, perpetuate the vulgar Marxist notion of Nazis and fascists as merely the agents of big capital, acting on instructions issued by their economic bosses.

UNORTHODOX MARXIST INTERPRETATIONS

While all Marxist analyses shared the assumption that fascism was a product of the contradictions and crises of capitalism, Marxist historians not bound by the party line offered a variety of more dialectical interpretations that challenged the Comintern's superficial "agent theory" of fascism. Some dissident Marxists, such as August Thalheimer (1884–1948), Leon Trotsky (1879–1940), and the Austrian Otto Bauer (1882–1938) in the early 1930s, sought to provide a more persuasive explanation of the relationship between fascism and capitalism by invoking Marx's analysis of the Bonapartist state in *The 18th Brumaire of Louis Napoleon* (1852). According to this analogy to Bonapartism, fascism results from a situation of political stalemate when the ruling capitalist class is no longer able to maintain its rule by constitutional and parliamentary means (whether because of dissension within the ruling class or because of the strength of the proletarian challenge), but the working class is not yet able to establish its dominance either. The Bonapartist state exercises power by mediating between the classes and thus ensuring the smooth operation of capitalist society.[7]

In contrast to the official Comintern view of the Nazis as merely agents and tools of the bourgeoisie, "Bonapartist" analyses assumed that bourgeois capitalists did in fact cede political power to the Nazis in order to retain economic control of society. While the political power of the bourgeoisie was thus destroyed under Nazism, its social and economic power remained intact. Such an analysis did greater justice to the evident autonomy of the Nazi movement and the Nazi state than the orthodox party line. Nazism's function was to guarantee the stability of capitalist society (through terror against the labor movement, propaganda to win over the masses, and repression of civil liberties). In such an interpretation Nazis did not just slavishly serve the interests of capital but pursued their own specific political and ideological goals as well, first and foremost the creation of a racial utopia. Racial ideology and anti-Semitism did not just serve the instrumental function of diverting anti-capitalist grievances into channels that did not threaten the economic elites, they also represented a substantive program of racial restructuring that the Nazis pursued as their top priority.

The most serious challenge to the official Comintern line from within the Marxist camp came from Trotskyists who had long accused Stalin of underestimating the fascist adversary and of betraying the cause of social revolution. While the Stalinist Comintern was deriding Social Democrats as "social fascists" in the early 1930s, Trotsky was calling for a united front with Social Democrats to oppose Nazism. Perhaps the most notable Trotskyist interpreter was the French historian Daniel **Guérin**, who in his books, *The Brown Plague* (1934) and *Fascism and Big Business* (1936), took issue with Stalinists for dismissing Nazism as merely a stage on the way to the proletarian revolution. While recognizing that the main function of Nazism was to sustain the capitalist system, Guérin took Nazism seriously as a genuine mass movement. He acknowledged its popular appeal, the stability of the Nazi regime, and its success in atomizing the working class and in attracting the masses. But Trotsky and Guérin also opposed the abrupt about-turn in Communist strategy after 1935, when Stalin endorsed **Popular Front** coalitions with a wide spectrum of anti-fascist parties, even if this entailed renouncing revolution and suppressing grassroots revolutionary movements (as for instance in republican Spain). Trotsky and Guérin continued to call for a "united front from below," mobilizing the working-class rank and file while rejecting the tactical compromises of the Comintern with bourgeois parties in favor of promoting popular revolutions in countries in which fascism had not yet taken hold.[8]

Unorthodox Marxist scholars also pioneered sociological and psychological studies of Nazism that challenged and augmented the simplistic agent theory of the Soviet Comintern. The German émigré scholar Arthur Rosenberg (1889–1943), who wrote the first history of the Weimar Republic in 1935, was among the first Marxists to recognize Nazism as a genuine mass movement that drew support mainly from the lower middle class, both the "old" *Mittelstand* of small proprietors and the new *Mittelstand* of white-collar employees.[9] According to Rosenberg, lower-middle-class susceptibility to Nazism could not be attributed solely to capitalist manipulation. Among the most innovative Marxist scholars who tried to account for the "false consciousness" of the masses (i.e., their support for Nazism against their own economic interests) were the maverick psychoanalysts Wilhelm **Reich** and Erich **Fromm**, and the equally unorthodox philosopher Ernst **Bloch**, each of whom proposed alternatives to the exclusive focus on economic forces in orthodox Marxist interpretations.[10] These theorists reproached orthodox Marxists for underestimating the importance of irrational factors in the triumph of Nazism and in human motivation in general. Each identified special conditions that made Germans particularly susceptible to Nazism.

While they continued to view Nazism as primarily an economic and political problem, both Reich and Fromm sought to explain its hold over the German people on socio-psychological grounds. For Reich the key to the German receptivity to fascism lay in the traditional patriarchal and sexually repressive middle-class family structure. For Fromm, on the other hand, the failure of economic, social, and political conditions to offer a basis for the realization of full individual self-development led to the individual's attempt to escape from the burdens of freedom by seeking refuge in submission to authority and submersion in a larger collective. According to Bloch, it was the backwardness of parts of German society, the disproportionate survival of historical anachronisms – pre-capitalist and pre-democratic ideas, attitudes, and institutions – that made the German public susceptible to fascism and ready to embrace Nazi mythology and destructiveness. The founders of the Frankfurt School, too, Horkheimer and Theodor Adorno (1903–1969), initiated a number of studies that sought to account for the irrational attraction of so many Germans to Nazism and for the fact that Germany developed the most radical and genocidal form of fascism. One of the most influential of such studies was *The Authoritarian Personality*, completed in American exile and published in 1950.

The political scientist Franz **Neumann**, on the other hand, saw the "authoritarian personality" not as an antecedent to or cause of Nazism so much as the result of Nazi rule. Like Fromm before him and Hannah **Arendt** after him, Neumann identified the atomizing of society to isolate its individual members and the creation of a uniform sadomasochistic character type as central Nazi techniques to form a malleable collectivity. Neumann's classic study *Behemoth*, published in American exile in 1942, offered a far more variegated and sophisticated analysis of Nazism than the mono-causal "agent theory" of the Comintern. Neumann regarded the Nazi state as an ally of heavy industry, not merely its instrument, and he acknowledged that relations between them were sometimes antagonistic. In identifying four major groups – the state bureaucracy, the party elite, industry, and the army – in competition with each other in directing the Nazi state and society, Neumann anticipated post-war structural studies that often corroborated the makeshift rather than monolithic administrative structure of the Nazi regime.

AFTER THE WAR: CONSERVATIVE GERMAN INTERPRETATIONS

When the war came to a close the focus of explanations of Nazism shifted from "What is to be done?" to "How could this have happened?" In Germany total defeat spawned a number of soul-searching attempts to explain how Germans could have fallen for a movement that turned out to be so ruinous for their nation. It was perhaps inevitable that even the best of these early attempts to come to terms with Nazism, written by distinguished historians who had remained in Germany during the **Third Reich**, struck an apologetic note that betrayed their nationalist and conservative values. Historians who had remained in Germany during the Nazi era were understandably anxious to absolve their national history and culture of culpability for Nazi crimes. In 1946 the dean of German historians, Friedrich **Meinecke**, published a pamphlet, *The German Catastrophe*, which, while critical of Prussian militarism and power politics, de-emphasized social, cultural, economic, and ideological factors in the rise of Nazism and put primary emphasis on international relations as the arena in which the main causes of the Nazi catastrophe had to be sought.

His conservative colleague Gerhard **Ritter** defended the Prussian monarchical tradition and went even further than Meinecke in attributing the origins of Nazism to European-wide developments. According to Ritter Nazism had its source in Enlightenment doctrines and the democratic revolutions of the late eighteenth and early nineteenth centuries. For Ritter "Hitler's proletarian movement," like the many other single-party dictatorships in twentieth-century Europe (Ritter listed Russia, Italy, Poland, Spain, Portugal, Turkey, and several Balkan states), was an outgrowth of industrial mass society and the materialist discontents it bred.[11] According to Ritter, Hitler's precursors were the populist non-German demagogues Robespierre and Lenin, not the German aristocrats Bismarck or Wilhelm II. Ritter even went so far as to claim that the notion of *Lebensraum* was not a Hitlerian invention, but originated in the Darwinian revolution in biology. For Ritter, Nazism represented a complete rupture with the authentic German past.

Meinecke and Ritter established the framework for numerous published attempts by German conservatives to explain the Nazi experience without implicating their own conservative values. Two tropes predominated: first, Nazism was seen as part of a general Western moral and political crisis, and, second, it was viewed as an avoidable accident brought on by a small group of immoral and unrepresentative villains taking advantage of an innocent and gullible nation. For Ritter and Meinecke, Nazism was an expression of the cultural and spiritual crisis of Western civilization under the hubris of the idea of worldly progress. Blaming the modern trend toward secularism and materialism became a favorite way of diverting attention from the role played by the organized churches and members of both Catholic and Protestant faiths in facilitating and perpetuating Nazi rule. Nietzsche's vitalist anti-Christian philosophy, which had indeed been a source of inspiration for many individual Nazis (though not for the Nazi leadership), became a favorite scapegoat for the Nazi catastrophe, especially for Christian writers.

Stressing the role of modern technology in the Nazis' propagandistic successes, Ritter portrayed the Germans as a people seduced and oppressed by a resolute minority of criminal activists with no essential connection to German traditions. In this view, embraced by most German conservatives, Nazism was a historical accident, a pathological aberration in German history brought on by a small clique of political gangsters taking advantage of popular discontents to seize power. In identifying the left with its emphasis on distributional equality and class struggle as the source of the discontents that led to popular demands for dictatorship, Meinecke and Ritter also pointed the way to totalitarianism theory, in which fascism is seen as the mirror image of communism. Their interpretation received unexpected support from conservative Jewish émigré historian Hans Rothfels (1891–1976), who resumed his university career in West Germany after the war. According to Rothfels, Nazism arose in Germany because the Weimar

Republic had been too democratic, permitting the masses to elevate the Nazis to power. His highly laudatory history of the aristocratic resistance designated German conservatives, rather than the left, as the true antipodes of Nazism.[12]

A general feature of conservative apologetics was the attribution to Nazism of the very egalitarian or leveling traits that the Nazis were ostensibly fighting against. This enabled conservatives to explain what had attracted them to Nazism in the first place or had persuaded them to collaborate with the Nazis, but did not require any fundamental disavowal of their views. The philosopher Martin **Heidegger**, for instance, could denounce Nazism as part of the nihilistic Western tradition of calculative thinking, even though it was precisely the Nazis' promise to eradicate Western nihilism that had attracted Heidegger to Nazism in the first place. Although Heidegger had joined the Nazi Party as, in his view, the only reasonable alternative to communism and materialism, he later contended that the Nazis were simply part of the general corruption of the Western tradition that they claimed to be fighting against. Thus by conceding that they had misjudged the true nature of Nazism, conservatives could retain the views and the values that had caused them to collaborate with the Nazis.

With a handful of exceptions, most German historians active during the Nazi era successfully navigated the **denazification** process after 1945 and resumed their university positions, bringing with them the time-honored principles of German historicism: the narrative reconstruction of a course of events based on an understanding of the motives and intentions of leading historical actors as the principal task of historians; the uniqueness of all historical events and decisions, which should only be judged by the standards that obtained at the time in which they occurred; the conflict between states for power on the international stage as the central concern of historians and the reliance on documents of state as the keys to historical reconstruction and explanation; the priority of facts over concepts or theory; and the priority of diplomatic and political over social and economic history.[13] German historians also avoided contemporary history and preferred to deal with events safely embedded in the past. After the war, Germany's leading historical journal, the *Historische Zeitschrift*, published only one article on National Socialism before 1950.[14] The first major critical history of Nazism in Germany was produced not by a scholar working in the historicist tradition but by a political scientist, Karl Dietrich **Bracher**, employing the analytical methods of the social sciences to explain the collapse of the Weimar Republic and the success of the Nazi seizure of power.[15]

TOTALITARIANISM THEORY

Bracher was also, however, an adherent of conservative totalitarianism theory. The term "totalitarianism" was used polemically as early as the 1920s by opponents of Mussolini's statism, and in the 1930s by opponents of Nazism as well as critics of the Soviet Union. It also was used in a positive sense by fascists to describe the penetration of their values and institutions into all areas of social life. As a serious scholarly effort to understand and explain both fascist and communist regimes and to stimulate comparative research, totalitarianism theory came into its own after the Second World War. Although the **Nazi–Soviet Pact** of 1939 had already converted many disillusioned liberals and socialists to the view that the Soviet Union was as much a totalitarian enemy of Western democracy as Nazi Germany was, the major catalyst for the wide dissemination of totalitarianism theory in the West was the cold war between the two military superpowers after the Second World War.

Undoubtedly the most influential and philosophically ambitious attempt to develop an explanatory theory of fascist and communist states was the three-part *Origins of Totalitarianism* by the social philosopher Hannah **Arendt**, published in 1951. In the first two parts, written in the mid-1940s under the impact of Nazism, Arendt traced the antecedents of totalitarianism in nineteenth-century anti-Semitism and imperialism. In the third part, however, written under the impact of the emerging cold war in the late 1940s, Arendt concluded, somewhat inconsistently, that the totalitarian societies of the twentieth century were an entirely unprecedented historical phenomenon characterized by the pervasive atomization of the masses. According to Arendt, in totalitarian societies the relationship of individuals to the state completely overshadowed their relationships to each other. Totalitarian policy destroyed the neutral zone in which the daily lives of human beings are ordinarily lived. The destruction of all traditional bonds between people and of all independent interest groups and voluntary citizen organizations allowed the mobilization of the masses around a simple-minded utopian ideology and facilitated a form of rule in which bureaucrats could perform murderous deeds with a clear conscience (an organizing theme of Arendt's controversial 1962 book, *Eichmann in Jerusalem: The Banality of Evil*). By fragmenting society into a mass of isolated individuals, each with their own narrow tasks without responsibility for the larger whole, totalitarianism created the conditions for the annihilation of superfluous or unintegrated population groups. Arendt was less concerned with tracing the history of totalitarianism than with counteracting what she regarded as the dangerous tendency of modern societies to discourage citizen participation in political decision-making and responsible civic engagement. Writing under the impact of her direct experience of Nazism, and against a cold war background of "both reckless optimism and reckless despair," she identified this abdication of moral and political responsibility as the ultimate source of modern totalitarianism.[16]

The more systematic theory developed by political scientists Carl **Friedrich** and Zibigniev Brzezinski (b. 1928) in their 1956 study, *Totalitarian Dictatorship and Autocracy*, was much more overtly driven by anti-communism. Friedrich and Brzezinski identified a set of six criteria that defined modern fascist and communist states: first, a state-sponsored millenarian ideology; second, a single-party system; third, a secret-police apparatus; fourth, a monopoly of propaganda and means of communication; fifth, a monopoly of arms; and sixth, a centrally controlled or planned economy. Friedrich and Brzezinski were particularly critical of Marxists or liberals who denied or downplayed the similarities between fascism and communism or between Nazism and Stalinism. As the analogy to Nazism was a useful way of discrediting the Soviet system, totalitarianism theory soon attained something approximating official status in the West. It was politically particularly useful at a time when West Germany was being asked to rearm under the auspices of NATO to meet the Soviet threat in the 1950s.

Totalitarianism theory was strongly contested, however, by critics who pointed to changes in the post-Stalinist Soviet Union and protested against the ideologically driven oversimplifications of the totalitarianism model. Friedrich and Brzezinski were criticized for having produced a static mechanistic model that neglected the social dynamics of totalitarian movements and failed to take into account the very different origins, goals, values, and class character of fascism and communism. Indeed, Friedrich and Brzezinski had deliberately limited their study to a general description "of a novel form of government" rather than attempting to explain how or why such governments came about, "for the authors are convinced that such an explanation is not feasible at the present time."[17] Unwilling to examine the class character of fascist and communist regimes, which might have helped to explain the origins of these regimes and their different aims, most adherents of totalitarianism theory confined themselves to describing the very similar ways in which fascist and communist regimes mobilized the masses, wielded power, and maintained control.

CRITICAL HISTORIOGRAPHY OF THE 1960s AND 1970s: THE FISCHER CONTROVERSY

The turn of German historians away from historicism to more critical social-scientific methods may be dated to the publication of the Hamburg scholar Fritz **Fischer**'s landmark study in 1961 of Germany's responsibility for the First World War, translated into English as *Germany's Aims in the First World War* (1967). Although Fischer did not deal with the Nazi era itself, his studies of the expansionist policies of the German Empire had profound implications for the Nazi period.[18] On the basis of a thorough examination of the German Foreign Office documents, Fischer showed that there was indeed far greater continuity between German ambitions in the two world wars than conservative historians like Gerhard Ritter had been willing to concede. Fischer argued that Germany's expansionist aims were not just a result of the revanchism generated by German defeat in the First World War, and the punitive Versailles Treaty, but actually predated the war. Fischer's work made it impossible to cordon off the Nazi period as an accidental aberration in the otherwise untarnished course of German history. His pioneering effort spawned numerous critical studies of the role of German elites in promoting policies that eventually led to the rise and triumph of the Nazis.

Fischer's methodology, influenced by several years of study in Britain and the United States, led to a break with the venerable nationalist and conservative historical tradition in Germany, which had survived the Nazi trauma and persisted into the post-war era. Fischer's analysis of the domestic factors that helped to shape aggressive German policies reversed the previously dominant historical paradigm of "the primacy of foreign policy," according to which German policies were dictated by the threats from rival European states. Ritter, for instance, had rationalized the Prusso-German authoritarian and militarist tradition as unavoidable in a centrally located nation surrounded on all sides by potential foes. The primacy of foreign policy had traditionally served conservative political purposes by providing a reason to subordinate demands for liberalizing or egalitarian social reform to the needs of national security. Fischer, however, argued that it was not Germany's exposed geographical position that was decisive in German policy formation but, rather, the exaggerated ambitions of its undemocratic leadership elites.

The "opening to the left" in the 1960s that brought to an end the conservative post-war era amidst world-wide protests against United States involvement in the Vietnam War inevitably affected the historiography of Nazism as well.[19] As the premises of official cold war ideology were increasingly challenged in the West under the impact of the Vietnam War, a new critical historiography emerged that was also bound to question prevailing conservative or cold war interpretations of Nazism. The paradigm shift in Germany corresponded to the leftward turn in West German politics after Adenauer's resignation as chancellor in 1963. Influenced by Fischer's iconoclastic approach, a younger generation of historians challenged the apologetic tendencies of the early post-war era with critical reinterpretations of the place of Nazism in German history. They questioned the inherited principles of German historicism and the rationalizations of the nationalist-conservative historical school. Younger historians were far more ready to explore and acknowledge continuities in German history in stark contrast to the tendency in the immediate post-war years to treat the Nazi period from 1933 to 1945 as both a historical accident with no true connection to the earlier German past or as the fault of a small clique of gangster leaders – above all Hitler personally – imposing their pathological visions and ambitions on a violated German public.

Perhaps the most important group of younger critical historians in the 1960s and 1970s was the so-called "Bielefeld School" of social historians under the leadership of Hans-Ulrich **Wehler** and Jürgen Kocka (b. 1941). Wehler revived the work of the short-lived dissident historian of the Weimar era, Eckart Kehr (1902–1933), who emphasized the primacy of domestic policies over foreign affairs and stressed the significance of material interests and socioeconomic factors in the formation of German naval policy before the First World War. Wehler and Kocka applied the methods of structural history first introduced by Kehr and Fischer in revising the history of Imperial Germany. Although the Bielefeld School was mainly concerned with German social and political history in the nineteenth and early twentieth centuries, their findings and methodology had important repercussions for the historiography of Nazism as well.

THE *SONDERWEG* CONTROVERSY

Wehler developed the hypothesis of the German *Sonderweg*, according to which the catastrophic developments in Germany from 1914 to 1945 could be best explained by Germany's failure, in contrast to Western European nations, to develop liberal and democratic institutions in the course of the nineteenth century.[20] Variants of the *Sonderweg* thesis, which emphasized continuities rather than ruptures in German history, had long informed Anglo-American historiography, especially in studies of Nazi ideology, as in the works of émigré historians Francis **Carsten**, Fritz **Stern**, George **Mosse**, and Hans Kohn (1891–1971).[21] Wehler's model focused more on social and economic forces and on the disproportionate political power of predominantly agrarian aristocratic elites hostile to liberalism and democracy. From Wehler's unabashed liberal perspective, the striking imbalance between Germany's rapid economic development and its retarded social and political structure (due to the failure of liberal revolution in German history) was the major source of the tensions that led to Germany's aggressive and regressive policies in the twentieth century.

One function of the *Sonderweg* theory was to create a "usable past" for liberal democracy and democratic citizenship in the Federal Republic. Conservative critics of the *Sonderweg* thesis objected to the moral and political didacticism of this interpretation and rejected an approach that seemed to treat the history of Imperial Germany as merely the prehistory of Nazism. In 1976 an American historian of German liberalism, James J. Sheehan (b. 1937), warned that emphasis on the structural flaws of the German Empire was hardening into a rigid new orthodoxy that blocked understanding of the richness and diversity of Imperial society.[22] Wehler's model came under even more scathing attack from the left in the early 1980s by British and American historians who denied that the economic bourgeoisie was any less dominant in Germany than in Western Europe, despite the failure of liberal revolution in 1848 and Germany's consequently more authoritarian political structure.[23] Geoff **Eley** in particular objected to an interpretation that, by stressing German backwardness and its deviance from the British developmental norm, diverted scholarly attention from the crisis of the capitalist state as the most important source of fascism.[24] In a later reflection on the *Sonderweg* controversy, Eley noted the irony that Wehler's effort to develop a non- or even anti-Marxist interpretation of Germany's susceptibility to Nazism implied a positive concept of "bourgeois revolution." The irony lay in the fact that Wehler thus resurrected a staple of earlier Marxist interpretations of the French Revolution at the very time that these interpretations were coming under increasing attack from liberal historians.[25]

THE REVIVAL OF FASCISM THEORY

Numerous new works in the 1960s and 1970s challenged the totalitarianism model and revived interest in earlier Marxist models that had been ignored or rejected in the West during the cold war. A younger generation of German historians questioned the cold war rigidities of the West as well as the Stalinist heritage in the East. Even non-Marxist historians accepted the Marxist claims that Nazism could best be understood as part of a generic fascist movement opposed to socialism and liberal democracy and that fascism had its most important source in the political and economic crisis that afflicted capitalist societies in the inter-war years. Ernst **Nolte**'s *Three Faces of Fascism*, published in Germany in 1963, compared Nazism to Italian Fascism and the French Action Française and identified anti-Marxism as the defining principle of fascist ideology.[26] The American historian William Sheridan Allen's pioneering regional study, *The Nazi Seizure of Power: The Experience of a Single German Town, 1922–1945* (1965), used the concept of social class to explain the popularity of the Nazis among middle-class Germans in the north German town of Northeim. While Bracher remained committed to the totalitarianism paradigm in his work, *The German Dictatorship* (published in Germany in 1969), Martin **Broszat** and Hans **Mommsen** published works critical of the conventional notion of the Nazi regime as a rationally organized, structurally unified, and centrally controlled monolith.[27] Edward N. Peterson (b. 1925), too, stressed the institutional chaos of Nazi Germany in *The Limits of Hitler's Power* (1969).

There was also a perceptible shift in the 1960s and 1970s toward more theoretical explorations of Nazism, especially in West Germany. East German historians began to be taken seriously in the West, participating in debates in the West German Marxist journal *Das Argument*, despite the fact that the East German regime permitted only minor modifications of the 1930s agent theory in the GDR. East German historians agreed that the interests of monopoly capitalists remained the most important factor determining Nazi policies. While their research may have been politically motivated and circumscribed, such East German historians as Dieter Eichholtz, Kurt Gossweiler (b. 1917), and Kurt Pätzold contributed important empirical findings on the relationship between fascism and capitalism. Western Marxist scholars, on the other hand, influenced by the writings of the Frankfurt School, particularly Adorno, Horkheimer, and Herbert Marcuse (1898–1979), and such unorthodox Marxists as Walter Benjamin (1892–1940) and Wilhelm Reich, as well as the posthumously published *Prison Notebooks* of the Italian communist Antonio Gramsci (1891–1937), rejected simplistic interpretations that explained political ideologies and the rise of fascism solely on the basis of immediate economic class interests. Gramsci, who died in a Fascist prison, had developed the notion of "cultural hegemony" to describe the success of Fascists in gaining the active consent of various sectors of society by representing themselves as serving the interests of society as a whole. Western Marxists developed sophisticated theories to account for what the Greek-French political theorist Nicos Poulantzas (1936–1979) called the "relative autonomy" of the Nazis to pursue their own radical racial agenda free from the control of big capital, whose interests they nonetheless served. According to this interpretation, disunity within the ruling class itself provided the opening for the Nazis to perform the vital function of mediation between competing fractions while also mobilizing the mass constituency needed to legitimate capitalist rule in a time of economic crisis.[28]

The influential British social historian Tim **Mason** went even further in stressing the "primacy of politics" over the economic sphere, while nonetheless acknowledging the overriding importance of economic imperatives. Mason argued that while the Second World War was ultimately caused by the Nazi drive for *Lebensraum*, the inability of the Nazi regime to assure Germans a reasonable standard of living while simultaneously diverting huge funds into armaments determined the timing of war in 1939.[29] This view was challenged by Richard **Overy** in a debate carried on in the pages of the British journal *Past and Present* in the late1980s.[30]

HISTORIOGRAPHY OF THE HOLOCAUST

An important development of the 1960s and 1970s was renewed consciousness of and research into the atrocities of the Nazi regime, which had received little attention from historians in the 1950s when the cold war was at its height. The process of integrating the Federal Republic into the NATO alliance tended to divert public attention in the West from the crimes of the Nazi regime in order to maintain Western harmony and gain German support for rearmament. In the 1950s the horrors of the Nazi regime were almost completely excluded from public discussion in Germany. Drawing attention to the systematic mass murder of the Jews was widely seen as a communist tactic in the West and as Zionist special pleading in the East. Even in the nascent state of Israel, fighting to establish itself against Arab opposition, political imperatives worked against publicizing Jewish weakness and passivity during the Shoah. The dean of American Holocaust historians, Raul **Hilberg**, has recounted the barriers he faced in the 1950s in publishing his magisterial work, *The Destruction of the European Jews* (1961). Hilberg faced contradictory criticisms. On the one hand, he was accused of understating the extent of Jewish resistance; on the other, he had supposedly adopted an excessively prosecutorial tone toward the Germans.[31] While Hilberg's path-breaking book was finally published in the US in 1961, it was not translated into German until 1983 (and not into Hebrew until even later). The first German account of the Holocaust, by Helmut Krausnick, director of the **Institut für Zeitgeschichte** (IfZ) in Munich from 1952 to 1972, was published in the second volume of a book devoted to the *Anatomy of the SS State* in 1965.[32] Although the horrors of the concentration camps had been well publicized in the aftermath of the war and the Nuremberg trials, the scale and detail of the genocide of the Jews were slow to seep into world-wide public consciousness. The capture and trial of Adolf **Eichmann** in Jerusalem in 1961 and 1962 was probably the single most important event that brought into sharper public focus the extent to which the Nazi killing program had systematically targeted Jews, but it was only in the 1970s that the term "Holocaust" came into wide academic and public usage in the United States and Europe.

The generational transition of the 1960s may have played as important a role as the Eichmann trial in the renewal of scholarly and public attention to both Nazism and the Holocaust. The challenge of the various protest movements against the cold war policies of the 1950s brought with it a resurgence of interest in the crimes of the Nazi period and a new determination among German students to demand an accounting from their parents and grandparents of their roles in the Third Reich. Historians trained in Germany in the aftermath of the Second World War showed considerably less reluctance to tackle the difficult task of explaining the Nazi era than the generation that had come to maturity before the war. A renewed stress on *Vergangenheitsbewältigung* (coming to terms with the past) informed research on the Nazi era in Germany and generated an ever-increasing number of new publications on various aspects of Nazi rule, including the origins of the Holocaust.

The British historian Tim Mason introduced the historiographical concepts of "intentionalist" and "structuralist" (or "functionalist") in 1981, which for a time dominated the debate on how Nazi policies of destruction were formed and implemented.[33] Mason sought to adjudicate the differences between intentionalists such as Lucy Dawidowicz (1915–1990) or Gerald Fleming (1921–2006), who stressed the centrality of the Nazi program and ideology in the planning of the Holocaust, and structuralists such as Martin Broszat or Hans Mommsen, who contended that the Judeocide was not the result of a premeditated plan or long-term conspiracy but of a bureaucratic and systemic dynamic unleashed by increasingly urgent efforts to solve what Nazis identified as Germany's foremost problem, the so-called "Jewish question." After the start of the war, structuralists argued, SS and state administrators resorted to increasingly brutal methods to free their territories of Jews once the option of forced emigration was no longer considered practicable. The debate involved more than the origins of the Holocaust. It also concerned the mechanism of government in the Third Reich, the role of ideology, and the extent of Hitler's power. Intentionalists identified the ideology and goals of the Nazi leadership as the sole or primary determinants of Nazi policies, while structuralists stressed the importance of bureaucratic, regional, or local initiatives, competition between party and government, and other more or less contingent factors in the development and implementation of Nazi policies.

What gave the debate between intentionalists and structuralists its polemical edge was the question of historical responsibility. The issue was so contentious because interpretations that stressed contingencies, social structures, or bureaucratic dynamics seemed to disperse responsibility for the Holocaust and conceal the human actors within a bureaucratic structural system. Diminution of Hitler's central role and concentration on systemic or structural factors seemed to make responsibility for Nazi atrocities that much harder to pin down. If the road to Auschwitz was "twisted," not straight, it was more difficult to equate Nazism with absolute evil.[34] Attributing rational or utilitarian motives to the perpetrators, as the German historian Götz **Aly** did, also seemed to downplay

37

the question of personal responsibility.[35] Some leading historians, including Christopher **Browning** and Ian **Kershaw**, sought to reconcile these conflicting positions, the latter through his concept of "working towards the Führer." Browning adopted an interpretation he characterized as "moderate functionalism." In recent years a consensus has developed among historians of Nazism that the distinction is no longer fruitful and that both intentionalist and structuralist perspectives must be taken into consideration in explaining the origins of the Holocaust.[36]

NEO-CONSERVATIVE HISTORIOGRAPHY OF THE 1980s AND THE *HISTORIKERSTREIT*

The historiography of Nazi Germany inevitably reflected the shift in political climate to the right in the late 1970s and 1980s in the wake of a widening backlash against what many people came to consider an excessive swing to the left in the late 1960s and 1970s. The "new cold war" of the 1980s unleashed by the West following the elections of the hardline anti-communists Margaret Thatcher in Britain and Ronald Reagan in the United States found a historiographical echo in the renewed ascendancy of more right-wing interpretations of Nazism and renewed efforts to downplay its criminality or its centrality to German history. The furious debate among West German historians known as the *Historikerstreit* in 1986 offered a striking example of how political concerns can affect historical interpretations. It was no coincidence that this debate about the appropriate interpretation of Nazism and the causes of the Holocaust took place in the midst of a heated election campaign, in which conservative German chancellor Helmut Kohl narrowly won reelection on the promise of a more resolute defense against the dangers of Soviet and East German Communism than the left could be expected to provide.

The verdict of professional historians is that the *Historikerstreit* shed more heat than light on historical issues and that it contributed little of enduring value to historical scholarship. It was primarily a political conflict. Nonetheless, it must be included in any historiographical survey of Nazism for at least three reasons: first, it involved a wide array of influential historians (and other public figures) in West Germany, almost exclusively from the generation born before the Second World War; it also provided an important spur to detailed empirical investigations of the Holocaust in the 1990s; and third, it served as an object lesson of how closely linked historical interpretation often is to political ideology and how scholarship is sometimes at odds with personal memory and experience. The German historian Michael Stürmer (b. 1938), a leading spokesman for the ascendant conservatives, candidly admitted the political motive behind the conservative reinterpretation of Nazism: "The future is controlled by those who determine the content of memory, define the concepts, and interpret the past."[37] Stürmer believed that West Germans could not overcome the challenge posed by East German anti-fascism if they continued to labor under a burden of guilt about the Nazi past.

At the center of the dispute were two theses advanced by the historian Ernst Nolte, whose scholarly reputation rested on his widely praised study of fascist ideology in France, Italy, and Germany, *Three Faces of Fascism* (1963). Ironically, this book had contributed to the new wave of interest in generic fascism that challenged the ideologically driven totalitarianism theory of the cold war. Now, more than 20 years later, with the conservative backlash against the 1960s intellectual revolt in full swing, Nolte's publications helped to revive totalitarianism theory, although this time with an important and provocative modification. Nolte posited not only a parallelism between fascism and communism, a longstanding thesis on which all adherents of totalitarianism theory could more or less agree, but now also insisted that communism had caused the fascist reaction and had exceeded fascism in destructiveness and criminality.[38] For Nolte communism therefore bore greater responsibility for the atrocities of the twentieth century than National Socialism, which he presented as an understandable, albeit excessive, defensive reaction to the greater communist threat. According to Nolte, the racial murder of the Holocaust was an admittedly disproportionate, but not irrational, Nazi response to the class-based murders of the Soviet Gulag. Although Nolte denied any apologetic intent, he candidly admitted that his objective was to "normalize" National Socialism and free it of its stigma of unique criminality. He called for an end to the self-flagellating, anti-national "pedagogical historiography" of the 1960s with its left-wing didacticism and obsessive focus on German guilt.

The prominent left-liberal social philosopher Jürgen Habermas (b. 1929) unmasked the political motives behind Nolte's revisionism. Nolte's targets were feminists, pacifists, anti-imperialists, and leftists who, according to Nolte, had a vested interest in maintaining and manipulating the symbolic status of Nazism as absolute evil in order to achieve their left-wing political goals. Nolte found surprisingly numerous and vocal defenders among German historians anxious to reverse the leftward trend of the 1960s and 1970s. Nolte's defenders included conservative historians Joachim **Fest**, Klaus **Hildebrand**, Andreas **Hillgruber**, and Michael Stürmer. Fest, the author of a well-received biography of Hitler in 1975, pleaded for a tragic view of history, in which the Holocaust was only the most recent in a long sequence of historical catastrophes. Hildebrand commended Nolte for raising questions previously repressed by left-liberal ideological conformism. Hillgruber's book *Two Kinds of Downfall: The Destruction of the German Reich and the End of European Jewry* (1986) was written from a perspective sympathetic to the German soldiers fighting to hold back the Red Army in 1945 despite the fact that prolongation of the war kept the death factories working. Stürmer was concerned that the burden of German guilt about Nazism could weaken the West in the cold war.

Nolte's revisionism provided a new model for conservative apologetics. While previously conservatives could only hope to salvage their values and reputations by repudiating Nazism and denying any connection or relationship between their own conservative world-view and Nazism, Nolte boldly argued that Nazism, despite its extreme methods, was essentially redeemed by its fundamentally constructive and conservative goal of thwarting communism. Reversing the anti-fascist imagery of communists and socialists as the earliest victims of fascism, he portrayed conservatives and fascists as victims of the left, and communists as the original perpetrators of violence and repression. After the collapse of Communism in 1991 Nolte would claim that his positive juxtaposition of Nazism to Bolshevism had been borne out by history.

Nolte remained isolated in one respect, however, even among the many conservative historians who rose to defend him against the blistering critiques of liberal historians, including Hans and Wolfgang **Mommsen**, Eberhard **Jäckel**, Hans-Ulrich Wehler, and Heinrich **Winkler**, and the Marxist historian Reinhard **Kühnl**. What disquieted Nolte's fellow conservatives was not so much his rationalization of the Holocaust as a preventive action against the communist threat, but rather his frank avowal that fascism was a movement of the national or even international bourgeoisie against left-wing revolution. This was a greater concession to Marxist class analysis than most conservatives were willing to make. They welcomed the mitigation of the national stigma that Nolte's revisionism seemed to promise, but they objected to holding the bourgeoisie responsible for Nazism, as Nolte's description of Nazism as a bourgeois reaction to communism implied. Most of the younger historians of Germany's New Right, most prominently perhaps Rainer **Zitelmann**, preferred the older conservative interpretation advanced by Ritter, Meinecke, and Rothfels in the immediate aftermath of the war. These conservative historians had stressed the populist and revolutionary rather than the elitist and conservative nature of Nazism, thus implicitly taking the propertied and educated classes off the hook while incriminating the left-leaning working class.

THE NAZI CONSTITUENCY AND THE SOURCES OF NAZI POPULAR SUPPORT

Conservatives were able to draw on recent research on the Nazi constituency that had revised the long-accepted postulate, advanced by a number of Marxist and non-Marxist historians ever since the 1920s, that mass support for the Nazis came predominantly from the lower middle class of peasants and small proprietors opposed to both the liberal free market and the left-wing socialization of private property. Numerous studies since then have shown that the Nazis drew substantial support from sectors of the working class as well, thus giving greater credence to interpretations that denied the importance of bourgeois class interest in explanations of Nazism. While the middle classes were over-represented and the working class under-represented in both the Nazi Party and its electoral constituency, clearly the Nazis had succeeded in creating a broad-based party that could appeal to all sectors of society.[39]

Citing Hitler's "progressive" social policies, which included generous health, old-age, and family benefits, Zitelmann went so far as to argue that Hitler was more a revolutionary of the left than a counter-revolutionary of the right.[40] According to Zitelmann, Hitler's major motive in starting the war was to establish and defend a "socialist" social order in Europe. Zitelmann's interpretation allowed him to discredit the left by saddling it with Nazism and at the same time to embellish Nazism by linking it with modernizing and progressive forces. This was not an interpretation, however, that persuaded many historians, at least not until the appearance of a provocative book by the maverick German historian Götz Aly, *Hitlers Volksstaat*, in 2005. A critic of the Federal Republic's social policies, Aly argued that Hitler had bought the loyalty of his people by progressively taxing the rich, expanding the welfare state, and financing benefits to ordinary Germans by robbing Jews and the occupied peoples of Europe.[41] Aly's purpose, however, was not to incriminate socialism by tying it to Nazism nor to rehabilitate Nazism by demonstrating its progressive features, as Zitelmann had sought to do. Rather, as a former Marxist writing in the tradition of historical materialism, he sought to explain the German people's support for Hitler on the basis of their material interests, not their irrational racist ideology. Critics like Hans-Ulrich Wehler accused him of downplaying racism as a motivating factor in public support for Nazism; but this judgement was excessively harsh.[42] It would be more accurate to say that for Aly racism was not the only or even the principal factor in explaining the popular support the Nazis enjoyed in Germany up to 1945, despite the hardships of a war they would eventually lose.

A more telling critique of *Hitlers Volksstaat* was delivered by the young British economic historian Adam **Tooze**, who accused Aly of exaggerating German material prosperity during the Nazi era and using spurious accounting methods for measuring the costs of the war. According to Tooze, Aly overstated the proportion of German war costs financed by plunder and understated the financial demands made by the state on the German population. Aly's main mistake was to assume that through deficit financing the Nazis were able to postpone the costs of financing the war to future generations. In actual fact, military spending, however it was financed, could only come at the expense of other economic activity, including social services. Tooze convincingly showed that while Hitler's policies brought some material benefits to all sectors of the population at least until 1942, national income was redistributed away from the working population in favor of the owners of capital throughout the Nazi era.[43] The German historian Michael Wildt (b. 1954) accused Aly of associating social egalitarianism with Nazism in order to discredit the post-war German welfare state, the seeds of which were supposedly sown in the Nazi period. Not surprisingly, Aly's thesis of Nazism as a redistributive *Gefälligkeitsdiktatur* (conciliatory dictatorship) was triumphantly publicized in Germany's right-wing press.[44]

THE MODERNIZATION DEBATE

The relationship of Nazism to modernization is a question that cuts across many aspects of the historiography of Nazism. Was Nazism a modernizing movement or is it more accurately classified as anti-modern, dedicated to holding back the forces of modernity, especially the social and cultural effects of industrialization, including urbanization, demographic mobility, secularization, economic rationalization, liberalization, democratization, and openness to innovation and experimentation in the arts? Based on the Nazis' own avowed opposition to the ideals of the Enlightenment and the French Revolution, most historians have assumed that Nazism looked predominantly to the pre-industrial, pre-democratic, and pre-modern past for its social and cultural models. Certainly the Nazi ideology of "**blood and soil**," idealizing the aristocratic notions of pedigree, the chivalric warrior ethos, the Germanic tribal past, and the rural virtues of a stable agrarian society, seemed to be oriented toward the past. The arguments for Nazism as an anti-modernizing movement were summarized in the American historian Henry **Turner**'s article, "Fascism and Modernization" (1975).[45] On the other hand, the Nazis claimed to be ushering in a brave new world of scientific and technological innovation, sloughing off the detritus of the past, and reorganizing society to better meet the challenges of the future. American historian Jeffrey **Herf** coined the term "reactionary modernism" to describe the typically Nazi combination of reactionary ideology and innovative technology.[46]

Like so many other controversies about Nazism, the question of whether it should be classified as a modernizing or an anti-modern movement is politically freighted as well. Some scholars committed to totalitarianism theory, such as the right-wing political scientist A. J. Gregor (b. 1929), have argued that fascism was a developmental ideology, thus placing it into the same future-oriented category as communism.[47] The debate on the Nazis' modernizing proclivities was joined by the publication of the liberal German sociologist Ralf **Dahrendorf**'s *Society and Democracy in Germany* in 1965 and American historian David **Schoenbaum**'s *Hitler's Social Revolution* in 1966. Both of these texts argued that the Nazis had unintentionally contributed to Germany's modernization by destroying the traditional institutions that had blocked such social aspects of modernization as vocational mobility, the weakening of class status, the liberalization of the economy, and the loosening of traditional ties to region and religion. While Dahrendorf and Schoenbaum emphasized that modernization was the unintended consequence of Nazi rule, an outcome that contradicted the Nazis' own avowed aims, conservative historians like Gregor and Zitelmann insisted that modernization was a deliberate result of Nazi policy.[48] The American historian Peter Fritzsche (b. 1959), long an advocate of the view that Nazism was a revolutionary rather than counter-revolutionary movement, went even further, contending that the Nazis were not only modernizers but "modernists."[49] But even in the realm of technology, where Germans pioneered the construction of long-range missiles and jet aircraft toward the end of the war, Nazi Germany lagged behind the technological advances in the West, as pointed out by British historians Alan Milward (b. 1935) in *The German War Economy* (1966) and Richard Overy in *War and Economy in the Third Reich* (1994). Hans Mommsen, too, questioned "the myth of Nazi modernization," pointing out that the self-destructive Nazi regime failed to pave the way to modernity in any positive sense.[50]

The earlier consensus on Nazism as an anti-modern movement that effected modernizing changes (or at least cleared the ground for such changes) despite its atavistic ideological commitments was challenged by the sociologist Zygmunt **Bauman** in his 1989 book, *Modernity and the Holocaust*. Bauman wrote of "the gnawing suspicion" that the Holocaust (and by extension Nazism) "was not an antithesis of modern civilization" but rather that it "could merely have uncovered another face of the same modern society whose other, more familiar, face [its progressive features] we so admire."[51] For Bauman, a bureaucratic culture in which decisions are based on functional efficiency rather than moral values was a necessary (though not sufficient) precondition of the Holocaust. Bauman denied that anti-Semitism, however pervasive in Europe, would have culminated in genocide if the instrumental rationality so typical of the modern age had not blinded perpetrators to the ethical implications of their actions.

POSTMODERN APPROACHES

In demonstrating how the complex dialectic of supposedly civilizing rationality could pervert and stifle the claims of morality and lead to unprecedented evil, Bauman may have been influenced by postmodernist critiques pioneered in particular by theorists in France. Implicit in postmodern analyses is a critique of the legacy of the Enlightenment, the intellectual revolution that ushered in the modern age. While postmodernists celebrated the emancipating features of the Enlightenment – its values of individual liberty and social equality – they contended that its rationalistic claims to universal truth and validity had the (perhaps unintended) effects of excluding dissent and difference and of marginalizing "the other." In Bauman's description the Holocaust appears as a thoroughly modern product of "rational" social engineering.

The German historian Detlev **Peukert** likewise traced the origins of the Holocaust to modern "scientific" eugenic schemes and other forms of social planning closely linked to modernization. Peukert argued that modern fantasies of omnipotence and confidence in the powers of rationality led not (or not only) to liberal democracy but also to bureaucratic repression and control. His critique challenged the modernization theory (the notion that lack of modernization made Germany susceptible to a particularly violent form of modernization) that underlay Dahrendorf's work and the Bielefeld School's narrative of Germany's deviant development. "Many non-democratic tendencies in Germany," Peukert wrote, "did not so much go back to a persisting reactionary tradition as arise quite functionally out of the structures and problems of modern civilization."[52] It was Germany's very modernity, Peukert contended, not its backwardness, as adherents of modernization theory claimed, that gave rise to Nazi atrocities. Influenced both by Horkheimer and Adorno's seminal *The Dialectic of Enlightenment* (1946) and by Michel Foucault's (1926–1984) analyses of how power and control were exercised through rational discourse and the instrumentalization of reason and knowledge in the modern era, Peukert explored the "crises" and "pathologies" of modernity in studies of Weimar and Nazi Germany and insisted that the horrors of Nazism required the "skeptical de-coupling of modernity and progress."[53]

Peukert was also a proponent of cultural – as opposed to exclusively socio-political – history and a critical practitioner of a multi-perspectival approach known in Germany as *Alltagsgeschichte* (everyday history). This informal movement of historians focusing on local studies and the day-to-day experiences of ordinary people gained adherents in the 1970s and 1980s, especially among younger historians looking for alternatives to the traditional preoccupation of historians with ruling elites and leading individuals. One of the models for everyday history was the "Bavaria Project" of social history under the direction of Martin Broszat, a multi-volume exploration of various forms of popular reaction to Nazi rule.[54] Among the most successful practitioners of this innovative genre were Lutz Niethammer (b. 1939) and Alf Lüdtke (b. 1943), who published several detailed studies of working-class culture in nineteenth- and twentieth-century Germany.[55]

The shift to *Alltagsgeschichte* also marked a generational shift, propelled as it was by younger historians born during and after the war and no longer as worried as the "Bielefeld generation" that exploring and revealing the complexities of German society in the Nazi years might impede democracy in the Federal Republic by attenuating the German public's sense of responsibility for the evil of Nazism. The new cultural history of the 1980s and 1990s stressed the human dimension of history – how people perceived and experienced historical situations, a dimension supposedly neglected by social historians whose primary interest lay in analyzing the structural elements of history and society to educate the nation in democracy. Not surprisingly, such prominent social historians as Hans-Ulrich Wehler reacted critically to *Alltagsgeschichte*, questioning whether its micro-historical approach could ever adequately explain major historical developments.[56]

Critics of *Alltagsgeschichte* also worried that focusing on the everyday experiences of ordinary people might normalize and trivialize the Nazi period and gloss over its terrible crimes. This was a topic of dispute in an important exchange between the German historian Martin Broszat and the Israeli-American historian Saul **Friedländer** in *Vierteljahrshefte für Zeitgeschichte* in 1988.[57] While Broszat called for the "historicization" of Nazi Germany, based on the assumption that moral sensitivity to Nazi crimes can only come from the same careful historical reconstruction and understanding that historians bring to other historical topics, Friedländer warned of the dangers in any approach that did not implicitly or explicitly acknowledge the unique criminality of Nazism. Friedländer was skeptical both of Broszat's summons to investigate the Nazi period with the same detached scholarly methods as any other period of history and his demand to incorporate the Nazi period more fully into German history by tracing the long-term social continuities that bridged the Nazi era. Friedländer particularly objected to the kind of empathetic treatment of **Wehrmacht** soldiers that Hillgruber had demonstrated in his controversial book, *Two Kinds of Downfall* (1986).

The most controversial aspect of postmodern influence on the historiography of Nazism has been postmodern skepticism about whether history of the past can ever be reliably objective or fully known. What is sometimes referred to as the "linguistic turn" – the notion that the language historians use to communicate their findings and perceptions does not necessarily signify any essential reality – potentially undermines confidence in the ability of historians ever to render a fully authoritative or truthful account of the past. A representative example of such postmodern skepticism about "master narratives" was the collaborative effort of historians Konrad R. Jarausch (b. 1941) and Michael Geyer (b. 1947), *Shattered Past: Reconstructing German Histories* (2002). Jarausch and Geyer debunked both Marxist and non-Marxist "metanarratives," encouraging historians instead to "reassemble the fragments of the central European past into new patterns" from diverse perspectives.[58]

Since all narrative accounts of the past are lingually constructed from a particular perspective, no narrative can lay claim to the exclusive truth. Some postmodern theorists even doubted the possibility of distinguishing historical facts from historians' interpretations, thus questioning one of the traditional axioms of objective historical method. The British historian Richard **Evans** launched a strong attack on this form of relativism in his book *In Defense of History* in 1997. Evans worried that postmodernism offered no position from which Holocaust denial could be effectively refuted. This was contradicted by defenders of postmodernism, such as the British historian Kevin Passmore (b. 1958), who pointed out that while all historical narratives may be fallible attempts to make sense of the past, some *do* make greater sense than others. Factually correct histories cannot be used arbitrarily to serve any political cause. Even postmodernists do not deny the possibility of distinguishing between historical statements and moral or political judgements. Historical method does not lose its validity, even if ultimate truth is unknowable, bias of some kind is unavoidable, or the empirical evidence is subject to differing interpretations. Just because truth claims cannot be established absolutely does not mean that none can be established beyond a reasonable doubt. Holocaust denial is illegitimate because the historical methods of Holocaust deniers are defective. Since Holocaust deniers operate on conspiratorial assumptions – they dismiss any evidence that refutes their claims as part of a wider conspiracy of deception – their hypotheses are ultimately impossible to falsify and therefore fail to pass the most rudimentary test of scientific method.[59]

THE GOLDHAGEN CONTROVERSY

Postmodern approaches to the historiography of Nazism and the Holocaust have been particularly controversial, because skepticism about "master narratives," the constructedness of history, and the validity of any single historical perspective seemed to undermine the possibility of a definitive explanation of the causes of the major catastrophe of the twentieth century. Postmodern emphasis on wider developments in Western civilization as explanatory factors in the history of Nazism and the Holocaust seemed to dilute the specifically German responsibility for the catastrophe as implied in more linear *Sonderweg* interpretations. Daniel **Goldhagen**'s best-selling book, *Hitler's Willing Executioners* (1996), may be read as a stinging rebuke both to Ernst Nolte's denial of the unique criminality of Nazism in the *Historikerstreit* and to postmodern "relativizing" approaches in general. Goldhagen attributed the Holocaust exclusively to an allegedly uniquely German "eliminationist" anti-Semitism that had supposedly informed German history and culture for centuries and reached its climax in the Nazi era.

Goldhagen's blanket rejection of any interpretation that might seem to diminish specifically German responsibility for the Holocaust led him to the opposite extreme of an overly narrow determinism. While acknowledging the value of his empirical findings on the Nazi labor camps, the death marches in the late stages of the war, and the extent of complicity of ordinary Germans, Goldhagen's critics rejected his monocausal explanation of the Holocaust.[60] Goldhagen's extreme version of Germany's ideological and cultural *Sonderweg* failed to explain the far greater prevalence of anti-Semitism in the Russian Empire before the First World War or the sometimes enthusiastic participation of other nations and ethnic groups in the Holocaust. It also failed to offer a convincing explanation of why the Nazis successfully rose to power after the First World War. As the American historian Doris Bergen (b. 1960) wrote in a searching critique, "Goldhagen neglects both the non-German perpetrators and the non-perpetrator Germans."[61] His exclusive focus on German anti-Semitism led him to oversimplify perpetrator motivation, reducing it almost entirely to hatred of Jews while rejecting the situational and contingent motives set forth in Christopher Browning's path-breaking book, *Ordinary Men* (1992).[62] Nonetheless, the Goldhagen controversy did lead to renewed and productive research in the 1990s, both on the motivation of perpetrators and on the experiences of victims. It reinforced public consciousness of the specificity of Jewish suffering and reemphasized the importance of ideology in understanding the Holocaust.

Goldhagen's focus on a uniquely German anti-Semitism, although much less original than he claimed it to be, also breached some of the constraints placed on interpretations of the Third Reich by cold war politics. The Western interest in courting West German support for the NATO alliance was not well served by incriminating ordinary Germans or burdening them with an undue sense of guilt about their past. Goldhagen himself understood this potential damage to Western unity by assuring his readers that Germany's endemic anti-Semitism had not survived beyond 1945.[63] Ironically, in reaching this conservative and somewhat inconsistent conclusion, Goldhagen pleased the German nationalist right while disappointing German progressives who had welcomed Goldhagen's book for galvanizing public attention on German responsibility for Nazi atrocities and thus strengthening the ethos of democratic citizenship in the Federal Republic.[64]

HISTORIOGRAPHY OF THE NAZI ERA AFTER THE COLLAPSE OF COMMUNISM AND GERMAN REUNIFICATION

The end of the cold war and the collapse of Communism from 1989 to 1991 was bound to give more conservative historical perspectives on the Third Reich at least a temporary boost while diminishing the credibility of Marxist interpretations. In the 1990s, as the Goldhagen controversy attested, the trend that had started in the 1980s away from structural social history toward a reemphasis on ideology and culture also continued. The emphasis on class analysis in the 1960s and 1970s was supplanted by a renewed emphasis on the overriding importance of race, perhaps most authoritatively in Michael **Burleigh** and Wolfgang **Wippermann**'s *The Racial State* (1991). This book, however, bucked the generally conservative trend by contesting the right-wing revisionist efforts of Zitelmann and others to exploit the putative modernity of the Third Reich and the demand for the "historicization" of Nazism for conservative purposes. The transition of 1989–1990 also led to a revival of totalitarianism theory as historians focused attention on the failed East German regime, which was often compared to the Third Reich, especially by Noltean conservatives anxious to discredit communism and draw a *Schlussstrich* (bottom line) under the "negative nationalism" that had supposedly distorted the historiography of Nazism in the Federal Republic as a result of the 1960s turn to the left.

Another conservative trope, Nazism as a "political religion" (first put forth in 1938 by the German-American political philosopher Eric Voegelin [1901–1985] in his book *Die politischen Religionen*, which blamed Nazism and communism on secular humanism), was also revived in Germany and Britain, most notably in Michael Burleigh's vividly written *The Third Reich* (2003). According to this analysis, Nazism (like Soviet Communism) operated as a religious cult, generating fervent belief among its followers by adopting the rituals and liturgical practices of organized religion to appeal to a population in which Christianity was losing its hold. In implying that Nazism (like communism) was a consequence of secularization and the abandonment of true religion, Burleigh rehearsed a familiar argument of religious conservatives. While not denying the power of Nazi rituals, critics of this theory, particularly younger scholars such as the American historian Richard Steigmann-Gall (b. 1965) and the British historian Neil Gregor (b. 1969), questioned the usefulness of "political religion" as an analytical concept, recommending the notion of "religious politics" as a better way of understanding the relationship of Nazism to religion. Viewing Nazism as a political religion had the effect of de-politicizing Nazism by diverting attention from its ideological content to its ceremonial form and style. It also had the perhaps unintended effect of explaining Nazism as a consequence of secularization and the loss of faith in "true religion" (i.e., Christianity).[65] In his provocative book, *The Holy Reich: Nazi Conceptions of Christianity* (2003), Steigmann-Gall provided a needed corrective to the conventional view of Nazism as a predominantly atheistic, neo-pagan, or secular movement. Instead, Steigmann-Gall argued, it is better understood as a movement that sought to transcend confessional differences in rallying Germans and Christians against the "godless" secularism of the Weimar Republic and the Soviet Union.

GERMANS AS PERPETRATORS

As was the case in the Goldhagen controversy, the end of the cold war reopened questions that had previously been neglected or taboo, such as the extent of support of ordinary Germans for Nazism and the degree of involvement of ordinary Germans in Nazi atrocities. One result of the eclipse of Marxist historiography was the recognition that Nazism was much more broadly anchored in German society than Marxist notions of economic determinism, especially the ritualized anti-fascism of the former German Democratic Republic, would permit. Robert **Gellately**'s widely discussed book, *Backing Hitler: Consent and Coercion in Nazi Germany* (2001), spoke of Hitler's Germany as a dictatorship based on consensus in which coercion and terror was directed against outsiders, but not against the vast majority of law-abiding Germans. By focusing his attention mainly on the period after the Nazis' violent consolidation of power in 1933 and 1934, however, Gellately may have understated not only the role that coercion played in assuring the submissiveness of the German population in the first place but also the full range of tensions between populace and party-state that obtained throughout the period of Nazi rule.[66]

Omer **Bartov**'s 1992 book, *Hitler's Army*, dispelled the post-war myth of the Wehrmacht as a professional army operating under a chivalric military code. Bartov documented Wehrmacht war crimes as well as the wide-ranging cooperation between regular army units and the SS killing squads in the campaign against the Soviet Union. Bartov also criticized West German historiography of the Wehrmacht in the immediate post-war era for perpetuating the legends of "the army's aloofness from the regime, the soldiers' professionalism, 'correctness,' and devotion (to the Fatherland, not the Führer), the generals' abhorrence of and opposition to the crimes of the SS, their rigidly upright conduct and their strict adherence to moral codes and soldierly standards . . ."[67] While acknowledging that this apologetic view had changed significantly in the 1960s and 1970s, Bartov criticized the mammoth and authoritative multi-volume history of the Second World War begun in 1979 by the semi-official Militärgeschichtliches Forschungsamt (Research Office for Military History) in Freiburg and Potsdam for failing to incorporate any perspectives of the new cultural history or any discussion of the Holocaust in its remarkably detailed account of the war.[68]

The controversy surrounding a traveling photographic exhibit of Wehrmacht crimes sponsored by the Hamburg Institute for Social Research in 1995 attested to the fact that the myth of the untainted Wehrmacht was slow to die. The exhibit drew protests from the nationalist right for allegedly insulting the reputation of honorable German soldiers. The exhibit was forced to shut down in 1999 when several photographs of mass killings in the Polish-Ukrainian town of Zloczow in early July 1941 were mistakenly attributed to the Wehrmacht rather than the Soviet NKVD. During their occupation of Polish territory in accordance with the Nazi–Soviet Pact, Soviet secret police had executed a number of anti-communist Ukrainian and Polish nationalists. Right-wing critics of the exhibit seized on these inaccuracies to discredit the exhibit and dispute Wehrmacht involvement in the Holocaust. Careful analysis of the photographs showed, however, that the vast majority of Zloczow photographs were indeed of Jews killed by the Nazis. Moreover these 1941 photographs had been deliberately manipulated by local German commanders at the time who had falsely claimed that this visual evidence of the killing of Jews actually showed the murder of Ukrainians by Jewish citizens favoring Soviet rule. By linking the Jewish population to Communist aggression and brutality, Nazi commanders deliberately sought to encourage Wehrmacht soldiers to continue murdering Jews.[69]

GERMANS AS VICTIMS

Growing German self-confidence after German reunification was also reflected in a new kind of revisionism, the increasing tendency to portray ordinary Germans not as perpetrators but as victims of war crimes, thus breaking an unspoken taboo in the Federal Republic since the 1960s. German suffering, formerly personified by the millions of German refugees expelled from their homelands in Poland, Czechoslovakia, and other Eastern European states at the end of the war, was now evoked in a number of publications that drew attention to Germans as victims of the brutal Allied strategy of carpet bombing civilian targets. The Anglo-German writer W. G. Sebald's (1944–2001) 1999 book, *The Air War and Literature* (misleadingly translated into English as *The Natural History of Destruction* [2003]), had called attention to the fact that German writers had largely ignored the ordeal of bombing victims in their literary output after the war. Sebald traced this apparent failure of German authors to empathize with civilian suffering to their fear of appearing to exculpate Germany from responsibility for the start of murderous aerial warfare.

Although Sebald exaggerated this alleged repression of German memory (the air war had in fact been the subject of a number of studies beginning in the 1950s), his strictures did spawn several books that graphically described the destructiveness of Allied bombing, at times using the kind of language usually reserved for descriptions of the Holocaust. The works of military historian Jörg Friedrich (b. 1944), particularly *The Fire: The Bombing of Germany, 1940–1945* (2002; English translation, 2006), were particularly controversial, popularizing the notion that the Allies had deliberately applied excessive force against German civilians at a time when Germany was already effectively defeated. However, in the debate that followed it became clear that renewed emphasis on German victimization had not diminished Germany's official acceptance of moral responsibility for Nazi crimes or the Second World War. If anything the culture of remembrance and contrition is even stronger in a united Germany than it was before.[70]

GERMANS AS HISTORIANS OF NAZISM AND THE HOLOCAUST

Contrary to widely expressed fears at the time, the transition of 1989–1990 has not had the effect of displacing Nazism either in public memory or in the field of historical studies. Scholarly research into the Nazi era continued unabated in Germany throughout the 1990s and shows no sign of slowing in the twenty-first century. In contrast to the 1960s and 1970s, when the years from 1933 to 1939 were generally viewed as paradigmatic of Nazism, the focus of academic scholarship has dramatically shifted to the war and the Holocaust. **Auschwitz** is now generally deemed as embodying the core of Nazism. Younger German historians, notably Christian **Gerlach**, Dieter Pohl (b. 1964), Thomas Sandkühler (b. 1962), and Wolf Gruner (b. 1960), have contributed thoroughly researched monographs on various aspects of the Holocaust. The discovery of new documents in the archives of the former Soviet bloc has also given an enormous boost to research on the Third Reich, resulting in particular in numerous detailed local or regional studies on the implementation of the Holocaust in Eastern Europe. Gerlach, for instance, discovered that Hitler had announced the onset of the extermination program to a closed meeting of Nazi Party district leaders on December 12, 1941, one day after the German declaration of war against the United States. Gerlach thus reopened the much-debated and still unsettled question of when (or even whether) Hitler made the decision to kill all Jews under German control. Other important documents surfacing after the collapse of the Soviet system included **Himmler**'s personal appointment calendar and previously undiscovered sections of **Goebbels**'s diary.

Numerous private corporations in Germany, as well as government agencies, have sponsored independent historical inquiries into their institutional histories during the Second World War, some of them by non-German historians.[71] Even the Foreign Ministry, the government agency that had perhaps the highest proportion of holdovers from the Third Reich, has now launched an independent examination of its compromised past by an international team of historians headed by Eckart Conze (b. 1963). The historical profession in Germany had been slow to address its own Nazi past, but that has changed as well. The generation of German historians born after the war, notably Götz **Aly**, Michael Fahlbusch, Ingo Haar, Peter Schöttler (b. 1950), and Willi Oberkrome (b. 1959), have turned a critical eye on their own profession, excoriating the alleged reluctance of the first post-war generation of historians (the "1945ers," also sometimes referred to as "the Hitler Youth generation") to delve into the Nazi background of their own mentors, many of whom, it turned out, had actively collaborated with the Nazi regime before and during the war.[72] Prominent historians such as Dieter Erdmann (1910–1990), and particularly Werner Conze (1910–1986) and Theodor Schieder (1909–1984), both of whom had studied under Hans Rothfels before the war and served as mentors to Hans-Ulrich Wehler, Hans Mommsen, and Jürgen Kocka's generation of social historians after the war, got their start in the service of the Nazi regime.

At a dramatic session of the biennial conference of the German Historical Association in 1998 the younger cohort of German historians accused Wehler's generation of failing to challenge their mentors' involvement with Nazism. At the heart of this generational dispute were questions about historical method and the interpretation of Nazism. Putting social structures and processes at the center of historical explanation supposedly made it possible for Wehler's generation to avoid issues of personal agency or belief.[73] Aly and his fellow critics went so far as to suggest, rather implausibly, that the social history of Wehler's generation was directly derived from the politicized *Volksgeschichte* (ethnohistory) practiced by their mentors in the Nazi era. While Conze and Schieder's generation of historians lent their expertise to validating German racial supremacy and the Nazis' claims to foreign territory, Wehler's social history was based on a firm commitment to liberal democracy. However questionable their substantive conclusions about their predecessors may have been, there is no doubt that the attack on structural social history by the younger generation of cultural historians reinforced the absolutely central role that the history and memory of Nazism continues to play in the formation of German national identity.

The younger historians also insisted, in contrast to Wehler's interpretation, that Nazism was a product of modernizing, not anti-modern, forces. In contrast to the period immediately after the war, Nazism is no longer understood as primarily the consequence of Germany's political backwardness, but more as a phenomenon of modernity. Another positive achievement of this latest dispute among German historians was to document lines of continuities that bridged the end of the Second World War in Europe. The notion that the study of Nazism can be limited to the years of the Third Reich between 1933 and 1945 is no longer tenable. Just as the first post-war generation of historians demonstrated continuities across the year 1933, so later generations have refused to accept 1945 as a barrier hermetically sealing off Nazism from the German successor states. Denazification, *Vergangenheitsbewältigung*, and the history of memory have attracted scholarly attention as discrete fields that have the potential of opening up new perspectives on Nazism and its role in history.[74] After 1990 the historiography of Nazism has not only been extended into previously neglected areas but also enriched by the new methods of cultural studies. As Marxist social and economic analyses fell out of fashion they were replaced – or at least augmented to some extent – by critical cultural and gender studies based on the post-structuralist theories of Michel Foucault and Jacques Derrida. The new cultural history has given rise to many studies dealing not directly with the Nazi period but with the way Nazism has been represented and remembered.[75]

NEW SYNTHESES

The many new findings of a host of historians from Germany and other nations in the last decade and a half have contributed to the scope and authority of several new large-scale syntheses of the Nazi era in English. These include Ian Kershaw's definitive two-volume biography of Hitler (1998 and 2000), based on Max Weber's concept of "charismatic leadership"; Michael Burleigh's *The Third Reich* (2000), highlighting the Nazis' irrational racial fanaticism while perhaps unduly dismissing rational explanations for genocide based on economic interests; the first two volumes of Richard Evans's comprehensive and judicious history of Nazism, *The Coming of the Third Reich* (2003) and *The Third Reich in Power, 1933–1939* (2005); Götz Aly's *Hitler's Beneficiaries* (2006); and Christopher Browning's (with contributions by Jürgen Matthäus) authoritative *The Origins of the Final Solution* (2004), the first volume of a comprehensive history of the Holocaust published under the auspices of Yad Vashem, the Holocaust memorial museum established in Jerusalem in 1953. The long-awaited second volume of Saul Friedländer's *Nazi Germany and the Jews* will appear in English in 2007, giving due attention to victim perspectives of the Holocaust. A number of German syntheses, most notably perhaps Peter **Longerich**'s *Politics of Destruction* (1998), will soon appear in English translation as well.

Perhaps the most provocative recent historical synthesis of scholarship on Nazism is the young British economic historian Adam Tooze's *The Wages of Destruction: The Making and Breaking of the Nazi Economy* (2006), which proposes a new paradigm explaining the Nazi regime in terms of the rising challenges posed to Germany's position in the global system both by the enormous potential military power of the United States and by the seductive appeal of American affluence and economic dynamism to the German population. Tooze offered an explanation that accounted for the stunning contradiction between the Nazis' reckless genocidal practices and their urgent need for additional labor to fight the war successfully. While traditional accounts have interpreted this contradiction as evidence of the absolute primacy of Nazi racial ideology over pragmatic economic interests, Tooze suggested that Nazi policies are more usefully interpreted as "a compromise between the more and less ideological elements of the Nazi regime." Tooze identified the looming food crisis in Germany in 1942 as one connecting link between economic pragmatism and genocide. "The overriding need to improve the food situation," he wrote, "actually created a perverse functional connection between the extermination of the Jewish population of the General Government and the improvement in food rations that was necessary to sustain the labor force working in the mines and factories of the Reich."[76]

The growing library of works on the Nazi era all attest to the widely acknowledged need to integrate the history of Nazism not only into German history but into European, Western, and world history in ways that can help to explain this extraordinary historical experience but do not understate its uniquely genocidal features. The extreme nature of Nazi racial policies and the Holocaust will continue to provide the greatest challenges to the powers of historiographical explanation. Divergent interpretations are likely to continue to generate controversy, not only because such divergences often reflect present-day discontents and political differences but also because efforts to understand, explain, and contextualize Nazism cannot entirely avoid running the risk of appearing to mitigate moral condemnation by making it comprehensible. In the case of Nazism, however, to understand is in no way to excuse. Historians must assume that rational explanations of past catastrophes are possible if they are to retain confidence in their craft and hope for the future. An argument can be made that as a result of the many thorough investigations into the Nazi experience world opinion has today become more sensitive to the extraordinary destructiveness of right-wing movements based on assumptions of national, racial, or cultural supremacy and bent on national, racial, or cultural dominance over other peoples. Heirs to the unparalleled stigma of Nazism, Germans have perhaps learned the bitter lessons of national hubris better than the citizens of any other nation. United Germany's positive national identity today is based in good part on repudiation of any apologetics for the Nazi past, on vigilance against recurrences of Nazi attitudes and practices in the present, on a shared sense of obligation to remember the millions of victims of Nazism, and on a continued commitment to conscientious scholarly investigations into its causes, its crimes, and its consequences.

4

A–Z OF HISTORIANS

- *This list is necessarily highly selective, restricted mainly to historians born before 1960. It includes only a small number of younger historians whose research has had a particular impact on the historiography of Nazism.*
- *Most of the works cited have been published in English. Titles of untranslated books are given in their original language or are otherwise identified as not having been translated into English.*

A

ALY, GÖTZ (b. 1947) One of the most innovative and provocative of German historians, Aly stirred up controversy in the 1980s and 1990s by arguing that there were rational, economic motives driving the murder of the Jews in the **Holocaust**. In the eyes of his critics (such as the British historian Michael **Burleigh**), attributing rational, utilitarian motives to Nazi perpetrators risked diluting the "absolute evil" of Nazism. Aly's revelations of the complicity of mid-level academic and bureaucratic officials in the planning of the **Final Solution**, however, were based on thorough research and have gained general acceptance among historians. His 1991 book, co-authored with Susanne Heim (b. 1955), *Architects of Annihilation: Auschwitz and the Logic of Destruction* (English trans. 2002), dealt with the *Schreibtischtäter* (desk-bound perpetrators) who drew up plans for population transfers in Eastern

Europe in the early 1940s to combat the perceived problem of agrarian "over-population" and create space for German colonization. Although Aly and Heim may have exaggerated the influence of population planners on Nazi decision-making, their research revealed the close linkage between German settlement policies in the east and the Holocaust. Their interpretation – epitomized in their provocative phrase, "the economy of the final solution" – was controversial because in emphasizing bureaucratic plans aimed at economic modernization and rationalization in the causation of the Holocaust, Aly and Heim seemed to downplay the significance of irrational racial ideology. Aly summarized his findings in his major work, *"The Final Solution": Nazi Population Policy and the Murder of the European Jews*, translated into English in 1999.

In the late 1990s Aly, along with his younger colleagues Ingo Haar, Michael Fahlbusch, Willi Oberkrome (b. 1959), and Peter Schöttler (b. 1950), prodded the German historical profession into examining its own complicity in the Nazi regime. They were particularly critical of the generation of German historians who had entered the profession immediately after the war (including the renowned social historian Hans-Ulrich **Wehler**) for failing to acknowledge or question the Nazi backgrounds of their own mentors, among them such prominent post-war historians as Werner Conze (1910–1986) and Theodor Schieder (1909–1984). Aly's latest book, *Hitlers Volksstaat* (translated as *Hitler's Beneficiaries*), published in 2005, again aroused controversy by suggesting that the Nazis implemented progressive social policies such as universal health insurance and higher old-age pensions to gain and retain the allegiance of the German people. Aly's main contribution, however, was to have shown how these policies were made possible by ruthless expropriation and exploitation of Jews and the conquered people of Europe. Ordinary Germans, not just elites, profited from Nazi conquests. Aly argued that the economic benefits derived from Nazi conquests and persecution of the Jews accounted for the low level of popular opposition, let alone resistance, in the **Third Reich** after the consolidation of the regime. His materialist analysis offered a corrective to what he regarded as excessively apologetic or misleading explanations for the popularity of the Nazi dictatorship. He denied that Germans were forced into compliance by terror or that the German populace was seduced by Hitler's uncanny charisma or racial **propaganda**. However, the accuracy of Aly's calculations of how the war was financed was disputed by Adam **Tooze**. Aly understated the material sacrifices required of the German people and overstated the generosity of Nazi welfare policies.

ARENDT, HANNAH (1906–1975) One of the leading political thinkers of the twentieth century, Arendt was born of Russian-Jewish parents in Germany, studied Christian theology at the University of Marburg (and philosophy with Martin **Heidegger**), and completed a dissertation on St Augustine under Karl Jaspers at the University of Heidelberg in 1929. In 1933 she sought refuge from the Nazis in Paris, eventually coming to the US with her husband Heinrich Blücher in 1941. Two of her many works have exercised particular influence on the historiography of Nazism: *The Origins of Totalitarianism* (1951) and *Eichmann in Jerusalem* (1963). Arendt traced the origins of **totalitarianism** to nineteenth-century racism and imperialism. Her work helped to popularize the notion of totalitarianism as a novel form of twentieth-century dictatorship by pointing to parallels in the tyrannies of **Hitler** and Stalin, despite their ideological differences. By mobilizing the atomized masses around their respective ideologies both regimes adopted a form of rule that made unprecedented mass murder possible, thus marking a radical break in European history and Western civilization. Yet in *Eichmann in Jerusalem*, a report on the trial of Adolf **Eichmann** in Israel in 1961 that drew on the research of Raul **Hilberg**, Arendt struck a different note, emphasizing "the banality of evil" and the potentially pernicious effects of bureaucratic careerism. Her portrait of Eichmann as a colorless but ambitious bureaucrat scrupulously following orders, rather than as a demonic sadist or virulent **anti-Semite**, aroused controversy by seeming to diminish his wickedness; her purpose, though, was not to trivialize the evil of the **Holocaust** but rather to warn that the failure to understand the "normality" of many perpetrators was to ignore the dangers of similar horrors occurring in other states under different historical conditions. Her critics accused her of slighting anti-Semitism as a driving factor in the Holocaust so as to emphasize the genocidal potential residing in modern states. Her criticism of the role of some members of the **Jewish Councils** in collaborating with the Nazis aroused controversy as well, but it also stimulated further research that has borne out some of her contentions.

B

BANKIER, DAVID (b. 1947) Head of Research at Yad Vashem, the **Holocaust** memorial in Jerusalem, Bankier is a leading authority on **anti-Semitism** in German public opinion during the Nazi era. In *The Germans and the Final Solution* (1992) Bankier concluded that awareness of the Holocaust was widespread among the German public, in part because the Nazi leadership itself chose to break the secret to create shared liability and "to make people realize that there was no way back."[1] Bankier has also edited and co-edited several volumes on the Holocaust, including *Probing the Depths of German Antisemitism* (2000), *The Holocaust: History and Memory* (2001), *Nazi Europe and the Final Solution* (2003), and *The Jews Are Coming Back* (2005).

BARKAI, AVRAHAM (b. 1921) Israeli historian whose books, *Nazi Economics: Ideology, Theory, and Policy* (1990) and *From Boycott to Annihilation: The Economic Struggle of German Jews* (1989), are standard works on the Nazi economy

and the "**aryanization**" of Jewish property. Barkai stressed the importance of the ideology of *Volksgemeinschaft* in legitimating the economic extrusion of the Jews and ultimately the "**final solution**." Barkai has also contributed essays to a number of collections on the Nazi economy, the Jewish experience in Nazi Germany, and the **Holocaust**.

BARTOV, OMER (b. 1954) In his books on the German military, *The Eastern Front, 1941–1945* (1986) and *Hitler's Army* (1991), Bartov described the barbarous nature of the Nazi war against the Soviet Union and the role of the **Wehrmacht** as an integral part and willing tool of the Nazi regime. In subsequent collections of essays, *Murder in Our Midst* (1996), *Mirrors of Destruction* (2000), *Holocaust: Origins, Implementation, Aftermath* (2000), *In God's Name* (with Phyllis Mack, 2001), *Crimes of War* (with Atina **Grossmann** and Mary Nolan, 2002), and *Germany's War and the Holocaust: Disputed Histories* (2003), Bartov challenged the post-war myth of the Wehrmacht as an unpolitical professional force and demonstrated the army's complicity and close involvement in the genocidal program of the regime. Bartov maintained that German soldiers fought out of conviction, believing themselves to be part of a redemptive project to create a better world. Bartov has been critical both of **Goldhagen**'s monocausal explanation of the **Holocaust** as the product of a collective German "eliminationist antisemitism" and of German functionalist or structuralist historians, such as **Mommsen** or **Aly**, who seem to downplay the importance of **anti-Semitic** ideology and the role of moral choice in the causation of the Holocaust. Bartov has also explored and revealed the connections between the mass industrialized killing of the First World War and the readiness to commit genocide in the Second World War. The destruction of war came to be widely viewed in Germany as sweeping away the weak and degenerate, and seemed to confirm the adage that life was war and war was life. German military history cannot be separated from the history of the Holocaust, according to Bartov, nor can the Holocaust be adequately represented or explained without integrating the perspectives of victims with those of the perpetrators. Bartov has also made important contributions to the growing scholarship on how Nazism, the Second World War, and the Holocaust have been remembered and represented differently in Germany, Western Europe, the United States, and Israel. His latest book is *The "Jew" in Cinema: From the Golem to Don't Touch my Holocaust* (2005).

BAUER, YEHUDA (b. 1926) Czech-born Israeli historian whose comprehensive *History of the Holocaust* was first published in 1982. Bauer has argued forcefully for the uniqueness of the **Holocaust** in the history of genocide, but he has also criticized mythical representations that treated the Holocaust as outside the realm of history and beyond human understanding. Bauer has criticized interpretations that implicated Jews in their own destruction by exaggerating the collaboration of **Jewish Councils** or understating the extent of Jewish resistance. Although Bauer has been critical of structuralist or functionalist explanations that minimized **Hitler**'s personal role in the origins of the Holocaust or the role of racist ideology (as, for instance, in **Mommsen**'s or **Aly**'s interpretations), he has himself modified his earlier interpretation of the Holocaust as primarily the result of the Nazi leadership's long-standing intention to destroy the Jews physically. In *Rethinking the Holocaust* (2001) Bauer concluded that while pragmatic decisions by local officials certainly played an important role in the process of destruction, the initiative for the radicalization of policies came from Berlin. According to Bauer, the basic motives for the killings were not bureaucratic or pragmatic, but ideological.

BAUMAN, ZYGMUNT (b. 1925) The sociologist Zygmunt Bauman's importance for the historiography of Nazism rests primarily with his book *Modernity and the Holocaust* (1989). Rejecting the notion that Nazism was an atavistic regression to pre-modern barbarism and animality in the modern world, Bauman argued that it was instead the product of the very same modern, rational, bureaucratic ordering processes that are generally prized in their progressive forms. According to Bauman, it was the bureaucratic division of labor and its instrumental rationality – the use of reason to achieve maximum efficiency at the expense of ethical self-reflection – that made the **Holocaust** possible. Bureaucrats develop no guilt feelings because bureaucratic decisions are not based on moral values. Like **Hilberg** and **Arendt**, Bauman believed that bureaucracy develops its own logic and momentum. Given a purpose or a goal, bureaucratic logic will seek ways to best accomplish that purpose or goal without questioning their moral legitimacy. Bauman's thesis was challenged by **Bauer**, **Goldhagen**, and others for underestimating the importance of anti-Semitic ideology in motivating the perpetrators and for failing to explain why the Holocaust developed in Germany and not in other industrialized countries. At issue here, too, is the specificity of the targeted population of the

Holocaust and the wider question as to whether the meaning and the lessons of the Holocaust are applicable to all real or potential victim groups, or whether they apply primarily or even exclusively to Jews. Bauman pleaded for an interpretation that would give the Holocaust a universal meaning as a warning against the dangers of large-scale social engineering projects that intentionally or unintentionally exclude, marginalize, or destroy the weakest members of a given society.

BENZ, WOLFGANG (b. 1941) German historian who has written extensively on Nazism, **anti-Semitism**, the history of Jews in the **Third Reich**, and the post-war era. With Hermann Graml and Hermann Weiss, Benz co-authored the *Encyclopedia of National Socialism*, published in Germany in 1997. His best-known work in English is probably the brief volume *The Holocaust* (1995; English trans. 1999), written for a general audience without endnotes. Benz is a member of the first generation of post-war German historians for whom scholarship on the Third Reich is inseparable from the pedagogical task of strengthening German democracy and combating the residues of the Nazi era in German society today. His *Concise History of the Third Reich* was published in English in 2006.

BESSEL, RICHARD (b. 1948) The author most recently of *Nazism and War* (2004), Bessel has contributed numerous publications to the study of political violence, paramilitary formations, and the police in twentieth-century Germany. He has contributed chapters on these subjects to numerous anthologies and has edited several important collections himself, including *Life in the Third Reich* (revised edn 2001) and *Fascist Italy and Nazi Germany:*

Comparisons and Contrasts (1996). Bessel has been critical of **Wehler**'s *Sonderweg* interpretation, which traces the origins of Nazism to an inherited set of social structures peculiar to Germany. He has also been critical of Marxist interpretations and of both **totalitarianism** theory and modernization theory. In his view Nazism did indeed mark the culmination of a long tradition of European racism, but not one confined to Germany. What was unique to Germany was the fact that the specific conditions resulting from the First World War and German defeat allowed a band of political thugs imbued with racist ideology to capture power in a highly developed industrial nation. The memory of the humiliating end of the First World War and a determination not to permit a repetition remained powerful influences on Nazi policies right up to 1945. Bessel has also made a sharp distinction between the "revolutionary" Nazis and the inept "counter-revolutionary" elite that helped them to gain power and shared many of their goals.

BLOCH, ERNST (1885–1977) Unorthodox Marxist thinker whose major contribution to the study of the origins of Nazism was his notion of "asynchronism," the coexistence of "non-contemporaneity and contemporaneity" (*Ungleichzeitigkeit* and *Gleichzeitigkeit*), first put forth in his book, *Heritage of our Times* (1935). In his account, a major factor in the success of Nazi ideology in Germany was the disproportionate survival in a rapidly modernizing German society of anachronistic institutions and attitudes. Bloch took issue with the orthodox Marxist premise that people were only motivated by rational economic interests. Instead he called on Marxists to apply dialectical analysis and critique not only to the bourgeois–proletarian class antagonism, but also to other social and cultural contradictions in German society. According to Bloch, irrational drives inherited from a pre-capitalist era led the peasantry, young people, and sectors of the bourgeoisie to identify so readily with Nazism. Bloch's major work was the radically optimistic *The Principle of Hope* (1959), which envisioned a redeemed world at the end of a historical process driven by recurring struggles for a better, more rational society.

BOCK, GISELA (b. 1942) Leading German feminist historian and author of *Zwangssterilisierung im Nationalsozialismus* (Compulsory Sterilization in Nazi Germany) in 1986, which linked Nazi racial policy to Nazi policy toward women in general. Bock argued that "compulsory sterilization affected women more than men . . . because women's identities were more closely connected to their sexual fertility."[2] Her contention that women in Nazi Germany should be seen primarily as victims rather than collaborators was challenged by Claudia **Koonz**, who disputed Bock's claim that the Nazis' anti-abortion policies could be compared to forcible sterilization (in the sense that both policies were based on the stereotype of women as mere breeding machines). Koonz also denied that the Nazis' anti-natalist policies, directed primarily against Jewish women, could be generalized to the female population of the **Reich**. While Bock's argument that women were more adversely affected than men by the Nazis' **eugenic** practices has been generally accepted, her conceptual equation of anti-feminism with **anti-Semitism** as two sides of the same deadly racial policy remains controversial. Bock acknowledged that some women had contributed to Nazi crimes in their functions outside the home, but she continued to deny any "specifically female guilt" in the traditionally separate private sphere. Bock was a contributor to the pioneering feminist work on women in Nazi Germany, *When Biology Became Destiny* (1984), edited by Renate Bridenthal (b. 1935), Atina **Grossmann**, and Marion A. Kaplan (b. 1946). Bock is also the author of *Women in European History* (2000) and most recently the editor of *Genozid und Geschlecht* (2005; Genocide and Gender), a collection of essays on Jewish women in Nazi camps.

BRACHER, KARL DIETRICH (b. 1922) Trained as a political scientist, Bracher came to international attention with his first major work, *Die Auflösung der Weimarer Republik* (The Dissolution of the Weimar Republic), in 1955, written from a liberal perspective and critical of the authoritarian governments of Brüning, Papen, and Schleicher for their roles in the collapse of the republic. He co-authored (with Wolfgang Sauer and Gerhard Schulz) the massive, detailed *Die nationalsozialistische Machtergreifung* (The National Socialist Seizure of Power) in 1960. His best-known work, *The German Dictatorship* (1969; English trans. 1970), perhaps the most representative German history of Nazism within the framework of **totalitarianism** theory, was published at a time when this interpretative model was coming under increasing attack from a younger generation of left-oriented historians in Germany. In works on contemporary historical controversies, including *The German Dilemma* (1971; English trans. 1974), *Zeitgeschichtliche Kontroversen* (Contemporary Historical Controversies, 1976), and *The Age of Ideologies* (1982), Bracher defended the totalitarianism paradigm, blurring the distinction between extreme left and extreme right. He was critical of the notion of a generic fascism, which failed in his view to do justice to the totalitarian features that Nazism shared with Soviet Communism. He also stressed **Hitler**'s central governing role, rejecting Martin **Broszat**'s and Hans **Mommsen**'s "**polycratic**" models of the Nazi political system and the notion of Hitler as a "weak dictator" constrained by the bureaucratic institutional dynamic of Nazi Germany. "It was indeed Hitler's *Weltanschauung* and nothing else that mattered in the end," Bracher wrote, thus striking a note similar to Gerhard **Ritter** though without the same apologetic intent.[3] Bracher's collection of essays, *Turning Points in Modern Times* (1992), was translated into English in 1995. Despite his background in the social sciences, which seek to develop general conclusions, Bracher favored a traditional version of historical narrative in which events were not caused by impersonal structural forces (such as in Hans-Ulrich **Wehler**'s account of the German *Sonderweg*), but rather by conscious human decisions and choices.

BREITMAN, RICHARD (b. 1947) Best known for his biography of **Himmler**, *The Architect of Genocide* (1991), the American historian Richard Breitman has recently focused his research on the United States response to the **Holocaust**, particularly the knowledge of the genocide on the part of US intelligence, and the links between US and Nazi intelligence operatives after the war. Co-author, with Walther **Laqueur**, of *Breaking the Silence* (1986) on reception of information about the Holocaust in the West and contributor to a volume entitled *FDR and the Holocaust* (1996), Breitman published *Official Secrets: What the Nazis Planned, What the British and Americans*

Knew in 1998 and co-authored *U.S. Intelligence and the Nazis* in 2005. He is also the author of *German Socialism and Weimar Democracy* (1981).

BROSZAT, MARTIN (1926–1989) Early member and director (from 1972 to 1989) of the Munich-based **Institut für Zeitgeschichte** (IfZ) (Institute for Contemporary History), Broszat was one of the most influential historians of the Federal Republic of Germany in the post-war era. Under his editorship the IfZ's quarterly *Vierteljahrshefte für Zeitgeschichte* (VfZ), first published in 1953, became the most important scholarly journal for research on Nazi Germany. Broszat provided the leadership for the so-called "Bavaria Project," *Bayern in der NS-Zeit* (Bavaria in the Nazi Period), published in six volumes from 1976 to 1983. This project marked one of the earliest attempts to write a history of society in the **Third Reich** "from below," anticipating the historiographical movement known as *Alltagsgeschichte* (the history of everyday life) and opening up research into various forms of consent and dissent, support and alienation, conformity and nonconformity, with which people adjusted to Nazi rule. Broszat introduced the novel concept of *Resistenz* to describe a passive kind of nonconformity that was far more widespread in the Bavarian population than active resistance (*Widerstand*) to Nazi rule.

In a widely cited article in the German journal *Merkur* in 1985 Broszat called for the "historicization" of National Socialism, a plea to integrate the Third Reich within the continuity of German history rather than treating it as an episode outside of history and thus inaccessible to historical understanding. Broszat warned that routine and ritualistic moral condemnation of Nazism for didactic reasons stood in the way of full understanding, which he believed could only be achieved by applying the same rigorous and objective scholarly methodology as historians applied to other periods of history. Conservative historians such as Ernst **Nolte** seized on Broszat's appeal to reinforce their call for the "normalization" of Nazism in 1986, thus precipitating the fierce *Historikerstreit*, in which, however, Broszat sided with Nolte's critics. Broszat's call for historicization was disputed by Saul **Friedländer** in 1988, who argued that the unique criminality of Nazism made it impossible to approach this topic with the same methods as "normal" history. Friedländer considered *Resistenz* to be too amorphous a concept to be useful, and he feared that the "historicization" of Nazism would lead to a trivialization of Nazism and a revival of the uncritical methods of German historicism, which placed a premium on empathizing with leading historical actors. Friedländer maintained that the history of Nazism called for judgement and critique rather than empathetic understanding. Broszat responded in an exchange published in VfZ in 1988. He argued that scholarly historicization of Nazism would enhance and deepen moral awareness of its criminality in a way that rote demonization of the Nazis could not. He denied that use of normal historical methodology would inevitably lead to a more favorable evaluation of Nazism. In perhaps his most important book, *The Hitler State: The Foundation and Internal Structure of the Third Reich* (German edition 1969), Broszat introduced the notion of "**polycracy**" to describe the often chaotic Nazi administrative system characterized by personal rivalries, jurisdictional disputes, power struggles, overlapping competencies, and bureaucratic confusion.

BROWNING, CHRISTOPHER (b. 1944) A leading American historian of the **Holocaust**, Browning (with the assistance of German historian Jürgen Matthäus [b. 1959]) published what has come to be recognized as the most authoritative work of synthesis on the early stages of the Holocaust, *The Origins of the Final Solution: The Evolution of Nazi Jewish Policy 1939–1942* (2005). The book, part of Yad Vashem's multi-volume *History of the Holocaust*, is divided into two parts. The first part describes successive "resettlement" plans under which Jews were to be expelled, first to the "**Lublin** reservation," then to a reservation to be established on the island of **Madagascar**, and finally to the Siberian or Arctic wastelands of the Soviet Union. The second part of the book shows how planning for a "war of destruction" against the Soviet Union radicalized Nazi policies, eventually leading to the systematic mass murder of all Jews under Nazi control. In explaining the origins of the "**final solution**" Browning took a middle position between **functionalism** and **intentionalism**, contingency and determinism, as he had already done in his essay collections *Fateful Months: Essays on the Emergence of the Final Solution* (1985) and *Paths to Genocide: Essays on Launching the Final Solution* (1992). Browning's first book was *The Final Solution and the German Foreign Office* (1978). Browning did not believe that the Nazis pursued a master plan aimed at the physical extermination of the Jews from the very start; but Browning was also critical of historical interpretations that portrayed the Holocaust as motivated predominantly by rational or economic goals, such as modernizing agriculture in eastern Europe by reducing the "surplus population" (see **Aly**) or combating food shortages by destroying "useless eaters" (see **Gerlach**). According to Browning the Holocaust can only be explained as a consequence of the Nazis' ideological obsessions and extreme anti-Semitism.

In the debate on the importance of local initiatives in the origins of the Holocaust, Browning also took a middle position, arguing that the decision-making that led to the "final solution" should be understood as the product of the interaction between local and central authorities in which, however, the central authorities played the predominant role. Browning contended that the decision for the "final solution" must have been reached by October 1941, for in that month plans for the deportation of Jews from the German **Reich** were developed, all Jewish emigration from areas controlled by Germany was prohibited, and construction of the **Belzec** extermination camp was under way. More controversially, Browning argued that it was the euphoria of battlefield success in the Soviet Union, not the prospects of impending defeat or the entry of the United States into the war (as argued by Gerlach), that led Nazi leaders to take the decisive step to the physical annihilation of all European Jews.

The equally controversial question of perpetrator motives was the topic of a bitter dispute with Daniel J. **Goldhagen**. In his book, *Ordinary Men: Reserve Police Battalion 101 and the Final Solution in Poland* (1992), Browning considered situational and organizational factors (peer pressure, careerism, opportunism, the brutalization of war, subservience to authority) just as important as ideology in explaining the willingness of German perpetrators to kill their victims. Browning agreed with **Hilberg** that hatred of Jews was not a necessary condition for Germans' participation in killing operations in time of war. In his

Nazi Policy, Jewish Workers, German Killers (2000), however, he acknowledged that among the perpetrators there were a significant minority (10 to 20 percent) of ideologically motivated killers ready to murder Jews from the start. The majority of perpetrators, however, did not fall into the category of eager killers.

BULLOCK, ALAN (1914–2004) British historian whose scholarly interests extended well beyond German history and the Nazi era. His importance as a historian of Nazi Germany rests on his influential *Hitler: A Study in Tyranny* (1952), the first comprehensive biography of the Nazi leader. However, his portrait of **Hitler** as an opportunist without principles or convictions motivated primarily by the desire to wield power is no longer widely shared. Bullock himself revised his earlier interpretation in his book, *Hitler and Stalin: Parallel Lives* (1991), in which he stressed the importance of ideology and Hitler's commitment to the basic ideas he expressed in ***Mein Kampf***.

BURLEIGH, MICHAEL (b. 1955) Trained as a medievalist, Burleigh developed an interest in Nazi Germany as a result of work on his first book, a history of the Teutonic Order in the fifteenth century, published in 1984. Among his important books on Nazi Germany are *Germany Turns Eastward: A Study of Ostforschung in the Third Reich* (1988); with Wolfgang **Wippermann**, *The Racial State* (1991); *Death and Deliverance: "Euthanasia" in Germany 1933–1945* (1994); and a collection of essays, *Ethics and Extermination: Reflections on Nazi Genocide* (1997). His opus magnum, *The Third Reich*, a comprehensive history, was published in 2000. Written in a tone of moral outrage, it described the unique criminality of the

Third Reich in grim detail. Its interpretation of Nazism, however, fell well within the conventional parameters of totalitarianism theory and shared the weaknesses of that paradigm, highlighting the similarities between Nazism and communism, while neglecting their significant differences. Burleigh invoked the excessively vague concept of "political religion" as his main explanatory trope, attributing the force of Nazism (like communism) to its utopian urge to create a new kind of man and a heaven on earth based on the triumph of the master race (rather than, as in communism, the triumph of the underclass). In contrast to structural interpretations of Nazi Germany, especially ones that implicate Western rationalism or bourgeois capitalist society in Nazism or in the **Holocaust**, Burleigh stressed the uniquely irrational, racist, and anti-modern aspects of the Nazi regime and the personal responsibility of **Hitler** and his leading henchmen for Nazi atrocities.

C

CARSTEN, FRANCIS L. (b. 1911) An Austrian refugee from Nazism who settled in Britain in 1939, Carsten was first attracted to early modern German history in the hope of explaining the roots of the Nazi debacle. His books *The Origins of Prussia* (1954) and *Princes and Parliaments in Germany* (1959) traced the process by which Prussian monarchism and Junker dominance blocked the emergence of a strong middle class, but took issue with the then-prevailing view among German historians that the German Estates had impeded the constructive state-building of the German territorial rulers. His landmark book *Reichswehr and Politics, 1918–1933* (1964) refuted another prevailing myth – the one that the German military leadership was untainted by involvement in the destruction of **Weimar** and the rise of the Nazis. His later books, *The Rise of Fascism in Europe* (1968), *Revolution in Central Europe, 1918–19* (1972), and *Fascist Movements in Austria* (1973), were written in the empirical, descriptive tradition of British social history, thus limiting their impact at a time when interest in the historical profession was shifting to more generalizing, theoretical approaches to the study of Nazism.

D

DAHRENDORF, RALF (b. 1929) In his path-breaking book, *Society and Democracy in Germany* (1965), Dahrendorf, a German sociologist who became a British citizen, berated his fellow Germans for their lack of social consciousness and sought to educate them in the principles of liberal democracy. Its importance for the historiography of Nazism lies in its structural analysis of the long-range anti-democratic trends in German society that made the Nazi seizure of power possible. According to Dahrendorf, four characteristics in particular distinguished German society from the classical liberal model. First, the persistence of inequalities in class status, educational opportunities, and social advancement. Second, repression of social conflict in the name of national harmony rather than resolution of conflicts through compromise and open debate. Third, the self-preservation and durability of

Germany's social elite, which retained its unity through inherited authoritarian patterns of behavior and a "cartel of fear" even in the critical years after the First World War. And fourth, a preference for private virtues rather than public political participation, leading to escapism and timidity. According to Dahrendorf, Imperial Germany missed the road to modernity and consolidated itself as an industrial feudal society and an authoritarian welfare state. The failure of Germans to develop the liberal civic consciousness necessary for the responsibilities of citizenship explained the demise of democracy in 1933. Dahrendorf's analysis thus presaged the *Sonderweg* interpretation put forth a few years later by the so-called Bielefeld School of social historians led by Hans-Ulrich **Wehler**. But while the absence of a modern liberal society made the triumph of Nazism possible, Dahrendorf also insisted on the modern characteristics of the Nazi movement and their hostility to tradition above all else. The Nazis, Dahrendorf claimed, gained their legitimacy in the eyes of the German public by carrying out the modernizing social revolution that Germany's illiberal social structures had previously prevented. The Nazi revolution took such a catastrophic form precisely because German social realities made peaceful social reform impossible even in the democratic **Weimar Republic**. His analysis of Nazism, however, was criticized by Hans **Mommsen** and other historians for overstating the revolutionary features of Nazism and understating its anti-modern thrust.

E

ELEY, GEOFF (b. 1949) Leading British-American historian of German nationalism, advocate of a culturally informed critical social history, and critic of Hans-Ulrich **Wehler**'s *Sonderweg* thesis. In *The Peculiarities of German History* (1984), co-authored with David Blackbourn (b. 1949), Eley rejected the notion that Nazism could be explained by Germany's "deviant" development in the nineteenth century. According to the *Sonderweg* interpretation, Germany's democratic development was fatally retarded by the continued political domination of agrarian aristocratic elites and the failure of the German bourgeoisie to bring about a liberal revolution in 1848. Eley and Blackbourn objected to this thesis for a number of reasons: it understated the modernization of German society, the liberalization of its economy, and the degree to which the German bourgeoisie was able to secure its interests through an authoritarian system of government; it exaggerated the degree of manipulation of events by feudal elites while understating the political agency and participation of the lower and middle classes; it extolled the Western liberal model of development as normative for all nations; and it diverted attention from analysis of the crisis of the capitalist state as the source of fascism and Nazism. Eley has also contributed important theoretical writings to the historiography of Nazism as exemplified by his defense of cultural studies in *A Crooked Line: From Cultural History to the History of Society* (2005). Eley intervened in the **Goldhagen** controversy by pointing out that the significance of Goldhagen's book lay not so much in its substantive historical arguments as in its effect of countering pressures in Germany to bring public debate on Nazism to a close. Eley has also written a definitive history of mass nationalist mobilization in the Wilhelmian Empire, *Reshaping the German Right* (1980), and a monumental history of the left in Europe from 1850 to 2000, *Forging Democracy* (2002).

EVANS, RICHARD (b. 1947) Originally a specialist in nineteenth-century German social history, British historian Richard Evans has become one of the leading authorities on Nazi Germany with his three-volume history of the **Third Reich**, the first two volumes of which are *The Coming of the Third Reich* (2004) and *The Third Reich in Power, 1933–1939* (2005). Evans adopted a less Hitler-centered or moralistic approach than earlier comprehensive histories of Nazism in English (such as those by **Kershaw**, **Burleigh**, or **Shirer**), and he also challenged the *Sonderweg* notion that Germany was by tradition or history uniquely susceptible to **Hitler**'s racist message or totalitarian rule. Evans's narrative is especially effective in portraying the complexities and ambiguities of the Nazis' seizure of power, Nazi rule, and popular reactions to the Nazis. Evans's book, *Lying about Hitler: History, Holocaust, and the David Irving Trial* (2001), resulted from his testimony in American historian Deborah Lipstadt's (b. 1947) successful defense in a libel suit brought by British historian David Irving (b. 1938), whom Lipstadt had accused of denying the **Holocaust**. Evans has also published extensively on German historiography, especially in *Rethinking German History: Nineteenth-Century Germany and the Origins of the Third Reich* (1987), *In Hitler's Shadow: West German Historians*

and the Attempt to Escape from the Nazi Past (1989), *Rereading German History: From Unification to Reunification, 1800–1996* (1998), and *In Defense of History* (1999). The latter book contains a critique of postmodernist theories that question the usefulness or legitimacy of traditional historiographic methods.

F

FEST, JOACHIM C. (1926–2006) Conservative journalist and historian best known for his detailed biography of **Hitler** (1973), the first major biography of Hitler by a German historian, stressing his misguided idealism and nationalism. Taking issue with **Bullock**'s contention that Hitler was driven only by the desire for power, Fest emphasized the importance of Hitler's strong ideological convictions. "The problem was not one of criminal impulses but of a perverted moral energy."[4] Fest answered in the affirmative his own question as to whether Hitler would have been considered "one of the greatest German statesmen" if he had died in 1938. For Fest the "negative greatness" of Hitler's personality explained Nazism better than did social or economic developments. Fest also published *The Face of the Third Reich: Portraits of the Nazi Leadership* (1963), *Plotting Hitler's Death: The Story of German Resistance* (1994), and a biography of Albert **Speer** (1999), whom he had previously assisted in writing his autobiography. Late in life Fest admitted that he had been wrong to have taken Speer at his word when Speer insisted that he knew nothing about the death camps of the **Holocaust**. Fest's account of the last days of the **Third Reich**, *Inside Hitler's*

Bunker (2002), provided the basis for the film *Der Untergang* (The Downfall) in 2004. As an editor of West Germany's leading conservative newspaper, *Frankfurter Allgemeine Zeitung*, Fest came to the defense of Ernst **Nolte**'s revisionism in the *Historikerstreit* of 1986–1987. Denying the singularity of Nazi crimes, Fest professed a tragic view of history in which the Holocaust was unique only for its technical innovations. He accused progressives like Jürgen Habermas (b. 1929) of excessive optimism about human nature, advocating instead a realistic pessimism that viewed Nazi destructiveness as part of the human condition. Fest agreed with Nolte's contention that in the murderous process of history Nazi atrocities were no worse than the Stalinist atrocities that preceded and allegedly inspired them.

FISCHER, FRITZ (1908–1999) Influential German historian whose landmark book *Germany's Aims in the First World War* (first published under the title *Griff nach der Weltmacht* [Grasp for World Power] in 1961) precipitated a controversy in Germany and led to a new awareness of German responsibility for the outbreak of war in 1914. An older generation of German historians, chief among them Gerhard **Ritter**, rejected Fischer's assertion that the German leadership had taken advantage of the assassination of the Austrian crown prince by Serbian nationalists in June 1914 to pursue policies that they knew were likely to result in war. Fischer repudiated the prevailing consensus among Germans that war had been forced on their nation and that Germany bore no greater responsibility for the conflict than the other European powers. Fischer's thesis that the German leadership consciously risked war because of their confidence in

the superiority of German arms in a continental war has been widely accepted and was corroborated by historian Mark Hewitson in his book on the origins of the First World War in 2004. The "Fischer thesis" did not change the historical consensus on Germany's guilt for the Second World War, which was never in doubt in any case. Its main effect on the historiography of Nazism was to have revealed continuities linking the expansionist goals of the Wilhelmian Empire to those of the Nazis. Fischer provided further evidence for such continuities in his subsequent books, *War of Illusions: German Policies from 1911 to 1914* (1969) and *From Kaiserreich to Third Reich: Elements of Continuity in German History, 1871–1945* (English trans. 1986). By demonstrating the influence of economic and social forces on foreign policy, Fischer also helped to launch a methodological change in German diplomatic history, which had traditionally treated foreign policy in relative isolation from domestic policies. His work helped to inspire the **Sonderweg** (special path) interpretation of social historian Hans-Ulrich **Wehler**.

FREI, NORBERT (b. 1955) Leading member of the younger generation of German historians who have entirely accepted liberal democratic values and are highly critical not only of Nazism but also of the post-war "politics of the past" (the title of Frei's 1997 book, *Vergangenheitspolitik*, translated into English in 2002 as *Adenauer's Germany and the Nazi Past: The Politics of Amnesty and Integration*). Frei linked the widespread German demands for the curtailment of **denazification** and the rehabilitation of former Nazis, including convicted war criminals, to a still pervasive, though muted, nationalism in the early years of the Federal Republic. Frei credited Adenauer for helping to create an anti-Nazi consensus in the late 1940s and 1950s, but also pointed out how ever more forceful repudiation of Nazi ideology could serve to cover up the growing retreat from denazification and the prosecution of war criminals. Frei also stressed the role of Allied pressure in blocking German efforts to free convicted war criminals, at least until the Allies themselves lost interest in prosecuting Nazi war crimes during the Korean War. It was not until the 1960s that a serious confrontation with the Nazi past finally emerged in the Federal Republic. In his earlier book, *National Socialist Rule in Germany: The Führer State, 1933–1945* (1987), Frei seconded his generational colleague Detlev **Peukert**'s stress on the modern, technocratic aspects of Nazism, an implicit warning against the potential for barbarism in modern industrial societies. Frei's book, *1945 und wir: Das Dritte Reich im Bewusstsein der Deutschen* (2005) (The Third Reich in German Consciousness since 1945), traced *Vergangenheitsbewältigung* in Germany through various phases to the institutionalizing of **Holocaust** memory and the simultaneous rediscovery of German victimization (at the hands of Allied bombers) at the start of the twenty-first century.

FRIEDLANDER, HENRY (b. 1930) A survivor of the Nazi camps, Friedlander is author of a thorough study of *The Origins of Nazi Genocide* (1995), which described the continuity between the **Aktion T-4 euthanasia** program, launched in 1939, and the "**final solution**," the killing of the Jews. In contrast to Jehuda **Bauer**, Friedlander advocated expanding the definition of the **Holocaust** to embrace not only Jewish victims but all victim groups defined in biological terms, which would include the gypsies (Roma and Sinti) and the mentally and physically disabled. In Friedlander's explanation the Holocaust resulted from the conjunction of two main strands of Nazi ideology – **anti-Semitism** and **eugenic** selection – under the favorable conditions for systematic murder created by total war. Friedlander also co-edited with Sybil Milton the 26-volume documentary series *Archives of the Holocaust* (1988–1993). The post-war prosecution of Nazi war criminals is another area of research to which Friedlander has made important contributions.

FRIEDLÄNDER, SAUL (b. 1932) In his most important book to date, *Nazi Germany and the Jews* (1997), the first of a projected two volumes tracing the persecution of the Jews under Nazism (volume II is to be published in English in 2007), Friedländer introduced the concept of "redemptive" **anti-Semitism**, a radical form of Jew-hatred resulting from the convergence of racial anti-Semitism and a pseudo-religious ideology of redemption (or perdition). "Redemptive" anti-Semitism was based on a vision of an apocalyptic struggle to the death between the Jews and "**Aryan**" humanity" and served an integrating and mobilizing function in the Nazi system. While Friedländer differed with "intentionalists," who argued that extermination of the Jews had always been **Hitler**'s goal, he did insist that the "redemptive" anti-Semitism of Hitler and the core of the Nazi Party was the key to the origins of the **Holocaust**. Friedländer recognized the role of technocratic rationality in the extermination program, but insisted on the centrality of Hitler and his ideological goals. Unlike **Goldhagen**, who posited an "eliminationist" anti-Semitism throughout

German society and history, Friedländer differentiated the Nazis' extreme anti-Semitism from traditional *völkisch* or religious anti-Semitism, which he viewed as necessary, but not sufficient causes of the Holocaust. In addition to books on Pius XII and Kurt **Gerstein**, the **SS** officer whose graphic description of the extermination camps helped to reveal the extraordinary criminality of the Nazi regime, Friedländer has also published widely on the history and memory of the Holocaust. He helped to found the new journal *History and Memory* in 1989, and has edited the influential volume *Probing the Limits of Representation: Nazism and the "Final Solution"* (1992). Friedländer raised the question whether an unproblematic representation of so unique an event as the Holocaust was possible. He also engaged in an important scholarly debate with Martin **Broszat**, the German historian who called for the "historicization" of the Nazi era in the late 1980s. While Friedländer agreed with Broszat that the Nazi era should be treated with the same rigorous scholarship and objectivity as other historical eras, he cautioned against the kind of normalization that Ernst **Nolte** had advocated in the *Historikerstreit*. Friedländer also warned against the kind of "historicization" that Andreas **Hillgruber** had practiced in empathetically identifying with German soldiers on the eastern front in the closing stages of the Second World War.

FRIEDRICH, CARL J. (1901–1984) German-born political scientist and co-author with Zibigniev Brzezinski of the influential study, *Totalitarian Dictatorship and Autocracy* (1956), which gave scholarly respectability to the concept of "**totalitarianism**," a category under which communism, fascism, and Nazism were subsumed. Although Friedrich conceded that communism and fascism were quite different in their proclaimed purposes and intentions, and that fascism appealed to the middle classes precisely because of their fear of communism, he nonetheless considered their similarities to be more important than their differences. Among these similarities he included a chiliastic ideology, a mass party led by a dictator, police control by means of terror, control of communications, control of arms, and a centrally planned economy. Totalitarian governments, Friedrich claimed, transformed classes into masses, supplanted a party system with a mass movement, shifted the center of power from the army to the police, and pursued a foreign policy aimed at world domination. Friedrich contrasted totalitarian societies to traditional tyrannies that supposedly pursued less ambitious goals and left the private sphere intact. Friedrich's totalitarianism theory enjoyed wide appeal in the US during the cold war as it provided a useful tool to tar the Soviet Union and other communist societies with the fascist brush. It was severely criticized by many historians, however, for failing to differentiate communist from fascist movements. Totalitarianism theory occluded differences in their origins, their economic systems, their relationship to private property, and the coalition of forces that sustained them. Totalitarianism theory fell out of favor in the 1960s and 1970s only to reemerge in somewhat more sophisticated form after the demise of the Soviet Union in the 1990s.

FROMM, ERICH (1900–1980) Fromm's 1941 book, *Escape from Freedom*, offered a socio-psychological explanation for the origins of Nazism combining both Marxist and Freudian insights. According to Fromm, freedom becomes an unbearable burden for individuals when social, economic, and political conditions do not permit self-realization, and family ties no longer offer the security they once did. Traumatized by the collapse of the Empire, impoverished by the Great Inflation, and aggrieved by the loss of parental authority, the lower middle classes in Germany were particularly susceptible to an immature longing to escape from the responsibilities of freedom by dissolving their individuality in a larger whole. Fromm believed that this servile attitude was formed by a combination of social relations and family structure. Submission to authority satisfied both masochistic and sadistic urges, resulting in conformism and destructiveness and paving the way to Nazi domination. **Hitler**'s own personal traits, his love of the strong and hatred of the weak, his pettiness, hostility, and asceticism, symbolized, reflected, expressed, and strengthened typically lower-middle-class attitudes.

G

GELLATELY, ROBERT (b. 1943) Canadian-American historian whose most important contributions to the historiography of Nazism to date have been his studies of popular cooperation in the totalitarian Nazi regime, *The Gestapo and German Society: Enforcing Racial Policy 1933–1945* (1990) and *Backing Hitler: Consent and Coercion in Nazi Germany* (2001). These studies marked a shift in emphasis from public dissent and non-cooperation in earlier literature on Nazi Germany (such as Sarah Gordon's *Hitler, Germans, and the "Jewish Question"*

[1984] and the six-volume Bavaria project of Martin **Broszat**) to an emphasis on the participation, compliance, and accommodation of ordinary German citizens. Gellately concluded that the efficient functioning of the understaffed secret police was dependent on the continuing cooperation of ordinary Germans in denouncing their fellow citizens. Gellately argued, however, that loyalty to the regime, ideological fanaticism, or fear of **Gestapo** reprisal were less important as motives for denunciation than opportunism, conformism, professional rivalries, personal grudges, and conflicts between neighbors.

Gellately also refuted conventional wisdom on the make-up of the secret police. Not only was it far smaller than had previously been assumed, but its personnel were drawn mainly from the professional police force that predated the Nazi regime. Gellately debunked what remained of the popular conception of the Nazi regime as a police state imposed by force on an unsuspecting population, which then found it too late to resist. His image of a widely accepted and popularly supported police state corroborated similar findings by Ian **Kershaw**, Detlev **Peukert**, and the German sociologist Reinhard Mann. Gellately's conclusions about the "auto-surveillance" of German society, as well as his profiles of Gestapo personnel, were in turn largely corroborated by the German scholars Gerhard Paul (b. 1951), Klaus-Michael Mallmann (b. 1948), and Nikolaus Wachsmann (b. 1971), as well as in Eric Johnson's (b. 1948) *Nazi Terror: The Gestapo, Jews, and Ordinary Germans* (1999) and (with Karl-Heinz Reuband) *What We Knew: Terror, Mass Murder, and Everyday Life in Nazi Germany* (2005). Both Gellately and Johnson, however, disputed **Goldhagen**'s contention that ordinary Germans were driven by a unique "eliminationist" **anti-Semitism**. What makes Gellately's findings on Nazi Germany particularly relevant to contemporary concerns is the implication that a **totalitarian** system can function effectively even without the use of large-scale coercion. Totalitarianism thus constitutes an insidious potential threat even in societies that perceive themselves as democratic. Gellately's edited volume, *The Specter of Genocide* (2003), identified state-sponsored mass murder as one of the defining characteristics of the twentieth century.

GERLACH, CHRISTIAN (b. 1963) Young German historian whose discovery of Heinrich **Himmler**'s appointment calendar in a newly opened Soviet archive in 1997 led to a reappraisal of the long-disputed question about whether and when **Hitler** made the decision to launch the "**final solution**." Based on several of Himmler's entries, as well as newly discovered pages of **Goebbels'** diary, Gerlach concluded in 1997 that Hitler announced his decision to exterminate all European Jews to a meeting of **Reichsleiter** and **Gauleiter** in Berlin on 12 December 1941, one day after the German declaration of war on the United States. The **Wannsee Conference**, originally intended to decide the fate of the German Jews, was now assigned the function of coordinating the implementation of the **Final Solution** and deciding whether German *Mischlings* and Jews married to Germans should be included in the extermination program. Gerlach published his findings in an important article, "The Wannsee Conference, the Fate of the German Jews, and Hitler's Decision in Principle to Exterminate All European Jews," in *The Journal of Modern History* in 1998. Gerlach's dating of Hitler's deci-

sion to early December ran counter to Christopher **Browning**'s contention that Hitler's decision to extend the killing program to include all European Jews had already been made by October 1941. Gerlach also disputed Browning's hypothesis that Hitler's decision was the result of the euphoria that accompanied German battlefield successes in the east in late summer 1941, arguing instead that the US entry into the war was the crucial catalyst of Hitler's decision. Gerlach's book *Krieg, Ernnährung, Völkermord* (War, Food, Genocide [1998]) explored the role of food shortages in the origins of the **Holocaust**. His book *Kalkulierte Morde* (Calculated Murder [1999]) is the authoritative account of the Holocaust in Byelorussia. With Götz **Aly** he also published *Das letzte Kapitel* (The Last Chapter [2002]), a history of the Holocaust in Hungary in 1944 and 1945.

GOLDHAGEN, DANIEL J. (b. 1959) Goldhagen's best-selling book, *Hitler's Willing Executioners: Ordinary Germans and the Holocaust* (1996), became the subject of a fierce controversy among historians about the causes of the **Holocaust**, the participation of ordinary people in atrocities, and the motivation of the perpetrators. Goldhagen contended that the Holocaust was a German "national project" perpetrated with the full knowledge and approval of the German public. As the ultimate cause of this "voluntary barbarism" Goldhagen identified an "eliminationist" anti-Semitism so deeply rooted in German history and culture as to have become part of the common sense of the average German. In collapsing the distinction between Nazis and Germans, Goldhagen violated a taboo that had been useful in reintegrating the post-war Federal Republic in the Western cold war alliance.

Goldhagen called for an anthropological approach to understanding how radically different pre-war German culture and society had been from Western norms.

Goldhagen was roundly criticized by fellow-historians for overstating German exceptionalism, offering an overly simplistic, monocausal explanatory model for the origin of the Holocaust, neglecting the political context in which Nazism arose, insisting that anti-Semitism was more pervasive in Germany than in other countries without providing any comparative data, and for exaggerating the novelty of his thesis that anti-Semitism was the root cause of the Holocaust. The empirical sections of his book did break new ground, however, drawing the attention of researchers to areas of Holocaust studies previously neglected – namely, the auxiliary police battalions, the ubiquitous labor camps, and the death marches at the end of the war.

As the deliberate use of the phrase "ordinary Germans" in his title made clear, Goldhagen directly challenged Christopher **Browning**'s findings on perpetrator motivation in his book *Ordinary Men* (1992). Browning had concluded that ordinary men became brutal killers, not because they were ideological fanatics or bloodthirsty sadists but because of situational factors such as peer pressure, conformism, careerism, deference to higher authority, the brutalization of war, and the routinization of killing. Goldhagen argued instead that German killers were decisively motivated by passionate hatred of Jews, a hostility shared by virtually all Germans as a result of their socialization in a specifically German culture of "eliminationist" **anti-Semitism**. The Goldhagen controversy did have the effect of putting the question of personal and national responsibility back on the research agenda, thus spurring numerous detailed studies, especially in Germany, into the killing process in different regions of Europe. Goldhagen's book attacking the Catholic Church for its tradition of anti-Semitism and complicity in the Holocaust, *A Moral Reckoning: The Catholic Church during the Holocaust and Today* (2002), was widely criticized for its prosecutorial approach and did not enjoy the same wide reception and prominence as his earlier book.

GROSSMANN, ATINA (b. 1955) Co-editor with Renate Bridenthal (b. 1935) of the pioneering feminist work, *Becoming Visible: Women in European History* (1977), and with Bridenthal and Marion A. Kaplan (b. 1946) of *When Biology Became Destiny: Women in Weimar and Nazi Germany* (1984). Grossmann has also written the definitive *Reforming Sex: The German Movement for Birth Control and Abortion Reform 1920–1950* (1995). With Omer **Bartov** and Mary Nolan (b. 1944) she co-edited the essay collection *Crimes of War* (2002). Grossmann has also written extensively on the post-war era, which is the subject of her forthcoming book, *Victims, Victors, and Survivors: Germans, Allies, and Jews in Occupied Germany 1945–1949.*

GUÉRIN, DANIEL (1904–1988) French Marxist historian who supported Leon Trotsky's call for a united working-class front against Nazism in opposition to the official **Comintern** policy in the late 1920s and early 1930s, which gave priority to the Communist competition with the Social Democrats for the working-class vote. *The Brown Plague* (1934) recorded Guérin's travels in Germany in 1932 and 1933, both before and after **Hitler**'s takeover. Guérin rebuked Soviet Communists for underestimating the fascist danger and undermining proletarian unity. Acknowledging that the Nazis had successfully consolidated power by exploiting proletarian militance and despair, Guérin regretted that the opportunity for mass socialist resistance had been squandered by official Communist and **SPD** policies. Guérin's most important contribution to the historiography of Nazism was his book *Fascism and Big Business* (1936), in which he again supported Trotsky against the Comintern, now in opposition to the official **Popular Front** strategy (formally adopted in 1935) of forming coalitions with bourgeois liberal parties at the expense of a revolutionary socialist program. Guérin linked the rise of Nazism not just to the general crisis of capitalism but more specifically to differences between light and heavy industry. According to Guérin it was above all the latter that supported fascism because of heavy industry's narrower profit margins, labor intensiveness, and lesser dependence on foreign trade. The function of fascism was to tame the proletariat and attract it into the national camp. One of the most important services the Nazis performed for industry was to transform the anti-capitalism of their middle- or lower-class followers into anti-Semitism.

H

HAFFNER, SEBASTIAN (1907–1999) Trained as a lawyer, Sebastian Haffner (a pseudonym adopted to avoid endangering his family in Germany) spent the war years as a journalist in England, returning to become an influential writer in West Germany after the war. His contributions to the historiography of Nazism include *Germany: Jekyll and Hyde* (1940), *Failure of the Revolution of 1918–19* (1968), *The Meaning of Hitler* (1978), *The Ailing Empire: Germany from Bismarck to Hitler* (1987), and *Defying Hitler* (2000), a personal memoir of his experiences from 1914 to 1933 written before the war but not published until after his death. His works are valuable for historians of Nazism not only for their psycho-social and political analysis of events from a self-critical, left-liberal perspective, but also as unusually clear and detailed primary sources of the Nazi seizure and consolidation of power.

HERBERT, ULRICH (b. 1951) Leading German specialist on forced labor in Germany during the Second World War. His most important book in English is the authoritative *Hitler's Foreign Workers: Enforced Foreign Labor in Germany under the Third Reich* (1997), originally published in German in 1986. Herbert is also the author of an important biography of the **SS** official Werner **Best** in 1996 (English trans. 2001). His edited volume, *National Socialist Extermination Policies: Contemporary German Perspectives and Policies* (2001), is a useful compendium of the latest German research into how the **Holocaust** was implemented. With Karin Orth (b. 1963) and Christoph Dieckmann (b. 1956), Herbert edited two volumes on German **concentration camps** in 1998. He has also written extensively on foreign guest workers in the Federal Republic of Germany after the war.

HERF, JEFFREY (b. 1947) American historian, the title of whose book, *Reactionary Modernism: Technology, Culture and Politics in Weimar and the Third Reich* (1984), added a phrase to the historiography of Nazism that is often used to designate the combination of advanced technological proficiency and reactionary ideology typical of the radical right in Germany. His book, *Divided Memory: The Nazi Past in the Two Germanys* (1997), contrasted the use of West and East German interpretations of Nazism for political purposes. His latest book, *The Jewish Enemy: Nazi Propaganda during World War II and the Holocaust* (2006), examined consistent Nazi efforts to legitimate mass murder as a retaliation against a putative international Jewish conspiracy against Germany. Although Herf concluded that leading Nazis were fanatics who truly believed their own propaganda, he recommended skepticism and restraint in any judgements about what "most Germans in Nazi Germany really believed, because the evidence is insufficient to support assertions on that score."[5]

HILBERG, RAUL (b. 1926) Trained in political science under Franz **Neumann**, Hilberg pioneered the field of **Holocaust** studies with his now classic work, *The Destruction of the European Jews*, first published in 1961 after more than a decade of painstaking research and revision. His book chronicled the complex machinery and process of destruction through various stages of definition, segregation, concentration, expropriation, deportation, and killing in stark, chilling detail. An expanded three-volume second edition was published in 1985. His work was finally translated into German in the 1980s as the ranks of perpetrators and former Nazis, many of whom had returned to high positions after the war, began to thin. Publication in Israel was delayed as well, because Hilberg's focus on the perpetrators, his reliance on

mainly German sources, and his implicit critique of the age-old Jewish strategy of accommodation as a response to persecution did not fit the image of heroic victims that was officially cultivated by the embattled Jewish state. Hannah **Arendt** relied heavily on Hilberg's work in her controversial book, *Eichmann in Jerusalem: The Banality of Evil*, to develop her critique of the unemotional, small-minded, bureaucratic mentality of so many ordinary German perpetrators. Hilberg's findings gave support to structuralist interpretations of the origins of the Holocaust, emphasizing the organizational complexity of decision-making and planning and the participation of virtually the entire nation in some capacity in the killing process. In his later book, *Perpetrators, Victims, Bystanders* (1992), Hilberg widened his focus from the bureaucratic killing apparatus to illuminate the wide variety of individual experiences and reactions in the era of the Holocaust. His memoir, *The Politics of Memory: The Journey of a Holocaust Historian*, appeared in 1996.

HILDEBRAND, KLAUS (b. 1941) Conservative German historian specializing in diplomatic, political, and military history. His books include *The Foreign Policy of the Third Reich* (1970), *The Third Reich* (1979), and *German Foreign Policy from Bismarck to Adenauer: The Limits of Statecraft* (1989). In his 1995 book *Das vergangene Reich: Deutsche Aussenpolitik von Bismarck bis Hitler* (The Past Reich: German Foreign Policy from Bismarck to Hitler), Hildebrand dismissed most of Fritz **Fischer**'s claims about Germany's responsibility for the outbreak of the First World War as unfounded. Hildebrand was criticized by **Wehler** for failing to take social forces and domestic constraints into account in analyzing foreign policy and for failing to discuss or justify his own antiquated historiographical methods and assumptions. Hildebrand's "**Hitler**-centric" interpretation of Nazism, like those of his colleagues **Hillgruber**, **Bracher**, **Fest**, and **Jäckel**, shares the "intentionalist" assumption that Nazi policies, both domestically and externally, were crucially determined by Hitler's own long-standing but clear-cut ideological program. Hildebrand also took issue with the polycratic model of the Nazi system put forth by "functionalists" like **Broszat** and **Mommsen**, arguing instead for a "monocratic" totalitarian system very different from Italian Fascism. Not surprisingly, Hildebrand found himself on the opposite side of Broszat, Mommsen, and Wehler in the *Historikerstreit*. Hildebrand defended his mentor Hillgruber, as well as Nolte, against Habermas's critique.

HILLGRUBER, ANDREAS (1925–1989) Prominent West German diplomatic and military historian of the generation just old enough to have been drafted into the German army in the closing stages of the Second World War. In his interpretation of Nazism Hillgruber upheld a strongly "intentionalist" view in which the course of the **Third Reich** and the Second World War were almost exclusively attributed to **Hitler**'s personal and ideological goals. In his most important books, *Hitler's Strategie* (1965) and *Germany and the Two World Wars* (1967; English trans. 1981), Hillgruber retracted his earlier contention that the German invasion of the Soviet Union had been a "preventive war" (a contention successfully refuted by the American historian Gerhard **Weinberg** in 1954). Hillgruber now attributed the attack on Russia to Hitler's fanatical racist beliefs and desire for *Lebensraum*. Hillgruber's

stress on the primacy of foreign policy in his traditional approach to diplomatic history drew criticism from Hans-Ulrich **Wehler** and put him partly at odds with Fritz **Fischer**. While Hillgruber agreed with Fischer that the German leadership brought about the First World War by its high-risk diplomatic strategy, he discounted the role of domestic factors in the German government's decisions. Hillgruber's pronounced Hitler-centrism also left him open to the charge of indirectly exculpating the German elites by making Hitler solely responsible for the **Holocaust** and other Nazi atrocities. Hillgruber's book *Two Kinds of Downfall: The Destruction of the German Reich and the End of European Jewry* (1986) was particularly controversial. In the bitter *Historikerstreit* that followed its publication, the liberal philosopher Jürgen Habermas criticized Hillgruber for openly identifying with German soldiers fighting to defend Germany's eastern borders against the Red Army.

HOFFMANN, PETER (b. 1930) German-Canadian historian Peter Hoffmann is a leading historian of the German military and bureaucratic resistance to **Hitler**. His *History of the German Resistance 1933–1945* (1969; English trans. 1977) is generally considered the standard work on the conservative resistance. Unlike Peter **Steinbach**, the leading German historian of the German resistance, Hoffmann did not devote the same attention to the much earlier and stronger resistance to Hitler from the left. Hoffmann has also written the history of *Hitler's Personal Security* (1975) and several biographical studies of Claus Schenk von **Stauffenberg**. In contrast to Theodore Hamerow (b. 1920), who in *The Road to the Wolf's Lair* (1997) criticized the conservative resistance for failing to oppose Hitler until the war was lost, Hoffmann defended the July 20 plotters and denied that their opposition to Nazism was based on expediency and patriotism rather than on principled opposition to Nazi goals.

J

JÄCKEL, EBERHARD (b. 1929) German historian known primarily for his books *Hitler's Weltanschauung: A Blueprint for Power* (1969) and *Hitler in History* (1984), which offer a highly **Hitler**-centric interpretation of Nazism. Jäckel is a leading representative of the **"intentionalist"** school of thought, according to which the **Final Solution** and the Nazi expansionist program were primarily launched and driven by Hitler's long-standing worldview. Jäckel believed that Hitler's worldview was formed in the aftermath of the First World War and aimed for the physical destruction of the Jews as early as 1924. According to Jäckel, extermination of the Jews was an essential German war aim from the start of the Second World War. The essential political decisions were taken by Hitler alone as the logical consequence of his ideological obsessions, justifying in Jäckel's judgement his labeling of the Nazi regime as *Alleinherrschaft* (Hitler's sole rule). Jäckel believed that Hitler's ultimate aim was continental, not global domination. Unlike other leading intentionalists, such as **Hildebrand, Hillgruber,** or Joachim **Fest**, all of whom defended Ernst **Nolte** in the *Historikerstreit*, Jäckel took the liberal side, affirming the unique criminality of the **Holocaust** as the only historical example of a modern state using all of the vast technological means at its disposal to seek to kill all the members of a particular ethnic group.

K

KATER, MICHAEL H. (b. 1937) Prolific German-Canadian historian who has published important monographs on subjects ranging from music to medicine in the **Third Reich**. His detailed 1966 study of the **Ahnenerbe** (ancestral inheritance), a teaching and research group of the **SS** founded in 1935, anticipated the later theses of Hans **Mommsen** and Martin **Broszat** describing the highly competitive "institutional chaos" of the Third Reich. Kater's findings that careerist motivations were at least as important as ideological fanaticism among the scholars and scientists affiliated with the Ahnenerbe also anticipated the later debate about perpetrator motivation between Christopher **Browning** and Daniel **Goldhagen**. Kater's books include *The Nazi Party: A Social Profile of Members and Leaders* (1983), *Doctors under Hitler* (1989), *Different Drummers: Jazz in the Culture of Nazi Germany* (1992), *The Twisted Muse: Musicians and their Music in the Third Reich* (1997), and *Hitler Youth* (2004).

KERSHAW, IAN (b. 1943) Leading British historian of Nazi Germany, whose two-volume biography of **Hitler**, *Hitler: Hubris* (1998) and *Hitler: Nemesis* (2002), has been widely recognized as the most reliable account of Hitler's life and rule to date. It is not so much a personal biography as it is a study of how Hitler interacted with German society and exploited and mirrored the fears and resentments of the German population after the First World War. Kershaw introduced the innovative concept of "working towards the Führer" in the journal *Contemporary European History* in 1993 to explain why so many Nazi policies originated on the local or regional levels and how an apparently dysfunctional Nazi administrative system of competing authorities, personal rivalries, and overlapping competencies was nonetheless able to carry out the murder of the Jews efficiently and obsessively. Hitler, who showed little interest in the day-to-day business of government or in administrative detail, needed only to establish the broad parameters of policy. Subordinate leaders and their underlings were encouraged to exercise their own initiative in fulfilling Hitler's perceived objectives.

Kershaw got his start as a member of the historical team working on Martin **Broszat**'s "Bavaria Project," an in-depth investigation of popular attitudes toward and relations with Nazism in the South-German *Land* (province or state). Kershaw's contribution to this project was his *Popular Opinion and Political Dissent in the Third Reich: Bavaria, 1933–1945*, published in 1983. Kershaw concluded that the main core of the Nazi program, **anti-Semitism** and the quest for *Lebensraum*, enjoyed only limited support among the mass of the population. He followed this with an influential book on *The Hitler Myth: Image and Reality in the Third Reich* (1987), in which he applied Max Weber's notion of charismatic leadership to explain how the Führer myth of a wise, omniscient, and all-powerful leader could serve to integrate and unify German society, generating enthusiasm for the regime and concealing underlying social contradictions. Kershaw also published the best short discussion of

historiographical controversies about the **Third Reich** in English, *The Nazi Dictatorship: Problems and Perspectives of Interpretation* (3rd edn, 1993). His most recent book, *Making Friends with Hitler* (2004), critically examined the political record of Lord Charles Londonderry, one of the most prominent proponents of **appeasement** in the 1930s.

KITCHEN, MARTIN (b. 1936) Prolific British-Canadian historian and author of *The Cambridge Illustrated History of Germany* (2000) and *A History of Modern Germany* (2006). Kitchen's research specialty is German military history, but he has been particularly adept in making history accessible to a general readership by dispensing with an elaborate scholarly apparatus. His works include *A Military History of Germany from 1860 to the Present Day* (1976), *Fascism* (1976), *The Coming of Austrian Fascism* (1980), *Nazi Germany at War* (1995), *Europe between the Wars* (2nd edn, 2006), and his short history of the Second World War, *A World in Flames* (1990). His book *The Political Economy of Germany 1815–1914* (1978) explored the question as to why economic modernization did not lead to social modernization in Germany, echoing many themes of the then-dominant model of German social history pioneered by **Fischer** and **Wehler**.

KOONZ, CLAUDIA (b. 1940) Leading American feminist historian of Nazism whose book *Mothers in the Fatherland: Women, the Family, and Nazi Politics* (1987) offered a salutary corrective to the earlier tendency to view women only as passive victims while ignoring their role as historical actors in Nazi Germany. Koonz described women as active participants in the Nazi system despite their restriction to the private sphere. While men were responsible for public policy, women provided the emotional support in domestic life that helped to stabilize the regime. In contrast to Gisela **Bock**, whose work focused on German women as victims of Nazi gender policies, Koonz emphasized the role of German women as willing accomplices and contributors to Nazi power. Their differences led to an exchange in the pages of the prestigious journal *Geschichte und Gesellschaft* (History and Society) in 1989 and 1992, referred to in Germany as the *Historikerinnenstreit* (the debate among women's historians). Koonz's widely acclaimed *The Nazi Conscience* (2003) identified "ethnic fundamentalism," the notion that the welfare of one's own ethnic group defines what is morally good, as the major reason why large sectors of the German public could see nothing morally wrong about Nazism.

KÜHNL, REINHARD (b. 1936) West German Marxist historian who has written extensively on Nazi Germany, the **Weimar Republic**, and right-wing extremism in the Federal Republic. Following a pioneering study of *The National Socialist Left* (1966) on Gregor **Strasser**'s efforts to commit the Nazi Party to greater social reform, Kühnl's most important contributions to Nazi historiography have been in the realm of theory. His *Forms of Bourgeois Dominance* (1971), however, was criticized for eliding crucial differences between fascism and liberal capitalism. Kühnl's work was representative of the revival of theories of fascism and the rejection of **totalitarianism** theory in the 1960s and 1970s. Pointing out the political consequences of historical interpretations, Kühnl intervened actively in the *Historikerstreit*

on the side of **Nolte**'s and **Hillgruber**'s critics in 1987. A leading authority on the neo-Nazi **NPD**, Kühnl turned his scholarly and political attention to right-wing radicalism in Europe in the 1990s.

L

LAQUEUR, WALTER (b. 1921) Founder and editor with George **Mosse** of the *Journal of Contemporary History*, Laqueur is a specialist in Russian history and Russian–German relations. He has also written extensively on German history, with books on the Youth Movement (1962), the **Weimar Republic** (1974), and the **Holocaust** (*The Terrible Secret: Suppression of the Truth of the "Final Solution"*, 1980). Among his most important contributions to the historiography of Nazism are his edited book, *Fascism: A Reader's Guide* (1976), and *Fascism: Past, Present, Future* (1996).

LONGERICH, PETER (b. 1955) A leading member of a younger generation of German historians (see Götz **Aly** and Christian **Gerlach**) who have used the opening of East European archives after the collapse of the Soviet Union to make important contributions to the historiography of the **Holocaust**. Before turning to the history of the Holocaust, Longerich had published books on the history of the **SA** (1989) and the Nazi Party chancellery under **Hess** and **Bormann** (1992). In *The Unwritten Order: Hitler's Role in the Final Solution* (2001) Longerich summarized the findings of his comprehensive investigation into the decision-making process leading to the Holocaust, *Politik der Vernichtung*

(The Politics of Extermination), published in 1998 (a translation is forthcoming). Longerich concluded that **Hitler** played a central, hands-on role in the origins and implementation of the Holocaust, even though there probably was no written order or even a single basic decision (*Grundsatzentscheidung*), as asserted by Gerlach. Longerich traced the extermination policy through several stages, beginning with the resettlement of Jews into ghettos after the defeat of Poland in October 1939. Although the ethnic cleansing of Soviet Jews began with the German invasion of the Soviet Union in the summer of 1941, Longerich believed that it was not until May 1942 that the "**final solution**" was extended to all European Jews under German control. Unlike Christopher **Browning**, Longerich did not consider the construction of killing centers, the deportation of Jews from the **Reich**, or the prohibition of Jewish emigration in October 1941 as compelling evidence that a basic decision to include all European Jews in the extermination program had already been made in 1941. "The history of the Holocaust," Longerich argued, "is not the history of an extermination program that progressed without deviation as a result of a single order, but is rather the history of a process, in the course of which various interests were weighed, priorities established, and decisions made – a process that was, in short, the result of a policy, but shaped by politics."[6] The function of the annihilation policy changed over time as well, according to Longerich, becoming by 1942 a tool for strengthening the radical forces (party and **SS**) in the German occupation administrations engaged in the reordering of the European continent. Like Browning and Richard **Evans**, Longerich appeared as an expert witness in the successful defense of Deborah Lipstadt against David Irving's suit for libel (Lipstadt had called Irving a Holocaust denier in her book, *Denying the Holocaust*, 1993). Longerich testified that Hitler ordered and directed the Holocaust, thus refuting Irving's claim that Hitler never planned or approved a systematic program to kill Jews. In his 2006 book "*Davon haben wir nichts gewusst!*" ("We knew nothing about that") Longerich addressed the paradox that Nazi leaders spoke openly about the destruction of the Jews in public speeches but treated the details of the death camps as a state secret. By announcing the extermination program without revealing its full scale and barbarity, the Nazis ensured the complicity of the German public while avoiding the potentially demoralizing effects of that knowledge. The purpose of this double strategy of treating the Holocaust as an "open secret" was to convince the German people that there was no alternative to fighting the war to the bitter end. Longerich thus confirmed the earlier findings of David **Bankier** and documented them with detailed evidence.

M

MAIER, CHARLES S. (b. 1939) Maier's major contribution to the historiography of Nazism is his authoritative work on *Vergangenheitsbewältigung*, *The Unmasterable Past: History, Holocaust, and German National Identity* (1988), a critique of Ernst **Nolte**'s theses in the *Historikerstreit* and a useful survey of postwar debates on Nazism. He has also written extensively on the period following the First World War, particularly *Recasting Bourgeois Europe* (1975), and on the cold war and the division of Germany. More recently he has turned his attention to the larger context of global imperialism, particularly in *Among Empires: American Ascendancy and its Predecessors* (2006).

MARRUS, MICHAEL R. (b. 1941) Marrus, a Canadian specialist on French Jewry and **anti-Semitism**, is the author of the important historiographical work, *The Holocaust in History* (1987), and the editor of the nine-volume series, *The Nazi Holocaust: Historical Articles on the Destruction of European Jews* (1989). With Robert O. Paxton (b. 1932) he co-authored *Vichy France and the Jews* (1981), which argues that anti-Semitism was not forced on the Vichy regime by the Nazis but originated from domestic sources and was marked by unusual brutality. As a member of a joint Catholic–Jewish commission to examine the eleven volumes of published Vatican documents relating to the Second World War, Marrus was critical of Pius XII's reluctance to assist non-Catholic Jews and his failure to publicize reports of the **Holocaust** or of the plight of the Polish Church. Marrus has also issued a documentary history of *The Nuremberg War Crimes Trials* (1997), pointing out the importance of these trials.

MASON, TIMOTHY (1940–1990) Mason is perhaps best known as the historian who introduced the distinction between **intentionalism** and **functionalism** (or structuralism) in 1981 in a famous essay entitled "Intention and Explanation: A Current Controversy about the Interpretation of National Socialism." At issue was the question whether the peculiar destructiveness and self-destructiveness of the **Third Reich** could best be understood through an analysis of systemic social and economic structures and processes (the structuralist method represented by historians such as Martin **Broszat** or Hans **Mommsen**), or whether the purposes and decisions of the Nazi leadership, particularly **Hitler** himself, were ultimately the crucial factor in explaining the criminality of Nazism (the intentionalist position of historians such as Andreas **Hillgruber** or Klaus **Hildebrand**). At stake was nothing less than the moral responsibility of historians, as both sides accused each other of misrepresenting and understating the evil of Nazism. Mason was particularly critical of the intentionalist interpretative model, which in his view gave far too much explanatory weight to Hitler's own program and rhetoric, but he also criticized functionalist approaches that failed to attach sufficient importance to economic factors or class analysis. He conceded that earlier Marxist approaches had tended to neglect unduly Hitler's purposes and intentions, thus failing to offer a convincing explanation for why the Third Reich generated such genocidal destructiveness. But more serious in Mason's view was the failure of intentionalists to investigate the larger context of capitalist accumulation and imperialism in which the Third Reich was situated.

Mason's own unorthodox Marxist interpretation, which acknowledged the primacy of political over economic interests in the Nazi era, sought to avoid the shortcomings of both approaches. Mason pleaded for retention of the concept of "fascism," which could yield general conclusions rather than merely specific descriptions of the extreme peculiarities of German Nazism. Mason's major, posthumously published work, *Social Policy in the Third Reich: The Working Class and the "National Community"* (1993; a shorter version was originally published in German in 1977), consists of a long essay (first published in German in 1975) along with later revisions and reflections. It documented the failure of the Nazis to gain the active compliance of the working class or to end the class struggle, which continued in the form of apathy, absenteeism, insubordination, work slowdowns, and other forms of disruptive behavior throughout the Nazi era. Mason's most controversial conclusion was that the outbreak of war was strongly conditioned by the internal problems of the regime. According to Mason, the timing of the war could not be adequately explained through Hitler's long-term intentions alone but had to take into account the imperatives and contradictions of an economic system geared to war rather than the satisfaction of consumer demands. The war economy, Mason contended, absorbed the economic resources that might have been used to placate the working class, and the resulting crisis induced Hitler to start his war of conquest sooner than he had planned. Mason did not argue that Hitler launched the war specifically to extricate his regime from economic crisis. Rather, he sought to explain why Hitler was willing to run the grave risk of provoking British and French intervention in September 1939. In a debate carried on in the journal *Past & Present* in the late 1980s, Richard **Overy** disputed Mason's conclusion that war in 1939 was (in part) a response to an insoluble domestic crisis brought about by rearmament. Overy's conclusion that Germany did not face an economic crisis in 1939 was corroborated by Adam **Tooze**. Tooze did, however, corroborate Mason's claim that economic pressures played a key role in Hitler's decision to risk war with the West in 1939.

MEINECKE, FRIEDRICH (1862–1954) Distinguished historian and long-time editor of Germany's most important historical journal *Historische Zeitschrift* until his removal by the Nazis in 1935, Meinecke was important for the historiography of Nazism mainly as a result of his postwar attempt to explain what he called *The German Catastrophe* (1946). Meinecke was trained in the conservative German historicist tradition, which stressed the primacy of the state and the centrality of politics, but he was more liberal than most of his colleagues in the historical profession. He was critical of one-sided power politics, which he characterized as the triumph of Machiavellianism over morality, and he supported the **Weimar Republic**. Nonetheless, like Gerhard **Ritter**, he struck an apologetic and evasive note in *The German Catastrophe*, viewing the rise of the Nazis as a European phenomenon resulting from the growth of rationalism, materialism, utilitarianism, technology, and democracy. True to his own conservative upper-middle-class values, Meinecke equated Nazism with the unwillingness of the restive lower classes to stay in their proper places. The moral degeneration of European society was rooted in "the mistaken striving after the unattainable happiness of the masses of mankind."[7] While more critical of the Prussian military tradition than Ritter, Meinecke attributed the perversion of that tradition to the Western Enlightenment cult of reason, which he paradoxically held responsible for generating irrationality by impoverishing the "spirit." He identified the causes of Nazism in the misguided pursuit of happiness (leading to unsatisfiable expectations of a better life), the Industrial Revolution, excessive population growth, and the rise of socialism. Like Ritter, he failed to appreciate that the Nazis only coopted the rhetoric of socialism to undercut the socialist workers' movement. Meinecke also insisted that chance was a major factor in **Hitler**'s assumption of power, thus implicitly diluting the responsibility of the German elites for bringing him to power.

MOMMSEN, HANS (b. 1930)   Member of a famous family of historians (his great-grandfather Theodor, a classical historian, won the Nobel prize for literature in 1902, and his twin brother Wolfgang, who died in 2004, was a prominent historian of Bismarckian and Wilhelmine Germany), Hans Mommsen is the leading representative of the left-liberal "functionalist" interpretation of Nazism that emerged to prominence in Germany in the 1960s and 1970s. In numerous books and articles on the **Weimar Republic** and the Nazi regime, Mommsen stressed the culpability of Germany's conservative economic and military elites both in **Hitler**'s rise to power and in his system of rule. He has been critical of potentially apologetic interpretations that overemphasize Hitler's personal role in the Nazi system, thus neglecting the complicity of collaborating elites as well as the conditions and structures that allowed Hitler to gain such indisputable overall control. Mommsen corroborated **Broszat**'s notion of the Nazi regime as a **"polycracy"** of competing authorities attributable in good part to Hitler's rejection of orderly bureaucratic procedures and reliance on improvisation and *ad hoc* institutions to achieve his policy objectives. Hitler's haphazard style of leadership contributed to what Mommsen called the typically Nazi process of "cumulative radicalization" in which bureaucratic agencies and party officials competed with each other to carry out the perceived will of the Führer.

According to Mommsen, anti-Semitic ideology and Hitler's intentions are not enough to account for the **"final solution,"** which was conceived as a sequence of emergency measures to solve the self-created "Jewish problem" rather than as the realization of a master plan for extermination. Mommsen certainly did not slight ideological factors in his interpretation of Nazism, however. Ideology provided the indispensable motor of "cumulative radicalization." Mommsen attributed Germany's fanatical resistance at the end of the war to the Nazis' ideological mobilization and their belief that a resolute will could make up for lack of material resources. In his account of Nazi policies in the Second World War, Mommsen gave great weight to Nazi leaders' determination to avoid the perceived mistakes of German leaders in the First World War, who had failed to secure the unity of the home front. Mommsen was critical of **totalitarianism** theory, which located Nazism closer to revolutionary movements of the left than to counter-revolutionary movements of the right (e.g., Joachim **Fest**). Mommsen also rejected interpretations that depicted Nazism as a modernizing movement, whether intentionally or unintentionally (e.g., **Zitelmann, Dahrendorf**). Mommsen played a leading role in the *Historikerstreit*, in which he defended the left-liberal critique launched by the prominent social philosopher Jürgen Habermas against the conservative apologetics of Ernst **Nolte** and his supporters. Mommsen's most important books in English are *From Weimar to Auschwitz* (1991), *The Rise and Fall of Weimar Democracy* (1989; English trans. 1996), *Alternatives to Hitler: German Resistance under the Third Reich* (2003), and the edited volume, *The Third Reich between Vision and Reality* (2001).

MOSSE, GEORGE L. (1918–1999) Grandson of the founder of Berlin's most prestigious press empire before 1933, Mosse was a prolific cultural historian whose contributions to Nazi historiography included books on *The Crisis of German Ideology: The Intellectual Origins of the Third Reich* (1964), *Nazi Culture* (1966), *Germans and Jews: The Right, the Left, and the Search for a "Third Force" in pre-Nazi Germany* (1970), *The Nationalization of the Masses: Political Symbols and Mass Movements in Germany from the Napoleonic Wars through the Third Reich* (1975), *Toward the Final Solution: A History of European Racism* (1977), and *Nationalism and Sexuality: Morality and Sexual Norms in Modern Europe* (1985). Mosse pioneered research into the *völkisch* and cultural antecedents of Nazism, but moved steadily toward wider, more comprehensive themes. Mosse's scholarly trajectory, itself symptomatic of a wider trend in the historiography of Nazism, brought him full circle. From his interpretation of Nazism in his early works as a specifically German anti-Jewish, anti-liberal, anti-bourgeois, and fundamentally irrational ideology, a product of Germany's deviant path to modernity, Mosse turned to a more postmodern interpretation that traced the sources of Nazi criminality not just to a uniquely German **anti-Semitism** but to the European-wide hatred, intolerance, and exclusion resulting from the marriage of bourgeois nationalism and morality. He came to see Nazism not as a revolt against middle-class values but rather as a corruption and radicalization of those very values. Persecuting all those who violated society's norms, Nazism represented the most destructive expression of the "bourgeois" drive to dominate and cleanse the world in the name of morality and respectability.

It was the integration of anti-Semitism into this more systematic structure of racism and denigration of outsiders that according to Mosse unleashed the full genocidal potential of Nazism. Anti-bourgeois and bourgeois motifs merged to produce the peculiar destructiveness of Nazism.

N

NEUMANN, FRANZ (1900–1954) A former trade union activist in the **Weimar Republic**, Neumann emigrated to the US, where his landmark analysis of Nazism, *Behemoth*, was published in 1942. The title, a reference to the monster of chaos (juxtaposed to the *Leviathan*, Thomas Hobbes's symbol of the state as guarantor of power and order), was deliberately chosen to symbolize the anarchic and destructive nature of the Nazis' peculiar form of "totalitarian monopoly capitalism." Rejecting the **Comintern**'s simplistic notion of the Nazi state as merely the instrument of monopoly capitalists, Neumann described the **Third Reich** as a more complex system in which four main elite groups collaborated and competed to direct the state and society: the bureaucracy, the party elite, industry, and the army. In the cold war climate after the Second World War, Neumann's unorthodox Marxist analysis, based on his commitment to a democratic and constitutional form of socialism, was politically marginalized, although it continued to open up new avenues of research to historians and has withstood the test of time remarkably well.

NOAKES, JEREMY (b. 1941) Noakes is the editor (with Geoffrey Pridham) of the most important collection of Nazi documents in English, *Documents on Nazism*, first appearing in 1974 and ultimately expanded into a four-volume set covering *The Rise to Power* (1983), *State, Economy and Society* (1984), *Foreign Policy, War and Racial Extermination* (1988), and *The German Home Front in World War II* (1998). Noakes is also the author of the pioneering regional study *The Nazi Party in Lower Saxony 1921–1933* (1971) and of numerous shorter publications on such diverse aspects of Nazism as the German resistance, the **eugenics** program, the terror apparatus, policy toward *Mischlings*, the Nazi constituency, Nazism in the universities, and Nazism in the provinces.

NOLTE, ERNST (b. 1923) The leading representative of right-wing historical revisionism in Germany seeking to "normalize" the history of Nazism, Nolte achieved public notoriety in the *Historikerstreit* (historians' debate) in 1986–1987 with his assertion that Nazism must be understood as an at least partially justified response to the greater evil and destructiveness of Soviet Communism. Nolte denied the unique criminality of the **Holocaust**, portraying it instead as a radical defensive reaction to the perceived genocidal threat posed by "Asiatic Bolshevism" and the Russian Revolution. According to Nolte, Nazi plans to destroy an entire race, the Jews, were modeled on the precedent established by the Bolsheviks in their efforts to destroy an entire class, the bourgeoisie. Nolte attributed ultimate responsibility for the atrocities of the twentieth century to the communist revolutionaries, without whose provocation there would have been no Nazi counter-revolution. This was the main thesis of the concluding volume of his "tetralogy on the history of modern

ideologies," *The European Civil War: Bolshevism and National Socialism* (1987), which has not been translated into English.

Nolte's scholarly reputation, however, rests on the first volume of this series, *Three Faces of Fascism: Action Française, Italian Fascism, National Socialism* (1963; English trans. 1966), which had already put anti-Marxism at the center of fascist ideology. Nolte's right-wing bias and apologetic purposes became increasingly apparent in his subsequent volumes, *Marxismus und die industrielle Revolution* (Marxism and the Industrial Revolution, 1983) and *Deutschland und der Kalte Krieg* (Germany and the cold war, 1985), both of which retained the interpretative framework of the Second World War as a preventive war against communism, thus linking **Hitler**'s cause with the Western cause in the cold war. A collection of essays, *Marxism, Fascism, Cold War*, was published in Germany in 1977 and translated into English in 1982. Unlike adherents of traditional **totalitarianism** theory, Nolte gave due emphasis to the fundamental differences and mortal antagonism between left and right, but he insisted on the causal (and criminal) priority of the "eternal left," which he defined as the rejection of existing social arrangements in the name of a higher normative code of reason or justice. Nolte thus provided an interpretation that allows Nazism to be at least partially rehabilitated without denying its radical nature or genocidal crimes. In his most recent book on *The Weimar Republic* (2006), Nolte again attributed the destruction of democracy in Germany to the international struggle between communists and fascists.

In books on Nietzsche (1990) and **Heidegger** (1992) Nolte sought to give Nazism a philosophical pedigree to rival the

Marxist pedigree of communism. He resurrected the dubious notion of Nietzsche as the intellectual progenitor of fascism (thus also indirectly exculpating the traditional Christian conservatism that was so instrumental in bringing **Hitler** to power), and he defended Heidegger's option for Nazism in 1933 as a reasonable response to the perceived danger of a communist takeover. As a former student of Heidegger's, Nolte adopted what he called a philosopher's approach to history, seeking not so much to describe historical events as to discern their "inner" or "higher" truths. His "phenomenological" method sought to understand the internal logic of historical actors and events and freed him from having to provide empirical proofs for his assertions and conjectures. His influence on the "new right" in Germany in the 1980s and 1990s was somewhat limited, however, by his insistence (shared with many Marxist historians) that Hitler's movement represented a bourgeois counter-revolution. Some of his fellow-conservatives (see **Zitelmann**) rejected Nolte's linkage of the bourgeoisie to Nazism, preferring instead the older conservative argument that Nazism was an anti-bourgeois revolt, thus incriminating the masses not the elites.

O

ORLOW, DIETRICH (b. 1937) Known primarily for his thorough two-volume history of the Nazi Party (1969 and 1973), Orlow has also written a two-volume history of the state of Prussia in the **Weimar** era (1986 and 1991) and a widely used text on the *History of Modern Germany: 1870 to the Present* (1987, 4th rev. edn 1999). In recent years Orlow has branched out into comparative history with particular focus on Social Democratic parties in Holland, France, and Germany.

OVERY, RICHARD (b. 1947) British military and economic historian and one of the foremost authorities on the Second World War. His books include *The Air War, 1939–1945* (1980), *The Origins of the Second World War* (1987), *War and Economy in the Third Reich* (1994), *The Nazi Economic Recovery, 1932–1938* (1996), *Why the Allies Won* (1996), *Russia's War: A History of the Soviet Effort, 1941–1945* (1998), *The Battle* [of Britain]: *Summer 1940* (2000), and a documentary history of the **Nuremberg Trials**, *Interrogations: The Nazi Elite in Allied Hands* (2001). Overy engaged in a widely publicized debate with Tim **Mason** in the British journal *Past & Present* in 1987. He disputed Mason's claim that Hitler had been forced to go to war in 1939 to prevent an economic crisis. Overy contended that Hitler had only miscalculated the likelihood of Britain and France intervening in the war against Poland. Like Gerhard **Weinberg**, Overy rejected the notion that the German invasion of the Soviet Union in 1941 was a preventive war. In *The Dictators: Hitler's Germany and Stalin's Russia* (2004) Overy concluded that the similarities between the two regimes outweighed the differences. Both systems were based on utopian visions that were similar in form though divergent in purpose, and both regimes understood that their true enemy was the liberal West. Critics of Overy's revived **totalitarianism** model, however, questioned his failure to differentiate between the very different popular bases on which these two regimes rested.

P

PEUKERT, DETLEV J. K. (1950–1990)
Short-lived but highly influential German historian and part of the movement of *Alltagsgeschichte* (history of everyday life) in the 1980s to which he contributed a history of the experiences of ordinary Germans during the **Third Reich**. Peukert stressed the ambivalence of popular interactions with the regime, ranging from active collaboration to passive resistance, and revealed the ambiguous but unavoidable complicity even of Germans who did not share the Nazi ideology. Peukert's most significant contribution to the historiography of Nazism, however, was his critique of modernization theory (the notion that Nazism can best be understood as a product of inadequate modernization). In his two major works, *Inside Nazi Germany: Conformity, Opposition, and Racism in Everyday Life* (1982), and *The Weimar Republic: The Crisis of Classical Modernity* (1987), and in his untranslated study of child welfare policies, *The Limits of Social Discipline* (1986), Peukert took issue with the conventional notion (implicit in Hans-Ulrich **Wehler**'s *Sonderweg* model) that Nazism resulted from Germany's failure to modernize and argued instead that Nazism represented the dark side of Germany's extraordinary modernity (as also argued by Zygmunt **Bauman**). Nazism demonstrated "the pathologies and seismic fractures of the modern civilizing process."[8] Peukert's interpretation highlighted the technocratic and contradictory aspects of Nazi rule and suggestively linked the **Holocaust** and other Nazi atrocities to modern "scientific" **eugenic** schemes. In Peukert's view Nazi racial policy, including compulsory sterilization, eugenic abortion, **euthanasia** (the killing of the mentally and physically disabled), and the "**final solution** of the Jewish question," exemplified a central feature of modernity, *Machbarkeitswahn* (the illusion that anything is doable), the belief that society could be renovated and social problems resolved through the application of biological principles and practices. In Peukert's interpretation Nazism typified the murderous potential of modern social engineering projects.

In arguing that Nazism demonstrated the negative potential of modernization, the pathologies rather than the achievements of modernity, Peukert drew on postmodern critiques of Enlightenment rationality: the Enlightenment's claim to universal truth and the "pathologization" of difference contributed to the marginalization and dehumanization of anyone who did not conform to the "rational" norms of society. Peukert rejected the comforting notion that Nazi barbarism marked a relapse into the primitive past, warning that it might instead offer a preview of a potentially genocidal future. While his empirical studies of Nazi Germany have been widely praised, not all historians share Peukert's dark vision of modernity. The American historian Peter Fritzsche (b. 1959), for instance, in a review article "Did Weimar Fail?" (*The Journal of Modern History*, 1996), rejected the teleological view that modern eugenics and biopolitics necessarily led to the excesses of the Third Reich. While he agreed with Peukert that **Weimar** (and Nazi) Germany were thoroughly modern societies, he did not share Peukert's pessimistic conclusion that social manipulation and control were the inevitable byproducts of post-Enlightenment modernization.

R

RAUSCHNING, HERMANN (1887–1982) A prominent German conservative, veteran of the First World War, and member of the Nazi party in 1931, Rauschning became president of the Danzig city government in 1933 before a personal conflict with East Prussian **Gauleiter** Albert Forster forced him to resign. In 1938 Rauschning published *The Revolution of Nihilism* as a way of settling accounts with the Nazis. This widely read book provided an interpretation of Nazism shared by many of his disillusioned fellow conservatives. According to Rauschning **Hitler**'s movement was solely opportunistic, without consistent ideology, program, or principle. By describing the Nazis as only interested in exercising power, Rauschning in effect extricated his own anti-democratic and anti-communist values and goals from complicity in the Nazi project without denying them. In some respects Rauschning anticipated **totalitarianism** theory by situating the Nazi movement on the left rather than the right of the political spectrum. Many of the direct quotations in his 1939 book, *Hitler Speaks*, purportedly based on conversations with Hitler, were fabricated, and this book is no longer considered a reliable historical source.

REICH, WILHELM (1897–1957) Controversial Marxist psychoanalyst, whose main contribution to the interpretation of Nazism was his book, *The Mass Psychology of Fascism* (1934). Here Reich argued that fascism could not be explained solely on the basis of economics, as orthodox Marxists assumed. Understanding the nature of fascism was not possible without recourse to Freudian insights and categories. Ideology was not merely a reflection of economic processes but a "material force" in its own right, mediating between the economic conditions of society and the psychological structures of individuals who lived in that society. The hierarchical social system that led to Nazism was reproduced and transmitted through longstanding patriarchal practices and sexual repression, which led to a fixation on the collective "mother," the nation. Fascism was not just a counter-revolution against the proletarian movement for economic freedom but also against the revolutionary quest for sexual freedom. For downplaying economic struggle, Reich was expelled from the Communist Party; for his methodology of generalizing from individual case histories to a whole social group (in this case, the lower middle class that formed the Nazis' mass base) he was read out of the International Psychoanalytical Association; and for his alleged defrauding of the public he was imprisoned in the US. His advocacy of sexual revolution, however, made Reich something of a cult figure for the youthful cohort of the generational 1960s rebellion.

RITTER, GERHARD (1888–1967) Ritter's conservative ideology was very much determined by his formative years in the Wilhelmian Empire, and especially by his service at the front during the First World War. Like most German nationalists he rejected the **Versailles Treaty** and the **Weimar** parliamentary system, embraced the "stab-in-the-back" legend, and denied German guilt for the outbreak of the First World War. While rejecting the Nazis' extremism in the 1930s, particularly their violent persecution of the Jews, Ritter admired and celebrated **Hitler**'s foreign policy successes and supported German expansionism. These nationalist attitudes colored his historical works as well. His contacts to the leader of the conservative resistance, Carl **Goerdeler**, whose biography he published in 1947, enhanced Ritter's stature after the war and helped to give his conservative, apologetic interpretation of Nazism a certain credibility and wide resonance.

According to Ritter, Nazism was the product of mass politics and the revolutionary movements emanating from the French Revolution. He rejected attempts to trace the origins of Nazism to German history, attributing it instead to such European-wide aspects of modernity as industrialization, materialism, rationalism, Marxism, secularization, Darwinian science, and technology. In Ritter's view, Nazism was rooted not in monarchist absolutism but in the Rousseauian general will. However, the consensus today is that Ritter was simply wrong in identifying Nazism as a direct consequence of the rise of socialism rather than as a reaction to it. Ritter devoted his post-war professional career, including his major work, the four-volume *Staatskunst und Kriegshandwerk* (Statecraft and Military Craft, 1954–1968), to defending the Prussian monarchical and military traditions and denying any link between the Bismarckian Empire and the **Third Reich**. In the early 1960s he led the outraged conservative attack on Fritz **Fischer**, whose pioneering works demonstrated the culpability of German government officials in the events leading up to the outbreak of war in 1914. Very influential in their time, Ritter's works are remembered today mainly as examples of outdated conservative attitudes and methods.

ROSEMAN, MARK (b. 1958) Roseman's research interests originally focused on the post-1945 reconstruction and occupation of Germany, but more recently his interest has shifted to the Nazi era and the **Holocaust**. This shift resulted in the prize-winning book, *The Past in Hiding: Memory and Survival in Nazi Germany* (2000), a thoroughly researched case study of one Jewish family's fate in Nazi Germany. The book was highly praised as a pioneering contribution not only to the study of Jewish lives under the Nazis but also to the study of the tensions between history and memory. Roseman's book on the **Wannsee Conference**, *The Villa, the Lake, the Meeting* (2002), concluded that **Heydrich**'s major purpose in convening the conference was to establish shared complicity with civilian administrators in the planned genocide, even though the specific means by which the genocide was to be carried out had not yet been determined.

S

SCHOENBAUM, DAVID (b. 1935) Schoenbaum's importance for the historiography of Nazism rests with his 1966 book *Hitler's Social Revolution*, a path-breaking study that documented the many ways in which the Nazis modernized German society despite their commitment to an anti-modern ideology. Under the Nazis such features of modernity as social mobility and the breakdown of traditional class divisions received a decisive boost. His findings corroborated **Dahrendorf**'s view of the Nazis as unintentional modernizers. Critics such as Hans **Mommsen**, however, have taken issue with Schoenbaum's use of the term "revolution" to describe this change.

SHIRER, WILLIAM L. (1904–1993) Journalist turned historian, William Shirer is today primarily known for his massive best-seller, *The Rise and Fall of the Third Reich* (1960), a well-documented, richly detailed, non-academic narrative account written from a strongly anti-Nazi perspective. Shirer was thoroughly familiar with Germany and with the Nazi hierarchy, having served as a CBS radio reporter in Berlin at the start of the war before being forced to leave in December 1940. His *Berlin Diary*, published in early 1941, accurately predicted the German invasion of Russia and the outbreak of war with the United States. It also contained eye-witness accounts of the Nuremberg party rallies, the French capitulation on June 22, 1940, and numerous other events.

STACHURA, PETER (b. 1944) British historian and author of important monographs on *The German Youth Movement* (1981) and *Gregor Strasser and the Rise of Nazism* (1983). His books on the **Weimar Republic** include *The Weimar Republic and the Younger Proletariat* (1989) and *Political Leaders in Weimar Germany* (1992), as well as several edited volumes. In recent years the focus of his research has shifted to Polish history in the twentieth century.

STEINBACH, PETER (b. 1948) Prolific German historian of the resistance to National Socialism. His book on that subject was first published in Germany in 1985 and reissued in expanded form in 1994. In 1983 Steinbach was selected by Berlin mayor and later president of the Federal Republic Richard von Weizsäcker (b. 1920) to head a group of scholars to expand the permanent exhibit on the German resistance in the former army headquarters building in Berlin where the military conspiracy was crushed on July 20, 1944. Against the opposition of conservatives, including members of the **Stauffenberg** family, Steinbach decided to include members of the Communist resistance in the exhibit, which opened on July 20, 1989. The inclusion of such groups as the **Red Orchestra** and the "National Committee for a Free Germany," founded in July 1943 by German officers in a prisoner-of-war camp in the Soviet Union, remained controversial at least until the collapse of the **German Democratic Republic** some months later. The catalogue of the exhibition, written with Johannes Tuchel (b. 1957), was translated into English in 1990. Steinbach has written numerous essays on all aspects of the German resistance, as well as on subjects ranging from Nazi crimes and **concentration camps** to the post-war trials, historical memory, and the ***Historikerstreit***.

STEPHENSON, JILL (b. 1944) Leading British historian of the role of women and women's organizations (particularly the NSF [National Socialist Women's Union] and the **DFW** [German Women's Enterprise]) in Nazi Germany and of the Nazis' exercises in quantitative and qualitative "reproductive engineering" to reverse the declining birth rate and to produce more "racially valuable" children. Stephenson's works include *Women in Nazi Society* (1975), *The Nazi Organization of Women* (1981), *Women in Nazi Germany* (2001), and most recently *Hitler's Home Front: Württemberg under the Nazis* (2006). In her study of forced labor in southern Germany, Stephenson found that racial ideology often gave way to pragmatic considerations in rural areas as German farmers, many of them women, became increasingly dependent on the labor of foreign workers.

STERN, FRITZ (b. 1927) An émigré to the US in the late 1930s, Stern is the author of an influential study of the intellectual origins of Nazism, *The Politics of Cultural Despair: A Study in the Rise of Germanic Ideology* (1961). Its main thesis, reflecting to some extent the confident, affirmative political culture of the US in the 1950s, was that radical pessimism in late nineteenth- and early twentieth-century Germany about the putative decline of German civilization and high culture as a result of the spread of liberal and democratic values and institutions prepared the ground for the rise of Nazism. He pursued this theme in three volumes of essays published as *The Failure of Illiberalism* (1972), *Dreams and Delusions* (1989), and *Einstein's German World* (1999). The Nazis were heirs to a vulgarized idealist tradition that rationalized imperialism and power politics on the basis of a superior culture and spiritual values allegedly under attack from the spread of Jewish influence and the left. Stern unmasked the anti-democratic motives and materialistic class interests behind the disinterested pose of this "vulgarized idealism." By deprecating the realms of politics and utilitarian pragmatism and exalting the realms of spiritual ideals and "morality," Germany's elites ennobled their own class interests, sanctified social divisions, and maligned movements of social and political reform. Stern considered the rise of the Nazis neither inevitable nor accidental. One of his essays, "The Temptation of National Socialism," described the pseudo-religious appeal of Nazism, to which Germany's elites proved particularly susceptible. His memoir, *Five Germanys I Have Known*, appeared in 2006.

T

TAYLOR, A. J. P. (1906–1990) Popular but controversial British historian, whose major work was *The Struggle for Mastery in Europe, 1848–1918* (1954). His importance for the historiography of Nazism is based on two works, *The Course of German History: A Survey of the Development of Germany since 1815* (1946) and *The Origins of the Second World War* (1961). The former, written during the war and inevitably reflecting the hostile passions of that conflict, was a classic indictment of Germany's anti-democratic and militarist tradition. In his later book on the events leading up to the Second World War Taylor seemed to reverse course, blaming the outbreak of the war on Britain's disastrous policy of **appeasement**, thus seemingly taking some of the onus of guilt from Germany's leadership. By characterizing **Hitler**'s foreign policy as not significantly different from earlier German policies, Taylor did not intend to absolve Hitler of culpability, however. Instead, his assertion that Hitler's policies were consistent with those of mainstream German nationalists was intended as a rebuke to British leaders, whose miscalculations and policy of appeasement made war in September 1939 unavoidable. Taylor was particularly critical of the failure of the British government to follow up Soviet overtures for an anti-fascist military alliance in the 1930s. Only by resurrecting the grand alliance of the First World War, which in fact came about after the German invasion of the USSR and the Japanese attack on the US in 1941, might war have been prevented in 1939.

TOOZE, ADAM (b. 1967) Young British economic historian whose impressive tome, *The Wages of Destruction: The Making and Breaking of the Nazi Economy* (2006), interprets the Second World War as **Hitler**'s desperate response (in the context of his conviction that Germany was locked in a mortal racial struggle with the Jews) to the challenge posed by the allegedly Jewish-dominated United States, both as a rival to Germany for global power and as a seductive model of a way of life that threatened traditional European institutions by its affluence and gratification of material and sensual desires. The book describes in unprecedented detail the extraordinary mobilization of German resources during the war to overcome the material advantages of Germany's foes. Tooze places the genocide of the Jews within a framework that gives weight both to overarching ideological tenets and mundane pragmatic considerations. Tooze also challenged **Aly**'s contention that the Nazis bought German popular support by reducing their taxes and offering welfare-state benefits funded through the expropriation of Jews and the occupied peoples of Europe. While in no way denying the Nazis' predatory practices, Tooze showed that the Nazis would not have been able to finance the war solely by conquest and spoliation. Moreover, the sacrifices imposed on the German population were borne unequally by Germany's subordinate classes.

TURNER, HENRY A. (b. 1932) Author of *German Big Business and the Rise of Hitler* (1985) and leading American critic of Marxist interpretations attributing the rise of Nazism to capitalist interests. In Turner's view Marxist interpretations are politically motivated, aimed primarily at discrediting Western capitalist systems, and therefore illegitimate. By exaggerating business support for Nazism and providing false diagnoses for action, Marxist interpretations, according to Turner, had had the unintended result of paralyzing effective resistance to Nazism in the early 1930s. By eliding the differences between **Papen**, **Schleicher**, **Hugenberg**, and **Hitler**, later Marxist interpretations trivialized Nazism and underestimated its evil "elemental force." Yet Turner's own impressive empirical evidence implicated the German business community in the breakdown of the parliamentary system and the destruction of **Weimar** democracy. Although he found that corporate donations to the Nazis before 1933 had not been substantially greater than to other "bourgeois" parties and were designed mainly to protect business interests against all possible contingencies, he acknowledged the importance of massive business support for the Nazis after Hitler came to power. Turner adopted Tim **Mason**'s formula of the "primacy of politics," giving it a different twist, however, by arguing that economic interests played only a secondary role in Hitler's rise to power. In *Hitler's Thirty Days to Power: January 1933* (1996) Turner presented the Nazi seizure of power as a highly contingent event, brought about by the well-meaning but misguided actions of a few individuals. Turner's rigorously positivistic method, eschewing conceptual generalizations and structural analysis in favor of close descriptions of individual experiences and a strong emphasis on individual agency, contrasted sharply to the works of social historians such as **Mommsen** or **Wehler**. In 1984 Turner challenged not only the Marxist perspective but also the scholarly integrity of David Abraham, whose originally well-received book *The Collapse of the Weimar Republic*

(1981) turned out to have contained an unusually large number of inaccuracies in quotations and citations (most of them corrected in a second edition of his book in 1986). The dispute led to a rancorous but intellectually stimulating exchange between Abraham and Gerald D. Feldman (the leading American historian of the Great Inflation of 1924) on historical methods and practices in the pages of *Central European History* in 1985.

V

VERMEIL, EDMOND (1878–1964) French literary scholar who traced the origins of Nazism back to the tradition of Romanticism in Germany in a book first published in France in 1938, *Doctrinaire de la révolution allemande*. His essay, "Origin, Nature, and Development of German Nationalist Ideology in the 19th and 20th Centuries" (1955), represented a school of thought that enjoyed particular currency in the years immediately preceding and following the Second World War when hostility to Germany ran high in Europe. Strongly influenced by the passions of war, this particular interpretative model of a German ideological *Sonderweg* no longer commands much support among historians today.

W

WAITE, ROBERT G. L. (1919–1999) Canadian-American historian whose book, *Vanguard of Nazism* (1952), pioneered the study of the **Free Corps** as the forerunners of Nazism in the period following the First World War. Waite also authored a biography of **Hitler**, *The Psychopathic God* (1977), perhaps the most notable example of the genre of "psycho-history," which utilized psychoanalytical categories to explain Hitler's policies and practices. Waite's other relevant works included *Hitler and Nazi Germany* (1965) and *Kaiser and Führer: A Comparative Study of Personality and Politics* (1998).

WEHLER, HANS-ULRICH (b. 1931) Although Wehler's primary research interests lie in the history of the Second Empire, his work has exercised great influence on the historiography of Nazi Germany as well. Wehler's most important works included *Bismarck und der Imperialismus* (1969), *The German Empire, 1871–1918* (1973; English trans. 1985), and the monumental four-volume *Deutsche Gesellschaftsgeschichte* (German Social History, 1987–2003), the final volume of which covered the years 1918 to 1949. A leading member of the so-called "Bielefeld School" of socially critical historians that also included Jürgen Kocka (b. 1941) and Hans-Jürgen Puhle (b. 1940), Wehler set forth the so-called *Sonderweg* theory to help explain the rise and triumph of Nazism in Germany. According to this interpretation, sharply criticized by Geoff **Eley** and David Blackbourn, a key factor in Germany's susceptibility to fascism was the lack of a liberal bourgeois revolution in Germany (due to the failure of the revolution of 1848). The consequence of the weakness of liberalism was that the landed aristocracy continued to wield disproportionate power in German politics. According to Wehler, pre-democratic values and institutions predominated in Bismarckian and

Wilhelminian Germany. While the German economy was rapidly modernized, Germany's political system failed to keep pace with democratic reforms enacted in Western Europe. The resulting social tensions in Germany and differences from the Western European model of liberal democracy helped to account for the aggressive nature of German foreign policy in the twentieth century.

Wehler seconded Fritz **Fischer**'s thesis that the German political and military elites deliberately pursued expansionist policies to integrate the growing labor movement into the existing Imperial system and to combat Social Democratic initiatives for liberalizing or egalitarian reforms. In support of his interpretation Wehler reissued the previously ignored book of the short-lived progressive historian Eckart Kehr (1902–1933), *The Primacy of Domestic Policy*, in 1965. Kehr's thesis that German policies were primarily directed toward the containment of social democracy and preservation of the domestic status quo contradicted the traditional emphasis on the primacy of foreign policy by conservative historians such as Gerhard **Ritter** and, among the younger generation, Klaus **Hildebrand** or Andreas **Hillgruber**.

Wehler played a leading role in the transformation of traditional historical methodology in Germany in the 1960s and 1970s when the time-honored approach of German historicism – concentration on political events, the power relations between states, and the motivations of leading statesmen – was successfully challenged by a younger generation of historians. Their efforts to integrate the methods and findings of the social sciences – sociology, economics, and political science – in historical studies had a liberalizing effect on the German historical profession, which had

previously been biased in favor of the defense of existing social and political institutions. Wehler also urged historians to become more reflective and open about their own *"erkenntnisleitende Interessen"* (epistemological assumptions). Although conservatives denounced his socially critical approach as quasi-Marxist, Wehler's methodology was more indebted to Max Weber's theories of modernization, progressive rationalization, and charismatic leadership. Wehler controversially applied the latter concept both to Bismarck and to **Hitler**, leading his critics to accuse him of exaggerating the continuities between Bismarck's and Hitler's regimes and of failing to appreciate the degree to which Nazism represented a distinctive symptom of the major rupture produced by the First World War. Wehler's strong commitment to progressive liberal values was evident in the ***Historikerstreit***, in which he joined the fray on the side of Ernst **Nolte**'s critics with his polemic, *Entsorgung der deutschen Vergangenheit* (Unburdening the German Past) in 1988.

Wehler's method of structural socio-economic analysis was itself challenged by a younger generation of postmodernist cultural historians with left-wing sympathies, notably Detlev **Peukert**, in the late 1970s and 1980s. Their efforts to write history "from below" by describing the everyday experiences of ordinary people (*Alltagsgeschichte*) were implicitly critical of the allegedly abstract, impersonal, institutional, top-down approach of Wehler's socio-structural method. The generational conflict came to a head in 1998 when younger historians such as Götz **Aly** accused Wehler's generation of deliberately ignoring the Nazi affiliations of their own mentors, especially Theodor Schieder (1909–1984) and Werner Conze

(1910–1986), whose careers had begun in the **Third Reich**. The charge that Wehler's brand of social history had its roots in the kind of Nazi *Volksgeschichte* (nationalist-populist history) that Conze and Schieder practiced in their youth was misleading, however. The liberal, democratic, socio-critical premises of the Bielefeld School had little in common with the ethnographic methods of Schieder and Conze, whose purpose was to justify German supremacy and expansion.

WEINBERG, GERHARD L. (b. 1928) Leading American historian of Nazi foreign policy and the Second World War. His most important works are the two volumes of *The Foreign Policy of Hitler's Germany* (1970, 1980) and his massive *A World at Arms: A Global History of World War II* (1994), a revised edition of which was issued in 2005. A collection of Weinberg's essays was published in *Germany, Hitler, and World War II* in 1995. In contrast to A.J.P. **Taylor**'s portrait of **Hitler** pursuing a traditional foreign policy of continental dominance, Weinberg argued that Hitler was driven by global ambitions. In a debate carried on in the pages of Germany's leading journal for contemporary history, *Vierteljahrshefte für Zeitgeschichte*, in 1953 and 1954, Weinberg played an important role in debunking the thesis advanced by Andreas **Hillgruber** that the German invasion of the Soviet Union in 1941 had prevented a planned Soviet attack. As a result of the evidence put forth by Weinberg, Hillgruber retracted the preventive war thesis (although it continued to be propagated by right-wing nationalists in the course of the cold war). Weinberg also effectively refuted David Hoggan's contention in 1961 that war had been forced on Hitler by the hostile actions

of the West. It was Weinberg who first discovered *Hitler's Second Book* in the archives, a translation of which he published in 2003. His *Visions of Victory* (2005) examines the goals and hopes of eight principal leaders during the Second World War.

WELCH, DAVID (b. 1950) Author of *The Third Reich: Politics and Propaganda* (rev. edn 2002), Welch has concentrated his research on Nazi propaganda both in practice and in theory. Welch has investigated not only the specific rhetorical or psychological techniques of persuasion that **Hitler**, **Goebbels** and other Nazis used to achieve their desired effects (particularly in the new medium of film), but also the social and political context that enhanced or limited the power of **propaganda**. One key to the Nazis' propagandistic success was their skill in merging Nazi ideology with traditional themes of patriotism and religion. Rather than changing people's minds, they reinforced existing prejudices.

WINKLER, HEINRICH AUGUST (b. 1938) Important member of the generation of German historians that came of age shortly after the end of the Second World War. His *opus magnum*, The *Long Road West* (2006), first appeared in Germany in two volumes in 2000 and 2002. A history of Germany from 1806 to 1990, this book described the German *Sonderweg* as a belated triumph of Westernization, culminating in the establishment of a reunified democratic Germany in 1990. Winkler's main field of expertise is the **Weimar Republic**, on which he has published many books, including a three-volume history of the labor movement from 1918 to 1933 (1985–1990) and a comprehensive history in 1994. Winkler conceded that the **SPD**'s failure to enact thoroughgoing social reform in the aftermath of the First World War impaired the long-term viability of the Weimar Republic by strengthening the right and alienating the left, but he defended the SPD for pursuing the only course that could possibly have led to the establishment of a functioning parliamentary democracy under extremely adverse conditions. Most recently Winkler's interest has turned to the politics of historiography, possibly as a reaction to criticisms of the unapologetically left-liberal perspective of his own historical works.

WIPPERMANN, WOLFGANG (b. 1945) Co-author with Michael **Burleigh** of *The Racial State* (1991), a study that authoritatively refuted revisionist efforts to "normalize" Nazi Germany and to portray it as a modernizing regime (see **Nolte** and **Zitelmann**), Wippermann has contributed numerous publications to various aspects of Nazism. His specific expertise lies in the fields of theory and historiography, particularly Marxist interpretations of fascism. Unfortunately, his books on theories of fascism and **totalitarianism**, the latest editions of which appeared in Germany in 1997, have not been translated into English. His book, *Umstrittene Vergangenheit* (Disputed Past) (1998), provides a clear and thorough survey of historical controversies about Nazism from a strong left-liberal perspective.

phy of Nazism was his startling revival of the thesis that **Hitler** was a man of the left, not the right. Zitelmann set forth this dubious interpretation in his book *Hitler as Social Revolutionary* in 1987, and in his full-scale biography of Hitler in 1989. Zitelmann claimed that Nazi social programs like **Strength through Joy** were not intended merely to maintain social peace but rather genuinely to improve the conditions of the working class. For Zitelmann Hitler and the Nazis were modernizers who constructively sought to enhance social equality and mobility in Germany. His critics (including Wolfgang **Wippermann**) pointed out that wages remained disproportionately low in Germany and that the social benefits that Zitelmann touted were only available to racially pure "**Aryans.**" Zitelmann's ideologically motivated theses have not gained acceptance among historians of Nazism. Nonetheless he remains a representative figure for a younger generation of conservatives whose aim it is to counteract the "pedagogical historiography," "ritualized *Vergangenheitsbewältigung*," or "negative nationalism" of the 1960s generation. In the 1990s this New Right pursued the same goals as Ernst **Nolte**, but with different arguments. While Nolte sought to cast Nazism in a more positive light by portraying it as an understandable reaction to communism, the New Right depicted Nazism as itself a progressive and modernizing movement similar to communism.

Z

ZITELMANN, RAINER (b. 1957) Conservative publicist whose major claim to inclusion in a survey of the historiogra-

ILLUSTRATIONS

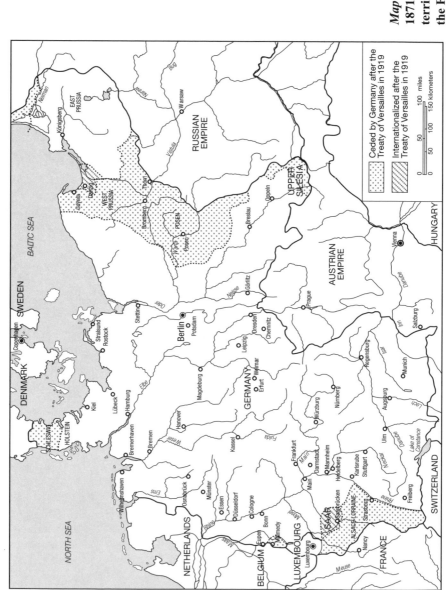

Map 1 **The German Empire, 1871–1919, showing territorial losses following the First World War**

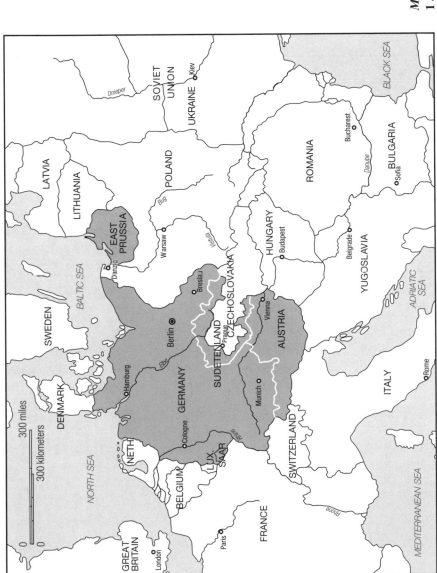

Map 2 **The German Reich, 1 January 1939**

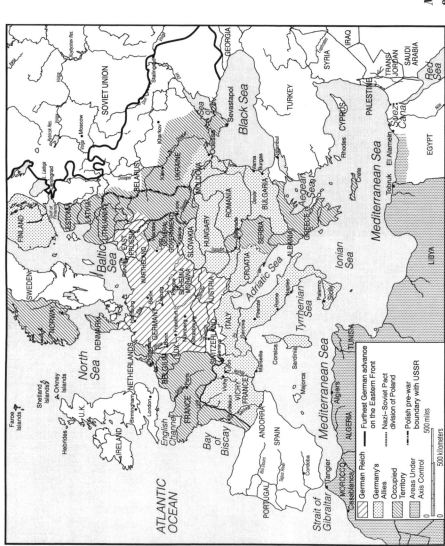

Map 3 **The height of German expansion, November 1942**

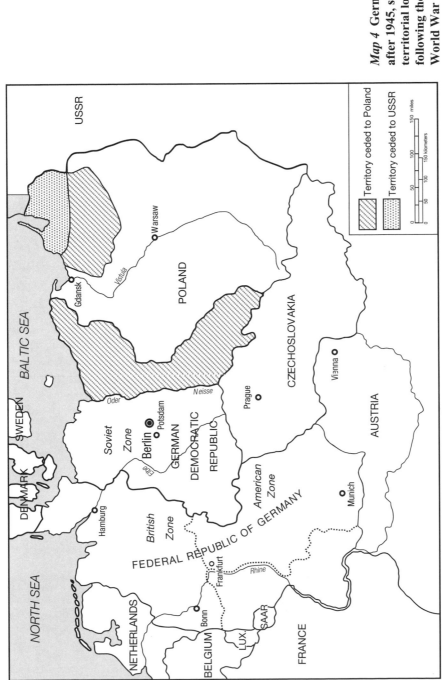

Map 4 Germany after 1945, showing territorial losses following the Second World War

Table 1 Reichstag elections, 1928–1933

Party	20 May 1928			14 September 1930			31 July 1932			6 November 1932			5 March 1933		
	Total votes	%	No. deputies	Total votes	%	No. deputies	Total votes	%	No. deputies	Total votes	%	No. deputies	Total votes	%	No. deputies
No. eligible voters	41,224,700			42,957,700			44,226,800			44,373,700			44,685,800		
No. valid votes cast	30,753,300	74.60	491	34,970,900	81.41	577	36,882,400	83.39	608	35,471,800	79.93	584	39,343,300	88.04	647
Social Democrats (SPD)	9,153,000	29.8	153	8,577,700	24.5	143	7,959,700	21.6	133	7,248,000	20.4	121	7,181,600	18.3	120
Communist Party (KPD)	3,264,800	10.6	54	4,592,100	13.1	77	5,282,600	14.6	89	5,980,200	16.9	100	4,848,100	12.3	81
Center Party	3,712,200	12.1	62	4,127,900	11.8	68	4,589,300	12.5	75	4,230,600	11.9	70	4,424,900	11.7	74
Bavarian People's Party	945,600	3.0	16	1,059,100	3.0	19	1,192,700	3.2	22	1,094,600	3.1	20	1,073,600	2.7	18
Democrats (DDP)	1,505,700	4.9	25	1,322,400	3.8	20	371,800	1.0	4	336,500	1.0	2	334,200	0.8	5
People's Party (DVP)	2,679,700	8.7	45	1,578,200	4.5	30	436,000	1.2	7	661,800	1.9	11	432,300	1.1	2
Wirtschaftspartei	1,397,100	4.5	23	1,362,400	3.9	23	146,900	0.4	2	110,300	0.3	1	—	—	—
Nationalists (DNVP)	4,381,600	14.2	73	2,458,300	7.0	41	2,177,400	5.9	37	2,959,000	8.8	52	3,136,800	8.0	52

Party	Votes	%	Seats	Votes	%	Seats	Votes	%	Seats	Votes	%	Seats	Votes	%	Seats
Christlich-soz Volksdienst	—	—	—	868,200	2.5	14	405,300	1.1	3	412,500	1.2	5	384,000	1.0	4
Landbund	199,500	0.6	3	194,000	0.5	3	96,900	0.2	2	105,200	0.3	2	83,800	0.2	1
Christlich-natl. Bauern u. Landvolk	581,800	1.8	10	1,108,700	3.0	19	90,600	0.2	1	46,400	0.1	—	—	—	—
Deutsch-Hannov. Partei	195,600	0.5	3	144,300	0.4	3	46,900	0.1	—	64,000	0.2	1	47,700	0.1	—
Deutsch Bauernpartei	481,300	1.5	8	339,600	1.0	6	137,100	0.3	2	149,000	0.4	3	114,000	0.3	2
National Socialists (NSDAP)	810,100	2.6	12	6,409,600	18.3	107	13,745,800	37.4	230	11,737,000	33.1	196	17,277,200	43.9	288
Other parties	1,445,300	4.8	4	1,073,500	3.1	4	342,500	0.9	1	749,200	2.2	—	136,646	0.3	—

Table 2 **Sociological structure of the NSDAP prior to 1933, by occupation groups**

Occupation	German Reich (1925 census)	NSDAP (Before 14 Sep 1930)	NSDAP (New members 9/14/30–1/30/33)	Percentage of NSDAP members among those employed (Before 1 Jan. 1933)
Blue-collar workers	14,443,000 (45.1%)	34,000 (28.1%)	233,000 (33.5%)	1.9%
Self-employed (a) Farming	2,203,000 (6.7%)	17,100 (14.1%)	90,000 (13.4%)	4.9%
(b) Industry and crafts	1,785,000 (5.5%)	11,000 (9.1%)	56,000 (8.4%)	3.9%
(c) Commerce	1,193,000 (3.7%)	9,900 (8.2%)	49,000 (7.5%)	4.9%
(d) Professions	477,000 (1.5%)	3,600 (3.0%)	20,000 (3.0%)	4.9%
Public employees (a) Teachers	334,000 (1.0%)	2,000 (1.7%)	11,000 (1.7%)	4.0%
(b) Others	1,050,000 (3.3%)	8,000 (6.6%)	36,000 (5.5%)	
White-collar employees	5,087,000 (15.9%)	31,000 (25.6%)	148,000 (22.1%)	3.4%
Domestic workers (mostly women)	5,437,000 (17.3%)	4,400 (3.6%)	27,000 (4.9%)	0.6%
Total	32,009,000 (100%)	121,000 (100%)	670,000 (100%)	2.5%

Table 3 **Nazi concentration and extermination camps**

Concentration camps	Date opened	Date evacuated or liberated	Satellite camps
Dachau	22 March 1933	29 April 1945	169
Sachsenhausen	August 1936	22 April 1945	61
Buchenwald	15 July 1937	11 April 1945	134
Flossenbürg	3 May 1938	23 April 1845	92
Mauthausen	June 1938	5 May 1945	56
Neuengamme	Fall 1938	29–30 April 1945	73
Ravensbrück	15 May 1939	30 April 1945	42
Stutthof (Danzig)	1 September 1939	after 27 January 1945	107
Auschwitz (I)	20 May 1940	27 January 1945	38
Gross-Rosen	2 August 1940	February 1945	99
Natzweiler-Struthof	1 May 1941	after September 1944	49
Lublin-Majdanek	October 1941	22–24 July 1944	10
Auschwitz II (Birkenau)	26 November 1941	27 January 1945	
Auschwitz III (Monowitz)	31 May 1942	27 January 1945	
Herzogenbusch-Vught	5 January 1943	5–6 September 1944	13
Riga (Latvia)	15 March 1943	after 6 August 1944	17
Bergen-Belsen	April 1943	15 April 1945	
Dora-Mittelbau	27 August 1943	9 April 1945	29
Warsaw	15 August 1943	after 24 July 1944	
Kauen (Lithuania)	15 September 1943	after 14 July 1944	8
Vaivara (Estonia)	15 September 1943	3 October 1944	10
Klooga (Estonia)	September 1943	19 September 1944	3
Krakaw-Plaszow	11 January 1944	15 January 1945	

Extermination camps	Dates gas chambers or vans in operation	Number of victims (minimum numbers)
Kulmhof/Chelmno	8 December 1941–March 1943, Summer 1944	152,000
Auschwitz-Birkenau	January 1942–November 1944	over 1,000,000
Belzec	17 March 1942–Spring 1943	over 600,000
Sobibór	7 May 1942–Fall 1943	250,000
Treblinka	23 July 1942–October 1943	700,000–900,000
Lublin-Majdanek	Summer 1942–July 1944	200,000, including 60,000 Jews

II
NAZI GERMANY
The major topics

5

ORIGINS AND CONSOLIDATION OF NAZI GERMANY

SOCIAL AND INTELLECTUAL ORIGINS OF NATIONAL SOCIALISM: THE *VÖLKISCH* MOVEMENT

What role did the German past play in the rise of National Socialism? A much-debated issue in the history of Nazi Germany is the degree to which it was prefigured by earlier events. Another way of framing this issue is to ask whether the onset of Nazism should be dated to the founding of the National Socialist German Workers Party (**NSDAP**) after the First World War or whether its beginnings should be traced to German Imperial politics of the late nineteenth century, or to an even more distant past. Does the history of Nazi Germany begin with the emergence of Adolf **Hitler** as a political leader and the formation of his world-view? Should its ideological origins be sought as far back as the early nineteenth century in the conservative ideological reaction in Germany (and other countries) against the Enlightenment and the liberal and egalitarian values of the French Revolution? In an obvious sense, of course, history is a seamless web of sequential events, and it is impossible to pinpoint the precise starting point of any major historical development. On the other hand, history is always more or less open-ended at any given time, and the historian must guard against the fallacy of assuming that what actually transpired was the only possible course that history could have taken. In tracing historical genealogy and causation, caution is always advised. But Nazism cannot be properly understood without taking into account its nineteenth-century antecedents.

National Socialism was the culmination of a diffuse political and ideological movement of German exceptionalism and supremacism with roots in the nineteenth century. While the explanatory power of Germany's special historical development ("the German *Sonderweg*") remains subject to considerable dispute (see Chapter 3 on "Historiography"), historians agree that much of Nazi ideology was anticipated by radical right-wing groups and organizations opposed to the allegedly too moderate foreign and domestic policies of the Wilhelmian Empire. These organizations, often in competition with one another, were part of a diffuse movement of nationalist opposition to foreign influences and modernizing trends that came to be known as the *völkisch* movement, named after the German term for nation or people, the Volk. *Völkisch* publicists celebrated the uniqueness and superiority of the German language, history, spirituality, and "race" (a synonym for ethnic group in nineteenth-century usage). *Völkisch* racial mythology represented a form of nationalism designed to overcome the many social, political, religious, cultural, and regional divisions in the recently unified German Empire and thus create a popular consensus for predominantly conservative but often contradictory policies. The goals of late nineteenth- and early twentieth-century *völkisch* publicists and organizations were to abolish the parliamentary system, viewed as an un-German institution; suppress the recently founded liberal and social democratic parties and the partisan politics they supposedly fostered; restore a pre-capitalist economic system based on native agriculture, handicrafts, and small proprietorship; "reform" German institutions allegedly corrupted by commercialism and materialism; create a specifically German religion (whether Protestant Christian or **Nordic** pagan); regenerate the nation through "**racial hygiene**"; strengthen the hierarchical, authoritarian, militaristic state; unite all Germans in a greater **Reich**; conquer and colonize foreign territories; and eliminate Jews from German society. The *völkisch* movement remained on the fringes of German political culture up to 1914, although it had continued to gather adherents throughout the 1890s and 1900s as the result of the social consequences of rapid industrialization, including economic fluctuations and dislocations, urbanization and the decline of rural traditions, and growing class differentiation and conflict. *Völkisch* ideology appealed particularly to groups and individuals that felt threatened by the growth of the Marxist Social Democratic Party (**SPD**) and worker militancy in Germany. The catastrophic experience of the First World War provided the catalyst that moved the ideas and goals of the *völkisch* movement into the mainstream of political conservatism during the era of the **Weimar Republic**.

The main objective of this nationalist, populist, and racist movement was to reinforce Germans' sense of national solidarity through appeals to the mystical notion of a racial blood bond between all members of the ethnic community. Racial **anti-Semitism** constituted the negative core of *völkisch* ideology. *Völkisch* nationalists attributed the modernizing trends of the Wilhelmian Empire, including the growth of liberalism, democracy, rationalism, secularism, capitalism, and socialism, to the subversive influence of Jews, who supposedly lacked loyalty to the German nation and pursued only their own economic and political advantage at the expense of commercially unsophisticated Germans. Right-wing hatred of the Jews also rested on the recognition that German Jews overwhelmingly supported the progressive and emancipatory movements of the left that promised all individuals, including Jews, full civil rights and equality of opportunity. Because the process of transformation of a static agrarian society into a dynamic-competitive, urbanized industrial system – the ultimate source of the *völkisch* reaction – coincided with the legal emancipation of Jews in Germany in the period of German unification, *völkisch* ideologues attached overriding significance to the "Jewish Question," defined as a problem of racial incompatibility. From the *völkisch* perspective revocation of Jewish citizenship rights and expulsion of the Jews from Germany was the key to achieving the *völkisch* project of national regeneration and German expansion.

Völkisch ideas were also disseminated in such economic and political interest groups as the Agrarian League, the national union of white-collar employees, the Eastern Marches Society, the League of Industrialists, and the German Naval League, all founded in the decade of the 1890s as the German Empire sought to match its European rivals in expanding its colonial empire. In the years before the First World War such militant *völkisch* organizations as the **Pan-German League**, founded in 1891, took an increasingly critical stance toward the regime of Kaiser Wilhelm II, under whose reign the modernization, commercialization, and "Judaization" of German society came to appear irreversible. There were *völkisch* student and youth groups, women's organizations, and movements for *völkisch* "reform" in the arts, education, and the professions. The most extreme *völkisch* organizations joined to form the *Deutschvölkische Vereinigung* (German *Völkisch* Association) in 1913, whose nationalist, authoritarian, militaristic, anti-Semitic, and anti-democratic program anticipated the Nazi **Twenty-five Point Program** issued in 1920.

HOW DID THE FIRST WORLD WAR LEAD TO THE RISE OF NAZISM?

The rise of Nazism and the origins of the Second World War can only be understood against the background of the catastrophic First World War. *Völkisch* radicalism no doubt contributed to the aggressive mood that characterized the policies of the German leadership in 1914, but if war had not broken out the *völkisch* movement would in all likelihood have remained on the margins of German political life. The outbreak of war gave enormous impetus to the nationalist, authoritarian, and militarist ideology of the radical right and muted the voices of the pacifist, internationalist, and democratic German left, at least until 1917 when supporters of a compromise peace were able to pass a Reichstag resolution calling on the government to renounce any expansionist aims. German defeat in 1918 had the effect of discrediting the Imperial government, as for a time at least public opinion favored the empowerment of the German left whose warnings of the catastrophic effects of militantly nationalist policies had been borne out by events. But soon a popular backlash against revolutionary upheaval, the new republican form of government, and the alleged lack of patriotism of democrats, socialists, and Jews set in. Ultimately, German defeat and humiliation served to strengthen the German right and to move *völkisch* radicalism into the mainstream of post-war German conservatism.

German defeat in the First World War set the stage for the rise of the Nazis in a number of ways. All the trends of the pre-war era that had led to war were aggravated and reinforced by the war itself. The start of war led to public expressions of patriotic enthusiasm in all the combatant countries, not least in Germany where the *Augusterlebnis* (the experience of August 1914) became part of a national mythology that fueled the radical right after the war. While recent research has shown that national enthusiasm for war was not as widespread or fervent as post-war nationalists claimed, the myth of unified national support for the war became a powerful ingredient in right-wing ideology during and after the war. Nazism can be understood as a movement that sought to revive and perpetuate the unity of purpose that most Germans felt in the early stages of the World War before setbacks and war weariness again exposed the divisions in German society. Nazis also sought to revive the comradeship and solidarity that many soldiers experienced in serving the national cause.

War also reinforced the authoritarianism that was part of the political legacy of the German monarchical past. In Germany liberal and democratic institutions had never grown the strong roots that they had in Western Europe. After the promotion in 1916 of generals Paul **von Hindenburg** and Erich **Ludendorff** to the posts of commander-in-chief of the army and army chief of staff, respectively, Germany was ruled as a virtual dictatorship by the Army High Command. The leadership principle at the heart of any military chain of command became the model for fascist organizations after the war. At the center of the Nazi project was the attempt to reorganize society along hierarchical lines to enable the nation to develop the same ruthless efficiency the German army had demonstrated during the war. The territorial ambitions of the High Command, particularly evident in the Treaty of Brest-Litovsk imposed on **Bolshevik** Russia in March 1918, anticipated the Nazis' drive for *Lebensraum* in the East.

The war reinforced militarism in many ways. As the first industrial war in history, and the first "**total war**" involving the entire population, it inured people to mass destruction and mass murder. The war provided a precedent for genocide, the destruction of an entire population group. For front-line soldiers it had a particularly brutalizing effect, but it also generated a sense of comradeship and noble self-sacrifice that fascists would try to revive and continue after the war. It appeared to legitimate the use of force and violence in achieving political goals. But it also gave new vitality to the ancient martial and aristocratic values of duty, discipline, obedience, courage, and heroism, values that constituted one of the major sources of fascist appeal. The war also gave rise to modern **propaganda**, the deliberate manipulation of information by the state to influence and control public opinion. The war led to a huge escalation of xenophobic prejudices and the unprecedented demonization of enemies and opponents.

As a result of German defeat and humiliation, the war remained more traumatic in German collective memory than elsewhere and formed the indispensable background to the rise of the Nazis. Numerous public rituals commemorated the dead and celebrated their sacrifices, which could only retain meaning and purpose in public consciousness if the results of the war could be reversed and a mightier German Empire could be established the next time round. The Nazis benefited from the *Totenkult* (the cult of death) and the *Trauerkultur* (the culture of mourning) that the First World War helped to generate. They used the commemoration of the war to mentally prepare the public for a resumption of war when the conditions for likely victory in a new round of fighting were right. They believed that the Second World War could be won by avoiding the mistakes of the first war, the most important of which in the Nazi view was the failure to maintain unified public support for the war and to sustain the will to fight to the death.

THE RISE OF THE NAZIS

Already by 1917, as the war dragged on, opposition to the refusal of the High Command to pursue a negotiated settlement emerged in the **Reichstag**, which had no control over policy but did have considerable influence on public opinion. In July 1917 the parties of the left and the Catholic **Center Party** passed a peace resolution that called on the government (in effect, the High Command) to seek a compromise peace and abjure all annexationist aims. In response, the High Command supported the creation of the right-wing **Fatherland Party** to rally popular support for a more vigorous prosecution of the war. This party registered more than a million members before the end of the war.

The Bolshevik revolution in Russia in November 1917 had the dual effect of emboldening left-wing opposition in Germany and hardening the commitment of the government to military victory. The growing polarization of German society was further aggravated by the humiliating end to the war. In August 1918 the High Command secretly conceded to civilian leaders that the war was lost and instructed the government to sue for an armistice. On 11 November 1918 the fighting came to an end. In June 1919 the German constitutional assembly, meeting in the central German city of Weimar to avoid revolutionary unrest in Berlin, was forced to sign the **Versailles Treaty**. Dubbed the Versailles **Diktat** by the radical right, the treaty deprived Germany of territory, restricted its military capability, imposed reparations, and forced Germans to accept full responsibility for the war.

Unwillingness to accept the results of the war, including the Versailles Treaty and the liberal Weimar constitution, was undoubtedly the single most important factor promoting the growth of the radical right after the war. Hitler, a veteran of four years of combat, shared the frustration of many of his fellow soldiers at the unsatisfactory outcome of the war. Had four years of bitter fighting been in vain? Were they now to accept parliamentary democracy, the enemy's form of government, as the legitimate system in Germany? Appalled by left-wing revolution and by the prominent role that liberals, Social Democrats, and Jews played in the new government, many veterans signed on to the **Free Corps** and other right-wing organizations committed to the suppression of democracy and the restoration of strong authoritarian government in Germany. Assigned by the army to monitor revolutionary organizations after the war, Hitler joined the German Workers' Party, which he renamed the National Socialist German Workers Party in 1920 and mobilized for counter-revolutionary ends. The main objective of Hitler's party was to build mass support for the *völkisch* goals of overthrowing the Weimar Republic, establishing a nationalist dictatorship, and expanding German territory in the quest for *Lebensraum* in the East. Nazis believed that this could only be achieved through stringent policies to purify the race and eliminate the presence of the Jews in the new unified *Volksgemeinschaft* (people's community) that they hoped to create.

The Party's Twenty-five Point Program was designed to appeal to a wide constituency, very much including industrial workers who traditionally supported the parties of the left. The Nazis hoped by a variety of promises, including the purely rhetorical "abolition of the slavery of interest" (which would have abolished the credit and banking system), the confiscation of war profits, the nationalization of trusts, the expropriation of land for public use, and restrictions on the rights of Jews, to attract workers to the right-wing nationalist cause. On Hitler's orders this program was never changed or expanded, despite efforts by **Gregor Strasser** to spell out the Nazi social policies more concretely in a detailed program drafted in 1926. In 1928 Hitler did issue an explanatory codicil assuring the Nazis' middle-class constituency and its corporate supporters that the party would respect and defend the right to private property. Hitler was determined, however, to avoid any policy debates in the party in order to preserve his own freedom of action. He was convinced, as he explained with remarkable candor in his book *Mein Kampf* in 1926, that the masses were most readily swayed by statements and slogans that were constantly repeated, whether they were true or not. He insisted that the public would swallow even deliberate lies if they were repeated often enough.

Hitler's tiny Munich-based Nazi Party emerged as the strongest of the many organizations that vied for leadership of the *völkisch* movement after the war for a number of reasons. Its deliberate appeal to the working class made it appear less tied to the wealthy bourgeoisie than its *völkisch* rivals. Its populist, anti-socialist, anti-Semitic, and anti-establishment rhetoric and program enjoyed the growing support of mainstream conservatives in what the right derogatorily labeled "the Jewish Weimar Republic." The banning of the *Deutschvölkischer Schutz- und Trutzbund* (German Völkisch Defense and Protection League, **DSTB**), the largest of the post-war extra-parliamentary *völkisch* organizations, under special legislation adopted in 1922 after the DSTB's involvement in the assassination of German foreign minister Walther Rathenau (1867–1922), left the field clear for the Nazis to absorb much of its membership. The Nazis enjoyed the protection of the Bavarian state government, which refused to implement the Weimar government's laws restricting right-wing organizations, thus encouraging Hitler to attempt to seize power in the so-called "beer hall putsch" in November 1923. Hitler hoped to take control of the national government with the help of the army, the police, and the economic elites, as Fascist leader Benito Mussolini had done in Italy by threatening a "march on Rome" in 1922. Hitler's attempt failed as the **Reichswehr** leaders refused to support his putsch for fear of French and British intervention, and Bavarian government leaders declined to follow through on their earlier promises to Hitler despite their hostility to the liberal Weimar regime.

Hitler learned from his failed putsch attempt to take a more legal, constitutional route to power. After serving a brief prison sentence, he refounded the Nazi Party in 1925, stressing organizational discipline, political pragmatism, and practical propaganda. Nonetheless, in the 1928 Reichstag election, at the height of the most prosperous phase of the Weimar era, the Nazis could do no better than 2.6 percent of the vote, with fewer than a million votes, translating into only 12 parliamentary seats (out of 491). Only two years later, however, the onset of the Great Depression created the conditions that allowed the Nazi Party to develop into a mass party. As growing unemployment induced increasing numbers of workers to vote for the radical German Communist Party (**KPD**), the threat of revolution radicalized increasing numbers of middle-class voters to the right. The depression also led to the breakdown of the governing coalition of **SPD** and **DVP** (German People's Party) in March 1930 on the issue of employers' contributions to the overburdened state unemployment fund, which the liberal DVP wished to reduce over SPD objections.

HOW WERE THE NAZIS ABLE TO TAKE POWER?

The appointment of Center Party leader Heinrich **Brüning** as Chancellor in March 1930 marked the effective end of normal parliamentary government, according to which all legislation must receive the approval of a parliamentary majority. Unable to obtain parliamentary approval for austerity measures (to balance the budget and pressure the Allies into ending reparations), Brüning called for new elections that led to a dramatic gain in Nazi votes in September 1930. With more than 18 percent of the vote the Nazis increased their electoral support more than eightfold, becoming the second largest party in the Reichstag behind the SPD (with 24 percent). Unable to build a majority governing coalition, Brüning received authorization from President **Hindenburg** under Article 48 of the Weimar constitution to create a *Präsidialkabinett* (presidential cabinet) independent of the Reichstag and to rule by presidential decree. His successors, Franz von **Papen** (June to December 1932) and General Kurt von **Schleicher** (December 1932 to January 1933), ruled in the same way, as did Hitler in the first two months of his chancellorship.

Brüning's failure to solve the economic crisis and his dependence on the SPD to block no-confidence votes in the Reichstag, which would have forced new elections, enraged German nationalists who wished to replace the Weimar system with a national dictatorship. In this quest for a more permanent authoritarian form of government the economic and military elites of the mainstream-right Nationalist Party (**DNVP**) as well as some leaders of the **DVP** were willing to make common cause with the Nazis, thereby enhancing Nazi respectability in the eyes of the general public. Nazis and traditional conservatives differed in temperament, tactics, and background, but not in their essential goals, which were to crush Marxism and democracy, reverse Versailles, and restore Germany's military and economic might. Conservatives regarded the Nazis as a particularly useful counter-force to the radical **KPD**. In the so-called **Harzburg Front**, named after the site of a giant right-wing rally in October 1931, the DNVP, led by industrial and media tycoon Alfred **Hugenberg**, formed a virtual alliance with Hitler that redounded to the latter's advantage. The apparent populism of the Nazis and the lower-middle-class origins of many of their leaders and functionaries gave them a considerable advantage over traditional conservatives whose upper middle-class or aristocratic status limited their popular appeal. Hitler also gained credibility in his unsuccessful run for the presidency against the aged Hindenburg in April 1932. The presidential election was in effect a referendum on the Weimar constitution. In a reversal of the presidential election of 1926, when Hindenburg, an avowed monarchist, was elected as the candidate of the nationalist right (with support from Hitler and the Nazi Party), Hindenburg was now the reluctant candidate of the defenders of the Weimar Republic. Although the revered war hero won the 1932 election in a run-off against Hitler, Hindenburg resented the fact that his main political support now came from the pro-Weimar Catholic Center and the SPD.

Hindenburg sympathized with the "national opposition" of Nazis and DNVP, but he distrusted Hitler's populism and his militantly anti-establishment following. Like many of his fellow conservatives, Hindenburg hoped to include Hitler in a nationalist government without turning over the full reins of power to him. Brüning's unwillingness to cooperate with the Nazis, as attested by his 1932 decree prohibiting the wearing of uniforms in public demonstrations (a decree aimed at reducing the street violence of the **SA**, the Nazis' paramilitary troop), was a major factor in his dismissal as chancellor in May 1932. His successor, the Catholic aristocrat Franz von **Papen**, lifted the ban on the SA in the hopes of persuading the Nazis to join his government in subordinate positions, thus giving his administration greater popular legitimacy. In an effort to further ingratiate himself with the Nazis, who had won a plurality in the Prussian state parliamentary election in April 1932, he also deposed the SPD-dominated Prussian state government and placed this oversized state, embracing almost two-thirds of the German population, under the direct control of the national government.

The Nazis did indeed benefit from Papen's courtship as they emerged the big winners in the Reichstag elections at the end of July 1932. With 37.4 percent of the vote and 230 seats (out of 608) the Nazis achieved their greatest electoral success before Hitler's assumption of power, well ahead of the second place SPD (21.6 percent). Their gains came mainly from the now virtually defunct middle-class parties, the **DVP** and the **DDP** (Democrats), as well as from conservative special-interest parties and new voters radicalized by the continuing economic crisis. As the Communists, who sought to establish a "dictatorship of the proletariat," won 14.6 percent of the vote and 89 seats, the two parties most committed to the destruction of the Weimar system now held a majority and were in a position to block parliamentary government. The Communists fought the Nazis in the streets, but the two parties effectively combined forces in their efforts to end liberal democracy.

The Weimar parliamentary system was now practically defunct, and the major questions remaining were what kind of system would succeed it and who would be in charge. Chancellor Papen and fellow conservatives of the Nationalist Party also wanted constitutional changes to strengthen the authority of the executive and weaken the Reichstag in a powerful "non-partisan state" (a euphemism for the abolition of political parties), but their lack of broad popular support made them dependent on the Nazis to give public legitimacy to any change toward a more dictatorial form of government. On Papen's and his minister of war General **Schleicher**'s urgings, President Hindenburg invited Hitler, as the leader of the strongest Reichstag party, to join a nationalist government under Papen's leadership in August 1932. Hitler, however, held out for the chancellorship and refused to support a Papen government. Forming a parliamentary majority for a nationalist government might result in the survival of the Weimar system, an outcome Hitler was determined to prevent. To avoid a no-confidence vote that he was certain to lose, Papen dissolved the Reichstag and scheduled new elections, hoping that Hitler's obduracy would persuade voters to shift their support to the DNVP and make Hitler more amenable to compromise.

In November 1932 the Nazis did indeed lose more than 2 million votes, although they remained the largest party with 33.1 percent of the vote and 196 Reichstag seats. Their tactical decision to support the Communist-initiated strike of Berlin transit workers shortly before the election (in the expectation of attracting worker support) had benefited only the Communists, who had increased their share of the vote to 16.9 percent. Together the two Marxist parties, the Social Democrats and the Communists, actually had a higher percentage of the vote than the Nazis had received at their height in July, but the bitter rift between SPD and KPD, a result of the SPD's suppression of revolution after the First World War, made a united front against Nazism unachievable. The disunity on the left was particularly tragic in view of the fact that the prospects of preventing the Nazis from gaining power seemed otherwise quite good. The Nazis appeared to have passed the peak of their popular support and were now on a downward slope (confirmed by further losses in state elections in Thuringia in early December, where the Nazis had already entered a coalition government in 1930). In addition, they now faced internal conflict, a post-election loss of morale among some Nazi functionaries, and a funding crisis. Nazi Organization leader Gregor Strasser challenged Hitler's all-or-nothing strategy and called for Nazi participation in a coalition government with the Nationalists and possibly the Center Party, even if this meant accepting subordinate ministerial roles. Sensing an opportunity finally to achieve what his two predecessors had been unable to bring about – a nationalist government with Nazi support – General Kurt von Schleicher persuaded Hindenburg to dismiss the unpopular Papen. Schleicher's plan was to form a viable government with Strasser's support without turning power over to Hitler. On 4 December 1932 Schleicher became the last chancellor of Germany before the Nazi takeover.

But Schleicher was no more successful in forming a coalition government with the Nazis than Papen had been before him. Hitler asserted his authority as party Führer to block Strasser's proposal to join the Schleicher government in a subordinate role. Despite the likelihood of a further deterioration of the Nazis' electoral strength if they continued their stonewalling tactics, Hitler ruled out any compromise. He speculated that the conservative elite, disdainful of parliamentary democracy and fearful of a resurgent left, would eventually have no choice but to turn over full power to him. He realized that conservatives desperately needed the Nazis' popular backing, and he knew that the economic and military elites feared the dissolution of the Nazi Party lest the break-up of the Nazi constituency lead to the defection of working-class Nazi voters to the Communists. Hitler did worry that his ambitions might yet be thwarted by a military dictatorship, which Schleicher was willing to lead. Hindenburg, however, was unwilling to authorize a measure that was likely to further undermine the government's legitimacy, narrow its popular base, and possibly lead to civil war.

These were the circumstances that led to Papen's fateful decision to join a Hitler government as vice-chancellor in January 1933. Agreement on a presidial government under Hitler was reached at a secret meeting between the two at the home of a prominent Rhineland banker on 4 January 1933. Conservatives hoped to retain control of the government by holding on to important ministerial positions and limiting the number of Nazis in the cabinet to three (Hitler as chancellor, Wilhelm **Frick** as minister of the interior, and Hermann **Göring** as Prussian minister of the interior). Papen's assurances that conservatives would be able to control the government's agenda helped to persuade Hindenburg to appoint Hitler as chancellor on 30 January 1933. Some conservatives viewed this as only a stop-gap solution until a more permanent authoritarian government could be established or the monarchy restored. Hitler's strategy of gaining power with the help of the authorities had finally paid off ten years after his failed attempt to gain power by force.

There was nothing inevitable about Hitler's accession to power. He was not elected to office as he never had close to a majority of Reichstag seats and was unwilling to make the necessary compromises to form a coalition government with the DNVP and/or the Center Party. Coalition with other parties might have given him a parliamentary majority but would have left him subject to constitutional constraints and would have circumscribed his freedom of action. If Hindenburg, acting on the advice of conservative leaders, had not authorized him to head a presidial government, the Nazis would have been, for the time being at least, effectively stalled. The key to Hitler's success was the determination of conservative leaders to replace the Weimar system with an authoritarian regime. Only the Nazis could provide the mass support for such a regime, and the only way to coopt that mass support, so it seemed to the conservative elites, was to give in to Hitler's demand for the chancellorship.

Several factors account for Hitler's popularity and hence his utility to the conservative elites. The fear of the growing appeal of communism to workers radicalized by the depression produced a backlash that benefited the populist Nazis more than the elitist Nationalists. Hitler also gained mass support through his promises to stand up to the Western Allies and defend German interests more effectively than his conservative counterparts seemed able or willing to do. Enthusiasm for a government that promised a national awakening and a resurgence of power was widespread and genuine. Popular revulsion against partisan politics and the seemingly unending gridlock of party government led many people to put their hopes in the personal leadership of a heroic figure at the head of a youthful, dynamic movement.

Hitler's tactical decision not to spell out his economic plans in any detail also worked to his advantage as farmers, artisans, and small proprietors – as well as the economic elites – could reasonably expect to improve their prospects under his rule. Among his staunchest supporters were career officers and soldiers, who looked forward to enhanced career opportunities through the revival of German militarism. Although anti-Semitism was not the main factor in Hitler's success, he did give expression to the prejudices and frustrations of millions of his followers. Many middle-class Germans in particular were also attracted by the prospects of a return of "law and order." The Nazis' left-wing opposition was demoralized and divided by the feud between SPD and KPD, which had its main source in the repression of Communist revolutions by the SPD-led government shortly after the end of the First World War. In any case, the left represented only a minority (albeit more than a third) of the German public. Even members of the SPD had lost faith in the possibility of retaining the crisis-ridden parliamentary system, although they remained the only party to fight for its survival until the end. Most Germans felt the need for a new start that promised to bring about German recovery, a government more willing to stand up to the Allies for German national interests, and an end to partisan conflicts and divisions.

HOW WERE THE NAZIS ABLE TO ESTABLISH HITLER'S PERSONAL DICTATORSHIP?

One of the sources of Nazi popularity was their perceived transcendence of partisan politics in uniting the country behind a "Government of National Concentration." The first official statement read by Hitler on the day after his appointment as chancellor played to the widespread hopes for national renewal, restoration of national harmony, and a revival of national pride. He promised that his government would preserve and protect Christianity and "human culture and civilization," restore stability to the family unit, disregard class distinctions and overcome class conflict, promote reverence for Germany's glorious past, and eradicate Marxism (a code word for social democracy) and communism. He invoked the memory of the World War in calling on his countrymen to rally behind President Hindenburg "to fight under him once more as we had at the front, this time at home, in unity and loyalty, for the salvation of the Reich."[1] The internal enemies against whom Hitler sought to mobilize the country were the German left, especially Communists and Social Democrats, and Jews, whom the Nazis accused of disloyalty and political subversion.

Hitler's strategy was to gain dictatorial powers legally by changing the Weimar constitution (thus also freeing his government from dependence on presidential approval under Article 48). To do this he needed a two-thirds majority in the Reichstag, which he hoped to gain in a special election scheduled for 5 March

1933. The election campaign was accompanied by repression of the left, officially authorized by an "Emergency Decree for the Protection of the German People" on 4 February 1933. The banning of Communist, Social Democratic, and liberal publications under this decree led also to self-censorship and greater readiness to tone down criticism of the government by the mainstream German press. Repression was greatly escalated in the wake of the **Reichstag fire** one week before the election. This spectacular event provided the pretext for a special decree suspending basic civil liberties and giving the government enhanced powers of search, surveillance, seizure, and arrest.

Yet with all the levers of power and propaganda at their command the Nazis were able to gain only 43.9 percent of the vote in the March election. Despite this disappointing result, the Nazis succeeded in gaining passage of the so-called **Enabling Act** on 23 March, which gave Hitler dictatorial powers for the duration of four years. Two days earlier, at the official opening of the newly elected Reichstag in the venerable Garrison Church in **Potsdam**, the Nazis had staged a stirring patriotic ceremony that linked Hitler's government with the glorious Prussian monarchical and military tradition. The Nazis made much of the fusion of Germany's old right personified by President Hindenburg, the aristocratic field marshal who had led the German forces during the war, with Germany's new right, represented by the Austrian corporal who had fought in the trenches for four years.

Passage of the Enabling Act by the necessary two-thirds majority was only made possible by the arrest, on the grounds of the Reichstag fire decree, of all 81 elected Communist deputies, who were not permitted to cast their votes. Only the 94 SPD deputies voted against the establishment of dictatorship. The crucial margin of victory was provided by the Catholic Center Party, which offered its support of Hitler's dictatorship in return for a Nazi guarantee to respect the independence of the Church. This arrangement was formalized in a **Concordat** signed by the Nazi government and the papacy on 20 July 1933. In return for the right to govern the German Church without state interference, Pope Pius XI promised the Church would abstain from any political activity or criticism of the Nazi regime.

Armed with the power to rule by decree without constitutional constraints, the Nazis moved rapidly to stamp out all diversity and dissent in a process officially termed *Gleichschaltung* (bringing all institutions under Nazi control). The first official **concentration camp** to "reeducate" political prisoners had already been opened at **Dachau** near Munich under the head of the Bavarian police and chief of the paramilitary **SS**, Heinrich **Himmler**, who would soon extend his authority over the law enforcement apparatus of the entire country. Jews and political dissenters were barred from all public employment in the **Civil Service Act** of 7 April 1933. Euphemistically entitled "Law for the Professionalization of the Civil Service," this Act contained the notorious **Aryan Paragraph**, which called for the expulsion of all "non-Aryans," defined as anyone with one or more Jewish grandparents. This clause was soon applied by professional, cultural, and social organizations all over the country, even before it became mandatory under law.

Organizations in all fields purged their ranks of Jews, leftists, and liberals in their eagerness to align themselves with the national revolution and ingratiate themselves with the new regime. The bandwagon effect that had already enabled the Nazis to attract millions of voters in 1932 now caused a veritable stampede among ambitious members of the professions to join the party. So great was the onrush of new members in the spring of 1933 that the party imposed a temporary moratorium, lest the avalanche of new members who joined for opportunistic reasons dilute the party's ideological zeal. The same combination of official pressure, legal sanction, and voluntary conversion led to the dissolution of all non-Nazi political parties during the first six months of the new regime. While the Communists and Social Democrats, the only parties to openly oppose the Nazi regime, were abolished by law, the Nationalists, the Center Party, and the formerly liberal parties of the middle, none of which had a firm commitment to democracy in any case, eased the task of the Nazis by formally voting to disband. In July 1933 the government designated the **NSDAP** as the only legal party in the land.

Reichsstatthalter (Reich governors), appointed by Hitler, took over the functions of the elected governments of the various states as power was increasingly centralized in the hands of the national government. On 2 May 1933, one day after the traditional labor day celebration, deputized storm troopers of the SA seized the headquarters and property of the independent labor unions, which were replaced by the Nazi-controlled **German Labor Front** (DAF) under the leadership of Robert **Ley**. The task of the DAF was not to represent workers' interests but to ensure labor peace. The dramatic book-burning ceremonies conducted on various university campuses, including the Friedrich Wilhelm University in Berlin on 10 May 1933, were organized by the Nazi student organization **NSDStB**, an example of how *Gleichschaltung* did not necessarily require a direct government mandate. These literary *autos-da-fé* were designed to purge German education and its intellectual and cultural life of "un-German" influences and to bring the German public into line with Nazi ideology. Joseph **Goebbels**, the newly appointed minister of propaganda, was the featured speaker at the book burning in Berlin. He also took an active role in imposing ideological conformity on German cultural life by organizing practitioners of the arts and journalism into occupational chambers that controlled the right to work in these vocations. But the smooth integration of autonomous organizations into the Nazi fold was usually made possible by the initiative and consent of organizational leaders and members themselves.

Why were ordinary Germans so willing to cooperate with or accommodate to a regime that did not conceal its contempt for democracy or its goal of suppressing dissent? For a number of reasons the mass of the German population rallied behind the new government despite its evident disdain for the rights of German citizens. Hitler seemed to embody a long-established middle-class ideological consensus opposed to Marxism and committed to restoring German power and reversing the results of the World War. One reason the judicial system did not require major overhaul, aside from the establishment of special courts, including the *Volksgerichtshof* (people's court) in April 1934 to try crimes of treason, is because for years the courts had been dominated by judges sympathetic to the parties of the political right. The economy was improving (it could hardly get worse), and on the surface, at least, it seemed that the government's strong-armed methods had succeeded in restoring public order and respect for authority. Significant sectors of the public welcomed the concentration of power in the hands of an apparently selfless, charismatic ruler who would cut through the bureaucratic obstructions of the Weimar system to finally overcome the apparent paralysis of government. The leadership principle extolled by the radical right had a long tradition in Germany's extensive monarchical and militaristic past. Perhaps the most important factor in the Nazis' consolidation of popular support was their appeal to *Volksgemeinschaft* (people's community), the promise of unity and solidarity in a nation badly riven by class divisions and partisan conflicts. By placing the interests of the nation ahead of individual and class interests, the Nazis seemed to offer an antidote to the divisiveness that was widely blamed on liberals and socialists. Middle-class Germans could bask in a feeling of organic community and civic parity with less fortunate fellow citizens (mainly the working class) without having to make any concessions to equality that would reduce their own property or wealth. The exclusion of liberals, Marxists, and Jews from public life and the body politic was widely accepted as the necessary means to restore social harmony.

WHY DID HITLER PURGE THE SA?

Even after the **Enabling Act** had given Hitler dictatorial powers, his rule was not entirely secure. The government still formally required President Hindenburg's approval to carry out its policies. The conservative economic and military elites who had facilitated the Nazis' rise to power distrusted the potentially disruptive radicalism of the Nazi rank and file. Much of this radicalism was concentrated in the mass membership of the SA, who frequently took the law into their own hands and continued to hound Jews even after the official **boycott** of Jewish stores on 1 April 1933 was called off by the government to avoid disruption to the economy and to forestall foreign retaliation. Conservatives feared the "second revolution" that some disgruntled storm troopers demanded to oust conservative elites from their positions in government and society and replace them with genuine Nazis. Attuned to fighting the "establishment" in the long years of the struggle for power, many storm troopers found it difficult to adjust to cooperation with the civil service elites. Military leaders were particularly worried about the aspiration of some storm troopers to convert the SA into an official militia that would eventually absorb the Reichswehr. Ernst **Röhm**, the head of the SA, aroused the generals' suspicions by failing to counter the talk of a "second revolution." Indeed, he seemed to encourage it as a means to enhance the status of the SA and the power and privileges of its leadership.

Vice-Chancellor Franz von Papen gave voice to conservative fears in a surprisingly critical address at the University of Marburg in June 1934. Papen applauded the break with the principle of popular sovereignty and the return to "natural and divine rule" that the "German Revolution" had supposedly inaugurated. But from a traditionally Christian conservative perspective he called for an end to the revolutionary dynamic and for the strengthening of the state against the arbitrary actions of the party and its affiliated organizations. While professing his admiration for Hitler and National Socialism, he called on the party to rein in the socially revolutionary lower-class activists who acted as if they were outside the law. National Socialism, he warned, was itself threatened by a continuing revolt from below. "The time of emancipation of the lowest social orders against the higher orders is past."[2]

Papen's speech apparently triggered Hitler's decision to crack down on the SA. Hitler had no sympathy for cautious conservatism but was pragmatic enough to realize that he had to maintain conservative – and especially military – support for his regime. With Himmler's connivance members of the SS fanned out across Germany on 30 June 1934 to arrest and murder close to a hundred top leaders of the SA, including Röhm who was summarily executed without trial in a Munich prison. Many conservative leaders were shot in the "night of long knives" as well, as Nazi leaders used the opportunity to settle old scores. The list of victims included former chancellor General Kurt von Schleicher, Gregor Strasser, and Edgar Jung (1894–1934), the young conservative intellectual who had written Papen's Marburg speech.

Despite the extra-legal nature of the purge and its brutality, many Germans regarded it as evidence that the Nazis repudiated the extra-legal violence associated with the SA, as well as the well-known homosexuality and extravagant lifestyle of some of its leaders. Hindenburg sent congratulatory telegrams to both Hitler and Göring, who had helped to carry out the purge in his capacity as Prussian interior minister. Military leaders demonstrated their gratitude by requiring all military personnel to swear a personal oath of allegiance to the Führer after the death of President Hindenburg on 2 August 1934. Hitler used this opportunity to abolish the office of presidency, thereby assuming the role not just of head of government but also of head of state. This action, ratified by **plebiscite**, signaled the completion of the Nazi consolidation of power. Hitler's dictatorship was now firmly in place. With Hindenburg's death and the pledge of allegiance to Hitler by German army leaders, the last institutional constraints on Hitler's power had been removed. At the annual Nazi Party rally in Nuremberg in September, celebrated under the watchword of "unity," Hitler assured the nation that there would be no more revolution in Germany for a thousand years.

6

DICTATORSHIP IN ACTION

HOW DID THE NAZIS GOVERN?

In the months and years following his accession to power, Hitler gained full independence from the conservative elites who had helped him to power but who were then gradually displaced by party members in leadership positions in the institutions of Nazi Germany. Under the process of *Gleichschaltung* all independent associations were brought under direct Nazi control. Hitler's powers expanded throughout the 1930s as a result of the compliance and collaboration of conservative elites and the muted responses of the Western democracies under the policy of appeasement, but also because the Nazi leader was genuinely popular among wide sectors of the German public. The perception of Hitler as executor of the will of the people and as guarantor of national unity and purpose was not just a triumph of Nazi propaganda but also reflected long-standing public longings for strong national leadership that would effectively get things done. Yet close investigation of how Germany was ruled under Hitler has challenged the conventional image of the **Third Reich** as an efficient bureaucratic monolith directly subject to Hitler's authority. Historians have adopted Martin **Broszat**'s term "polycracy" to describe a system of rule characterized by competing authorities, personal rivalries, overlapping jurisdictions, a multiplication of offices, and administrative confusion.[1] Bureaucratic overlap, the tendency to improvise, and sometimes bitter personal disputes among leading Nazis were typical features of the Nazi regime. This was not a static system of rule, but one subject to constant alteration and modification.

While the Nazis created numerous new offices, and the **SS** eventually became the most powerful organization in Nazi Germany, there was no sweeping elimination of the existing framework of government when the Nazis came to power. Old and new existed side by side. The state's administrative functions were left largely in the hands of the existing civil service, purged of its Jewish and left-leaning members, just as industry was left in control of the capitalist elites, large-scale agriculture remained in the hands of the landed aristocracy, and the army continued to be run by professional officers. The political scientist Ernst Fraenkel (1898–1975) coined the notion of the "dual state" in which a "normative" legal system continued to coexist with the growing "prerogative state" of extra-legal party and SS rule.[2] The legal apparatus was in fact a "fundamental pillar of the Nazi dictatorship" and helped to legitimize the regime.[3] Yet the *Führerprinzip* (leadership principle), eventually implemented at every level of government, societal institution, and party organization, created a kind of feudal system in which regional bosses, secure in their fiefdoms, often enjoyed considerable independence from central control. "Empire-building" by party and government leaders and agencies was one of the forces driving the ceaseless dynamism of Nazi rule. Party bosses enjoyed considerable scope for initiative, experimentation, and activity. Historian Dietrich **Orlow** referred to the Nazi administrative system as "bureaucratized romanticism," which "neither differentiated between the party functionary's role as a private individual and as a public person, nor did it seek to separate decision-makers from decision-administrators."[4] Although bonds of personal loyalty played an important role in the Nazi system, personal ambitions often clashed, adding to the administrative confusion.

Reich press chief Otto **Dietrich** may have been deliberately exaggerating Hitler's sole responsibility for policy-making when he wrote in his self-serving post-war memoirs that "Hitler created in the political leadership of Germany the greatest confusion that has ever existed in a civilized state," but the personal intrigues among Nazi leaders and sub-leaders that he describes were characteristic of a personalized bureaucracy.[5] Dietrich suggested that Hitler deliberately cultivated rivalry among his subordinates in order, if necessary, to play one person off against another, thus enhancing his own power as final arbiter. Certainly the Social Darwinist ethos of competition and struggle for power that pervaded the party promoted friction and jurisdictional disputes, often resulting in inefficiency, duplication of tasks, and conflicting priorities. The system offered plentiful opportunities for self-promotion in the name of the national interest. Nazi officials were often personally corrupt, using the powers of their offices for material gain. Hitler's own unbureaucratic style of working, his aversion to official routine, and his indifference to detail added to the incoherence of the system. Reliance on secret Führer decrees rather than on the organs of the state also impeded an orderly legislative or administrative process. Orders were often only given orally in face-to-face meetings. Hitler's biographer Ian **Kershaw** concluded that "a party leader and head of government less bureaucratically inclined, less committee man or man of the machine, than Hitler is hard to imagine."[6]

The dichotomy between Nazi party and state apparatus was never clearly defined. It was not until 1937 that all public officials were expected to join the party if they were not yet members. Hitler's own official titles of Führer and Reich chancellor (he rejected the title of Reich president because of its republican connotations) designated his dual role as head of party and government. By 1939, however, he was almost exclusively referred to only as the Führer, reflecting the dominant role that the party had come to play in government affairs. After April 1933 each German state (*Land*) was headed by a **Reichsstatthalter** nominally subject to the Interior Ministry of the Reich. The party had its own administrative districts (not necessarily identical with state boundaries), each headed by a **Gauleiter** (district leader).

Party offices and agencies paralleled governmental bodies and often interfered in their work. The same person usually held the offices of Reichsstatthalter and

Gauleiter simultaneously, creating in this double function a kind of personal union between state and party. This was not, however, necessarily matched at other levels of government, at least not until the war when the party, and especially the **SS**, increasingly dominated and even eclipsed the state bureaucracy. But recent research has also confirmed that orders passed down by the **Reichsleitung** (Reich leadership) from party headquarters in Munich were frequently modified or ignored by officials on the regional or local levels.[7] The sphere of the state expanded during the Nazi era, but so did the extra-legal sphere carved out by the SS and the **Gestapo** (secret state police) and typified by the notorious **concentration camp** system. As a result the lines of authority and areas of competence were not as clear as the notion of a monolithic totalitarian dictatorship might suggest. Although on 26 April 1942 Hitler announced to the Reichstag his authority to override judicial decisions, the regular legal system did survive and function to the very end. However, to counter the arbitrary power of the SS to seize an accused individual if he had been acquitted by the courts or given too lenient a sentence, the judiciary escalated its conviction rates and increased the severity of its sentences, thus surrendering its own objectivity and independence and undermining the rule of law.

Hitler discouraged any form of democratic or collective decision-making. The Reich Cabinet of ministers, which had frequently convened before **Hindenburg**'s death, met for a last time in early 1938. Thereafter the only central coordination of legislation was provided by the Reich Chancellery, whose head, Hans-Heinrich **Lammers**, controlled the information that reached the Führer and served as the main liaison between the dictator and his government ministers. Hitler also refused to approve the creation of a party senate, and the relations between the party's political organization, headed by Rudolf **Hess** until his flight to Scotland in 1941, and the state bureaucracy remained undefined. The influence of the party expanded, especially after the start of the war when Martin **Bormann**, Hess's successor as head of the Party Chancellery, took over the function previously reserved for the head of the Reich Chancellery of screening access to Hitler and passing on his orders to the executing organs in the party or state bureaucracy. Hitler removed himself more and more from domestic affairs as he assumed personal command of the **Wehrmacht** during the war. Even before the start of the war the party increasingly intervened in government affairs, particularly to pressure a bureaucracy that was often perceived by party militants as too moderate or conservative in carrying out the will of the Führer.

HOW GREAT WAS HITLER'S POWER?

To what extent was Hitler personally responsible for policy decisions? This was an issue raised in the debate between **intentionalists** and **structuralists** on the origins of the "**final solution**" of the Jewish question. Intentionalists tended to stress Hitler's role as all-powerful leader, whose goals, plans, and ideology crucially determined all policies, including the murder of the Jews. Structuralists (sometimes referred to as **functionalists**), on the other hand, stressed more contingent factors, especially the bureaucratic dynamic that led to increasingly radical policies ultimately culminating in genocide under the conditions of total war. Independent initiatives of competing ministers and party or SS leaders contributed to the "cumulative radicalization" of policies.[8] Some structuralists, such as the historian Hans **Mommsen**, went so far as to describe Hitler as a relatively weak dictator whose policies were driven and constrained by institutional forces often beyond his control. In his view Hitler operated more as a regulator than as a systematic planner of governmental measures.

Kershaw offered a convincing way of reconciling these two interpretative extremes of an all-powerful dictator, in full command of all policy decisions, and a weak leader, often merely reacting to initiatives launched by his immediate subordinates or by lower echelons of the party and government bureaucracy who were frequently in competition with each other. The key to understanding how the command system worked in Nazi Germany was the readiness, encouraged at all levels of government and party, "to work toward the Führer" by initiating measures that lower-ranking Nazis understood as implementing Hitler's over-all political and ideological goals.[9] Nazi followers competed with each other in realizing their leader's vision in "anticipatory obedience" to the Führer's will. Thus laws, directives, and regulations were usually launched without requiring the dictator's direct mandate or intervention, but only his retroactive approval. Hitler could thus remain above the fray of day-to-day politics, embellishing his popular image as omniscient and infallible savior of his people. This image was the central element of his charismatic leadership and of the political myth that held the Nazi system together.

The personality cult of Hitler, not as despot or dictator but as heroic leader carrying out the German will against a host of internal and external enemies, played a crucial role in the Nazi system of governance. Hitler's role as a symbol and source of inspiration may, in fact, have played a more important role in the Third Reich than his actual leadership. According to Kershaw, the "Hitler myth" served three primary functions. Perhaps most importantly it served as a means of integrating the disparate and sometimes opposing forces both within the party and among the conservatives in the army, the administration, and the economy, and to bind them to the regime. The revered leader personified the "idea" of the movement, the hopes for a unified people's community, a strengthened nation, and a Greater Germany that millions of Germans shared. A second function of the Führer cult was to mobilize public enthusiasm and serve as a stimulus for action against designated enemies of the regime, especially the Jews. And lastly the authority of the Führer was invoked to authorize and sanction even the most extreme measures that subordinates might take under the pretext of furthering the goals of the leader. Among these latter measures were the **euthanasia** program launched in 1939 and the "final solution" put into effect in 1941. In the closing phase of the war the Führer myth still provided the most powerful ideological incentive for Nazi loyalists to fight on to the bitter end.[10]

The myth of the heroic leader who took personal responsibility to overcome the bureaucratic obstacles that blocked the realization of German dreams thus helped to conceal the contradictions inherent in the chaotic and fragmented system of Nazi rule. The main function of the Hitler cult was to generate and to simulate public solidarity in support of Nazi rule. This reliance on a myth of personalized Messianic leadership entailed a dynamic of escalating radicalism that depended as much on popular collaboration as on coercion. Various studies on the role of the Gestapo in Nazi Germany have shown that contrary to the conventional perception of an all-embracing, omnipresent surveillance apparatus, the Gestapo had limited personnel and resources and depended much more than previously recognized on the cooperation of the German public in carrying out its policing functions. The willingness of members of the German public to spy and inform on each other was crucial to the ability of the Gestapo to enforce the racial laws enacted by the Nazis, as well as other ordinances and decrees. To be sure, the myth of Gestapo omnipresence and efficiency, as well as the brutal persecution of communists, Jews, and other outsiders, helped to create the climate of fear that encouraged popular compliance and cooperation. But after 1934 coercion probably played less of a role in inducing collaboration than the widespread consensus that supported Nazi rule. Historian Robert **Gellately** concluded that "the population at large internalized the norms of the regime to the point where they acted as unofficial extensions of the terror by keeping their eyes and ears open."[11]

In cases of petty offenses the Gestapo largely reacted to public denunciations in initiating its investigations. Denunciations of fellow citizens played a major role in the prosecution of *Rassenschande* (racial crime) after the criminalizing of sexual relations between Germans and Jews in 1935 and between Germans and foreign workers after the start of the war. By the late 1930s freely proffered denunciations had become so frequent that the authorities tried to discourage them by penalizing intentionally false leads. Although denunciations were often motivated by personal grudges, petty resentments, and other self-serving and opportunistic reasons rather than ideological convictions, there can be no doubt that the repressive measures of the Nazi regime against outsiders were more widely accepted and popularly supported than the conventional image of a totalitarian "police state" would suggest. Because Nazi terror was directed at specifically targeted groups of victims, ordinary law-abiding Germans had little reason to fear the Gestapo, which was generally seen as a force for law and order. According to historian Eric Johnson (b. 1948), "Most of the ordinary German population supported the Nazi regime, did not perceive the Gestapo as all-powerful or even as terribly threatening to them personally, and enjoyed considerable room to express frustration and disapproval arising out of minor disagreements with the Nazi state and its leadership."[12] The police state was not imposed on an unwitting population by force; it was built on a popular consensus that was largely indifferent to the fate of targeted victims, such as communists, socialists, "political priests," homosexuals, pacifists, Jews, and gypsies, and of foreign workers in Germany during the war. In the early years of the regime up to the start of the war, the Nazis' punitive practices, including the creation of concentration camps for political "reeducation," were not conducted in secret. Indeed, unlike the **extermination camps** during the war, their existence was well-publicized and even advertised by the regime to deter opposition and dissent. Gellately concluded that the Nazis' "coercive practices, the repression, and persecution won far more support for the dictatorship than they lost."[13] The idea that the majority of ordinary Germans were terrorized into submission by Nazi thugs is a myth, despite the apologetic function that this account of events served after the war. Nazi Germany offers incontrovertible evidence that even a brutal police state can enjoy substantial popular support.

THE POLITICAL ECONOMY OF THE THIRD REICH

The Nazi economic system shared some superficial features of a socialist planned economy, but despite the strong supervisory role played by the state in the economy, an organized capitalist market and private ownership of the means of production remained in place throughout the Nazi era. Just as Nazi ideology harked back to a pre-liberal, pre-democratic era, so Nazi economic thinking revived the statist ethos of autocratic conservatism while adopting or retaining policies that aimed at maximum productivity and technological progress. Unlike the liberal, more market-driven economies of the West, organized to facilitate business and commerce, the Nazis placed the ideological objectives of the party, state, and nation ahead of the economic interests of individual businesses or corporations when these interests were in conflict with Nazi priorities (which they sometimes were). If the fundamental principle of Western economic organization may be said to have been, at least in theory, the creation of a system in which individuals (and corporations) can make maximum profits, the fundamental principle of Nazi economic organization was to maximize state power and to guarantee the ability of the state to wage war. Individual profit (the guiding principle of liberal economies) or social welfare (the guiding principle of socialist economies) were viewed by the Nazis not as ends in themselves, but only as means to stabilize and strengthen the state.

The Nazis adopted pragmatic policies and avoided major structural changes to ensure maximum industrial productivity. Corporatism (the division of society into self-governing vocational chambers made up of employers and employees in particular industries), a program advocated by fascist intellectuals in the 1920s as a more efficient alternative to a potentially unstable liberal economy, remained a dead letter in practice (in Italy as well as Germany). In the period immediately following Hitler's seizure of power, Nazi efforts to realize their ideological goals were perhaps most pronounced in agriculture, which had always occupied a privileged position in Nazi doctrine. Yet it was precisely in this sector of the economy that the Nazis were least successful in achieving their aims. Rhetorical promises to small farmers and small business notwithstanding, the trend toward concentration in agriculture and business continued in the interests of efficient production. Ideologically driven economic measures, such as the **Hereditary Farm Law** of September 1933, gave way to more practical measures when the former failed to achieve the goal of increased productivity. Intended to protect the viability and continuity of family farms by prohibiting their mortgaging or sale, the Hereditary Farm Law actually reduced the standard of living of small farmers and spurred internal migration into the cities – trends the Nazis had earlier vowed to stop.

Notwithstanding the rhetorical and tactical use of the term "socialism" in Nazi propaganda, and notwithstanding their call for the "nationalization of all businesses that have previously been formed into trusts" in their 1920 party program, German industry and business property remained in private hands.[14] More businesses were nationalized in the Weimar era than under the Third Reich. If anything, the trend in Nazi Germany favored the reprivatization of publicly owned businesses rather than further nationalization. After the adoption of the **Four-Year Plan** in 1936 to prepare Germany for war, the government did establish state-run enterprises, most notably the **Hermann-Göring Works**, but only for the production of war-related goods that could not be manufactured profitably by private businesses (such as the extraction of metals from inferior ores or the creation of synthetic products). Nazi public enterprises were specifically designed to complement, not to compete with, private business. Industrialists did very well under the Nazis as war-related government orders helped to stimulate demand. Freed from the pressures of labor union demands, business owners saw their profits rise at a much higher rate than wages, productivity, or the general standard of living.

The Nazi principle of the primacy of politics meant that the economy was to serve the interests of the state, not the other way round as in liberal doctrine. The Nazi government undertook innovative measures to counter the effects of the Great Depression earlier than the liberal governments of the West, which were hampered by their traditional suspicion of any government interference in the "free market." Building in part on initiatives already begun under Hitler's predecessor Kurt von **Schleicher**, the Nazis introduced deficit financing and greatly increased public spending on such mammoth projects as the construction of the **Autobahn**. The Nazis also used tax incentives and subsidies to encourage economic expansion and stimulate public demand. As a means of combating unemployment a six-month work service, introduced on a voluntary basis even before the Nazis came to power, was made obligatory for all young men in 1935 and for young women in 1939 under the auspices of the Reich Work Service (**RAD**). This not only made labor available for menial tasks in construction and agriculture but also helped to prepare German youths for military service and war. The RAD also provided a model of what the Nazis meant by "German socialism." Rather than signifying a classless society, "socialism" as envisioned by the Nazis stood for the comradeship of members of all classes in the fulfillment of their common duty to the nation.

Although the Nazis had no intention of expropriating private businesses or the owners of capital, the German economy was subjected to increasingly stringent regulations designed to achieve the military objectives of the state. Prices, salaries, wages, rents, imports, and exports were all subject to varying degrees of state control. The government regulated not only interest rates, credit policy, and currency trading, but also set production goals and determined the percentage of net receipts that businesses were obligated to reinvest in expanded production. Since business owners enjoyed the rewards of increased production, they had little reason to object to these constraints on their independence in making production and investment decisions. German business people appreciated the lucrative contracts and freedom from union pressures for higher wages that the Nazi regime provided. Under the leadership principle business owners obtained a free hand to run their firms as they saw fit as long as they filled government orders.

There was a good deal of continuity in social policy after 1933 as well, along with specifically Nazi organizational and ideological changes. The public health insurance and old-age pension plans originally introduced in the Bismarck era were left in place, but the independent decision-making powers of insurance boards and committees were curtailed by the introduction of the leadership principle at all levels of management. Except for minimal government support for the destitute, welfare programs were left in the hands of private charities, all of which were eventually incorporated in the party's own welfare agency, the **NSV**. Ideologically, however, social policy under the Nazis underwent a crucial change. Only members of the *Volksgemeinschaft* – ethnic Germans certified as "healthy" on the basis of race and genetics – were eligible for welfare assistance of any kind. The NSV, originally founded in 1931 to help unemployed and indigent party members, gave financial assistance only to genetically healthy "**Aryans**." Its purpose was not so much to alleviate personal suffering as it was to demonstrate ethnic solidarity and encourage an ethos of service to the German race. The **German Labor Front** (DAF), too, the largest of the party's mass organizations, had its own "office of social self-reliance," as well as a program touted as "**Strength through Joy**" (KdF) that provided organized leisure activities to workers who would otherwise not have been able to afford them. The **Volkswagen** (people's car) was first developed as part of a KdF project to make affordable automobiles available to all Germans; but even before the outbreak of war the Nazis converted the VW plant to military production.

The development of Nazi economic policy occurred in three major phases. From 1933 to 1936 the major priority was to overcome the adverse effects of the depression and to restore the economic stability that was crucial to the projection of national power. The leading economic policy-maker in this period was former president of the **Reichsbank** Hjalmar **Schacht**, a representative of the conservative elite who strongly supported Hitler's rise to power. Schacht was restored to his post at the Reichsbank in 1933 and became Hitler's minister of economics from 1934 to 1937. He advocated a traditional export-oriented policy designed to attract foreign exchange, which could be used not only to restore prosperity but also to finance the rearmament that began in earnest in 1934. Schacht successfully concluded bilateral trade agreements with a number of countries, particularly in south-east Europe and Scandinavia, to secure markets for German manufactured products and raw materials for German industry, but his cautious monetary policies and his opposition to deficit financing ran into trouble with more militant Nazis who wished to free Germany from any dependence on international trade or the world market. For his part, Schacht feared the inflationary consequences of a precipitous shift from the production of consumer goods to the production of armaments.

Autarky (economic self-sufficiency) was the main goal of the second phase of Nazi economic policies, which began with the official introduction of the Four-Year Plan at the annual party rally in September 1936. Directives for the plan came from Hitler himself in a confidential memorandum drawn up in August 1936. The goals of the plan were to make the German army and the economy ready for war within four years. The threat of Soviet Communism served as the pretext for forced rearmament. But Hitler also wrote that the "final solution" of Germany's economic problems lay in the extension of the "living space of our people and/or the sources of its raw materials and foodstuff." He spoke of the need of the state to assist in the production of fuel, synthetic rubber, light metals, and other goods necessary for waging war. Under the plan the state was to play a larger role in the economy, but not at the expense of private industry. "It is for the Ministry of Economics simply to set the national economic tasks," he wrote, "and it is for private industry to carry them out."[15] As newly appointed head of the Four-Year Plan, Hermann **Göring** now became the most powerful figure in the management of the German economy, overshadowing Walther **Funk**, Schacht's successor as minister of economics. The transformation of the German economy for war undoubtedly hastened the coming of war as it not only gave Germany a temporary advantage in technologically advanced armaments, and thus an added incentive to go to war, but also because it created potentially long-term economic problems (how to provide both guns and butter) that could only be solved by conquest and the seizure of foreign assets. The degree to which domestic economic problems determined Hitler's decision to go to war in 1939 was the subject of an important debate between British historians Tim **Mason** and Richard **Overy** in the 1980s.[16]

Despite the introduction of the Four-Year Plan, whose managers were largely drawn from the I. G. Farben cartel, no central planning agency was created until the appointment of Albert **Speer** as minister of armament and munitions production in April 1942 as Germany prepared for **total war**. But even in this third and final phase of Nazi economic development German industry retained its rights of private ownership and self-management, although enterprises were increasingly forced to follow production decisions made by the state. Indeed, Speer's success in raising arms production was partly due to his willingness to allow considerable flexibility to private enterprise on how best to meet the government's production goals. Production of arms rose dramatically during the war. The foreign workers forcibly recruited by the newly appointed plenipotentiary for the allocation of labor, Fritz **Sauckel**, made up for the loss of German workers conscripted into military service. Efforts to mobilize women for war work fell short of projected goals, however. The Nazis' ideological categorization of women as homemakers and caregivers ran counter to the practical needs of the war industry. The generous allowances paid to military families made it unnecessary for women to supplement their income. The war was funded by a variety of measures, including the ruthless exploitation of occupied countries as well as the confiscation of Jewish property throughout Europe. The spoils of war allowed the Nazi regime to continue to offer German citizens a higher standard of living than its defeated neighbors. Historian Götz **Aly** even contended that through low taxation, generous health insurance, and other social benefits the Nazi regime in effect bought the continued allegiance of its citizens, thus preventing the popular disaffection that the Nazis believed had contributed to German defeat in the First World War. Aly's thesis was effectively disputed, however, by Adam **Tooze**, who pointed out that Aly vastly understated the sacrifices required by the German war economy.[17]

NAZI CULTURE

Control of the arts was central to Nazi totalitarian rule. The basic principle governing the Nazis' cultural policies was that all aspects of aesthetic culture had to serve the national cause – the cause of national regeneration. The Nazis understood their revolution, after all, not merely as a political changing of the guard but as a cultural transformation ultimately intended to unify the nation behind the Nazi project of national expansion and domination. The Nazis understood art and literature as the expression of race and the national community, not as the product of isolated individuals or as the expression of a particular age. The truths revealed in the art of a people supposedly expressed the eternally valid ideals of that people, not the fads or fashions of a particular time. The Nazis' cultural program appealed to popular tastes and prejudices. They viewed the aestheticism epitomized in the slogan "l'art pour l'art" (art for art's sake) as an abomination. Art that was not comprehensible to the common man was considered to be without value. Nazi cultural policies appealed to wide sectors of the public as a way of protecting the natural cultural order seemingly under attack by a self-appointed liberal cultural elite. This conservative attitude enjoyed considerable resonance in a population dismayed by the innovative experimentalism of the Weimar era and the esotericism of the artistic avant-garde.

In the German "culture wars" of the first four decades of the twentieth century, the Nazis and their *völkisch* forebears posed as the defenders of the cultural values of "the people" against the assaults of "pathological" aesthetic movements accused of subverting natural and traditional standards of beauty. To many ordinary citizens, modernism in music, literature, painting, and architecture represented a decline in traditional standards of beauty and form, a decline the Nazis promised to reverse. To be sure, there were some differences among the Nazi elite in their attitudes toward modernism. **Goebbels**, for instance, was more open to innovative trends than **Rosenberg**, who, as the founder of the **Combat League for German Culture** in 1928 and as "Delegate of the Führer for the Supervision of all Spiritual and Worldview-related Schooling and Education of the NSDAP" in 1934, wielded considerable influence in the cultural sphere. In music, the Nazis favored the traditional melodic style of the Classical and Romantic eras; in literature they promoted the traditional narrative form and heroic themes of the nineteenth-century novel and conventional rhyme and meter in poetry; in painting and sculpture they insisted on clarity and literal representation. "'Works of art' which cannot be comprehended," Hitler declared at the dedication of the newly constructed House of German Art in Munich in July 1937, "will no longer be foisted on the German people!"[18] In the Nazi view, the proper function of art was to idealize the German peasant and soldier and to affirm the mythical value of the Germanic race and its *Bodenständigkeit* (rootedness in the soil) as the source of all cultural creativity. Nazi "purification of the arts" was directed at art criticism as well. Henceforth only straightforward reporting and positive evaluation of officially sanctioned art would be permitted.

The Nazis posed as the defenders of the integrity of the fine arts against their political misuse by the left. They understood the usefulness of works of art as expressions and instruments of power, yet they denied that their own esteem for the arts had any political motive other than the edification of the Volk. It was the engaged artists of the left, they claimed, who politicized art and misused it to disseminate egalitarian and democratic ideology. By "depoliticizing" the arts, offering the public an illusory retreat from the ruthless world of politics to the harmonious realm of aesthetics, the Nazis not only blunted the socially critical function of art but also concealed or embellished their own radically conserva-tive political agenda. Their sponsorship of "high culture" (as well as apolitical mass entertainment to divert the populace from thinking about political issues) enhanced their claim to non-partisanship as the arbiters of the true national taste above the fray of partisan politics. The philosopher Walter Benjamin coined the phrase "the aestheticizing of politics" to describe this typically fascist process of depoliticization. Masters of gestures, pageantry, and symbols, the Nazis practiced politics as theater. Political events, most notably the annual party rallies, were staged as theatrical spectacles to overawe and mesmerize the citizenry – and to *prevent* their actual political participation in decision-making. The Nazis were quite willing to adopt aspects of modernism as well as advanced production techniques to achieve maximum aesthetic effects. Albert Speer, for instance, Hitler's favorite architect and wartime head of arms production, created a "cathedral of light" at the annual party rallies in Nuremberg by using anti-aircraft searchlights to cast beams of light into the sky to a height of 25,000 feet.

The aestheticization of politics did not just apply to the staging of bombastic rituals and ceremonies. The entire polity was to be shaped according to aesthetic principles of order, symmetry, and beauty. The arts helped the Nazis celebrate the national and racial preeminence of Germany and to convey the illusion of benign change in a society transformed by Nazi rule. Art served to conceal the contradictions and divisions in German society and to project an image of social harmony, community, and unified national purpose. As in most other fields, the ready collaboration of professionals made Nazification of the arts possible. The Nazis gave lavish support to artists who were willing to turn their talents to promoting the aesthetic policies of the regime. Artists, art dealers, and museum directors, many of whom considered themselves "apolitical," took advantage of the new opportunities opened to them.

Their hostility to artistic innovation notwithstanding, the Nazi leadership, and particularly Hitler (who earned his living as a young man from the sale of his scenic Vienna watercolors), were obsessed with the arts and presented themselves as men of culture. Many of them amassed huge art collections of their own, robbing the treasures of occupied countries for that purpose. Even at the height of the war Hitler pursued his pet project of creating a "Führer museum" in the Austrian city of Linz where he had grown up. "The intensity of the Führer's longing for music, theater, and cultural relaxation is enormous," Goebbels wrote in his diary at the height of the war in January 1942. Nazi patronage of "high art" fed the Nazi conceit of German cultural superiority and their sense of Germany's civilizing mission in the world. Art provided "the painted veil behind which they could commit whatever horrors they pleased."[19]

The Nazis attributed degeneracy in art, as in all other areas of culture, to impurity of blood. They sought to halt the perceived decline in traditional standards by purging German cultural life of all Jewish influence. The alleged preoccupation of Jewish artists with disease and deformity was supposedly responsible for the "nihilism" and defective vision of modern art. This tendency to equate modernism in the arts with biological decline and disease was not limited to Nazis, though they added their own racist emphasis on the Jews as the biological agents of degeneration. The linkage of racial and cultural degeneration with egalitarian political movements had a long pedigree in racial doctrines of the nineteenth and early twentieth centuries. Oswald Spengler's post-First World War best-seller *Decline of the West* treated civilizations as organisms and identified symptoms of biological degeneration in modernist trends in the arts as well as in democratic political ideologies. In the 1920s right-wing critics coined the phrase "cultural bolshevism" to denounce the transgression of conventional norms of artistic representation in innovative movements such as cubism, expressionism, or surrealism. The Nazis revived this notion as part of their political campaign against international communism. Nazi ire was directed not only against any socially critical or politically revolutionary art but also against all abstract, non-objective art. From the Nazi point of view art had to be "healthy," positive, morally edifying, and patriotic, offering an idealized picture of the German national community to uplift and divert the masses. Ironically, this meant that in practice Nazi art bore a considerable resemblance to the "socialist realism" imposed on Soviet artists under Stalinism, except that while the subjects of Soviet art tended to be industrial proletarians, Nazi artists romanticized the soldier, the artisan, and the peasant-farmer tilling the soil. Typical subjects of fascist art were "muscular figures in aggressive poses."[20]

As in other areas of policy, Nazi cultural policies grew more radical in the later 1930s. Up to the mid-1930s even modernism had its champions among the Nazi elite, and some modernist artists and architects, such as Emil Nolde (1867–1956), Ernst Barlach (1870–1938), and Ludwig Mies van der Rohe (1886–1969), sympathized with the Nazi regime until their own works came under fire from cultural conservatives, who emerged triumphant in their struggle to dominate the arts. Hitler's own personal aesthetic predilection for nineteenth-century Bavarian genre painting may have doomed the modernist cause. Nazi rejection of modern art was dramatically demonstrated by the Exhibit of Degenerate Art staged as the opening exhibition in the new **House of German Art** in 1937. Ironically, this exhibit generated far greater public attendance than the staid collection of officially approved German art exhibited the following year.

Nazi control over the arts was exercised by Propaganda Minister Josef Goebbels through the **Reich Chamber of Culture** (*Reichskulturkammer*) founded in September 1933. It comprised seven separate chambers for the visual arts, literature, music, theater, film, radio, and the press, respectively. Since by law only members of a chamber were permitted to be professionally active in their respective fields, the Chamber of Culture provided a means to enforce both racial homogeneity and ideological conformity in the cultural sphere. No independent cultural associations of any kind were permitted. Architecture, subsumed under the Chamber of Visual Arts (*Bildende Künste*), was particularly important to the Nazis. Hitler, whose boyhood dream was to become a master-builder, considered architecture, along with music, as one of the two queens of the arts.[21] He took a personal role in designing the new Reich chancellery, constructed under Speer's direction in 1938. Architecture was meant to manifest the glory, power, and dominance of the nation, state, and party. The monumental neo-classical edifices favored by the Nazis were deliberately intended to underscore the authority and durability of the "thousand-year Reich." Speer's monumental, neo-classical German Pavilion at the Paris World's Fair in 1937, parts of which were destined to become permanent fixtures at the Nuremberg site of the annual party rallies, was planned to express "security, pride, self-confidence, clarity, discipline, and thereby the concept of the new Germany."[22] In the last days of the war, isolated in the Führer bunker beneath the chancellery that now lay in ruins, Hitler took comfort by contemplating his model of a grandiose new Berlin, to be renamed "Germania" and designed to serve as the capital of a fascist Europe. The "Great Hall" that was to become the centerpiece of the new capital was to have a 300-foot-high ceiling and be capable of seating 180,000 persons.

The relentlessly affirmative cultural policies of the Nazis (affirming the positive qualities of life in the Third Reich, the legitimacy of existing social and political arrangements, and the superiority of the German nation, race, and culture) were evident in other areas as well, such as science, education, and religion. Jews were associated with negativism, irreverence, and social and cultural criticism, which supposedly corroded the healthy attitudes and instincts of the people and under-mined morality, patriotism, and religion. Just as the "Jewish press" was accused of purveying editorial opinion in the guise of factual reporting (thus displaying the putative "liberal bias" of Jewish journalists), so Jewish scientists were accused of mixing theory with fact. Nazi defenders of "Aryan physics," led by the Nobel Prize-winning physicists Johannes **Stark** and Philipp **Lenard**, attacked Albert Einstein's theory of relativity as a typical example of Jewish materialism in the realm of science. Einstein's challenge to the Newtonian principle that the mea-surement of space and time was fixed in absolute terms was equated by Nazis with skepticism about the existence of a spiritual sphere of moral absolutes. To combat such moral and physical relativism, Nazi scientists promoted a common-sense approach that rejected any conclusions not verified by the senses. Although Stark, Lenard, and their Nazi cohort in the sciences were ascendant in the early years of the Third Reich and succeeded in driving Jewish and liberal scientists and scholars from their academic and research posts (about a fifth of university faculties, including no fewer than 24 past or future Nobel Prize-winners in all fields, lost their positions in the purge), the tide swung against the advocates of "Aryan physics" as war approached. The practical exigencies of war eventually trumped the mandates of Nazi ideology at least in the "hard sciences." The regime increased its support for conventional science when this offered greater promise of useful results than "Aryan physics."

As in other areas of culture, anti-intellectualism defined Nazi attitudes and practices in the field of education as well. The officially proclaimed principal aim of education was to build character, not merely to improve the mind through greater knowledge or better reasoning skills. Critical thinking was regarded with distrust as a liberal Jewish trait that subverted popular faith in God, nation, and state. Character-building meant inculcating the military virtues of duty, obedience, discipline, respect for authority, and unquestioning willingness to serve one's country as a soldier and, if necessary, to die for it. The Nazi stress on physical education had an obvious military motive as well. The Nazi curriculum focused on the teaching of celebratory national history and placed particular emphasis on racial biology and **eugenics**, the "science" of upgrading a population group by selective breeding. In higher education the dubious field of "racial science" became academically respectable and received preferential government support. The Nazis exercised ideological control of education not only through various party and governmental agencies, such as the so-called **Amt Rosenberg** (office of the party ideologist Alfred Rosenberg) and the Reich Education Ministry (REM) under Bernhard **Rust**, but also through their mass organizations for teachers, the National Socialist Teachers' League (**NSLB**) and the National Socialist League of University Teachers (**NSDDB**), and for students, the National Socialist German Student League (**NSDStB**) as well as, of course, the **Hitler Youth** (HJ) and the League of German Girls (**BDM**).

WHAT ROLE DID RELIGION PLAY IN NAZI GERMANY?

The Nazi ascendancy to power in 1933 was accompanied by a huge increase in church membership in Germany, reversing a trend of declining church memberships throughout the Weimar years. "There could have been no clearer sign," historian Richard Steigmann-Gall has written, "that national renewal and religious renewal were believed to be deeply connected."[23] In their 1920 Party program the Nazis had expressed their support for a "positive Christianity," by which they meant a militant, non-denominational form of Christian creed tied to German nationalism and opposed to the "Jewish-materialist spirit in us and around us." Hitler's government reiterated this commitment to religion in its first official proclamation on 1 February 1933: "[The national government] will extend its firm protection to Christianity as the basis of our moral system, and to the family as the nucleus of our Volk and state."[24] At the first meeting of the Reichstag after the elections in March 1933, Hitler declared that he viewed the two major confessions, Protestant and Catholic, as essential to maintaining the German national character (*Volkstum*).[25]

These avowals of support for organized religion, though no doubt motivated by the need to retain the support of the church-going public, were entirely consistent with the party's long-proclaimed mission to suppress "godless communism," "Marxist Social Democracy," "cultural bolshevism," and "moral nihilism." In the late Weimar era the Nazis had appealed to the church-going public by asserting that the liberal parliamentary state was not capable of defending either religion or the institutional rights of the churches. The Nazi victory in 1933 was welcomed by many Germans as not just a political turn but also as a moral turn against the secular humanist values of the Enlightenment and French Revolution. Although before 1933 a number of radical Nazis, such as Erich **Ludendorff**, made no bones about their opposition to Catholicism, and others, such as Rosenberg, tried to develop an alternative anti-Jewish, nordic-pagan *völkisch* creed for popular consumption, all Nazi factions joined in professing belief in divine providence and moral rearmament, and in repudiating atheism. Determined to show their support for religion, Nazi and SA groups frequently attended church in uniform before and after the takeover of power, and members of the SS were explicitly prohibited from professing a disbelief in God. Opportunism no doubt played a part in these displays of religious faith, but they also reflected the convictions of many Nazis and their leaders. They understood their movement as embodying traditional morality and religion against the "evil" forces of the Jewish-led liberal, socialist, and secular left.

Nazi appeals to the devout were reciprocated by substantial sympathy for the Nazis' patriotic agenda among the church-going German public. Within the German Protestant churches in particular there had long been strong support for a nationalist form of Lutheran doctrine and for National Socialism. Many German Protestants shared the Nazis' anti-democratic, illiberal, and racist goals. Protestant Nazis and Nazi sympathizers helped to form the movement of **German Christians** within a number of the 28 separately governed state churches in the late 1920s and early 1930s, as the Nazis were gaining strength. In the elections of 1930 and 1932 the Nazis did particularly well in the overwhelmingly Protestant rural and semi-urban districts of northern, central, and eastern Germany. Well aware of the importance of his religious base, Hitler increasingly distanced himself from the *völkisch* sectarians in his party. Ludendorff had already left the party in 1928 to form his own extreme nationalist cult. In deference to church leaders Hitler also refused to give Rosenberg's anti-clerical tract, *The Myth of the Twentieth Century*, official party approval. Opponents of Christianity who tried to gain official recognition for a neo-Germanic **German Faith Movement** after Hitler's accession to power enjoyed a considerable following in the party, but received no encouragement from the pragmatically oriented Nazi state.

After Hitler's accession to power, the Nazi strategy to assume control of the Protestant (or Evangelical) Church in Germany was to try to unite the separate state churches into a single nation-wide church under German Christian dominance. That strategy seemed to have succeeded with the election of Ludwig **Müller** as the first *Reichsbischof* of the newly formed *Reichskirche*, the German Evangelical Church, at a national synod in September 1933. However, the attempt by the German Christians to introduce the **Aryan paragraph** into the Church constitution provoked the formation of a clerical opposition movement within the Evangelical Church that ultimately constituted itself as the **Confessing Church**. Under the leadership of Pastor Martin **Niemöller** this movement rejected the efforts of the German Christians to meld *völkisch* principles with traditional Lutheran doctrine. In the ensuing **Church Struggle** between the two contending sides, adherents of the Confessing Church successfully resisted attempts by the German Christians to oust converted Jews from church membership and to dispense with the Old Testament in church services. Although leaders of the Confessing Church insisted that theirs was a theological, not a political movement, they invoked the traditional Lutheran distinction between the temporal and spiritual realms and denied the right of the state to intervene in doctrinal matters or in the self-administration of the German Evangelical Church.

Anxious not to alienate their strong support among all factions of German Protestantism, and conscious of the potentially damaging results that a heavy-handed response to the Church Struggle could provoke both at home and in the eyes of the world, the Nazi government sought to reconcile the contending factions within the German Evangelical Church. In 1935 a new Ministry for Church Affairs was created under the leadership of the former Prussian minister of justice Hanns **Kerrl**. His efforts to conciliate the contending factions failed, however, to settle the dispute within the Church, and his goal of blending Christian faith with National Socialist ideology also ran into increasing opposition from Nazi radicals, who feared the moderating influence of Christian principles on the Nazi program.

Nazi policy toward the churches was never uniform. The polycratic nature of the Nazi system affected religious policy formation as well, as advocates of organized Christianity, those who were neutral toward religion, and those who were hostile to the churches competed with each other from their various institutional perches. In 1940, after the start of the war, Martin **Bormann**, at the time still **Hess**'s deputy as head of the Party Chancellery, ordered the end of all efforts to fuse Christianity with National Socialism in religious and ideological instruction in schools. "It will not be possible to create a Christian doctrine that would be completely compatible with the point of view of National Socialist ideology," he wrote, "just as the communities of Christian faith would never be able to accept the ideology of National Socialism in its entirety."[26] Among the reasons he cited for the impossibility of achieving a Christian–Nazi synthesis were the Christian reluctance to embrace the Nazi racial doctrine and the inability of the various Christian denominations to agree on a common doctrine. Hitler's "table talk" during the war, though more anti-clerical than anti-Christian in tone, also indicated that the ultimate Nazi goal was to suppress the organized churches in Germany after the war.

Nazi relations with the Roman Catholic Church underwent similar fluctuations. Although a high proportion of leading Nazis, including Hitler, Goebbels, and Himmler, had been raised as Catholics, they were also heirs to a long tradition of anti-Catholicism among German nationalists, for whom international Catholicism represented a threat to the unity and sovereignty of the German Reich. In Austria, where Hitler had grown up, pan-German nationalists saw both the Habsburg monarchy and the Catholic Church as barriers to Austria's incorporation in a Greater German Empire. *Völkisch* sectarianism within the Nazi Party always had a specifically anti-Catholic edge. Catholics made up only about a third of the population of Germany, mainly concentrated in Bavaria, the Rhineland, and the south-west, but the Catholic Center Party and its Bavarian affiliate (the Bavarian People's Party) consistently out-polled the Nazi Party in Catholic areas. On the other hand, Catholic distrust of the liberal Weimar government made Bavaria a hospitable location for radical right-wing groups to organize and conspire against the central government in the 1920s and early 1930s. A number of Catholic clerics actively promoted the early Nazi movement in Munich. The Catholic hierarchy in Germany, however, declared Nazi racial doctrines to be incompatible with Catholic teachings in 1931, and in a number of dioceses Catholics were forbidden from joining the Nazi Party.

All this changed abruptly after Hitler's accession to power in 1933. The Center Party, eager to demonstrate its support for the movement of national awakening, provided the margin of victory for the Enabling Act in the Reichstag in March 1933. The Vatican, anxious to maintain the independence of the Church in Germany and the authority of the pope within the German Church, signed a **Concordat** with the Reich government in July 1933, in which the Church pledged to refrain from all political activity, thus also obligating the Church not to oppose the anti-Semitic legislation of the state. The Concordat failed to end tensions between Church and state, however. Although according to its terms the Church had the right to operate "charitable, cultural, or religious" organizations, the Nazis refused to recognize the independence of Catholic social and professional organizations. In the process of *Gleichschaltung* the Nazis sought to abolish long-standing Catholic youth and worker groups and force their members into Nazi organizations. Members of the German Faith Movement also openly sought to recruit Catholics, an initiative that many party members supported. German bishops responded to what they regarded as violations of the Concordat by persuading the pope to issue the encyclical, *Mit brennender Sorge* (with burning anxiety), in March 1937. This document repudiated Nazi efforts to impose their racial doctrine on the Church and to encourage the defection of German Catholics. However, in conformity with the Church's pledge to abandon political activity, the encyclical failed to criticize the anti-Semitic **Nuremberg Laws** or even mention the plight of German Jews. Nonetheless, the Nazis responded by prohibiting dissemination of the encyclical and confiscating as many published copies as they were able to seize. The Nazis also sought to discredit the Church in the eyes of the public by prosecuting priests for sexual offenses and imprisoning priests who criticized the Nazis from the pulpit.

Strong Church antagonism to communism was one of the factors moderating the Church's aversion to the Nazis both before and after the start of the war, despite the ascendancy of anti-religious hard-liners within the Nazi Party. In the Polish territory annexed to Germany as the **Wartheland**, the German administration restricted the prerogatives and the financial resources of the Catholic Church. Within the borders of Germany as well the Nazis introduced harsher penalties for dissident priests after the start of the war. In the **Dachau** concentration camp alone more than 400 dissident Catholic priests were interned during the war (as well as a smaller number of Protestant pastors). The source of greatest tension between church and state during the war was the active opposition of both churches to the Nazis' murderous campaign against the mentally and physically handicapped launched at the start of the war. Widely publicized sermons preached by the Catholic bishop Clemens Graf von **Galen** in Münster (as well as protests by the Protestant bishop Theophil **Wurm** of the Confessing Church) contributed to Hitler's decision to order a halt to the program in August 1941. Already before the war the Catholic Church in particular had unsuccessfully sought to halt the practice of compulsory sterilization introduced in 1933. The Church's strong opposition to "negative eugenics," however, did not lead to any public Church protest against the murder of the Jews, despite the request for papal intervention by the bishop of Berlin, Konrad Graf von **Preysing**, who sought to persuade the pope to break off diplomatic relations with the Nazi government in 1943. Fearful of any actions that might harm the interests of the Church, Pius XII made no effort to share his own information on the ongoing Holocaust with the German bishops, who failed to approve a statement of public protest at a national conference in Fulda in 1943. Courageous individual clerics, however, such as Prior Bernhard Lichtenburg (1875–1943) of Berlin or the Jesuit priest Alfred Delp (1907–1945), publicly condemned the persecution of the Jews and paid for their resistance with their lives.

In his Christmas message in December 1942 Pope Pius XII called attention to the plight of "hundreds of thousands of persons, who, without any fault on their part, sometimes only because of nationality and race, have been consigned to death or to a slow decline."[27] However, he failed to mention Jews or Poles or any other nationality by name. The pope's failure to issue any public protest against the Holocaust has generated a large literature, both critical and apologetic. Critics attribute the pope's silence mainly to his fear of thereby facilitating a communist victory in Europe. "In his mind," historian Michael Phayer has written, "Germany was and would remain the European bulwark against Russian communism."[28] As papal nuncio in Munich at the end of the First World War Eugenio Pacelli (later Pius XII) had become convinced that Jews played a disproportionate role in the aborted revolution in that city in 1919. Pius's defenders have argued that a public protest against the killing of the Jews would in all likelihood have intensified the Nazis' crackdown on Jews, as indeed seemed to have been the case after protests by Catholic leaders of Nazi-occupied Holland against the deportation of Jews in February 1942. The Vatican also seems to have feared that protests against Nazi mistreatment of Poles would have the opposite effect than the one intended. The pope's defenders have also pointed out the role of the Church in saving hundreds of Italian Jews from deportation. However, the beneficiaries of Church protection were mainly Jewish converts to Catholicism. The Vatican did not publicly condemn German deportations of the Jews of Rome in October 1943, ostensibly for fear of a German retaliatory attack on Rome or on the Vatican itself.

The pope's major concern throughout the war seems to have been to preserve the unity and universality of the Church against encroachments by any of the warring parties. The pope feared that the Church would not be permitted to continue its public religious functions in a murderous war in which the Church was responsible to Catholics on both sides of the conflict. No doubt this fear reinforced the pope's reluctance to issue a public statement specifically denouncing the Nazis' genocidal policies toward the Jews. Since the end of the religious wars in Europe the Vatican had traditionally sought to play the role of impartial peacemaker between nations and had resisted pressures to join any of the warring sides. In the early stages of the war Pius XII hoped to mediate a peace between the British government and members of the German resistance. In the latter stages of the war he seems to have hoped that a separate peace with the Western Allies would prevent the total destruction of Germany and the consequent triumph of communism. Whatever his specific objectives may have been, Pius XII clearly preferred behind-the-scenes diplomacy as a means of influencing events to any overt attempts to mobilize public opinion. Although it is highly unlikely that an open papal protest would have succeeded in halting the killing program, failure to issue such a protest could not help but tarnish the image of the Church in the eyes of those who considered its fundamental moral obligations to be more important than its immediate institutional interests.

7

FOREIGN POLICY, WAR, AND THE HOLOCAUST

WHAT WERE HITLER'S FOREIGN POLICY GOALS?

Hitler and leading Nazis were determined to achieve three long-range foreign policy goals. The first goal was one that virtually all Germans shared and could therefore be openly proclaimed: reversal of the results of the **Versailles** settlement, which had deprived Germany of territory, restricted the size and weaponry of its armed forces, and saddled it with a large reparations debt. The second goal was also shared by a majority of Germans, but because of the risks of Allied intervention it could not, at first, be publicly acknowledged: creation of a Greater German **Reich** that would include not only the territories lost in the First World War but also the millions of ethnically German former subjects of the Habsburg Empire, particularly those residing in Austria and in the newly formed state of Czechoslovakia. Hitler was himself of Austrian birth and his world-view was shaped by the strong pan-German movement in the Austrian Empire before the First World War.

Hitler's third long-range goal entailed the virtual certainty of conflict with the victors of the First World War and was never publicly acknowledged until the war actually started: the conquest of *Lebensraum* (living space) in the east, territories that had never been part of Germany and were not populated by ethnic Germans. It seems clear, however, that Hitler was committed to this goal from the very start of his political career following Germany's defeat in the First World War. In *Mein Kampf*, published in 1926, he had written, "The right to possess soil and territory can become a duty, if decline seems to threaten a great nation unless it extends its territory."[1] The driving force behind Nazi policies, both domestic and foreign, was their Social Darwinist notion of unavoidable and unceasing struggle between people and races, a struggle in which nature and providence favored the "superior" races to win. This bleak and bellicose attitude was not limited to the Nazis or even to fascists, but had its roots both in the First World War and in the age of imperialism that preceded it.

One way to understand Nazi expansionism is to view it as the displacement of European colonizing efforts from Africa and Asia to the European continent. Extreme German nationalists had long regarded the Slavic-populated areas of Eastern Europe as the proper field for German colonization. Here a new order based on racial hierarchy was to be created. But an open avowal of this aim would not only have alerted the Allies to take preventive measures but would also have risked provoking opposition among Germans who feared that such a reckless policy would lead to the over-extension of German power and resources and eventual ruin. Hitler, therefore, made every effort to conceal his true long-term aim of eastward expansion both from the German public and from the victor powers (although he made no effort to conceal it from his generals, most of whom supported his plans, if only because it would result in a huge expansion of the armed forces). What Hitler had written in *Mein Kampf* was not taken particularly seriously by Western statesmen, because it was assumed that its sole purpose was to gain political advantage in the partisan struggle for power in Germany. Perhaps British statesmen were also lulled by Hitler's illusory pursuit of an alliance with his fellow **Nordics** in the Anglo-Saxon kingdom. The victor powers of the First World War confidently assumed that the responsibilities and realities of power would eventually moderate Hitler's stated aims.

HOW AND WHY WERE THE NAZIS ABLE TO DISMANTLE THE VERSAILLES TREATY?

Nazi diplomatic triumphs were made possible by a British and French policy of wary accommodation of German demands, a policy that came to be known as **appeasement**. This policy had its source not in cowardice or pacifism but in a determination to avoid another fratricidal war that would leave the European nations even weaker than after the First World War. Appeasement was partly the result of a history lesson too well learned. Mindful that the great powers had resorted to war in 1914 without fully exhausting the possibilities of diplomacy, Western statesmen resolved not to repeat this mistake in the 1930s. To prevent another round of bloodletting, the consequence of which could only be to further weaken European preeminence in the world, supporters of appeasement insisted that differences between nations must be resolved by negotiation, not war. They put their faith in the peacekeeping machinery established by the **League of Nations,** which required its members to submit disputes to international arbitration before resorting to military force. If historians in the 1920s seemed to confirm that the Great War could have been prevented by more willingness on all sides to negotiate, it made sense to rely on negotiations and compromise to prevent a second world war.

Appeasement was not generally motivated by sympathy for National Socialism as a system of rule. Rather, it was motivated more by the hope of moderating Nazi radicalism by addressing certain German grievances. A decade after the end of the war some German grievances had come to seem reasonable and justified. Some members of the British establishment came to believe that the Versailles Treaty had indeed been excessively harsh and served French hegemonic aims. Certainly this was the perception of the overwhelming majority of Germans, whose embrace of the radical right could be explained as an understandable reaction to the injustices of Versailles. If this diagnosis was correct – the harsh terms of Versailles as the root cause of German extremism – it made sense to modify these terms as a way of ending Germany's pariah status, mitigating German resentments, and restoring normalcy to the German political system. This strategy for moderating German nationalism and thus preventing another war was also in keeping with the principles of national self-determination, mutual disarmament, and peaceful conflict resolution embodied in the covenant of the League of Nations.

Although appeasement as an active policy in pursuit of peace enjoyed popular support in Britain and, to a lesser extent, in France, it was not a policy that went unchallenged. The left was far more perspicacious than liberals or conservatives in recognizing the Nazis' long-term expansionist aims and in warning that appeasement would lead to war. By encouraging Nazi ambitions, appeasement seemed to be playing into Nazi hands. The left-wing alternative to appeasement was the **Popular Front** strategy, adopted by the **Comintern** after Hitler's accession to power in 1933. Communists now belatedly called for the formation of a united anti-fascist front that would include not only the previously maligned reformist Social Democrats but also liberals of the left-of-center bourgeois middle. The Communists pledged to put their revolutionary goals on hold and to unite behind a liberal democratic program for the duration of the fight against fascism. Short-lived popular front coalition governments were indeed elected in France and Spain in 1936, but liberal and Social Democratic suspicions of Communist aims and motives and conservative hostility to popular front domestic and foreign policies doomed these governments to ineffectiveness, and, in the case of Spain, to a right-wing military rebellion that led to the **Spanish Civil War**.

Soviet efforts to commit Western European nations to an anti-fascist front by promoting a **collective security** policy in the League of Nations after the USSR joined the League in 1934 were met by similar skepticism from supporters of appeasement. Both the Soviet Union and the Western European nations suspected the other side of wanting to involve them in war with Nazi Germany. From the Soviet perspective Western appeasement was designed to encourage the Nazis to go to war against the USSR. Western advocates of appeasement, on the other hand, suspected the Soviet Union of wanting to unleash a war among the capitalist countries in order to pave the way for communism. Fear of communism was an important factor in mobilizing and rationalizing support for the appeasement policy. Some defenders of appeasement argued that fascism was preferable to communism and that a strong Nazi Germany was essential to stemming the expansion of the Soviet Union. The alleged Soviet threat was frequently invoked by Nazi leaders as a way of justifying their defiance of the terms of Versailles. Hostility to communism also muted Western criticisms of the brutal Nazi crackdown on the left, the suspension of civil liberties in Germany, and the persecution of Jews (carried out in the name of combating left-wing political subversion) in the early months of the Nazi regime.

Notwithstanding the seemingly compelling arguments for appeasement, the victorious Allies were understandably reluctant to lift the military restrictions imposed on Germany by the Versailles Treaty until they could be certain that

Germany would pose no threat to them. Hitler took advantage of the Allies' unwillingness to grant Germany full parity in arms to scuttle the disarmament conference conducted under League of Nations auspices in Geneva in 1932/1933. The Nazi government seized on this pretext to resign from the League in October 1933, following the example of Japan, which had left the League in response to its protest against their invasion of Manchuria in 1931. In March 1935, strengthened by the return of the coal-rich **Saar** to German control after an internationally supervised **plebiscite**, Hitler announced the reintroduction of military conscription and the expansion of the army beyond the limits prescribed by the Versailles Treaty. Rearmament was necessary, Hitler asserted, to counter the Soviet threat as well as the failure of France to disarm in accordance with the League covenant. At the same time he revealed the existence of a German air force, the **Luftwaffe**, secret construction of which had begun years earlier in violation of Versailles.

Britain and France responded to these provocations with a League of Nations resolution condemning German rearmament, but failed to follow this up with significant sanctions. France did conclude a defensive treaty with the Soviet Union and made territorial concessions to Italy in Africa to win Mussolini's support for containing Germany, but the British pursued a contrary policy by concluding a **naval agreement** that allowed Germany to exceed the limits on naval construction established at Versailles. Both Britain and France were reluctant to take stronger stands against German rearmament for fear that this would give the Germans all the more reason to refuse to cooperate in international efforts to maintain peace. Mussolini, who had pledged his support to Allied efforts to contain Germany in a meeting at **Stresa** in April 1935, took advantage of the climate of appeasement to launch an attack on the African state of **Ethiopia** in October 1935 and to annex it in May 1936. Although Britain and France again failed to apply effective sanctions, their protests against Mussolini's aggression drove Italy further into the German embrace. One result of the rapprochement between Italy and Germany was to give the Nazis a free hand to intervene in Austrian affairs, despite the failure in July 1934 of a Nazi attempt to seize power from the government of dictator Engelbert Dollfuss (1892–1934). Dollfuss lost his life in the Nazi putsch attempt, but his quasi-fascist government remained in power.

In February 1936, after long and bitter debate between supporters of appeasement and supporters of the left, the French parliament finally ratified the Franco-Soviet Security Pact signed in April 1935. This provided the pretext for Hitler to send a token military force into the **Rhineland** on 7 March 1936, in violation not only of Versailles but also of the 1925 **Locarno Treaty**, which had confirmed the status of the Rhineland as a demilitarized buffer zone between Germany and France. Hitler gambled that the French would not risk a military conflict. He ordered his troops to make a fighting withdrawal if the French should intervene. However, the French government, weakened by the fall of Premier Pierre Laval (1883–1945) as a result of his inept diplomacy in the Ethiopian crisis, was in no position to intervene. Polarized between parties of the right and the left, the French were in the midst of a bitter campaign that would lead to the election of a Popular Front government under socialist Leon Blum (1872–1950) in May. British foreign secretary Anthony Eden (1897–1977) protested against the German troops in the Rhineland, but announced that the British government would not support military action to expel them. In the eyes of most of the British public, the Germans were only reclaiming their own back yard. But by failing to take stronger action the British and French had tacitly endorsed Germany's unilateral revision of the post-war settlement. Hitler's popularity soared to new heights. A plebiscite on 29 March 1936 gave him a 99 percent vote of confidence. More importantly, Hitler's successful Rhineland gamble shifted the balance of power in Germany's favor. Smaller European nations such as Belgium and Holland loosened their ties to Britain and France so as not to invite a German attack.

The Nazi regime gained further respectability by hosting the elaborately staged Olympic games in Garmisch-Partenkirchen and Berlin in 1936. Many supporters of appeasement expressed their admiration for the new Germany. The appeasement policy was also evident in the Western refusal to offer aid to the democratically elected Popular Front government in the Spanish Civil War that broke out as a result of a military rebellion led by the right-wing general Francisco Franco (1892–1975) in July 1936. The Western arms embargo left the Spanish government dependent on the Soviet Union for assistance against the fascist-supported rebel forces. Italy sent ground troops to fight on Franco's side, while Germany used the opportunity to test its new Luftwaffe and other technologically advanced weaponry in battle. Neither the murderous German aerial assault on civilians in the city of **Guernica** in April 1937 nor fascist gains against the republican government dissuaded the Western powers from continuing their non-intervention policy. Hitler hoped that the civil war in Spain would further widen the breach between Mussolini and the West. It would also distract the world's attention from the Nazis' expansionist plans in the east. Hitler outlined these plans to the heads of the **Wehrmacht** and the foreign ministry in the notorious **Hossbach memorandum** in November 1937.

HOW DID THE NAZIS ACHIEVE THEIR GOAL OF CREATING A GREATER GERMAN REICH?

The replacement of Stanley Baldwin (1867–1947) by Neville Chamberlain (1869–1940) as British prime minister in May 1937 brought to power the political leader most closely identified with the appeasement policy. Chamberlain's minister of war and later foreign secretary, Lord Edward Halifax (1881–1959), met with Hitler at his mountain retreat in Berchtesgaden in November 1937 and assured him that Britain would not oppose a modification of Germany's eastern borders as long as this was achieved by peaceful means. In France, too, appeasement gained ground with the formation of a more conservative and strongly anti-communist government under Edouard Daladier (1884–1970) in April 1938. Hitler, meanwhile, took steps to remove potential critics or lukewarm supporters of his aggressive course from the military leadership and foreign ministry. He shored up his control of the Wehrmacht in February 1938 by eliminating the position of minister of war held by General Werner von **Blomberg** and creating a new supreme command (**OKW**) directly subject to Hitler's authority. The obsequious General **Keitel** became head of the OKW. Walther von **Brauchitsch** replaced Werner von **Fritsch** as head of the army command (**OKH**). Most importantly, the staunch Nazi Joachim von **Ribbentrop**, Hitler's ambassador to Britain and special envoy for foreign affairs, replaced the old-school conservative Konstantin von **Neurath** as foreign minister. The stage was now set to achieve the second of Hitler's major foreign policy goals – the annexation of the German-speaking territories of the former Habsburg Empire into a Greater German Reich.

Taking full advantage of appeasement the Nazis moved swiftly to annex German Austria in March 1938. The **Anschluss** followed a desperate effort by Austrian Chancellor Kurt von Schuschnigg (1897–1977) to avoid German intervention by holding a plebiscite on Austrian independence. To avoid defeat in a popular referendum the Nazis were likely to lose, Hitler sent troops across the border on 13 March. The following day Hitler returned in triumph to Vienna, the city where he had struggled to earn a living as a youthful sidewalk artist years before. The Allied reaction was muted by the fact that the annexation of Austria was neither unexpected, nor entirely unjustified on the basis of the principle of national self-determination. After all, the rump German Austria that emerged from the collapse of the Habsburg Empire and the founding of new ethnic states in the region had voted for union with Germany immediately following the First World War, a move that the Allies had blocked as part of the peace settlement.

Appeasement reached its apogee in the Czechoslovakian crisis that followed in the wake of the Anschluss. Acting through the Nazi front man in Czechoslovakia Konrad **Henlein**, leader of the Sudeten-German Party, the Nazis exploited the discontent among the ethnic German majority in the Czech border province of the **Sudetenland** to demand its independence from the Prague government. Hitler's true, though unacknowledged, purpose was to destroy the Czech state as the first step in Germany's eastward expansion. Emboldened by a mutual assistance pact signed with France and the Soviet Union in 1935, the Czech government refused to be intimidated. Czech resolution and the fear of Allied intervention led Hitler to rein in the German troops poised at the Czech borders in May 1938, but left him all the more determined to crush the Czech state as soon as it became militarily feasible.

The threat of becoming embroiled in war as a result of France's treaty obligations prompted Chamberlain to take extraordinary measures to find a peaceful solution. Three times he flew to Germany to meet personally with the Führer to negotiate a compromise. In the face of Hitler's obduracy, however, Chamberlain saw no other way to avoid war than to give in to all of the Führer's demands. In the **Munich Agreement** brokered by Mussolini, Chamberlain and Daladier acquiesced in the German military occupation of the Sudetenland beginning 1 October 1938. Neither Czechoslovakia nor its Soviet ally (which was committed to come to the defense of the Czechs only if France did so, too) were invited to the Munich Conference. Deprived of its border fortifications and left to defend itself on its own, the Czech government was forced to back down. In England Chamberlain was celebrated for his dramatic diplomatic initiative, which seemed to have brought, as Chamberlain put it, "peace to our time."[2]

HOW AND WHY DID THE NAZIS START THE SECOND WORLD WAR?

If appeasement had a saving virtue, it was that it tested Hitler's trustworthiness and ultimately revealed his true goals. When Hitler marched into Prague on 15 March 1939, thereby flouting the pledge he had made at Munich not to seek further territorial aggrandizement in Europe, Chamberlain and the British public were finally disabused of the notion that Hitler's aims were limited to regaining the territories lost in the First World War or that his intent was to achieve his aims peacefully. The Nazis proceeded to dismember the Czechoslovak state, establishing the **Protectorate of Bohemia and Moravia** in the Czech lands and a pro-Nazi dictatorship under the Catholic cleric Josef Tiso (1887–1947) in a nominally autonomous Slovakia.

Chamberlain took Hitler's violation of his "gentleman's agreement" at Munich as a personal affront. He responded by issuing an unconditional guarantee of military support to Poland, the next likely target of German aggression. Chamberlain thus offered the authoritarian and militarily weak Polish state, the primary beneficiary of territory ceded by Germany in the Versailles settlement, the kind of commitment he had refused to make the year before to support a democratic and militarily more defensible Czechoslovakia, none of whose territory had been part of Germany before the First World War. This abrupt reversal of the failed appeasement policy, while morally laudable and undoubtedly overdue, entailed serious practical difficulties. For one thing, it encouraged the Polish government not to negotiate German demands for the restoration of territories lost in the First World War, including the city of **Danzig** (Gdansk). Despite its overwhelmingly German population, Danzig had been placed under League of Nations control after the First World War to give the newly founded state of Poland an outlet to the sea. The Germans also demanded extra-territorial rights in the so-called **Polish Corridor**, the strip of territory that separated the German homeland from East Prussia. Fearful that concessions would only encourage German aggression, and assured of British support in case of war, the Polish government rejected the German demands.

The only realistic possibility of deterring Germany or of defending Poland against German attack would have been to involve the Soviet Union in the British military guarantee to Poland. However, a military alliance with the USSR was entirely unacceptable to the Polish government, whose eastern provinces had been gained by force during the Russian Civil War and contained large numbers of Ukrainians and Belorussians within their borders. Seeking Soviet military support also ran counter to one of the main aims of British policy since the end of the

First World War, which was to contain the spread of communism. Committed to appeasement, Britain had never warmed to Soviet efforts to forge an anti-fascist front after joining the League of Nations in 1934. Hence the British government reacted with little enthusiasm to renewed Soviet overtures for military cooperation against Nazi Germany in the summer of 1939. Fear of Soviet designs on the independent Baltic states (Lithuania, Latvia, and Estonia), formerly part of the Russian Empire, reinforced the British reluctance to enter into serious negotiations with the USSR. Having rejected the defense of Czechoslovakia despite (or perhaps even because of) its defensive alliance with the Soviet Union, Chamberlain now committed Britain to the defense of Poland without prospect of Soviet support.

Whether a more energetic British effort to revive the military alliance of the First World War might have deterred German aggression is an open question. Stalin may already have decided after Germany's uncontested seizure of Prague in March 1939 that his best chance of avoiding war and preventing the formation of an anti-Soviet front was not by concluding an alliance with Britain but by reaching an understanding with Nazi Germany. His appointment of Vyacheslav Molotov (1890–1986) as foreign minister in May 1939 to replace the Jewish Maxim Litvinov (1876–1951), a champion of collective security with the West, signaled Stalin's readiness to negotiate with the Third Reich despite the bitter ideological differences between the two totalitarian states. Hitler had responded to Chamberlain's guarantee to Poland by renouncing both the 1934 German–Polish non-aggression pact and the 1935 naval treaty with Britain, signing the so-called **Pact of Steel** with Italy, and instructing his generals to plan an attack on Poland to be launched in late August 1939. He now saw the practical advantages of a temporary neutrality pact with the Soviet Union. Surely this would dissuade Britain and France from intervening on behalf of Poland. A successful military defense of Poland was hardly feasible without Soviet cooperation in any case. Since the Western powers had failed to fight for Czechoslovakia with the promise of Soviet aid the year before, how likely was it that they would fight for Poland without prospects of military success?

The **Nazi–Soviet Non-Aggression Pact**, signed in Moscow on 22 August 1939, set the stage for the German invasion of Poland on 1 September 1939. Although Britain and France reaffirmed their commitment to Poland in a formal military alliance on 25 August, Hitler would not be deterred. He would certainly have preferred to avoid war with Britain, but he was determined not to let British opposition stand in the way of German eastward expansion. To overcome the misgivings of some of his military leaders Hitler pointed out that even if Britain and France declared war (which they did when Germany failed to respond to their ultimatum to halt its attack on Poland), the pact with the USSR put Germany in a far more advantageous position than in the Great War from 1914 to 1918. Secret trade and territorial provisions of the Nazi–Soviet Non-Aggression Pact assured the Germans of a steady flow of supplies from the Soviet Union. Britain could no longer pin its hopes on the kind of economic blockade that had proved so effective in the First World War. Tacit Soviet support for the Nazis meant that conditions for the rapid conquest of Poland could hardly be more ideal. Hitler was determined to take advantage of the opportunity afforded by Soviet neutrality to achieve his goal of eastward expansion one step at a time. From Hitler's point of view, his pact with Stalin was only a tactical maneuver to facilitate the conquest of Poland. His long-range goal remained the conquest of *Lebensraum* at the expense of the Soviet Union. Control of the Eurasian heartland would give the German Reich the territorial base from which to challenge the United States for world dominance.

HOW WERE GERMAN AMBITIONS DEFEATED, AND WHY DID GERMANY LOSE THE WAR?

In pursuing the goal of eastward expansion and continental hegemony Hitler and his war planners overestimated German capabilities, although this was certainly not apparent at the start of the war. The Germans lost the war because they underestimated the willingness and ability of Britain, Russia, and the United States to resist German military expansion. Perhaps Hitler's most fundamental misjudgement was to assume that Britain would eventually give Germany a free hand on the continent once the British became convinced that they had no chance to gain military victory at an acceptable cost. Hitler would have preferred to have come to some arrangement with Britain short of war, but he would not let British opposition deter him from his long-range goal. Years of British appeasement led him to assume that Britain would be unwilling to fight a long war that might put its world-wide empire at risk. This fundamental misjudgement meant that after launching the invasion of Poland Hitler would never again have full control of events. As Winston Churchill (1874–1965) acidly remarked at the time, Hitler had been free to start the war at a time of his choosing, but he was not free to choose the time for its end, except by surrender.

British refusal to come to terms after the German conquest of Poland in 1939 and after the fall of France in 1940 forced Hitler to revise his original plan of attacking the Soviet Union only after peace with Britain. His miscalculation of the Russians' willingness and capacity to fight for their country was Hitler's second egregious mistake. The unexpected failure of Operation **Barbarossa**, the invasion of the Soviet Union, in the autumn of 1941 in effect forced Hitler to play the "Japanese card" against the United States in the hope that Japan would prevent the US from tipping the balance against Germany in the European theater. Hitler's third and fatal misjudgement was to have underestimated the determination and resources that the United States would bring to the war. In late 1941 Germany sought to persuade its treaty partner Japan to enter the war by promising to declare war on the US in support of a Japanese attack. Three days after Pearl Harbor Hitler made good on this promise.

From the start of the war in 1939 to the end of the Battle of **Stalingrad** in early 1943 the German Wehrmacht was the strongest and technologically most advanced fighting force in the world. One of the reasons Hitler was determined to go to war in 1939 was to take advantage of Germany's relative lead in state-of-the-art weaponry and aircraft, as well as to exploit its perceived superiority in resolute leadership and the will to fight. As a relatively small country with limited natural resources, however, German plans were predicated on fighting short wars, isolating their opponents, and rapidly defeating them one at a time. This **Blitzkrieg** strategy worked to perfection against Poland, which found itself having to fight a two-front war when Soviet forces invaded from the east in accordance with the secret protocol of the Nazi–Soviet Pact. Poland was forced to surrender in early October 1939. In the West the **Phony War** that resulted from the reluctance of France or Great Britain to launch any offensive action in the hope that full-scale war might yet be avoided came to an end in May 1940 when the German armies overran Holland, Belgium, Luxemburg, and France within six weeks. The British managed to extricate their forces at **Dunkirk** in early June 1940, but were now reduced to preparing a desperate defense of their home island against a threatened invasion. Germany appeared to have won the war.

But Britain, now under the defiant leadership of Winston Churchill, a long-term foe of appeasement, refused to accept the German conquest of Poland or to accede to German domination of the continent. German failure to gain air supremacy in the **Battle of Britain** in the summer of 1940 forced the postponement and eventual cancellation of **Operation Sea Lion**, the plan to invade Britain across the English Channel. Instead, Hitler gave his long-range foreign policy goal, conquest of *Lebensraum* in the east, top priority. The time seemed right for the invasion of the Soviet Union, as Britain was in no position to contest a German campaign in the east, and the US, despite the unconcealed antipathy of President Franklin D. Roosevelt (1882–1945) to Hitler's regime, was badly divided on the wisdom of active American intervention in the war. Here was the window of opportunity to achieve what Hitler had always considered his primary mission: the destruction of the Soviet regime and the seizure of its territory for German colonization. Mutually reinforcing racial and ideological assumptions about the evil of "Jewish Bolshevism" lay behind the Nazis' contempt for the Soviet Union and their decision to violate their pledge of non-aggression a full eight years before it was scheduled to run out. Vast stretches of rich and fertile lands sparsely populated by what the Nazis defined as *Untermenschen* (subhumans) seemed ripe for Germany's taking. Defeat of the Soviet Union would also end the potential danger of a Soviet–British alliance and greatly strengthen Germany's position in the coming showdown for global primacy with the Anglo-American powers. A campaign against Communist Russia would enjoy the full support of Germany's allies and co-belligerents, Italy, Hungary, Romania, Finland, Vichy France, and Franco's Spain, who had always regarded the Nazi–Soviet Pact as a breach of fascist principles.

At the heart of the German decision to attack the Soviet Union lay the assumption of Soviet weakness. Stalinist purges in the late 1930s had not only sown fear and dissension in the Soviet population but had also decimated the ranks of the officer corps of the Red Army and the Soviet navy. The Red Army's poor performance in the 1939–1940 **Winter War** against Finland seemed to confirm its lack of fighting strength. Imperial Germany had soundly defeated the Russian forces in the First World War. The Nazis could not believe that the communists, the "peaceniks" of the First World War, could effectively rally the Russian population behind an egalitarian ideology that championed the interests of the "inferior" proletarian masses and restricted the enterprise of "superior" individuals. Soviet military technology and economic production lagged well behind German levels. German military leaders confidently expected Russian resistance to collapse within a matter of weeks. Although the **Balkan Campaign** to pacify Yugoslavia and Greece delayed the invasion of Russia until 22 June 1941, there was no reason to believe that Moscow would not be captured by the end of the year. And even if German forces were to take longer to conquer the USSR than expected, the possibility that they could be defeated by so backward and "primitive" an enemy seemed out of the question.

But Hitler and his paladins had miscalculated the strength of Soviet resistance. Informed by their intelligence sources that Japan, with whom the Soviets had signed a non-aggression treaty in April 1941, would not join the German attack on the USSR, the Soviets were able to mass some three million soldiers for the **Battle of Moscow** in December 1941. The overstretched German front, hampered by severe winter weather, was forced to retreat. The Germans now had to prepare for a much longer war than expected. The news of the Japanese attack on Pearl Harbor on 7 December 1941, however, lifted German morale. The Japanese entry into the war seemed to mark the successful culmination of Hitler's global strategy. On 11 December 1941 Hitler honored his commitment to Japan under the **Tripartite Pact** by declaring war on the US.

In retrospect this declaration of war appears to have been Hitler's greatest mistake. At the time, however, it represented the climactic realization of Hitler's plan of using Japan to tie down American and British forces in the Pacific. A Japanese–American settlement that would enable the US fully to engage its forces in Europe was the one eventuality that the Nazis sought to prevent at all costs. True, a Japanese attack on the US would have the effect of bringing the potentially formidable American foe fully into the war sooner than Hitler might have wished. But from the German perspective a formal declaration of war was a small price to pay for Japanese entry into the war, which promised to relieve the military threat to Germany from the US. The US was after all already fully engaged in the war in the Atlantic against the German navy, to whom the thankless task of preventing American supplies from reaching Britain and the USSR was assigned. German naval leaders pressured the Nazi government for a formal declaration of war against the US to give the navy the same legitimate claim to supplies and resources as the army that was fighting in Russia. A formal declaration of war against the US would also presumably give Japan a boost in morale and enable Germany to share in the credit for the expected Japanese victories.

The year 1942 was indeed one of **Axis** ascendancy as German **Panzer** units conquered the Ukraine and rolled through the southern Russian steppes on their way to the Volga River and the beckoning oilfields of the Caucasus. In the Pacific theater Japan conquered the Philippines, Indonesia, and Malaya, including the British fortress at Singapore, before losing its naval supremacy at the Battle of Midway in June 1942. The turn of the year 1942/1943 brought the turning of the tide in Europe. In the battle of **El Alamein** in November 1942 British forces turned back the German–Italian campaign under General Erwin **Rommel** to capture Egypt and the British possessions in the Middle East. That same month Anglo-American troops landed in the French colonies of Algeria and Morocco in an operation codenamed **Torch**. The most significant German defeat occurred at Stalingrad on the Volga River in the winter of 1942/1943. After some of the most savage fighting in the history of warfare, an entire German army was forced to surrender to the Soviets on 1 February 1943. The crushing of the last major German offensive in the east in the Battle of **Kursk** in July 1943 spelled the end of the German military initiative on the eastern front.

From 1943 on Germany fought a defensive war as its armies began the long-drawn-out, more than 1,200-mile retreat from its forward positions in Russia that ended in the battle for Berlin in April 1945. The remnants of the German **Africa Corps** and the Italian troops in North Africa surrendered to the Allies at Tunis in May 1943. In July 1943, after the Allied capture of Sicily and the landing of Allied forces on the Italian mainland, Mussolini was deposed by the Fascist Grand Council. Italy formally joined the Allied side in October of that year. Allied naval supremacy forced German submarines on the defensive in the Atlantic as well. Increasing Allied superiority in aircraft and weaponry brought the air war home to the Reich, culminating in the devastating bombing of **Dresden** in February 1945 with the loss of thousands of civilian lives.

The long-anticipated **D-Day** landing of Allied forces in Normandy on 6 June 1944 (**Operation Overlord**) doomed the Nazi regime, which now had to fight for its very survival in Russia, Italy, and France. On each of these fronts the Allies mounted major offensives in the summer of 1944. The Allied forward thrust on the Western front was slowed but not stopped by an unexpected counterattack in the Ardennes in December 1944, known as the **Battle of the Bulge**. The hope that "wonder weapons" developed by German engineers might yet turn the tide in Germany's favor came to an end when Allied troops overran the launching sites of the **V1** flying bombs and **V2** long-range missiles aimed at London and Antwerp. Jet-powered aircraft, operational by early 1945, could not be used for lack of fuel.

With Soviet troops only a few city blocks away, Hitler committed suicide on 30 April 1945 in his fortified bunker under the ruined Reich Chancellery, constructed and dedicated with much fanfare in 1939. The European phase of the war officially ended on 8 May 1945 after the German government under Admiral Karl **Dönitz**, Hitler's successor, surrendered to the Allied and Soviet commands. In his last testament Hitler refused to recant Nazi principles and expressed no remorse for the untold suffering that Nazi aggression had brought upon the world.

The Nazis' supremacist ideology had led to German defeat by blinding Nazi leaders to the realities of power in the world and to the readiness of peoples threatened by German domination to defend their liberty and sovereignty. In retrospect, Germany was doomed by a hubris that could not help but lead to tactical and strategic misjudgements. Germany's defeat was not the result of any single mistake in military tactics, though undoubtedly there were a number of these. One such unsound tactical decision was Hitler's refusal to permit the German Sixth Army to break out of its encirclement at Stalingrad in late 1942. He could not bring himself to authorize a tactic that would contradict his oft-proclaimed conceit that German soldiers never retreat. By the end of the war German forces had retreated some 2,000 miles from their positions on the Volga.

In what remains a classic example of historical justice, Nazi Germany fell victim to its own odious Social Darwinist conviction that military might was the only principle that counted in international relations. "I shall give a propa-gandist reason for starting the war, whether it is plausible or not," Hitler had told his military commanders in Berchtesgaden to overcome their skepticism on the eve of the war in August 1939. "The victor will not be asked afterwards whether he told the truth or not. When starting and waging a war it is not right that matters, but victory."[3] Nazi militarism was based on the fascist conviction that stronger peoples have the right to rule over the weak. Their belief that their supposed cultural superiority was sufficient grounds for a war of colonial conquest left the Nazis with no moral or material resources for the defense of their own country against the Allies' superior strength at the end of the war. Nazism equated the power, the interests, and the welfare of the German nation and racial community with the highest moral good. It was a system of belief that allowed its adherents to commit the most horrible atrocities with good conscience.

HOW AND WHY DID THE NAZIS COMMIT GENOCIDE AGAINST THE JEWS?

No Nazi crime has so discredited the German cause in the eyes of posterity as the Holocaust, the mass murder of the European Jews. This signature event of the twentieth century continues to offer the single greatest challenge to the explana-tory powers of historiography. Historians continue to debate the origins and meaning of the Holocaust. Was the killing program always part of the Nazi plan (**intentionalism**) or was it the result of the specific circumstances of the war (**functionalism**)? Was the "road to Auschwitz" twisted or straight?[4] Were its causes primarily ideological and irrational or did rational economic and social factors contribute to the decision for genocide? Without question anti-Semitism – hatred of the Jews – was a necessary cause of the Holocaust, but was it a sufficient cause, as controversially argued by Daniel **Goldhagen** in 1996? Complicating the historiography of the Holocaust is the fact that interpretations of its causes and meaning, like interpretations of Nazism itself, are inevitably morally and politically charged. The obvious horror and irrationality of mass murder seem to require a correspondingly irrational motivation. So closely is the Holocaust linked to the notion of absolute evil that the very attempt to find a rational explanation for the genocide may seem morally perverse. If practical reasons and utilitarian judgements contributed to the process that led to the destruction of the Jews, the Nazi leaders who launched the killing program may no longer appear as the monsters that they were. While it may be reassuring to believe that large-scale atrocities can only be committed by primitive savages in the grip of irrational emotions, the Holocaust shows that genocide can also be committed by rational people pursuing what seemed to them to be rational goals by the most efficient and technologically advanced means available.

There is no simple explanation for why the Holocaust happened. Historians have, however, been able to identify some of its necessary conditions. The Holocaust marked the confluence of three separate but related strands in German history. The first and arguably most important strand was the long tradition of anti-Semitism, which permeated every aspect of Nazi ideology, program, and policy. The second contributing factor was the Nazi determination to implement a program of **racial hygiene**, eugenic measures to purify and strengthen the German "race." As lethal as these two long-term trends turned out to be, a third condition was necessary for the launching of systematic genocide. That third necessary condition was total war. Killing of Jewish (as well as Polish) intellectuals and political leaders by SS and Wehrmacht commenced shortly after the invasion of Poland in September 1939. But it was the total war that began with the savage German invasion of the Soviet Union in June 1941 and spread across the globe after the Japanese surprise attack on the US in December 1941 that set the stage for the **Final Solution** – the systematic murder of all Jews under German control.

Anti-Semitism

Nazi anti-Semitism fed on long-standing prejudices against Jews dating back to ancient times. It was not, however, based solely on irrational hatred, nor was it just a politically expedient means of scapegoating a visible but vulnerable minority for the many problems facing German society after the First World War. Anti-Semitism was also rooted in the Nazis' long-term ambition of national expansion and domination. Nazi leaders were well aware that they could only achieve their imperialist goals by eliminating all liberal and democratic opposition in Germany. They also realized that they would not be able to achieve their goals without recourse to war. The emergence of popular dissent against German imperialism in the closing phase of the First World War had taught them that national unity was the most important prerequisite for success in war. The major aim of the Nazi regime after Hitler's accession to power in 1933 was to create the kind of ethnic and ideological unity and top-down authority that would prepare Germans for the war they would have to wage to achieve their long-term objectives of restoring German power and gaining *Lebensraum*. **Gleichschaltung** – the suppression of democratic process, diversity, and dissent – was a policy primarily designed to remove all obstacles to the successful prosecution of a war of expansion. The primary objective of *Gleichschaltung* was to purge all Jews and other potential opponents of National Socialism from positions of influence and to drive them out of Germany. The Nazis no doubt exaggerated Jewish power and influence in Germany, but their assumption that the removal of Jews would fatally weaken the liberalizing or egalitarian political forces that blocked their expansionist aims was not completely unfounded.

Official Nazi policy throughout the 1930s sought to eliminate the Jewish presence in Germany by encouraging, provoking, and eventually mandating Jewish emigration. Anti-Jewish policy evolved through various stages of restriction, extrusion, definition, segregation, expropriation, and concentration. The ultimate objective of all anti-Jewish measures before the start of the war was to expel all Jews from Germany. The first major anti-Jewish legislation, the **Civil Service Act** of April 1933, excluded "non-Aryans," defined as persons with one or more Jewish grandparents, from public employment, including German universities. Many private professional and cultural organizations followed suit by applying the **Aryan paragraph** to their members, in some cases even before this became mandatory by law.

The purge of Jews (and non-Jewish dissidents) led to the mass exodus of highly educated, highly skilled professionals, many of whom were readily received in Britain, the United States, and other countries. The same welcome was not, however, extended to indigent Jews or to those without marketable skills or guaranteed means of support. For the large number of Jews who earned their living in the business sector, as small business owners, executives, or salaried employees, there was little choice but to make do in Germany as long as this was legally possible. Emigration was often financially unfeasible, especially in view of the severe restrictions on the amount of capital or other assets that emigrants were allowed to take out of the country. Despite the **Haavera Agreement** between the German Economics Ministry and the Jewish Agency in Palestine, which permitted Jews emigrating to Palestine to use part of their assets to pay for German exports to Palestine in return for the equivalent value in goods or lodging on arrival, Palestine offered only a limited haven for persecuted German Jews. Up to 1935 the **Zionist Association for Germany** accepted for emigration only younger Jews with skills needed in the Jewish settlements. Increasing British restrictions on Jewish immigration also limited the option of settling in Palestine. In any case, most German Jews considered themselves to be Germans of Jewish faith, not a separate nation or race, and had little desire to form a Jewish state in Palestine. The majority of German Jews believed that by defining Jewishness in purely confessional terms they could gain acceptance in German society, retaining their rights as German citizens while practicing their own religion.

This illusion came to an end with the promulgation of the **Nuremberg Laws** of September 1935, which deprived German Jews of their civil rights, in effect relegating Jews to their legal status before emancipation in 1869. Jews were no longer allowed to call themselves Germans, to display the official German **swastika** flag, or to claim membership in the German nation in any way. The euphemistically named "Law for the Protection of German Blood and Honor" prohibited marriage and sexual relations between ethnic Germans and Jews. The Nuremberg Laws spawned a series of regulations that defined a Jew as a person with three or four Jewish grandparents (in contrast to the earlier definition of a "non-Aryan" as anyone with one or more Jewish grandparents) and created two categories of *Mischlinge* for persons of mixed ancestry.

The effect of the Nuremberg Laws was to segregate the Jewish community in Germany and to further undermine their means of livelihood. This legal assault on the rights of Jews also intensified the social stigma under which those who had no means of emigrating were forced to live. Jews were increasingly shunned by Germans, who feared the social, professional, or legal consequences of any show of sympathy or social contact with Jews. Although existing marriages were not subject to the Nuremberg Laws (partly due to the opposition of the churches to the dissolution of the sacred marriage bond), many Germans married to Jewish spouses sued for divorce. The progressive internalization of anti-Semitic prejudices by the German population and the dehumanization of Jews in official propaganda set the stage for the destruction that followed.

As war approached, the campaign to expel the Jews from Germany reached a preliminary climax in 1938/1939. One faction of hard-line anti-Semites, headed by the Nuremberg Gauleiter Julius **Streicher**, had long called for the use of force, if necessary, to create a **judenrein** Germany (a Germany free of Jews). Streicher headed the **boycott** of Jewish-owned businesses in 1933 that was called off after one day for fear of economic disruption and foreign retaliation. In 1938 the Nazi regime escalated pressures to force Jews out of the German economy as they already had been forced out of professional, cultural, educational, and social institutions. On 9 November of that year, ostensibly in retaliation for the assassination of a German diplomat in Paris, the regime unleashed an orgy of violence against Jews popularly known as *Reichskristallnacht* (crystal night) because of the shards of broken glass that littered the streets in front of Jewish-owned businesses and homes. The destruction caused by this "November pogrom" in turn became the pretext for introducing mandatory **aryanization** of Jewish-owned businesses. Many of the properties destroyed in November 1938 turned out to have been insured by German-owned insurance companies, who protested the liability they now faced. Göring thereupon decided to levy a collective fine on the Jewish community to cover the costs of the pogrom. To eliminate the need for further "spontaneous" popular demonstrations with its attendant damage of property, Jews were now required by law to divest themselves of their businesses on terms established by the German Ministry of Economics. Jews were to be left with no alternative but to seek refuge abroad.

By 1938 the SS, which prided itself on its efficiency and rational approach to the solution of the "Jewish Question," had assumed control of the program of forced emigration. After the *Anschluss* of Austria in March 1938, the SS established the Reich Central Emigration Bureau in Vienna under the direction of Adolf **Eichmann**, who sought to force the pace of Jewish emigration by a variety of coercive techniques. Similar offices were subsequently opened in Prague and Berlin. In January 1939 **Göring** officially delegated to Reinhard **Heydrich**, head of the SD, the security service within the SS, the task of resolving "the Jewish question by emigration and evacuation in the most favorable way possible, given present conditions."[5]

The two main obstacles to Jewish emigration were the penury of potential emigrants, made worse by the increasingly punitive economic restrictions imposed on the Jewish community, and the difficulty of obtaining permission to enter other countries. The Swiss government, for instance, overwhelmed by the number of Jews who sought refuge after the *Anschluss*, insisted that the German government identify emigrants as Jewish by stamping the letter J on their passports. The United States State Department, operating under a system of immigration quotas imposed in 1924, adopted a go-slow policy in issuing visas to Jews. Nonetheless, in the last six months of 1938 some 100,000 Jews managed to leave the Reich. By the outbreak of war in September 1939 about half of the Jewish population of Germany, Austria, and the Protectorate of Bohemia-Moravia had managed to emigrate. More than 250,000 Jews remained within the borders of the Greater Reich. After the start of the war emigration, while still permitted, became ever more difficult, and only a few thousand Jews were able to leave German-controlled areas before emigration was officially prohibited in October 1941 in anticipation of the "final solution of the Jewish Question" – the physical extermination of all Jews under German control.

Racial hygiene

The Social Darwinist notion that human life, as part of the natural world, involved a struggle for existence in which superior peoples survive and prosper at the expense of inferior races formed an integral part of Nazi ideology. According to this ideology the "superior" German race had not only the right but the duty to fight against potential rivals for control of resources, territory, and the spread of its political and cultural ideals. The inevitable struggle between cultures, nations, and races seemed to call for eugenic measures to strengthen the German Volk and to eliminate not only disease but any elements that might weaken the Volk in its competition with other nations for supremacy. Improvement of Germany's genetic substance by selective breeding was the goal of the racial hygiene movement founded in Germany in 1905 at a time when the Darwinian revolution in biology made hereditary determinism scientifically credible and intellectually fashionable throughout Europe. Adherents of racial hygiene believed that it was necessary to reverse the modern humanitarian and democratizing trends that seemed to favor the weak and the poor at the expense of the strong and the rich. If medical advances, progressive social policies, and democratic empowerment led to the disproportionate survival and reproduction of the handicapped, the lower classes, and other racial "inferiors," as eugenicists feared, then state intervention was needed to restore nature's proper balance. Although not all racial hygienists believed that Jews were racially inferior to ethnic Germans (indeed many were convinced that Jews were intellectually superior), the close association of Jews with precisely the democratizing and modernizing trends that seemed to make corrective eugenic intervention necessary helped to persuade most German racial hygienists that Jews were an obstacle to strengthening the German Volk.

German defeat in the First World War led to more than just a resurgence of anti-Semitism, as liberals, socialists, and Jews were blamed for "stabbing the German army in the back." The loss of the war also led to renewed calls for eugenic measures to regenerate and revitalize the German people. Eugenicists argued that care for chronically ill or mentally disabled persons constituted an unacceptable burden for society. Some recommended the medical killing of "worthless lives," cloaked as "mercy killing" (**euthanasia**). Already in the First World War mental patients in public hospitals had been allowed to die of starvation to make food and hospital space available for soldiers and civilians actively engaged in the war effort. "A new age will arrive," the prominent psychiatrist Alfred Hoche predicted in 1920, "operating with a higher morality and with great sacrifice – which will actually give up the requirements of an exaggerated humanism and overvaluation of mere existence."[6] At the very least, he asserted, "defective people" should not be allowed to reproduce. In Nazi ideology the anti-Semitic and eugenic traditions merged in a lethal combination as both racism and racial hygiene became official state policies. Jews and gypsies came to be defined as carriers of social diseases, and the sick and socially disadvantaged came to be classified as being of lesser racial value than healthy or prosperous Germans.

Nazi racial and eugenic legislation involved both "positive" selection, designed to give preferential treatment to the racially "valuable" members of the population, and "negative" selection, designed to eliminate "useless eaters" and "racial inferiors" from the gene pool and from society. An essential element of the Nazi mindset was the conviction that all social problems were ultimately hereditary and racial in nature, and hence could be solved by regulating breeding and reproduction. This tendency to apply principles of biology and race to the solution of social problems such as crime, poverty, and economic inequality contrasted diametrically to the practice of communists of looking to social conditions and class analysis for explanations and remedies for these problems. Fascists and communists were at odds not only on economic policies; in the debate on the relative importance of heredity and environment ("nature vs. nurture") they were also at opposite poles.

Under the Nazis only the "biologically valuable" members of the German population were to receive public support. Through pro-natal policies, such as the "Law for the Reduction of Unemployment" of June 1933, the Nazi government encouraged healthy "Aryan" women to give up their jobs to start families. This law provided marriage loans to racially pure German women that could be paid off by having children. In a number of other ways, including generous maternity benefits, tax benefits for large families, special medals for women with four or more children, easy divorce for childless marriages, and harsh penalties for abortion the regime tried to increase the "Aryan" German population. In 1936 Heinrich Himmler, head of the SS, announced the founding of *Lebensborn*, an agency to care for unmarried mothers of good racial stock and their children. "Let us never forget," Himmler wrote in an order to the SS shortly after the start of the war, "that the victory of the sword and the spilled blood of our soldiers remains fruitless, if it is not succeeded by the victory of the child and the colonizing of conquered soil."[7] He reminded the soldiers of the SS of their duty to procreate before leaving for the front and promised that if they were killed in battle the state would assume the care of their children.

The purpose of negative selection was to "purify" the "Aryan" German *Volksgemeinschaft* by preventing the reproduction of those deemed to be racially inferior. In July 1933 the "Law for the Prevention of Genetically Diseased Offspring" (otherwise known as the Reich **Sterilization Law**) provided for compulsory sterilization of various categories of mentally or physically disabled persons and obligated physicians and teachers to register persons under their care who showed symptoms of mental retardation, hereditary disease, or chronic illness, including alcoholism. Registration requirements were later extended to include people of "alien races" or of "lesser racial value." After the passage of the Nuremberg Laws a certificate of fitness was required for the right to marry. The power to mandate sterilization was granted to newly created **Hereditary Health Courts**.

Predisposed to consider not only diseases but also criminality, alcoholism, and vagrancy as hereditary conditions, the Nazis eventually applied the sterilization law to habitual criminals, long-term welfare recipients or unemployed, transients, and others defined as "asocial" as well. From 1933 to 1945 some 400,000 persons were forcibly sterilized in Germany, most of them recipients of some sort of public support. The extent to which the sterilization law was based on a consensus in favor of eugenics may be seen from the fact that it was modeled on a 1932 draft law in the state of Prussia, which had, however, still called for parental consent for the sterilization of handicapped children. Compulsory sterilization laws introduced in a number of states in the United States as early as 1907 also served as models for the Nazis, who then went well beyond American laws in defining the groups subject to sterilization. Many American eugenicists, in turn, admired the German law, which they hoped would serve as a model for similar legislation on the federal level in the United States.

The Nazis also sought to drum up popular support for the euthanasia of severely handicapped patients, including children, in public institutions. Their purpose, however, was not to reduce the suffering of the victims, but to cleanse the population eugenically and to reduce the economic burden on the state. To avoid any public protest against euthanasia, the program for the systematic killing of handicapped children and adults was launched in secret by Hitler's personal order shortly after the start of the war. The euthanasia program was code-named **Aktion**

T-4 after the address in Berlin, Tiergartenstrasse 4, from which it was directed by the head of the Führer's chancellery, Philipp **Bouhler**, and Hitler's personal physician, Dr Karl **Brandt**. The killings were carried out by lethal injection and other means at several specially equipped hospitals or nursing homes. As the number of targeted victims increased, the T-4 program introduced the method of mass killing by carbon monoxide gas in chambers disguised as shower rooms that was later used in the "final solution."

It was not possible, however, entirely to conceal the killings from the general population or from other government agencies. The Ministry of Justice, to which a growing number of suspicious relatives of euthanized victims appealed, had to be informed of the program, as did the Ministry of the Interior. Officials of both the Protestant and Catholic churches also launched official protests in 1941. In August 1941, shortly after a series of highly critical public sermons by the Catholic bishop Clemens von **Galen**, Hitler officially ended the program. Killings of handicapped newborns, however, went on in secret until the end of the war. It is estimated that some 200,000 handicapped children and adults were killed in the course of the war.

The killings had already been extended to include handicapped Jewish concentration camp inmates in 1940 under the code name **Aktion 14 f 13**. Just at the time the T-4 program was officially winding down in Germany in late 1941, preparations for the mass murder of Jews were being finalized in the east. Approximately a hundred T-4 personnel, including the notorious Christian **Wirth**, who became head of the **Operation Reinhard** extermination camps, and Franz **Stangl**, commandant of the **Sobibór** and **Treblinka** death camps, were transferred to occupied Poland where they supplied the technical expertise for the systematic killing by gas of approximately three million Jews at specially established killing sites at **Chelmno**, **Belzec**, **Treblinka**, **Sobibór**, **Majdanek**, and **Auschwitz**. Here the largest systematic, state-sponsored genocide of all time was carried out under the cover of war.

Total war

Speaking to the Reichstag on 30 January 1939, two and a half months after the deadly pogrom of November 1938, Hitler announced that if there were another world war, "then the result will not be the Bolshevization of the earth, and thus the victory of Jewry, but the annihilation of the Jewish race in Europe."[8] War justified – indeed glorified – the killing of "enemies" and provided the conditions under which the Holocaust could be carried out without fear of public scrutiny or humanitarian protests. War also changed the scope of the "Jewish problem" from the Nazi perspective by bringing millions of European Jews under German control. More than two million Jews came under German control at the end of the Polish campaign. After the fall of France in June 1940 hundreds of thousands of West European Jews fell into German hands as well. Well over a million Jews lived in the German client states in the Balkans, most of which came under

German control by April 1941. While the Nazi–Soviet Pact was still in force and there was still a prospect of victory over Britain, the Nazis apparently planned a "territorial solution," the creation of a giant Jewish reservation under German military control, either in the Lublin area of the **Generalgouvernement** (German-occupied Poland) or, after the fall of France, on the French colonial island of **Madagascar**. Meanwhile Jews were herded into ghettos and camps pending the implementation of resettlement plans after the end of the war with Britain. The largest of these ghettos, the **Warsaw ghetto**, was walled in in late 1940 and cut off from all contact with the outside world except through SS administrators.

Hitler's decision to invade the Soviet Union even before the end of the war with Britain led to a further escalation of Nazi policies against Jews. Hitler's decision was reached in December 1940 after the failure of the **Battle of Britain** and the refusal of the British to submit to German terms. The war against the Soviet Union was planned from the start to be waged as a war of extermination against Soviet Jews. Specially trained SS death squads, the notorious *Einsatzgruppen*, were to follow on the heels of the front-line Wehrmacht troops to kill all partisans, Soviet commissars (political officers), and Jews. While at first the death squads targeted only men, by the end of July 1941 they were killing women and children as well. In one such action by an SS *Sonderkommando* at **Babi Yar** on the outskirts of Kiev on 29–30 September 1941, 33,771 Jews were shot and buried in mass graves in the bloodiest two-day massacre of the war. Approximately half a million Soviet Jews fell victim to the *Einsatzgruppen* by the end of the year.

In the months that followed the German invasion of the Soviet Union, the decision was made to carry out the "final solution," the killing of all the Jews under German control in Europe. Although there is no doubt that the killings were authorized by Nazi leaders at the highest echelons, initiatives came from the field as well, as SS administrators sought ways to reduce the populations in the overcrowded ghettos, and regional officials, such as Hans **Frank**, the governor-general of Poland, and Arthur **Greiser**, the governor of the territory annexed to the Reich as the **Wartheland**, competed with each other for primacy in clearing their areas of Jews. While no written Führer order has ever surfaced, historical evidence suggests that the decision was made between August and October 1941 and was implemented in the months that followed. On 23 October 1941 all emigration of Jews from German-controlled areas was prohibited, reversing the Nazis' long-standing forced emigration policy. In occupied Poland preparations for systematic gassing operations got under way, and within the Reich preparations were launched for the deportation of German Jews to the east. The transports from the Reich began on a systematic basis two months later. On 12 December 1941, one day after the German declaration of war against the United States, Hitler informed his assembled **Gauleiters** in Berlin that the "final solution" of physical annihilation was now to be put into force. Jews had lost their potential value as hostages to deter American entry into the war.

The organization and implementation of the "final solution" came under the direction of SS general Reinhard Heydrich, who had been appointed to head of the newly created **Reich Security Main Office** (RSHA) shortly after the beginning of the war in September 1939. The RSHA incorporated the **Gestapo**, the criminal police, and the Security Service (SD) of the SS in a single mammoth policing organization. Heydrich had already been put in charge of the program of forced emigration in January 1939. On 31 July 1941 his authority was extended by Göring to include "making all necessary preparations in regard to organizational and financial matters for bringing about a total solution of the Jewish question in the German sphere of influence in Europe."[9] In January 1942, after several delays occasioned by German military reverses in the outskirts of Moscow and by the Japanese attack on Pearl Harbor in December 1941, Heydrich convened leading officials of various government and party ministries and agencies to secure their cooperation in a comprehensive plan for the deportation and resettlement of Jews throughout occupied Europe and Germany's client states. The surviving minutes of the **Wannsee Conference** cloaked the specifics of the killing program in the euphemistic language of "special treatment," but the proceedings could have left none of its participants in doubt about the ultimate fate intended for the European Jews. The Nazi goal of freeing their realm of Jews was now to be extended to all of Europe by means of systematic murder.

The killing of Jews by carbon monoxide poisoning in mobile gas vans at Chelmno, located in the Wartheland, began on 8 December 1941. Shortly before, construction had begun on a large stationary extermination camp at Belzec, which went into operation in March 1942. Further killing sites were established at Sobibór in the eastern portion of the Generalgouvernement in March 1942 and at Treblinka near Warsaw in June 1942 for the killing of all Polish Jews under the codename **Aktion Reinhard**. The name originally derived from the official in the Reich Finance Ministry, Fritz **Reinhardt**, who was in charge of administering the valuables, including dental gold, extracted from the victims before or after their death. SS officials in charge of the killing program seized the opportunity to commemorate their chief Reinhard Heydrich after his assassination by the Czech underground in June 1942. More than one and a half million Jews were killed at the three Aktion Reinhard camps before they were closed in the course of 1943 as the SS attempted to erase the evidence of their crimes. The largest of the killing sites, established in late 1941 at **Auschwitz-Birkenau**, began systematic gassings in early 1942 that continued until late 1944. Up to 1.5 million victims, including more than a million Jews from all over Europe, were killed in Birkenau with the use of the lethal pesticide, **Cyclon B**, which was also used at **Majdanek** in the outskirts of the Polish city of Lublin. Some 200,000 victims, including at least 60,000 Jews, were murdered at Majdanek before its liberation by Soviet troops in July 1944.

The Aktion Reinhard camps were established for the sole purpose of killing. Auschwitz-Birkenau and Majdanek (officially named the **Lublin** camp in 1943) also served as holding camps for workers whose labor could be exploited for industrial or military purposes. Able-bodied workers interned at Birkenau were pressed into labor at the giant synthetic rubber plant constructed by the I. G. Farben corporation at **Auschwitz-Monowitz** in 1941 and at a number of other industrial sites. Those no longer able to work were condemned to the gas chambers. The overall toll of Jewish victims who died by gas in the killing centers of occupied Poland numbered close to 3 million, approximately half of the total number of Jewish victims in the Holocaust. Up to 1.5 million Jews were shot to death by units of the *Einsatzgruppen*, Order Police, Security Police, and the Wehrmacht in the course of the war. An additional 1.5 million Jews fell victim to execution, deprivation, disease, exhaustion, and brutal treatment in the ghettos and the concentration camps of the Reich. Inmates still deemed capable of work were driven by their SS guards to interior locations to evade the rapidly encroaching Allied armies at the end of the war. Thousands perished on these death marches. Thousands more succumbed to disease or the lingering effects of their internment after the German surrender.

Hundreds of thousands of ordinary German citizens were involved directly or indirectly in the planning, logistics, and implementation of the "final solution." A dispute between historians Daniel **Goldhagen** and Christopher **Browning** in the late 1990s about the motives of the perpetrators involved some major issues of the intentionalist–functionalist debate (see Chapter 3, on "Historiography"). While Goldhagen insisted that only Germany's allegedly unique "eliminationist" anti-Semitic tradition could explain the unusual readiness of Germans to kill Jews, Browning pointed out that situational factors, such as conformism in the face of peer pressure, selfish career ambitions, subservience to authority, and progressive brutalization and military routinization could turn even normal persons into killers in time of all-out war. Both interpretations coincided in stressing dehumanization and demonizing of the victims as necessary conditions for mass murder. Since 1933 the Jews had been singled out in official propaganda as the most dangerous internal and external enemies of Germany's legitimate nationalist aspirations. The confluence of anti-Semitism, "racial hygiene," and total war made the Holocaust possible. For the Nazi leadership the killing of the Jews became a major aim after the start of the war, the only aim, as it turned out, that the Nazis were able to achieve even in defeat.

8

OPPOSITION AND LEGACY

WHY WAS THERE SO LITTLE EFFECTIVE OPPOSITION TO THE NAZI DICTATORSHIP?

Among the many open questions about Nazi Germany are the extent of public knowledge about the atrocities of the regime, the reasons why there was so little popular resistance or opposition to the regime after 1934, and why the military conspiracy to oust the regime did not act until 20 July 1944. There was, of course, fierce opposition to the regime before 1933, and in clandestine form throughout the period of the **Third Reich**, but it came almost exclusively from Communists, Social Democrats, and left liberals, the particular targets of brutal repression in 1933 and 1934. Hitler's accession to power in 1933 had been welcomed with general enthusiasm by those Germans – more than two-thirds of the population – who had no affiliation with the parties of the left, and his popularity grew as a result of his economic and diplomatic successes during the 1930s. The vast majority of middle-class Germans did not oppose the destruction of parliamentary democracy and gave their assent to the Nazi Party dictatorship as the necessary condition for the suppression of the perceived socialist and communist threat. The euphoria of national revival generated a bandwagon effect that continually added to **Hitler**'s popular support until it reached its zenith after the fall of France in June 1940. Even Germans who would never have voted for Hitler's party came to appreciate a regime that seemed to guarantee stability, full employment, and the step-wise restoration of German power and prestige on the international stage. Germans who were not politically active on the left felt protected, not threatened, by the Nazi assault on civil liberties, which, while in fact restricting everyone's personal freedoms, seemed to most Germans to be directed only against the enemies of the state.

The history of Nazi Germany offers plentiful evidence that most people who make a comfortable living can be readily persuaded to exchange their political freedoms in return for security and order. Although Nazi **totalitarianism** restricted the personal rights of citizens, in practice ordinary people not involved in political activity generally experienced Nazi controls as guaranteeing a private sphere in which law-abiding individuals could safely go about their personal lives and enjoy consumer products and popular entertainments without government interference. Ordinary Germans had little to fear from the authoritarian state as long as they stayed out of trouble. A similar passivity and indifference to the plight of the persecuted marked most Germans' attitudes toward the **anti-Semitic** policies of the regime. Many, perhaps most, Germans deplored violent attacks on Jews, although sometimes only because these caused undue property damage and violated law and order; but most Germans were at best indifferent to legal measures restricting Jews' political rights and public activities. Repressive legal measures could be rationalized as necessary restrictions on the freedom of an exclusive and tight-knit ethnic minority whose loyalty to the German nation was widely questioned. Jews were also popularly perceived to have enjoyed disproportionate income, wealth, and influence in pre-Nazi Germany. In the early years of the regime no one, except perhaps the leading Nazis themselves, could have foreseen or even imagined the coming **Holocaust**. Hitler's foreign policy successes, too, encouraged the widespread illusion that Germany would achieve its national aspirations short of war. Although the German public was clearly unenthusiastic about going to war in 1939, in contrast to the patriotic fervor that accompanied the start of the First World War in 1914, the spectacular victories on the western front in 1940 made Hitler more popular than ever.

COMMUNIST AND SOCIAL DEMOCRATIC RESISTANCE

In the early years of the regime resistance was almost exclusively confined to the left. The Social Democrats and the Communists, which together enjoyed the voting support of about a third of the German electorate in 1932/1933, strongly opposed Hitler's appointment as chancellor, but the **SPD** in particular was not prepared to go beyond parliamentary means to resist a regime that had come to power by constitutional means. Communist leaders did call for a general strike after Hitler's appointment to head the government, but their call went unheeded in the face of massive Nazi repression. Although most wage-earning workers probably opposed the Hitler government in 1933, continuing mass unemployment limited the potential effectiveness of a strike as a political weapon. Union leaders, too, justifiably concerned about their institutional survival, feared that a strike would only give the regime the pretext they needed to suppress the labor movement. This suppression occurred in any case only three months later when the independent unions were forcibly dissolved and replaced by the **German Labor Front (DAF)** under Robert **Ley**.

From the start of Hitler's rule the **KPD** (Communist Party) was the target of massive and ruthless repression. Many Germans genuinely believed the government's announcement that the Reichstag fire signalled the start of a Communist uprising. Most Communist leaders and many mid-level functionaries were either killed or forced to leave Germany in the months that followed Hitler's accession to power. By July 1933 some 12,000 to 15,000 Communist activists were imprisoned or interned in concentration camps. KPD leader Ernst Thälmann (1886–1944) was interned for many years before his execution on Hitler's specific orders at **Buchenwald** on 18 August 1944. Despite the murder, internment, or forced exile of its leadership, the KPD remained active in the underground, issuing numerous calls to resist the Nazis and continuing to publish its party newspaper clandestinely until 1935. Notwithstanding massive repression and **Gestapo** infiltration, small Communist-organized resistance circles continued to operate secretly until well into the war. One of the more effective of these was the so-called **Red Orchestra** under the leadership of Arvid **Harnack** and Harro **Schulze-Boysen**, who were able to provide the Soviet Union with useful information by radio before the group was discovered and suppressed in late 1942.

In the cold war climate of the 1950s there was some reluctance in West Germany to grant the Communist underground the status of a legitimate resistance movement because of their espionage activities. But the line between resistance and espionage was fluid. Even the conservative military resistance passed classified information on to the Allies in the hopes of shortening the war. Social Democratic cells continued to operate clandestinely until late in the war as well. Their secret reports (**SOPADE**) of the public mood in Germany, collated from 1934 until 1940 by SPD leaders in exile in Prague and Paris, attest to continuing anti-Nazi attitudes and passive resistance especially among German workers, but they also document the success that the Nazis had in manufacturing consensus, integrating industrial workers into the *Volksgemeinschaft*, and neutralizing potential opposition in Germany. Several SPD leaders who remained in Germany did, however, join or make contact with the conservative resistance during the war and participated in the planning for the post-Nazi government that the 20 July military conspiracy hoped to establish.

THE MILITARY RESISTANCE

The dynamic young war hero Claus Schenk von **Stauffenberg**'s failed attempt to assassinate Hitler at his East Prussian field headquarters, the *Wolfschanze* (Wolf's Lair), on 20 July 1944 marked the single greatest challenge to the regime in the 12 years of Nazi rule. The bomb planted under a briefing table killed three high-ranking military officers, but Hitler survived the blast with only minor injuries. The conspirators' plan to seize military control of the government, code-named Operation **Valkyrie**, collapsed when it became known, several hours after the assassination attempt, that Hitler had survived. Stauffenberg and other leading co-conspirators were executed by firing squad in the courtyard of the army headquarters building in Berlin that same night. In the months that followed, the Nazi dragnet rounded up hundreds of persons, some only loosely connected with the military conspiracy. Most of the members of the plot, mainly career officers and civil servants, were subjected to show trials by the *Volksgerichtshof* (People's Court) under the jurisdiction of the fanatical Roland **Freisler** and condemned to death.

While the courage and self-sacrifice of the participants in the 20 July conspiracy have never been in doubt, their motives and political goals have been the object of some criticism and controversy among historians. At the center of the controversy is the question whether the conspirators acted mainly to avert the consequences of defeat, as the Allies claimed during the war, or whether they were motivated by dedication to universal principles of freedom and justice, in accordance with the view that gained general acceptance in the West for political reasons (as a way of integrating West Germany into the Western alliance) during the cold war in the 1950s and after. Did they act out of fundamental opposition to National Socialism, as was certainly the case with the left-wing opposition, or only because Germany was losing the war? While the attitude of the left toward Nazism was one of uncompromising hostility, the attitudes of most conservative resisters to National Socialism was marked by ambivalence, and their conversion from supporters of the regime into its opponents typically came late in the war when Germany's military prospects had become bleak. Even then, according to their own testimony, they opposed the murderous excesses of the regime and its failed policies, not its fundamental military and political aims. Compounding the ambivalence of the conservative resistance were the scruples of military officers who had taken a personal oath of loyalty to the Führer and the hesitations of a number of high-ranking officers who were prepared to accept a change of regime but were unwilling to take the lead in bringing it about.

The debate about the motives of the conservative resistance helps to illuminate the appeal of the Nazi movement to so many high-minded and well-meaning German conservatives before it became clear that this movement would lead their nation to ruin. With the exception of some religiously inspired conservatives, most notably, perhaps, the Protestant theologian Dietrich **Bonhoeffer** and the aristocratic lawyer Helmut von **Moltke**, leader of the resistance circle known as the **Kreisau** Circle, none of the leading members of the conservative resistance considered Nazism inherently evil. Rather, they opposed the movement for failing to live up to its own stated ideals. Most of the military, administrative, and clerical officials who eventually conspired against Hitler had bitterly rejected the Weimar parliamentary system and democratic culture, had welcomed Hitler's accession to power with hardly less enthusiasm than those who defended Hitler to the bitter end, had supported the Nazi goals of curbing the allegedly excessive influence of Jews in German society, and had approved of Germany's withdrawal from the League of Nations, the **Röhm purge**, and the remilitarization of German society.

From 1935 to the **Reichskristallnacht** (crystal night) pogrom in November 1938, which did mark a turning point, there was little difference in political attitude between those who later turned against the regime and those who did not. The military and political resistance that formed at the height of the Czechoslovakian crisis under General Ludwig **Beck**, who resigned as army chief of staff in August 1938, was not based on opposition to Hitler's avowed goals or his domestic policies but rather on his fear that the use of force would provoke a major European war before the German army was ready. In fact, anti-Nazi military conspirators, including most notably Admiral Wilhelm **Canaris** and General Hans

Oster of the counter-intelligence office in the newly established **OKW**, as well as the later field marshal Erwin von **Witzleben**, did not initially seek to oust the Hitler regime but only to dissuade it from starting a war that Germany was likely to lose. The leading civilian member of the 20 July conspiracy, Carl **Goerdeler**, mayor of Leipzig until his resignation in 1937 and the conspirators' choice for chancellor in the post-Hitler government they were hoping to establish, believed that Hitler imperiled the realization of Germany's justified territorial demands by eschewing patient diplomacy.

When war broke out most of the small minority of military officers who had harbored doubts about Hitler's leadership rallied behind the war effort and helped to prepare his military successes in Poland and the west. The high point of national solidarity was reached with the invasion of the Soviet Union in 1941. Even church leaders who protested the regime's **euthanasia** policy, including Catholic bishops Clemens von **Galen** and Michael von **Faulhaber** and the Protestant bishop Theophil **Wurm**, enthusiastically endorsed the Nazis' defense of morality and idealism against godless communism. Even **Confessing Church** leader Martin **Niemöller**, interned at **Sachsenhausen** and **Dachau** for opposing the state's intervention into ecclesiastical self-governance, supported the German cause in 1941. Although disenchanted with Nazism after the 1938 Reichskristallnacht pogrom, Stauffenberg declined to join the resistance while the war was at its height in the winter of 1941. His attitude was that the war must be won before the "brown pestilence" could be dealt with.[1]

If German victories had continued, it is very unlikely that there would have been a military revolt. Impending defeat created the conditions for the growth of resistance in the army and lent urgency to the military plot. Major-General Henning von **Tresckow**, chief of the operations staff of Army Group Center in the east, planned an assassination attempt as early as March 1943 when Hitler visited front-line troops shortly after the German defeat at **Stalingrad**. However, the bomb planted on Hitler's plane failed to go off. Similar misadventures thwarted several further attempts before 20 July 1944. The planned coup was also delayed by the insistence of some conspirators that **Himmler**, who was rarely present at military briefings, had to be assassinated at the same time as Hitler. By the time Stauffenberg made his failed assassination attempt Anglo-American forces in the west were preparing to break out of their beachheads in northern France and the Red Army had launched the powerful summer offensive that would bring it to the borders of the Reich by the end of the year. Yet the conspirators continued to pursue unrealistic expansionist goals. A Stauffenberg memo from May 1944 called for the 1914 Reich borders in the east, retention of Austria and the Sudetenland, autonomy for Alsace-Lorraine, and acquisition of the disputed area of South Tyrol.[2]

Ultimately, however, most of the leading military and civilian conspirators of the conservative resistance understood that even if they were unlikely to achieve their objectives, they had to act if they were to avert the total destruction of their country. They hoped that their action, even if it failed, would help to salvage what was left of German honor in the eyes of the world and thus contribute to the rehabilitation of their nation in defeat. This unusually heroic attitude did indeed have lasting symbolic significance, demonstrating to the world that not all Germans in leadership positions were Nazis and that some were prepared to risk their lives to rid their country of the Nazi scourge. Equally exemplary courage was displayed by the unsuccessful student resistance group centered in Munich and calling itself the **White Rose**. Under the leadership of the young medical student Hans **Scholl** and his sister Sophie, this group printed and distributed a series of six leaflets from late summer 1942, while the German armies were still advancing, to January 1943, as the battle of Stalingrad was nearing its bitter end. Appalled by the *Einsatzgruppen* murders of Jews that some of its members had witnessed while on duty on the eastern front, the White Rose called for uncompromising resistance and acts of sabotage in hopes of inciting a popular revolt against the Nazi regime. In February 1943 members of the group were arrested while distributing anti-Nazi leaflets, condemned by the *Volksgerichtshof*, and executed.

Neither the White Rose nor the military revolt was able to mobilize support among the public at large. Most Germans remained at least passively loyal to the regime in a time of **total war**. The growing number of Germans who lost their confidence in the Nazi regime preferred "inner emigration" – retreat into the private sphere – to highly risky and seemingly hopeless opposition. *Wehrkraftzersetzung*, the undermining of the will to fight, was a criminal offense, and as the war progressed even off-hand remarks that could be construed as defeatist resulted in penalties of death. The apparently successful seven-day **Rosenstrasse protest** by over 150 German women in Berlin against the deportation of their Jewish husbands in February–March 1943 did seem to indicate that a public display of collective dissent could effect a change in Nazi policies. Other historians, however, have argued that the Nazis never planned to deport the Jewish husbands in question and that their release therefore cannot be construed as evidence of the potential effectiveness of public protest in Nazi Germany.[3] Overestimation of the effectiveness of the Rosenstrasse protest runs the danger of exaggerating the possibilities of dissent and opposition, let alone resistance, and understates the degree to which the Nazi regime rested on a broad public consensus.

RESISTANCE IN OCCUPIED COUNTRIES

In forcibly opposing their government's policies in the midst of war, the German resistance operated under a huge handicap that resistance movements in occupied countries did not have to face. Here the anti-Nazi resistance did not have the stigma of treason as it was directed against a foreign oppressor. Unlike the German resistance, which was forced to operate in isolation from the public, resisters in occupied countries could count on widespread support from their compatriots. Moreover, the Allies supported resistance groups in occupied countries but withheld support for the German resistance – both for fear of giving rise to another stab-in-the-back legend after the war and because of their commitment to a policy of **unconditional surrender**. Yet even in occupied countries the extent of resistance was crucially determined by the fortunes of war. In France, for instance, where the resistance eventually grew into a formidable force, collaborators initially outnumbered resisters. The collaborationist government established under General Henri-Philippe Pétain at **Vichy** in June 1940, while refusing to join in the war against England, cooperated with the Nazis in implementing anti-Semitic measures and in supporting their anti-communist crusade against the Soviet Union. The balance of power between collaborators and resisters changed after the war turned in the Allies' favor in November 1942, when the Germans occupied Vichy France in reaction to the Anglo-American landing in North Africa and the subsequent defection of the French colonial government in Algeria. From then on the French resistance grew in strength and militancy, contributing decisively to the liberation of their country in the late summer of 1944.

All over Europe the anti-Nazi resistance was divided into communist and non- or anti-communist factions, which occasionally fought each other (most ferociously, perhaps, in Yugoslavia) but usually acted in concert against the foreign occupiers. Everywhere communists tended to be more militant and uncompromising in their resistance to the Nazi invaders than their non-communist counterparts. **Partisan** resistance movements played important military roles, particularly in Yugoslavia, Poland, the occupied territories of the Soviet Union, and in Greece and Italy toward the end of the war. The resistance movement under Marshal Tito (1892–1980), one of the founders of the Communist Party in Yugoslavia, succeeded in liberating the country before the arrival of Soviet troops in 1944. The **Warsaw Uprising** launched by the anti-communist Polish Home Army, loyal to the government in exile in London, failed to liberate the country in August 1944 but did force the diversion of numerous German units from the front before its defeat in October of that year. Partisan resistance, however, provided the pretext for the Nazi government to ignore the Geneva conventions on the rules of war in taking preventive or retaliatory action. Demonized as bandits, criminals, and terrorists, patriotic insurgents in occupied countries faced ruthless and disproportionate retaliatory measures, including the deliberate killing of innocent civilian hostages in areas where resistance fighters were active. The notorious **Night-and-Fog Decree** of July 1941 authorized the abduction and "disappearance" of persons suspected of resistance activities in the occupied areas of Western Europe.

Even among the most persecuted and defenseless population groups, including the Jews, there were courageous acts of resistance despite the hopeless odds against them. The Jews of the **Warsaw Ghetto** staged a heroic last-ditch uprising to avoid deportation to **Treblinka** in April and May 1943. It took well-armed German SS units four weeks to quell the revolt in fierce house-to-house fighting. There were revolts under even more hopeless conditions in some of the death camps as well, including Treblinka in August 1943 and **Sobibór** in October 1943. Although the failure of such rebellions was a virtually foregone conclusion, resistance to Nazi persecution and repression provided inspirational if tragic examples of courage and valor under the most adverse conditions imaginable.

HOW SUCCESSFUL WERE THE VICTOR POWERS IN STAMPING OUT NAZISM AFTER THE WAR?

The victor powers were determined to stamp out Nazism in Germany after the war both by judicial prosecution and punishment of war criminals as well as by the permanent removal of all former Nazis from positions of influence and leadership in German society. At the **Yalta Conference** in February 1945 the Allies declared that **denazification** would be a primary goal of their policy toward a defeated Germany. At the **Potsdam Conference** in July–August 1945 the Allies agreed to dissolve the Nazi Party and all its subsidiary organizations, ban all Nazi publications, abolish all Nazi laws, intern all party leaders, remove all party members from public office, and eliminate all Nazi instructional materials from schools (which in practice involved the temporary closing of all schools). Punitive measures were to be supplemented by a campaign to reeducate the German public in the ideology and principles of democratic government.

In 1945 the victor powers were united in their adoption of punitive policies, their rejection of Nazism, and their determination to eliminate its vestiges in postwar Germany. However, in their respective plans for Germany's future government and economy, and in their notions of what constituted true democracy (whether liberal or socialist), the Western powers and the Soviet Union were very much at odds. One of the consequences of the long and bitter cold war that grew out of these differences was increasingly to deflect both Allied and German energies from efforts to stamp out Nazism. The growing breach among the victor powers in 1947 and 1948 led to the division of Germany and, at least in the West, to the abandonment of punitive policies, a change of course that redounded to the benefit of many former Nazis whose services were now enlisted by both sides in the escalating cold war between East and West.

THE NUREMBERG TRIALS

Although agreement on the need to punish the leading Nazi perpetrators was reached as early as 1942, the Allies did not agree to hold a formal trial until a few days before the end of the war in Europe in May 1945. Churchill would have preferred to forgo a formal judicial proceeding to avoid the anticipated legal difficulties of proving a Nazi conspiracy to wage war and of convicting leading Nazis of acts that were not necessarily illegal at the time or in the place they were committed. While Stalin insisted on some official public proceeding that would display the guilt of the accused to the world, he obviously preferred a kind of show trial to any procedure that assumed the possibility of innocence on the part of the defendants. Eventually, however, it was American notions of justice, including "the right for defendants to defend themselves against clearly stated charges," that prevailed.[4] The **International Military Tribunal (IMT)** established to conduct the trials was made up of one judge and one chief prosecuting counsel from each of the four victor powers (France having been added after its liberation). The

Nuremburg Trials of major war criminals from November 1945 to October 1946 led to the conviction of 19 top Nazi leaders, 12 of whom were sentenced to death (including, *in absentia*, Martin **Bormann**, whose death while attempting to escape from Berlin in the last days of the war was not yet known at the time). **Hitler, Goebbels, Himmler,** and **Ley** had committed suicide, the latter while already in detention at Nuremberg.

Of the 22 leading Nazis tried by the International Military Tribunal at Nuremberg, 12 were condemned to death, three received life imprisonment, four received sentences between ten and 20 years, and three were acquitted. Of the five organizations indicted at Nuremberg, only the SS and the Leadership Corps of the Nazi Party (including national, regional, and local party leaders) were found guilty of criminal activity. Over strenuous Soviet objections, the **SA**, the Reich governmental bureaucracy, and, most controversially, the **OKW** and the General Staff of the army were acquitted. In the view of the Western powers crimes committed by military forces were the responsibility of individual officers, not of the Wehrmacht or the High Command. Twelve subsequent trials under the auspices of the American Military Government at Nuremberg against leading medical, judicial, military, industrial, administrative, and SS and **Gestapo** officials led to 144 convictions and 35 acquittals. Numerous trials of individual war criminals were also held in the Soviet, British, and French occupation zones, and in the occupied countries in which the Nazis had committed war crimes.

The significance of the Nuremberg Trials of major war criminals went far beyond the relatively small number of convictions. They provided a precedent for the prosecution of human rights abuses and war crimes under international law. Codified by the United Nations in 1950, the Nuremberg Principles, like the Geneva Conventions on the rules of war, have been adopted as the law of the land in most major nations in the world today. Beyond this, the Nuremberg Trials fulfilled a major function in documenting the horrors of Nazi crimes. The atrocities revealed at the trials helped to discredit and stigmatize Nazism and thus to prevent a revival of Nazi ideology in Germany. The 42-volume record of the trial (as well as the largely unpublished interrogations that preceded the trial) provide a major resource for historians of Nazism.

DENAZIFICATION

Denazification represented a much broader effort to ensure that even Nazis who were not accused of war crimes would be barred from returning to positions of influence both in the public and private sectors of a reconstituted German society. The task the victor powers faced was formidable. Over 15 million Germans had either joined the Nazi Party or one of its affiliated organizations such as the SS. Thousands of mid-level perpetrators implicated in Nazi crimes had changed their identities at the end of the war. Denazification rested on decrees issued by the four-power **Allied Control Council** that governed Germany until the establishment of separate West and East German states in 1949, but appeals boards consisting of non- or anti-Nazi Germans were entrusted with implementing the denazification process. In the Western occupation zones over 6 million former Nazis were divided into five categories of major offenders, offenders, lesser offenders, fellow travelers, and exonerated, respectively. Only the first three categories were subject to penalties ranging from criminal prosecution to occupational restrictions.

For a number of reasons the goal of denazification, the elimination of former Nazis from public and semi-public offices, was not achieved. The ease of obtaining a so-called *Persilschein* (certificate of innocence) from one of the churches or other authorities – as well as the leniency of the appeals boards, which accepted a wide range of extenuating arguments to exculpate even mid-level Nazi leaders – led to the exoneration of the vast majority of former Nazis. Arguing that they had merely obeyed orders, most old Nazis refused to face the horrors of the past. The post-war public mood of collective amnesia and self-pity played its part in undermining denazification efforts. Because so many former Nazis were exonerated, the term "denazification" came to mean not "elimination of Nazis from positions of power" (its original meaning) but rather "rehabilitation of former Nazis." To be "denazified" meant to be certified as not, or at least no longer, a Nazi. The process was nonetheless highly unpopular in Germany; not surprisingly so, since hundreds of thousands of people found themselves in the uncomfortable position of having to explain away their past collaboration with Nazism or face the end of their public or professional careers.

Another reason for the failure of denazification was the growing shortage of qualified personnel for public administration in each of the occupation zones. A series of amnesties decreed by the Western powers greatly reduced the number of former party members subject to denazification in 1947 and 1948. But the most important reason why denazification was slowed down and eventually halted in both the Western and Soviet zones was the incipient cold war, which induced the Western powers, under US leadership, to shift from a punitive policy toward Germany to a policy of restoring prosperity in a separate West German state aligned with the Western side. Former Nazis with useful skills were also recruited by the American armed forces for military projects or covert operations against the Soviet Union. Denazification ground to a halt with the founding of the Federal Republic of Germany in May 1949. The West German constitution authorized the return of former Nazis to the civil service unless they had been convicted of war crimes. In the Soviet-backed German Democratic Republic, founded in October 1949, merely nominal Nazi Party membership was no longer a hindrance to obtaining high positions, except in politically sensitive fields. Surveying the situation in West Germany in the late 1950s, one US war crimes investigator came to "the inescapable conclusion that the Nazis have had a quiet comeback almost everywhere."[5]

The failure of denazification to achieve its original purpose of barring former Nazis from positions of influence in post-war West Germany did not, however, mean that the larger Allied project of stamping out Nazi ideology had failed. Indeed, the retreat from denazification was accompanied by ever more forceful repudiation of Nazi doctrine and condemnation of the Nazi past. Though ineffective in barring former Nazis from public office or the professions, the denazification process, by inducing former Nazis to deny any allegiance to Nazi values, contributed to the further discrediting of Nazism in the eyes of the public and to the elimination of Nazi ideas, particularly anti-Semitism, from public discourse. In eliciting protestations of innocence and disavowals of Nazi doctrines from former Nazis as a condition of their rehabilitation, denazification helped to reinforce the public perception of Nazism as an odious and criminal movement.

In offering former Nazis the opportunity for rehabilitation by publicly distancing themselves from Nazism, denazification served an integrating function after the war. Although undoubtedly some former Nazis retained their commitment to Nazi ideas in private, even unreconstructed Nazis knew that they had no chance to revive Nazism as a political movement in the post-war environment. Most former Nazis were happy publicly to embrace liberal-democratic ideas in the West (and socialist ideas in the East), thus preventing the formation of an alienated and potentially powerful right-wing opposition to democracy in West Germany. Though for many former Nazis the repudiation of Nazism may have been more a ritualistic expedient than a genuine conversion, the result nonetheless was to invest Nazism with the public stigma of criminality and evil.

CONFLICTING INTERPRETATIONS OF NAZISM IN THE COLD WAR

The two post-war German states competed with each other in demonstrating their rejection of and difference from Nazism. Precisely because Nazism provided such a negative foil against which to define the superiority of their respective social systems, the interpretation of Nazism was hotly contested in the cold war. The imputation of Nazi traits to the opposing side became a powerful political weapon. Continuing the long-standing **Comintern** definition of fascism as an extreme, terrorist form of capitalism, publicists for the East German state sought to link the West German economic system with the Nazi regime. West German publicists, in turn, linked communism with fascism as essentially similar forms of totalitarian rule, thus in effect de-emphasizing the striking differences in communist and fascist social policies. While the East German official consensus identified anti-communism as the essential feature of Nazi ideology, thus linking the liberal anti-communism of the West to fascism, West Germans designated anti-Semitism (and anti-liberalism) as the defining Nazi traits, thus enabling the West German state to dissociate itself from Nazism by making restitution to Jewish victims of Nazism and by supporting the Jewish state in Israel, while condemning the East German state for failing to make similar amends for the Nazi past.

There were important differences, too, in their respective attitudes toward the German resistance to Nazism. East Germans pointed with pride to the record of Communist resistance in the Third Reich, while in West Germany the Communist resistance was widely equated with treason. Instead, West Germans valorized the conservative military resistance that had wished to continue the war against the Soviet Union in the East. While anti-fascism emerged as the integrating ideology in the much smaller and weaker East German state, it was anti-communism that provided the integrating ideology in the prosperous West. In 1955 the Western powers decided to rearm their half of the nation that only 14 years earlier had launched a war of annihilation against the Soviet Union. Former Nazis had little difficulty refurbishing their anti-communist ideology for use in the cold war. But while the two German states both sought to use interpretations of Nazism and the Holocaust to their advantage, their instrumental use of Nazi ideology as a negative foil to profile their respective ideologies shared the common premise that Nazism was an unmitigated evil without any redeeming value.

NEO-NAZISM

Nonetheless, Nazi ideas in the form of neo-Nazism reemerged in the liberal, but anti-communist political landscape in West Germany, particularly as a backlash against the emancipatory, anti-authoritarian, anti-establishment, and anti-war protest movements of the 1960s. Neo-Nazism also gained support in the former East Germany in the wake of the Communist collapse in 1989 and 1990. Typically projecting a benign image to the public by appropriating the language of democracy, radical right-wing parties, most importantly, perhaps, the National Democratic Party (**NPD**), have become fixtures in German politics (as elsewhere in Europe) without, however, up to now gaining enough electoral support to be represented in the national parliament of a reunited Germany, the Bundestag.

Beginning with the economic downturn in the early 1970s, hostility to foreign immigration, particularly from Eastern Europe, Africa, and Asia, became the chief source of appeal of radical right-wing parties, some of which gained enough votes to enter state parliaments in West Germany in the 1980s, and in the reunited Federal Republic in the 1990s and the 2000s. While they echo some of the xeno-phobic, authoritarian, and hyper-nationalist values of Nazi ideology, there are also significant differences that limit the threat that they represent to the liberal order in a reunited Germany. So discredited are Nazism and anti-Semitism in Germany today that any profession of allegiance to these doctrines disqualifies the individual or party in question from political office by general public consensus.

PROSPECTS FOR THE FUTURE

Does that mean that fascism and Nazism can be safely relegated to the "dustbin of history," to use the phrase with which Leon Trotsky famously derided the defeated anti-Bolshevik parties in Soviet Russia in 1918? While it is impossible to predict the future, it is safe to say that as specific ideological products of the political conditions in Europe in the first half of the twentieth century fascism and Nazism will never recur in their historically specific forms, except perhaps as secretive cults confined to the extremist political fringe. But the conditions that gave rise to fascism or Nazism in the first place, mainly frustrated national-ism, economic deceleration, and the public perception of a left-wing threat, continue to harbor the potential for breeding a radical right-wing backlash against foreign immigration, economic instability, or egalitarian social policies, especially those that are perceived to favor excluded minorities disproportionately. The catastrophic end of the Third Reich, the totality of German defeat, the abruptness of the change of systems that occurred in 1945, and the subsequent disrepute of Nazism may also have had the effect of obscuring possible continuities beyond the apparent caesura in 1945. History is after all a dialectical process in which the newly dominant consciousness after a conflict is constituted not just by the ideas and values of the victorious side – in the case of the Second World War, the shared egalitarian values of the victor powers – but usually represents a synthesis of winning and losing ideas.

A question that goes beyond the range of this book but merits serious thought and investigation is the degree to which the victor powers may have incorporated some of the anti-egalitarian political and social values (as well as structural components) of the defeated side after the Second World War. The liberal synthesis that emerged in the United States and in the West more generally after the war incorporated the conservative culture that had produced pro-fascist sympathies in certain sectors of Western society before the war. In the cold war that followed the Second World War, the political culture of the United States in particular changed in subtle and tenuous ways to meet the new threat from the East. The newly founded Central Intelligence Agency, for instance, did not hesitate to recruit former SS agents and right-wing terrorists for covert operations against the Soviet Union right up to the collapse of Communism in 1991.[6] From a power that championed the egalitarian values of the left in the fight against fascism, the United States changed into a power that regarded the egalitarian principle as potentially threatening to its interests. If in the fight against the Nazis the United States fought on the side of communists for equality for the weak and the poor, after the war it willingly incorporated former fascists, Nazis, neo-Nazis, and right-wing terrorists in Third World countries (particularly Latin America) in what many poorer nations perceived as a world-wide counter-revolutionary struggle in defense of the privileges of the strong and the rich that continues today. It is the American shift to the right in the latter half of the twentieth century and the militarization of American policies in the effort to spread American-style democracy world-wide that have led some left-wing critics to raise fears of the emergence of a modified form of fascism that would turn out to be as specifically American as Nazism was specifically German.

Despite the eclipse of both fascism and communism and the apparent victory of liberal democracy in the twenty-first century, the battle of ideas and political values continues. Although it is most unlikely that Nazi-style fascism or Soviet-style communism will ever reappear in their earlier incarnations, the forces they represent will undoubtedly continue to exert influence in the world, not least in the form of conflicting evaluations of the Nazi past. Efforts on the part of the revisionist historian Ernst **Nolte** to cast Nazism in a more favorable historical light as a counter-movement to the allegedly more extreme international communist movement led to a bitter dispute among German historians, known as the *Historikerstreit*, in 1986 and 1987. The issue was not just the historical question as to whether fascism or communism constituted the greater evil, but involved the larger question of German and European political identity. The equation of communist atrocities with Nazi atrocities became a favorite right-wing technique to influence future policy. As the European Union continued to expand, for instance, anti-fascism and anti-communism represented (broadly speaking) the two contending sides of an emerging European liberal-democratic identity. In the aftermath of the Second World War, and as a preventive measure against the revival of neo-Nazism, Germany and other European nations criminalized anti-Semitism, the display of Nazi flags, slogans, or insignia, and other overt expressions of allegiance to Nazi ideas to demonstrate their commitment to democracy. In the aftermath of the collapse of the Soviet Union, European conservatives sought to extend this ban to the paraphernalia of communism as well, as if Nazi and communist values presented equivalent threats to European societies.

At stake here is nothing less than the priority of the contending social ideals of left and right. The Western consensus on the superior merits of liberal democracy does not necessarily guarantee that democratic values will prevail over the authoritarian and militaristic values of the right in the policies that liberal democracies pursue. The notion of Nazism as a uniquely aberrant historical movement that cannot be repeated may be a comforting delusion. The visibility of neo-Nazism on the fringes of liberal democratic societies may even have the perverse function of fostering fascist and imperialist tendencies within these societies by offering a ready target while more insidious right-wing tendencies free of the stigma of Nazism grow unhindered. The history of Nazi Germany should at the very least serve as a warning of the danger and destructiveness of the nationalist, authoritarian, and militarist values that are latently present in all societies but present particular dangers in nations that command great military power. Although neo-Nazism remained a fringe phenomenon in Europe and the US at the start of the twenty-first century, fears of mass democracy and of movements that favor greater equality among nations and individuals, fears that have historically bred right-wing extremism, are still very much present.

III
KEY ACTORS AND TERMINOLOGY

9

BIOGRAPHIES

- *This section includes brief biographies of the top leaders in Nazi Germany, a minuscule percentage of the leadership in Nazi Germany as a whole.*
- *It also includes non-Nazis and anti-Nazis who played a significant role in the advent or course of the Third Reich. The aim is to provide a representative sampling of typical careers of leading figures.*
- *Biographies include post-war careers whenever that information is available and relevant in order to document the uneven prosecution of Nazi crimes.*

A

AMANN, MAX (1891–1957) Nazi press baron, honorary **SS** general, a *Reichsleiter*, and president of the Reich Press Chamber from 1933 to 1945. Amann owed his career in the Nazi Party to the trust placed in him by **Hitler**. They had served together as non-commissioned officers in the same regiment during the First World War. Despite Amann's lack of education, Hitler appointed him the party's business manager in 1921 (until 1923). As director of the party's publishing firm, Eher Verlag, from 1922 until the end of the **Third Reich**, Amann was responsible for publishing the party newspaper *Völkischer Beobachter* and numerous other party publications, including *Nationalsozialistische Monatshefte*. For his part in the **Hitler Putsch** Amann served one month in prison. In 1924 he was elected to the Munich city council, on which he served until 1932. After Hitler's ascent to power Amann

became president of the Association of German Publishers and in December 1933 the president of the newly founded Reich Press Chamber. Amann had little competence as a writer, relying instead on his able assistant Rolf Rienhardt (b. 1903) to write his articles and speeches, but did have considerable business acumen and accumulated enormous personal wealth as the press tsar of the Third Reich. He played a leading role in the *Gleichschaltung* of the press, eventually absorbing virtually all independent German newspapers into what became the world's largest publishing empire. Although he frequently clashed with other Nazi leaders in jurisdictional disputes, especially with Reich press chief Otto **Dietrich**, party culture tsar Alfred **Rosenberg**, and Minister of Propaganda Joseph **Goebbels**, Amann retained Hitler's favor. Amann handled Hitler's royalties from *Mein Kampf* and paid huge fees to Hitler and other Nazi leaders for articles they published in the Nazi press. Amann was classified as a "major offender" by a **denazification** court and sentenced to a ten-year term in 1948.

AXMANN, ARTHUR (1913–1996) Successor to **Schirach** as Reich Youth Leader from 1940 to 1945. Axmann entered the **Hitler Youth** in 1928 and became Nazi Youth Leader in a working-class section of Berlin that same year. After joining the Nazi Party in 1931 he was appointed to a leadership position in the national Hitler Youth in 1932 and head of social affairs for the Reich Youth Leadership organization in 1933. In that capacity he organized the annual Nazi national vocational competitions and chaired the committee that drew up the law for compulsory youth work sevice in 1939. After Schirach assumed governing duties in Austria in 1940, Axmann replaced him as Reich Youth Leader. Wounded on the eastern front in 1941, Axmann nonetheless retained his fanatical loyalty to Hitler until the end. Having organized military units from under-age Hitler Youth cohorts for the last-ditch defense of Berlin, Axmann was one of the last functionaries to escape the Führer bunker in April 1945. He testified at the **Nuremberg trial**, but was not arrested until December 1945, apparently while engaged in organizing a secret Nazi cell. In 1949 he was classified as a "major offender" by a **denazification** court and sentenced to a three-year term. He was immediately released as his sentence was considered to have been served while waiting for his case to be heard. He then went on to a successful business career.

B

BACH-ZELEWSKI, ERICH VON DEM (1899–1972) SS general, Higher SS and Police Leader (HSSPF) attached to Army Group Center in the east, and **Himmler**'s plenipotentiary for anti-partisan warfare on the eastern front from October 1942. Of Prussian aristocratic extraction, Bach-Zelewski served in the First World War and remained as an officer in the **Reichswehr** until 1924 before returning to his hereditary estate. He joined the Nazi Party in 1930, the SS in 1931, and served as a Nazi delegate to the **Reichstag** in 1932. In his capacity as Higher SS and Police Leader in Russia from 1941 and as chief of anti-partisan warfare from 1942, Bach-Zelewski was deeply involved in the massacre of Jews and partisans by SS *Einsatzgruppen* and military and police units. In August 1944 Bach-Zelewski commanded the troops that suppressed the **Warsaw Uprising** and accepted the surrender of Polish resistance fighters. Bach-Zelewski's willingness to testify for the prosecution at the war crimes tribunal at **Nuremberg** saved him from being put on trial himself and from extradition to the Soviet Union. He thus became one of the most prominent perpetrators of the Nazis' murderous racial crimes who was never prosecuted by the Allies. Although sentenced to a ten-year term by a Munich **denazification** court in 1951, he was released that same year. He did however serve prison terms in the 1960s for his involvement in the **Röhm Purge** and in the murder of six Communists shortly after Hitler came to power. Bach-Zelewski died in a Munich prison hospital in 1972.

BACKE, HERBERT (1896–1947) Permanent secretary in the Ministry for Food and Agriculture (1933), Food commissioner for the **Four-Year Plan** (1936), successor to **Darré** as Reich farm leader (1942), and Reich minister (1944). Born into a family of German colonists in Russia, Backe was schooled in Tiflis but managed to escape to

Germany after being interned at the start of the First World War. After military service he received a degree in agriculture from Göttingen University. He joined the **SA** in 1922 and the Nazi Party in 1923. Backe was instrumental in bringing the *Landbund*, a farmers' organization, under Nazi control. In October 1933 he became the leading official under Darré in the Ministry for Food and Agriculture. Backe's practical competence made him more useful to the Nazis than his ideologically driven boss, who frequently pursued unrealistic policies. Backe's powers grew as he became the primary coordinator of food production in Germany. His expertise on agricultural problems in Russia and his commitment to racial resettlement policies in the east led to his appointment in 1942 as Reich farm leader with ministerial rank in April 1944. He retained his position as Reich food minister in **Dönitz**'s cabinet. Backe committed suicide in prison while awaiting trial in **Nuremberg** in 1947.

BECK, LUDWIG (1880–1944) Army chief of staff 1935 to 1938 and leading member of the military resistance to **Hitler**. Beck joined the army in 1898, became a member of the German general staff in 1911, served on the Western front in the First World War, and joined the **Reichswehr** after the war where he rose to the rank of lieutenant-general in 1932 and second in command of the army under Werner **Fritsch** in 1934. As chief of staff Beck was responsible for operational planning. Although he welcomed Hitler's accession to power as an opportunity to reestablish military parity with other European powers, Beck became increasingly concerned both by the repressive nature of the regime and by Hitler's reckless foreign policy. Having tried without success to persuade his fellow officers to

oppose Hitler's march to war, for which he felt the German army was not sufficiently prepared, Beck resigned his position in August 1938 and was succeeded by Franz **Halder**. Beck established contacts with the leader of the conservative civilian resistance Carl **Goerdeler** and eventually came to the conclusion that the Nazi government could only be overthrown through Hitler's assassination. Beck was slated to become head of state if the 20 July assassination attempt had succeeded. After learning that Hitler had survived Beck committed suicide at army headquarters in Berlin in the evening of 20 July 1944.

BERGER, GOTTLOB (1896–1975) SS general, head of the recruitment office of the **Waffen-SS** (the military arm of the SS) from 1939, and chief of the SS Main Office (the SS administrative headquarters) from 1940 to 1945. Wounded as an officer in the First World War, Berger became a physical education teacher in the southwest German state of Württemberg and joined the Nazi Party in 1931. Originally with the **SA**, he shifted to the SS in 1936 where he headed the recruitment office in 1938 and helped to build up the Waffen-SS. In 1940 he was promoted to chief of the SS administrative headquarters where he oversaw offices for leadership, personnel, recruitment, training, security, intelligence, procurement, logistics, medical services, and welfare. In 1942 he became **Himmler**'s liaison officer to the Ministry for the Occupied Eastern Territories, where **Rosenberg** entrusted him with the direction of the political operations staff. In August 1944 Berger was responsible for the suppression of an anti-Nazi rising in Slovakia. In October 1944 Himmler put him in charge of all prisoner-of-war camps. Sentenced in one of the secondary **Nuremberg** trials to 25 years in 1949, Berger was pardoned and released in 1951.

BEST, WERNER (1903–1989) SS general, leading official of the Security Service (**SD**), and Reich plenipotentiary for occupied Denmark from 1942 to 1945. Best, whose father was killed in the First World War, joined the Nationalist party (**DNVP**) after the war and was imprisoned by the French for resistance activities during the French occupation of the **Ruhr** (1923–1924). In 1927 he earned a law degree at the University of Heidelberg, but was forced out of the judicial service in the state of Hesse in 1931 after the discovery of the **Boxheim Documents**, the blueprint for a Nazi putsch written by Best. Best had joined the Nazi Party in 1930 and the **SS** in 1931. Elected to the Hesse state parliament from 1931 to 1933, Best became police commissioner in Hesse after the Nazi seizure of power. In 1935 he became head of the department for administration and legal affairs in the SD, where he worked closely with **Heydrich** in consolidating the SD (including the **Gestapo**), the security police, and the criminal police into the Reich Security Main Office (**RSHA**) in 1939. Although Best performed valuable services in expanding the SS's extra-legal authority under legal cover, Heydrich considered him to be too concerned about legal niceties. From 1940 to 1942 Best served as head of civil administration in occupied France until his appointment as the top German occupation official in Denmark. Here Best oversaw the repression of Danish sovereignty, but there is some evidence that he tacitly permitted the escape to Sweden of most of Denmark's 7,000 Jews, only 477 of whom were ultimately rounded up for the "**final solution**." After testifying in the war crimes trials at **Nuremberg**, Best was

extradited to Denmark, where he was condemned to death in 1949. However, he was pardoned and released in 1951 and joined the West German Stinnes industrial concern as legal counsel, later becoming office manager for a neo-Nazi parliamentary deputy in Hesse. In 1969 Best was arrested again on charges of having ordered the murder of over 8,700 Poles in 1939 and 1940, but the case was dropped in 1972 on grounds of ill health.

BLOBEL, PAUL (1894–1951) SS *Sonderkommando* commander in the rank of colonel; responsible for the massacre of Jews at **Babi Yar**. Trained as an architect and a veteran of the First World War, Blobel joined the Nazi Party and the **SA** sometime before 1931 and transferred to the **SS** in 1932. From 1933 to 1941 he was active with the police and **SD** in Düsseldorf. As commander of *Sonderkommando* 4a of *Einsatzgruppe* C, active in the Ukraine, Blobel commanded the unit that murdered 33,771 Jewish men, women, and children in a ravine near Kiev on 29–30 September 1941, the largest single massacre perpetrated by the *Einsatzgruppen*. In June 1942 he was named commander of the task force responsible for the exhumation of victims and the removal of all traces of the extermination action. Directly responsible for the murder of approximately 60,000 Jews, Blobel was sentenced to death in the Sonderkommando trial at **Nuremberg** in 1948 and executed in 1951.

BLOMBERG, WERNER VON (1878–1946) Field marshal (1936) and war minister from 1933 to 1938. Of Pomeranian aristocratic extraction, Blomberg was a highly decorated officer during the First World War and continued in the **Reichswehr** after the war, where he rose to the rank of general by

1928. He was one of the chief organizers of Reichswehr collaboration with the Red Army in training and the secret testing of weapons in violation of **Versailles**. In 1932 Blomberg led the German military delegation to the disarmament conference in Geneva. On **Hindenburg**'s recommendation **Hitler** named him Reichswehr minister on 30 January 1930. In that capacity Blomberg proved to be highly useful to Hitler in bringing the army into a virtual coalition with the Nazi Party to promote German rearmament. In 1934 Blomberg welcomed the **Röhm Purge**, refused to condemn the murder of General **Schleicher**, and took the initiative in dismissing Jewish officers and introducing a personal oath of loyalty to Hitler in the army. In 1935 the Reichswehr Ministry was renamed the Ministry of War, and Blomberg became commander-in-chief of the newly expanded **Wehrmacht**. In February 1938 Blomberg was forced to resign his post when his young bride turned out to have been a prostitute with a police record. Hitler took the opportunity to abolish the office of war minister, to establish a new supreme command (the **OKW**) headed by **Keitel**, and to take personal control of the Wehrmacht. Blomberg died in American captivity in 1946.

BLUNCK, HANS-FRIEDRICH (1888–1961)
Völkisch author and novelist; president of the Reich Chamber of Literature from 1933 to 1935. An officer in the First World War, Blunck became a best-selling writer in the 1920s and 1930s, specializing in fiction based on Nordic sagas, historical novels of the Germanic past, and political tracts rejecting the **Weimar Republic**. He acquired an estate in the north-German state of Holstein, whose rural lifestyle and ethnic traditions he celebrated in his works. Although he did not join the Nazi Party until

1937, he shared and disseminated the Nazis' *völkisch* world-view and was rewarded for his services with high decorations. Classified as a *Mitläufer* (fellow traveler) after the war, Blunck denied any complicity in the Nazi regime but continued to advocate his right-wing views.

BONHOEFFER, DIETRICH (1906–1945)
Leading theologian of the **Confessing Church** and active member of the conservative resistance to the Nazis. Trained in theology in Berlin, Bonhoeffer studied at the Union Theological Seminary in New York in the late 1920s. He was one of the few resistance leaders not associated with the left who opposed the Nazis from the very start on the basis of morality and principle. Upon **Hitler**'s ascent to power in 1933, Bonhoeffer took up a position in London, but felt impelled by a sense of responsibility to return to his homeland in 1935. Bonhoeffer was one of the most active members of the Confessing Church movement from 1935 to 1937, opposing both the right-wing **German Christian** faction in the Church and the Nazi bureaucracy's efforts to impose racist doctrine and practices on the Church. In 1936 he was forbidden to teach, in 1940 he was no longer allowed to speak or conduct services in public, and in 1941 he was prohibited from publishing. Through his brother-in-law Hans von Dohnányi (1902–1945) Bonhoeffer and his brother Klaus (1901–1945) were recruited into the intelligence and counter-espionage section of the **OKW** under Admiral Wilhelm **Canaris**. Here Bonhoeffer was introduced to the military resistance circle around General Hans **Oster**. In 1942 Bonhoeffer transmitted concrete proposals for peace from Oster, General Ludwig **Beck**, and Carl **Goerdeler** to British Foreign Office officials in

Sweden, but received no positive response. Arrested in April 1943, Bonhoeffer was interned in **Buchenwald** after the failure of the July plot in 1944. From here he was transferred to **Flossenbürg**, where he, Oster, and Canaris were hanged in April 1945 shortly before the arrival of Allied troops. That same month his brother Klaus was shot by the Gestapo in Berlin and Dohnányi was murdered in **Sachsenhausen**.

BORMANN, MARTIN (1900–1945) Successor to Rudolf **Hess** in 1941 as deputy Führer of the party, head of the party Chancellery, and **Hitler**'s personal secretary. As the official who controlled access to Hitler and was responsible for issuing and implementing Hitler's orders and mediating all contacts with the government, Bormann exercised enormous power during the war, especially over appointments and personnel. A veteran of the First World War and the **Free Corps** movement, Bormann served a year in prison in 1924 for involvement in **Feme murders** by right-wing vigilantes. He joined the **NSDAP** in 1927, and was appointed chief of staff to Hess and a **Reichsleiter** of the party in 1933. One of his important roles was to administer Hitler's personal finances. As deputy minister for Church affairs in 1935, Bormann was one of the driving forces behind the Nazis' struggle with the churches. The most anti-clerical fanatic among the top Nazi leadership, Bormann viewed Christianity as incompatible with Nazi ideology and advocated its destruction after the war. Bormann was condemned to death *in absentia* at **Nuremberg**. For years he was suspected of having escaped to South America. In 1972, however, his remains were positively identified and a German court decided that he had been killed while trying to escape from Berlin on 2 May 1945.

BOUHLER, PHILIPP (1899–1945) Honorary **SS** general, **Reichsleiter**, and chief of the Führer's private chancellery from 1934. A wounded veteran of the First World War, Bouhler was active in the Völkisch Protection and Defense League (**DSTB**) before joining the Nazis in 1922. After participation in the **Hitler Putsch** Bouhler became the party's business manager in 1925, a post he held until 1935. In 1934 Hitler chose Bouhler to head his private chancellery to complement the functions of **Lammers** as head of the Reich Chancellery, into which Bouhler's office was eventually absorbed during the war. Bouhler found himself in constant friction with Martin **Bormann**, chief of staff under Rudolf **Hess** and after 1941 the head of the party chancellery, who succeeded in reducing Bouhler's functions primarily to processing clemency and **euthanasia** appeals and forwarding them to Hitler. It was in this capacity, however, that Bouhler succeeded in taking charge, along with Hitler's personal physician Karl **Brandt**, of the compulsory euthanasia program launched in secret under the code name **Aktion T-4** at the start of the war. Bouhler committed suicide in May 1945 to avoid capture by American troops.

BRACK, VIKTOR (1904–1948) SS colonel responsible for organizing and selecting medical personnel for the **Aktion T-4 euthanasia** program. The son of a physician, Brack was trained in economics and joined the Nazi Party and the **SS** in 1929. After joining Philipp **Bouhler**'s party management office in 1932, Brack became Bouhler's chief of staff at the Führer's chancellery in 1934, and Bouhler's deputy in 1936. In 1939 Brack took over the administrative and technical implementation of the secret Aktion T-4 euthanasia program.

Under his direction carbon monoxide gas was first used for mass killings of the disabled. In 1941 Brack provided technical expertise and euthanasia personnel to set up mobile gas vans and killing centers for the **Final Solution** in the east. Brack was sentenced to death in the doctors' trial at **Nuremberg** and executed in 1948.

BRANDT, KARL (1904–1948) SS general, **Hitler**'s accompanying physician, and commissioner for medicine and health services, 1942–1945. The son of a military officer, Brandt completed his medical studies in 1928 and joined the Nazis in 1932. In 1934 he was named Hitler's physician with the obligation of being available to Hitler at all times. With Philipp **Bouhler**, Brandt was entrusted with the task of implementing the **euthanasia** of the mentally and physically handicapped when that program was launched in secret in October 1939. As commissioner for medical and health services in 1942 Brandt was responsible not only for coordinating medical research but also for authorizing human experimentation on **concentration camp** inmates. His competencies overlapped with those of Reich health Führer Leonardi Conti (1900–1945), whose authority Brandt superseded when he was named Reich plenipotentiary for medical services in 1944. Later that year, however, Brandt was dismissed as Hitler's physician after questioning the unorthodox practices of Dr Theo Morell (1886–1948), who prescribed a variety of potent drugs for Hitler in the last stages of the war. Brandt was sentenced to death at the doctors' trial at **Nuremberg** and executed in 1948.

BRAUCHITSCH, WALTHER VON (1881–1948) Field marshal and commander-in-chief of the army from 1938 to 1941. Born into a professional military family,

Brauchitsch joined the army in 1900 and participated in the First World War as a staff officer. He was rapidly promoted in the **Reichswehr** after the war, achieving general officer rank in 1931. In February 1938 Brauchitsch was named to replace Werner von **Fritsch** as commander-in-chief of the army as **Hitler** moved to consolidate his personal control over the **Wehrmacht**. Brauchitsch was more amenable to Hitler's plans for war than the more skeptical Fritsch. Brauchitsch, however, was forced to take the blame for the failure of the German army to win a quick victory in Operation **Barbarossa**. After German setbacks in the **Battle of Moscow** in December 1941 Hitler dismissed Brauchitsch and assumed personal operational command of the army. Brauchitsch died in British captivity in 1948.

BRAUN, WERNHER VON (1912–1977) Rocket scientist responsible for the development of the **V1** and **V2** weapons. The precocious son of a minister in **Papen**'s short-lived government in 1932, Braun was trained as an engineer in Berlin and developed a lifelong fascination for space travel. He joined the experimental rocket program of the army's weapons office in 1932 and was named to head the army's rocket research facility at **Peenemünde** on the Baltic Sea in 1937 under the command of General Walter Dornberger (1895–1980). Under Braun's direction army technicians developed the first prototype of a ballistic missile with a range of 11 miles in 1938. After the successful testing of a V2 missile in October 1942, **Hitler** ordered mass production of this secret "reprisal" weapon. To escape Allied air raids elaborate facilities for the production of missiles were constructed in a mountainside in Thuringia. **Concentration camp** inmates were forced to labor in these facilities under inhuman conditions. The V2 weapon was first used against London in September 1944. Attacks continued until the launching sites in Belgium and Holland were captured by Allied forces. Braun and about a hundred members of his technical team were captured by American troops at the end of the war and brought to the US to provide their expertise to the American missile and space programs. Braun became a US citizen in 1955 and played a leading role in the Apollo project that successfully landed a man on the moon in 1969. In 1970 Braun reached the pinnacle of his career as planning chief for the National Aeronautics and Space Administration.

BRÜNING, HEINRICH (1885–1970) German chancellor from 1930 to 1932. The son of a Westphalian Catholic industrialist, Brüning served as a company commander in the First World War. From 1920 to 1930 he served as business manager of the Catholic trade unions and was elected to the **Reichstag** in 1924. Head of the Catholic **Center Party** in 1929 and an avowed monarchist, Brüning was named chancellor after the fall of the coalition government under **SPD** leader Hermann Müller (1876–1931) in March 1930. Unable to gain legislative approval for his austerity budget intended to counter the deepening depression, Brüning dissolved the Reichstag in July 1930, called new elections, and imposed his budget by decree under provisions of Article 48 of the constitution, which granted the president temporary dictatorial powers in times of emergency. The election of September 1930 made the Nazis the second-largest party in the Reichstag behind the SPD and forced Brüning to continue governing by decree. Brüning sought to overcome the depression by reducing

government expenditures and scaling down reparations obligations, but his deflationary measures only aggravated the hardship caused by the depression. In an effort to control growing street violence Brüning prohibited the wearing of paramilitary uniforms in public in April 1932, thus effectively preventing **SA** marches and demonstrations. His refusal to bring the Nazis into the government or to cooperate with them in any way, and his investigation into the embezzlement of agricultural subsidies to east-Elbian estate owners, led **Hindenburg** to replace Brüning with **Papen** in May 1932. This marked an important waystation in the collapse of the Weimar Republic and its replacement by the Nazi dictatorship. Brüning left Germany in 1934, accepting a position on the faculty of Harvard University.

C

CANARIS, WILHELM (1887–1945) Admiral of the navy and chief of German military intelligence from 1935 to 1944. Canaris joined the navy in 1905 and commanded a U-boat in the Mediterranean during the First World War. An officer in the **Free Corps** movement after the war, Canaris participated in the **Kapp Putsch** in 1920. His rejection of the **Versailles Treaty** and the Weimar Republic, as well as his anti-communism, made him sympathetic to the Nazi movement. In 1935 he was appointed chief of counter-intelligence in the War Ministry, an office converted into chief of foreign intelligence and counter-intelligence in the newly created supreme command of the Wehrmacht (**OKW**) in 1938. In this position Canaris came to view

Hitler's preparations for war with growing concern and apparently tolerated the secret activities of his subordinate General Hans Oster's resistance circle without participating in them directly. Canaris was typical of a number of high-ranking officers who opposed Hitler's potentially ruinous course but could never make up their minds to take decisive action against him. After Oster's dismissal in April 1943 Canaris came under increasing surveillance, and in February 1944 he was dismissed and his office was absorbed by the **SS** into the Reich Security Main Office (**RSHA**). Although Canaris was not directly involved in the 20 July plot, his contacts to **Beck** and the discovery of incriminating documents in counter-intelligence office files led to his arrest in August 1944. He, Oster, and the theologian Dietrich **Bonhoeffer** were killed at **Flossenbürg** in April 1945.

D

DALUEGE, KURT (1897–1946) SS general, **Himmler**'s deputy as chief of the German police 1936, and **Heydrich**'s successor as deputy protector of Bohemia and Moravia, 1942–1943. Severely wounded in the First World War, Daluege joined the **Free Corps** movement after the war. He joined the Nazis in 1923, serving as **Hitler**'s representative in Berlin at the time of the **Hitler Putsch**. From 1926 to 1928 Daluege was chief of the **SA** in Berlin, and in 1930 he helped to restore party control over the SA in the wake of the rebellion of deputy SA leader Walter Stennes (1895–1973), who resisted Hitler's strategy of gaining power by electoral politics. In 1932 Daluege was elected to the Prussian parliament and in 1933 to the **Reichstag**. After Hitler's takeover he became police chief in Prussia in 1933. A member of the **SS** since 1928, Daluege played a leading part in purging **Röhm** and other SA leaders in 1934. In 1936 he became Himmler's deputy chief of police for the Reich and head of the order police (combining all municipal and special police forces). In that capacity Daluege played a leading role in the organization of the SS police state in Germany. After **Heydrich**'s assassination in 1942, Daluege took over as Reich protector of Bohemia and Moravia, where he was responsible for savage reprisals, including the killing of all the male residents of the Czech village of **Lidice** on 9–10 June 1942. Daluege was sentenced to death and executed in Prague in 1946.

DARRÉ, RICHARD WALTHER (1895–1953) Reich farm leader from 1933 to 1945 and minister of food and agriculture from 1933 to 1942. Born into a German-Argentinian merchant family, Darré was schooled in Germany and served as an officer in the First World War. After the war he earned a degree in agronomics and livestock breeding. He served as an agricultural advisor on the staff of the German legation in Riga, Latvia, in the late 1920s. Here he became convinced that the solution to the problems of rural decay and foreign threats lay in a revival of rural **Nordic** values and Nordic blood. He set forth his program in two influential tracts, *The Peasantry as the Source of Life of the German Race* (1929) and *The New Nobility of Blood and Soil* (1930). Through membership in the *völkisch* agrarian youth organization Artamanen, Darré had made the acquaintance of Heinrich **Himmler**, whose views overlapped with Darré's in many respects. Darré joined the Nazi Party in 1930 as head of the party's agricultural section and helped to draw up the party's agricultural program. From 1931 to 1938 he also headed the Racial and Settlement Main Office in the SS. After Hitler's assumption of power Darré was named Reich farm leader and in June 1933 **Hugenberg**'s successor as Reich minister of food and agriculture. Darré also headed the Reichsnährstand (Reich Food Estate), the Nazi organization that absorbed all agricultural interest groups and controlled all agricultural production, processing, and marketing. Darré sought to implement his ideological goals in the **Hereditary Farm Law** of September 1933, which sought to maintain small farmsteads by prohibiting their division, mortgaging, or sale. The practical results of this legislation, however, were to dampen agricultural production without raising farmers' standard of living or slowing migration from the countryside. For this reason Darré increasingly lost influence and authority, not only to **Göring** as head of the **Four-Year-Plan** but also to his own more practical and efficient subordinate Herbert **Backe**, who assumed Darré's duties in 1942. Darré was sentenced to prison at **Nuremberg** for sponsoring German settlements in Poland, but was released in 1950.

DIELS, RUDOLF (1900–1957) Founder and first head of the Prussian **Gestapo**, 1933–1934. A veteran of the First World War, Diels was trained in the law and joined the Prussian interior ministry in 1930 while it was still under **SPD** control. In August 1932 he was promoted to head of the political police in Prussia, responsible for combating the communist movement. In April 1933, after the Nazi takeover, **Göring** appointed him to head the newly created Gestapo (secret police), formed from the Prussian political police office. Here Diels led the crackdown on communists and leftists while at the same time attempting to contain the extra-legal violence of the **SA**, some of whose members were deputized as police officers. When **Himmler** gained control over the Prussian police in 1934, the Gestapo was incorporated into the SS under **Heydrich** and its reach extended nationwide. Diels was transferred to head the municipal government in Cologne in 1934 and in Hannover in 1936. He was briefly arrested after the failure of the 20 July plot, but freed through his connections to Göring into whose family he had married. After testifying at **Nuremberg** for the prosecution, Diels wrote his self-justifying memoirs *Lucifer ante portas* and worked in the West German interior ministry until 1953. He was killed in a hunting accident in 1957.

DIETRICH, OTTO (1897–1952) SS general, Reich press chief of the Nazi Party (1931–1945) and press chief of the Nazi government (1937–1945). A decorated veteran of the First World War, Dietrich received a doctorate in political science in 1921 and pursued a career as a journalist, becoming an editor of the *Essener Nationalzeitung*. He joined the Nazi Party in 1929 and the SS in 1932. As the party's press chief in 1931, Dietrich generated publicity for the Nazis and helped to organize Nazi election campaigns. After the Nazi takeover he headed the Reich Press Association and the press chamber in the Reich Chamber of Culture, playing a leading role in the regimentation of the press. In 1937 he became permanent secretary in the Ministry of Propaganda and replaced **Funk** as the government's press chief in 1938. In 1940 he began issuing daily directives to the press. Dietrich was also active as a publicist, authoring a number of propagandistic books that celebrated **Hitler**, Nazism, and the German victory in

Poland. At **Nuremberg** he was sentenced to a seven-year term in 1949 but was released in 1950. His self-serving memoirs, *Twelve Years with Hitler*, were published posthumously. While they must be used with caution, they also contain much first-hand information on the jurisdictional struggles among leading Nazis.

DIETRICH, SEPP (JOSEPH) (1892–1966) SS general and commander of the Sixth SS Army. A decorated veteran of the First World War, Dietrich was a member of the Bavarian police from 1919 to 1927. As a member of Bund Oberland, a Bavarian paramilitary organization that started as a **free corps** in 1919, Dietrich took part in the **Hitler Putsch** in 1923. He joined the Nazi Party and the **SS** in 1928, taking over command of the SS unit that served as **Hitler**'s personal bodyguard. In 1930 Dietrich was elected to the **Reichstag** as a Nazi deputy from lower Bavaria. As commander of the Leibstandarte-SS Adolf Hitler, an elite regiment formed in 1933, Dietrich played a leading role in the execution of Ernst **Röhm** and other **SA** leaders in June 1934. Dietrich's reputation for loyalty, ruthlessness, and courage led to his rapid promotion in the **Waffen-SS**, into which the Adolf Hitler regiment was incorporated. He commanded an SS division on the eastern front from 1941 to 1943, took command of an SS tank corps in Normandy in 1944, and commanded an SS army in the **Battle of the Bulge** in December 1944 and in Hungary and Austria in 1945. In 1946 a US military court sentenced Dietrich to life imprisonment for his role in the execution of American prisoners of war at Malmédy in Belgium during the Battle of the Bulge. The sentence was commuted to 25 years, and Dietrich was released from prison in 1955 on the recommendation of a joint Allied–German clemency board. He was arrested by West German authorities in 1956 for his role in the **Röhm Purge**, but again released in February 1959. Thereafter Dietrich applied his energies on behalf of **HIAG**, a West German support group for SS veterans and former Nazis.

DÖNITZ, KARL (1891–1980) Grand admiral and last leader of the **Third Reich**, appointed by **Hitler** as Reich president and commander-in-chief of the armed forces on 30 April 1945. It was left to Dönitz to negotiate the German surrender on 7 May after futile efforts to make a separate peace with the Western Allies and continue the war in the east. Dönitz was convicted at **Nuremberg** for "crimes against peace" and served a ten-year term. Dönitz joined the German navy in 1910, served as a submarine officer in the First World War, and continued his naval career in the Weimar Republic despite his hostility to the republican regime. An ardent advocate for an expanded submarine fleet, he was appointed to command the new submarine program launched by the Nazis in defiance of the **Versailles Treaty** in September 1935. It was under Dönitz's command that the temporarily successful strategy of operating in "wolf packs" to prey on Allied shipping was implemented during the war. Unconditionally loyal to Hitler, Dönitz was appointed to succeed Erich **Raeder** as commander-in-chief of the navy in January 1943. By November 1943, however, Allied successes in tracking down German submarines with the use of radar forced Dönitz to withdraw his fleet from the Atlantic. Defeats in the naval war did not shake Dönitz's confidence in or admiration for the Führer. As late as 1944 he supported the indoctrination of the officer corps with Nazi ideology. It was this fanatical loyalty that led Hitler to choose him as his successor. In that capacity Dönitz helped to establish the apologetic narrative adopted by German military leaders after the war. His condemnation of Nazi ideology and denial of any personal responsibility for or knowledge of Nazi atrocities while retaining a key element of the Nazi world-view – the crusade against communism – as the ultimate justification of Germany's role in the Second World War helped to facilitate West German integration into the cold war alliance against the Soviet Union in the 1950s.

DORPMÜLLER, JULIUS HEINRICH (1869– 1945) Reich minister of transportation from 1937 to 1945. A trained engineer who spent a decade between 1907 and 1917 with the Chinese state railroad system, Dorpmüller returned to Germany at the end of the First World War. From 1926 to 1945 he was director-general of the German *Reichsbahn*. In 1933 he was named chairman of the commission overseeing the construction of the Autobahn. In 1937 Dorpmüller became minister of transportation, succeeding Paul von Eltz-Rübenach (1875–1943) who had held that position since his original appointment by **Papen** in 1932. Dorpmüller died in early June 1945. As the leading German transportation official he bore formal responsibility for providing the means to transport millions of Jews to the extermination camps in the east.

E

EICHMANN, ADOLF (1906–1962) Head of the "Jewish desk" of the **Gestapo** at the Reich Main Security Office (**RSHA**) and chief organizer of the deportation of over three million Jews from German-controlled Europe to the killing centers of the "**final solution.**" Eichmann first joined the Austrian Nazi Party in 1932 and the **SS** after moving to Bavaria in 1933. In 1934 he was assigned to the Jewish Department of the SS Security Service (**SD**) in Berlin. His special area of expertise was Zionism, and in 1937 he briefly negotiated with Zionist officials in Palestine to explore the possibility of increasing Jewish emigration from Nazi Germany. Eichmann established the Central Office for Jewish Emigration in Vienna in August 1938, five months after the *Anschluss*, in order to force the pace of emigration. His office became a model for similar offices in Berlin and in Prague after the occupation of Czechoslovakia in March 1939. In October 1939 Eichmann was put in charge of Jewish emigration throughout the **Reich**, and after the outbreak of war he extended his operations into Poland. In December 1939 Eichmann was transferred to the newly created **RSHA**, serving in the rank of Lieutenant-colonel of the SS as head of the department in charge of all Jewish affairs from 1941 to 1944. In July 1941 he was instructed by Reinhard **Heydrich** to submit an overall plan for the implementation of a "desired final solution of the Jewish question." Eichmann's department organized, managed, and scheduled the deportation of Jews to the killing centers in Eastern Europe. Eichmann provided the demographic and bureaucratic expertise at the **Wannsee Conference** convened in early 1942 to implement the program to annihilate European Jewry. After the Nazi overthrow of the Hungarian government in March 1944 Eichmann played a hands-on role as head of a special detachment dispatched to Budapest to coordinate the "final solution" in Hungary. After the war Eichmann managed to escape his American captors and lived under an assumed name in Argentina from 1946 to 1960. On 11 May 1960 he was captured by Israeli agents and transported to Jerusalem, where he was tried, convicted, and executed in 1962. The quintessential *Schreibtischmörder* (desk-bound perpetrator), Eichmann exemplified Hannah **Arendt**'s concept of "the banality of evil."

EICKE, THEODOR (1892–1943) SS general, commandant at **Dachau**, and inspector of **concentration camps**. A decorated war veteran, Eicke was forced to leave police service in 1923 because of anti-republican activities, but was hired by I. G. Farben as their security specialist from 1923 to 1932. He joined the Nazi Party and the **SA** in 1928, transferring to the **SS** in 1930. Eicke fled to Italy in 1932 to escape a prison sentence for right-wing terrorism, but returned to Germany after **Hitler**'s accession to power. In June 1933 Eicke was named as commandant of the Dachau concentration camp and in April 1934 was promoted by **Himmler** to inspector of concentration camps and chief of the SS **Death's Head units** that provided the camp guards. The brutal methods first adopted by Eicke at Dachau became paradigmatic and obligatory for the entire camp system. In 1939 Eicke commanded the Death's Head division of the **Waffen-SS**, notorious for its ruthlessness and unconditional obedience. Eicke was killed in a plane crash on a reconnaissance mission on the eastern front in February 1943.

F

FAULHABER, MICHAEL (1869–1952) Archbishop of Munich 1917 to 1952. Faulhaber entered the priesthood in 1892, was named archbishop of Munich in 1917, and raised to the rank of cardinal in 1921. As a convinced monarchist he was critical of the **Weimar Republic** and ambivalent toward Nazism after 1933. In this his attitude was representative of the Catholic Church hierarchy, which condemned Nazi racial doctrine in the early 1930s but accepted the legitimacy of **Hitler**'s government and concluded a **Concordat** with that government in 1933, renouncing all Catholic political opposition to the regime. In December 1933, however, Faulhaber denounced racial hatred and stressed the Jewish origins of Christianity in his so-called Advent sermons. In the years that followed he protested against Nazi violations of the Concordat and met with Hitler in 1936 in an effort to defend Church interests. He participated in drawing up the papal encyclical "With Burning Anxiety" in 1937, but offered a thanksgiving mass to celebrate Hitler's survival of an assassination attempt by the Munich carpenter Georg Elser (1903–1945) in November 1939. Faulhaber protested against the Nazis' secret **euthanasia** program, but remained loyal to what he regarded as God-given secular authority; he failed to protest the murder of the Jews.

FEDER, GOTTFRIED (1883–1941) Early Nazi economics expert without influence in the **Third Reich**. A Bavarian engineer, Feder was an early member of the **NSDAP** who advocated "breaking the interest slavery" of international capitalism, a phrase included in the original 25-point

Nazi program in 1920. Feder represented the "anti-capitalist" wing of the Nazi Party whose influence declined after **Hitler** assumed full control of the party in 1926 and definitively ended after the ousting of Gregor **Strasser** in 1932. Feder nonetheless fulfilled a valuable function for the Nazis before 1933 by helping to secure the Nazis' disgruntled lower-middle-class constituency, many of whom were attracted to the party by Feder's eccentric economic ideas. In 1933 Feder received only a subordinate position in the Economics Ministry, from which he was soon dismissed by **Schacht**. In 1936 Feder was relegated to an economics professorship at the Technical University in Berlin.

FISCHER, EUGEN (1874–1967) Director of the state- and industry-financed Kaiser Wilhelm Institute for Anthropology, Human Genetics, and Eugenics (one of several institutes of the Kaiser Wilhelm Society devoted mainly to research in the natural sciences) from 1927 until his retirement in 1942. An anthropologist and proponent of **racial hygiene**, Fischer was co-author (with Erwin Bauer and Fritz **Lenz**) of the influential text, *Human Heredity and Racial Hygiene*, in 1921. A professor at the University of Berlin and rector from 1933 to 1935, Fischer served as judge on the Court for Hereditary Health in Berlin that approved compulsory sterilizations after the passage of the Law for the Prevention of Genetically Diseased Offspring in July 1933. A member of the Prussian Academy of Science from 1937 to 1945, Fischer was named an honorary member of the German Anthropological Society in 1952 despite his record of providing medical and biological legitimation for Nazi racial policies.

FLICK, FRIEDRICH (1883–1972) Wealthy industrialist and founder with coal baron Emil Kirdorf (1847–1938) of the United Steelworks cartel in 1926. Although not a member of the Nazi Party until 1937, Flick was a regular financial contributor to the party from 1932 and fund-raiser after 1933. As a member of the Circle of Friends of Heinrich **Himmler**, he also made regular contributions to the **SS**. Flick profited enormously from rearmament and the "**aryanization**" of Jewish businesses. During the Second World War his enterprises employed approximately 60,000 slave laborers with a high mortality rate. Sentenced by an American military court to a seven-year term in 1947, Flick was freed under an amnesty by American High Commissioner for Germany John J. McCloy (1895–1989) in 1950. Rebuilding his industrial empire in the 1950s, Flick became the richest man in Germany. In the early 1960s he refused to pay the 6.5 million marks demanded by the Conference of Jewish Material Claims against Germany as compensation for 1,300 Jewish **concentration camp** inmates used as slave laborers during the war. His name was in the news again when protests greeted an exhibit of the family's large art collection mounted by his grandson Friedrich Christian Flick in Berlin in September 2004.

FRANK, HANS (1900–1946) Leading Nazi Party jurist and governor-general of occupied Poland during the Second World War. A veteran of the First World War and of the **Free Corps** movement after the war, Frank joined the Nazi Party and took part in **Hitler's Putsch** attempt in November 1923. After completing his legal training in Munich in 1926, Frank became **Hitler's** personal lawyer and Nazi Party counsel. Frank headed the party's organization for jurists from 1928 on, served as Bavarian minister of justice from March 1933 until December 1934, and accepted the title of Reich minister without portfolio in 1934. His apparent commitment to legal norms and the primacy of law (albeit in the form of Germanic common law) led to some tensions with **Himmler** and other leading Nazis who did not wish to be bound by any law. Nonetheless, Hitler appointed Frank to head the **Generalgouvernement** in occupied Poland from the provincial capital of Cracow in 1939. Here he continued to clash in turf wars with **SS** and party rivals, particularly the SS general in charge of the police in the Generalgouvernement, Friedrich Krüger (1894–1945). Differences with the SS about questions of authority and competency did not, however, extend to opposition to the extermination of the Jews. "They must be done away with," he told his cabinet in December 1941. Although replaced by Otto **Thierack** as Reich commissioner of justice in 1942, Frank retained his position as governor-general of Poland where he oversaw the deportation and killing of the Jewish population. He was tried at **Nuremberg**, where he showed remorse for his actions and converted to Catholicism. He was executed for crimes against humanity in October 1946.

FRANK, KARL HERMANN (1898–1946) Permanent secretary in the Reich **Protectorate of Bohemia and Moravia** from 1939 to 1945, and Reich minister for Bohemia and Moravia from 1943. A Sudeten-German politician, member of the Czech parliament, and member of the SS from 1937, Frank was second in command to Konrad **Henlein** in the Sudeten Nazi Party. He was appointed deputy **Gauleiter** to Konrad Henlein after the incorporation of the Sudetenland into Germany in October 1938 and deputy to Reich Protector **Neurath** after the incorporation of Bohemia and Moravia into the **Reich** in 1939. In that capacity he also served through the successive tenures of Reinhard **Heydrich**, Kurt **Daluege**, and Wilhelm **Frick**. Under the latter it was Frank who exercised true authority and was responsible for the repression of Czechs and Jews. He was sentenced to death by a Prague court and executed in May 1946.

FRANK, WALTER (1905–1945) Leading Nazi historian who headed the newly founded Reich Institute for the History of the New Germany from 1935 until his dismissal in 1941 after the flight to England of his patron Rudolf **Hess**. Editor of the nine-volume *Researches on the Jewish Question* (1937–1944), the most notorious publication of the Reich Institute, Frank lost influence as a result of his rivalry with Alfred **Rosenberg**, who established his own anti-Semitic institute in Frankfurt. Frank committed suicide on the day of the German surrender in 1945.

FREISLER, ROLAND (1893–1945) Permanent secretary in the Reich Ministry of Justice in 1935 and president of the *Volksgerichtshof* (People's Court) from 1942 to 1945. A Russian prisoner of war from 1915 to 1920, Freisler received a law degree at Jena in 1922 and represented a *völkisch* party in municipal and regional government in Kassel and Hesse-Nassau. In 1925 he joined the Nazi Party, acting as defense attorney for party members in numerous criminal trials. In 1933 he was named to the Prussian Ministry of Justice, where he played an active role in drafting a new criminal code with racial provisions and bringing the judicial system into line with Nazi ideology. After the centralization of all judicial functions in the Reich

Ministry of Justice in 1935, Freisler became the leading official under Minister of Justice Otto **Thierack**. Freisler's ideological fanaticism made him the ideal candidate to replace Thierack as president of the *Volksgerichtshof*, the special court for "political crimes," in 1942. Under Freisler's presidency the death sentences issued by the *Volksgerichtshof* rose from 102 in 1941 to 2,097 in 1944. The principle Freisler applied in his decisions was, "How would the Führer himself judge this case?" Freisler was killed in an Allied air raid while conducting a trial in February 1945.

FRICK, WILHELM (1877–1946) Reich minister of the interior from 1933 to 1943. Trained in the law, Frick joined the Munich police department in 1904 where as head of the criminal police he protected Nazis and other right-wing extremists from prosecution in the early 1920s. At the time of **Hitler**'s putsch attempt in November 1923 he used his office to block police interference in the putsch. For his role in the **Hitler Putsch** he served four months in prison, but retained his post with the Munich police from 1926 to 1930. In May 1924 he became the first Nazi deputy elected to the **Reichstag**. From 1928 on he led the Nazi parliamentary faction. In January 1930 he became the first Nazi to hold a ministerial post in a German state. Frick became minister of the interior and education in the state of Thuringia, where the Nazis had gained enough parliamentary seats to join a governing coalition. Here he introduced measures that would be extended to the whole nation when the Nazis came to power in 1933: a purge of liberal and republican civil servants and police officers, introduction of anti-Semitic prayers in schools, prohibition of *Negerkultur* (Negro and jazz music), and creation of a chair for racial

science at the University of Jena (filled by ideologist Hans **Günther**). Forced to resign in April 1931 as a result of a parliamentary no-confidence vote, Frick devoted his energies to facilitating the Nazi takeover of power on the national level. In January 1933 he was one of only three Nazis in Hitler's first cabinet (along with Hitler and **Göring**). As minister of the interior he was responsible for quelling all political opposition and introducing **anti-Semitic** racial legislation. His value to the party, however, consisted mainly in providing quasi-legal cover for the Nazi police state. Although nominally superior to **Himmler** (until the latter's appointment as Reich minister of the interior in 1943), Frick in fact exercised no authority over the **SS** after Himmler became head of the national police in 1936. Frick's last appointment was as Reich protector of Bohemia and Moravia in August 1943, although real power was wielded by his deputy Karl Hermann **Frank**. Frick was tried, convicted, and executed at **Nuremberg** in October 1946 for crimes against humanity.

FRITSCH, WERNER VON (1880–1939) Chief of the High Command of the army from 1934 to 1938. A professional soldier from 1898, Fritsch joined the General Staff in 1911, served as a staff officer in the First World War, and was retained in the **Reichswehr** after the war. Rising rapidly in the officer ranks, Fritsch became commander of the Berlin military district in 1932 and was named by President **Hindenburg** to replace Kurt von Hammerstein-Equord (1878–1943) as chief of the Army Command in January 1934 (the position was renamed commander-in-chief of the **Wehrmacht** in May 1935). In that capacity Fritsch took part in the **Hossbach** conference in November 1937, at which

Hitler informed the commanders of the armed services about his plans for war against Czechoslovakia. Fritsch, however, expressed his reservations about a possible clash with the Western powers before the German army was ready. That may have induced Hitler to dismiss him in February 1938 on a trumped-up charge of homosexuality (a military court of honor cleared him of all charges in March 1938). Fritsch was replaced by the more amenable **Brauchitsch** in a general shake-up that also included the dismissal of Minister of War **Blomberg**, Foreign Minister **Neurath**, and about sixty senior officers. Fritsch, however, refused to join his chief of staff General **Beck** in halting Hitler's rush to war. Fritsch's attitude was typical of conservative nationalists who generally shared Nazi strategic goals while disdaining their tactics, style, and methods. Fritsch was killed in the assault on Warsaw in September 1939 after apparently deliberately exposing himself to enemy fire.

FRITZSCHE, HANS (1900–1953) Head of Radio Broadcasting in the Reich Ministry of Propaganda from 1933 to 1945. A veteran of the First World War, Fritzsche joined the Nationalist Party (**DNVP**) in 1923 and worked as an editor and journalist in the international news service of **Hugenberg**'s huge media empire. In 1932 he became the news service director for the German state broadcasting company. In May 1933 Fritzsche joined the Nazi Party and was recruited by **Goebbels** as director of the news service and later head of the press division of the newly formed Ministry of Propaganda. In this capacity Fritzsche was responsible for coordinating all news outlets in Germany and for controlling all news published or broadcast in Germany and all information released to the outside

world. In 1942 Fritzsche reached the pinnacle of his power as plenipotentiary for the political supervision of broadcasting in Greater Germany. Since 1937 Fritzsche had also become a well-known radio personality, whose seemingly balanced and objective expert commentaries on the news contributed to the credibility and effectiveness of Nazi propaganda. As the highest-ranking surviving official of the Propaganda Ministry Fritzsche was tried with the major war criminals at **Nuremberg**, but like **Speer** he expressed remorse for his role in the **Third Reich** and was able to convince the court that he had put his professional skills at the service of the regime without sharing its criminal aims or knowing of its crimes. Fritzsche was acquitted in October 1946 over Soviet objections. A **denazification** court imposed a prison sentence in 1947, but Fritzsche was released in 1950.

FUNK, WALTHER (1890–1960) Reich economics minister from 1938 to 1945, president of the **Reichsbank** from 1939, and plenipotentiary for the war economy. Born in East Prussia, Funk turned from a career as a business-oriented economic journalist to politics, joining the Nazi Party in 1931. From 1922 to 1930 he was editor-in-chief of the leading conservative market-oriented newspaper *Berliner Börsenzeitung*. His main services to the Nazis were to collect funds from **Ruhr** industrialists and to reassure the business community, some of whose members were suspicious of the economic radicalism of Gottfried **Feder**. Appointed Reich press chief in January 1933, Funk was shifted to the newly established Propaganda Ministry in March, and became vice-president of the **Reich Chamber of Culture**. From 1933 to 1938 he also held the post of press chief of the

Reich government. In January 1938 he replaced **Schacht** as the minister of economics, in effect downgrading the importance of that position as **Göring** took over control of the German economy as head of the **Four-Year Plan**. Despite his exalted titles as president of the Reichsbank, plenipotentiary for the war economy, and in 1943 member of the Central Planning Board, his decision-making roles in economic affairs were minor compared to those of Göring, **Speer**, and **Rosenberg**. At **Nuremberg** Funk was sentenced to life imprisonment, but released in 1957 due to ill health.

G

GALEN, CLEMENS AUGUST VON (1878–1946) Catholic bishop of Münster and critic of the **euthanasia** policy. A conservative nationalist, Galen signed a loyalty oath to the **Reich** constitution in 1933 and welcomed the **Concordat** in 1933 and the remilitarization of the Rhineland in 1936, but continued to express his opposition to Nazi racial doctrine, even going so far as to distribute a pamphlet in his diocese critical of **Rosenberg**'s *Myth of the Twentieth Century* in 1934. In 1937 he again defied the authorities by distributing the papal encyclical *Mit brennender Sorge*. His finest acts of defiance came in July and August 1941 when he preached three successive sermons denouncing the police state and the **Aktion T-4** euthanasia program to destroy "life unworthy of living" and filed a criminal complaint of murder with the Reich Ministry of Justice. His protests gained him popular renown as the "lion of Münster" and probably induced the Nazis to reduce the

rate and visibility of the **euthanasia** program, which nonetheless continued in secret until the end of the war. **Himmler** favored Galen's arrest, and **Bormann** even proposed his execution, but **Hitler** decided, on **Goebbels'** advice, to postpone punitive action until the end of the war for fear of losing the support of Rhineland Catholics. Galen did not issue any public protest against the "**final solution**," however. He was arrested after the collapse of the 20 July conspiracy, in which, however, he was not involved. After the war Galen protested against the harsh occupation measures imposed by the British in their zone. A month before his death Galen was raised to the rank of cardinal by Pope Pius XII.

GEHLEN, REINHART (1902–1979) Chief of Army Intelligence on the eastern front from 1942 to 1945 and head of West German intelligence until 1968. A professional soldier, Gehlen entered the military in 1920 and served in numerous staff positions, including as adjutant to army chief of staff **Halder** in 1940. In April 1942 he was appointed to head the army's intelligence service on the eastern front, achieving the rank of general in 1944. After the war Gehlen was held as a prisoner of war in the United States before being recruited by American intelligence to gain information about the Red Army. From his network of agents he created the so-called Organisation Gehlen, funded by the CIA from 1948 to 1956. It became the official West German intelligence service (BND) after Germany was allowed to rearm and join NATO in 1955. Gehlen had recruited as many as a hundred former Nazi Party members, **SS** men, and even **Gestapo** operatives for his organization, which numbered about 4,000. In the late 1960s Gehlen was accused of illegally using his service to gather domestic intelligence. Gehlen's career offers a striking example of the ready rehabilitation of Nazi officials whose services could be put to use in the cold war. In his memoirs, published in 1971, he justified the German invasion of the USSR as a necessary war against communism.

GERSTEIN, KURT (1905–1945) SS engineer in the rank of lieutenant-colonel who sought to alert the world to the Holocaust. Trained as an engineer, Gerstein joined the Nazi Party in 1933 but remained an active member of the oppositional **Confessing Church**. He lost his civil service position, was twice briefly imprisoned, and was expelled from the party in 1938. Gerstein enrolled in medical school, but after the loss of his handicapped sister-in-law in the **euthanasia** program in 1940 he decided to join the **Waffen-SS** to find out what was going on in the euthanasia centers and in the **concentration camps**. In 1941 he succeeded in gaining an appointment with the Hygienic Institute of the Waffen-SS. His responsibilities included distribution of chemical disinfectants and supervision of their use. In August 1942 he was sent to the **Operation Reinhard** camps (**Belzec, Treblinka, Sobibór**, and **Majdanek**) to deliver shipments of **Cyclon B** to the **SS** officers in charge, Odilo **Globocnik** and Christian **Wirth**. At Belzec and Treblinka Gerstein was able to see the killing operations at first hand. He reported his findings to a Swedish diplomat and a member of the Dutch underground, as well as to the Protestant leader of the Confessing Church, Otto Dibelius (1880–1967), the Catholic bishop of Berlin Konrad von **Preysing**, and the papal envoy in Berlin, but none of them acted on the information they received (although after the war they acknowledged having received it). Gerstein gave a detailed

written account of his experience in French captivity in May 1945. Shortly thereafter he was found hanged in his prison cell. The official verdict was suicide, but he may have been the victim of fellow prisoners from the SS. The accuracy of his report has been repeatedly confirmed in judicial proceedings against former SS guards.

GLOBOCNIK, ODILO (1904–1945) SS general, head of the **SS** and police for the **Lublin** district of occupied Poland, and the official in charge of **Operation Reinhard**, the extermination of the Jews of the **Generalgouvernement**. Trained as a construction engineer, Globocnik was active in Austrian radical right-wing politics after the First World War. He rejoined the Austrian Nazi Party in 1931, the SS in 1932, and became deputy **Gauleiter** of the Austrian province of Carinthia in 1933. Sentenced to prison at least four times for illegal activities with the outlawed Austrian Nazi Party, Globocnik served as a liaison official with party headquarters in Munich. After the *Anschluss* he was named Gauleiter of Vienna, but was removed from office in January 1939 for corruption and replaced by Josef Bürckel (1895–1944). Despite, or perhaps because of, his criminal background Globocnik was named by **Himmler** as SS and police leader (**SSPF**) of the **Lublin** district and promoted to general rank in November 1939. In August 1941 he became Himmler's plenipotentiary for the establishment of SS and police bases in the conquered eastern territories. Notorious for his brutality and amorality, Globocnik was assigned responsibility for implementing Operation Reinhard in May 1942. In that capacity he oversaw the killing of 1,750,000 Polish Jews at **Belzec, Treblinka**, and **Sobibór**. After the official completion of Operation Reinhard in November 1943,

Globocnik was named higher SS and police Führer (**HSSPF**) for the Adriatic region with headquarters in Trieste. He committed suicide shortly after his capture by British troops on 31 May 1945.

GOEBBELS, **JOSEPH** **(1897–1945)** Gauleiter of Berlin (1926), party Reichsleiter for propaganda (1930), Reich minister of propaganda (1933–1945), and general plenipotentiary for total war (1944). A Rhineland Catholic of working-class background, Goebbels was rejected for military service in the First World War because of a foot crippled by polio in childhood. After completing a doctorate at the University of Heidelberg he wrote a romantic novel *Michael: A German Destiny in Pages of a Diary* in 1923. Originally affiliated with Erich **Ludendorff**'s *völkisch* party, Goebbels joined the Nazi Party in 1925, initially aligning himself with Gregor Strasser's socially revolutionary northern wing. He helped to write the more socially oriented draft program that Strasser put forward in 1925. After **Hitler** successfully vetoed **Strasser**'s reform proposal in 1926 Goebbels became convinced that only Hitler had the personal charisma and political skills to lead the party to power. For his support of Hitler's leadership Goebbels was appointed **Gauleiter** of "Red Berlin" in 1926. Although temporarily banned from public speaking in 1927 for incitement to violence, Goebbels successfully applied his propagandistic skills in his newly launched party newspaper *Der Angriff* (Attack), relentlessly assailing the Weimar "system" and Jewish "sedition." In 1928 he was elected to the **Reichstag** despite his vow to use the instruments of democracy to abolish the democratic system. From 1930 he headed the propaganda section of the party, helping to create the

heroic "Führer myth" that boosted Hitler to power and augmented his popularity throughout the era of the **Third Reich**. Goebbels became Reich minister of propaganda when that office was established by the Nazis in March 1933. Here he played a leading role in the *Gleichschaltung* of the arts, radio, journalism, and publishing. Goebbels was the main speaker at the official book-burning ceremony on the campus of the University of Berlin in May 1933, designed to purge the "un-German spirit" from German culture. As head of the **Reich Chamber of Culture** Goebbels clashed with other high-ranking Nazi officials for control of ideological questions and cultural activities, including **Ley**, **Rosenberg**, and **Frick**. Goebbels also played a leading role in instigating the **Reichskristallnacht** anti-Jewish pogrom in November 1938. With a rousing speech in Berlin on the need for "total war"after the German defeat at Stalingrad in early 1943 Goebbels regained some of the influence he had lost to the **Wehrmacht**'s propaganda offices at the start of the war. In the later stages of the war he became the primary spokesman for "staying the course," despite overwhelming military reversals. Although perhaps the most fanatically loyal of the Nazi leaders, he also was more realistic and pragmatic than other leaders in developing the most effective means of rousing the public and gaining popular support for Nazi decisions. The full extent of his fanatical loyalty was displayed in the last days of the war. Although appointed by Hitler as his successor (to be followed by **Dönitz** in the event of Goebbels' death), Goebbels and his wife Magda chose to die with Hitler in the Führer's bunker. Before committing suicide they poisoned their six children to spare them from having to live in a post-Nazi world. Goebbels' multi-volume diary from

1924 to 1945 provides an invaluable source of information for historians on the motives and goals of the Nazi leadership.

GOERDELER, CARL FRIEDRICH (1884–1945) Mayor of Leipzig 1930 to 1937 and civilian leader of the conservative resistance to **Hitler**. Born into a conservative East Prussian family, Goerdeler studied law and served as an administrative official in occupied Russian territory during the First World War. In 1920 he was elected deputy mayor of Königsberg (today Kaliningrad) on the Nationalist Party (**DNVP**) ticket. Already in the 1920s Goerdeler was involved with former head of the **Reichswehr**, General Hans von Seeckt (1886–1936), in drawing up plans for a corporative authoritarian constitution that would ban political parties and labor unions and replace the Weimar constitution. In 1930 Goerdeler became mayor of Leipzig, retaining his post after the Nazi takeover in 1933. In 1931 Chancellor **Brüning** named Goerdeler as Reich commissioner of prices, a watchdog position to which he was reappointed by the Nazis in May 1934. He resigned as price commissioner the following year, however, because of his opposition to deficit financing. In April 1937 he also stepped down as mayor of Leipzig because of differences with local Nazi leaders about the removal of a monument to the Jewish composer Felix Mendelssohn from the main square in front of the city hall. As a representative of the Stuttgart-based industrial firm of Robert Bosch (1861–1942) Goerdeler undertook extensive foreign travels in 1937 and 1938 with the approval of Hermann **Göring**, the head of the **Four-Year Plan**, to whom Goerdeler submitted regular reports on German economic interests abroad. Increasingly disenchanted with Nazi rule

and worried about the prospects of war, Goerdeler established contact with generals **Beck**, **Fritsch**, **Halder**, **Witzleben**, and Georg Thomas (1890–1946), chief of the armaments office of the **OKW**, as well as conservative civilian dissidents Johannes Popitz (1884–1945), Prussian minister of finance until 1943, and Ulrich von Hassell (1881–1944), ambassador to Italy until 1938. After the start of the war he extended his contacts to include other conspirators against Hitler, including counter-intelligence official Hans-Bernd Gisevius (1904–1974), former Social Democratic union leader Wilhelm Leuschner (1890–1944), former Catholic union leader Jakob Kaiser (1888–1961), leader of the **Kreisau** Circle Helmut von **Moltke** (1907–1945), as well as leaders of the military resistance **Stauffenberg** and **Tresckow**. Goerdeler played a leading role in the planning for a post-Hitler government and was prepared to assume the post of Reich Chancellor in the event of a successful coup. His demand for a return to Germany's 1914 borders, however, had little chance of acceptance by the Allies, nor did his plans to establish a quasi-authoritarian government. Goerdeler went into hiding after the failure of the 20 July assassination attempt, but was arrested in August and condemned to death in September 1944. As the Nazis hoped to use his testimony to implicate other conspirators, his execution was postponed until February 1945. Goerdeler and his fellow conspirators were strangled in particularly gruesome fashion on meat-hooks at Berlin-Plötzensee.

GÖRING, HERMANN (1893–1946) Commander-in-chief of the **Luftwaffe**, **Hitler**'s deputy for all governmental affairs, head of the German economy from 1936, and Hitler's designated successor after the start of the war. Göring entered the army as lieutenant of the infantry eight months before the start of the First World War. Transferred to the air force as a combat pilot, he was commander of the Manfred von Richthofen fighter squadron and distinguished himself as an air ace. He was credited with shooting down 22 enemy aircraft. Discharged from military service in 1920, he was employed as a stunt pilot in Sweden before returning to Munich as a student and member of a **Free Corps** in 1922. He joined the Nazi Party in November 1922, was appointed commander of the **SA** in December of that year, and suffered a serious injury in the **Hitler Putsch** in November 1923. To escape prosecution he fled to Italy, and in 1925 to Sweden where he became temporarily addicted to morphine as a result of treatments for his injuries. Göring returned to Germany in October 1927 after charges for high treason against him were dropped. In 1928 he was elected to the **Reichstag** on the Nazi ticket. After the Nazis' strong electoral showing in July 1932 he was elected president of the Reichstag. With an aristocratic wife and contacts to high society, Göring helped to gain support for Hitler in conservative circles. On 30 January 1933 he was named to Hitler's cabinet as minister without portfolio and Prussian minister of the interior with full control over the Prussian police. In April 1933, in the course of the *Gleichschaltung* of the German states, he was appointed Prussian prime minister with full governing authority (although Hitler formally retained the title of **Reich commissioner** in Prussia). Göring played a key role in deputizing members of the SA and SS and leading the Nazis' vicious campaign of repression against the left, particularly after the **Reichstag fire**. As Reich minister

of aviation he was entrusted with the secret expansion of the Luftwaffe, becoming its commander-in-chief after Hitler's public announcement of rearmament in March 1935. Göring advanced rapidly in military rank, becoming a general field marshal at the time of the formation of the **OKW** in 1938 and Germany's highest-ranking officer, Reich marschall, after the fall of France in July 1940. Despite his lack of professional qualifications and addiction to personal enrichment, Göring was put in charge of Germany's economic and military preparations for war as plenipotentiary for the **Four-Year Plan** from 1936 until 1945. His influence waned in the later stages of the war as the Luftwaffe failed to achieve the objectives Göring had promised in the Battle of Britain, the invasion of Russia, and in the defense of the **Reich** from aerial bombardment. Göring's functions as head of the war economy were taken over by the far more competent Albert **Speer** in 1942. Göring continued, however, to indulge his taste for personal luxury in his roles as Reich forest chief, Reich hunt master, and protector of the Prussian Academy of Arts until his fall from grace in April 1945. The last straw was his request for permission to take over power from Hitler, who had decided to remain in Berlin to defend the capital. Hitler dismissed Göring from all offices and expelled him from the party. At **Nuremberg** Göring assumed the leadership of his fellow defendants, exhorting them to remain loyal to the Nazi idea. He was convicted of all four counts and sentenced to death. Two hours before his scheduled execution he committed suicide by swallowing a poison capsule that he had successfully concealed in a tube of toothpaste.

GREISER, ARTHUR (1897–1946) SS general and **Gauleiter** as well as **Reich**

commissioner for the **Wartheland** from 1939 to 1945. Wounded in the First World War, Greiser co-founded the veterans' organization **Stahlhelm** in the city of **Danzig** in 1924. He joined the Nazi Party in 1929, becoming the party's business manager in Danzig and a **Reichstag** deputy in 1930. From 1933 to 1939 he served as deputy **Gauleiter** of Danzig to Albert Forster (1902–1952). As leader of the Nazi faction in the Danzig parliament and Hermann **Rauschning**'s successor as president of the senate from 1934, Greiser helped to stir up popular demonstrations for the return of the **League of Nations**-governed city to Germany. As senator for the interior Greiser controlled the Danzig police, and with Forster he carried out the policy of *Gleichschaltung* in the city. After the start of the war Greiser became chief of the civil administration with the **Wehrmacht** in Poland and the leading Nazi official in the Polish territories incorporated into Germany as the Wartheland. Here he was responsible for the **ghettoization** of Jews in **Lodz** in 1939, the sealing of the ghetto in April 1940, the deportation of thousands of Jews and ethnic Poles into the **Generalgouvernement**, the systematic murder of Jews at **Chelmno** beginning in November 1941, and the settlement of approximately 350,000 ethnic Germans on formerly Polish land. Although at his trial after the war Greiser claimed to have only been carrying out **Hitler**'s and **Himmler**'s orders, in actual fact he frequently took the initiative in imposing ruthless Germanization policies in his domain. He also imposed repressive anti-Catholic measures, closing more than 90 percent of the churches in the Wartheland and executing or interning hundreds of Polish priests. At the end of the war he fled from his post to escape advancing Soviet troops, but was extradited to Poland and tried and executed in front of his former headquarters in Poznan in 1946.

GROSS, WALTER (1904–1945) Founder and director of the Office of Racial Policy of the Nazi Party from 1933 to 1945. Trained as a physician, Gross joined the Nazi Party in 1925, helped to found the Nazi Student League (**NSDStB**) at the University of Göttingen, and from 1932 was active in the leadership of the **NSDÄB** (National Socialist German Physicians' League). He was named honorary professor for racial science at the University of Berlin, served as a member of the **Reichstag** from 1936 to 1945, as editor of the leading Nazi journal of racial biology from 1936, as a board member of the Kaiser Wilhelm Society (the leading scientific research organization in Germany) from 1937 to 1945, as director of the Science Division of the **Amt Rosenberg** (Office for Ideology) from 1942 to 1945, and authored *The Racial and Political Preconditions for the Solution of the Jewish Problem* (1943). Gross committed suicide in Berlin shortly before the German surrender in 1945.

GUDERIAN, HEINZ (1888–1954) Four-star general and inspector-general of Germany's armored forces in 1943. An officer in the Signal Corps and the General Staff in the First World War, Guderian was retained in the **Reichswehr** after the war and posted to General Rüdiger von der Goltz's (1865–1946) **Free Corps** in Latvia, where he absorbed some of the extreme anti-communist philosophy that would henceforth dominate his views. Guderian supported **Hitler**'s rise to power and became the driving force behind the development of Germany's motorized forces after 1933. Guderian appeared at Hitler's side when German troops moved into

Vienna in 1938 and Prague in 1939. His greatest triumphs came in the **Blitzkrieg** campaigns in Poland in 1939 and in France in 1940. In December 1941, however, Guderian was dismissed for advocating the retreat of German forces in the **Battle of Moscow**. He was recalled as head of the German **Panzer** armies in February 1943, accepting a 2,000 acre estate in the **Wartheland** as a gift from Hitler for his services. After the failure of the 20 July plot, Guderian succeeded Kurt Zeitzler (1895–1963) as chief of the General Staff, issuing an order to his officers informing them that there was no future for Germany without National Socialism. As a member of a military "court of honor" he referred officers suspected of participating in the 20 July plot to the *Volksgerichtshof* rather than granting them military courts-martial. He was again dismissed by Hitler in March 1945 after unsuccessfully trying to persuade Hitler to sue for peace with the West. After the war his American captors refused to turn him over to Poland for prosecution of war crimes. Instead he was encouraged to write his memoirs, which turned into a self-serving apologia.

GÜNTHER, HANS F. K. (1891–1968) Leading propagator of Social Darwinism and racial hygiene in Germany. A veteran of the First World War and the **Free Corps** movement, Günther was trained in anthropology and biology and pursued a career as a racial publicist in the 1920s. He popularized the notion of *Aufnordung* ("Nordicizing") of the German nation by strengthening its **Nordic** elite, raising the birthrate of Nordic families, and adopting a Nordic Protestant faith to counteract the alleged racial degeneration ushered in by racial mixing and humanitarian and democratic values that fostered the survival of the weak and the sick. Author of the influential *Rassenkunde des deutschen Volkes* (Ethnology of the German People) in 1922 and its best-selling abridged version in 1929, Günther was appointed to a newly created chair in racial anthropology at the University of Jena by Wilhelm **Frick**, the Nazi interior minister of the state of Thuringia, in 1930. In 1935 Günther taught at the University of Berlin and from 1939 to 1945 at the University of Freiburg. Barred from teaching after the war, he continued to publish books calling for the *Aufartung* (upgrading of the species), denouncing the growth of "mass society," and lamenting the counter-selective forces allegedly undermining the white races in Europe.

H

HALDER, FRANZ (1884–1972) Chief of the army general staff from 1938 to 1942. Halder joined the military in 1904, served on the general staff during the First World War, and was retained in the **Reichswehr** after the war. During the Czech crisis in September 1938 he replaced Ludwig **Beck** as chief of the army general staff under the command of Walther von **Brauchitsch**. A talented military strategist, Halder was responsible for planning and leading the German campaigns against Poland, Denmark, Norway, the Benelux countries, France, the Balkan countries, and the Soviet Union. Halder came into increasing conflict with **Hitler**, however, after Hitler took over direct operational command of the army from Brauchitsch in late 1941. Halder was relieved of his duties in September 1942 just as the battle for **Stalingrad** was being joined. Despite his contacts with Beck and

Witzleben, Halder refused to join the active resistance, but was nonetheless arrested and interned after the failure of the 20 July military conspiracy against Hitler in 1944. From 1946 to 1961 Halder served as German director of the historical division of the US army in Germany, under whose auspices Halder's daily war diary was translated into English and published in 1962. It remains an important source for German military affairs during the war.

HARNACK, ARVID (1901–1942) Leader with **Schulze-Boysen** of the Communist resistance organization designated by German counterintelligence as the **Red Orchestra** (Rote Kapelle). Nephew of the famous liberal Protestant theologian Adolf von Harnack (1851–1930) and son of a well-known literary scholar, Harnack obtained a law degree and received a Rockefeller Foundation stipend to study economics at the University of Wisconsin from 1926 to 1928. Here he met and married the American Mildred Fish (1902–1943), who accepted a position as lecturer in American literature at the University of Berlin in 1931. That same year Harnack completed his doctoral dissertation on the American labor movement. After the Nazis came to power the Harnacks developed a circle of like-minded friends in government positions to prepare the ground for a post-Nazi government. Harnack himself obtained a position in the Reich Ministry of Economics and even joined the Nazi Party in 1937 to gain cover for his anti-Nazi activities. Through his cousin Ernst von Harnack (1888–1945), a member of the Social Democratic Party, he and Mildred also developed contacts with members of the **Kreisau** resistance circle. In an effort to end the war and remove the Nazi regime Harnack and Schulze-Boysen began trans-

mitting information to Soviet intelligence in 1940, including a warning of an impending German attack. Harnack was arrested in September 1942, condemned to death by the Reich Military Court, and executed at Berlin-Plötzensee in December. Mildred Harnack was first sentenced to a six-year prison term, but on Hitler's personal orders the sentence was changed to death by hanging. She was executed in February 1943.

HEIDEGGER, MARTIN (1889–1976) Influential existentialist philosopher and author of *Being and Time* (1927) who joined the Nazi Party in 1933, and as rector of Freiburg University from April 1933 until April 1934 played a leading role in the *Gleichschaltung* of German academic life. Attracted to Nazism by the humiliation of German defeat in the First World War, which he saw as the triumph of modern Western nihilism (rationalism, liberalism, commercialism, consumerism, individualism, egalitarianism, pacifism, cosmopolitanism), Heidegger grew increasingly disenchanted with Nazism when he realized that party leaders did not share his goal of bringing about a radical transformation in the Western metaphysical tradition of calculative thinking and technological control over nature and being. Although he rejected the Nazis' biological racism and imperialism, Heidegger's basic commitment to Germany's anti-Western cultural mission did not change, however. His philosophy became idyllic and quietist after the war, but Heidegger evaded taking responsibility for his involvement with National Socialism by assuming an apolitical stance. He was barred from teaching from 1945 until 1951.

HEISENBERG, WERNER (1901–1976) Director of the Kaiser Wilhelm Institute for

Physics from 1941 to 1945 and head of Germany's nuclear weapons research program. Born into an academic family, Heisenberg's political views were formed in reaction to German defeat in the First World War and the revolutionary uprising in Bavaria. A brilliant physicist whose contributions to quantum mechanics and discovery of the indeterminacy principle in 1927 earned him the Nobel Prize in physics in 1932, Heisenberg was professor at Leipzig from 1927 to 1942. Although he defended Einstein's relativity theory and theoretical physics in general against the vicious attacks of Johannes **Stark** and other Nazis, who labeled him a "white Jew," Heisenberg chose to remain in Germany and contribute his services to the German army's underfunded "uranium project" during the war. Post-war speculations that Heisenberg may have deliberately sought to block the development of a German atomic bomb appear unfounded. German research was more seriously hampered by the Nazi bias against theoretical physics as a "Jewish science." After the war Heisenberg became the director of the Max Planck Institute for Physics, the successor organization to the Kaiser Wilhelm Institute.

HEISSMEYER, AUGUST (1897–1979) SS general in charge of the NAPOLA – secondary schools for future Nazi Party leaders. A veteran of the First World War, Heissmeyer entered the Nazi Party and the **SA** in 1925, advancing temporarily to deputy **Gauleiter** of Westphalia. He transferred to the **SS** in 1930 and was elected to the **Reichstag** on the Nazi ticket in March 1933. He became chief of the SS main office until his replacement by Gottlob **Berger** after the reorganization of the SS into 12 separate main offices in 1940.

Since 1935 Heissmeyer headed the national political education institutions known by the acronyms NPEA or NAPOLA. In that position he reported directly to Reich Education Minister **Rust** and in 1940 received his own SS main office in the general consolidation of state and SS functions. Heissmeyer also served as higher SS and police Führer (**HSSPF**) for Berlin-Brandenburg. Divorced from his first wife, Heissmeyer married Nazi women's leader Gertrud **Scholz-Klink** in 1940. After the war he was classified as a "major offender" by a **denazification** court and sentenced to a three-year prison term.

HENLEIN, KONRAD (1898–1945) Founder of the Sudeten-German Party, **Gauleiter** and head of the civil government of the **Sudetenland** from May 1939, and **SS** general. A First World War veteran of the Austro-Hungarian army, Henlein founded the Sudeten-German Homeland Front (later renamed the Sudeten-German Party) after the dissolution of the Sudeten-German Nazi Party by the Czech government in 1933. Henlein's party was subsidized by the German Nazi Party and operated as a "fifth column" in Czechoslovakia. In a secret agreement with **Hitler** in March 1938 Henlein pledged to always make greater demands than the Czech government could satisfy in order to give the Nazis a pretext for war. After the annexation of the Sudetenland following the **Munich Agreement** in September 1938, Henlein was appointed Reich commissioner for the Sudetenland, and Gauleiter. Although he retained these posts until the end of the war, in reality he wielded little power after the establishment of the **Protectorate of Bohemia and Moravia** in 1939. He committed suicide in an Allied POW camp on 10 May 1945.

HESS, RUDOLF (1894–1987) Deputy Führer of the Nazi Party and minister without portfolio in the **Reich** cabinet from 1933 to 1941. Today Hess is best known for his flight to Scotland in May 1941 in an attempt to persuade Britain to make peace prior to the German invasion of the Soviet Union. Hess's main qualification for leadership was an unquestioning dedication to **Hitler** and the idea of National Socialism. His early biography is representative of many so-called *alte Kämpfer* (old fighters) who joined the Nazi Party even before Hitler's "beer-hall putsch." Hess volunteered for military service at the start of the First World War. He rose to the rank of lieutenant, received pilot training in 1918, and participated in aerial combat on the western front in the last weeks of the war. In 1919 he joined the **Free Corps** in Bavaria, became a member of the secretive nationalist **Thule Society**, and, after hearing Hitler speak, joined the Nazi Party in early January 1920 as member number 1,600. Hess studied history and geography at the University of Munich until his participation in the **Hitler Putsch** as a leader of an **SA** company in November 1923. Tried for his part in the putsch in April 1924, Hess served eight months in prison in Landsberg where he transcribed *Mein Kampf* from Hitler's dictation. From 1925 until his appointment as deputy Führer in April 1933 he acted as Hitler's private secretary and head of the Führer's party chancellery. Hess also held the rank of *Obergruppenführer* (general) in the **SS**, but no longer used that title after becoming Hitler's deputy in 1933. In 1939 Hess was named second in line after **Göring** as Hitler's successor in case of his death. Acting entirely on his own, Hess piloted a Messerschmitt fighter plane to Scotland on 10 May 1941 in an attempt to reach the residence of the Duke of Hamilton, whom he had known as a supporter of the appeasement policy in the 1930s. Arrested before he could make contact with the duke, Hess was interned in Britain throughout the war. The German government dissociated itself from Hess's effort and declared him insane. At the **Nuremberg trial** he was sentenced to life imprisonment for conspiracy to wage war and crimes against peace. Imprisoned at Berlin-Spandau, Hess attempted suicide several times before finally succeeding at the age of 92 in 1987. Hess became a martyr in the eyes of neo-Nazis who turned his burial site in Bavaria into a shrine.

HEYDE, WERNER (1902–1964) SS physician in the rank of colonel in charge of the **Aktion T-4 euthanasia** program in 1939. After completing his medical studies Heyde entered the Nazi Party in 1933 and the **SS** in 1934. A professor of psychiatry and neurology at the University of Würzburg, Heyde headed the German Association of Hospitals and Sanatoria and was deeply involved in planning compulsory euthanasia. When the Aktion T-4 program was secretly launched at the start of the war, Heyde was named as its medical director. In this capacity he was responsible for approximately 100,000 killings perpetrated by lethal injection, starvation, and carbon monoxide gas at special hospitals, including **Bernburg**, **Sonnenstein**, and **Hartheim**. Heyde also headed a mobile commando of **concentration camp** physicians who selected disabled and Jewish inmates for killing in the **Aktion 14 f 13** program that used the medical facilities and personnel of the Aktion T-4 program. Heyde escaped from captivity in 1946 and practiced medicine under an assumed name in Schleswig-Holstein, where he enjoyed the protection of key state government officials. His identity was revealed and he was arrested in

1959. He committed suicide in prison while awaiting trial in 1964.

HEYDRICH, REINHARD (1904–1942) Head of the SS Security Service (**SD**) in 1932, the German Security Police in 1936, the Reich Security Main Office (**RSHA**) in 1939, Reich protector of Bohemia and Moravia in 1941, second in command to **Himmler** in the **SS**, and leading organizer of the "**final solution**." A veteran of the **Free Corps** movement, Heydrich joined the navy in 1922 but was forced to resign his commission after jilting his fiancée in 1931. That same year he joined the **NSDAP** and the SS, participating in the organization of its intelligence and police apparatus. He worked closely with Himmler in gaining control of the Bavarian police and played a leading role in the purge of the SA in 1934. In May 1936 Heydrich was appointed as head of the German Security Police (**SIPO**), combining SD, **Gestapo**, and the criminal police. He played a leading role in organizing the anti-Jewish pogrom of November 1938. After the start of the war Heydrich was put in command of the RSHA, amalgamating all state and SS security functions. Already charged with expediting forced Jewish emigration before the war, Heydrich assumed the task of implementing the "final solution" in July1941. Known as the "blond beast," Heydrich oversaw the formation of SS *Einsatzgruppen* (death squads), the concentration of Jews in ghettos, and the murder of Soviet Jews after the start of Operation **Barbarossa**. In January 1942 Heydrich convened the **Wannsee Conference** to gain the cooperation of German ministries in the deportation and murder of Jews from German-controlled Europe. Named Reich protector of Bohemia and Moravia to replace the old-school diplomat **Neurath** in 1941, Heydrich directed the ruthless pacification of the Czech lands before his assassination by members of the Czech underground in May 1942. After his death on 4 June 1942, the Germans launched a vicious reprisal by shooting all the male inhabitants of the Czech mining village of **Lidice**. Heydrich received a lavish state funeral. In his honor the campaign to eradicate all Polish Jewry was officially renamed **Aktion Reinhard**.

HIERL, KONSTANTIN (1875–1955) Chief of the Reich Labor Service (**RAD**) from 1933, Reich labor leader in 1935, and Reich minister in 1943. A professional soldier, Hierl joined the army in 1892, served as an officer in the First World War, and commanded his own **Free Corps** in Bavaria after the end of the war. Hierl was dismissed from the **Reichswehr** in 1923 for his subversive activities as a member of **Ludendorff**'s radical right-wing *Tannenbergbund*. He joined the Nazi Party as its second-ranking organization leader in 1929, was elected to the **Reichstag** in 1930, and directed the development of the party's labor service in 1931. After **Hitler**'s takeover of power Hierl became a leading official in the Reich Ministry of Labor as **Reich commissioner** for Voluntary Labor Service. After the introduction of compulsory labor service in 1935, Hierl was given the title of Reich labor leader. The Reich Labor Service was organized in military fashion to inculcate militant nationalism, absolute obedience, and total subordination to the state and the Führer. To enhance the status of the labor service Hierl was elevated to the rank of Reich minister in 1943, no longer subordinate to Reich Minister of Labor **Seldte**. After the war Hierl was classified as a "major offender" and sentenced to a five-year term in 1949. After his release in 1950 Hierl published several books of memoirs in which he continued to defend his *völkisch* world-view.

HIMMLER, HEINRICH (1900–1945) Reichsführer of the **SS** from 1929, chief of the German police from 1936, head of the entire Nazi system of repression and terror, **Reich commissioner** for the consolidation of German ethnicity from 1939, Reich interior minister in 1943, and commander of the German reserve army in 1944. Brought up as a strict Catholic like **Goebbels**, **Heydrich**, and many other leading Nazis, Himmler volunteered for the army in 1918, too late to see combat at the front. He received a degree in agronomics in Munich in 1922 and took part in the **Hitler Putsch** as a member of Ernst **Röhm**'s paramilitary organization in 1923. He rejoined the **NSDAP** after its reestablishment in 1925 as deputy **Gauleiter** for Bavaria and deputy propaganda leader. In 1927 he managed a poultry farm in Bavaria, but failed to weather financial difficulties. Himmler helped to organize the SS in Bavaria, and in January 1929 was named its national leader. At that time still only a 280-man personal protection squad subordinate to the **SA**, the SS became a powerful elite organization under Himmler's leadership with more than 50,000 members in 1933. After **Hitler**'s accession to power, Himmler became the chief of police in Munich and head of the political police in Bavaria. It was in this capacity that he established the first **concentration camp** for political prisoners in the Munich suburb at **Dachau** in March 1933. Himmler's authority over the police was gradually extended to other states as well, including Prussia, where he was appointed **Göring**'s deputy in 1934. By 1936 Himmler had consolidated full control over all police forces throughout Germany. Himmler provided the death squads to carry

out the purge of Röhm's SA in June 1934, thereby removing a dangerous rival, freeing the SS from its nominal subordination to the SA, and allowing Himmler to construct a vast SS empire – a state within the state not subject to normal legal controls. With Walther **Darré** Himmler established the scientific research organization **Ahnenerbe** in 1935 to generate scientific evidence for German racial supremacy. That same year Himmler established the *Lebensborn* agency within the SS Race and Settlement Main Office (**RuSHA**) to encourage unmarried women to give birth to **Nordic** children. In the years that followed Himmler issued several directives instructing SS members to father at least four children with Nordic women. He assured SS men leaving for the front in 1939 that any children left behind would be cared for. The military arm of the SS was officially named the **Waffen-SS** in 1940.

Himmler established strict racial criteria for membership in the SS, including proof of "**Aryan**" ancestry for at least three generations. The so-called **Death's Head** units of the SS served as guards for Himmler's expanding concentration camp system. After the start of the war Himmler took charge of the population resettlement and Germanization programs in the conquered areas of Poland and the Soviet Union. As commissioner for the consolidation of German ethnicity, Himmler commissioned and approved the notorious **General Plan for the East**, which called for massive population transfers in Eastern Europe that were expected to entail at least 30 million deaths. Himmler authorized the murders carried out by shooting by the *Einsatzgruppen* in the Soviet Union. To combat his executioners' disaffection and increase their productivity Himmler ordered the establishment of gassing facilities as an allegedly more efficient and humane way of killing. In a notorious speech to SS leaders in Poznan in 1943 Himmler described the **Holocaust** as a glorious chapter of German history, albeit one that would never be recorded in writing. In that same speech he praised his minions for their idealism and ruthlessness in carrying out the mass murder of the Jews while still retaining their "decency" in abstaining from petty theft. Although already exercising power second only to Hitler's in the **Reich**, Himmler was formally named Reich minister of the interior to replace the less unscrupulous **Frick** in 1943. After the failure of the 20 July plot against Hitler in 1944, Himmler took over command of the reserve army, the institutional base of many the leading conspirators. Although coldly efficient in overseeing the **Final Solution** and suppressing all forms of dissent, Himmler pursued the fantasy of a negotiated settlement with the Western powers at the end of the war. Hoping to use the few surviving Jewish captives as hostages in negotiations, he tried to persuade the Allies to continue the war against the USSR on Germany's side. For his attempts to come to some arrangement with the Western Allies he was stripped by Hitler of all his offices in late April 1945. After trying to escape detection under an assumed identity at the end of the war, Himmler was captured by British forces in the disguise of a common soldier and committed suicide on 23 May 1945.

HINDENBURG, PAUL VON (1847–1934)
Field marshal and Reich president, 1925 to 1934. Wounded as a young Prussian lieutenant in the Austro-Prussian war of 1866, Hindenburg commanded enormous respect and prestige in Germany in the 1920s and 1930, not only as former chief of the German High Command in the First World War but also as one of the last active surviving veterans of Germany's wars of unification. With his chief of staff Erich **Ludendorff**, Hindenburg exercised virtually dictatorial control over Germany from 1916 to 1918 and emerged from the war as a national hero. A member of an ancient east-Elbian estate-owning family and a lifelong monarchist, Hindenburg was elected president of the **Weimar Republic** to succeed Social Democrat Friedrich Ebert (1871–1925) in 1925. Hindenburg's election reflected the shift to the right and the growing strength of anti-democratic forces in the late years of the Weimar era. Although the presidency was a largely ceremonial position, the Weimar constitution did give the president the authority to suspend the **Reichstag** and rule by decree in times of emergency. In 1930 this article of the constitution was invoked to give chancellors **Brüning**, **Papen**, and **Schleicher** authority to rule by decree and effectively suspend parliamentary process. Like many members of Germany's economic, bureaucratic, and military elites Hindenburg disdained the Nazi Party leaders as social inferiors lacking the qualifications for high office, but he shared their goals of creating an authoritarian state and restoring German military power. In April 1932, at the age of 84, Hindenburg reluctantly agreed to run for reelection as president of the republic to block **Hitler** from gaining that office. After defeating Hitler in a run-off election, however, Hindenburg replaced Brüning with Papen as chancellor in a bid to reduce the influence of the republican parties, especially the Social Democrats (**SPD**), and to court Nazi support for a conservative nationalist restoration without turning full power over to the Nazis. This strategy backfired when the Nazis won an overwhelming plurality in the Reichstag elections of July

1932. Unable to persuade Hitler to enter the government in a subordinate position, Papen and Hindenburg called another election in November 1932 in which the Nazis lost two million votes but again emerged as the strongest party. Schleicher made one more unsuccessful attempt to entice the Nazis into the government under his chancellorship in December 1932 before Hindenburg finally relented in his opposition to a Nazi-led government. Pressured by industrial, agrarian, and military leaders and by his own entourage, Hindenburg gave his approval to a Hitler government with Papen as vice-chancellor in January 1933. After the passage of the **Enabling Act** in March 1933, Hitler no longer needed Hindenburg's approval to rule by decree. When Hindenburg died in August 1934 Hitler abolished the office of presidency, combining the functions of head of government and head of state in his own person as Führer. Hindenburg's last testament gave thanks for Germany's revival and called on Germans to support the Nazi regime.

HINKEL, HANS (1901–1960) SS general, business manager of the Reich Chamber of Culture, and head of the film division of the Reich Ministry of Propaganda. A member of the **Free Corps** Oberland, Hinkel joined the Nazi Party in 1921 as one of its earliest members. He worked as a journalist for various Nazi newspapers, including the *Völkischer Beobachter* in Berlin. A leading ideologue in **Rosenberg**'s *Kampfbund für die deutsche Kultur* (Combat League for German Culture), Hinkel was elected to the **Reichstag** on the Nazi slate in 1930. After the Nazi accession to power he played a leading role in the *Gleichschaltung* of German cultural institutions in the Reich Ministry of Propaganda under **Goebbels**, where he ultimately became responsible for

all matters involving the **Reich Chamber of Culture**. As Reich film director in 1944 he was given the task of filming the *Volksgerichtshof* trials of the members of the 20 July military conspiracy and their grisly executions in Berlin-Plötzensee. After the war he was imprisoned in Poland for several years before being deported to Germany in the 1950s.

HITLER, ADOLF (1889–1945) Founding leader of the Nazi Party, chancellor and Führer of the **Third Reich**, supreme commander of the armed forces, and absolute dictator of Nazi Germany. Born in the Austrian provincial town of Braunau, Hitler pursued a career as an artist in Vienna from 1908 to 1913, supporting himself by painting watercolor scenes for tourists. His rejection at the Vienna Academy of Arts may have reinforced his vehement anti-Semitism, an ideology that pervaded the right-wing political culture of the pan-German opposition to the Habsburg Empire. Here Hitler developed a fanatical hostility to Marxism, liberalism, trade unionism, and Social Democracy, and absorbed the xenophobia, intolerance of ethnic diversity, and Germanic supremacism characteristic of the *völkisch* movement in Austria-Hungary and Germany. In 1913 he emigrated to Munich where he volunteered for German military service at the start of the First World War. Though never promoted beyond the rank of corporal, he served with distinction and was awarded the Iron Cross. Wounded in a gas attack at the end of the war, Hitler, like so many of his contemporaries, was dismayed by the German surrender and the outbreak of revolution in November 1918. Convinced that Germany had been betrayed by the "inner enemy" on the left, Hitler joined one of the many *völkisch* groups that sprang up at the end of the war. He transformed the minuscule German Workers Party (**DAP**) into the National Socialist German Workers Party (**NSDAP**) in 1920. He used this party and affiliated *völkisch* organizations to launch an attempted putsch in Munich in November 1923, where the conservative Bavarian state administration had provided hospitality to anti-Weimar paramilitary groups. The plot, however, was thwarted by the failure of Bavarian government officials, and particularly the commander of the **Reichswehr**, to cooperate with the planned "march on Berlin." Hitler was tried and convicted of high treason, but served only eight months of the minimum five-year sentence required by law. After his release in 1925 he refounded the party and henceforth sought to gain power by electoral and constitutional means. In 1926 he consolidated his control over the party by rejecting a new expanded social program proposed by Gregor **Strasser**. Henceforth the *Führerprinzip* (leadership principle) prevailed in the formation of party policy. Hitler's party gained millions of votes in the Depression, becoming the largest party in Germany in July 1932 with over 37 percent of the vote. But Hitler's "all or nothing" strategy, opposed by Strasser, cost the party more than two million votes in the November 1932 elections, and the Nazi star appeared to fade. It was at this crucial juncture that traditional conservatives in the military, industry, agriculture, and state bureaucracy persuaded President **Hindenburg** to appoint Hitler chancellor on 31 January 1933.

Hitler consolidated his dictatorial power over the next one and a half years, becoming head of state and commander-in-chief of the armed forces after Hindenburg's death on 2 August 1934. German economic recovery through public works projects, deficit financing, and rearmament increased Hitler's popularity. A succession of improbable foreign policy successes, culminating in the **Munich Agreement** in 1938, gave him an aura of infallibility and a free hand to pursue his ultimate goals, already outlined in *Mein Kampf* (1925): the racial purification of the German Volk, the conquest of *Lebensraum* in the east, and German domination of Europe and eventually the globe. Faced by Britain's refusal to acquiesce in Germany's continental supremacy after the fall of France, Hitler made the decisive mistake of ordering the invasion of the Soviet Union in June 1941, contrary to his original plan not to seek continental expansion until after the end of the war in the west. The failure of the **Blitzkrieg** in Russia forced Hitler to go for broke. To stanch the continuing flow of United States aid to Britain and Russia and to fulfill his promise to Japan, Hitler declared war on the US three days after the Japanese attack on Pearl Harbor on 7 December 1941. On Hitler's orders the war in the east was fought with utmost ruthlessness. Aware that he had now burned all his bridges behind him, Hitler gave his approval in late 1941 to the "**final solution**," the program to murder all the Jews under German control. As Soviet troops closed in on Berlin, Hitler committed suicide with his new wife Eva Braun (1912–1945) in the bunker of the Reich Chancellery on 20 April 1945. In his political testament Hitler showed no remorse for his actions, denied any responsibility for the war, urged Germans not to give up the struggle, and forecast the "radiant renaissance of the National Socialist movement."

HÖSS, RUDOLF (1900–1947) Commandant of **Auschwitz**, the largest **concentration camp** and killing center of the "**final**

solution." A much-decorated veteran of the First World War and a member of the **Free Corps** movement, Höss joined the Nazi Party in 1922 and was sentenced to ten years in prison for his involvement in a right-wing vigilante murder in 1923. After his release under a general amnesty in 1928, Höss was active in a number of rural colonization projects sponsored by *völkisch* organizations in eastern Germany. He joined the **SS** in 1934 as a camp guard supervisor in **Dachau** and in 1938 was transferred to **Sachsen-hausen**. In May 1940 he was appointed commandant of the newly created camp at Auschwitz where he oversaw its expansion into a forced labor and death camp in 1941 and 1942. Höss presided over the first experimental use of **Cyclon B** gas on Soviet prisoners of war in September 1941 and its use in the murder of approximately a million Jewish victims from all over Europe from 1942 to 1944. In November 1943 he was promoted to head the concentration camp department of the SS Economics and Administration Main Office (**WVHA**), returning to Auschwitz temporarily to oversee the mass murder of Hungarian Jews in the summer of 1944. Raised as a strict Catholic, Höss considered fulfillment of duty and obedience to orders to be the highest virtues. In his memoirs written in prison after the war he prided himself in having maintained a normal family life while presiding over an efficient and "hygienic" extermination program. Along with **Eichmann**, Höss represented the prototype of the bureaucratic murderer who never participated in the actual killings and retained his self-image of personal virtue and conscientious service. He was discovered and arrested in northern Germany in March 1946 and extradited to Poland, where he was executed in April 1947 in front of the house in which he had lived with his wife and five children at Auschwitz.

HOSSBACH, FRIEDRICH (1894–1980) Hitler's personal adjutant from 1934 to 1938. A professional soldier, Hossbach served as an officer in the First World War and was retained in the **Reichswehr** after the war. He was appointed adjutant of the **Wehrmacht** to the Führer and Reich chancellor in August 1934, achieving the rank of colonel in 1937. It was in this capacity that he transcribed the minutes of **Hitler**'s November 1937 meeting with Foreign Minister **Neurath**, War Minister **Blomberg**, and the commanders of the three branches of the armed services, **Fritsch**, **Göring**, and **Raeder**, in what became known as the **Hossbach Memorandum**, a document submitted as evidence of Hitler's aggressive war plans at the **Nuremberg trials**. Hossbach lost his position as Hitler's adjutant after the dismissal of Fritsch as army commander in February 1938, but continued his military career as a staff officer, division commander, and finally as commanding general of the German Fourth Army in 1944.

HUGENBERG, ALFRED (1865–1951) Industrial tycoon, press baron, head of the Nationalist Party (DNVP) from 1928 to 1933, and minister of economics and agriculture in **Hitler**'s first cabinet. A founding member of the Pan-German League while still a student in 1890, Hugenberg became the chief executive of the giant Krupp metalworks in Essen from 1909 to 1918. After the war he acquired a media empire (including newspapers, magazines, advertising companies, and Germany's largest film producing firm, Ufa), which he used to propagate his conservative and imperialist world-view. A member of the conservative

German National People's Party from 1919, and a member of the **Reichstag** from 1920, Hugenberg took over the chairmanship of the party in 1928 and steered it in a rightward, authoritarian direction. Determined to overthrow the **Weimar** democratic system, he openly courted the Nazi Party, whose popular appeal in the Depression far exceeded that of the Nationalists. After cooperating with the Nazis in an unsuccessful attempt to defeat a national referendum on the **Young Plan** to reschedule reparations payments in 1929, Hugenberg succeeded in persuading the Nazis to join the **Harzburg Front** in 1931. His goal was to form a large nationalist movement in opposition to the **Brüning** government and the Weimar constitution. Hugenberg used his media monopoly to give the Nazis favorable publicity and respectability. Ironically, the Nazis benefited far more from this tactical alliance than Hugenberg's own party, which lost some business support as a result of its opposition to Brüning and was widely identified in the public mind with reactionary monarchism. Hugenberg joined the Hitler–**Papen** government in 1933 as minister of economics with the expectation of controlling Hitler's policies in the interests of big business. He lost his political base, however, after the wholesale defection of Nationalist Party members to the Nazis in spring 1933 and the official dissolution of his party in June of that year. Hugenberg resigned his cabinet post, but continued as a Reichstag deputy until the end of the war. Hugenberg lost control of his media holdings during the Nazi period, but was honored as an elder statesman with the Order of the Eagle. Arrested by the British in September 1946, Hugenberg was eventually exonerated by a **denazification** court in 1949 and was never held responsible for enabling the Nazis to take power.

J

JECKELN, FRIEDRICH (1895–1946) SS general and higher SS and police leader (**HSSPF**) in the occupied eastern territories from 1941. After a stint in the **Free Corps** movement, Jeckeln joined the Nazi Party and the **SS** in 1929, rising rapidly to high offices in the police and security systems. From his headquarters in Riga he presided over the murder of hundreds of thousands of Jews in his domain. He was condemned to death by a Soviet military court in February 1946 and executed on the grounds of the former Riga ghetto.

JODL, ALFRED (1890–1946) Chief of the operations staff of the Wehrmacht High Command (**OKW**) from 1939 to 1945. Born into a Bavarian military family, Jodl earned the Iron Cross in the First World War and was retained in the **Reichswehr** after the war. An admirer of **Hitler**, Jodl was entrusted with increasing responsibilities for war planning in the 1930s, becoming second in command to the chief of the OKW Wilhelm **Keitel** after the reorganization of the **Wehrmacht** command in 1938. Throughout the war he and Keitel were Hitler's closest advisors on strategy and operations. For his loyalty and achievements he was awarded the Golden Party Badge in 1943. Jodl and Hans Georg von Friedeburg (1895–1945), the last commander-in-chief of the German navy, signed Germany's surrender to the Allies at Rheims on 7 May 1945 on behalf of the **Dönitz** government. Tried as a major war criminal at **Nuremberg** after the war, Jodl defended himself by insisting that it was not the task of a military officer to judge his commander-in-chief. He was nonetheless sentenced to death and executed in October 1946. A German **denazification** court, however, exonerated him posthumously of the crimes for which he had been executed.

JOHST, HANNS (1890–1978) Author, and president of the Reich Chamber of Literature from 1935 to 1945 with the honorary rank of **SS** general. The son of a schoolteacher, Johst served in the First World War and began his literary career as a writer in the expressionist style. Although his first play had struck an anti-war theme, Johst wrote increasingly nationalistic and anti-democratic dramas after the war. His greatest success was *Schlageter*, a play based on the life of Albert Leo Schlageter (1894–1923), a German **Free Corps** fighter executed for resisting the French occupation of the **Ruhr**. Dedicated to **Hitler**, the play became a huge hit in 1933, was the most frequently performed play in the **Third Reich**, and was included as compulsory reading in secondary school texts. Although Johst did not join the party until 1932 he was active in **Rosenberg**'s *Kampfbund für deutsche Kultur* (Combat League for German Culture) from the time of its founding in 1928. A close friend of **Himmler**'s, Johst churned out propagandistic celebrations of Nazism and the SS, for which he received many honors and rapid promotion in the SS ranks. He also used his positions as artistic director of the Berlin Theater and president of the Reich Chamber for Literature to denounce fellow writers whose style deviated from conventional Nazi norms. Johst was among the high-ranking SS officers present in Poznan in 1943, when Himmler referred to the destruction of the Jews as a "page of glory that has never been written and is never to be written." Interned after the war, Johst underwent a lengthy **denazification** process that led to a temporary publishing ban but culminated in his full rehabilitation in 1955.

K

KALTENBRUNNER, ERNST (1903–1946) SS general and **Heydrich**'s successor as chief of the Reich Security Main Office (**RSHA**). Born in Austria and trained as a lawyer, Kaltenbrunner joined the Austrian Nazis and the **SS** in the early 1930s. He was disbarred from the practice of law in Austria and served two prison terms for subversive activities after the banning of the Austrian **NSDAP** in 1934, but continued clandestine preparations for the *Anschluss* in March 1938. Kaltenbrunner served as chief of security under **Seyss-Inquart**, became a member of the **Reichstag** in 1938, and took the initiative in establishing the **concentration camp of Mauthausen** near Vienna. Appointed to head the RSHA in January 1943 after Heydrich's assassination, Kaltenbrunner also incorporated the counter-intelligence office of the **OKW** into the RSHA after the dismissal of Admiral **Canaris** in February 1944. In July 1944 Kaltenbrunner played a leading role in the commission investigating the 20 July military conspiracy against **Hitler**. Although as head of the RSHA he controlled the **Gestapo**, the police, and the concentration camp system, Kaltenbrunner denied all responsibility for the **Holocaust** at the **Nuremberg trials**, claiming that he was a powerless functionary who only followed higher orders. He was hanged in October 1946.

KAUFMANN, KARL (1900–1969) SS

general and **Gauleiter** of Hamburg from 1929 to 1945. The son of a Catholic textile merchant, Kaufmann fought in the First World War and joined naval officer Hermann Ehrhardt's (1881–1971) **Free Corps**, one of the formations participating in the **Kapp Putsch** in 1920. Kaufmann joined the Nazi Party in 1921, helped to found local Nazi groups in the **Ruhr** region, and participated in the **Hitler Putsch** in Munich as a member of the **SA** in 1923. After serving a short prison term he was named by **Hitler** as Gauleiter of the **Ruhr** district in 1926 and was elected to the Prussian parliament in 1928 and the **Reichstag** in 1930. Kaufmann also edited several Nazi publications, including the *Nationalsozialistische Briefe* in 1927 and *Die Neue Front* in 1928. Originally an adherent of the **Strasser** wing of the party, he disassociated himself from Strasser in 1932. Gauleiter of Hamburg, a stronghold of the left, since 1929, Kaufmann was named **Reich commissioner** of Hamburg after Hitler's accession to power in 1933. Sentenced by a British military court to a 14-month term after the war, Kaufmann was released in 1949. Unrepentant, he was again arrested in 1953 for participating in Werner **Naumann**'s illegal organization of former Nazis, as well as in the **SS**-aid organization Bruderschaft, but was released shortly thereafter.

KEHRL, HANS (1900–1984) Industrialist and head of the planning office in the Reich Ministry of Economics 1942. Son of a cloth manufacturer in the central German city of Cottbus, Kehrl took over the family firm in 1926. As president of the regional chamber of industry and trade, Kehrl acted as economic advisor to the **Gauleiter** of Brandenburg. A member of the **Keppler** circle of "Friends of Heinrich **Himmler**,"

Kehrl contributed funds to the party and **SS**. As a leading official in the Reich Ministry of Economics Kehrl was responsible for the exploitation of raw materials from the occupied countries after the start of the war. In 1943 he became chief of planning in the Reich Ministry of Armaments and War Production under Albert Speer. Kehrl was sentenced to a 15-year term in the so-called Wilhelmstrasse trial of major civil administrators at **Nuremberg** after the war, but was amnestied in 1951.

KEITEL, WILHELM (1882–1946) Field marshal and chief of the **Wehrmacht** High Command (**OKW**) from 1938 to 1945. The son of an estate owner, Keitel joined the German army in 1902, was wounded in the First World War, and continued as a career officer in the **Reichswehr** after the war. From 1935 to 1938 Keitel headed the Armed Forces Office in the Reich War Ministry under **Blomberg**. After Blomberg's fall in 1938, which gave **Hitler** the opportunity to abolish the war ministry and assume direct command of the armed forces, Keitel became chief of the newly established OKW. His loyalty and subservience were greatly valued by Hitler who used Keitel to transmit his orders to military commanders. Keitel's obsequiousness gained him the designation *Lackeitel*, a play on the word "lackey," among fellow officers. A recipient of the Golden Party Badge in 1939, Keitel pronounced Hitler "the greatest military commander of all time" after the fall of France in 1940. Although skeptical about some of Hitler's military decisions, Keitel never contradicted his commander-in-chief and assisted in the progressive nazification of the German armed forces. He was sentenced to death at **Nuremberg** for crimes against humanity and executed in October 1946.

KEPPLER, WILHELM (1882–1960) Economic advisor and fund-raiser for **Hitler** and **Himmler** in the rank of **SS** general. The director of a chemical factory since 1921, Keppler joined the Nazi Party in 1927 and was appointed the party's economic advisor in 1931. As the organizer of the Keppler Circle of leading bankers and industrialists, including **Schacht**, **Vögler**, and the banker Kurt von Schröder (1889–1966), in whose house **Papen** and Hitler had met to agree on their "government of national concentration" in 1933, Keppler played a key role in building support for the Nazis in the business community. After Hitler's assumption of power this circle evolved into the much-larger Friends of Heinrich Himmler Circle, which channeled funds from the private sector to the party and the SS. In 1933 Keppler was named commissioner for economic questions in the Reich Chancellery with special responsibility for the procurement of raw materials, until these functions were taken over by **Göring** as plenipotentiary for the **Four-Year Plan** in 1936. As an administrator in the Foreign Ministry Keppler was entrusted with preparations for the *Anschluss*, the administration of the **Protectorate of Bohemia and Moravia**, and the integration of **Danzig** into the **Reich**. During the war his main responsibility was to oversee the administration of the industrial firms confiscated by the SS in occupied eastern areas. Keppler was sentenced to ten years in the Wilhelmstrasse trial in **Nuremberg** in 1949, but was released in 1950 and amnestied in 1951.

KERRL, HANNS (1887–1941) Reich minister for Church affairs from 1935 to 1941. Son of a Lutheran schoolteacher and a decorated veteran of the First World War, Kerrl joined the Nazi Party in 1923. Elected to the Prussian state parliament in 1928, he became its president after the Nazi electoral victory in 1932. Unable to form a majority government despite the Nazi plurality, Kerrl induced Chancellor **Papen** to oust the **SPD**-led minority government in Prussia on 20 July 1932. After **Hitler**'s rise to power Kerrl was appointed Prussian minister of justice in 1933. In 1935 he was selected to fill the newly created office of Reich minister for Church affairs. Kerrl sought to overcome the conflict between the **German Christian** faction and the **Confessing Church** by uniting the separate state churches into a single Reich Evangelical Church by administrative means, but his efforts failed to overcome the opposition of the Confessing Church to any outside intervention in Church government. Hitler was unwilling to jeopardize the unity of the *Volksgemeinschaft* and his support in the Protestant community by forcing Church leaders to submit to the government's will. Kerrl was forced to drop his scheme and accept the traditional form of Church organization. Kerrl also attempted to use his office to weaken the rights of the Catholic Church under the **Concordat**. Despite Kerrl's open sympathy for the nazified German Christians and his effort to bring the churches into the Nazi fold, Kerrl ran into opposition from Nazi radicals who rejected Kerrl's premise that Christianity and National Socialism were in principle compatible. **Bormann**, in particular, rejected the notion that Christian doctrine could ever be reconciled with Nazi ideology. The fact that no successor was named to Kerrl after his death in 1941 was a sign that leading Nazis had lost confidence in Kerrl's conciliatory policies.

KESSELRING, ALBERT (1885–1960) Chief of staff of the air force in 1936, chief of two air fleets and field marshal in 1940, and commander-in-chief of German forces in the south from 1941 to 1945. Kesselring joined the Bavarian army in 1904, served in the First World War, and was retained as an officer in the **Reichswehr** after the war. Kesselring directed the undercover expansion of the **Luftwaffe** in 1933, becoming chief of staff in 1936. After the outbreak of war Kesselring commanded air fleets in the campaigns against Poland, Holland, Belgium, and France and in the **Battle of Britain**. Named commander-in-chief of German forces on the southern front in 1941, Kesselring helped to direct **Rommel**'s campaign in North Africa, the German withdrawal from Tunisia in 1943, and Germany's defensive war in Italy from 1943 to 1945. In March 1945 he was also appointed commander-in-chief of German forces in the west to replace **Rundstedt** in Hitler's last desperate efforts to stem the Allied advance. Although Kesselring was approached by members of the military resistance in 1944, he remained loyal to the regime until the end. For his role in the murder of 355 Italian hostages in the Ardeatine caves in Italy in March 1944, and other war crimes, Kesselring was sentenced to death by a British military court in 1947. The sentence was commuted to life imprisonment, and Kesselring was released in 1952. He published his memoir *Soldat bis zum letzten Tag* (Soldier to the Last Day) in 1953, translated into English as *A Soldier's Record* in 1970.

KOCH, ERICH (1896–1986) Honorary **SS** general, **Gauleiter** of East Prussia 1928 to 1945, and **Reich commissioner** of the Ukraine from 1942 to 1944. A veteran of the First World War and the **Free Corps** movement, Koch joined the Nazi Party in 1922 and participated in the resistance to the French occupation of the **Ruhr** in 1923. As Gauleiter of East Prussia from 1928,

Koch was elected to the provincial parliament, the Königsberg city council, and in 1930 to the **Reichstag**. After the Nazis came to power he also headed the government of East Prussia. He was also active in Church affairs, supporting the **German Christians** as the elected president of the East Prussian Protestant Church synod. As commissioner for the occupied Ukraine, with his headquarters in Rovno, Koch implemented some of the most brutal policies in the entire Nazi realm, incurring the wrath of Alfred **Rosenberg**, who wanted to exploit the anti-communism of Ukrainian nationalists. Having returned to Königsberg after the liberation of the Ukraine by the Red Army in 1944, Koch refused to permit the evacuation of the civilian population in advance of the Soviet troops – though he did transfer his own staff to safety. In April 1945 he escaped to Denmark and lived under an assumed identity in northern Germany until his arrest by British forces in 1949. Extradited to Poland, he was sentenced to death in 1959 but was not executed because of ill health. He died in a Polish prison in 1986 at the age of 90.

KOCH, ILSE (1906–1967) Wife of Karl Koch (1897–1945), commandant of **Buchenwald** from 1937 to 1942. Born Ilse Köhler, Koch joined the Nazi Party in 1932, married in 1936, and bore three children. At Buchenwald she developed a reputation for cruelty. She and her husband were arrested in 1943 by Josias von Waldeck-Pyrmont (1896–1967), higher SS and police Führer (**HSSPF**) for the central German region. The charges against the Kochs were private enrichment, embezzlement of funds, and the murder of prisoners to prevent their testimony in the case. Ilse Koch was acquitted for lack of evidence in 1944, but her husband was found guilty and executed in early 1945. An American military court condemned Ilse Koch to death in the Buchenwald trial in 1947, in which she was the only female defendant. Her sentence was commuted to four years in prison in 1948. However, under the pressure of public opinion she was retried by a German court and sentenced to life imprisonment in 1951. At the **Nuremberg trials** she and her husband had been accused of having prisoners killed to make lampshades out of their skin, but these charges were never proved and are probably false. Ilse Koch committed suicide in prison in 1967.

KRIECK, ERNST (1882–1947) Nazi publicist and professor of education at the University of Heidelberg from 1934 to 1945. Krieck joined the **NSDAP** in 1932 and became the first Nazi Party member to be named rector of a German university (at the University of Frankfurt from 1933 to 1934). He also served as rector of the University of Heidelberg from 1937 to 1938. As a leading member of the **NSLB** (National Socialist Teachers' League) and various other Nazi educational organizations, he played an active role in formulating Nazi educational policy and introducing racial teachings into primary and secondary school curricula. His book *National Political Education* (1932) served as the standard Nazi pedagogical text. Krieck died in an internment camp in 1947, but was posthumously **denazified** as a "fellow traveler."

KRUPP VON BOHLEN UND HALBACH, GUSTAV (1870–1950) Industrialist and head of the Reich Association of German Industry from 1931 to 1945. Through his marriage to Bertha Krupp (1886–1967) in 1906 Gustav von Bohlen und Halbach took over the Krupp industrial works, Germany's

major arms conglomerate. Krupp played a major role in organizing the Adolf-Hitler-Spende in 1933, a huge fund contributed by German businesses to the Nazi Party. Krupp also contributed funds to the "Friends of Heinrich **Himmler**" and was named a *Wehrwirtschaftsführer* (military economy leader) in 1937. During the war the Krupp works employed approximately 100,000 slave laborers interned in camps in the **Ruhr** guarded by the **SS**, and for a time also maintained a munitions plant at **Auschwitz**. Gustav Krupp received the Golden Party Badge in 1940. Although classified by the Allies as a major war criminal, Gustav Krupp was exempted from trial because of ill health. His son Alfried Krupp von Bohlen und Halbach (1907–1967), to whom Gustav had turned over direction of the company in 1943, was prosecuted in a secondary trial at **Nuremberg** and sentenced to a 12-year term in 1948. Amnestied by American high commissioner John J. McCloy in 1951, Alfried Krupp was able to resume direction of his firm in 1953 and rebuilt his family fortune in West Germany's "economic miracle" in the 1950s. In 1959 he belatedly agreed to pay some compensation to victims of forced labor, but only to victims of Jewish origin.

L

LAMMERS, HANS-HEINRICH (1879–1962) Chief of the Reich Chancellery from 1933 to 1945. A recipient of the Iron Cross in the First World War, Lammers was trained as a lawyer and pursued a career in the civil service both before and after the war. A nationalist and conservative, Lammers joined the DNVP in 1922 but shifted to the

Nazis in 1932. In 1933 he was appointed to head the Reich Chancellery, first as permanent secretary and after 1937 with ministerial rank. In that capacity he became an indispensable link between **Hitler** and the governmental administrative apparatus. Lammers provided the bureaucratic competence and legal expertise to offset Hitler's distaste for administrative process and detail. During the war he was a member of the "committee of three" with **Bormann** and **Keitel**, whose approval was necessary for all orders and legislation submitted to Hitler for signature. His authority to control access to Hitler, however, diminished as Bormann's powers increased in the later stages of the war. Lammers' support for **Göring**'s bid to take over the functions of head of government due to Hitler's isolation in Berlin in April 1945 led to Lammers' arrest, but he was saved from execution by the arrival of Allied troops. At the **Nuremberg trial** of leading civil servants in 1949 he was sentenced to a prison term of 20 years, but was amnestied in 1951.

LANGE, HERBERT (1909–1945) Commandant of **Chelmno** extermination camp in the rank of **SS** major. After failing to complete his legal studies, Lange joined the Nazi Party and the **SA** in 1932 and the SS in 1933. Throughout the 1930s he was a member of the criminal police force. In 1940 he headed an SS *Sonderkommando* equipped with mobile gas wagons to murder thousands of disabled patients from hospitals in the newly annexed **Wartheland** in Poland. In 1941 and 1942 he was responsible for the murder of approximately 152,000 Jewish victims in mobile gas wagons at Chelmno (known to the Germans as Kulmhof). Transferred to the **Reich Security Main Office** in 1942, Lange was killed in the battle for Berlin in April 1945.

LENARD, PHILIPP (1862–1947) Physicist at the University of Heidelberg closely associated with the school of "**Aryan** physics" in the **Third Reich**. Lenard won the Nobel Prize in physics in 1905 for his experimental work with cathode rays. Embittered by German defeat in the First World War and an opponent of the **Weimar Republic**, Lenard became increasingly **anti-Semitic** and openly supported the Nazi movement in the 1920s. Denouncing Einstein's relativity theory as a form of mechanistic materialism, Lenard lent his prestige to the view that race was the determining factor in scientific innovation as in any other field of human endeavor. He believed that "Jewish physics" failed to heed the proper boundaries of scientific research by denying the existence of a higher spiritual sphere beyond material reality. Only Aryan scientists possessed the sound metaphysical perspective necessary for true scientific achievement. Lenard was a member of the board of the Kaiser Wilhelm Society from 1933 to 1945. Although acclaimed by the Nazis, Lenard's influence was greater in the ideological realm than in formulating scientific policies in practice.

LENZ, FRITZ (1887–1976) Prominent racial theorist and eugenicist. Lenz was a disciple of Alfred Ploetz (1860–1940), founder of the German Society for Racial Hygiene in 1905. The members of this society advocated **eugenic** practices to strengthen the German race in its competition with other races. From 1913 to 1933 Lenz edited the leading journal of scientific racism, *Archiv für Rassen- und Gesellschaftsbiologie*. Lenz publicized the doctrine of racial and biological determinism in the influential text *Human Heredity and Racial Hygiene*, co-authored with

Erwin Bauer (1875–1933) and Eugen Fischer in 1921. In 1923 Lenz was named to a newly established chair for **racial hygiene** at the University of Munich. From 1933 to 1945 he headed the eugenics department of the Kaiser Wilhelm Institute for Anthropology in Berlin. His works provided a justification for the so-called elimination of "life unworthy of living," a eugenic movement that under the Nazis led to the **Sterilization Law** of 1933, to the "euthanasia" of the disabled in 1939, and to the "**final solution** of the Jewish Question." After the war Lenz returned to teaching "human genetics" at the University of Göttingen from 1946 to 1953.

LEY, ROBERT (1890–1945) Leader of the **German Labor Front** (DAF) from 1933 to 1945. Ley came from a prosperous peasant background, was wounded in the First World War, and interned in a French POW camp until 1920. He joined the Nazis in 1924 after reading **Hitler**'s speech at his trial following the failed "beer hall" putsch. Ley was dismissed from his employment at the I. G. Farben works in 1928 for his Nazi activities and drunkenness (both of which led to numerous arrests and jail time). His coarse and violent demagoguery, however, had Hitler's support, and in 1930 he was elected as one of the party's **Reichstag** deputies from the Rheinland. After Gregor **Strasser**'s resignation from the party in December 1932, Ley took over his functions as **Reich** organization leader. In May 1933 Ley oversaw the Nazi takeover of the trade unions and the creation of the DAF, which under Ley's leadership became the largest Nazi organization with more than 25 million members by 1942. Its function was to foster a quiescent labor force by various programs, such as beautifying the workplace, sponsoring cultural events, and providing recreational opportunities and inexpensive consumer goods for workers. The DAF's **Strength through Joy** leisure-time organization made subsidized tours and vacations available to workers. Ley was frequently at odds with other party or government leaders, including **Rosenberg**, **Darré**, **Schacht**, and **Seldte**, particularly in jurisdictional disputes about the authority to set wages and working conditions. In 1940 Ley expanded his administrative empire to include the elite Nazi schools, the *Ordensburgs*. During the war, however, his power waned as he increasingly had to yield jurisdiction over labor matters to **Todt**, **Speer**, and **Sauckel**. At **Nuremberg** Ley was to be tried as a major war criminal, but he succeeded in committing suicide in his prison cell before the trial began.

LIEBEHENSCHEL, ARTHUR (1901–1948) Commandant of Auschwitz I and Majdanek in the rank of SS lieutenant-colonel. A professional soldier discharged from the **Reichswehr** in 1931, Liebehenschel joined the Nazi Party and the **SS** in 1932. Liebehenschel joined the **Death's Head Units** in 1934, rising in the ranks to become chief of staff to the inspector of concentration camps and chief official in the SS Economic and Administrative Main Office (WVHA) in 1940. He was appointed commandant of the Auschwitz main camp in 1943 and commandant at Majdanek in 1944. At the end of the war he was chief of the SS Main Office for Personnel. Handed over to Poland after the war, Liebehenschel was sentenced to death for crimes against humanity in 1947 and executed in Poznan in 1948.

LOHSE, HINRICH (1896–1964) Gauleiter of Schleswig-Holstein, **SA** general, and

Reich commissioner for the Ostland (Baltic States and White Russia) from 1941 to 1944. A wounded veteran of the First World War, Lohse joined the Nazi Party in 1923, became a **Gauleiter** in 1925, a member of the Prussian parliament in 1928, a **Reichstag** deputy in 1932, and Reich defense commissioner in 1939. In 1941 he was appointed Reich commissioner of the conquered Baltic states and Byelorussia, with his headquarters in the Latvian capital of Riga. Lohse questioned some aspects of the "**final solution**" in the areas under his administrative control, particularly the shooting of women and children and of Jews capable of work, but raised no further objections to the killing of Jews when told by **Rosenberg**'s Ministry for the Eastern Territories in December 1941 that economic considerations were to be ignored in the extermination program. Lohse was sentenced to a ten-year prison term by a **denazification** court in 1948 but was released in the 1951 amnesty.

LORENZ, WERNER (1891–1974) SS general in charge of the Volksdeutsche Mittelstelle (**VOMI**: Ethnic German Coordinating Office) responsible for the resettlement of ethnic Germans in Poland and other eastern territories. After serving as an officer in the First World War, Lorenz acquired property in what had become the "free city" of **Danzig** after the war. A veteran of the **Free Corps** movement, he joined the Nazi Party in 1929 and the **SS** in 1931. He served as head of the SS in the northwestern sector of Germany before his appointment to head the central office for ethnic Germans outside the **Reich** in 1937. As head of this office Lorenz was directly subordinate to Heinrich **Himmler**, who after the outbreak of war in 1939 expanded his powers as Reichsführer SS to

include the title of **Reich commissioner** for the strengthening of German Ethnicity. Lorenz was responsible for the relocation of hundreds of thousands of ethnic Germans from the Baltic states, southeastern Europe, and Poland to land and properties seized from Poles and Jews deported from the newly annexed **Wartheland** to ghettos, camps, or the **Generalgouvernement**. He was also responsible for the Germanization of Poles, especially children identified as having a sufficient proportion of **Nordic** ethnicity. Lorenz was sentenced to a 20-year term at **Nuremberg**, but was released in 1955.

LUDENDORFF, ERICH (1865–1937) Quartermaster-general of the German army in the First World War and co-leader of the **Hitler Putsch** in 1923. Son of a Pomeranian estate owner, Ludendorff joined the German army in 1881. As chief of staff under **Hindenburg** on the eastern front in 1914 he organized the German victories over the Russian army at Tannenberg and the Masurian Lakes in East Prussia. When Hindenburg became the chief of the German High Command in 1916, Ludendorff joined him as second in command. Together they dominated not only the military but also the domestic policies of the German government. Their commitment to victory at all costs prevented them from developing a successful strategy for ending the war. Instead, their decision to unleash unrestricted submarine warfare in January 1917 brought the United States into the war. The trauma of defeat led Ludendorff to join the most radical segments of the *völkisch* movement after the war. He supported the **Kapp Putsch** in 1920 and was slated to take command of the army in the government that he and **Hitler** planned to establish if their coup attempt had succeeded in 1923.

In 1925 Ludendorff was the Nazi Party candidate for the presidency of the **Weimar Republic** (won by Hindenburg), but received little more than one percent of the vote. Ludendorff served as a deputy for the Völkisch Freedom Party (a party created to replace the temporarily outlawed Nazi Party) from 1924 to 1928, but his rabid anti-Catholicism and sectarianism led to growing friction with Hitler after the latter's adoption of a pragmatic electoral strategy for gaining power. Ludendorff founded his own right-radical organization, the Tannenbergbund, in 1925 and a **Nordic** pagan religious sect in 1930, both of which were banned when Hitler came to power in 1933. Ludendorff had no public influence after 1933, but he was given a state funeral in 1937. His wife Mathilde (1877–1966) tried to carry on the Ludendorff movement in West Germany after the war, asserting that Hitler had been part of the Jewish world conspiracy. Her movement was eventually banned in 1961.

LUTZE, VICTOR (1890–1943) Chief of the **SA** to succeed Ernst **Röhm** after his purge in June 1934. A wounded veteran of the First World War, in which he served as an officer, Lutze joined the Nazis in 1922 and helped to found the volunteer corps in which the Nazi martyr Leo Schlageter (1894–1923) – killed by the French during the **Ruhr** occupation – served as a member. Lutze became an SA general and deputy **Gauleiter** of the Ruhr in 1928, a member of the **Reichstag** in 1930, and police president and *Oberpräsident* of the province of Hannover in March 1933. Lutze played an active role in the purge of Röhm, whom he replaced as leader of the SA at **Himmler**'s suggestion. However, Lutze became embittered by the SA's loss of prestige and power under his leadership

and engaged in numerous rivalries with SS leaders. He died in a car crash in May 1943.

M

MANSTEIN, ERICH VON (1887–1973) Field marshal and commander of Army Group South on the eastern front from 1942 to 1944. Born into a military family, Manstein was commissioned in 1906, served on the General Staff during the First World War, and was retained in the **Reichswehr** after the war. At the start of the Second World War, Manstein was chief of staff of Army Group South and was named its commander in 1942. Considered one of the most effective German military strategists of the war, Manstein is credited with developing the "sickel plan" used in the invasion of France and with consolidating the Ukrainian front after the German defeat at Stalingrad in January 1943. Because of disagreements with **Hitler** on strategy he was transferred to the army reserve in March 1944. Manstein refused, however, to join the military resistance despite his disillusionment with Hitler's leadership. Indeed, he shared some of the tenets of Nazi ideology, including the need to "root out the Jewish-Bolshevik system once and for all," as one of his directives put it in November 1941. Manstein also issued commands that justified Germany's harsh occupation policies. Because of the inhumane treatment of Soviet prisoners of war and the brutal murders of the *Einsatzgruppen* in the areas under his command, the Soviet Union demanded his extradition after the war. Instead, he was tried by a British military court in 1949 and sentenced to an 18-year prison term. In 1953 he was released on probation. In 1955 Manstein published his self-serving memoirs, *Lost Victories*, in which he blamed Hitler for losing a war that Germany could have won if the generals had been given a free hand. In 1956 he served as an advisor to the West German government on issues of rearmament.

MENGELE, JOSEF (1911–1979) Head physician at **Auschwitz** in charge of selection of victims for gassing. The son of a factory owner, Mengele studied medicine at Frankfurt University and joined the research staff of the newly founded Institute for Hereditary Biology and Racial Hygiene in 1934. He joined the Nazi Party in 1937 and the **SS** in 1938, serving as a medical officer in the **Waffen-SS** after the start of the war. Wounded on the eastern front, he was named chief physician at Auschwitz in 1943. Here he became notorious for his experimentation on inmates, subjecting his victims to painful procedures that often resulted in death. His particular interest was in the study of twins with special characteristics such as retarded growth, spinal curvature, or other unusual physical traits. He was also responsible for selecting for the gas chambers inmates deemed incapable of work or incapacitated by illness or exhaustion. After the war Mengele escaped from British captivity and fled via Rome to Buenos Aires with the help of falsified papers. In 1959 he became a citizen of Paraguay under a new identity. The West German government unsuccessfully sought his extradition from 1962 on. In 1979 Mengele drowned accidentally in Brazil and was buried under the name of Wolfgang Gerhard. In 1985 his body was exhumed, and a panel of forensic experts conclusively identified Mengele's remains.

MEYER, ALFRED (1891–1945) SS general, **Gauleiter** of northern Westphalia 1931, **Reichsstatthalter** of Lippe and Schaumburg-Lippe 1933, *Oberpräsident* of Westphalia 1938, and **Rosenberg**'s deputy in the Reich Ministry for the Occupied Eastern Territories 1941. A professional military officer, Meyer was wounded and decorated in the First World War. After his release from French captivity in 1920 Meyer studied law and became a mining official in Gelsenkirchen in the **Ruhr** valley. He joined the Nazi Party in 1928 and was elected to the **Reichstag** in 1930. During the war Meyer served first as chief of civil administration with the German army in the west and then joined the newly created Reich Ministry for the Occupied Territories as Rosenberg's deputy in 1941. Here he helped to implement Germany's brutal occupation and Germanization policies. Meyer committed suicide in 1945.

MEYER, KONRAD (1901–1973) As planning director for the "Reich Commissioner for the Strengthening of German Ethnicity," one of Heinrich **Himmler**'s many offices, Meyer was responsible for drawing up the **General Plan for the East (Generalplan Ost)** in 1941, which served as the basis for population resettlement schemes in the conquered territories of the Soviet Union. An agronomist by training, Meyer taught at the University of Göttingen and Berlin and was vice-president of the **DFG** (German Research Institute) from 1935 to 1937, as well as a leading member of the staff of the **Race and Settlement Main Office** of the **SS** from 1935 to 1939. He rose to the rank of brigadier-general (*Oberführer*) of the SS in 1942. Acquitted of war crimes at **Nuremberg** in 1948, Meyer returned to teaching land use planning at the University of Hannover in 1956.

MILCH, ERHARD (1892–1972) Field marshal, **Göring**'s deputy as **Reich commissioner** of German aviation in 1933, and inspector-general of the air force in 1939. The son of a naval pharmacist and a Jewish mother, Milch joined the German armed forces as an officer in 1911 and served as an aircraft pilot in the First World War. After the war he continued his career in civil aviation, becoming a member of the board of directors of the Lufthansa company in 1926. Appointed deputy Reich commissioner for aviation in 1933, Milch joined the Nazi Party and played a key role in the clandestine rebuilding of the German air force. His half-Jewish origins were no obstacle to his rapid promotion as Göring arranged for his "**aryanization**" with the notorious pronouncement, "I determine who is a Jew." Ambitious, competent, and hard-working, Milch was named inspector-general of the air force in 1939 and promoted to field marshal in 1940. After the suicide of First World War air ace General Ernst Udet (1896–1941), whom Göring had blamed for the failures of the Luftwaffe in the **Battle of Britain** and Operation **Barbarossa**, Milch took over Udet's functions as chief ordnance officer responsible for all air force armaments programs. Göring, however, opposed Milch's proposal to shift the Luftwaffe to a more defensive posture and held him responsible for the loss of control of German air space in 1943 and 1944. By early 1945 Milch had been relieved of all his duties. Sentenced by an American military court to a life sentence in 1947, Milch was released from prison in 1954.

MOLTKE, HELMUTH JAMES VON (1907–1945) Leader of the resistance group, the **Kreisau** Circle. The great-grandnephew of Field Marshal Helmuth von Moltke (1800–1891), chief of the Prussian and later German General Staff, Moltke was trained in international law. He opened a law office in Berlin in 1935, but his plan to transfer his practice to London after passing his examination for entrance to the English bar in 1938 was prevented by the outbreak of war. As an expert in international law and the rules of war Moltke was recruited by the **OKW** counter-intelligence agency under Admiral **Canaris** and General **Oster**. In 1940 Moltke organized a group of dissidents who held irregular meetings at Moltke's Silesian estate of Kreisau and at **Yorck von Wartenburg**'s Berlin apartment to plan for a post-Nazi German state. The Kreisau circle was made up of representatives from various political camps, including Moltke's fellow aristocrats Fritz-Dietlof von der Schulenburg (1902–1944), Ulrich Wilhelm Schwerin von Schwanenfeld (1902–1944), and Adam von Trott zu Solz (1909–1944), as well as the Jesuit priest Alfred Delp (1907–1945), the Protestant theologian Dietrich **Bonhoeffer**, and Social Democrats Julius Leber (1891–1945), Carlo Mierendorff (1897–1943), Theodor Haubach (1896–1945), Adolf Reichwein (1898–1944) and Wilhelm Leuschner (1890–1944). What united the conspirators was a commitment to Christian and pacifist principles and a rejection of Nazism. Although originally opposed to **Hitler**'s assassination on religious grounds, Moltke developed contacts to the military–civilian conspiracy around **Beck**, **Goerdeler**, **Stauffenberg**, and former diplomat Ulrich von Hassell (1881–1944) in 1943. Moltke was arrested in January 1944 for warning fellow dissidents Otto Carl Kiep (1886–1944) and Elisabeth von Thadden (1890–1944) that they were under **Gestapo** surveillance. The full extent of his links to the military conspiracy came out after the failure of the plot on 20 July 1944. Moltke was sentenced to death by the *Volksgerichtshof* in January 1945 and executed at Berlin-Plötzensee.

MÜLLER, HEINRICH (1900–1945?) SS general and head of the **Gestapo** (section IV of the RSHA) from 1939 to 1945. A veteran of the First World War, Müller began his career with the Bavarian police after the war, specializing in the surveillance of communists. **Heydrich** recruited him for the **SD** in 1934 because of his professional expertise and technical knowledge of the Soviet secret police. Known for his coarseness, brutality, and unscrupulousness, but also for his professional competence and doggedness, "Gestapo-Müller," as he was called, was regarded with some suspicion even within the Nazi Party. As a member of the Bavarian state police he had fostered close ties to the **Center Party** and had opposed the Nazi takeover of the police apparatus as late as 1933. He was not admitted to the party until 1939, the same year he was named by Heydrich to head the Gestapo. In this capacity Müller was one of the major officials responsible for the deportation of Jews to the extermination camps. Müller attended the **Wannsee Conference** at which the implementation of the **"final solution"** was organized. In 1943 he traveled to Italy to pressure the Italian government to cooperate more fully in the deportation of its Jews. Müller was last seen in the Führerbunker on 29 April 1945 and is believed to have been killed trying to leave Berlin, although his remains have never been identified.

MÜLLER, LUDWIG (1883–1945) Reich bishop of the Lutheran Evangelical Church from 1933 to 1935. Ordained in 1908, Müller served as a naval chaplain in the First World War and continued as a military chaplain after the war. Müller supported the conservative **German Christian** movement within the Lutheran Church, which sought to combine Christian theology with German nationalism. At the *Vaterländischer Kirchentag* (Patriotic Church Convention) in Königsberg in 1927 Müller met Hitler, who appointed him his plenipotentiary and advisor for questions regarding the **German Evangelical Church**. Buoyed by the Nazi takeover of power, the German Christians made a concerted effort to take over the Evangelical Church in 1933 by uniting the 28 regional Evangelical churches in Germany into one centralized Reich Church. This government-supported strategy appeared to have succeeded when Müller was elected Reich bishop at a national synod in September 1933 to replace Friedrich von Bodelschwingh (1877–1946), whom representatives of the regional churches had previously elected to block a German Christian takeover. Müller's triumph was short-lived, however, as more moderate pastors and theologians, led by Martin **Niemöller**, formed the **Confessing Church** to prevent the introduction of the "Führer principle" and the **"Aryan paragraph"** into the Church constitution and to defend the Church from government interference. When Müller unilaterally transferred the Evangelical youth organization into the **Hitler Youth** in December 1933, the conflict within the Church could no longer be reconciled. Although Müller did not formally resign as Reich bishop, his office was effectively stripped of its powers by the appointment of Hanns **Kerrl** as Reich minister for Church affairs in 1935.

N

NAUMANN, WERNER (1909–1982) SS general and **Hitler**'s appointee as **Goebbels**' successor as minister of propaganda. A member of the "Friends of Heinrich **Himmler**" organized by Wilhelm **Keppler** and a leading official in the Propaganda Ministry, Naumann was named Goebbels' successor in Hitler's last testament. Naumann gained notoriety after the war as a member of the Bruderschaft, an organization of former party and SS members founded in Hamburg in 1949, and as the leader of the so-called Gauleiter-Kreis, which also included Karl **Kaufmann** and former Reich student Führer Gustav Adolf Scheel (1907–1979). Naumann was briefly arrested in January 1953, but this did not prevent him from running as a candidate for the neo-Nazi Deutsche Reichspartei that same year. Nor did it impede a successful business career that culminated in the directorship of a metalworking factory in Lower Saxony.

NEBE, ARTHUR (1894–1945) SS general, head of the German criminal police (**Kripo**), *Einsatzgruppen* leader, and member of the military conspiracy against **Hitler**. A lieutenant in the First World War, Nebe joined the Prussian criminal police after the war. Opposed to Weimar democracy, Nebe joined the Nazi Party and the **SA** in 1931, acting as undercover Nazi liaison within the police. In 1933 he transferred to the **SS** and became a leading official in the Prussian secret police (**Gestapo**). In 1936 he was named head of the German criminal police with the title of Reich criminal director in 1937. With the integration of all SS police functions in the Reich Security Main Office (**RSHA**) in 1939, Nebe headed the department in charge of the criminal police and acted as technical advisor to the **Aktion T-4** program. His contacts with the anti-Hitler generals **Beck** and **Oster** may have begun as early as 1938. Nebe volunteered as a leader of one of the *Einsatzgruppen* in Russia in 1941 and was apparently persuaded by Beck and Oster to remain as leader of *Einsatzgruppe* B, which was responsible for the liquidation of more than 45,000 Jews and partisans before Nebe returned to Berlin in November 1941. Although not originally a suspect, Nebe's abandonment of his post at the RSHA on 27 July 1944 alerted investigators to his role in the 20 July plot. Captured at his hideout in Berlin in January 1945, he was sentenced to death by the *Volksgerichtshof* in March 1945. Whether Nebe's contradictory roles as a member of the resistance and as a commander of an *Einsatzgruppe* were motivated by principled opposition or cynical opportunism remains in dispute.

NEURATH, KONSTANTIN VON (1873–1956) Reich foreign minister from 1932 to 1938. The son of the court chamberlain to the king of the southwest German state of Württemberg, Neurath studied law and entered the consular and diplomatic service in 1903. Although German ambassador to Italy from 1921 to 1930 and to England from 1930 to 1932, Neurath was hostile to Weimar democracy and harbored resentments against Jewish colleagues in the foreign service. At President **Hindenburg**'s behest he was named foreign minister in **Papen**'s government in 1932 and retained his post in the **Schleicher** and **Hitler** governments that followed. Neurath was accepted into the Nazi Party in 1937 and given the honorary rank of general in the **SS**. Although Neurath supported German withdrawal from the **League of Nations** in 1933, the remilitarization of the Rhineland in 1936, and revocation of the **Versailles Treaty**, his reservations about Hitler's expansionist *Lebensraum* policies led to his replacement with Hitler's personal plenipotentiary for foreign affairs Joachim **Ribbentrop** in 1938. Neurath retained his ministerial rank without specific portfolio until the occupation of Prague in March 1939 when he was named protector of Bohemia and Moravia. He was replaced by **Heydrich** in September 1941, officially because of Neurath's age, but in fact because his occupation policies were deemed too moderate, despite the fact that he presided over the introduction of the **Nuremberg racial laws** into the former Czech republic. At the **Nuremberg trials** of major war criminals after the war Neurath was sentenced to a 15-year term, but was released in 1954 because of ill health.

NIEMÖLLER, MARTIN (1892–1984) Protestant pastor in Berlin-Dahlem and leader of the **Confessing Church**. Commander of a U-boat in the First World War, Niemöller studied theology after the war and was ordained in 1924. True to his conservative nationalist upbringing, Niemöller was critical of the Weimar Republic and initially welcomed the Nazi regime. However, he turned against the efforts of the **German Christians**, Reich Bishop **Müller**, and the Nazi regime to impose *völkisch* and anti-Semitic measures on the **German Evangelical Church**. In September 1933 he founded the Pastors' Emergency League, which evolved into the Confessing Church in 1934. After several fiery sermons as pastor of the Berlin-Dahlem parish Niemöller was sentenced to nine months in jail in July 1937 for alleged misuse of his position for political ends and defamation of Minister for Church Affairs Hanns **Kerrl**. On **Hitler**'s orders Niemöller was incarcerated throughout the war, first at **Sachsenhausen** and in 1941 at **Dachau**. Here he was imprisoned in a block with Catholic priests in an apparent effort to encourage his conversion to Catholicism and thereby demoralize his Protestant supporters in the Confessing Church. After his liberation by Allied troops he participated in drawing up a "Confession of Guilt" promulgated by Evangelical Church officials at Stuttgart in October 1945. As a peace activist after the war he coined the famous saying, later circulated in varying versions: "First they came for the Communists, but I remained silent, because I was not a Communist; then they came for the Social Democrats, but I remained silent, because I was not a Social Democrat; then they came for the trade unionists, but I remained silent, because I was not a trade unionist; then they came for the Jews, but I remained silent, because I was not a Jew. When they came for me, there was no one left to speak up."

O

OHLENDORF, OTTO (1907–1951) SS general and chief of *Einsatzgruppe* D in the Ukraine. Born into a farming family, Ohlendorf studied law and joined the Nazi Party in 1925 and the **SS** in 1926. Well educated in economics, Ohlendorf worked as a research assistant in the Institute of World Economics in Kiel in 1933 and 1934, and as a departmental head in the Institute for Applied Economics in Berlin in 1935 and 1936. In 1936 Ohlendorf became an official in the **SD**, rising to the post of chief of Section III for domestic intelligence in the Reich Security Main Office (**RSHA**) from 1939 to 1945. From May 1941 to June 1942 he was transferred to Russia as leader of the SS *Einsatzgruppe* responsible for the liquidation of partisans and Jews in southern Russia and the Ukraine. Under his command some 90,000 persons were killed, including women and children. Ohlendorf was sentenced to death at the **Nuremberg** *Einsatzgruppen* trial in 1948 and executed in 1951.

OLBRICHT, FRIEDRICH (1888–1944) Chief of the General Army Office of the Army High Command (**OKH**) in 1940, head of the Troop Replacement Office of the High Command of the Armed Forces (**OKW**) in 1943, and leading organizer of the 20 July military conspiracy against Hitler. A general staff officer in the First World War, Olbricht became chief of the Foreign Armies department in the **Reichswehr** ministry in 1926. From 1933 to 1939 Olbricht held several troop commands, receiving a decoration for his command of an infantry division in the rank of major-general in the campaign against Poland. Increasingly disenchanted with the Nazi regime after 1941, Olbricht used his post as chief of the General Army Office (responsible for the replacement of troops and *matériel* for all ground forces) to organize the military resistance, maintain contacts with civilian resistance leaders **Beck** and **Goerdeler**, and to recruit sympathetic officers for the cause, including Claus von **Stauffenberg** as his chief of staff in 1943. With Stauffenberg he reworked the plans for Operation **Valkyrie**, originally intended to enable the reserve army to suppress an internal revolt, in order to serve as a cover for an attempt to overthrow the Nazi government. This was the plan put into operation on 20 July 1944. Implementation of the plan was fatally delayed by several hours, however, as Olbricht waited to hear whether Stauffenberg's assassination attempt had succeeded before putting the plan into action. Five days earlier Olbricht had barely managed to disguise an abruptly canceled coup attempt as merely a military exercise. On 20 July the operation did not commence until Stauffenberg had returned to Berlin more than three hours after his assassination attempt. When word of **Hitler**'s survival was received in Berlin, Olbricht was unable to persuade his immediate superior Friedrich Fromm (1888– 1945), commander of the reserve army, to continue to support the coup. After the collapse of the coup attempt Olbricht, Stauffenberg, and their fellow officers Albrecht Mertz von Quirnheim (1905– 1944) and Werner von Haeften (1908– 1944) were shot by a hastily assembled firing squad in the courtyard of army headquarters in Berlin in the night of 20–21 July.

OSTER, HANS (1887–1945) Brigadier-general, chief of staff of the counter-intelligence office of the **OKW** under **Canaris** from 1941 to 1943, and a leading member of the military resistance. A professional soldier since 1907, Oster served at the front in the First World War and joined the **Reichswehr** after the war. From 1933 he served in the counter-intelligence department of the War Ministry, which was reorganized as a department of the newly established OKW in 1938. Opposed to **Hitler**'s war plans, he was already part of the incipient military resistance under General Beck at the time of the Czechoslovakian crisis in September 1938. After 1941 Oster provided the explosives for several attempts to assassinate Hitler. His efforts to shield his subordinate and fellow conspirator Hans von Dohnáyi (1902–1945), who was accused of helping Jews to escape from Germany disguised as counter-intelligence agents, led to his forced resignation in April 1943 and constant **Gestapo** surveillance. One day after the failure of the 20 July plot Oster was arrested. In April 1945 he was hanged at **Flossenbürg** with fellow conspirators Canaris and **Bonhoeffer**.

P

PAPEN, FRANZ VON (1879–1969) Chancellor of Germany in 1932 and vice-chancellor in **Hitler**'s first cabinet from 1933 until 1934. A Catholic Rhineland aristocrat who originally pursued a military career, Papen played a key role in Hitler's accession to power in 1933 and continued to serve the regime loyally after his dismissal as vice-chancellor in July 1934. Papen served as military attaché in the German embassy in Washington during the First World War, but was expelled from the US for espionage activities in 1915. He became military attaché to Mexico and later joined the staff of a Turkish army unit in Palestine. After the war he turned to politics, joining the **Center Party** in 1920, serving as its deputy in the Prussian parliament until 1932, and using his influence to steer the party to the right. Papen also exercised influence as a founding member of the right-wing Herrenclub (Gentleman's Club) in Berlin. Despite his lack of administrative experience and the opposition of his own party, Papen was named by **Hindenburg** to replace **Brüning** as chancellor on 1 June 1932. Lacking popular or parliamentary support, he failed in his mission of enticing Hitler into his government in a subordinate position, which would have given Papen a parliamentary majority and at the same time would have enabled him to control the Nazis. Papen's efforts to court Nazi cooperation by rescinding Brüning's ban on paramilitary demonstrations and ousting the **SPD** minority government in the state of Prussia on 20 July 1932 failed to persuade Hitler to support his government. On 3 December 1932 Papen was replaced as chancellor by his war minister Kurt von **Schleicher**, who had recommended Papen to Hindenburg as Brüning's replacement earlier that year. Determined to get back at Schleicher, Papen now gave in to Hitler's demands, offering to join Hitler's government as vice-chancellor in January 1933. Papen played an important role in negotiating the **Concordat** with the Vatican in July 1933. However, he had misjudged his ability to restrain Nazi extremism. His speech at Marburg University in June 1934 criticizing Nazi Party radicals and calling for a relaxation of censorship and a return to Christian values induced Hitler to launch the so-called "night of the long knives," the purge of the **SA** leadership, on 30 June 1934. The purpose of the purge of **Röhm** and other SA leaders was to mollify military leaders, but also to stifle conservative dissent by depriving conservatives of any grounds for opposing Hitler's regime. Among the victims of the blood purge was the young conservative revolutionary Edgar Jung (1894–1934), who had written Papen's Marburg speech. Papen himself was forced to resign as vice-chancellor, but continued to serve the regime as ambassador to Austria (where he prepared the ground for the *Anschluss*) and ambassador to Turkey. Despite his services in paving the way for the Nazi regime, Papen was acquitted at **Nuremberg**. He was convicted as a major offender by a **denazification** court in 1947, but the decision was overturned on appeal in 1949.

POHL, OSWALD (1892–1951) SS general and chief of the SS Main Office of Economic Administration (**WVHA**) from 1942 to 1945. A professional naval officer, Pohl joined the Nazis and the **SS** in 1929. In 1933 **Himmler** made him chief of administration in the SS Main Office with responsibility for the administration of **concentration camps** and armed SS units. In this capacity he oversaw the expansion of SS-owned and operated economic enterprises utilizing the labor of concentration camp inmates. Pohl was also a member of the "Friends of Heinrich Himmler," a group of financial backers of the SS from industrial, banking, and insurance corporations, originally organized by Wilhelm **Keppler**. The WVHA was created in early 1942 through consolidation of the SS offices of "Economics and Administration" and "Budget and Construction." Pohl was primarily responsible for implementing Himmler's policy of "destruction through labor." Pohl became one of the most powerful functionaries in the SS empire, allocating labor both to SS-run enterprises and to private industry. Some 500,000 camp prisoners are estimated to have died at forced labor. Among the projects he oversaw were the construction of **V2** weapons in underground factories at **Dora** and Nordhausen in central Germany, exploiting the labor of inmates from nearby **Buchenwald** and other camps. Pohl was sentenced to death by an American military court at **Nuremberg** and executed in June 1951.

PREYSING, KONRAD VON (1875–1950) Catholic bishop of Berlin. Descended from a Bavarian aristocratic family, Preysing was ordained in 1912 and received his doctorate in theology in 1913. As bishop of Eichstätt, the smallest Catholic diocese in Germany, in 1932, Preysing viewed the Nazi takeover with foreboding. The Nazis in turn boycotted his installation as bishop of heavily Protestant Berlin in September 1935. Preysing was critical of the German Bishops' Conference under the leadership of Cardinal Adolf Bertram (1859–1945), whose attitude toward the Nazi regime was too accommodating in Preysing's eyes. In 1937 Preysing was a member of the five-man commission that assisted Pius XI in drawing up the papal encyclical, "With Burning Anxiety." Although he shied away from public confrontation, Preysing criticized Nazi violations of the **Concordat** and supported the efforts of his subordinate, Canon Bernhard Lichtenberg (1875–1943), to help the Jewish victims of Nazi persecution. After Lichtenberg's imprisonment and death at the hands of the Nazis, Preysing continued his relief efforts. Preysing also maintained contact with several members of the **Kreisau** Circle resistance group led by Helmuth von **Moltke**. Preysing was unable, however, to persuade the Catholic Church to take a public stance against Nazi atrocities. In 1946 Preysing was elevated to the rank of cardinal.

R

RAEDER, ERICH (1876–1960) Grand admiral and commander-in-chief of the navy from 1935 to 1943. Raeder joined the navy in 1897, became chief of the central department of the Reich Naval Office in 1918, and continued his naval career in the **Reichswehr** after the war. Even before his appointment as commander-in-chief of the newly constituted German navy in 1935, Raeder supported clandestine rearmament and expansion of naval construction. Conscious of Germany's naval inferiority to Britain, Raeder favored ending the war in the west before undertaking expansion to the east, but was overruled by **Hitler**. Raeder also clashed with Hitler on naval strategy, opposing excessive reliance on submarine warfare. This led to his replacement as commander-in-chief by **Dönitz** in 1943. At **Nuremberg** Raeder was a defendant in the trial of major war criminals. Although sentenced to life imprisonment in 1946, he was released on ill-health grounds in 1955.

REICHENAU, WALTER VON (1884–1942) Field marshal and commander of Army Group South on the eastern front. The son of a career military officer, Reichenau joined the army in 1903, served on the General Staff in the First World War, and continued his career in the **Reichswehr** after the war. Welcoming the Nazi takeover of power, Reichenau became chief of staff in the Reichswehr Ministry under **Blomberg** in 1933 (renamed the **Wehrmacht** Office in March 1935). Reichenau supported the purge of the **SA** leadership in 1934, whom he suspected of wanting to supplant the army as the nation's primary fighting force, but he raised no objections to the introduction of military training for the **Waffen-SS** in 1935. Reichenau fully supported the Nazis' racial and ideological goals. While commander of the Sixth Army on the eastern front (later destroyed at Stalingrad), Reichenau issued an order to his troops calling for full understanding of the need for revenge against "subhuman Jewry." He described the major aims of the war as the destruction of "the Jewish-Bolshevistic

system" and elimination of "Asiatic influence" on European culture. Shortly after his appointment as commander of Army Group South in December 1941 Reichenau suffered a heart attack and died.

REINHARDT, FRITZ (1895–1969) Gauleiter, SA general, and state secretary in the Reich Ministry of Finance from 1933 to 1945. While pursuing training in business administration in the Latvian capital of Riga at the outbreak of the First World War in 1914, Reinhardt was interned as an enemy alien in Siberia until the end of the war. After his return to Germany he was employed as director of a trade school in his native state of Thuringia. Already a member of a *völkisch* organization before the war, Reinhardt joined the Nazi Party in 1923. In 1929 the Nazis converted the business school that Reinhardt had founded in 1924 into the official school to train prospective Nazi Party orators. From 1928 to 1930 Reinhardt was Gauleiter of the upper Bavarian district and joined the party's **propaganda** department as deputy leader in 1930. That same year he was elected to the **Reichstag**. After **Hitler**'s ascent to power Reinhardt joined the Finance Ministry as the highest-ranking civil servant under Reich Minister **Schwerin von Krosigk**, while also retaining his party functions as plenipotentiary for economic policies. Reinhardt was the finance official responsible for administering the proceeds from the valuables, including dental gold, extracted from Jewish victims before or after their murder in the extermination camps. Reinhardt was imprisoned by the Allies after the war and testified as a witness at the **Nuremberg trials**, but was released in 1949. He was, however, classified as a "major offender" by a **denazification** court in Munich in 1950.

REITSCH, HANNA (1912–1979) Leading woman aircraft pilot in Nazi Germany. Reitsch set a number of records as a glider pilot in the 1930s and became the first woman test pilot in the newly established **Luftwaffe** in 1937, surviving a number of minor crashes and forced landings. In 1942 she became the first woman to receive the Iron Cross military decoration. An avid admirer of **Hitler**, she and Field Marshal Robert Greim (1892–1945) were among the last visitors to the Führer's bunker in late April 1945. As personal pilot for Greim, whom Hitler named as the last commander-in-chief of the air force to replace **Göring**, Reitsch managed to fly out of Berlin on 29 April despite the fierce battle then raging in the city center. Classified as "exonerated" by a **denazification** court after the war, Reitsch continued her career as glider pilot and wrote her memoirs in 1951.

RIBBENTROP, JOACHIM VON (1893–1946) Ambassador to England from 1936 to 1938 and foreign minister from 1938 to 1945. Ribbentrop spent four years in Canada and the United States before returning to Germany to serve in the First World War, in which he received the Iron Cross. After the war he married into the Henkell family, the largest producers of champagne in Germany. Establishing his own wine-exporting business in Berlin, Ribbentrop accumulated considerable wealth. A monarchist in the 1920s, Ribbentrop did not join the Nazi Party until 1932. His wealth, social graces, knowledge of languages, and his Nazi convictions made him attractive to **Hitler**, who authorized him to establish his own party-based foreign affairs department in direct competition with the German foreign ministry in 1933. Other Nazi leaders, however, saw Ribbentrop as vain, pretentious, arrogant, and ignorant, and resented his efforts to use his personal relations with Hitler to widen his power and authority. **Goebbels** wrote in his diary that Ribbentrop "bought his name, married his money, and swindled his way into office." Ribbentrop's success in getting England to agree to a naval treaty in 1935 that allowed Germany to exceed the limits on naval construction established at **Versailles** led Hitler to appoint him ambassador to England in 1936. He failed, however, to impress the English or to persuade them to give up their opposition to German eastward expansion. British snubs left Ribbentrop embittered and determined to pursue an anti-British course. In February 1938 Ribbentrop replaced **Neurath** as foreign minister as Hitler sought to consolidate his control of the military and diplomatic services. Ribbentrop helped to convince Hitler that English opposition could be safely ignored in pursuing war against Poland. Ribbentrop's greatest success came in August 1939 when he negotiated a non-aggression pact with the USSR intended to deter England and France from entering the war to defend Poland. During the war Ribbentrop's power and influence waned as all his optimistic prognostications proved to have been wrong. Hitler held him in increasing contempt, and in his last testament he named **Seyss-Inquart** to replace him as foreign minister in the government under **Dönitz**. Ribbentrop was tried and convicted on all four counts of the indictment at **Nuremberg** and was the first of the prisoners there to be hanged in October 1946.

RIEFENSTAHL, LENI (1902–2003) Film director. Trained as an actress and dancer in Berlin, Riefenstahl turned to film producing and directing in 1932. Her documentary film of the 1934 annual Nazi Party rally, *Triumph of the Will*, which earned a gold medal at the Venice film festival in Fascist Italy, is today regarded as notorious **propaganda**, but it was not so perceived at the time. Her documentaries of the Olympic games in Berlin in 1936, *Festival of Nations* and *Festival of Beauty*, also gained acclaim for their technical innovations and received an award from the International Olympic Committee in 1948. For her film *Lowlands* in 1940, however, Riefenstahl recruited 60 gypsies from **concentration camps** with unfulfilled promises of compensation and exemption from further deportation. Claiming to have been disinterested in politics, she successfully contested these charges in court in 1949, but was forced to concede their truthfulness when further evidence became public in the 1980s. Her collaboration with the Nazis did not, however, impede her post-war career. Exonerated by a **denazification** court in 1948, she went on to publish numerous books of photographs on the Nuba tribe of southern Sudan, celebrating the natural beauty of the human body.

RÖCHLING, HERMANN (1872–1955) Leading figure in the German coal and steel industry. Heir to the family's large iron foundry holdings in the **Saarland**, Röchling was sentenced *in absentia* by a French court to ten years' imprisonment for alleged war crimes after the First World War. At **Hitler**'s request Röchling created the German Front in the Saar after the Nazi assumption of power in 1933 to promote the restoration of the Saar territory to Germany, which was achieved by plebiscite in 1935. After the conquest of France in 1940 the family's industrial holdings in Lorraine were temporarily restored to Röchling as well. A **Reich** military economy leader during the war, Röchling also headed the Reich Iron Association in 1942. After the war he was sentenced by a French military court to a ten-year prison term for mistreatment of prisoners of war and foreign workers. His release in 1951 was contingent on his pledge never to enter the Saarland again. He did not live to see the second restoration of German control of the Saar in 1957.

RÖHM, ERNST (1887–1934) Head of the SA until his purge in the "night of the long knives" on 30 June 1934. Severely wounded in the First World War, Röhm was one of **Hitler**'s closest associates in the build-up of the Nazi Party and its paramilitary arm the SA. As a captain in the **Reichswehr** until his dismissal as a result of his participation in the **Hitler Putsch** in 1923, Röhm helped to channel weapons and resources to the **Free Corps** and paramilitary formations. He participated in the crushing of the Soviet Republic in Munich by forces under Franz Ritter von Epp (1868–1947) in May 1919. Röhm was typical of a generation of combat veterans who found readjustment to normal civilian life both difficult and unappealing. Opposing Hitler's shift to legality after 1925, Röhm accepted a position as military advisor and instructor in Bolivia in 1928. In 1930 Hitler personally appealed to him to return to Germany to resolve a crisis precipitated by the revolt of a socially revolutionary SA faction under Walter Stennes (1899–1973) against Hitler's electoral politics and readiness to collaborate with Germany's conservative elites. Under Röhm's leadership the SA rapidly expanded to a mass organization of 445,000 by August 1932 and several millions by 1934. Many of the new members were recruited from the unemployed worker constituency of the left. Röhm's power grew after Hitler's accession to power, and in December 1933 he joined the cabinet as minister without portfolio. But growing disagreement about the role of the SA with Hitler, **Göring**, and **Himmler**, who was still nominally subordinate to Röhm, and growing concerns of German military leaders and conservative elites about Röhm's military ambitions, led Hitler to decide on his elimination, despite the fact that Röhm's loyalty to Hitler was never seriously in doubt. Röhm did, however, advocate the upgrading of the SA into an official national militia potentially absorbing or eclipsing the army. His demagogic rhetoric of the need for a "second revolution" to unseat the conservative elites from positions of authority in government and society put further pressure on Hitler to take action against him. Röhm's homosexual proclivities gave his rivals in the party and the army an additional pretext for his arrest and execution, which took place at the hands of an SS firing squad in a Munich prison on 1 July 1934.

ROMMEL, ERWIN (1891–1944) Field marshal, commander of the German **Africa Corps** from 1941, and commander of Army Group B on the western front in 1943. A highly decorated veteran of the First World War, Rommel pursued a military career after the war. Originally sympathetic to the Nazi regime, Rommel was named as the liaison officer for the Reich youth leadership in the Armed Forces Ministry in 1935. In 1938 he became the commander of the temporary Führer headquarters established for **Hitler**'s visits to the **Sudetenland** in 1938, and to Prague, Memel, and the Polish front in 1939. In the invasion of France Rommel commanded a tank division known as the "ghost division" because of its rapid surprise attacks. In February 1941 he commanded army units dispatched to North Africa to assist the Italian army against advancing British forces. Rommel's tacti-

cal successes and skillful maneuvering in the African campaign made him Germany's most admired field commander and gave him his reputation as the "desert fox." Lack of necessary supplies and equipment, however, led to German defeat at **El Alamein** in Egypt in November 1942 and to the subsequent withdrawal of German forces from the African continent. Rommel left Africa in March 1943 to organize the defense of Italy. In December 1943 he was transferred to the western front to assist **Rundstedt** in preparing for the coming Allied invasion. On 15 July 1944, five and a half weeks after the successful Allied invasion, Rommel informed Hitler that the war was lost and had to be ended to avoid unnecessary further losses. Two days later, however, Rommel was wounded and incapacitated by Allied aircraft. Although Rommel was not involved in the 20 July assassination attempt, his designation as commander-in-chief of the armed forces in a prospective post-Nazi government led to Nazi reprisal. Faced by trial before the **People's Court** for treason, Rommel chose to commit suicide and was given a formal state funeral.

ROSENBERG, ALFRED (1893–1946) Chief Nazi ideologue and minister for the occupied eastern territories from 1941 to 1944. Of Baltic-German and Protestant extraction, Rosenberg formed his worldview in bitter opposition to the Russian Revolution, which forced him to flee from Estonia, the Russian imperial province where he was born and educated. In Rosenberg's mind the **Bolsheviks** were inextricably linked with Jews, who in his view propagated communism in order to gain world domination. An early member of the Nazi Party, Rosenberg met **Hitler** through the Bavarian *völkisch* publicist

Dietrich Eckart (1868–1923), to whom Hitler would later dedicate the first volume of *Mein Kampf*. Rosenberg succeeded Eckart as editor of the Nazi Party newspaper *Völkischer Beobachter* in 1923 and participated in Hitler's failed putsch attempt in November of that year. In 1929 Rosenberg founded the **Combat League for German Culture** with the purpose of cleansing Germany of "degenerate" literature and art. In 1930 he published the anti-Catholic and anti-Semitic tome *Myth of the Twentieth Century*, based on the racial interpretation of history set forth by Houston Stewart Chamberlain (1855–1927) in his *Foundations of the Nineteenth Century* (1899), a book that Rosenberg greatly admired. Although disparaged by many Nazi leaders for its obscurity and pedantry, and disavowed by Hitler because it alienated the Catholic Church, Rosenberg's *Myth* nonetheless sold more than a million copies by 1942. In 1934 he received the title "The Führer's Delegate for the Supervision of all Intellectual and Ideological Education and Indoctrination in the Nazi Party." In his role as chief party ideologue and censor Rosenberg frequently clashed with **Rust**, **Goebbels**, and **Bormann** on matters of jurisdiction and policy. As head of the Nazi Party's Foreign Policy Office Rosenberg also clashed with **Ribbentrop** and the German foreign ministry. Rosenberg, however, was not a member of Hitler's inner policy circle, and he exercised less authority than other major Nazi leaders. In 1940 Rosenberg's special task force to confiscate works of art from Jewish collections and public museums in France and other occupied countries came into conflict with **Göring**, who insisted on securing the best pieces for his villa Karinhall. Rosenberg seemed to have reached the apex of his power when he was appointed minister for the occupied eastern territories after the invasion of the USSR in 1941. In fact, however, he had little control over **Reich commissioners Lohse** (eastern territories) and **Koch** (Ukraine). Rosenberg's proposal to mobilize anti-communist sentiment among Soviet subject nationalities by creating independent satellite states in the conquered areas was rejected by Hitler, who continued to insist that they remain under direct German control. For his role in the **Holocaust** Rosenberg was sentenced to death at **Nuremberg** and executed in October 1946.

RÜDIN, ERNST (1874–1952) Leading **eugenicist** and chairman of the German Society for Racial Hygiene from 1933 to 1945. Trained as a physician, Rüdin was one of the co-founders with Alfred Ploetz (1860–1940) of the German Society for Racial Hygiene in 1905 and editor of its journal for racial and population policy. An early supporter of eugenic sterilization of the mentally ill, Rüdin headed the genealogical and demographic department of the German Research Institute for Psychiatry in Munich (converted into a Kaiser Wilhelm Institute [KWI] in 1924) from 1916 and became managing director of the KWI in 1931. Rüdin welcomed the Nazi takeover of power as the long-sought opportunity to transform eugenic dreams into reality. After 1933 he became plenipotentiary for Reich Interior Minister Wilhelm **Frick** on questions of **racial hygiene** (the German term for eugenics). In this capacity he participated in drawing up and implementing the Law for the Prevention of Genetically Diseased Offspring in 1933 that legalized the compulsory sterilization of mentally or physically disabled patients. Rüdin described this law as "the most humane deed of mankind" and participated as a judge on the highest hereditary health court in deciding who would be affected by this law. He also promoted eugenic policies as publisher of the journal *Volk and Race* and collaborated with the **SS** institution **Ahnenerbe** (Ancestral Heredity). During the war he collaborated with the **Luftwaffe** in experiments on inmates of **concentration camps**, including the effects on the brain of prolonged deprivation of oxygen.

RUNDSTEDT, GERD VON (1875–1953) Field marshal and commander-in-chief of German forces in the west from March 1942 to July 1944 and again from September 1944 to March 1945. The son of an army officer, Rundstedt received his officer's commission in 1893. Rundstedt had retired in October 1938 in the rank of general, but was reactivated as commander-in-chief of Army Group South in the Polish campaign in September 1939. In the campaign against France he commanded Army Group A in the central part of the front. It was his chief of staff Erich von **Manstein** who developed the plan for Rundstedt's army group to attack through the Ardennes, resulting in a decisive victory despite Rundstedt's cautious order to halt the German advance outside of **Dunkirk**. Rundstedt commanded Army Group South in the campaign against the Soviet Union, but was relieved of his command in December 1941 after ordering a tactical withdrawal that **Hitler** countermanded. As commander-in-chief of the western front, Rundstedt overruled Rommel's plan to deploy tank divisions on the coastline to prevent an Allied invasion, opting instead to maintain reserve forces in the rear. Although relieved of his command by Hitler in July 1944 for alleged pessimism in the face of the Allies' Normandy campaign, Rundstedt nonetheless presided over the so-called army "court of honor" that turned over officers accused of involvement in the 20 July plot to the **People's Court** for trial. He also gave the official eulogy at Rommel's state funeral in October 1944. Reinstated as commander-in-chief in the west in September 1944 after the suicide of Field Marshal Hans Günter Kluge (1882–1944), who had failed to report his knowledge of the resistance plans of officers under his command, Rundstedt presided over the last-ditch German offensive in the **Battle of the Bulge**. Rundstedt was interned as a prisoner of war for four years after the end of the war.

RUST, BERNHARD (1883–1945) Minister of education from 1934 to 1945. A veteran of the First World War and a secondary school teacher by profession, Rust joined the Nazi Party and the **SA** (eventually reaching the rank of general) in 1925 and served as **Gauleiter** of Hannover-Braunschweig and as a member of the **Reichstag** from 1930 to 1945, having been elected on the Nazi ticket despite his dismissal from his teaching post in Hannover for "mental imbalance" in 1930. Rust founded the so-called national political educational institutions (NAPOLA) in 1933 as elite training schools based on the Italian Fascist formula of "believe, obey, fight," and oversaw the introduction of Nazi curricula in German primary and secondary education. He was frequently involved in struggles with other agencies claiming competence on educational matters, particularly the office of Reich youth leader Baldur von **Schirach**, the **DAF** under Robert **Ley** (which was responsible for the elite Adolf Hitler Schools and the **Ordensburgs**, special schools for training party leaders), and the SS (which ran its own special schools for training SS leaders). Rust committed suicide after learning of the German surrender in 1945.

S

SAUCKEL, FRITZ (1894–1946) SS general and plenipotentiary for the mobilization of labor from 1942 to 1945. A prisoner of war in France during the First World War, Sauckel joined the Nazi Party in 1923 after the banning of the Völkisch Defense and Protection League **(DSTB)** as a result of the assassination of Foreign Minister Walter Rathenau (1867–1922). In 1927 Sauckel became **Gauleiter** of the state of Thuringia, a Nazi deputy in the Thuringian parliament, and after Nazi electoral gains in July 1932 minister of the interior in the Thuringian state government. After **Hitler**'s accession to power he became *Reichsstatthalter* (governor) of Thuringia. His unshakable personal loyalty to Hitler may have been a factor in his appointment to head the ruthless recruitment of forced labor for German industry in 1942. More than five million foreign workers were deported from occupied territories to Germany during the war. If **concentration camp** workers and prisoners of war are included, the number of slave laborers in Germany reached a total of well over seven million in 1944. Housed in over 22,000 labor camps, they were forced to work under often brutal conditions. At least 500,000 forced workers died during the course of the war. For these crimes Sauckel was sentenced to death and executed at **Nuremberg**. Ironically, his better-educated and more articulate superior Albert **Speer**, who established the labor quotas that Sauckel had to meet, escaped the death penalty.

SCHACHT, HJALMAR HORACE GREELEY (1877–1970) President of the **Reichsbank** from 1923 to 1929 and again from 1933 to 1939, and minister of economics from 1934 to 1937. Schacht spent his childhood in the United States, where his parents had emigrated, his father becoming an American citizen. Schacht returned to Germany to complete his doctorate in economics in 1903 and pursue a banking career. He was a founding member of the liberal German Democratic Party **(DDP)** in 1919 but left the party in 1926 as his views shifted to the right. During the Great Inflation in November 1923 he was appointed Reich currency commissioner under Finance Minister Hans Luther (1879–1962) and helped to introduce the *Rentenmark*, the new currency that stemmed the inflationary tide. As president of the Reichsbank from December 1923 he participated in drawing up the Dawes Plan that restored the stability of the German economy until the onset of the **Great Depression**. Although he had helped to negotiate the **Young Plan** in 1929, he turned against the government's reparations policies and resigned as president of the Reichsbank in 1930. In 1931 he joined the **Harzburg Front** of nationalist opponents to the government of Heinrich **Brüning**. As a member of the circle of business leaders around Wilhelm **Keppler** he promoted the Nazi cause among associates in the business world. In November 1932 he organized a petition of business leaders to **Hindenburg** to appoint **Hitler** as chancellor. Hitler in turn reappointed Schacht as president of the Reichsbank in 1933, minister of economics in 1934, plenipotentiary for the war economy in 1935, and as first director of the **Four-Year Plan** in 1936. Schacht's opposition to Nazi plans for **autarky** and to what he believed was excessive deficit financing for rearmament led to his replacement by **Göring** as head of the Four-Year Plan and by **Funk** as economics minister in 1937, although Schacht continued to hold cabinet rank as minister without portfolio until 1943. Increasingly disenchanted by Nazi radicalism, Schacht resigned as Reichsbank president in 1939 and established contacts with **Goerdeler** without formally joining the resistance. Nonetheless he was arrested after the failure of the 20 July 1944 assassination attempt and interned at **Sachsenhausen** and **Flossenbürg** until the end of the war. As a result he was acquitted of war crimes at **Nuremberg** over Soviet objections. His classification as a "major offender" by a **denazification** court was reversed on appeal in 1948. Schacht pursued a successful career as banker and economic advisor to such developing countries as Indonesia, Egypt, and Libya in the 1950s and 1960s.

SCHELLENBERG, WALTER (1910–1952)
SS general, head of domestic counterintelligence from 1939, and head of foreign intelligence in the **RSHA** from 1941 to 1945. Trained in the law, Schellenberg joined the Nazi Party and the **SS** in May 1933 to further his career. Elegant, well-mannered, and ambitious, he joined the administrative staff of the SS Security Service (**SD**) under **Heydrich** in 1934. Schellenberg played a leading role in the consolidation of all police and security functions in the Reich Security Main Office (RSHA) in 1939. From head of domestic counterintelligence in Department IV (**Gestapo**) of the RSHA he was promoted to chief of department of Department VI (Foreign Intelligence) in 1941. He played a leading role in crushing the Communist resistance group **Red Orchestra** in 1942 and in exposing the military resistance group around the chief of military intelligence Wilhelm **Canaris** in 1944. Schellenberg assumed the functions of Canaris's office after the latter's arrest. In the closing stages

of the war Schellenberg prodded **Himmler** into seeking a separate peace with the West through the Red Cross, using Jewish internees as bargaining chips. In the trial of leading SS functionaries at **Nuremberg** he was sentenced to a six-year term for his role in the murder of Soviet POWs in 1949, but was pardoned and released in 1950.

SCHIRACH, BALDUR VON (1907–1974)
Reich youth leader of the Nazi Party from 1933 to 1940 and *Reichsstatthalter* (governor) as well as **Gauleiter** of Vienna from 1940 to 1945. Having joined the party at age eighteen in 1925, Schirach took over responsibility for the leadership and management of the **Hitler Youth** in 1936. As a student at the University of Munich in 1928 he became a member and, as of 1932, the official leader of the **NSDStB** (National Socialist German Student League). Schirach was first elected to the **Reichstag** in 1932. He also rose to the rank of general in the **SA** and was a member of the **Reichsleitung** of the party. An idealistic and enthusiastic advocate of the Nazi cause, Schirach published numerous books exalting Hitler, exhorting young people to join the party, and extolling the martial values of loyalty, discipline, and obedience. Tried at **Nuremberg** in 1945/1946 for crimes against humanity, Schirach was sentenced to a 20-year term for his role in overseeing the deportation of 65,000 Jews from Vienna during the war. Unlike most of the other defendants, Schirach acknowledged his personal responsibility and expressed remorse for supporting the murderous Nazi regime. He denounced Nazi atrocities, but insisted that he had not known about the extermination camps in the east.

SCHLEICHER, KURT VON (1882–1934)
Last German chancellor of the **Weimar**

Republic before **Hitler**. Born into a military family, Schleicher joined the army in 1900, served on the General Staff in the First World War, and became one of the most influential **Reichswehr** officers in the closing years of the Weimar Republic. Schleicher's extraordinary political influence was partly a function of the fact that Reichswehr support was an absolute precondition for governments ruling without a parliamentary majority under authority given to the president of the republic under Article 48 of the Weimar constitution. As chief of staff in the office of Reichswehr minister Wilhelm Groener (1867–1939) from 1929 to 1932 and as Reichswehr minister in **Papen**'s government in 1932, Schleicher worked behind the scenes to bring the Nazis into the government in subordinate roles after their electoral triumph in September 1930. A personal friend and classmate of President **Hindenburg**'s son Oskar von Hindenburg (1883–1960), Schleicher was able to persuade the aged president to dismiss both Groener and Chancellor **Brüning** in 1932 because of their reluctance to cooperate in Schleicher's project of bringing the Nazis into the government. When Papen failed in his effort to persuade Hitler to join his cabinet in a subordinate position, Schleicher decided to assume the chancellorship himself. In December 1932 he offered the position of vice-chancellor to Nazi Organization Leader Gregor **Strasser**, who was known to be critical of Hitler's strategy of holding out for full power. When this final effort to bring the Nazis into the government under a non-Nazi chancellor also failed, Schleicher saw no viable alternative to a Hitler government. His willingness to accept Hitler as chancellor in January 1933, however, did not spare him from Hitler's wrath for having previously opposed Hitler's appointment to the highest governing office in the state. In the "night of long knives" (the **Röhm** purge) on 30 June 1934 Schleicher, his wife, and his former chief of staff in the Reichswehr ministry, General Ferdinand von Bredow (1884–1934), as well as Strasser, were murdered by the SS.

SCHMITT, CARL (1888–1985) Right-wing political thinker and leading authority on constitutional law who joined the Nazi Party in 1933 and played an important role in providing legal justification for Nazi rule until his fall from favor in 1936. Defining politics as the ability of the state to distinguish between its friends and enemies, and political sovereignty as the control of decision-making in emergency situations, Schmitt wrote several acclaimed works highly critical of liberalism, parliamentarism, and the "weak" **Weimar** constitution in the 1920s. Although he advocated an authoritarian executive, he supported the governments of **Papen** and **Schleicher** rather than the Nazis in 1932. After the passage of the **Enabling Act** in March 1933, however, he jumped on the Nazi bandwagon. His legalistic tracts justifying the Nazis' extra-legal measures earned Schmitt the label of "crown jurist of the **Third Reich**" from a Nazi newspaper. In 1934 he provided the legal justification for **Hitler**'s murderous purge of the leadership of the **SA**. In 1936, however, Schmitt came under attack from hardliners of the **SS** for his earlier Catholic-tinged political theory and for the fact that he had displayed little overt **anti-Semitism** until 1933. Although he continued to teach at the University of Berlin until the end of the war, his direct influence on Nazi policies waned. He was barred from teaching after the war, but continued publishing works that gained a strong following among conservatives. Unexpectedly, his critique of liberalism also gained favor among sectors of the left dissatisfied with traditional welfare state policies and attracted by Schmitt's personal "decisionism" as a more effective way to bring about change than liberal process.

SCHOLL, HANS (1918–1943) and SOPHIE SCHOLL **(1921–1943)** Founders and leaders of the student resistance movement the **White Rose** in Munich. Raised in a liberal home, Hans Scholl began the study of medicine at Munich University in 1939. In May 1940 he took part as a medic in the campaign against France. Back in Munich to resume his medical studies, Hans and his younger sister Sophie, who had already been questioned by the **Gestapo** as early as 1937 about their critical stance toward the regime, organized the dissident group the White Rose and prepared and distributed a series of four mimeographed leaflets in the summer of 1942. Together with fellow dissident medical students Alexander Schmorell (1917–1943) and Willi Graf (1918–1943), Hans Scholl served on temporary duty on the Russian front from June to October 1942. Horrified by what they had seen at the front and by the murderous siege of Stalingrad in the winter of 1942/1943, the group issued two more leaflets calling for active and passive resistance to the Nazi regime. Apprehended while distributing the last of these leaflets on the university campus, the Scholls and fellow conspirator Christoph Probst (1919–1943) were arrested, sentenced to death by the **People's Court**, and executed by guillotine in February 1943. Schmorell, Graf, and the Catholic philosophy professor Kurt Huber (1893–1943), who had helped to prepare the last leaflets, were apprehended and executed later that same year.

SCHOLTZ-KLINK, GERTRUD (1902–1999) Reich women's leader and head of the National Socialist Women's Union (**NSF**) from 1933 to 1945. Born into the family of a minor civil servant in the southwest state of Baden, Scholtz-Klink joined the Nazi Party in 1928. In 1934 she was named to head the Nazi *Frauenschaft* (NSF) for women leaders and the German Women's Enterprise (*Deutsches Frauenwerk –* **DFW**) for the rank and file under the nominal direction of the head of the National Socialist Welfare Organization (*NS-Volkswohlfahrt – NSV*) Erich Hilgenfeldt (1897–1945). Her many offices also included leadership of the Women's Labor Service under Reich Labor Service Leader Konstantin **Hierl**, the Women's Office in the German Labor Front under Robert **Ley**, and the Reich Women's League of the German Red Cross. Although she had little influence on policy decisions, Scholtz-Klink fully embraced Nazi ideology, including the belief in "separate spheres" for men and women. She promoted motherhood as women's primary task, not just through advocacy but also by example, giving birth to 11 children in three marriages. Married to the leading **SS** official August **Heissmeyer** in 1940, she joined him in forging a new identity after the war. Discovered in 1948, Scholtz-Klink was sentenced to 18 months in prison by a French military court. A German **denazification** court barred her from political activity for life and from employment as a journalist or teacher for ten years. She remained committed to Nazi ideas, however, as became clear in her 1978 book, *Die Frau im Dritten Reich* (The Woman in the Third Reich), which she dedicated to the "victims of the Nürnberg trials."

SCHULENBURG, FRIEDRICH WERNER VON DER (1875–1944) German ambassador to the Soviet Union from 1934 to 1941 and member of the 20 July assassination plot. The son of a Prussian officer, Schulenburg entered the diplomatic service in 1901 as a consular official in Barcelona, Lemberg, Prague, Naples, Warsaw, and, during the First World War, in Beirut and Damascus. After the war he represented Germany in Teheran and Bucharest before being named German ambassador to Moscow in 1934. In this role Schulenburg sought to normalize economic and political relations with the Soviet Union and emphasized the essentially defensive character of Soviet arms in his reports to the German government. Schulenburg was closely involved in drawing up the **Nazi–Soviet Non-Aggression** Treaty of August 1939 and apparently tried as late as April 1941 to dissuade **Hitler** from attacking the Soviet Union. After the German invasion, Schulenburg headed the Russian desk in the German Foreign Office, where he helped to prepare propaganda to be used to turn the Soviet Union's many ethnic groups against the Soviet government. Disgusted by Germany's brutal occupation policies in the east, Schulenburg got in touch with conservative resistance circles, including the **Kreisau** Circle of Helmuth von **Moltke**, and the military resistance in which his nephew Fritz-Dietlov von der Schulenburg (1902–1944) was closely involved. In **Goerdeler**'s plans Werner Schulenburg was to have become foreign minister in a post-Hitler government, entrusted with the task of negotiating peace with the Soviet Union. Schulenburg was arrested in August 1944, sentenced to death by the **People's Court**, and executed in November 1944.

SCHULTZE-NAUMBURG, PAUL (1869–1949) Leading Nazi architect, artist, and publicist. An advocate of traditionalist

architecture, Schultze's greatest achievement before the First World War was as architect of the Cecilienhof Palace in Potsdam, constructed from 1913 to 1917 for the Hohenzollern crown prince (and the site of the conference of the heads of the three victor states of the Second World War in July 1945). One of the earliest proponents of removing "degenerate" modern art from public museums, Schultze-Naumburg published the book *Art and Race* in 1928 in which he called for a national art and architecture based on an appreciation of "blood and soil." Schultze-Naumburg served on the executive board of **Rosenberg**'s *Kampfbund for German Culture*. As director of the School for Architecture in Weimar from 1930 he played a leading role in the closing of the politically progressive and modernistic Bauhaus in Dessau by local officials after the Nazi electoral victory in the state of Thuringia in 1932. During the **Third Reich** he served on the Expert Advisory Committee on Population and Racial Policies of the Ministry of the Interior. His influence was limited, however, partly by his advanced age and partly because **Hitler** preferred the architectural designs of the Munich architect Paul Ludwig Troost (1878–1934) and Albert **Speer**.

SCHULZE-BOYSEN, HARRO (1909–1942) Resistance fighter and leading member of the **Red Orchestra** espionage group. The great-nephew of Admiral Alfred von Tirpitz (1849–1930), "father" of the Imperial German navy, Schulze-Boysen participated in the nationalist resistance to the French occupation of the **Ruhr** in 1923. After completing law school he moved ever further to the left in his political allegiance, actively opposing Nazism after 1933. Through his wife Libertas Haas Heye (1913–1942), whose family was related to **Göring**, Schulze-Boysen obtained a position in the Reich Aviation Ministry and in 1941 on the **Luftwaffe** headquarters staff with access to secret documents. Together with Arvid **Harnack**, head of the American desk in the Economics Ministry, Schulze-Boysen transmitted warnings of the impending German attack on the Soviet Union to Soviet officials. Their resistance groups, integrated into the Soviet espionage network in Europe (labeled "Red Orchestra" by the **Gestapo**), were uncovered in the summer of 1942. Schulze-Boysen and his wife were arrested, sentenced to death by a military court, and executed with Harnack and Rudolf von Scheliha (1897–1942) at Berlin-Plötzensee in December 1942.

SCHWERIN VON KROSIGK, LUTZ (1887– 1977) Reich minister of finance from 1932 to 1945. Although not a member of the Nazi Party, Schwerin von Krosigk was retained by **Hitler** as one of the holdovers from the **Papen** and **Schleicher** cabinets at the express wish of President **Hindenburg** in 1933. Trained in law and political science, Schwerin von Krosigk had joined the Prussian civil service in 1909 and had served in various capacities in the Finance Ministry during the Weimar Republic, including as German representative at a number of international reparations conferences, before joining Papen's government as Reich finance minister in 1932. Schwerin von Krosigk was representative of the type of old-fashioned monarchist and nationalist willing to collaborate with the new Nazi regime. He shared responsibility for financing Germany's rearmament in the 1930s and the war in the 1940s. After **Hitler**'s suicide in 1945, Schwerin von Krosigk was appointed foreign minister by **Dönitz** in his short-lived government. At the so-called

Wilhelmstrasse trial of leading civil servants at **Nuremberg** Schwerin von Krosigk was sentenced to ten years in prison, but was released in the general amnesty of 1951. He wrote several books, including his memoirs, after his release.

SELDTE, FRANZ (1882–1947) Reich minister of labor from 1933 to 1945. The son of a soda water plant owner, Seldte lost his left arm in the First World War. In December 1918 he founded the **Stahlhelm** (Steel Helmet), an organization of veterans of the front later closely aligned with the Nationalist Party (**DNVP**). As leader of the anti-Republican Stahlhelm he helped to initiate the nationwide referendum against the **Young Plan** (rescheduling reparations), which was defeated in 1929. With Hitler and Alfred **Hugenberg**, head of the DNVP, Seldte co-founded the **Harzburg Front** in opposition to the **Brüning** government in 1931. As minister of labor, Seldte's authority was limited by the competing jurisdictional claims of the German Labor Front under Robert **Ley**, the **Four-Year Plan** under **Göring**, and, during the war, the office of labor mobilization under Fritz **Sauckel**. Seldte died in Allied captivity in 1947 shortly before his trial for war crimes was to begin.

SERAPHIM, PETER-HEINZ (1902–1979) Economist and leading academic specialist on the "Jewish question" in Nazi Germany. A member of a well-known Baltic German family that moved to Germany after Latvia gained its independence from the Russian Empire after the First World War, Seraphim was trained as a specialist on Eastern European economic questions. His 732-page tome on *Jewry in Eastern Europe* made his reputation in 1938. A compendium of statistical data on Jewish demography, social structure, occupational patterns, and political organization, this book provided practical information that could be applied to anti-Jewish policy. After the publication of his *opus magnum* Seraphim was much in demand as a consultant, contributor to journals, and speaker at conferences. Seraphim edited the journal of Alfred **Rosenberg**'s Institute for Research on the **Jewish Question**, founded in Frankfurt in March 1941. Seraphim favored the mass deportation of Jews to an unspecified overseas destination. He rejected a Jewish reservation in Europe and criticized the mass killing of Jews in the Soviet Union on economic grounds. Although his work gave official **anti-Semitism** an intellectual, social scientific legitimacy, he had little direct influence on policy formation. After the war Seraphim taught economics at a civil service academy in West Germany.

SEYSS-INQUART, ARTHUR (1892–1946) SS general and **Reich commissioner** for the occupied Netherlands 1940 to 1945. A veteran of the Austro-Hungarian army in the First World War, Seyss-Inquart practiced law in Vienna during the 1920s. He joined the Austrian Nazi Party in 1931, supporting its more moderate wing after 1933. Under German pressure Austrian chancellor Kurt von Schuschnigg (1897–1977) appointed Seyss-Inquart as Austrian minister of the interior in February 1938. In that position he prepared the ground for *Anschluss*. On the day the German army invaded, 11 March 1938, Seyss-Inquart replaced Schuschnigg as chancellor and welcomed the German troops. In October 1939 Seyss-Inquart became deputy governor-general of occupied Poland under Hans **Frank**. In May 1940 Seyss-Inquart assumed control of the occupied Netherlands, where he implemented ruthless policies of repression

and deportation. **Hitler** named him to succeed **Ribbentrop** as German foreign minister in 1945, but **Dönitz** shunted him aside, appointing the less criminally encumbered **Schwerin von Krosigk** instead. Seyss-Inquart was sentenced to death as a major war criminal at **Nuremberg** and executed in October 1946.

SKORZENY, OTTO (1908–1975) SS commando leader and head of special operations in the Reich Security Main Office (**RSHA**) from 1943 to 1945. An Austrian by birth and a protégé of Ernst **Kaltenbrunner**, Skorzeny joined the Nazi Party in 1930. After taking part in the French, Balkan, and Russian campaigns as a member of the **Waffen-SS**, Skorzeny achieved enormous notoriety as leader of several daring commando raids, including the rescue of Mussolini from Italian captivity in September 1943 and the capture of Hungarian head of state Miklós Horthy (1868–1957) in October 1944. In the **Battle of the Bulge** in December 1944 he commanded a tank brigade of 2,000 German soldiers disguised in American uniforms. Acquitted by an American military tribunal of violations of the laws of war in 1947, Skorzeny escaped from a German detention camp in 1948 and fled to Spain. Here he enjoyed the protection of the Franco government and played a key role in organizing an escape and support network for incriminated **SS** officers and other Nazis under the cover of an export and import business in Madrid.

SPEER, ALBERT (1905–1981) Hitler's favorite architect and Reich minister for armaments and munitions from 1942 to 1945. The son and grandson of architects, Speer was fascinated by **Hitler**'s oratory and joined the Nazi Party in 1931. Hitler regarded him as his personal protégé and entrusted him with major architectural projects, including the Nazi Party rally site in **Nuremberg** and the new Reich Chancellery in Berlin in 1939. Responsible for planning and designing Nazi mass rallies and ceremonies, Speer created the innovative "cathedral of light" spectacles that helped give the annual Nazi Party rallies their religious aura. As leader of the "workplace beautification" office of the German Labor Front's **Strength through Joy** program, Speer supervised the remodeling of numerous German industrial and commercial work sites. He also developed plans for the prospective reconstruction of Berlin according to Hitler's gargantuan specifications. In 1942 Speer was named to replace Fritz **Todt** as minister of armaments and munitions (renamed the Reich Ministry for Armaments and War Production in September 1943). In this position Speer exercised full control over the German economy. Hitler appointed him minister of economics in the successor government under **Dönitz** in May 1945 despite Speer's failure to carry out Hitler's order to destroy the German infrastructure in the face of the Allied advance. By expressing remorse for Nazi crimes and claiming ignorance of the **Holocaust** Speer was able to avoid the death penalty at Nuremberg despite his responsibility for a war economy that exploited millions of slave laborers. Sentenced to 20 years in prison, Speer used the time to work on his memoirs, *Inside the Third Reich* (1970). In this apologetic work Speer explained the Nazi regime as the consequence of modern technology and technocratic practices, thus mirroring in his interpretation of Nazism the anti-modern bias of Nazi ideology. Scholars have long since determined that Speer was lying when he claimed to have known nothing about the

Nazis' extermination program or the fate of the Jewish victims consigned to the camps.

STAHLECKER, WALTER (1900–1942) SS general and chief of SS *Einsatzgruppe* A. Trained as a lawyer, Stahlecker was a member of the leading post-First World War *völkisch* organization **DSTB**, gravitating to the Nazis after this organization was outlawed in the wake of the assassination of Foreign Minister Walter Rathenau in 1922. He formally joined the Nazi Party in 1932. As head of the Security Police (**SD**) in the **Protectorate of Bohemia and Moravia** Stahlecker assisted **Eichmann** in the attempted deportation of Austrian and Czech Jews across the new Soviet border along the San River in Poland in October 1939. The project had to be halted due to objections by the Soviet Union as well as German officials in the **Generalgouvernement** (who did not want to have to cope with an influx of Jews) and **Wehrmacht** officials (who did not want to spare the rolling stock). In June 1941 Stahlecker was named to command the SS *Einsatzgruppe* operating in the Baltic states and northern Russia. On 15 October 1941 Stahlecker reported the murder of 135,567 Jews, Communists, and mentally handicapped patients in the previous two months. It was Stahlecker's task force that murdered the first trainloads of Jews deported from inside Germany to Riga and Minsk in November and December 1941. Stahlecker was killed by Soviet partisans in March 1942.

STANGL, FRANZ (1908–1971) Commandant of **Sobibór** and **Treblinka** in 1942 and 1943. A career police officer in Austria, Stangl formally joined the Nazi Party after the *Anschluss* in 1938. As police superintendent Stangl presided over the mass killing of mentally and physically handicapped patients at the **euthanasia** institutions **Hartheim** and **Bernburg**. Transferred to **Lublin** in March 1942, Stangl assisted his fellow-Austrian Odilo **Globocnik** in preparing and implementing **Aktion Reinhard**, the mass murder of the Jews of Poland. As commandant at Sobibór and Treblinka, Stangl earned **Himmler**'s commendation as the "best leader" of the killing program. In August 1943 Stangl was assigned to Trieste to organize the campaign against Yugoslav partisans. Here he was arrested by US forces at the end of the war. Unaware at the time of Stangl's activities in Poland, American authorities turned Stangl over to Austria for prosecution of his euthanasia crimes. Stangl was able to escape from Austrian internment in 1948 and made his way to Brazil via Syria with the aid of the Nazi-helper Bishop Alois Hudal (1883–1963). Tracked down by Nazi-hunter Simon Wiesenthal (1908–2005) in 1967, Stangl was extradited to Germany and sentenced to life imprisonment in 1970 for the murder of hundreds of thousands of Jews.

STARK, JOHANNES (1874–1957) Leading representative, with Philipp **Lenard**, of "German Physics," a school of scientists that embraced Nazism and rejected theoretical physics as "Jewish." Stark won the Nobel Prize in physics in 1919 for his experimental work in electro- magnetism, but his increasingly vitriolic attacks on Einstein's relativity theory and quantum mechanics brought about his forced resignation from the University of Würzburg in 1922 and temporary retreat into private business. He joined the Nazi Party in 1930, and after **Hitler**'s accession to power he was named president of the Reich Institute for Physics and Technology (until 1939) and head of the **DFG** (the state institution supporting scientific research) until 1936. Stark published several books arguing that only **Aryans** were capable of disinterested observation of natural phenomena, while Jewish scientists supposedly disregarded facts or bent the truth for selfish or commercial advantage. He lost influence because most of his colleagues in the physics community, including some with Nazi affiliations, came to realize that Stark's opposition to modern theoretical physics hindered innovation and put German scientific research at a disadvantage in competition with other nations. For his role in the Nazi regime Stark was sentenced to four years' imprisonment in 1947, but the sentence was suspended in 1949.

STAUFFENBERG, CLAUS SCHENK VON (1907–1944) Leader of the military resistance to **Hitler**. Descended from a prominent south German Catholic aristocratic family, Stauffenberg became a professional soldier in 1926. His pronounced aesthetic interests crucially determined his mental and psychological development. With his older brother Berthold (1905–1944) he became a member of the inner circle of the conservative poet Stefan George (1868–1933), dedicated to a high-minded *völkisch* creed. Stauffenberg originally welcomed the Nazi takeover of power as an opportunity for national regeneration and the restoration of German power and pride. He began to have serious doubts about the regime, however, after the so-called *Reichskristallnacht* pogrom of November 1938. Stauffenberg participated in the German occupation of the Sudetenland, the successful military campaigns against Poland and France, and the invasion of the Soviet Union. In April 1943 he was badly wounded on the North African front, losing an eye, his right hand, and two fingers of his left hand. It was in September of that year that he decided to join the military conspiracy which already included such high-ranking active and retired officers as generals **Beck, Witzleben, Treskow, Stülpnagel, Olbricht**, Helmuth Stieff (1901–1944), and Erich Hoepner (1886–1944). A brave, energetic, and talented leader, Stauffenberg organized the secret alteration of the military contingency plan against domestic unrest, "Operation **Valkyrie**," into a plan to unseat the Nazi government. As chief of staff of the reserve army Stauffenberg was one of the few members of the military resistance to have direct access to Hitler. For that reason he was forced not only to lead the military coup but also to carry out the assassination attempt himself. The bomb planted at Hitler's East Prussian headquarters on 20 July 1944 failed to kill the Führer, however, and Stauffenberg's long flight back to Berlin fatally delayed the implementation of the plan. When **Goebbels**, the highest-ranking government official in Berlin, persuaded Major Otto Ernst Remer (1912–1997), the officer sent to arrest him, to disregard his orders, the plot collapsed. Stauffenberg was executed by firing squad in the courtyard of the High Command that same evening with his fellow conspirators **Olbricht**, Albrecht Mertz von Quirnheim (1905–1944), and Werner von Haeften (1908–1944). Stauffenberg's brother Berthold was executed on 10 August. For his part in thwarting the coup attempt Remer was promoted to major-general. After the war he founded the neo-Nazi Socialist Reich Party (SRP), which was banned in 1952. Remer continued, however, to advocate neo-Nazi views and was forced to flee to Spain in 1993 to avoid arrest for **Holocaust** denial.

STRASSER, GREGOR (1892–1934) Reich organization leader of the Nazi Party from 1928 to 1932 and **Hitler**'s main rival for leadership. A highly decorated veteran of the First World War, Strasser opened a pharmacy in his native Bavaria after the war, but soon became embroiled in right-wing politics. He joined the Nazis in 1921 and participated in Hitler's "beer hall" putsch in November 1923. After serving a brief prison term, Strasser was elected to the **Reichstag** as a member of the National Socialist Freedom Party, a stand-in for the Nazi Party while Hitler was in prison. With his younger brother Otto (1897–1974) Strasser represented the socially revolutionary wing of the Nazi Party. The Strassers failed, however, in their attempt to expand the 1920 25-point program to include more specific economic reforms. Hitler steered the party in a more conservative, business-friendly direction. After **Goebbels'** defection to Hitler in 1926 the "anti-capitalist" wing of the party became more and more marginalized. Otto Strasser was expelled from the party in 1930. Gregor Strasser accommodated himself to Hitler's course and took over the functions of building up the party organization. Tension between Hitler and Strasser came to a head in December 1932, however, over the best tactics to achieve power. Believing that the Nazis had reached the limits of their electoral strength in the November 1932 elections, Strasser advocated joining a broad conservative coalition government under Chancellor **Schleicher**. Repudiated by Hitler, who insisted on holding out for full power, Strasser resigned his party offices and retired to his home in Bavaria. Here he was gunned down by an **SS** squad in the purge that followed the alleged putsch by Ernst **Röhm** in June 1934.

STREICHER, JULIUS (1885–1946) **Gauleiter** of Franconia from 1925 to 1945 and publisher of the **anti-Semitic** *Der Stürmer*. A primary school teacher by profession, Streicher served in the First World War and joined the Nazi Party in 1922 with the entire 2,000-person membership of the *völkisch* splinter group he had founded two years earlier. As editor and publisher of the weekly *Der Stürmer* from April 1923 until 1945, Schteicher preached hatred and violence against Jews. After serving a one-month prison term for his participation in the **Hitler Putsch** Streicher was elected to the Bavarian Landtag in July 1924. Valued by Hitler for his Jew-baiting propensities, Streicher was named Gauleiter of Franconia in 1925. As leader of the "Central Committee to Counter Jewish Atrocity and Boycott Agitation" Streicher helped organize the one-day boycott of Jewish businesses on 1 April 1933 and continued throughout the 1930s to publish the names of ethnic Germans who had any business or social contact with Jews. Increasingly notorious even within the party for his corruption, crudity, pornography, and slander, Streicher was suspended from his party offices in 1940 by order of the party court under Walter Buch (1883–1949). Even then, however, he was permitted to retain his title as Gauleiter and his editorship of *Der Stürmer*, apparently at Hitler's express wish. Streicher was tried as a major war criminal at **Nuremberg**, sentenced to death for crimes against humanity, and executed in October 1946.

STROOP, JÜRGEN (1895–1952) SS general and commander in charge of the suppression of the **Warsaw ghetto** uprising in April–May 1943. The son of a policeman, Stroop served with distinction in the First World War and joined the Nazi Party and the **SS** in 1932. As SS police leader in Warsaw, Stroop was entrusted with the liquidation of the Warsaw ghetto in April 1943. After the brutal suppression of the ghetto uprising in May 1943, Stroop issued a lengthy report under the title "The Jewish Ghetto in Warsaw Is No More," complete with photographs of the operation. Stroop was extradited to Poland after the war and executed as "the hangman of Warsaw" in March 1952.

STÜLPNAGEL, CARL-HEINRICH VON (1886–1944) Commanding general of occupied France from 1942 to 1944 and member of the military resistance. The son of a general, Stülpnagel joined the army in 1904, served in the First World War, and participated in the unsuccessful **Kapp Putsch** in 1920. In June 1940 he chaired the Franco-German Armistice Commission that drew up the terms for the French surrender. Appalled by the murder of Jews on the eastern front, Stülpnagel asked to be relieved of his command of the Seventeenth Army in Russia in November 1941. In March 1942 he was named to replace his older cousin Otto von Stülpnagel (1878–1948) as military commander of France. Together with his adjutant Cäsar von Hofacker (1896–1944), a cousin of Claus von **Stauffenberg**, he maintained contact with the military resistance in Berlin. On 20 July 1944 Stülpnagel ordered the arrest of leading Nazis and **SS** officers in Paris. After the failure of the plot he and Hofacker were arrested, tried by the **People's Court**, and executed.

T

TERBOVEN, JOSEF (1898–1945) Reich commissioner for occupied Norway from

1940 to 1945. A veteran of the First World War, Terboven was an early Nazi Party member and participated in **Hitler**'s abortive 1923 putsch. In 1928 he was appointed **Gauleiter** of Essen in the **Ruhr** Valley. Appointed **Reich commissioner** for Norway in April 1940, Terboven supported the fascist government of Vidkun Quisling (1887–1945), while at the same time directing the exploitation of Norwegian resources for the German military effort. Terboven committed suicide in May 1945, and Quisling was executed after trial in Norway.

THIERACK, OTTO GEORG (1889–1946) Reich minister of justice from 1942 to 1945. After service in the First World War, Thierack pursued a career as public prosecutor and joined the Nazi Party in 1932. From 1933 to 1935 he was minister of justice in the state of Saxony. In 1936 **Hitler** appointed him the first president of the *Volksgerichtshof*, a special court founded in 1934 to try cases of treason and sedition. Its jurisdiction was broadened to cover *Wehrkraftzersetzung* (undermining of military strength) in 1938. Although not as brutal as his successor Roland **Freisler**, Thierack oversaw the systematic elimination of procedural guarantees and legal norms. In August 1942 Hitler appointed Thierack Reich minister of justice with specific authorization to override existing law in the interests of Nazi racial and political goals. Thierack continued efforts begun under his predecessors Franz Gürtner (1881–1941) and Franz Schlegelberger (1876–1970) to Nazify the judicial system by increasing the severity of penalties, issuing confidential evaluations of judges' decisions, and purging judges unwilling to bend the law to achieve Nazi goals. After consultation with **Himmler**, Thierack agreed to turn over to the **SS** for "destruction through labor" all Jews, gypsies, Russians, and Ukrainians convicted of any crime, as well as Polish convicts sentenced to terms of three years or longer and German convicts sentenced to terms of eight years or longer. Thierack committed suicide while awaiting trial at **Nuremberg**. Schlegelberger received a life sentence, but was released in 1951.

TODT, FRITZ (1891–1942) Reich minister for armaments and munitions from 1940 to 1942. After training as a civil engineer and service in the First World War, Todt joined the Nazi Party in 1922. In 1933 he was named general inspector for German highway construction. Under his auspices the *Autobahn* network was constructed. In 1938 he was placed in charge of coordinating all German construction under the **Four-Year Plan**. That same year he founded the Organisation Todt (OT), a quasi-military organization of some 350,000 workers, including slave laborers, first used in constructing the series of fortresses and bunkers on the western frontier known as the Atlantic Wall and in English as the Siegfried Line. During the war the OT used slave labor for military projects and reconstruction of damaged roads, bridges, and railway lines. A competent technocrat, Todt was named Reich minister of armaments and munitions in March 1940. He died in an airplane crash in February 1942 and was succeeded by Albert **Speer**.

TRESCKOW, HENNING VON (1901–1944) Leading member of the military resistance in the rank of major-general. After volunteering for service in the First World War at the age of sixteen, Tresckow rejoined the **Reichswehr** in 1926. Hostile to the

Weimar Republic, Tresckow initially welcomed **Hitler**'s takeover of power. His disillusionment with the Nazis began in 1938 and ripened into the conviction that Hitler had to be removed. Yet as late as June 1944 as chief of staff of Army Group Center on the eastern front Tresckow signed orders for the deportation of thousands of orphaned children for forced labor in the **Reich**. It was their involvement in actions such as these that has led some historians to question the motives of the military resistance, which seemed more determined to avert the consequences of defeat than to stop Nazi crimes. According to Tresckow's aide Fabian von Schlabrendorff (1907–1980), however, Tresckow acted out of principle. Tresckow planned to assassinate Hitler on his visit to the eastern front in March 1943, but the bomb planted in Hitler's plane failed to go off. According to Schlabrendorff, the sole source for this account, Tresckow helped to convince **Stauffenberg** that an attempt to oust the Nazis from power had to be made, despite the likelihood of failure, in order to salvage German honor in the eyes of the world. After the failure of the 20 July 1944 plot Tresckow blew himself up with a hand grenade, disguising his suicide as an enemy attack in order to throw the **Gestapo** off the track of fellow conspirators. His involvement in the plot came to light, however, in the subsequent investigation. His brother Gerd also committed suicide in prison.

V

VÖGLER, ALBERT (1877–1945) Prominent industrialist and general manager of the United Steel Works in Düsseldorf from 1926 until 1939, when he became chairman of the board. Vögler was elected to the National Assembly (which wrote the Weimar Constitution) in 1920 as a delegate of the **German People's Party** and served in the **Reichstag** for four years. Although not a member of the Nazi Party, he raised funds for the party after 1930 and was present at a meeting with **Hitler** in February 1933 where he and his fellow industrialists pledged three million marks for the party in the March election campaign. From 1933 to 1945 Vögler was again a member of the **Reichstag**, which had now become a rubber-stamp body. He was chairman of the Rhenish-Westphalian Coal Syndicate from 1925 to 1927, president of the Association of German Ironworks from 1926 to 1936, and a member of the board of directors of numerous manufacturing firms. Trained as an engineer, Vögler also played a leading role in the formation of Nazi policy toward scientific research, serving as treasurer (until 1941) and chairman of the board (until 1945) of the Kaiser Wilhelm Society for the Promotion of Science. Vögler committed suicide in American captivity in April 1945.

W

WEIZSÄCKER, ERNST HEINRICH VON (1882–1951) Leading civil servant in the Foreign Ministry and ambassador to the Vatican from 1943 to 1945. A former naval officer, Weizsäcker joined the Foreign Ministry in 1920 and served as ambassador to Norway and Switzerland before joining the Nazi Party and accepting an appointment as state secretary in **Ribbentrop**'s Foreign Ministry in 1938. A conservative nationalist, Weizsäcker disapproved of

Nazi excesses but supported **Hitler**'s assertive foreign policy. He helped to write the Munich agreements that enabled the Western powers to avoid war over Czechoslovakia. During the war, however, Weizsäcker signed documents endorsing the deportation of Jews from occupied France. As ambassador to the Vatican Weizsäcker supported the efforts of Pope Pius XII to declare Rome an "open city" to spare it from Allied bombing. Weizsäcker was sentenced to a seven-year term at the so-called Wilhelmstrasse trial of civil servants in **Nuremberg** in 1947, but was released in 1950. His memoirs were edited and published in 1950 by his son Richard (b. 1920), who served two terms as president of the Federal Republic of Germany from 1984 to 1994.

WESSEL, HORST (1907–1930) Official martyr of the Nazi movement. A member of the Nazi Party from 1926, Wessel was the leader of an **SA** unit in a heavily communist working-class district in Berlin. A dispute with his communist landlady led to his shooting death in 1930. **Goebbels** seized upon this incident to portray Wessel as a hero who had sacrificed his life for the cause. A poem he had published in the **SS** journal *Der Angriff* (The Attack) in 1929, "Die Fahne hoch" (The Flag Raised), set to the tune of a sailors' march, was officially titled the "Horst Wessel Song" and elevated to the status of a second national anthem after 1933.

WIRTH, CHRISTIAN (1885–1944) Head of all **euthanasia** institutions in Germany (1940–1941) and head of the **Operation Reinhard** killing centers in occupied Poland (1942–1943). A decorated veteran of the First World War, Wirth served with the criminal police in the state of Württemberg after the war. Wirth originally joined the Nazi Party in 1923, rejoining it after a hiatus in 1931. After the Nazis came to power he continued his career with the criminal police, a body eventually absorbed into the **SS** security empire. In 1939 he was posted to the euthanasia institution **Grafeneck**, where he carried out the first mass gassings of chronic mental patients under the secret **Aktion T-4** program headed by **Bouhler** and **Brack**. In 1940 Wirth was promoted to command all euthanasia institutions. In late summer 1941 Wirth headed a team of approximately one hundred Aktion T-4 personnel dispatched to Poland to oversee the construction and operation of the Operation Reinhard killing sites at **Belzec**, **Treblinka**, and **Sobibór**. As inspector of the Operation Reinhard camps under SS and police leader **Globocnik** in **Lublin**, Wirth oversaw the killing of over 1.5 million Jews in 1942 and 1943. Transferred to Trieste to fight Yugoslav and Italian partisans in 1943, Wirth was apparently killed by insurgents in May 1944.

WITZLEBEN, ERWIN VON (1881–1944) Field marshal and highest-ranking member of the military resistance to **Hitler**. Witzleben joined the German Imperial Army in 1901 and was retained in the **Reichswehr** after the First World War. Already a major-general at the time of Hitler's appointment as chancellor in 1933, Witzleben was involved in tentative plans with generals **Beck** and **Olbricht** to oust the Nazis from power should the Czech crisis lead to war against the West in 1938. After the outbreak of war in 1939, however, he commanded armies in both the Polish and French campaigns and was promoted to field marshal in July 1940. He was commander-in-chief of Germany's armies in the west from May 1941 until his retirement in

March 1942. Witzleben remained active, however, in the military conspiracy and was projected to become supreme commander of the **Wehrmacht** in the event of a successful coup. Arrested after the failure of the 20 July plot, Witzleben was sentenced to death by the *Volksgerichtshof* and executed in August 1944.

WOLFF, KARL (1900–1984) SS general and highest-ranking German military official in Mussolini's republic of **Salò** from 1943 to 1945. Decorated for courage in combat in the closing stages of the First World War, Wolff headed a **Free Corps** in the state of Hesse before opening his own advertising firm in Munich in 1925. Wolff joined the Nazi Party and the **SS** in 1931, rapidly rising in the officer ranks. From 1933 he advanced from **Himmler**'s personal adjutant to chief of Himmler's personal staff in 1936 to Himmler's liaison officer with **Hitler** in 1939. After Italy concluded an armistice with the West in September 1943 Wolff became German military governor of occupied northern Italy and plenipotentiary to Mussolini's puppet government at Salò. Without authorization from either **Hitler** or Himmler, Wolff negotiated the early surrender of German forces in Italy with Allen Dulles (1893–1969), the head of the American Office of Strategic Services in Switzerland. As a result he was not indicted at **Nuremberg** as originally planned, but appeared instead in SS uniform as a witness for the prosecution. A German court subsequently sentenced him to four years in prison, but he was released in 1949. A successful business career enabled him to build a lavish villa on the banks of the Starnberger See in Bavaria in the 1950s. In 1962, as more information about his war-time activities came to light, he was tried again by a Munich court for his role in the deportation of Jews to **Treblinka**. Sentenced to a ten-year term in 1964, he was again released in 1971.

WURM, THEOPHIL (1868–1953) State bishop of the Lutheran Church in Württemberg from 1933 to 1949. Ordained as a Lutheran minister in 1899, Wurm was a conservative theologian who welcomed the Nazi government in 1933. However, his opposition to Nazi efforts to control the Lutheran Church by creating a unified and centralized national church under the right-wing Protestant "Reich bishop" **Müller** in 1933 led to conflict with the government. To avoid disaffection among Church members, Hitler confirmed Wurm and his Bavarian counterpart Hans Meisner (1881–1956) in their offices as heads of their respective state churches, thus weakening Müller's role. For his opposition to Nazi efforts to intervene in Church government Wurm gained the support of **Confessing Church** leaders, but Wurm never became a formal member of the Confessing Church, seeking instead to play a conciliatory role in the **Church Struggle** between the Confessing Church and the Nazi faction, the **German Christians**. Wurm sent a letter of protest to the Ministry of Justice after the 1938 **Reichskristallnacht** pogrom, but affirmed the right of the state to combat Jewry as a "dangerous element." Wurm did, however, strongly protest the **euthanasia** killings in 1941 and, at least obliquely, the murder of the Jews. With Martin **Niemöller** Wurm drew up the post-war Stuttgart Declaration of Guilt in October 1945, accepting belated responsibility for the failure of Protestant clergymen to speak out more forcefully against the Nazi regime.

Y

Z

YORCK VON WARTENBURG, PETER (1904–1944) Leading member of the bureaucratic and military resistance. A descendant of the famous Prussian general who led German troops in the war against Napoleon in 1813, Yorck was trained as a lawyer and pursued a career as a civil servant despite his unwillingness to join the Nazi Party. He served in the office of price controls under Commissioner Josef Wagner (1899–1945) from 1936 to 1941 and was then transferred to the economic staff of the Supreme Command (**OKW**). With Helmuth von **Moltke** he founded the **Kreisau** Circle of dissidents and conspirators who met periodically at Yorck's home in Berlin and Moltke's estate in Silesia to make plans for a post-Nazi government. Through his cousin **Stauffenberg** Yorck also maintained close contact with the military resistance. After the failure of the attempt to assassinate **Hitler** on 20 July 1944 Yorck was arrested, tried, and executed in August 1944.

ZIEGLER, ADOLF (1892–1959) President of the Reich Chamber of Fine Arts from 1936 to 1943. A member of the Nazi Party since 1925, Ziegler was delegated by **Hitler** to organize the 1937 exhibition of degenerate art in Munich that attracted about 20,000 visitors a day. A year later an exhibition of officially approved art, including Ziegler's own technically proficient but unoriginal works, found far less public resonance. Ziegler's naturalistic female nudes gained him the sobriquet, "the master of the German pubic hair." As president of the Reich Chamber of Fine Arts, Ziegler was responsible for the removal of modern art from public museums. A law authorizing the purge of private as well as public collections led to the confiscation of more than 16,000 allegedly degenerate works.

10

GLOSSARY

- *This section lists and defines a broad range of terms and concepts relating to Nazi Germany.*
- *It includes the most important acronyms in use in Nazi Germany.*

ABWEHR Military counter-intelligence and counter-espionage service founded after the First World War. Headed by Admiral Wilhelm **Canaris** from 1935 to 1944, the Abwehr became a center of military resistance under General Hans **Oster**, chief of administration. The Abwehr was absorbed by the **SS**-run Reich Security Main Office (**RSHA**) in 1944.

ADOLF HITLER SCHOOLS Secondary schools founded in 1937 with the specific purpose of training Nazi Party leaders. Unlike the state-sponsored, public **NAPOLA** schools, the Adolf Hitler Schools were private schools under party control. Due to the war, however, the plan of opening an Adolf Hitler School in every Nazi **Gau** was never realized.

AFRICA CORPS Formed under the command of Erwin **Rommel** in February 1941, the Africa Corps came to the aid of beleaguered Italian troops in the Italian colony of Libya. Rommel drove the British eastward into Egypt, but was defeated in the Battle of El Alamein in November 1942 and forced to withdraw. As a result of the British victory and the Allied landings in Morocco and Algeria on 7–8 November 1942, the Africa Corps was driven back and forced to capitulate at Tunis on 13 May 1943.

AHNENERBE (ancestral heritage) An **SS** research institution founded by **Himmler** and **Darré** in 1937 to investigate German prehistory and folklore for evidence in support of the Nazis' racial world-view. It encompassed 40 separate departments and was headed by Wolfram Sievers (1905–1947), who was sentenced to death at the doctors' trial at **Nuremberg** in 1947 for his role in conducting experiments on concentration camp inmates.

AKTION REINHARD See **Operation Reinhard (T)**.

AKTION T-4 Camouflage designation for the **euthanasia** program directed from a villa in Berlin at Tiergartenstrasse 4 under the authority of the office of Viktor **Brack** in the Führer chancellery.

AKTION 14 F 13 Camouflage designation for the extension of **euthanasia** killings to inmates of concentration camps.

ALLIED CONTROL COUNCIL Central governing organization formed by the four occupying powers in Germany in 1945 with its seat in Berlin. It was made up of the military commanders of the four occupation zones. Because decisions had to be reached unanimously, the Allied Control Council proved ineffective, although it was not formally dissolved until September 1990.

AMT ROSENBERG Unofficial designation for the party office of **Reichsleiter** Alfred Rosenberg as "Plenipotentiary of the Führer for the Supervision of all Intellectual and Ideological Education and Indoctrination in the **NSDAP**." A task force created by this office in 1940 was responsible for the plunder of art works throughout occupied Europe.

ANSCHLUSS Designation for the union of the German-speaking parts of Austria with Germany. Demands for union dated back to the nineteenth century, but the term did not come into widespread usage until after the First World War. After the dissolution of the Habsburg Empire into its constituent national parts the rump German Austria that was created by the victors of the First World War was obligated by treaty to maintain its independence from Germany. Although *Anschluss* was one of the major Nazi goals, **Hitler** was forced to delay implementation until his support of the Italian invasion of Ethiopia in 1935 overcame Mussolini's opposition. *Anschluss* was effected in March 1938 when German troops marched into Austria to prevent an Austrian plebiscite on independence.

ANTI-COMINTERN PACT Anti-Soviet treaty negotiated in November 1936 without Foreign Ministry participation by the Japanese military attaché in Berlin and **Hitler**'s foreign policy specialist **Ribbentrop**. Renewed in 1941, the pact committed its signatories to cooperation in combating the Communist International (**Comintern**) and, in a secret protocol, to benevolent neutrality in the case of a Soviet attack. Italy signed on to the pact in 1937, Hungary and Spain in 1939, and Bulgaria, Croatia, Denmark, Finland, Nationalist China, Romania, and Slovakia in 1941.

ANTI-SEMITISM Term first widely used in the 1870s to designate a political ideology and a movement opposed to the presence and influence of Jews in European societies. Today it is used as a synonym for all forms of Jew-hatred, whether religious, economic, political, or racial. First popularized in Germany by the journalist Wilhelm Marr (1819–1904) in a book entitled *The Victory of Jewry over Germandom* (1879), modern anti-Semitism had a positive connotation for its adherents, standing for repudiation of materialism, commercialism, and immorality. Anti-Semites equated Jewishness or the "Jewish spirit" with selfishness, arrogance, intellectual cunning, worldliness, and a lack of Christian humility, self-restraint, and self-denial. As a political movement anti-Semitism was dedicated to reversing the legal emancipation of Jews in Germany in 1869. Anti-Semitism became a potent weapon of German conservatives and nationalists in their campaign against liberalism, democracy, and socialism – left-wing movements that anti-Semites defined as Jewish-led or Jewish-inspired efforts to undermine traditional institutions and subject German culture and society to Jewish control. Defining Jewishness in racial and biological terms gave anti-Semitism an aura of scientific validity. It also allowed anti-Semites to escape the charge of religious bigotry while at the same time blocking

Jewish assimilation through conversion to Christianity. Racial anti-Semitism was a central component of the Nazi program.

APPEASEMENT Term used to designate the British and French policy of meeting German territorial demands in the 1930s to avoid war. The policy is most closely associated with Neville Chamberlain (1869–1940), British prime minister from 1937 to 1940, who signed the **Munich Agreement** with **Hitler** in 1938.

ARDEATINE CAVES Site near Rome where on 24 March 1944 German **SS** soldiers executed 335 Italian hostages, including women and youths, in retaliation for an attack by communist partisans on a German unit resulting in the death of 33 German soldiers. The SS officer in charge, Herbert Kappler (1907–1978), was sentenced to life in prison by an Italian court in 1947.

ARMY HIGH COMMAND See **OKH** and **OKW**.

ARROW CROSS Strongest Hungarian fascist party originally founded in 1931 and repeatedly banned under the authoritarian regime of Admiral Miklós Horthy (1868–1957). After the German occupation of Hungary in March 1944, the Arrow Cross played a prominent role in the deportation of Hungarian Jews to **Auschwitz**. In October 1944 its leader Ferenc Szálasi (1897–1946) replaced Horthy as head of government with German support. Szálasi was executed in Budapest in March 1946.

ARYAN A term originally used to designate the parent language of the Indo-European family of languages. The idea of an "Aryan" race corresponding to the parent Aryan language was proposed by racial theorists in the nineteenth century, particularly the French aristocrat Joseph Arthur de Gobineau (1816–1882). The idea of Aryan racial superiority was revived by the Nazis and became part of Nazi anti-Semitic doctrine, despite the absence of any anthropological evidence for the existence of such a race.

ARYANIZATION Term for the transfer of property from Jewish to non-Jewish hands. This program became compulsory by law at the end of 1938.

ARYAN PARAGRAPH Provision in the **Civil Service Act** (1933) defining non-Aryans as any person with one or more Jewish grandparents. This definition was retained until the **Nuremberg Laws** (1935) defined a Jew as a person with three or four Jewish grandparents. Persons with one or two Jewish grandparents were defined as *Mischlings*.

ASOCIAL Nazi term for predominantly lower-class citizens who did not conform to the standards of the *Volksgemeinschaft*, including beggars, vagrants, prostitutes, habitually unemployed welfare recipients, alcoholics, and gypsies. Asocials interned in concentration camps were compelled to wear black triangles. Asocials were also subjected to compulsory **sterilization**.

ATLANTIC CHARTER Declaration signed by Prime Minister Winston Churchill and President Franklin D. Roosevelt aboard a British battleship off the American coast on 14 August 1941 outlining joint aims in establishing a new post-war international order. The declaration called for national self-determination, economic cooperation, unrestricted access to markets and raw materials, freedom from fear and want, freedom of the seas, renunciation of force and territorial annexations, and disarmament of aggressors.

AUSCHWITZ Largest Nazi concentration camp and killing center established near the Polish village of Oswiecim in May 1940. It consisted of three camps: the base camp, the holding camp and killing center of Auschwitz-Birkenau, and the industrial wing at Auschwitz-Monowitz, with approximately 40 satellite labor camps supplying workers to nearby industrial enterprises. Approximately 1.2 million victims, mostly Jewish, were systematically killed in gas chambers at Auschwitz-Birkenau using the pesticide **Cyclon B**. Auschwitz was liberated by Soviet troops on 27 January 1945.

AUTARKY Term denoting self-sufficiency in food and raw materials. This became one of the leading Nazi economic goals. Its purpose was to insulate Germany from the vagaries of the world market following the Great Depression and to avoid the possibility of the kind of Allied blockade that had led to defeat in the First World War. Autarky was closely related to military preparations for the acquisition of *Lebensraum* in the **Four-Year Plan**.

AUTOBAHN Network of limited access four-lane highways begun as the Nazis' most important public works project in 1933. By 1936 125,000 workers were employed in the construction of the road system. Military planners participated in selecting the routes to be constructed. By the start of the war only about half of the planned 4,278 miles of highways had been completed.

AXIS Term first used by Mussolini in 1936 to describe the close relationship with Germany that led to Italy's signing on to the **Anti-Comintern Pact** in 1937 and to the Italo-German military alliance known as the **Pact of Steel** in 1939. The alliance was extended to include Japan in the **Tripartite Pact** in September 1940. The term concealed a fundamental contradiction in the goals of the two partners, however. While Mussolini hoped to use Germany as a counterweight against Britain and France in the Mediterranean, **Hitler** hoped the Italian alliance would deter Britain and France from intervening to stop Germany's drive to the east.

B

BABI YAR The site of the worst single massacre of Jews by *Einsatzgruppe* C under the command of Paul Blobel. According to the official report filed in Berlin 33,771 Jews were murdered at Babi Yar on 29 and 30 September 1941, ten days after the capture of Kiev by German forces. Babi Yar continued to serve as a killing site until August 1943, when a task force of concentration camp inmates was ordered to exhume the bodies and remove evidence of the massacre.

BAEDEKER RAIDS Popular term for bombing raids conducted by the **Luftwaffe** against such cultural sites in England as Norwich, Bath, York, and Canterbury in 1942, ostensibly in retaliation for earlier British attacks on Lübeck and Rostock. Karl Baedeker (1891–1859) was the publisher of a series of authoritative German guidebooks for foreign travel.

BALKAN CAMPAIGN German attack on Greece and Yugoslavia on 6 April 1941 to offset the defeat of Italian forces that had invaded Greece in October 1940.

Yugoslavia surrendered on 17 April 1941, the same day that British forces vacated the Greek mainland. The German occupation of Greece was completed in early May 1941. The Germans captured the island of Crete in an airborne assault at the end of May, thus securing their southern flank before the planned launching of Operation **Barbarossa**.

BARBAROSSA Code name for the plan of attack against the Soviet Union, derived from the name of the red-bearded Hohenstaufen emperor Frederick I, who launched the Third Crusade against Islam in 1190. Operation Barbarossa was launched on 22 June 1941.

BARMEN DECLARATION Issued by leaders of the **Confessing Church** in May 1934 at the height of the **Church Struggle**, this declaration rejected the doctrines of the **German Christians** and denounced state intervention into the governance of the German Lutheran Church.

BATTLE OF BRITAIN Aerial battle fought for control of the air for the planned German invasion of Britain (**Operation Sea Lion**) after the fall of France in 1940. The most intense phase of the battle occurred in August and September 1940. The Royal Air Force succeeded in retaining control of the airspace over Britain and the English Channel, thus preventing a German invasion.

BATTLE OF THE BULGE The last desperate German offensive of the Second World War. It was launched in December 1944 in the Ardennes region in northeastern France and Belgium with the objective of capturing Antwerp and encircling Allied forces in the north. The attack petered out in January 1945 due to insufficient supplies of fuel to power the German tanks.

BATTLE OF MOSCOW Soviet counteroffensive in December 1941, preventing the German capture of Moscow and bringing about the failure of Operation **Barbarossa** to achieve its aims.

BAYREUTH Town in northern Bavaria, home of the great composer Richard Wagner (1813–1883), and site of an annual Wagner festival. Bayreuth was also a center for the dissemination of *völkisch* ideology by Wagner's followers both before and after 1933.

BDM (Bund Deutscher Mädels) League of German Girls with the same organizational structure as the **Hitler Youth** for boys. The aim of the BDM was to indoctrinate girls in the Nazi world-view, which identified child-bearing, family-rearing, and domestic service as women's most important functions.

BEER HALL PUTSCH See **Hitler Putsch**.

BELZEC First of the three extermination camps constructed in occupied Poland to carry out the destruction of Polish Jews (see **Operation Reinhard**). The other two were **Sobibór** and **Treblinka**. Construction of Belzec began November 1941. From March 1942 to early 1943 over 600,000 Jews were murdered at Belzec using carbon monoxide gas from diesel motors. The camp was liquidated in spring 1943.

BERGEN-BELSEN Concentration camp north of Hannover in Lower Saxony created in April 1943 to detain foreign Jews to be used as hostages in exchange for Germans interned abroad. Up to autumn 1944 approximately 6,000 Jews were held at Bergen. That same year separate sections for inmates from other concentration camps no longer capable of work and for female inmates were created. Bergen-Belsen was also the destination of numerous **death marches** in 1945. Among the victims who died at Bergen-Belsen was Anne Frank (1929–1945), whose moving diary gained world fame after the war. When British troops liberated the camp on 15 April 1945 they found 56,000 starving and ill inmates, 13,000 of whom died of their weakened condition in the following months. They also found 10,000 unburied corpses, which had to be bulldozed into mass graves to prevent epidemics. The graphic film of this operation brought the reality of Nazi terror home to millions around the world. The commandant of Bergen-Belsen, Josef Kramer (1906–1945), was sentenced to death by a British military tribunal and executed in December 1945.

BERGHOF Hitler's country estate on the Obersalzberg near Berchtesgaden, where he often received foreign dignitaries and conducted state business when not in Berlin. **Hitler** acquired the property in 1928 and had it remodeled and expanded over the years. **Goebbels**, **Göring**, and **Bormann** also built lavish villas close by.

BERNBURG Hospital converted into a **euthanasia** killing site for handicapped patients in northern Germany in late 1940. The killing site was used in both the **Aktion T-4** and **14 f 13** programs. It was not dissolved until 1943.

BIALYSTOK The largest ghetto in the Bialystok district occupied by German forces in July 1941. The ghetto was liquidated in August 1943 despite tenacious resistance, and surviving residents were deported to **Auschwitz** or **Treblinka**.

BIRKENAU See **Auschwitz**.

BLITZ Designation for the bombing of English cities by the **Luftwaffe** in the **Battle of Britain**.

BLITZKRIEG Term first used to describe the military doctrine of rapid surprise attack applied in the German invasion of Poland. It called for rapid advances of armored and motorized forces supported by aircraft to encircle and destroy enemy forces, while the infantry carried out mopping-up operations. Blitzkrieg tactics were designed to avoid the kind of war of attrition that had brought about German defeat in the First World War. These tactics were again successfully applied in the campaign in the west and in the **Balkan campaign**, but they failed to bring about the expected quick victory in the invasion of the Soviet Union (see Operation **Barbarossa**).

BLOOD AND SOIL (*Blut und Boden*) Slogan expressing the Nazi idea of the mystic union of a racially homogeneous indigenous people with the land on which their ancestors had originally settled. First introduced by the conservative philosopher of history Oswald Spengler (1880–1936) in *The Decline of the West* (1918–1922), the notion was appropriated by agricultural specialist Richard Walther **Darré** and other Nazis to contrast the rooted German peasantry to nomadic urban Jewry. The ideology of blood and soil also underpinned the alleged need for *Lebensraum*.

BOLSHEVIKS "Majority" faction of the Russian Social Democratic Party led by Vladimir Ilich Lenin (1870–1924) and Leon

Trotsky (1879–1940). It was this faction that seized power in Russia in November 1917 and established the Soviet state.

BOXHEIM DOCUMENTS Authored by Werner **Best** in 1931 and named after the location in the state of Hesse where they were drawn up, these documents revealed Nazi plans to transform the German state and society after their accession to power. The documents revealed that the Nazis expected an unsuccessful Communist uprising to give them the opportunity to seize power by force. Among the measures advocated in these plans were the introduction of a compulsory work service and extralegal elimination of political opponents. The Boxheim Documents gave the lie to **Hitler**'s assurances that a Nazi government would respect the law. They led to the dismissal of Best from the Hessian civil service.

BOYCOTT AGAINST JEWISH BUSINESSES AND PROFESSIONS The first official anti-Jewish action after the Nazi seizure of power. Scheduled to begin 1 April 1933 under the direction of Julius **Streicher**, the boycott was called off after one day to avoid disruptions to the economy, in which Jewish retailers and manufacturers still played a vital role as employers. German industrialists also opposed continuation of the boycott to avoid foreign retaliation against German exports. Nonetheless, the boycott continued on an unofficial basis in some regions. Party and **SA** members were forbidden to shop in Jewish-owned stores. Jewish businessmen came under increasing pressure to sell their businesses and leave Germany. In 1938 they were forced to do so by law (see **Aryanization**).

BRANDENBURG A former prison north of Berlin that was converted to a killing site for **euthanasia** in February 1940. Some 9,000 patients were killed here before the site was transferred to **Bernburg** in fall 1940.

BROMBERG BLOODY SUNDAY Nazi designation for the killing of ethnic Germans in the Polish city of Bromberg on 3 September 1939, two days after the German invasion. Approximately 1,100 ethnic Germans were killed. This was used as a pretext for the killing of thousands of Polish leaders by **SS** *Einsatzgruppen* in retaliation in the months that followed.

BROWN HOUSE Popular designation for the Nazi Party headquarters in Munich based on brown as the official color of the Nazi movement and the color of **SA** uniforms.

BUCHENWALD Concentration camp for political prisoners, pacifists, and "habitual criminals" opened in July 1937 near the city of Weimar. After the **Reichskristallnacht** pogrom close to 10,000 Jews were interned at Buchenwald with release made conditional on arrangements to emigrate. During the war Polish, French, and Soviet prisoners of war were also interned at Buchenwald. Inmates at Buchenwald and 129 satellite camps were forced to work in German munitions industries. In October 1942 most Jewish inmates were deported to **Auschwitz** to be murdered. Among the prominent victims at Buchenwald was the long-time German Communist Party head Ernst Thälmann (1886–1944), who was shot at the camp on **Hitler**'s orders in August 1944. American troops liberating Buchenwald in April 1944 found 21,000 survivors. Approximately 50,000 inmates had died at the camp. Karl Koch (1897–1945), first commandant at Buchenwald, was executed by the Nazis for corruption in April 1945. His wife Ilse **Koch** was known as the "witch of Buchenwald." Hermann Pister (1885–1948), commandant from 1941 to 1945, was condemned to death in 1947.

C

CASABLANCA CONFERENCE Meeting of President Roosevelt and Prime Minister Churchill with their military chiefs of staff in January 1943. It was here that the invasion of Sicily was given priority over opening a second front in France and agreement on a policy of "unconditional surrender" was reached.

CENTER PARTY Political party founded in 1870 to represent the interests of German Catholics. The party supported the **Weimar Republic**, but voted for the **Enabling Act** in 1933. It dissolved itself under Nazi pressure in July 1933.

CENTRALVEREIN (Central Association of German Citizens of the Jewish Faith) Organization founded in 1893 to combat growing **anti-Semitism** and to advocate equal rights for Jews. It sponsored numerous publications, refuted anti-Semitic lies, and provided legal assistance to victims of anti-Semitic attacks. In contrast to the **Zionist Association** it favored the full assimilation of Jews in German society while maintaining a separate Jewish identity. Its membership numbered approximately 300,000 in the 1930s. After 1933 the Centralverein increasingly supported Jewish emigration. After **Reichskristallnacht** in November 1938 the organization was forcibly dissolved by the Nazis.

CERTIFICATE OF DESCENT Certificate of Aryan descent (see **Aryan paragraph**) required of all civil servants in April 1933 and of all Germans as a result of the **Nuremberg Laws** in September 1935. For Nazi Party membership and membership in its auxiliary organizations proof of non-Jewish descent was required back to 1800.

CHANCELLOR German equivalent of prime minister, or head of government.

CHELMNO Polish village (renamed Kulmhof by the Germans) near Lodz that became a killing site as part of the **Final Solution** in November 1941. Killings were conducted in mobile gas vans using truck exhaust fumes. The camp operated until March 1943 and again between April and August 1944. Over 150,000 Jews were killed at Chelmno.

CHURCH STRUGGLE (*Kirchenkampf*) Conflict between the Nazi-backed **German Christians** and the dissenting **Confessing Church** for doctrinal and ecclesiastic control of the 28 regional Protestant churches in Germany. The term is also sometimes used to designate the struggle of the churches, both Protestant and Catholic, to remain independent from state control. As the Nazi-backed German Christians failed in their effort to control the German Evangelical Church under Reich bishop **Müller**, the Nazis created a new Ministry for Church Affairs under Hanns **Kerrl** in 1935. The Law for the Protection of the **German Evangelical Church** of September 1935 was intended to facilitate Nazi control, but failed to heal the schism. The Nazi Party was itself divided on Church policy. Kerrl hoped to reconcile the ideologies and interests of Church and state, while **Bormann** took an increasingly hard line against the churches, eventually asserting that Christianity and National Socialism were entirely incompatible. For pragmatic reasons, however, resolution of the conflict was tabled until the end of the war.

CIVIL SERVICE ACT Law issued on 7 April 1933 "for the Restoration of the Professional Civil Service" and the dismissal of "officials who entered the civil service after 9 November 1918 without possessing the required or usual training or other qualifications." Under this provision all civil servants who were members of a communist or communist-affiliated organization were dismissed. The **Aryan paragraph** (Article 3) called for the dismissal of all civil servants with one or more Jewish grandparents, with exceptions for civil servants who had already been in office before August 1914, veterans of the First World War, and sons or fathers of soldiers killed in the war. Article 4 provided for the dismissal of all civil servants "whose former political activity does not offer a guarantee that they will at all times without reservation act in the interest of the national state."

COLLECTIVE SECURITY Central doctrine of the **League of Nations** calling for the shared deterrence of aggression. It failed in the 1930s because of the lack of agreement among the major powers about how best to combat fascism, Nazism, and Japanese imperialism.

COMBAT LEAGUE FOR GERMAN CULTURE (Kampfbund für deutsche Kultur) Organization founded by Alfred **Rosenberg** in 1929 to oppose the "degenerate" art of modernism and to promote the conservative art of ethnic Germans. It did not originally have official party status, but became part of the "National Socialist Culture Community" in 1934, which in turn was absorbed by the **German Labor Front** in 1937.

COMINTERN The Third International, an organization founded by Communists in Moscow in 1919 to support the Russian Revolution and promote Communism. It was dissolved in 1943 in deference to the Soviet Union's Western allies.

COMMISSAR ORDER Decree issued on **Hitler**'s order on 6 June 1941 by the Army High Command (OKW) and distributed to army and air-force commanders with instructions to transmit the decree orally to lower commands. It called for the execution of all Communist commissars, officers attached to troop units for political indoctrination, who fell into German hands in the Soviet Union. Commissars apprehended behind the lines were to be turned over to **SS** *Einsatzgruppen* for execution.

COMMUNISM Also referred to as **Bolshevism**. Economic and social system dedicated to the public control of the means of production, including agriculture, industry, banking, commerce, and natural resources. The Nazis considered the destruction of communism to be their major political goal. Hostility to **liberalism**, democracy, and communism was one of the sources of the **Holocaust**, as the Nazis considered Jews to be the originators, disseminators, and beneficiaries of these egalitarian doctrines. See also **KPD**, the acronym for the German Communist Party.

CONCENTRATION CAMP Internment facility created in 1933 by Heinrich **Himmler** as head of the SS to confine opponents of the regime (see **Dachau**) or those defined as undesirable. Seven major camps were established in Germany before the war. Various categories of prisoners were identified by upside-down triangles of different colors: green for criminals, red for political prisoners, black for "asocials" and gypsies, pink for homosexuals, and purple for Jehovah's Witnesses. Jewish prisoners were identified by a yellow triangle sewn on top of the first one to form a Star of David. Inmates were subjected to brutal treatment and were forced to work in quarrying, mining, and other industrial projects. During the war the camp system expanded rapidly to include 24 major camps and more than a thousand satellite camps providing labor for the war effort. Six **extermination camps** were created in occupied Poland in 1941–1942 for the killing of Jews in the so-called "**final solution**."

CONCORDAT Treaty between Germany and the Vatican guaranteeing freedom of public worship, the independence of Catholic Church administration, Church property, and protection of Catholic religious, cultural, and charitable organizations. The question as to whether this included Catholic youth organizations later led to serious disputes between the Church and the Nazi government. Newly invested bishops were obligated to take a loyalty oath to the government. Provision was made for the opening of new Catholic schools and the continuation of religious instruction in public schools. Under Article 32 members of the clergy and religious orders were prohibited from membership and participation in political parties. This latter provision was particularly useful to the Nazis in that it greatly weakened Catholic opposition to Nazi rule.

CONFESSING CHURCH Theological movement in the **German Evangelical Church** opposed to the Nazi-supported **German Christians**. See **Church Struggle**.

CONSERVATIVE REVOLUTION An informal movement of right-wing German intellectuals in the 1920s that called for the redirection of the liberal and social democratic revolution of 1918–1919 into nationalistic and conservative channels. Aware that there was no turning back of the clock to the failed monarchy of the past, members of the "Conservative Revolution" called for a revolutionary upheaval to end Germany's subservience to Western values and institutions and to establish a distinctly German form of socialism – a solidarity based on common membership in the German Volk or race. Representative authors of this movement included the historian Oswald Spengler (1880–1936), the publicist Arthur Möller van den Bruck (1876–1925), the political theorist Carl **Schmitt**, and the novelist Ernst Jünger (1895–1998). Their call for a rebirth of a **Third Reich**, a euphemism for a realm in which selfish interests (liberalism and socialism) and partisan conflicts (parliamentarianism and democracy) had been purged, played into Nazi hands. On the one hand conservative intellectuals celebrated the apolitical nature of German culture and character; on the other hand they worried that this typically German (and conservative) aversion to politics gave a fatal advantage to the supposedly politicized and partisan left. Hence they were ready to support the Nazis, who promised to achieve nationalist and conservative objectives by the unavoidably ruthless means of political struggle.

CORPORATIVE STATE Model of society developed by Catholic and conservative theorists such as Othmar Spann

(1878–1950) as an alternative to the democratic principles of majority rule and "one person, one vote." According to the corporative model, society would be divided into vocational or professional "estates" with each estate electing its own representatives to the national legislature as a way of neutralizing the numerical majority of the lower classes and the labor movement. A version of this model was put into practice in the "Austrofascist" regime of Engelbert Dollfuss (1892–1934) and his successor Kurt von Schuschnigg (1897–1977). The Nazis paid lip service to the corporative state but repudiated it in practice in favor of a dictatorship in which representative bodies had only an acclamatory function.

CRYSTAL NIGHT See **Reichskristallnacht**.

CYCLON B Hydrogen cyanide tablets used as an insecticide and fumigant. Cyclon B gas in lethal doses were used at **Auschwitz** and **Majdanek** to supplant carbon monoxide exhaust fumes in the systematic killing of Jews and other victims in the **Holocaust**.

D

DACHAU Concentration camp near Munich opened by **Himmler** in his function as head of the Munich police on 20 March 1933 to house political prisoners, particularly Communists, Social Democrats, and labor union leaders, many of them Jewish. The camp was under direct **SS** control and not subject to judicial oversight. Under the command of Theodor **Eicke**, Dachau was organized as a model for all later camps.

In the course of the 1930s the camp was expanded to include Jews, Jehovah's Witnesses, oppositional clergy, gypsies, homosexuals, and criminals. After **Reichskristallnacht** approximately 10,000 Jews were interned at Dachau pending their emigration from Germany. During the war the majority of inmates came from conquered or occupied countries. Although a gas chamber was constructed at Dachau in 1942, it was not put into use. Mass murder did, however, take place at Dachau. In October 1941 several thousand Soviet prisoners of war were shot at Dachau. In 1942 more than 3,000 inmates classified as disabled were murdered by gas at **Hartheim** in the course of **Aktion 14 f 13**. In late 1942 Jewish inmates were deported to **Auschwitz** to be killed. A large number of inmates were also subjected to painful medical experimentation. Dachau and its 169 satellite camps provided forced labor for the German munitions industry. Allied troops liberated the camp on 29 April 1945. They found approximately 30,000 survivors. A far greater number had died.

DAF (Deutsche Arbeitsfront) See **German Labor Front**.

DANZIG (Polish *Gdansk*) City of approximately 380,000 predominantly German inhabitants put under **League of Nations** control after the First World War according to the terms of **Versailles**. Although the Nazis gained control of the city parliament in 1934, the status of Danzig as a "free city" remained unchanged under the terms of the **German–Polish Non-Aggression Pact** until the German renunciation of the pact in April 1939. German demands for the return of Danzig was one of the issues that led to the German invasion of Poland in September 1939.

DAP Acronym for Deutsche Arbeiterpartei (German Workers' Party). *Völkisch* party founded in May 1919 in Munich under Anton Drexler (1884–1942) to attract workers to the nationalist counter-revolutionary cause. **Hitler** attended a meeting of the DAP in September 1919 on behalf of the German **Reichswehr**. Hitler joined the party soon after and changed its name to the National Socialist German Workers Party (**NSDAP**) in February 1920.

D-DAY (Decision Day) Term used for the Allied invasion of Normandy on 6 June 1944.

DDP Acronym for Deutsche demokratische Partei (German Democratic Party). A liberal middle-class party originally part of the so-called **Weimar Coalition**. In the course of the Weimar era it moved steadily to the right, ultimately merging with the right-wing Young German Order in 1930 and changing its name to Deutsche Staatspartei (German State Party). Its voters increasingly defected to the Nazis.

DEATH MARCHES Term used to designate the forced evacuations of inmates of concentration camps in the closing months of the war under brutal conditions in which a high proportion of evacuees were murdered or died as a result of starvation, exposure, or disease. Death marches began in July 1944 with the evacuation of the concentration camp created in the ruins of the **Warsaw ghetto** in August 1943. At least 15,000 of the approximately 66,000 inmates evacuated from **Auschwitz** in January 1945 died en route to their destinations in Germany, where many of those who survived the original death marches were once again forcibly evacuated in April. Thousands of the approximately 47,000 evacuees from **Stutthof** and its satellite camps in January 1945 were massacred, either on death marches or while transported on barges in the Baltic Sea. The number of death marches grew in the months that followed as Allied armies closed in from all sides. Of approximately 43,000 inmates of **Buchenwald** forced on to death marches, at least 15,000 died. Tens of thousands of inmates were killed on death marches from **Dachau, Flossenbürg, Sachsenhausen, Neuengamme, Mauthausen**, and **Ravensbrück** in April 1945. Of the hundreds of **SS** guards who accompanied the death marches and participated in the murders only a small minority were ever prosecuted for their crimes.

DEATH'S HEAD UNITS Official designation after May 1939 of SS concentration camp guards under Theodor Eicke. After the start of the war the Death's Head units were included in the Death's Head Division of the **Waffen-SS**.

DEMOCRACY Form of government in which people participate directly in making laws (participatory democracy) or exercise power by electing legislators (representative democracy). Communists defined democracy as a form of government under which all people shared equally in the material benefits of a given society even if they did not participate in decision-making. Nazis shared the conservative hostility to democracy in all its forms because it gave power to the supposedly inferior masses rather than to the superior elites (however defined).

DENAZIFICATION Term used to designate Allied efforts to exclude former Nazi Party members from public offices and influential positions in post-war German society.

DEPORTATIONS Term used to designate the forced transfer of German Jews to the **Generalgouvernement** after the start of the war and the transfer of European Jews to the death camps of the **Final Solution** beginning in late 1941.

DFG Acronym for Deutsche Forschungsgemeinschaft (German Research Institute), an organization that determined the direction of scientific research by controlling its funding.

DFW Acronym for Deutsches Frauenwerk (German Women's Enterprise), an organization founded in October 1933 to bring previously independent women's associations under the Nazi umbrella. It was headed by Reich women's leader Gertrud **Scholz-Klink**, who also headed the **NSF**, the Nazi organization for women.

DIKTAT Term widely used by extreme right-wing groups to designate the **Versailles Treaty**.

DISPLACED PERSONS See **DP**.

DNVP Acronym for Deutschnationale Volkspartei (German National People's Party) founded as a successor to the defunct Conservative Party after the First World War. Under the leadership of Alfred **Hugenberg**, the party allied itself with the Nazis in the early 1930s and facilitated the Nazi assumption of power.

DORA (Dora-Mittelbau) Labor camp (originally a satellite camp of **Buchenwald**) near Nordhausen in the Harz region of central Germany established in August 1943 to provide workers for the subterranean factory constructed to assemble **V2** rockets after the bombing of the original

assembly site in **Peenemünde** on the Baltic Sea coast. Of the approximately 50,000 to 60,000 inmates, more than 10,000 died.

DP Acronym for "displaced persons." Used after the war to designate people forcibly removed from German-occupied territories, especially in Eastern Europe, as well as for the predominantly Jewish refugees and former concentration camp inmates no longer able or willing to return to their former homes in Eastern Europe.

DRANCY Originally a German internment camp for French and British prisoners of war near Paris, Drancy became a transit camp for French and foreign Jews under the command of **SS** captain Alois Brunner (b. 1912) in 1942. Between 1942 and August 1944 more than 60,000 Jews were deported from Drancy to death camps in the east, approximately half of them French citizens.

DRESDEN City in east-central Germany renowned for its culture and architecture. It was the target of a devastating series of Allied air raids on 13–14 February 1945, resulting in an estimated 35,000 deaths.

DSTB Acronym for Deutschvölkischer Schutz- und Trutzbund (German Völkisch Defense and Protection League), the most important *völkisch* umbrella organization formed in 1919. The Nazis were the beneficiaries of the dissolution of the DSTB in 1922 after its involvement in the assassination of the German foreign minister Walther Rathenau (1867–1922) was uncovered. The Nazis absorbed much of its membership.

DUNKIRK Port city in northern France from which the encircled British Expeditionary Force of 220,000 men and 120,000 French and Belgian soldiers were transported to England by the British navy between 26 May and 4 June 1940. Although Dunkirk was a defeat for British forces, the successful rescue operation represented a moral victory.

DVP Acronym for Deutsche Volkspartei (German People's Party), founded after the First World War as a successor to the pre-war National Liberal Party. Liberal in the European sense of favoring a free market, the party voted against the Weimar constitution. Its voters defected to the Nazis in the early 1930s.

E

ECONOMICS AND ADMINISTRATION MAIN OFFICE (WVHA) A main office of the **SS** established in February 1942 under the command of Oswald **Pohl** with responsibility for budget, payroll, procurement, construction, and all the economic enterprises of the SS. The WVHA was also given authority over the concentration camps that provided the slave labor for its industrial enterprises.

EINSATZGRUPPEN Mobile units of **SS** Security Police (**SIPO**) and Security Service (**SD**) deployed behind advancing **Wehrmacht** troops, particularly in Eastern Europe, to monitor political activity, secure government archives, and, above all, to execute alleged political opponents and "racial undesirables." Further subdivided into commando units, *Einsatzgruppen* were already deployed in Austria and Czechoslovakia in 1938. In the Polish campaign in 1939 their main task was to murder the Polish

intelligentsia, predominantly Jewish. Because of sporadic protests by the army leadership in the Polish campaign, the functions of the *Einsatzgruppen* in the invasion of the Soviet Union were already cleared with the **OKW** (Wehrmacht command) and **OKH** (army command) in the spring of 1941. Augmented by members of the criminal police (**KRIPO**), the **order police**, and the **Waffen-SS**, the *Einsatzgruppen* grew to a strength of 3,000 men. They were further subdivided into *Einsatzgruppen* A, B, C, and D, attached to army groups North, Middle, South, and the Black Sea coast, respectively. In the Russian campaign, their main function was to murder Jews, as well as Communist political officers, gypsies, mentally disabled persons, and others accused or suspected of resistance. Up to April 1942, when the mobile units were phased out in favor of stationary killing sites (except for *Einsatzgruppe* D, which continued to be deployed in "anti-Partisan" warfare), over 500,000 persons fell victim to the *Einsatzgruppen*, mainly in mass shootings and killings in mobile gas vans.

EINTOPF The German expression for a one-dish meal. In September 1933 the Nazis designated the first Sunday of every month from October to March as *Eintopf* Sunday. The difference in cost between a one-dish meal (soup or stew) and the usual elaborate Sunday dinner was supposed to go to charity.

EL ALAMEIN Village in northern Egypt 60 miles west of Alexandria where a British counterattack halted the forward march of the **Africa Corps** on 2 November 1942.

ENABLING ACT Euphemistically entitled, "Law to Remove the Distress of People and

State," the Enabling Act gave **Hitler** dictatorial powers for a period of four years. It freed him of dependence not only on the **Reichstag**, but also on the president, whose approval was needed for all legislation passed by decree under Article 48 of the Weimar constitution. The Enabling Act was passed on 24 March 1933 by the two-thirds majority required to change the constitution. The 444 to 94 margin was made possible by the arrest of all 81 Communist Party Reichstag members elected in March 1933 and by the crucial support of the Catholic **Center Party** (73 votes), which hoped to safeguard the independence of the Church in Germany by concluding a **Concordat** with the Reich government. Only the **SPD** voted against the Enabling Act. It was renewed for another four years in 1937 and extended indefinitely during the war.

ETHNIC GERMAN CENTRAL OFFICE (Volksdeutsche Mittelstelle – **VOMI**) Nazi Party office founded in 1936 under the direction of **SS** general Werner **Lorenz** to coordinate policies toward ethnic German minorities in foreign countries. With the appointment of Heinrich **Himmler** as **Reich commissioner** for the strengthening of German ethnicity in 1939, the VOMI became the agency in charge of resettling ethnic Germans on territory conquered from Poland.

ETHIOPIA (formerly Abyssinia) Country in East Africa that was the victim of a savage Italian attack in September 1935.

EUGENICS The "science" of improving the quality of a race or population group by breeding practices. See **racial hygiene**, **euthanasia**, **Sterilization Law**, and **Marital Health Law**.

EUTHANASIA Although the term means bringing about the humane death of persons suffering from incurable diseases, it was misleadingly used to designate the Nazi program to kill mentally and physically handicapped adults and children systematically. The Nazi aim was not to release persons from suffering but rather to strengthen the Volk by eliminating "lives unworthy of living." The euthanasia program was launched on **Hitler**'s secret order (in violation of the official penal code) at the start of the war under the code name **Aktion T-4**. Killings took place in special isolated "hospitals," including **Brandenburg**, **Bernburg**, **Grafeneck**, **Hadamar**, **Hartheim**, and **Sonnenstein**, as well as in occupied Poland. Victims were killed by starvation, lethal injection, and, beginning in 1940, by carbon monoxide gas in chambers disguised as shower rooms. Despite the secrecy of the euthanasia program, it could not be concealed from the public and provoked protests from Church officials, including Protestant bishop **Wurm** and Catholic bishop **Galen**. The program was officially called off in August 1941 after the killing of approximately 70,000 persons. It continued, however, in secret and was extended to include Jewish inmates of concentration camps under the code name **Aktion 14 f 13**. At least another 50,000 persons fell victim to "euthanasia" after the end of Aktion T-4. Euthanasia personnel played a leading role in providing the technical expertise for the mass murder of Jews in the **Final Solution**.

EVIAN CONFERENCE Convened at the urging of President Franklin D. Roosevelt in France in July 1938 in response to the refugee crisis caused by the expulsion of Jews from Austria after the *Anschluss*. Although delegates from 32 countries participated, the goal of providing greater opportunities for Jewish immigration was not achieved. Britain refused to place increased immigration into Palestine on the agenda, France insisted that host countries needed to be found for its own large number of foreign refugees, and the US refused to revise its strict quota system.

EXTERMINATION CAMPS Term sometimes used to designate the six main camps used for the systematic destruction of Jews in the **Holocaust**. The major camps, all located on occupied territory, were **Auschwitz**, **Belzec**, **Chelmno**, **Majdanek**, **Sobibór**, and **Treblinka**.

F

FASCISM Term derived from the Latin *fascis*, the bundle of rods and an axe used as a symbol of authority in ancient Rome and adopted by Benito Mussolini as the symbol of the Fascist movement and of the Italian state from 1926 to 1943. In a wider sense historians use the term to designate all ideologically related radical right-wing movements in Europe between the world wars, including Nazism. Ideologically related movements since 1945 have usually been called "neo-Fascist." Although historians disagree on the precise definition of fascism, it always includes nationalism, authoritarianism, militarism, and palingenesy – a dedication to the rebirth, regeneration, and reproduction of the ancestral racial type.

FATHERLAND PARTY Radical nationalist party founded in 1917 under the chairmanship of Admiral Alfred von Tirpitz (1849–1930) to rally popular support for continuation of the war. Its membership reached 800,000 in September 1918. Disbanded shortly after the end of the war, it nonetheless served as a model for right-wing mobilization. Two of its leaders were Heinrich Class (1860–1954), chairman of the **Pan-German League**, and Wolfgang Kapp (1858–1922), leader of the **Kapp Putsch** in 1920.

FEDERAL REPUBLIC OF GERMANY (FRG) Official name of the state formed in West Germany from the three Western zones of occupation in May 1949. The FRG eventually absorbed the states of the **German Democratic Republic** as well in 1990.

FELIX Code name for a planned military operation to capture the British base of Gibraltar in 1940. The operation was canceled when Spain decided not to enter the war on the German side in December 1940.

FEME MURDERS Term used to designate the summary justice meted out by the **Free Corps** and other right-wing vigilante organizations to members of the political left in the early1920s. The term derived from medieval secret courts

FINAL SOLUTION Code name for the deportation and physical annihilation of all Jews within the reach of the Nazi government. Although the term had already been used with various meanings in **anti-Semitic** literature for decades, the policy of systematic killing was not adopted until the height of the war in 1941. The term was used in this sense in **Göring**'s authorization to **Heydrich** in July 1941 and in the letters of invitation and the agenda of the **Wannsee Conference**. See also **Holocaust**.

FLAK Acronym for *Flugabwehrkanonen* (anti-aircraft artillery).

FLOSSENBÜRG Concentration camp in northern Bavaria opened in May 1938 to provide labor for a neighboring granite quarry. The camp also generated close to a hundred satellite camps principally for the exploitation of labor in armaments-related industries in the area. Flossenbürg was the site of the execution of some prominent members of the German resistance, including Admiral **Canaris**, General **Oster**, and the theologian Dietrich **Bonhoeffer**. The camp was liberated by US troops on 23 April 1945. Of the approximately 100,000 inmates of Flossenbürg, at least 30,000 were killed, hundreds of them on death marches in April 1945.

FOUR-YEAR PLAN Economic program introduced by **Hitler** at the annual Nazi Party rally in September 1936 to make Germany ready for war within four years. It was headed by **Göring**, with full powers to rule the economy by decree. The Office of the Four-Year Plan allocated resources, deployed labor, regulated wages and prices, and planned investments. The technical expertise was provided by the I. G. Farben cartel under its board chairman Carl Krauch (1887–1968). The goal of the plan was not to displace private industry but to augment and assist it in achieving economic self-sufficiency (**autarky**). The state-owned Hermann Göring Works, founded in 1937, produced iron and steel from the low-grade ore that the steel industry rejected as unprofitable. It also produced synthetic fuel, rubber, and other scarce resources. Göring's authority was extended for another four years in 1940, but after the failure of **blitzkrieg** in Russia revealed the inadequacies of the Four-Year Plan, Göring lost most of his authority in the economic sphere to Albert **Speer** in 1942.

FREE CORPS Volunteer military units formed in 1919 to evade demobilization requirements under the terms of the armistice on 11 November 1918 and later the **Versailles Treaty**. Free Corps units were used by the **SPD**-led post-war government to suppress left-wing revolution and strikes, despite the open hostility of Free Corps leaders to democracy. Free Corps soldiers provided the armed force for the failed **Kapp Putsch** in 1920 and participated in border skirmishes with Polish forces in Silesia and other border areas, as well as in efforts to hold the Baltic countries for the German **Reich**. After their formal dissolution in 1920 many Free Corps militants joined right-wing paramilitary groups such as the **SA**.

FRG See **Federal Republic of Germany**.

FÜHRER German term for leader.

FÜHRERPRINZIP See **Leadership principle**.

FUNCTIONALISM A term originally introduced by the historian Tim **Mason** to distinguish interpretations that explain the origins of the Holocaust on the basis of the structural dynamics of the Nazi regime from interpretations that explain the Holocaust as the implementation of **Hitler**'s long-term premeditated plan (see **intentionalism**). The issue that precipitated the debate in the 1970s was the question as to whether Hitler specifically ordered the start of the **Final Solution** or whether he simply allowed a killing process begun by independent lower-level bureaucratic initiatives to continue. Functionalist historians (**Broszat**,

Mommsen) viewed the Holocaust as the result of a contingent, unsystematic, and improvised series of decisions, often made by local and regional officials in their efforts to solve the "Jewish problem" in areas under their authority. An explicit Führer order was not required to set the killing process in motion. Functionalism also influenced other aspects of the interpretation of Nazism, particularly the structure of the Nazi regime, which functionalists viewed as a **polycracy** rather than as totalitarian monolith.

G

GAU Old German term for a geographical region. The Nazi Party organization was subdivided into 42 regions, each headed by a **Gauleiter** with full authority under the **leadership principle**. Each region was further subdivided into districts (*Kreis*), localities (*Ort*), cells (*Zelle*), and urban blocks (*Block*), each headed by a leader with full authority over subordinates in the party and, after the Nazis assumed power, over residents within their respective spheres of authority.

GAULEITER Regional leader of the Nazi Party directly subordinate to the **Reichsleitung**, the national party leadership.

GDR See **German Democratic Republic**.

GENERALGOUVERNEMENT (GG) The area of occupied Poland not annexed directly to the Reich (see **Wartheland**). The GG was originally divided into four districts, **Krakow**, Radom, **Warsaw**, and **Lublin**. After the invasion of the Soviet Union a fifth district, Galicia, was added.

The seat of the German occupation government under Governor-General Hans **Frank** was in Krakow.

GENERAL PLAN FOR THE EAST (Generalplan Ost) A memorandum on how to Germanize the conquered eastern territories of Poland and the Soviet Union drawn up under the leadership of **SS** colonel Konrad **Meyer** in May 1942 at the behest of **Himmler** in his capacity as **Reich commissioner** for the strengthening of German ethnicity. The plan called for the forcible transfer of Slavic populations to Siberia in a multi-year operation expected to cost over 30 million lives. In the course of 25 years the creation of 36 large Germanic settlement colonies were to lead to the transformation of the eastern territories into Germany's new *Lebensraum*. Representatives from the Ministry for the Occupied Eastern Territories and the Racial and Political Office of the Nazi Party participated in the planning. Although German defeats on the eastern front made the full implementation of the plan impossible, it contributed to the brutality of German occupation policies, which ultimately provoked increased resistance from the indigenous population.

GENEVA CONVENTIONS A series of four international agreements, drawn up in 1864, 1906, 1929, and 1949, respectively. The first two conventions regulated the protection of medical personnel and established the protective symbol of the red cross. The third convention regulated the treatment of prisoners of war. All three conventions were formally in force during the Second World War, but widely and deliberately violated, especially by German forces on the eastern front. The fourth convention, drawn up under the impact of the enormous civilian casualties of the Second World War, sought to protect the victims of war from mutilation, torture, and violations of human dignity.

GENOCIDE Term first coined in 1944 to denote the intentional and systematic destruction (both physical and cultural) of a racial, religious, or ethnic group. The statute governing the International Military Tribunal for the **Nuremberg trials** classified genocide as a "crime against humanity." In December 1948 the United Nations General Assembly unanimously adopted an Agreement for the Prevention and Punishment of genocide. West Germany ratified the agreement in 1954. The United States government refused to do so on the grounds that provisions for an international tribunal infringed upon national sovereignty.

GERMAN CHRISTIANS A Protestant movement that sought to combine Christianity with nationalist and racialist goals. As a formal group within the **German Evangelical Church**, the Faith Movement of German Christians was founded by the Nazi **Gauleiter** of Brandenburg Wilhelm Kube (1887–1943), who later became the general commissioner (governor) of White Russia in Minsk, where he was killed by Soviet partisans. At a national synod in July 1933 the German Christians were able to elect Ludwig **Müller** as Reich bishop. Their demands for dropping the Old Testament from the Bible, introducing the **Aryan paragraph** into the Church constitution, and excluding Jewish converts from church membership, provoked the formation of a counter-movement under Martin **Niemöller** known as the **Confessing Church**, which succeeded in thwarting the Nazi takeover of the Church in the so-called **Church Struggle**.

GERMAN COMMUNIST PARTY See **KPD**.

GERMAN DEMOCRATIC PARTY See **DDP**.

GERMAN DEMOCRATIC REPUBLIC (GDR) State formed in the Soviet occupation zone in October 1949. After the collapse of the East German government in 1989, the GDR was integrated into the **Federal Republic of Germany** (FRG) in October 1990.

GERMAN EVANGELICAL CHURCH Official name of the national Protestant church that the **German Christians** sought to establish by unifying Germany's 28 regional Protestant churches in July 1933. This effort to unify German Protestants under a centralized Church government was unsuccessful, however, as a result of the opposition of the **Confessing Church** both to the changes proposed by the German Christians and to state intervention in Church affairs. The efforts of Hanns **Kerrl**, Reich Church minister in 1935, to reconcile the opposing factions by centralizing its governing structure under Nazi control also failed, and the question of unifying the Protestant churches was tabled until the end of the war.

GERMAN FAITH MOVEMENT (Deutsche Glaubensbewegung) An umbrella group created in June 1933 under the leadership of theologian Wilhelm Hauer (1881–1962) and *völkisch* author Ernst zu Reventlow (1869–1943). It sought to combine a number of **nordic** pagan sects into a single movement to compete with the organized Christian churches. Its anti-Christian bias, however, undercut the Nazis' efforts to gain the support of Christian churchgoers. **SS** members were forbidden to join the German

Faith Movement in 1935, and in 1936 it was prohibited from conducting any rites or ceremonies in public.

GERMAN LABOR FRONT (DAF) Nazi Party organization founded in May 1933 to supplant the banned free trade unions. Under its leader Robert **Ley**, the DAF grew into a huge bureaucratic empire that played an important role in the German economy and the administration of labor and welfare policies. Although it claimed to represent the interests of workers, its membership also included employers and salaried management personnel, and its task was to implement wage and benefit policies established by the party or government without worker participation. Membership was officially voluntary, but the DAF was financed by compulsory withholding of a percentage of all workers' wages. Its many economic enterprises included housing construction, insurance, banking, publishing, retailing, shipbuilding, and even an automobile factory (see **Volkswagen**). The DAF was further subdivided into a number of offices responsible for job training, vocational competitions, workplace beautification, and leisure-time activities (see **Strength through Joy**). The main function of the DAF was to maintain labor peace and productivity by keeping workers content. Much of its activities were devoted to propaganda, in keeping with the Nazis' preferred strategy of combating worker disaffection through psychological rather than material compensation. With close to 25 million members, it was the largest mass organization in Nazi Germany.

GERMAN NATIONAL PEOPLE'S PARTY See **DNVP**.

GERMAN PEOPLE'S PARTY See **DVP**.

GERMAN–POLISH NON-AGGRESSION PACT Signed in Berlin in January 1934, this pact renounced the use of force between the two countries for a period of ten years. From the German point of view it provided security from Polish intervention to halt German rearmament and it drove a wedge between Poland and France. After the British guarantee of military support for Poland **Hitler** renounced the pact in April 1939.

GERMAN–SOVIET NON-AGGRESSION PACT Signed in Moscow on 23 August 1939 by German foreign minister **Ribbentrop** and Soviet foreign minister Vyacheslav Molotov (1890–1986), pledging each side to neutrality in case of war with a third power. The pact contained a secret protocol dividing Poland and Eastern Europe into spheres of influence. It paved the way for the German invasion of Poland on 1 September 1939.

GERMAN WORKERS' PARTY See **DAP**.

GERMANIC ORDER (Germanenorden) Secret *völkisch* organization founded in 1912 by the **anti-Semitic** publicist Theodor Fritsch (1852–1933) to combat Jewish influence. After the First World War the Germanic Order became part of the *völkisch* umbrella organization **DSTB**. One of its branches was the **Thule Society** in Munich.

GESTAPO Acronym for Geheime Staatspolizei (secret state police). Originally formed in the state of Prussia in April 1933 under the direction of Rudolf **Diels**, the Gestapo came under **Himmler**'s control in April 1934. In 1936 the Gestapo was merged with the criminal police into the Security Police (SIPO) under Reinhard

Heydrich, head of the **Security Service (SD)** of the **SS**. In 1939 all police and security agencies were integrated into the **Reich Security Main Office (RSHA)**.

GHETTOIZATION Program launched under the direction of Reinhard **Heydrich** in occupied Poland in September 1939 to concentrate Jews in cities and towns with railway connections to facilitate large-scale and rapid population transfers to as yet unspecified and undetermined destinations further east. In each ghetto **Jewish Councils** were formed to execute German orders. The largest such ghettos were formed in **Warsaw**, **Lodz**, and **Lublin**, and, after the German attack on the Soviet Union, in **Kovno** and **Vilna**. Ghetto inmates were forced to work for the German occupiers, and residents incapable of work were liquidated. After the decision for the "**final solution**" was made in 1941, ghettos in Eastern Europe were gradually dissolved and its surviving members deported to the **extermination camps**.

GLEICHSCHALTUNG (coordination or integration) The process of bringing all independent organizations in all fields into line with Nazi ideology and under Nazi control. The term was first used in a law passed by the **Reichstag** on 7 April 1933 excluding from political office all members of the individual state governments who did not belong to the **NSDAP** or the **DNVP** and dissolving state parliaments. This process of purging state governments and bringing them under control of the central government was eventually extended to all institutions and organizations in German society. In practice *Gleichschaltung* was equivalent to suppressing all dissent and diversity, with Jews, Communists, and Social Democrats as the principal targets.

The goal was to create ideological and ethnic uniformity.

GLEIWITZ City in Upper Silesia on the Polish border and site of a "false flag" operation under **SS** colonel Alfred Naujocks (1911–1966) to justify the German invasion of Poland. On 31 August 1939, one night before the planned invasion, Naujocks used SS personnel in civilian clothes to occupy the radio station in Gleiwitz and broadcast a message in Polish calling for war against Germany. The corpses of the Polish translator who read the message as well as a previously drugged concentration camp inmate were left behind for added credibility. Personnel of the SS Security Service (**SD**) secured the site before the arrival of the local police. That same evening feigned attacks were also staged at a German customs post at Hochlinden and a German forestry station at Pritschen. At both locations corpses of criminals previously condemned to death were left behind in Polish uniforms supplied by German counter-intelligence. These attacks were played up in the German press to justify the German invasion.

GRAFENECK First **euthanasia** institution opened in January 1940 in the state of Württemberg and equipped with a gas chamber as part of **Aktion T-4**. More than 10,000 victims were killed at Grafeneck before it was closed in December 1940 and its personnel shifted to **Hadamar**.

GREAT DEPRESSION Severe economic crisis precipitated by the US stock market crash of 1929. In Germany this economic disaster contributed both to growing working-class support for the **KPD** (German Communist Party) and to increased middle-class support for the Nazis.

GROSS-ROSEN Concentration camp opened in August 1940 in Silesia and expanded to include 99 satellite camps and a total of approximately 120,000 inmates, mostly Polish citizens and at least half of them Jewish. The Red Army liberated the abandoned camp in February 1945. An estimated 40,000 inmates were killed at Gross-Rosen and its satellite camps, many of them on death marches at the end of the war.

GUERNICA Town in the Basque area of northern Spain attacked and destroyed by German aircraft of the Condor Legion in April 1937 in support of Franco's anti-republican forces. German propaganda insisted that most of the damage had been self-inflicted by republican troops. Hundreds of civilians were killed in the raid. Guernica became a symbol of fascist savagery, commemorated in a famous painting by Pablo Picasso (1881–1973).

GURS Internment camp in the foothills of the Pyrenees in southern France originally established in 1939 as a camp for refugees and members of the International Brigades in the Spanish Civil War. After the fall of France it was converted into an internment camp for foreigners under the control of Vichy French police. In October 1940 the Jewish population of the German states of Baden and the Palatinate were deported to Gurs. Living conditions deteriorated rapidly. Beginning in 1942 approximately 3,000 Jewish inmates were deported via **Drancy** to the death camps in the east.

GUSEN See **Mauthausen**.

GYPSIES See **Roma and Sinti**.

H

HAAVARA AGREEMENT Agreement signed by the German Economics Ministry with the Jewish Agency in Palestine in August 1933 to permit emigrating German Jews to use a portion of their assets to purchase German products for export to Palestine. This agreement (and a similar one reached with Britain in 1936) stimulated German exports while allowing emigrating Jews to use assets they would otherwise have had to leave behind. From the German point of view it had the advantage of promoting Jewish emigration while restricting the outflow of Jewish capital. It also had the additional advantage of counteracting efforts to organize an international boycott of German goods to protest anti-Jewish persecution.

HADAMAR Killing site of the **euthanasia** program near Limburg opened in January 1941 to replace **Grafeneck**. Well over 10,000 patients were killed here with carbon monoxide gas and, after the official end of **Aktion T-4** in August 1941, by lethal injection or overdoses of medication.

HARTHEIM Killing site of the **euthanasia** program near Linz in Austria opened in May 1940. Over 18,000 victims were killed here under **Aktion T-4**. More than 5,000 inmates of **Dachau** and **Mauthausen** were killed here under **Aktion 14 f 13**.

HARVEST FESTIVAL Code name for a killing operation at the **Majdanek** camp in which approximately 42,000 Jews from Majdanek and surrounding labor camps were rounded up and shot. The killing operation took place in mid-October 1943 shortly after a revolt at **Sobibór** in which several inmates escaped.

HARZBURG FRONT A political rally of the "National Opposition" to the **Brüning** government and the **Weimar Republic** held at Bad Harzburg in October 1931. The rally was organized by the chairman of the **DNVP** Alfred **Hugenberg** in an effort to create a united nationalist front with the Nazis. Other participants were veterans' organizations such as the **Stahlhelm**, as well as prominent representatives of the economic and military elite. Hugenberg and Stahlhelm leader Franz **Seldte** joined **Hitler**'s first cabinet in January 1933.

HENDAYE French town on the Spanish border and site of a meeting between **Hitler** and Spanish dictator Franco and their respective foreign ministers in October 1940. Hitler's efforts to persuade the Spanish dictator to enter the war against Britain failed, leading Hitler to decide in favor of Operation **Barbarossa** on 18 December 1940.

HEREDITARY FARM LAW (Reichserbhofgesetz) Law issued in September 1933 prohibiting the division, sale, or mortgaging of all family farms between approximately 22 and 325 acres in size. Only owners of such farms were permitted to use the title *Bauer*. Only farmers who could trace their **Aryan** descent back several generations were eligible. The law, the brainchild of **Reich** peasant leader Walter **Darré**, was intended to ensure that farms remained within the family in accordance with the Nazi ideology of **blood and soil**. However, by denying owners the right to freely dispose of their property, the law had the effect of lowering the living standard of the small farmers it was meant to protect and worked to the advantage of large-scale farmers.

About 35 percent of German farmers were affected by the law.

HEREDITARY HEALTH COURT (Erbgesundheitsgericht) Judicial body created to implement the **Law for the Prevention of Genetically Diseased Offspring** of July 1933, which called for the compulsory **sterilization** of persons suffering from illnesses or conditions deemed to be hereditary, including blindness or alcoholism. Local and regional hereditary health courts consisted of a judge and two physicians, who decided whether patients should be subject to compulsory sterilization.

HERMANN-GÖRING WORKS State-owned industrial conglomerate to manufacture synthetic war-related products under the **Four-Year Plan**.

HERZOGENBUSCH-VUGHT A **concentration camp** with 13 satellite camps opened in the Netherlands in January 1943. Approximately 30,000 persons were interned here, including approximately 10,500 Jews deported via **Westerbork** to **Sobibór** and **Auschwitz**. The camp was closed in September 1944 as Allied troops advanced. Surviving inmates were shipped to **Sachsenhausen** and **Ravensbrück**.

HIAG Acronym for Hilfsgemeinschaft auf Gegenseitigkeit (Auxiliary Fellowship for Reciprocal Aid), a post-war organization of veterans of the **Waffen-SS** for mutual assistance in overcoming the stigma associated with the **SS** and obtaining the same privileges as veterans of the **Wehrmacht**.

HISTORIKERSTREIT (historians' dispute) Term used to designate the controversy among German historians generated by historian Ernst **Nolte**'s assertion in 1986 that the **Holocaust** should be understood as an understandable overreaction to earlier Stalinist crimes. He was challenged by the social philosopher Jürgen Habermas (b. 1929) and historians Hans **Mommsen**, Eberhard **Jäckel**, and Martin **Broszat**, among others. He was defended by historians Joachim **Fest**, Andreas **Hillgruber**, and Karl **Hildebrand**, among others.

HITLER PUTSCH Hitler's first attempt to seize power with General **Ludendorff** in Munich on 8–9 November 1923. Also sometimes referred to as the "Beer Hall Putsch" because it started at a nationalist rally sponsored by the Bavarian government under Gustav von Kahr (1862–1934) in a Munich beer hall. The putsch attempt failed when Bavarian government and army officials withheld their promised support. Sixteen putschists and three policemen were killed in a shoot-out in front of the war memorial in Munich on 9 November. At the trial that followed Ludendorff was acquitted and **Hitler** was given the minimum sentence allowed by law for high treason. Of that sentence he only served eight months.

HITLER–STALIN PACT See **German–Soviet Non-Aggression Pact**.

HITLER YOUTH Nazi youth organization under Reich youth leader Baldur von **Schirach**. Founded in 1922, the Hitler Youth encompassed all German boys' organizations by law in 1936. Membership became compulsory for all boys, beginning with the cohort of ten-year-olds in 1940. The Hitler Youth grew from a membership of 108,000 in 1932 to around nine million in 1939. The equivalent organization for girls was the Bund deutscher Mädel (**BDM**).

HIWIS Acronym for *Hilfswillige*, volunteers from Eastern Europe, particularly Russians, Ukrainians, Poles, and Latvians, ready to serve as auxiliaries for the **Wehrmacht**, police, and **SS** in Germany's eastern campaign.

HJ Acronym for Hitler-Jugend (**Hitler Youth**).

HOHENZOLLERN Royal family ruling in Prussia from 1525 and in Germany from 1871 to 1918. The most prominent member of the family to join the Nazi Party was **SA** general August Wilhelm (1887–1949), fourth son of Wilhelm II, the last kaiser.

HOLOCAUST Term originally meaning a sacrifice consumed by fire and applied historically to the mass murder of the Jews under the Nazi program of the "**Final Solution** of the **Jewish Question**." The term did not come into widespread usage until the 1960s. By the end of the Second World War approximately six million Jews had been systematically murdered by the Nazi regime. Approximately three million Jews were killed by poison gas (carbon monoxide and **Cyclon B**) at the killing sites of **Auschwitz**, **Belzec**, **Chelmno**, **Majdanek**, **Sobibór**, and **Treblinka**. Another 1.5 million were shot by the *Einsatzgruppen* of the **SS**, units of the **Order Police**, and the **Wehrmacht**. Approximately 1.5 million victims died of disease, starvation, or exposure in the ghettos and **concentration camps** of the **Third Reich**.

HOSSBACH MEMORANDUM Notes taken by **Hitler**'s adjutant Colonel Friedrich **Hossbach** of a meeting on 5 November 1937 at which Hitler informed his foreign minister, the war minister, and the heads of the three branches of the **Wehrmacht** of his intention to launch a war of conquest in the east in the near future.

HOUSE OF GERMAN ART Museum building in Munich designed by architect Paul Ludwig Troost (1878–1934) in the neo-classical design favored by **Hitler** and the Nazis. Hitler's speech at the opening of the museum in 1937 gave vent to the Nazis' hostility to modernism in the arts. The museum was the site of the well-attended exhibition of "degenerate art" staged under the direction of Adolf **Ziegler** in the summer of 1937.

HSSPF Acronym for *Höhere SS- und Polizeiführer* (higher **SS** and police leaders). Established in November 1937, the HSSPF were responsible for directing all policing functions in occupied Europe during the war.

I

INSTITUT FÜR ZEITGESCHICHTE (IfZ) Institute for contemporary history founded in Munich in 1951. It has become the most important scholarly organization for research on Nazism, publishing the quarterly *Vierteljahrshefte für Zeitgeschichte.*

INTENTIONALISM A term introduced by the historian Tim Mason to designate interpretations of Nazism that stress the importance **Hitler**'s specific intentions in the origins of the **Holocaust** (as opposed to **functionalism** or structuralism). Intentionalists explain the Holocaust as the result of long-term plans on the part of the Nazi leadership rather than more contingent

factors such as the circumstances of war. Although intentionalist historians differ in details of interpretation, they agree in their stress on ideology as the crucial factor in Nazi policy formation and on the centrality of Hitler's role in the Nazi system.

INTERNATIONAL MILITARY TRIBUNAL (IMT) Established at Nuremberg in 1945 for the trial of German and Austrian war criminals (see **Nuremberg trials**).

J

JASENOVAC The largest concentration camp in the **Ustasha**-controlled independent state of Croatia backed by the Nazis. The camp was established in August 1941. Of the approximately half a million victims killed at the camp the vast majority were Serbs, but also included at least 20,000 Jews and a lesser number of gypsies. The camp was liberated by Yugoslav **partisans** under Tito (1892–1980).

JEWISH COUNCIL (*Judenrat*) Administrative body mandated by the Nazis for the Jewish ghettos in the east and for Jewish communities in other German-occupied territories. Jewish councils, often made up of representatives of pre-war Jewish community leaders, were used by the German authorities to transmit and enforce German orders and regulations. Jewish councils were also responsible for the organization of medical services, schooling, the allocation of housing, the distribution of food, and related administrative functions. They were forced to collaborate in deportations to the death camps by selecting the victims to be deported.

"JEWISH QUESTION" Term used by German nationalists in the late nineteenth century and the early twentieth to designate the "problem" of Jewish "over-representation" in the professions and the economy, supposedly excessive influence on German society and culture, and alleged political subversion through leadership and participation in liberal, social democratic, and communist parties. Right-wing radicals, including the Nazis, advocated the reversal of Jewish emancipation and the segregation, legal restriction, expulsion, and eventual elimination of Jews as solutions to the "Jewish Problem."

JEWISH STAR Yellow star of David inscribed with "Jew" that all Jews were compelled to wear on their clothing as identification marks. First introduced in Poland and other occupied territories in 1939, it was made mandatory for all German Jews over the age of six on 20 August 1941. Similar identification of Jewish apartments and residences was also made compulsory in March 1942

JUDENREIN (*Judenfrei*) Term used to designate an area "cleansed of Jews" or "free of Jews."

KAPP PUTSCH Radical right-wing attempt to seize control of the **Weimar** government in March 1920 and introduce an authoritarian regime. The leaders of the putsch attempt were the Prussian civil servant Wolfgang Kapp (1858–1922) and General Walther von Lüttwitz (1859–1942), commander of military forces in the Berlin area.

The event that precipitated the putsch attempt was the government's decision, in compliance with the Treaty of **Versailles**, to disband **Free Corps** units. Captain Hermann Ehrhardt (1881–1971), the commander of one such unit, assembled 3,000 men to march on Berlin in support of the coup. The putsch also had the support of General **Ludendorff** and of **Hitler** and other leading Nazis, who traveled from Munich to Berlin to support the coup. They later blamed its failure on the reluctance of the new regime to carry out more extreme measures of repression, including the imprisonment of Jewish leaders. Despite the refusal of the **Reichswehr** to intervene to stop the coup, the Kapp Putsch failed because of its lack of widespread public support. After the failure of the Kapp Putsch, the center of counter-revolutionary conspiracy shifted from Prussia to Bavaria, where the Kapp Putsch had succeeded in installing an authoritarian government under Gustav von Kahr (1862–1934), which gave refuge to radical right-wing groups, including the **Oberland League** and the still minuscule Nazi Party.

KATYN Village near Smolensk in the Soviet Union and burial site of 4,400 Polish officers killed by Soviet secret police (NKVD) in 1940. The Germans discovered the killing site in April 1943, and their request for an investigation by the international Red Cross was supported by the Polish government in exile in London. The Soviets used the opportunity to break off diplomatic relations with the anti-communist Polish government and attributed the killings to the Germans. It was not until 1990 that the Soviet government officially acknowledged responsibility for the killings.

KAUEN (Polish, Kovno; Lithuanian,

Kaunas) Pre-war capital of Lithuania and site of mass killings of Jews from 1941 to 1944. In September 1943 the former Jewish ghetto was converted into a concentration camp on **Himmler**'s orders. More than 50,000 Jews were killed at Kauen by **SS** and Lithuanian collaborators. The Red Army found only 90 survivors when they liberated the camp in August 1944.

KDF Acronym for *Kraft durch Freude*. See **Strength through Joy**.

KOVNO See **Kauen**.

KPD Acronym for Kommunistische Partei Deutschlands (German Communist Party) Founded in January 1919, the KPD was banned by the Nazis following the **Reichstag fire** in 1933. Its leaders and functionaries were subjected to unrelenting persecution

KRAKOW-PLASZOW Concentration camp opened in 1942 in a suburb of Krakow. Survivors of the liquidation of the Krakow ghetto in March 1943 were interned here as forced labor in the German armaments industry. Under its commandant Amon Göth (1908–1946), this camp was the site of mass murder, torture, and severe maltreatment. Approximately 900 inmates were recruited by Oskar Schindler (1908–1974) for his munitions factory, thus saving them from almost certain death. This was the subject of Steven Spielberg's film *Holocaust* in 1992.

KREISAU Silesian estate of Helmuth and Freya von **Moltke** and the site of meetings of the resistance group known as the Kreisau Circle organized by the Moltkes as well as by Peter and Marion **Yorck von Wartenburg**.

KRIPO Acronym for *Kriminalpolizei* (criminal police).

KULMHOF See **Chelmno**.

KURSK Site south of Moscow of the largest tank battle in history from 5 to 13 July 1943, involving 2,000 German and 4,000 Soviet tanks. Defeat at Kursk marked the last major offensive action of German forces on the eastern front.

KZ Acronym for *Konzentrationslager* (concentration camp). KL was also used as an acronym.

L

LAND German term for federal state (US) or province (Canada), e.g., Prussia or Bavaria. The term also means "country" or "countryside."

LAW FOR THE PREVENTION OF GENETICALLY DISEASED OFFSPRING See **Sterilization Law**.

LAW FOR THE PROTECTION OF GERMAN BLOOD AND HONOR See **Nuremberg Laws**.

LEADERSHIP PRINCIPLE (*Führerprinzip*) The basic formula underlying the hierarchical chain of command in the government, party, economy, and society in Nazi Germany, described by **Hitler** in *Mein Kampf* as "authority over all subordinates and responsibility toward all superiors." The leadership principle was conceived as an alternative to the parliamentary principle of majority rule and participatory democracy. In practice, however, the leadership principle led to fierce rivalries between "leaders" and a chaotic proliferation of competing authorities (see **polycracy**).

LEAGUE OF GERMAN GIRLS See **BDM**.

LEAGUE OF NATIONS International organization founded on the initiative of US president Woodrow Wilson (1856–1924) in 1919 with 45 member states and its headquarters in Geneva, Switzerland. Its charter was incorporated into the **Versailles Treaty**, which was never ratified by the US, thus weakening the League from the start. Germany joined the League after signing the **Locarno Treaty** in 1926, but left the League in 1933 to gain the freedom to rearm.

LEBENSBORN (fount of life) **SS** agency founded 1935 to increase the national birthrate by encouraging racially pure unmarried German women to have children. *Lebensborn* provided free maternity care and care for racially pure children born out of wedlock. Approximately 8,000 children were born in *Lebensborn* facilities, the majority to unmarried women. During the war the organization was also used for the compulsory "Germanization" of children from occupied areas of Europe deemed to be "racially valuable." Although SS members were officially encouraged to father children, *Lebensborn* homes were not, contrary to legend, used as breeding facilities.

LEBENSRAUM (living space) Concept used to justify German conquest and settlement of territory in Poland and the Soviet Union. The term was popularized in the works of the geographical theorists Friedrich Ratzel (1844–1904) and Karl Haushofer (1869–1946), and was part of the geopolitical discourse of the **Pan-German League** before the First World War. Their basic assumption was that Germans were a "people without space" (the title of a 1926 novel by Hans Grimm [1875–1959]). While originally the concept was used to defend Germany's colonial aspirations, under the Nazis it was redirected to eastward expansion on the European continent. In *Mein Kampf*, **Hitler** criticized the objective of restoring Germany's 1914 boundaries as inadequate to its needs for new territory. The Nazis also added a racist dimension: because the coveted territory in the east was populated by inferior Slavic races, the Germans as a superior people claimed the right under the laws of Social Darwinism to seize it for themselves.

LEFT-WING/RIGHT-WING Conventional distinction between political movements and ideologies based on their advocacy or rejection of human equality as a social ideal. Movements advocating equality occupy the left side of the spectrum, movements advocating hierarchy and opposing equality are on the right. Fascism and Nazism are movements of the extreme right, resembling communism as a movement of the extreme left in their resort to extreme methods (violence, deception, **propaganda**, mass mobilization, suppression of individual rights) to achieve their respective goals. **Liberalism** is generally located in the center of the political spectrum as liberals reject the extremist principle that the ends justify the means.

LIBERALISM Political philosophy dedicated to the protection of individual rights, tolerance of individual differences, equality under law, representative and constitutional government, and free economic activity. Liberalism in the European sense is defined by the absence of government intervention, not by support for government social programs. The Nazis shared the conservatives' disdain for liberalism as a divisive and seditious ideology that supposedly undermined the authority of government, the solidarity of a people, the public role of religion, and the sense of duty and service of individuals to their nation, thus paving the way for international socialism or communism.

LICHTENBURG Concentration camp opened in 1933 in central Germany near Leipzig for political detainees. Its approximately 1,200 inmates were transferred to **Buchenwald** when it opened in 1937. Lichtenburg then became a concentration camp for women. In May 1939 its inmates were transferred to the newly opened **Ravensbrück** camp and Lichtenburg was closed.

LIDICE Czech town near Prague whose entire male population over the age of 15 (approximately 185 men) were shot by the **SS** on 10 June 1942 in reprisal for the assassination of Reinhard **Heydrich** by members of the Czech underground. Women and children were sent to **concentration camps**, where many of them died. The settlement was leveled on **Hitler**'s orders. Like **Oradour-sur-Glane** it became a symbol of resistance and of Nazi savagery.

LITTLE ENTENTE Alliance system launched on the initiative of Czech foreign minister Edvard Benes (1884–1948) uniting Czechoslovakia, Romania, and Yugoslavia against the revisionist aspirations of Italy, Austria, and Hungary in 1920. It enjoyed the support of France, but was gravely weakened by the **Munich Agreement** in 1938.

LOCARNO TREATY A pact signed by Germany, Britain, France, and Belgium in Locarno, Italy in October 1925 to guarantee the post-First World War borders in the west, thus relinquishing German claims to Alsace-Lorraine. Germany's eastern borders were not similarly guaranteed, although Germany did sign bilateral agreements with Poland and Czechoslovakia, mandating arbitration and the renunciation of force in border disputes. The pact also confirmed the demilitarization of the **Rhineland** and committed its signatories to seeking peaceful resolution of all disputes. The pact paved the way for German entry into the **League of Nations** in September 1926. **Hitler** renounced the pact in March 1936 in conjunction with the remilitarization of the Rhineland.

LODZ (German: Litzmannstadt) Largest Jewish ghetto in the areas of occupied Poland formally annexed to the German Reich as the **Wartheland**. Originally planned as a transit camp for deportation of Jews to the **Generalgouvernement**, the failure of that plan led to the enclosing of the ghetto in April 1940 and the use of ghetto residents as forced labor in German munitions factories. Between January 1942 and July 1944 over 80,000 Jews from the Lodz ghetto were gassed at **Chelmno**. The remaining 60,000 inhabitants were eventually deported to **Auschwitz** where most of them died. The Lodz ghetto was liquidated in August 1944.

LUBLIN-MAJDANEK Concentration camp erected by Soviet prisoners of war in a borough of the Polish city of Lublin in the **Generalgouvernement** in October 1941 for the incarceration of Jews and Poles to be used as forced labor. In the late summer of 1942 gassing facilities were added. Some

200,000 inmates were murdered, including at least 60,000 Jews, before the liberation of the camp by Soviet forces in July 1944. Lublin was also the site of Operation **Harvest Festival** on 3 November 1943 when 17,000 inmates were shot by **SS** perpetrators in a single day.

LUFTWAFFE German Air Force.

M

MADAGASCAR PLAN Plan to deport approximately four million European Jews to a German-run reservation to be created on the French colonial island of Madagascar off the East African coast after the fall of France in June 1940. The plan was drawn up by Adolf **Eichmann** in the **RSHA** at the behest of the Foreign Ministry. Its implementation, however, depended on a successful end of the war against Britain, which was not forthcoming. The plan was dropped in favor of deporting Jews to conquered territories in the USSR after the invasion of Russia in June 1941.

MAGINOT LINE Series of allegedly impregnable defensive fortifications built on the instructions of French minister of war André Maginot (1877–1932) between 1929 and 1932 along the French–German border from Switzerland to Belgium. In 1940, however, the Germans attacked through the unfortified Ardennes forest, which was considered impassable by tanks. The Maginot line symbolized the defensive mentality of French military leaders, who failed to prepare adequately for mobile warfare.

MAJDANEK See **LUBLIN-MAJDANEK**.

MARITAL HEALTH LAW Officially named "Law for the Protection of the Hereditary Health of the German People," the Marital Health Law was issued on 18 October 1935 as a supplement to the **Sterilization Law**. It prohibited mentally and physically handicapped persons from marrying unless they could produce a certificate of marital fitness issued by the Office of Health.

MARRIAGE LOANS In 1933 the Nazis issued a law, officially labeled the "Law for the Reduction of Unemployment," to encourage marriage by offering loans to women that could be paid off by bearing children on condition that they give up their employment. The main purpose was to increase the German birth rate. The ban on employment of women receiving marriage loans was revoked in 1937 to combat the growing labor shortage..

MAUTHAUSEN A **concentration camp** near Linz in Austria opened in August 1938 after the *Anschluss* earlier that year. This was the only camp classified as "category III" for "heavily incriminated, incorrigible . . . and untrainable prisoners," who were deliberately worked to death in neighboring quarries. In 1942 inmates from all over Europe were also used as forced labor in armaments factories. Mauthausen eventually spawned 56 satellite camps, the most important of which were at Gusen. In 1941/1942 approximately 5,000 prisoners were gassed at the **Hartheim** facilities before a gas chamber was put into service at Mauthausen itself in 1942. Mauthausen was liberated by US troops on 5 May 1945. At least 100,000 persons are estimated to have lost their lives at Mauthausen and its satellite camps.

MAY DAY Established by the Second

Socialist International in 1889 as the day of labor, the 1st of May was established as a legal holiday by the Nazis in 1933 to win over blue-collar workers. It was eventually renamed the "National Holiday of the German Volk."

MEIN KAMPF (My Struggle) Title of **Hitler**'s book, the first volume of which was written while he was confined in Landsberg prison in 1924. The autobiographical first volume, subtitled *A Settlement of Accounts*, was published in July 1925. A second volume, subtitled *The National Socialist Movement*, appeared in December 1926.

MEMEL East Prussian city on the Baltic Sea annexed by Lithuania in 1923 because of its large Lithuanian minority. It was returned to German control on 23 March 1939.

MISCHLING (mixed breed) Category created for persons of mixed descent in the first amendment to one of the **Nuremberg Laws**, the **Reich Citizenship Law**, in November 1935. A *Mischling* of the first degree was defined as any person with two Jewish grandparents. A person with one Jewish grandparent was designated a *Mischling* of the second degree. Germans in these categories retained some citizenship rights and were subject to milder discriminatory treatment and regulations than full Jews. German *Mischlinge* were generally excluded from deportations during the **Holocaust**. In occupied areas no such distinction was made.

MITTELBAU See **DORA**.

MITTELSTAND Archaic term for the "estate" of independent artisans, shopkeepers, and peasant farmers favored by the Nazis and theorists of the "**corporative state**." The "old" *Mittelstand* of pre-industrial small proprietors and producers and the "new" *Mittelstand* of lower and mid-level salaried employees, fearful of their loss of property and status under socialism, provided much of the mass support for the Nazis.

MONTOIRE Site of a meeting between **Hitler** and **Vichy** France president Henri Philippe Pétain (1856–1951) and Prime Minister Pierre Laval (1883–1945) on 24 October 1940, two days after Hitler's unsuccessful meeting with Franco at **Hendaye**. Hitler failed in his efforts to persuade the Vichy leaders to participate actively in the war against England.

MORGENTHAU PLAN Plan proposed by US Secretary of the Treasury Henry Morgenthau (1891–1967) in August 1944 for the permanent division of Germany into three states and the internationalization of the economies of the **Ruhr** and of the North Sea coast. The purpose was to establish an agrarian-based economy that would make any future aggression impossible. Although Roosevelt and Churchill gave this plan their tentative approval at their meeting in Quebec on 15 September 1944, their foreign ministers Cordell Hull (1871–1955) and Anthony Eden (1897–1977) successfully opposed the plan. One of its effects was to give some credibility to the Nazis' claim that the Allies intended to destroy Germany.

MOTHER'S CROSS Award introduced in 1938 for "**Aryan**" mothers to encourage them to bear many children. The bronze cross was awarded to mothers of four children, the silver cross for six children, and the gold cross for eight children.

284

MUNICH AGREEMENT Signed by **Hitler**, Mussolini, British prime minister Neville Chamberlain (1869–1940), and French prime minister Edouard Daladier (1884–1970) on 30 September 1938, this agreement ceded the **Sudetenland** to Germany and called for an internationally supervised plebiscite to determine the future Czech–German borders. Neither Czechoslovakia nor the Soviet Union were invited to participate in the Munich Conference. The Munich Agreement is generally regarded as the most flagrant example of the Franco-British **appeasement** policy.

N

NAPOLA Acronym for *Nationalpolitische Erziehungsanstalten* (National-Political Education Institutes). Specially selected elite secondary boarding schools designed to become models of Nazi instruction, emphasizing military sports, agrarian work service, and historical field trips as well as academic preparation. The **SS** managed to wrest control of these schools from the Ministry of Education through the appointment of August **Heissmeyer** to head the NAPOLA.

NATIONAL DEMOCRATIC PARTY See **NPD**.

NATIONAL SOCIALIST GERMAN STUDENT LEAGUE See **NSDStB**.

NATIONAL SOCIALIST GERMAN TEACHERS' LEAGUE See **NSLB**.

NATIONAL SOCIALIST GERMAN WORKERS' PARTY See **NSDAP**.

NATIONAL SOCIALIST WELFARE ORGANIZATION (NSV) Founded in Berlin in 1931, the NSV became the second-largest Nazi mass organization under its director **SS** captain Erich Hilgenfeldt (1897–1945) after 1933. Its 17 million members was second only to the 25 million members of the **German Labor Front**. All non-governmental welfare and charity organizations were eventually incorporated into the NSV. Its functions included annual charity collections (see **Winter Relief Agency**), social services such as the "Mother and Child Agency" to care for needy families, the evacuation of children from urban areas, and assistance to bombing victims during the war. Disbursement of benefits, however, was based on racial and **eugenic** principles. Only racially "healthy" "**Aryans**" were eligible to receive support.

NATIONAL SOCIALIST WOMEN'S UNION See **NSF**

NATIONALIST PARTY See **DNVP**.

NATZWEILER-STRUTHOF A **concentration camp** in Alsace opened in May 1941 to make forced labor available to neighboring quarries and for road and tunnel construction as well as armaments production. It had 49 satellite camps. Many **Night-and-Fog Decree** victims were interned here. The camp was closed in September 1944 to escape the advancing Allied armies. Surviving inmates were transferred to other camps, mostly to **Dachau**. Estimates of inmates killed at Natzweiler range from 6,000 to 12,000.

NAVAL AGREEMENT Treaty between Germany and Britain in June 1935 limiting German naval construction. The German navy was not to exceed one-third the strength and size of the British navy. However, the treaty in effect authorized Germany to disregard the limits set by the **Versailles Treaty**. It therefore retroactively sanctioned Germany's unilateral violation of the Versailles Treaty in reestablishing universal military training in March 1935 and undermined French efforts to prevent German rearmament by force if necessary. See **Appeasement**.

NAZI Popular and pejorative abbreviation for the **NSDAP** derived from the first two syllables of national as it is pronounced in German. Members of the **SPD** were often referred to as Sozis.

NAZI–SOVIET NON-AGGRESSION PACT See **German–Soviet Non-Aggression Pact**.

NEO-NAZISM Term used to designate ideas, groups, organizations, and parties that sought to revive Nazi ideology after the Second World War. The most important of these parties in the Federal Republic were the Sozialistische Reichspartei (SRP), which was banned in 1952; the **NPD**, which benefited from the backlash against the protest movements of the 1960s; and the Republikaner and Deutsche Volksunion (DVU), which capitalized on hostility to immigrants and foreigners in the 1980s and 1990s. No neo-Nazi party in Germany has so far gained enough support to enter the Bundestag (the national parliament). Regionally neo-Nazi parties have been more successful, particularly in the new states of the former German Democratic Republic after the fall of Communism. Racist violence remains a serious problem, especially among disaffected male youth in economically depressed areas of the east.

NERO ORDER Führer order of 19 March 1945 named after the Roman emperor Nero (who supposedly fiddled while Rome burned). **Hitler** demanded a "scorched earth" policy that would deny the enemy the infrastructure to govern the conquered areas of Germany. In a memo on 29 March 1945 minister for armaments and munitions Albert **Speer** sought modification of the order because of its destructive effects on the German civilian population. Although Hitler allegedly told him that if the war was lost, the German people did not deserve to live, Speer was able to persuade Hitler to leave his ministry in charge of implementing the Nero order. According to his postwar testimony Speer was able to block full implementation of the order.

NEUENGAMME Concentration camp opened as a satellite camp of **Sachsenhausen** in December 1938 in a village near Hamburg and converted into an independent camp in 1940 to provide forced labor for construction work in the Hamburg harbor. As the need for labor in the armaments industry grew during the war, Neuengamme eventually included 73 satellite camps. Of the estimated 106,000 inmates, approximately 55,000 were killed.

NIGHT-AND-FOG DECREE Führer order issued 7 December 1941 authorizing the secret rendition to Germany of any resistance fighters not sentenced to death by military courts in occupied areas. They were to be deported to Germany and tried by special courts. Those not sentenced to death were to be permanently detained in concentration camps. No contact with the home country was to be permitted. Approximately 7,000 resistance fighters fell victim to this decree, most of them French.

NIGHT OF THE LONG KNIVES Popular designation for the purge of Ernst **Röhm** and other **SA** leaders by members of the **SS** on 30 June 1934.

NORDIC IDEOLOGY Doctrine of Nordic racial superiority propagated in Nazi Germany.

NOVEMBER CRIMINALS Pejorative designation applied by the radical right in Weimar Germany to the signatories of the armistice that ended the First World War on 11 November 1918, such as Matthias Erzberger (1875–1921), as well as members of the Social Democratic Council of People's Representatives who assumed power after the abdication of the kaiser on 9 November 1918 and proclaimed a republic. Among the most prominent politicians denounced by the *völkisch* right were the **SPD** leaders Friedrich Ebert (1871–1925), first president of the **Weimar Republic**, and Philipp Scheidemann (1865–1939), first prime minister of the new republic. The Nazis made extensive use of the term to attack the "November republic" and the "November system."

NOVEMBER POGROM See **Reichskristallnacht**.

NPD Acronym for Nationaldemokratische Partei Deutschlands (National Democratic Party of Germany), a **neo-Nazi** party founded in November 1964 in West Germany. Although it gained representation in several state parliaments, it has never succeeded in obtaining the minimum 5 percent of the vote required for representation in the Bundestag, the national parliament.

NSBO Acronym for Nationalsozialistische Betriebszellenorganisation (National Socialist Workplace Cell Organization). Founded in 1928 for the purpose of recruiting workers, the NSBO lost whatever influence it had after the formation of the **German Labor Front**.

NSDÄB Acronym for Nationalsozialistischer Deutscher Ärztebund (National Socialist German Physicians' League).

NSDAP Acronym for Nationalsozialistische Deutsche Arbeiterpartei (National Socialist German Workers' Party). The **DAP**, forerunner of the NSDAP, was renamed on **Hitler**'s initiative in February 1920.

NSDDB Acronym for Nationalsozialistischer Deutscher Dozentenbund (National Socialist League of University Teachers).

NSDSTB Acronym for Nationalsozialistischer Deutscher Studentenbund (National Socialist German Student League). Nazi student organization founded in 1925 primarily for the purpose of campaigning against Jewish, liberal, and leftist professors. The NSDStB was formally integrated into the Nazi Party in 1934. Perhaps its most spectacular action was its sponsorship of the book-burning of the works of "degenerate and Jewish" writers in German university towns on 10 May 1933.

NSF Acronym for Nationalsozialistische Frauenschaft (National Socialist Women's Union). Founded in 1931, the NSF was integrated into the party structure as an official agency in 1935. Designed as an auxiliary of Nazi women leaders under the direction of Gertrud **Scholtz-Klink**, the NSF's role in decision-making was very limited. Its major activity was ideological indoctrination through special courses for women.

NSKG Acronym for Nationalsozialistische Kulturgemeinde (National Socialist Cultural Community) See **Combat League for German Culture**.

NSLB Acronym for Nationalsozialistischer Lehrer Bund (National Socialist Teachers' League). Founded in 1929 by Hans Schemm (1891–1935), **Gauleiter** of eastern Bavaria, for the purpose of indoctrinating teachers in the Nazi world-view.

NSV Acronym for Nationalsozialistische Volkswohlfahrt. See **National Socialist Welfare Organization**.

NUREMBERG LAWS Set of **anti-Semitic** laws passed by the **Reichstag** in September 1935, including the **Reich Citizenship Law**, restricting citizenship to ethnic Germans, and the **Law for the Protection of German Blood and Honor**, prohibiting marriage and sexual intercourse between ethnic Germans and Jews. A regulation to the Reich Citizenship Law was issued by the Interior Ministry in November 1935 defining a person with three or four Jewish grandparents as a Jew and a person with one or two Jewish grandparents as a *Mischling*. The Nuremberg Laws also prohibited Jews from flying the **swastika**, now designated as the official national flag.

NUREMBERG TRIALS Series of trials held before the International Military Tribunal established by the Allies in Nuremberg in August 1945. The US, the UK, the USSR, and France provided both judges and prosecutors. Representatives from countries occupied by Germany were also present at Nuremberg to assist in preparing cases for prosecution. The trial of major war criminals from October 1945 to October 1946 resulted in death sentences for **Göring, Ribbentrop, Rosenberg, Frick, Sauckel, Streicher, Seyss-Inquart, Kaltenbrunner, Keitel, Jodl,** Hans **Frank,** and **Bormann** (*in absentia*). **Ley** committed suicide before the start of the trial. **Hess, Funk,** and **Raeder** received life sentences. **Speer** and **Schirach** were sentenced to 20 years, **Neurath** and **Dönitz** 15 and ten years, respectively. **Papen, Schacht,** and **Fritzsche** were acquitted over Soviet objections. Major war criminals were tried on four counts: conspiracy to wage war, crimes against peace, war crimes in contravention of international agreements on the rules of war, and the newly established "crimes against humanity" for genocidal crimes. Twelve subsequent trials were conducted at Nuremberg by American occupation authorities against leading military, medical, and judicial figures of the **Third Reich**; leading industrialists and business executives; Foreign Office officials and leading civil servants; and **SS** officers involved in *Einsatzgruppen*, the administration of **concentration camps**, and slave labor programs. Of the 185 defendants indicted, 131 were convicted, 24 were sentenced to death, and 12 were executed.

O

OBERLAND LEAGUE (Bund Oberland) *Völkisch* paramilitary organization founded in 1921 after the forced dissolution of the Oberland **Free Corps**. Led by the Reich veterinary leader Friedrich Weber (1892–1956), the Oberland League participated in the **Hitler Putsch** in November 1923 and was merged into the Nazi Party after its refounding in 1925.

ODER–NEISSE LINE The boundary between Germany and Poland since the end of the Second World War along the Oder and (western) Neisse rivers. The border was formally recognized by international treaty in the settlements accompanying the reunification of Germany in 1990.

OKH Acronym for *Oberkommando der Heeres* (Supreme Command of the Army). The OKH, established in 1936, was headed by **Fritsch** (until February 1938), **Brauchitsch** (until December 1941), and then by **Hitler** in person.

OKL Acronym for *Oberkommando der Luftwaffe* (Supreme Command of the Air Force). Established in 1934 with **Göring** as its head until April 1945.

OKM Acronym for *Oberkommando der Kriegsmarine* (Supreme Command of the Navy). The OKM, established in 1935, was headed by admirals **Raeder** (until January 1943), **Dönitz** (until May 1945), and Hans Georg von Friedeburg (1895–1945).

OKW Acronym for *Oberkommando der Wehrmacht* (Supreme Command of the Armed Forces). The OKW, established in 1938 when **Hitler** took over the functions of minister of war, was headed by General **Keitel** until the end of the war, with General **Jodl** as chief of operations.

OPERATION OVERLORD Code name for the Allied invasion of Normandy on 6 June 1944.

OPERATION REINHARD(T) (Aktion Reinhard) Code name for the systematic murder of the Jews of Poland carried out at **Belzec**, **Sobibór**, and **Treblinka** in 1942 and 1943 as part of the "**final solution**." The name originally derived from the Finance Ministry official Fritz Reinhardt (1895–1969), who was responsible for converting assets and valuables collected from Jewish victims into revenues for the SS. After the assassination of Reinhard **Heydrich** in May 1942, the operation was dedicated to his memory. Operation Reinhard was prepared by Odilo **Globocnik**, the head of the SS police in the **Generalgouvernement**, with the technical aid of the **euthanasia** specialists under Christian **Wirth**. Approximately 1,750,000 Jews were killed in the Operation Reinhard death camps.

OPERATION SEA LION Code name for the planned German invasion of Britain in July 1940. The plan was not officially rescinded until 1942.

OPERATION TORCH Code name for the Anglo-American landings on French colonial territory in North Africa in November 1942.

ORADOUR-SUR-GLANE Village in southwestern France destroyed by troops of an SS armored division on 10 June 1944 in retaliation for partisan attacks; 642 persons were killed, with only 36 survivors. The ruins of the village were left as a memorial to the atrocity of war.

ORANIENBURG Site near Berlin of a **concentration camp** opened under SA auspices in March 1933 for political detainees arrested under the **Reichstag Fire Decree**. The camp was closed in March 1935. Oranienburg was also the site of the concentration camp **Sachsenhausen** opened in August 1936.

ORDENSBURG (Order Fortress) Special secondary schools run by the **German Labor Front** for the training of Nazi Party functionaries. Three such schools were established. They were to be run like religious orders with strict discipline, hierarchical structure, and communal goals to indoctrinate their members in the Nazi world-view.

ORDER POLICE (*Ordnungspolizei*) Placed under the command of **SS** general **Daluege** in 1936, the Order Police included all uniformed communal, regional, and local police forces, as well as firefighters, emergency medical teams, and non-uniformed administrative personnel such as building or health inspectors. Battalions of the Order Police participated in policing, and rounding up and killing Jews in occupied territories during the war.

ORPO Acronym for *Ordnungspolizei*. See **Order Police**.

P

PACT OF STEEL Term coined by Mussolini for the German–Italian friendship treaty and military alliance signed in Berlin on 22 May 1939, formalizing the **Axis** established by Italy's adherence to the **Anti-Comintern Pact** in 1937. The alliance was extended to include Japan in the **Tripartite Pact** of September 1940. **Hitler** sought the Pact of Steel to create optimal conditions for war against Poland. For Italy the main advantage was Germany's concession of sovereignty over the disputed territory of South Tyrol. The pact never led to full Italian–German military coordination. It ended when Italy signed an armistice with the Western powers in September 1943 and declared war on Germany.

PAN-GERMAN LEAGUE Founded in 1891, the Pan-German League advocated colonial expansion and the creation of a Greater Germany embracing all ethnic Germans in Europe. An important ideological forerunner of Nazism, the Pan-German League took a radically **anti-Semitic** turn under the leadership of Heinrich Class (1868–1953) in 1908. In a famous pamphlet entitled *If I Were the Kaiser* (1912) Class called for suppression of the **SPD**, abrogation of Jewish citizenship rights, and German expansion to the east. Its relatively small upper-middle class membership exercised disproportionate influence in the Wilhelmian Empire, but it was rapidly overtaken by the mass-based **NSDAP** after the First World War.

PANZER German term for tank.

PARTISANS Term to describe guerrilla forces or civilian combatants not part of regular armed forces resisting foreign occupation. Although entitled by the Hague Convention of 1907 to prisoner-of-war status when captured, partisans were designated by German occupation forces as "terrorists" and "bandits" not subject to the protections of the rules of war. Ruthless German occupation policies led to the growth of partisan forces, particularly in the Soviet Union, Yugoslavia, Italy, and France. Communist resistance was especially fierce. By 1944, according to German estimates, there were approximately 250,000 partisans operating behind German lines on the eastern front. Partisan forces in Yugoslavia under Josip Tito (1892–1980) inflicted heavy losses on the

German army, including at least 55,000 casualties in the first half of 1944 alone. The casualty rate among partisans was also extremely high.

PEENEMÜNDE Location on the Baltic Sea of the Army Weapons Office research and production facilities for the **V-weapons** under General Walter Dornberger (1895–1980) and Wernher von **Braun**. It was destroyed by the British Royal Air Force in August 1943. The rocket production facilities were then moved underground at **Dora**.

PEOPLE'S COURT (*Volksgerichtshof*) Special court established on 24 April 1934 for the prosecution of treason and political crimes, including pacifism and defeatism. Justices were appointed by **Hitler**, the rights of the defense were strictly limited, and there was no appeal from its verdicts. The court was headed by **Thierack** from 1936 to 1942 and by **Freisler** until February 1945. In the course of the **Third Reich** the People's Court meted out an estimated 5,200 death sentences.

PERSILSCHEIN Certificates attesting to the innocence of former Nazis in the **denazification** process after the war. The term, derived from the German detergent Persil, was used ironically as a euphemism for "whitewash."

PHONY WAR Term used to characterize (and ridicule) the inaction of Western troops between the start of the war in September 1939 and the German assault beginning 10 May 1940.

PLEBISCITE A referendum on a specific question repeatedly used by the Nazis to obtain popular ratification of controversial measures, such as withdrawal from the **League of Nations** or the *Anschluss* of Austria.

PLÖTZENSEE Prison in northwestern Berlin used as the site for the execution of political prisoners, dissidents, and members of the resistance condemned to death by the **People's Court**, including members of the 20 July 1944 conspiracy to assassinate **Hitler**. An estimated 2,500 victims were executed here, by guillotine or by hanging.

POLISH CORRIDOR Strip of land between the Vistula River and Pomerania ceded by Germany under the terms of the Treaty of **Versailles** to give Poland access to the Baltic Sea. More than half of the Corridor population were German-speaking. **Hitler**'s demand for control of the Corridor was one of the pretexts for the German invasion of Poland in September 1939.

POLYCRACY Term introduced by the historian Martin **Broszat** to describe the internecine bureaucratic conflicts, *ad hoc* procedures, and administrative confusion that characterized the Nazi system of rule, contrary to its reputation as a smoothly functioning, highly centralized, monolithic dictatorship (see **leadership principle**).

POPULAR FRONT A strategy originating with the French Communist Party and approved by the **Comintern** in 1935 to unite all left-of-center parties in an anti-fascist front. This reversed the previous Comintern policy of spurning coalition with the **Social Democrats** and condemning their leadership as "social fascists." Communist cooperation with the Popular Front government of socialist Léon Blum (1872–1950), elected in France in 1936, collapsed as a result of the French government's refusal to intervene on behalf of the Popular Front government in Spain.

POTSDAM City close to Berlin and traditional seat of the **Hohenzollern** monarchy. The Nazis staged an elaborate ceremony in Potsdam on the first day of spring in 1933 to demonstrate the linkage of the **Third Reich** to the Prussian and German monarchical tradition.

POTSDAM CONFERENCE Meeting of the three heads of government of the US, USSR, and the UK from 17 July to 2 August 1945 to coordinate the occupation of Germany and establish common policies. The three victor powers agreed on measures to demilitarize, **denazify**, and partially de-industrialize the defeated nation. The **Oder–Neisse** line was established as Germany's temporary eastern border pending a final peace settlement. The orderly transfer of German inhabitants residing to the east of that border was approved.

PROPAGANDA The process of manufacturing consensus and shaping and controlling public opinion. The etymological source of the term is the Congregation for the Propagation of the Faith, an office of the Catholic Church created at the height of the Counter-Reformation in 1622. The Nazis established a Ministry of Public Enlightenment and Propaganda under the direction of Josef **Goebbels** in March 1933. Goebbels believed that the best results in influencing the masses and manipulating public opinion were achieved by reducing social and political problems to the simplest terms and by constant repetition of simplified slogans and formulas, whether true or not.

PROTECTIVE CUSTODY Measure first introduced in a "Decree for the Protection of the German People" on 4 February 1933 permitting the arrest and detention of persons without judicial warrant for a period of three months. In the **Reichstag Fire Decree** on 28 February 1933 all temporal limits on protective custody were eliminated and detainees were no longer permitted any legal recourse or redress. This measure was applied by the Nazi paramilitary formations to imprison political opponents who had committed no crime. In April 1934, in an effort to reduce the huge number of arbitrary arrests, authority to detain persons for protective custody was withdrawn from the **SA** and **SS** and limited to official police agencies, particularly the **Gestapo**; but detainees were still left without any judicial rights.

PROTECTORATE OF BOHEMIA AND MORAVIA Czech provinces of Czechoslovakia incorporated into the Third Reich by decree on 16 March 1939. Former foreign minister **Neurath** was replaced by **Heydrich** in September 1941. After Heydrich's assassination in May 1941, Daluege took power until his replacement by former interior minister **Frick** in August 1943.

PROTOCOLS OF THE ELDERS OF ZION An **anti-Semitic** forgery originating in Imperial Russia around the turn of the twentieth century and carried to Western Europe and the US by Russian refugees from the **Bolshevik** revolution in 1918 and 1919. It was translated into many languages and widely disseminated by right-wing radicals in their efforts to discredit the Russian Revolution as a Jewish conspiracy to dominate the world. The Protocols purported to be the verbatim record of an unspecified Jewish leader addressing a secret Zionist meeting and detailing a strategy of undermining national governments through class conflict, revolution, and war to establish a world government under the control of "international Jewry." The Protocols gained credibility because they seemed to have foretold the Russian Revolution. Hence right-wing anti-Semites, including the publisher of the Protocols in the US, Henry Ford (1863–1947), discounted the question of their authenticity as irrelevant to their veracity. In Germany the Protocols helped to justify the Nazis' hostility to both Western liberal capitalism and to Soviet Communism by portraying these apparently incompatible social systems as two sides of the same Jewish world conspiracy.

QUEBEC CONFERENCES Meetings between President Roosevelt and Prime Minister Churchill in the Canadian city of Quebec in August 1943 and again in September 1944. At the first Quebec conference the decision to invade France in May 1944 was reached, while simultaneously continuing the Mediterranean offensive. At the second conference the war against Japan as well as the **Morgenthau Plan** were on the agenda.

RACE AND SETTLEMENT MAIN OFFICE (RuSHA) **SS** office founded in 1931 and upgraded to an SS Main Office in 1935. The RuSHA was responsible for racial

instruction of SS members, processing of certificates of descent, planning of racial settlements, and issuing of racial guidebooks. Under its first leader Walther **Darré** it propagated the ideology of **blood and soil**. Darré was succeeded by SS general Günther Pancke (1899–1973) in 1938, SS general Otto Hofmann (1896–1982), a participant in the **Wannsee Conference**, in 1940, and SS general Richard Hildebrandt (1897–1951) in 1943.

RACIAL HYGIENE Obsession with racial hygiene, broadly defined as the application of **eugenic** selection to the improvement of the German race, pervaded all public policy in the **Third Reich**. The German Society for Racial Hygiene was founded by the Social Darwinist Alfred Ploetz (1860–1940) in 1905. It viewed modern medicine and democratic, humanitarian values as contrary to natural selection, enabling the weak, the sick, and the poor to survive, thus weakening the race in its competition with other races. Hence the racial hygiene movement favored human intervention to restore the natural balance supposedly skewed by the growth of liberal, progressive movements on behalf of "inferior" groups and individuals. Two developments after the First World War put the racial hygiene movement in Germany on a particularly destructive course. First, the perceived need to regenerate the nation after its humiliating defeat made racial hygiene particularly attractive to the right wing of the political spectrum. Second, the growth of **anti-Semitism** as a result of widespread Jewish adherence to liberal and democratic values made Jews a particular target of efforts to purify and strengthen the German race. Among the most prominent advocates of racial hygiene in the 1920s and 1930s were the "racial scientists" Eugen **Fischer**, Fritz

Lenz, and Hans F. K. **Günther**. The Nazis wholeheartedly endorsed policies of both positive and negative selection, as manifested by the **Sterilization Law**, **marriage loans**, the **Hereditary Farm Law**, and the **Nuremberg Laws**, as well as the **euthanasia** program.

RACIAL POLICY OFFICE Nazi Party office founded in 1934 as a successor to the so-called Information Office for Population Policy and Racial Education under Walter **Gross**. Its task was to disseminate racial ideology through publications and propaganda. The office was dissolved in 1942 when its functions had been largely superseded by **Himmler**'s Office of the **Reich Commissioner for the Strengthening of German Ethnicity**.

RAD Acronym for Reichsarbeitsdienst (Reich Work Service). Compulsory work service for six months was introduced in June 1935 for all male youths between 18 and 25 and for female youths in 1939. The RAD was headed by Reich work Führer Konstantin **Hierl**.

RAPALLO TREATY Agreement signed in April 1922 in the northern Italian town of Rapallo by foreign ministers Walther Rathenau (1867–1922) of **Weimar** Germany and Georgi Chicherin (1872–1936) of Soviet Russia normalizing relations between the two countries. On the one hand the treaty paved the way for secret cooperation between the **Reichswehr** and the Red Army in the testing of weapons prohibited by the **Versailles Treaty**. On the other hand, despite its function of creating a counterweight to the western Allied powers, the diplomatic recognition of the Communist government outraged the radical right in Germany as well as monarchist Russian émigrés, providing one of the motives for the assassination of Rathenau on 24 June 1922 by right-wing conspirators. The Nazis abruptly ended all cooperation with the Soviet Union when they came to power in 1933.

RASSENSCHANDE (racial crime) Term used to designate sexual relations between Germans and Jews, which was criminalized in the **Nuremberg Laws**. It was also used to criminalize sexual relations between Germans and foreign workers during the war.

RASTENBURG See **Wolfschanze**.

RAVENSBRÜCK Largest Nazi **concentration camp** for women opened in May 1939 north of Berlin with 42 satellite camps for workers used mostly in armaments production. A separate smaller camp for men was added in 1941. A total of some 132,000 women and 20,000 men were interned at Ravensbrück. Toward the end of the war a gas chamber was installed in which an estimated 1,500 to 5,000 inmates were murdered. The total number of inmates who died at Ravensbrück is estimated at over 30,000, including most of the 800 infants born at the camp. Thanks to the intervention of Folke Bernadotte (1895–1948), head of the Swedish Red Cross and later United Nations commissioner in Palestine, approximately 7,000 women of different nationalities were transferred to Denmark and Sweden before the end of the war. Soviet troops liberated the camp on 28 April 1945.

RDI Acronym for Reichsverband der deutschen Industrie (Reich Association of German Industry).

RED FRONT Communist (**KPD**) paramilitary organization founded in 1924 as a counterweight to the right-wing veterans' organization **Stahlhelm**, the **SPD's Reich Banner**, and the Nazi paramilitary formations. It was banned in 1929 by **Weimar** government authorities after street clashes.

RED ORCHESTRA Gestapo designation for Communist resistance movement under **Harnack** and **Schulze-Boysen** broken up in fall 1942. Over 120 members were arrested, most of whom were tried by the **People's Court**. 49 members, including seventeen women, were executed.

REICH German term for empire.

REICH BANNER "BLACK-RED-GOLD" Organization for the defense of the republic founded by members of the **SPD** in 1924 and numbering at its height more than three million members. Black, red, and gold were the revolutionary colors of 1848 and the official colors of the **Weimar Republic**. Although the Reich Banner wore uniforms, they were not armed and did not receive military training. The Reich Banner failed to mount armed resistance to the Nazi regime and was disbanded in March 1933.

REICH CENTRAL OFFICE FOR JEWISH EMIGRATION Established in January 1939 in Berlin on the model of the Central Office for Jewish Emigration opened by Adolf **Eichmann**, the **SS** specialist for Jewish affairs, in Vienna on 26 August 1938. A similar office was opened in Prague in July 1939 and in Holland in 1940. Eichmann also headed the Berlin office, which was subordinated to Eichmann's office in the **Reich Security Main Office**. The offices for Jewish emigration were the only offices authorized to issue emigration permits. Up to the start of the war Jews were pressured into emigrating. After the prohibition of Jewish emigration at the start of the **"final solution"** in October 1941, the offices for Jewish emigration were used to organize Jewish deportations.

REICH CHAMBER OF CULTURE Founded in September 1933 under **Goebbels**, the **propaganda** minister, to regulate and synchronize all cultural activities in Germany. It was divided into seven chambers for literature, the press, broadcasting, theater, film, music, and the fine arts, respectively.

REICH CITIZENSHIP LAW See **Nuremberg Laws**.

REICH COMMISSIONER FOR THE STRENGTHENING OF GERMAN ETHNICITY Title and office assumed by **Himmler** in October 1939 with responsibility for the population resettlement and Germanization programs required to usher in the Nazis' New Order in Europe

REICH COMMISSIONERS Officials appointed by the national government with supervisory authority to represent the interests of the central government in regional matters. The position was created by the Weimar constitution and retained in the **Third Reich** as an instrument of *Gleichschaltung*.

REICH FLAG LAW Introduced at the same time as the **Nuremberg Laws** in September 1935, this law restored the Imperial colors of black, red, and white to official status and made the **swastika** the official national flag.

REICH FOOD ESTATE (Reichsnährstand) Corporatist organization established in 1933 to bring German agriculture under Nazi control. Membership was obligatory for all persons involved in agricultural production and distribution. Independent agricultural groups were absorbed or disbanded. The Reich Food Estate was headed by Minister of Food and Agriculture Richard Walter **Darré**.

REICH GOVERNORS (*Reichsstatthalter*) Officials appointed by the Reich government to head the individual German states as a means of bringing them under central Nazi control in the course of *Gleichschaltung*.

REICH LEADERS (*Reichsleiter*) Political leaders of the Nazi Party appointed by **Hitler** with specific spheres of responsibility and directly subordinate to Hitler. Unlike **Gauleiters**, Reich leaders did not have specific geographic areas under their command. Collectively they determined the policies and supervised the affairs of the Nazi Party from its headquarters in the **Brown House** in Munich.

REICH MINISTERS Heads of the sixteen ministries of the Reich government, including Foreign Affairs (**Neurath**, then **Ribbentrop**), Interior (**Frick**, then **Himmler**), Propaganda (**Goebbels**), Finance (**Krosigk**), Economics (**Hugenberg**, then **Schacht**, then **Funk**), Labor (**Seldte**), Justice (Franz Gürtner [1881–1941], Franz Schlegelberger [1876–1970], then **Thierack**), Postal Service (Wilhelm Ohnesorge [1872–1962]), Transportation (**Dorpmüller**), Aviation (**Göring**), Nutrition and Agriculture (**Darré**), Science and Education (**Rust**), Ecclesiastical Affairs (**Kerrl**), War (**Bromberg**, then **Keitel** as head of the **OKW**), Occupied Eastern Territories (**Rosenberg**), and Armaments and Munitions (**Todt**, then **Speer**).

Ministers without portfolio included Hans **Frank** and **Seyss-Inquart**.

REICH REPRESENTATION OF GERMAN JEWS Umbrella association of leading Jewish organizations founded in September 1933 as a response to the growing discrimination against and segregation of Jews. Led by Rabbi Leo Baeck (1873–1956), its executive committee consisted of representatives of the leading Jewish organizations in Germany, including the **Centralverein**, the **Zionist Association**, and the Association of Jewish Veterans, as well as representatives of the orthodox and liberal wings of German Jewry. Its tasks were to organize a separate Jewish education and vocational training system, provide economic assistance to indigent Jews, maintain a healthcare system, support cultural activities, and assist Jewish families to emigrate. The organization was financed by taxes, fund-raising, and contributions from foreign Jewish organizations, including the American Joint Distribution Committee and the British Council for German Jewry. In 1935 it was forced by the loss of citizenship mandated by the **Nuremberg Laws** to change its name to Reich Representation of Jews in Germany. It was further restricted in its activities in March 1938 when it was deprived of its right to levy taxes. It lost its independence in June 1939 when it was again forced to change its name (this time to Reich Association of Jews in Germany) and was forcibly integrated into the German Ministry of the Interior. Beginning in October 1941 the organization was forced to collaborate with German authorities in preparations for the deportation of German Jews. In 1943 the organization was forcibly dissolved, its property confiscated, and its remaining employees deported to **concentration camps**.

REICH SECURITY MAIN OFFICE (RSHA) Central administrative office created in September 1939 to integrate all police agencies with the Security Service (**SD**) of the SS under **Himmler**. The RSHA was both a part of the government and one of 12 "main offices" of the SS. The RSHA was headed by **Heydrich** until his assassination in May 1942. His successor was **Kaltenbrunner**. The RSHA was subdivided into seven offices: I, Personnel Matters (under Bruno Streckenbach [1902–1977]); II, Law and Administration (under **Best**, then Hans Nockemann [1903–1941]; III, Domestic Intelligence (under **Ohlendorf**); IV, **Gestapo** (under **Müller**, with **Eichmann** as head of the Jewish desk); V, Criminal Police (under **Nebe**); VI, Foreign Intelligence (under Heinz Jost [1904–1964], then **Schellenberg**); and VII, Ideological Research (under Franz Six [1906–1975], then Paul Dittel [b. 1907]).

REICHSBANK Germany's central bank.

REICHSKRISTALLNACHT (Reich Crystal Night) Popular designation for the pogrom unleashed by the Nazi Party on 9–10 November 1938. The term derived from the shards of glass that littered the streets in front of demolished Jewish stores, synagogues, and homes. The pretext for the pogrom was the assassination of the German consular official in Paris Ernst vom Rath (1909–1938) by the stateless Jewish expatriate Hershel Grynszpan (1921–1945?), who died at **Sachsenhausen** after being turned over to German authorities for prosecution in July 1940. Goebbels portrayed Grynszpan as an agent of world Jewry to whip up outrage in Germany against Jews. The purpose of the pogrom, carried out all over Germany by **SA** and party members, was to force Jews to leave Germany and turn over their wealth to ethnic Germans in what would become known as the **Aryanization** program. The pogrom, which took at least 35 Jewish lives, reflected growing Nazi indifference to world opinion in the wake of **Hitler**'s diplomatic triumph at **Munich** a few weeks earlier. The goal of Nazi policy was to expel all Jews from Germany and Austria to assure ideological unity on the home front prior to the launching of their planned war of conquest in the east.

REICHSLEITER See **Reich leaders**.

REICHSLEITUNG Top executive body of the Nazi party.

REICHSRAT Council of representatives of the individual German states. This was the upper legislative chamber under the **Weimar** constitution, equivalent to the Bundesrat in the post-war Federal Republic. The Reichsrat was officially disbanded in February 1934 as a part of the *Gleichschaltung* of the states.

REICHSSIPPENAMT (Reich Family Office) Originally part of the Interior Ministry, this office was responsible for issuing **Certificates of** (Aryan) **Descent**.

REICHSSTATTHALTER See **Reich governors**.

REICHSTAG German parliament elected by universal suffrage under the Imperial and **Weimar** constitutions, equivalent to the Bundestag in the post-war Federal Republic. The **Enabling Act** of March 1933 transferred all legislative powers to the executive, and the "Law Against the Formation of Parties" of 14 July 1933 eliminated all opposition to the Nazi Party.

Henceforth the Reichstag served a purely ceremonial function.

REICHSTAG FIRE DECREE Law issued by decree under Article 48 of the **Weimar** constitution on 28 February 1933, the morning following the Reichstag fire. Formally entitled "Decree for the Protection of Volk and State" and justified by the need "to counter Communist acts of violence threatening the state," the Reichstag Fire Decree suspended civil liberties, including freedoms of speech, the press, association, assembly, and postal and telephone communications, as well as freedom from arbitrary seizure, search, and arrest. This "emergency" decree was never revoked and formed the legal basis for *Gleichschaltung* and the Nazi police state.

REICHSTAG FIRE TRIAL Trial before the German Supreme Court, September–December 1933, in which the Nazi government unsuccessfully attempted to convict the German Communist Party (**KPD**) and **Comintern** officials of setting fire to the Reichstag. The court found no evidence to substantiate charges that the arsonist, the former Dutch communist Marianus van der Lubbe, had received aid from members of the KPD. Georgi Dmitrov, the Bulgarian head of the Comintern, and his aides were acquitted of any involvement in planning or carrying out the arson. Suspicion fell instead on the Nazis themselves. One result of this trial was the establishment of the **People's Court** as a more reliable Nazi instrument for prosecuting political crimes.

REICHSWEHR Official name of the German armed forces from 1919 to 1935. See **Wehrmacht**.

REICH WORK SERVICE See **RAD**.

REM Acronym for Reichserziehungsministerium (Reich Education Ministry).

RFSS Acronym for Reichsführer SS, **Himmler**'s official title.

RHINELAND German-speaking area between the Rhine River and the French border that was supposed to remain permanently demilitarized by the Terms of the **Versailles** and **Locarno** treaties. **Hitler** violated these provisions by sending troops into the Rhineland in March 1936.

RÖHM PURGE The extra-legal killing of Ernst **Röhm** and the top **SA** leadership by members of the **SS** with **Reichswehr** support in the "Night of the Long Knives," 30 June 1934. Röhm, whose top officers included veterans of the Imperial army who had never been part of the Reichswehr, was suspected of wishing to absorb the Reichswehr into the much larger SA and to supplant it as the official fighting force of the **Third Reich**. Many of the more than four million rank-and-file members of the SA also advocated a "second revolution" to unseat traditional conservatives from their positions of power. **Hitler** used the opportunity presented by conservative opposition to the SA not only to divest himself of the radical SA leadership but also to settle scores with conservative critics of the regime such as **Schleicher**, **Strasser**, and the Bavarian president during the **Hitler Putsch** Gustav von Kahr (1862–1934).

ROMA AND SINTI Formal names for the gypsy minority living in various parts of Europe. Gypsies were persecuted by the Nazis and formed the second largest ethnic group after the Jews to be killed in the **Holocaust**. It is estimated that as many as

500,000 Sinti and Roma fell victim to the Nazi killing machine.

ROSENSTRASSE PROTEST Demonstration by German women married to Jews against the arrest of their husbands in Berlin in late February to early March 1943. This was one of the very few instances of public resistance in **Hitler**'s Germany. The arrested Jews were eventually released to return to their families. This event became the subject of a dispute among historians after the publication of Nathan Stoltzfus's *Resistance of the Heart* in 1996. Stoltzfus argued that the Rosenstrasse protest proved that open protest could be effective under some circumstances in Hitler's Germany. Resistance was possible and could have made a difference. He was contradicted by other historians, in particular Wolf Gruner, who argued that the Rosenstrasse protest had played no part in the release of the prisoners. According to Gruner, the Nazis had never intended to deport Jews in mixed marriages because of its potential negative effects on public morale. Exaggerating the effect of the demonstration runs the risk of underestimating the total domination exercised by the Nazi regime.

RSHA Acronym for Reichssicherheitshauptamt. See **Reich Security Main Office**.

RUHR Industrial region in western Germany. French and Belgian occupation of the Ruhr to collect unpaid reparations in January 1923 precipitated the crisis that provided the context for the **Hitler Putsch** in November of that year.

RUSHA Acronym for Reich und Siedlungshauptamt. See **Race and Settlement Main Office**.

S

SA Acronym for Sturmabteilungen (storm troopers). A designation first used in November 1921 for the Nazis' paramilitary formations. From a troop of approximately 300 men in 1921, mostly veterans of the First World War, the SA membership grew to 1,500 in 1923, when its leadership and organization were entrusted to Captain Ernst **Röhm**. Dissatisfied with **Hitler**'s legalistic course after the failure of the **Hitler Putsch**, Röhm resigned in 1925. He was replaced by the **Free Corps** veteran Franz Pfeffer von Salomon (1888–1968) until Röhm's return from South America in 1930. Under Röhm's leadership the SA, members of which wore brown uniforms, developed into a brutal terrorist organization that targeted the political left and fought fierce street battles with supporters of the Communist **KPD**. Its membership grew from approximately 420,000 in early 1932 to more than four million by 1934. Although SA units were temporarily deputized in Prussia as an auxiliary police force after the Nazi seizure of power and took the lead in the repression of political opponents of the regime, their proclivity for extra-legal violence provoked a backlash among segments of the German public who had expected the Nazis to restore law and order in Germany. The military leadership, too, distrusted Röhm's apparent efforts to transform the SA into an official, state-sanctioned militia. Under **Göring**'s and **Himmler**'s prodding, Hitler moved against the SA leadership in the **Röhm Purge** in June 1934. Röhm was executed on the pretext of having planned a putsch against the state. Under Viktor **Lutze**, the SA was disarmed and membership limited to veterans and former members of the **Hitler Youth**. Thereafter the SA membership declined to 1,600,000 in 1935, 1,200,000 in 1939, and fewer than one million in 1940. Its functions were reduced to pre-military training for German youth, fund raising and other services for the party, and occasional public marches and demonstrations. Its terrorist activities were largely restricted to party-sponsored attacks on Jews, most notably the **Reichs-kristallnacht** pogrom of November 1938.

SAAR Territory of approximately 2,000 square miles formed from previously Prussian and Bavarian districts and placed under a **League of Nations** mandate exercised by France in accordance with the Versailles Treaty. The coal-rich Saar voted overwhelmingly in favor of reintegration into the German **Reich** in a popular referendum in January 1935.

SACHSENHAUSEN A **concentration camp** opened in August 1936 in **Oranienburg**, north of Berlin. The number of inmates grew to 12,000 by 1939. It is estimated that at least 135,000 and possibly as many as 200,000 prisoners from over 40 nations passed through Sachsenhausen and its 61 satellite camps during the war. The estimated 100,000 inmates killed included approximately 18,000 Soviet prisoners of war. Only 3,000 survivors had been exempted from the death marches that preceded the liberation of the camp by the Red Army on 22 April 1945.

SAINT-GERMAIN TREATY Peace treaty imposed by the Allies on Austria in September 1919. Modeled on the **Versailles Treaty**, the treaty of Saint-Germain restricted the Austrian state to the German-speaking territory of the former Austro-Hungarian Empire, excluding however the German-speaking areas of Bohemia and Moravia (awarded to Czechoslovakia) and South Tyrol (awarded to Italy). The treaty also imposed reparations, imposed military restrictions, and prohibited *Anschluss* with Germany except if approved by the **League of Nations**.

SALÒ Location of the Republic of Salò on Lake Garda in northern Italy established on 23 September 1943 under German military command with Mussolini as head of government after the collapse of the Fascist government in Italy on 25 July 1943.

SCHUPO Acronym for Schutzpolizei (literally, protective police). See **Order Police**.

SD Acronym for Sicherheitsdienst. See **Security Service**.

SECURITY POLICE (SIPO) Agency that included the **Gestapo**, the criminal police (**KRIPO**), and the border police. Originally under the control of the separate German states, these functions of the Security Police were centralized under the control of Reinhard **Heydrich** in 1936. The Security Police was merged into the **Reich Security Main Office** in September 1939.

SECURITY SERVICE (SD) Surveillance agency of the SS founded in 1931 under the direction of **Heydrich**. Originally formed for the gathering of intelligence on opposing parties and political opponents of the Nazis, its mission expanded after 1933 to include the surveillance of public attitudes and opinion. It issued periodic domestic intelligence "Reports from the Reich" evaluating the public mood and the extent of popular support for Nazi policies. It also evaluated the political reliability of individuals. In 1939 it was merged into the **Reich Security Main Office**, the central agency combining all governmental and party policing functions. Its foreign intelligence section, headed by **Schellenberg**, eventually absorbed the **Abwehr**, the military intelligence office, in 1944.

SED Acronym for Sozialistische Einheitspartei (Socialist Unity Party), comprised of Social Democrats and Communists in the German Democratic Republic in 1945.

SINTI See **Roma and Sinti**.

SIPO Acronym for Sicherheitspolizei. See **Security Police**.

SOBIBÓR An **extermination camp** operating from May 1942 to fall 1943 in the **Lublin** district of the **Generalgouvernement** under the command of **SS** generals Franz **Stangl** and Franz Reichleitner (1906–1944). Approximately 250,000 Jews were killed here under the program labeled **Operation Reinhard**. The camp was dismantled after an inmate revolt in October 1943. Special teams were then deployed to remove all traces of the camp.

SOCIAL DEMOCRATIC PARTY See **SPD**.

SONDERKOMMANDO Special unit (see *Einsatzgruppen*).

SONDERWEG (special path) Term used to describe the alleged exceptionalism and uniqueness of German history and culture. The historian Hans-Ulrich **Wehler** used the term to develop an explanation of Germany's susceptibility to Nazism. His theory was criticized by British–American historians Geoff **Eley** and David Blackbourn.

SONNENSTEIN Hospital near **Dresden** converted into a killing facility in April 1940 (see **Euthanasia**).

SOPADE Name formed from the first syllables of the Social Democratic Party of Germany (SPD) designating the exiled Social Democratic Party executive formed in Prague in 1934. Reports filed by Sopade agents within Germany during the Nazi era constitute a valuable resource for historians.

SPANISH CIVIL WAR Precipitated by a military revolt under Francisco Franco against the elected **Popular Front** government in July 1936, the war ended with the defeat of the government forces in April 1939. Franco's forces received military support from Fascist Italy and Nazi Germany.

SPD Acronym for Social Democratic Party of Germany. Originally founded in 1875 as the Socialist Worker Party, the SPD was renamed in 1890 and formally adopted a Marxist program in 1892. Although proclaiming the need for revolutionary change, the party adopted a reformist strategy in practice. In 1912 it became the largest party in the **Reichstag**. Despite the defection of its left-wing faction (known as the Independent Social Democrats or USPD) during the First World War because of the failure of the "majority Socialists" to oppose the war, and despite the formation of the Spartacist League and later the German Communist Party (**KPD**) after the war, the SPD remained the largest party in the Reichstag until July 1932, when for the first time it received fewer votes than the Nazi Party. The SPD voted unanimously against the **Enabling Act** in March 1933. As Nazi repression mounted, the SPD dissolved into three separate groups: those who sought to carry on legal opposition, a group that practiced open resistance, and a group that went into exile (see **Sopade**). The SPD was banned by the Nazis in June 1933, but the party continued to function underground for several years. The party was revived in 1945 and became one of the major parties in the **Federal Republic**. In the **German Democratic Republic** it was forcibly merged with the Communist Party into the Socialist Unity Party (**SED**) until 1989.

ss Acronym for Schutzstaffel (Protection Squad). Founded in 1925 as a successor organization to earlier bodyguard units dissolved by police order after the failed **Hitler Putsch**, the SS was originally formed as a personal guard sworn to loyalty to **Hitler** himself. Although officially part of and formally subordinate to the **SA**, the SS developed into an independent elite organization based on biological selection after **Himmler**'s appointment as its leader (**RFSS**) in 1929. Its motto was "loyalty is our honor." The SS grew exponentially after the Nazis came to power in 1933. **Göring**, as Prussian prime minister, ceded authority over the **Gestapo** to Himmler in 1934 because he needed the SS to disarm the SA leadership in the **Röhm Purge** on 30 June 1934. The SS grew into the most powerful organization in Germany with full control of the police, domestic (and eventually foreign) intelligence and surveillance, the **concentration camps**, and numerous economic enterprises utilizing slave labor. In 1944 the SS included twelve "main offices":

1 Himmler's personal staff (**RFSS**)
2 The administrative main office (**SSHA**)
3 Leadership office of the **Waffen-SS**, the military arm of the SS
4 **Race and Settlement Main Office** (RuSHA)
5 The SS court

6 SS personnel office
7 **Reich Security Main Office** (RSHA)
8 **Order Police** office (ORPO)
9 **Economic Administration Main Office** (WVHA)
10 Office for the National and Political Education Institutions (**NAPOLA**)
11 Office for Ethnic German Affairs (**VOMI**)
12 Office of the **Reich Commissioner for the Strengthening of German Ethnicity**

The SS and specifically the Reich Security Main Office under Reinhard **Heydrich** were responsible for carrying out the "**Final Solution** of the **Jewish Question**," the systematic murder of the Jews of Europe. The SS and its security arm, the **SD**, were formally designated criminal organizations by the International Tribunal at the **Nuremberg Trials** in 1946.

SSHA Acronym for SS-Hauptamt (SS Main Office).

SSPF Acronym for SS- und Polizeiführer (SS and police leaders). See **HSSPF**.

STAB IN THE BACK LEGEND Thesis disseminated by the radical right after the war, according to which the German army did not suffer defeat on the battlefield but was "stabbed in the back" by the **November criminals** and their leftist and Jewish supporters. In fact, however, the German government sued for peace in 1918 on the instructions of the German military leadership, who informed civilian leaders that the war was lost.

STAHLHELM (Steel Helmet) A veterans' organization formed on 25 December 1918 by Franz **Seldte**, also known as the League of Frontline Soldiers. The Stahlhelm, which had a membership of 400,000 in 1925, opposed the **Weimar Republic**. Although not formally affiliated with the Nationalist Party (**NDVP**), in effect it served as the party's paramilitary formation. Most of the Stahlhelm was integrated into the **SA** after **Hitler**'s seizure of power, and the Stahlhelm was officially dissolved in 1934.

STALINGRAD (Volgograd) City on the Volga River that was the site of a major battle on the eastern front from September 1942 until the German surrender of the city on 1 February 1943.

STERILIZATION LAW Officially named "Law for the Prevention of Genetically Diseased Offspring," the Sterilization Law was issued on 14 July 1933. It authorized the compulsory sterilization of the mentally and physically disabled as well as alcoholics whose condition was deemed to be hereditary. The law was to be administered through specially established **Hereditary Health Courts**. Under this law approximately 400,000 persons were sterilized in Germany between 1933 and 1945.

STRENGTH THROUGH JOY A subdivision of the **German Labor Front** responsible for organizing and subsidizing free or inexpensive leisure-time activities and vacation tours for workers. The purpose of this program was to win the allegiance of workers and to increase their productivity by making available privileges and perks previously reserved for higher-income groups. The KdF, as it was known by its German acronym, sponsored cultural activities and entertainments such as concerts, art exhibits, lectures, plays, and sporting events, as well as workplace beautification programs, cruises, vacation packages, and even an affordable automobile (the **Volkswagen**) for millions of German workers.

STRESA Site of a conference in northern Italy between representatives of Britain, France, and Italy in April 1935. The purpose of the conference was to agree on a common response to the reintroduction of compulsory military training in Germany in violation of the **Versailles Treaty** in March 1935. The three nations agreed to oppose all unilateral revocation of treaty obligations, specifically referring to the **Locarno Treaty** that prohibited the militarization of the **Rhineland**. The three nations proclaimed their commitment to collective security, Austrian independence, and international disarmament. The "Stresa Front" dissolved, however, after the conclusion of a **Naval Agreement** between Britain and Germany in June 1935 and the Italian invasion of Ethiopia in September 1935.

STRUCTURALISM See **Functionalism**.

STRUTHOF See **Natzweiler**.

DER STÜRMER Title of a notorious **anti-Semitic** weekly mass-circulation tabloid founded by Julius **Streicher** in 1923. Its circulation reached 20,000 by 1933, increased to over 500,000 in the years that followed, and declined to about 400,000 by 1944, after Streicher had been relieved of all party offices due to corruption. Although it never became an official party paper, its malicious caricature of "the Jew" set the standard for how Jews were portrayed in the Nazi press. Part of *Der Stürmer*'s mass appeal was due to the pornographic content of many of its defamatory articles allegedly exposing the crime of ***Rassenschande***. It called on Germans to denounce anyone suspected of a sexual relationship with a Jew.

STUTTGART CONFESSION OF GUILT (*Stuttgarter Schuldbekenntnis*) Formal declaration issued by the newly constituted Protestant Evangelical Church Council in post-war Germany in October 1945. The declaration regretted the Church's failure to speak out more courageously against the Nazi tyranny.

STUTTHOF Concentration camp east of the city of **Danzig** (Gdansk) that originated in September 1939 as a detention camp for Polish civilians. In 1942 it became a **concentration camp** that could also be included under the rubric "**extermination camp**" because of its extremely high mortality rate. Of the approximately 155,000 internees of many nationalities during the war, 65,000 died or were killed. The rate of execution was high, and in the last half of 1944 a gas chamber was activated for mass murder. Stutthof had more than 100 satellite camps. It was liberated on 27 January 1945 by Soviet troops. However, thousands more died in the **death marches** at the end of the war.

SUDETENLAND Border areas of Czechoslovakia with approximately 3.3 million ethnic German inhabitants. **Hitler**'s demand for the cession of this territory led to the crisis that ended with the **Munich Agreement** in September 1938.

SWASTIKA (*Hakenkreuz*) Official symbol of the Nazi Party adopted in 1920. Usually interpreted as a rotary solar disk, the swastika has been used as a symbol for dynamic transformation and good fortune in various Asian and European cultures for thousands of years. Its use as a symbol

by revolutionary nationalist movements began in the nineteenth century. Numerous *völkisch* organizations, including right-wing groupings of the **Youth Movement**, the **Free Corps**, and the **Thule Society**, adopted this symbol in the early twentieth century. **Hitler** may first have been exposed to the swastika as a symbol of **Aryan** racial supremacy through the racist pamphlets of **anti-Semitic** Austrian publicists such as Guido von List (1848–1919) or Jörg Lanz von Liebenfels (1874–1955). In 1935 the Nazis' swastika became the official national flag. It is still used as an anti-Semitic symbol by **neo-Nazis** today.

T

TABLE TALKS Conventional designation for **Hitler**'s commentaries and monologues on various subjects at lunch and dinner at the Führer's headquarters from July 1941 to 1944, beginning shortly after the German invasion of the Soviet Union. The table talks were not verbatim transcriptions but were based on notes made by Martin **Bormann**'s adjutant **SS** colonel Heinrich Heim (1900–1988) and then transcribed by headquarters clerks under his direction. During Heim's absence from March to August 1942, Hitler's monologues were summarized by Henry Picker (b. 1912), a senior civil servant assigned to headquarters. The table talks were published after the war.

TANNENBERG LEAGUE (Tannenbergbund) *Völkisch* umbrella group named after a famous First World War victory over the Russian army in East Prussia. The group was founded in 1925 by General

Ludendorff and Konstantin **Hierl** and dedicated to the creation of a pan-German military dictatorship to combat "supranational forces," including the Catholic Church, the Jesuits, Marxism, Jews, and Freemasons. Its anti-Christian orientation made it a liability for the Nazis and it was dissolved in September 1933.

TEHERAN CONFERENCE Meeting of the Big Three (Roosevelt, Churchill, and Stalin) in the Iranian capital in November 1943. The Western Allies pledged to open a second front in France in 1944. The USSR promised to join in the war against Japan after the end of the European war. Agreement was also reached on shifting the borders of post-war Poland to the west and on the division of Germany, as well as the creation of an international peacekeeping organization. The details were left to be worked out by separate commissions.

TEREZÍNE See **Theresienstadt**.

THERESIENSTADT Concentration camp established in an old Austro-Hungarian garrison town north of Prague in November 1941 as a detention camp for Jews from the **Protectorate of Bohemia and Moravia**. In July 1942 the non-Jewish population was evacuated and Theresienstadt was converted into an "old-age ghetto" for elderly German and Austrian Jews of various categories, including decorated veterans from the First World War and their spouses, prominent former civil servants, Jewish partners from terminated mixed marriages, and *Mischlinge* considered to be Jews under the **Nuremberg Laws**. Among its prominent inmates from 1943 to 1945 was Leo Baeck (1873–1956), president of the **Reich Representation of German Jews**. A façade of normality was created in

Theresienstadt on the occasion of a visit by delegates from the International Red Cross in July 1944 to create the illusion that its inmates were treated well. Theresienstadt also served as the setting of a **propaganda** film produced in 1944. In practice, however, living conditions were abominable, made worse by its use as a transit camp to the killing sites in the east, particularly **Auschwitz**. Of the approximately 141,000 Jews deported to Theresienstadt (not including the approximately 14,000 inmates evacuated to Theresienstadt from other **concentration camps** in the closing weeks of the war), only 23,000 survived. The camp was liberated by the Red Army on 8 May 1945.

THIRD REICH Term widely used to designate the period of **Hitler**'s rule in Germany from 1933 to 1945. The term itself dates back to millenarian medieval notions of an empire of the Holy Spirit following the empires of God the father and God the son, thus creating eternal harmony and fulfilling the promise of history. Its modern usage was revived by publicists of the **Conservative Revolution**, particularly Arthur Möller van den Bruck (1876–1925), who published a book under that title in 1923, calling for the revival of a *völkisch* empire to succeed the Holy Roman Empire and the Bismarckian Reich. Hitler did not mention the concept in *Mein Kampf*, but did refer to the newly established Nazi dictatorship as the Third Reich in September 1933 and promised that it would last for a thousand years. Nonetheless, **Goebbels** discouraged use of the term in 1939, instructing the press instead to refer to the Greater German Reich (Grossdeutsches Reich).

THULE SOCIETY Secret conspiratorial society founded by Rudolf von

Sebottendorf (pseudonym for Rudolf Glauer [1875–1945]) in Munich in early 1918 as a cover for the *völkisch* Germanic Order, whose activities were banned in the First World War to maintain domestic unity. Closely allied with the **Pan-German Society**, its membership of several hundred included many later Nazis, such as **Hess**, **Feder**, **Rosenberg**, **Eckart**, Hans **Frank**, and Anton Drexler (1884–1942), the founder of the German Workers' Party (DAP) from which the Nazi Party evolved. Thule Society members were involved in counter-revolutionary activities against the Social Democratic Bavarian government of Kurt Eisner (1867–1919), the Soviet republic that followed, and the **Weimar Republic** in Berlin. Thule Society members founded the Oberland **Free Corps** in 1919, precursor of the **Oberland League**, which participated in the **Hitler Putsch** in 1923. The Society's newspaper, the *Münchener Beobachter*, later became the *Völkischer Beobachter*, official paper of the Nazi Party. The Nazis also adopted the Society's emblem, the **swastika**.

TOTALITARIANISM Term first popularized in Mussolini's Italy to describe an authoritarian system of rule in which all institutions are subordinated to a government controlled by a single political party. It was used as an analytical concept in the works of political theorists Hannah **Arendt** and Carl **Friedrich**. It is generally contrasted to a liberal democratic form of government that guarantees the inalienable rights of individuals, a multi-party political system, and the independence of civil institutions from governmental control (see **liberalism**). Although Nazi Germany has generally been viewed as exemplifying totalitarian rule, some historians prefer to use the term

polycracy to describe the administrative confusion of the Nazi system.

TOTAL WAR Term popularized by Erich **Ludendorff** in a book of that title published in 1935 and revived by **Goebbels** after the Battle of **Stalingrad** to mobilize full public involvement in the war effort. As plenipotentiary for total war in July 1944, Goebbels oversaw the introduction of compulsory work service, the increased recruitment of forced labor, the formation of the **Volksturm**, the increased prosecution of all forms of defeatism, the summary execution of surrendering soldiers or deserters and incarceration of their families, propaganda for supposedly imminent miracle weapons (see **V-weapons**), and preparations for continued resistance after the war (see **Werewolf**).

TRAWNIKI Forced labor camp for Soviet prisoners of war and Polish Jews in the **Lublin** district of the **Generalgouvernement** established in fall 1941. Its Jewish inmates were killed in the course of Operation **Harvest Festival** in November 1943. Trawniki was also the site of a training camp for Ukrainian prisoners of war and personnel from other nations for service as auxiliary guards at the **Operation Reinhard** camps.

TREBLINKA Largest of the three killing centers of **Operation Reinhard**. Approximately 900,000 Jews and several thousand gypsies were murdered here between July 1942 and August 1943 through diesel exhaust fumes. Beginning in spring 1943 corpses originally buried in mass graves were exhumed and burned on metal grids constructed from railway tracks. After an abortive revolt by "work Jews" in August 1943 the camp was shut down and all traces of its former purpose removed in October 1943.

TRIANON TREATY Peace treaty between the victorious Allies and Hungary as a defeated power signed in June 1920 and modeled on the **Versailles** and **Saint-Germain** treaties. It contained a war-guilt clause, and imposed reparations, military restrictions, and territorial cessions on Hungary. As a result Hungary supported a revision of the peace settlement following the First World War and became a German ally in the Second World War.

TRIPARTITE PACT Treaty signed 27 September 1940 by Germany, Italy, and Japan committing each signatory to come to the aid of the others in case of attack by an outside power. The pact was directed against the US and specifically exempted the USSR, with whom Germany had signed the **German–Soviet Non-Aggression Pact**.

TWENTY-FIVE POINT PROGRAM Official Nazi Party program drawn up by Gottfried **Feder** and formally proclaimed in Munich in February 1920 under the mottos, "Abolition of the Slavery of Interest" and "The general interest above self-interest." It contained **anti-Semitic** and anti-capitalist provisions designed to attract workers and small proprietors, and it called for a strong central state, a national army, censorship, and "positive Christianity." The program remained unchanged except for an addendum in 1928, explaining that the provision for the expropriation of private property pertained only to Jewish property

U

UNCONDITIONAL SURRENDER Allied policy adopted at the **Casablanca Conference** in 1943 to reassure the Soviet Union that the Allies would not make a separate peace with Germany.

USTASHA Fascist Croatian movement supported by the Nazis. The movement sought the separation of Croatia from Yugoslavia. Its leader, Ante Pavelíc (1889–1959), headed the independent Nazi-backed state of Croatia from 1941 to 1945. Members of the Ustasha assassinated King Alexander I (1888–1934) of Yugoslavia while on a state visit to France in 1934 and his host, French foreign minister Louis Barthou (1862–1934). The Ustasha established the notorious concentration camp **Jasenovac** in which tens of thousands of Jews, Serbs, gypsies, and political opponents were killed.

V

V-WEAPONS Term used to designate the V1, a flying bomb, and the V2, a long-range missile. V stood for *Vergeltung* (retribution). These weapons, introduced in June and September 1944, respectively, were heralded as the wonder weapons that would turn the tide of war in Germany's favor despite its numerical and material inferiority to the Allies. **SS** officer Wernher von **Braun**, the guiding spirit behind the development of the V2, went on to develop the technology that landed a man on the moon in 1969.

VAIVARA A **concentration camp** with at least ten satellite labor camps opened near Narva in Estonia in September 1943. Its inmates were mostly survivors of the Kovno (**Kauen**) and **Vilna** ghettos, which were dissolved in 1943. The camp was shut down in August 1944 as Soviet troops approached, and its surviving inmates were transferred to other camps.

VALKYRIE (*Walküre*) Code name for a military plan drawn up in September 1943 to quell an internal uprising or popular unrest in Germany. It was subsequently used by members of the military resistance, particularly **Stauffenberg** and **Olbricht**, as the vehicle for mobilizing military units in support of the failed military coup on 20 July 1944. What made Operation Valkyrie so useful to military conspirators were its provisions for secrecy. Not even the police or the **SS** were to be informed of the existence of this plan. It would have given military commanders authority even over **Gauleiter** and all other party and government functionaries.

VERGANGENHEITSBEWÄLTIGUNG (coming to terms with the past) Term used to describe efforts in Germany to come to terms with the burden of guilt left by Nazi atrocities and to atone for Nazi crimes. The need for *Vergangenheitsbewältigung* – national self-reflection, self-criticism, and avowal of responsibility for the past – has helped to shape German identity in the **Federal Republic** since its formation in 1949.

VERSAILLES TREATY Settlement ending the First World War signed by the German delegation in June 1919 in the Hall of Mirrors of the Royal Palace where the Wilhelmian Empire had been founded by Bismarck in 1871. Popular revulsion against this treaty in Germany came to be one of the major sources of support for the radical right, which was committed to its reversal. Germans opposed the loss of territory to newly formed Poland, the restrictions imposed on their military forces, economic reparations, and the "War Guilt Clause," which forced Germans to accept full responsibility for having started the war. The Nazis benefited from the anti-Republican sentiments generated by the Versailles Treaty. Even before **Hitler** came to power the governments under **Papen** and **Schleicher** were able to gain the end of reparations and other concessions from the Allies. Hitler defied the treaty and rendered it obsolete by introducing universal military training in March 1935.

VICHY Seat of the authoritarian collaborationist French government under Marshal Philippe Pétain (1856–1951) from July 1940 until August 1945. Its territory was occupied by the Germans after the defection of the colonial French government in Algeria to the Allies in late 1942.

VILNA Jewish ghetto established in September 1941 in the Lithuanian city (now Vilnius). The approximately 60,000 Jewish inhabitants were subjected to repeated mass-shooting operations to cull out those no longer capable of work. Eventually virtually the entire Jewish population was killed, the last remaining residents shortly before the arrival of Soviet troops in July 1944.

VINNITSA Site in the Ukraine of **Hitler**'s military headquarters from July to September 1942, and again in February and March 1943.

VÖLKISCH Term used to describe an ideology that celebrated the uniqueness and superiority of the German language, history, spirituality, and race. The term, derived from *Volk* (a people), was first used in the 1870s by nationalists as a German substitute for the Latin-rooted word "national." The main objective of the *völkisch* movement – never unified until the Nazi era – was to deepen Germans' sense of national solidarity through appeals to the mystical notion of a racial blood bond among all members of the ethnic community, the *Volksgemeinschaft*. The hallmark of *völkisch* ideology was the significance it attached to the "**Jewish Question**," defined as a problem of racial incompatibility. From the *völkisch* perspective, revocation of Jewish citizenship rights and expulsion of the Jews were the keys to achieving the *völkisch* project of national regeneration and German expansion. In *Mein Kampf* **Hitler** scorned his *völkisch* precursors for their sectarianism, lack of realism, and political ineffectiveness. Nonetheless, the preparatory work of many *völkisch* organizations and publicists both in Germany and Austria was indispensable to Hitler's acquisition of power.

VÖLKISCHER BEOBACHTER (*Völkisch Observer*) The official Nazi Party newspaper, acquired by the party in 1920 and edited by Alfred **Rosenberg** after 1923.

VOLKSGEMEINSCHAFT (people's community) Ideal national community propagated by the Nazis in contradistinction to the allegedly artificial and un-German *Gesellschaft* (society) of Western liberalism and individualism. Derived from the **Youth Movement** of the early twentieth century and the *Kampfgemeinschaft* (battle community) of the First World War, the concept stood for the overcoming of class, denominational, occupational, and political divisions through the cultivation of a sense of ethnic solidarity (see *völkisch* ideology). It provided an egalitarian mask to conceal the continuing differences in wealth, property, income, and status in a hierarchical society.

VOLKSGERICHTSHOF See **People's Court**.

VOLKSTURM (People's Storm) People's militia founded by **Hitler**'s order in September 1944 to resist advancing Allied forces in the final stages of the war. Under party rather than military control, the Volksturm was recruited from men between the ages of 16 and 60 who had not been previously conscripted. It was subject to the command not of the **Wehrmacht** but of **Himmler** in his capacity as commander of the Reserve Army. The Volksturm was poorly trained, poorly equipped, and poorly led. Used primarily against the Red Army in the east, the Volksturm suffered high casualties. Approximately 175,000 members of the Volksturm were killed or missing in action.

VOLKSWAGEN Designed by Ferdinand Porsche (1875–1951), the "people's car" was produced, beginning in 1938, under the auspices of the **German Labor Front**. First known as the **KdF** car, its purpose was to make an affordable car available to millions of workers who were encouraged to save five marks a week toward its acquisition. At the onset of war, however, production was converted to military vehicles. Mass production for civilian use did not begin until after the war.

VOMI Acronym for Volksdeutsche Mittelstelle (Ethnic German Coordinating Office). Nazi Party office founded in 1935 and headed by Werner **Lorenz** with responsibility for coordinating policies, organization, financing, and other activities dealing with ethnic German minorities outside Germany.

WAFFEN-SS Term used for the military units of the **SS** after October 1939. The Waffen-SS incorporated the standby SS units (*Verfügungstruppe*) created after the **Röhm Purge** in 1934, the **Death's Head Units** used as **concentration camp** guards, and **Hitler**'s personal bodyguard (Leibstandarte "Adolf Hitler") commanded by Sepp **Dietrich**. In May 1939 Hitler ordered the creation of an SS division of 20,000 men. The Waffen-SS grew rapidly in the course of the war. By June 1944 the Waffen-SS included some 38 divisions with a total of 600,000 men. Originally an all-volunteer army of men who could meet the racial and ideological standards for SS membership, the Waffen-SS was forced to resort to conscription by the end of the war and included units recruited from Denmark, Holland, Flanders, and non-Germanic areas such as Bosnia. Units of the Waffen-SS were notorious for their brutality against prisoners of war, partisans, and civilians. A division of the Waffen-SS was responsible for the massacre of the inhabitants of the French village **Oradour-sur-Glane** in June 1944.

WANNSEE CONFERENCE Meeting of leading administrators from the Ministries of the Interior, Justice, Foreign Affairs, and the Occupied Eastern Territories with party and SS officials convened in a suburban Berlin villa by **Heydrich** on 20 January 1942 to coordinate plans for the **Final Solution**. Originally planned to convene in early December 1941, the meeting was postponed because of the **Battle of Moscow**, the attack on **Pearl Harbor**, and the US entry into the war. The 15 participants in the Wannsee Conference coordinated plans for the deportation and killing of Jews. Members of the bureaucracy did, however, successfully block Heydrich's plan to include German *Mischlings* in the "resettlement" plans.

WARSAW GHETTO The concentration of Jews in urban ghetttos was intended as an interim measure pending a decision on the final disposition of the Jewish population. The largest such ghetto was located in the pre-war Polish capital, home before the war of the second-largest Jewish community in the world after New York. As Jews from the countryside were forcibly relocated into ghettos, conditions grew progressively worse for their humiliated, impoverished, and savagely exploited inhabitants. The population of the Warsaw ghetto swelled to over 400,000. In November 1940 the Warsaw ghetto was walled in. Poverty, hunger, and disease drove up the mortality rate. Deportations from the Warsaw ghetto to the killing center at **Treblinka** began on 22 July 1942. Only about 50,000 inhabitants remained alive when **SS** and higher police leader Jürgen **Stroop** began the final clearing of the ghetto on 19 April 1943, thus precipitating the Warsaw ghetto uprising, an armed resistance movement led by the ghetto's Jewish Combat Organization. In the face of unexpectedly tenacious resistance, units of the **Waffen-SS** required more than three weeks to complete the clearing operation. The ghetto was razed to the ground and a **concentration camp** was erected on its site to house the few survivors still capable of work in armaments-related workshops and factories.

WARSAW UPRISING Operation by the underground Polish Home Army led by General Thadeusz Bór-Komorowski (1895–1966) in consultation with the Polish government in exile in London. The goal of the operation, launched on 1 August 1944, was to liberate the Polish capital before the arrival of Soviet troops. The uprising was crushed, however, by German forces under **SS** general von dem **Bach-Zelewski** with the loss of at least 150,000 civilian lives. Polish forces held out until 2 October 1944 in the hopes that the Red Army would relieve them. However, Warsaw was not liberated until January 1945.

WARTHELAND Designation for the Polish territories annexed to the German **Reich** after the conquest of Poland in October 1939. The Wartheland encompassed not only territories lost to Poland after the First World War but also additional territory that had never been part of Germany. Some 85 percent of its approximately 4.2 million inhabitants were ethnic Poles. Under **Gauleiter Greiser** the Wartheland was forcibly Germanized through the expulsion of Poles into the **Generalgouvernement**, the resettlement of ethnic Germans from the Baltic countries, and the destruction of virtually all Jews at **Chelmno** and other extermination sites.

WEHRKRAFTZERSETZUNG (Undermining of military strength). A broad capital offense introduced in August 1938, criminalizing all anti-war activities, conscientious objection to military service, draft-dodging, assisting deserters, malingering, criticism of the government's military policies, and various forms of defeatism.

WEHRMACHT Designation for the German armed forces introduced in 1935 to replace the earlier term **Reichswehr**. The High Command of the Wehrmacht was known as the **OKW** after 1938.

WEIMAR COALITION Coalition of the three parties, **SPD**, **DDP**, and **Center Party**, that supported the **Weimar Republic** and voted in favor of the Weimar Constitution in August 1919.

WEIMAR REPUBLIC Designation for the republic established in Germany after the fall of the monarchy on 9 November 1918. Although Berlin remained the capital of Germany, the new republic was generally referred to by the name of the city in which the elected National Assembly met to draw up the constitution for the new state in 1919. Weimar, in the central German state of Thuringia, was chosen as the site for the constitutional convention to escape the revolutionary turmoil in post-war Berlin. As the home of Goethe and Schiller in the age of German classicism, the city also symbolized the intention of republicans to restore the nation's links to its humanist rather than its militarist traditions.

WEREWOLF Code name for an underground resistance movement planned by the Nazis to be used against the Allied occupation. Except for isolated acts of murder by diehard Nazis against German civilians ready to cooperate with the Allies, Operation Werewolf lacked all public support and failed to mobilize any kind of effective resistance. "Werewolf" was also the code name of the Führer's headquarters near **Vinnitsa** in the Ukraine.

WESTERBORK Opened in October 1939 by the Dutch government as a camp for refugees from Germany, Westerbork was converted by the Nazis into a transit camp for Jews to be deported to the east. More than 100,000 persons, including approximately 69,000 Jews, passed through the camp. Only 900 inmates remained alive when the camp was liberated by Canadian troops in April 1945.

WHITE ROSE Resistance group founded by students at the University of Munich in the summer of 1942 under the leadership of Hans and Sophie **Scholl**. It was broken up by the **Gestapo** in February 1943.

WHW Acronym for Winterhilfswerk (**Winter Relief Agency**).

WILHELMSTRASSE Street in Berlin on which many German government buildings were located, including the Foreign Ministry. The trial of leading German civil servants at **Nuremberg** in 1947 is often referred to as the Wilhelmstrasse Trial.

WINTER RELIEF AGENCY Annual charity collection introduced in summer 1933 by the **National Socialist Welfare Organization** (NSV). Funds were collected from firms, organizations, contributions collected in residential areas, and withdrawals from wages and salaries. Although contributions were nominally voluntary, pressure to donate was intense. The purpose was not just to raise money but also to inculcate a readiness to make sacrifices for the national good. Funds were used to finance NSV functions as well as other party organizations

WINTER WAR War between the Soviet Union and Finland precipitated on 30 November 1939 by Soviet demands for additional territory to strengthen the Soviet

defenses around Leningrad. The Soviet Union attempted to seize some of the land allocated to it under secret provisions of the **German–Soviet Non-Aggression Pact**. The war ended in March 1940 when Finland was forced to accede to Soviet demands. However, the poor performance of the Red Army in the Winter War led **Hitler** and German military leaders to believe that the Soviet Union could not withstand a German attack.

WOLFSCHANZE (Wolf's Lair) Code name of **Hitler**'s military headquarters near Rastenburg in East Prussia from June 1941 to November 1944. It was here that an unsuccessful attempt on his life was made by military conspirators under **Stauffenberg**.

WVHA Acronym for Wirtschaftsverwaltungshauptamt. See **Economics and Administration Main Office**.

Y

YALTA CONFERENCE Meeting of the Big Three (Roosevelt, Stalin, and Churchill) at a Crimean resort from 4 to 11 February 1945 to decide on post-war policies. Germany was to be divided into temporary occupation zones (including a French zone to be drawn from territory of the US and British zones). Occupation policies were to be coordinated through an Allied Control Council in Berlin, which was to be divided into occupation sectors. The Soviet Union pledged to enter the war against Japan within three months after the end of the war in Europe. The Western Allies gave preliminary approval for the Soviet Union to retain the portion of Poland acquired under the **German–Soviet Non-Aggression Pact** and to move Poland's western borders to the **Oder–Neisse line**. The decision to recognize the Communist government in exile as the core of the Polish post-war government (to be augmented by members of the Polish government in exile in London) proved to be the source of greatest post-war contention. Roosevelt also gained Stalin's approval for the founding of a United Nations Organization, whose charter would call for member nations to settle their differences peacefully, refrain from the threat or use of force, respect the sovereignty of other nations, and cooperate in the solution of international political, economic, social, and cultural problems.

YELLOW STAR Identifying badge made compulsory for Jews in occupied Poland in October 1939, in other occupied areas in 1940, and mandated by law in Germany itself in September 1941. The badge was to be sown onto clothing on the upper left side and to be visible at all times. The purpose of this measure was to isolate Jews from the rest of the population and to facilitate their apprehension for deportation to the killing centers of the **Holocaust**.

YOUNG PLAN Program named after American banker Owen D. Young (1874–1962) to reschedule German reparations payments in 1929. The effort to defeat the plan by popular referendum was initiated by **Hugenberg** and supported by **Hitler**. Although the referendum was defeated, Hitler's cooperation with the established German Nationalist Party (**DNVP**) gave the Nazi Party national recognition and increased popular support.

$$\boxed{Z}$$

ZIONIST ASSOCIATION FOR GERMANY Organization founded in 1897 to foster Jewish settlements in Palestine and to reinvigorate a sense of Jewish national identity. Most German Jews, however, supported the assimilation policies of the **Centralverein**. The Zionist Association had a membership of approximately 20,000 in 1930. Its membership and influence grew after 1933, especially after the publication of its president Robert Weltsch's (1891–1982) article, "Wear it with Pride, the Yellow Badge," in the Zionist publication *Jewish Review* as a response to the Nazi economic **boycott** on 1 April 1933 (long before wearing the **yellow star** became compulsory for German Jews). The Zionist Association supported the **Haavara Agreement** with the German government to facilitate Jewish emigration to Palestine. The organization was forcibly dissolved by the Nazis after the *Reichskristallnacht* pogrom in November 1938.

NOTES

1 Introduction and background

1 An indispensable source on European fascism is *Fascism: Critical Concepts in Political Science*, 5 vols., ed. by Roger Griffin with Matthew Feldman, London and New York, Routledge, 2004.

2 For a provocative discussion of Jews as representatives of modernity, see Yuri Slezkine, *The Jewish Century*, Princeton, N.J., Princeton University Press, 2004.

3 Historiography

1 Pierre Ayçoberry, *The Nazi Question: An Essay on the Interpretations of National Socialism (1922–1975)*, New York, Pantheon, 1981, p. 37.

2 Edmond Vermeil, *Germany in the Twentieth Century*, New York, 1956, and "Origin, Nature, and Development of German Nationalist Ideology in the 19th and 20th Centuries," in International Council for Philosophy and Humanistic Studies, *The Third Reich*, London, Weidenfeld & Nicolson, 1955.

3 The most striking example of this genre was Rohan d'O. Butler, *The Roots of National Socialism, 1783–1933*, London, Faber & Faber, 1941. An American example is William M. McGovern, *From Luther to Hitler: The History of Fascist-Nazi Political Philosophy*, Boston, Mass., Houghton-Mifflin, 1941. The best of the wartime surveys of German history was A. J. P. Taylor, *The Course of German History*, London, 1945. Two other notable books identifying the roots of Nazism in the German cultural and intellectual tradition are Peter Viereck, *Meta-Politics: From the Romantics to Hitler*, New York, Knopf, 1941, and, almost twenty years later, Hans Kohn, *The Mind of Germany: The Education of a Nation*, New York, Scribner's, 1960.

4 Sir Robert Vansittart, *Black Record: Germans Past and Present*, London, Hamish, 1941.

5 Max Horkheimer, "Die Juden und Europa," *Studies in Philosophy and Social Science (Zeitschrift für Sozialforschung)*, Vol. 8 (1939), p. 115.

6 D. Renton, *Fascism: Theory and Practice*, London, Pluto, 1999, p. 109.

7 A good discussion of "Bonapartist" interpretations of the 1930s is Derek S. Linton, "Bonapartism, Fascism, and the Collapse of the Weimar Republic," in *Radical Perspectives on the Rise of Fascism in Germany, 1919–1945*, eds Michael N. Dobkowski and Isidor Wallimann, New York, Monthly Review Press, 1989,

pp. 100–27. See also, Robert S. Wistrich, "Leon Trotsky's Theory of Fascism," *Journal of Contemporary History* 11 (1976), pp. 157–84.

8 Daniel Guérin, *Sur le Fascisme*. Vol. II, *Fascisme et Grand Capital*, Paris, Gallimard, 1936; English translation, *Fascism and Big Business*, New York, Monad Press, 1973.

9 Arthur Rosenberg, *Der Faschismus als Massenbewegung: Sein Aufstieg und seine Zersetzung*, Karlsbad, Graphia, 1934. Also, *A History of the German Republic* (1935), London, Methuen, 1936, and *The Birth of the German Republic* (1928), Oxford, Oxford University Press, 1932.

10 Wilhelm Reich, *Massenpsychologie des Faschismus*, Copenhagen, Verlag für Sexualpolitik, 1934; English translation, *The Mass Psychology of Fascism*, New York, Farrar, Straus & Giroux, 1970. Erich Fromm, *Escape from Freedom*, New York, Rinehart, 1941. Ernst Bloch, "Ungleichzeitigkeit und Pflicht zu ihrer Dialektik," *Erbschaft dieser Zeit*, Frankfurt, Suhrkamp, [1935] 1962.

11 Gerhard Ritter, "The Historical Foundations of the Rise of National Socialism," in International Council for Philosophy and Humanistic Studies, *The Third Reich*, London, Weidenfeld & Nicolson, 1955, p. 385. See also, "The Fault of Mass Democracy," in *The Nazi Revolution: Germany's Guilt or Germany's Fate?*, ed. John Snell, New York, Heath, 1959.

12 Hans Rothfels, *The German Opposition to Hitler*, Hinsdale, Ill., Regnery, 1948. See Georg G. Iggers, "Refugee Historians from Nazi Germany: Political Attitudes toward Democracy," Occasional Paper of the Center for Advanced Holocaust Studies, Washington, DC, US Holocaust Memorial Museum, 2006, p. 13.

13 The best study of German historicism in English is Georg G. Iggers, *The German Conception of History: The National Tradition of Historical Thought from Herder to the Present*, Middletown, Conn., Wesleyan University Press, 1968.

14 Jane Caplan, "The Historiography of National Socialism," in Michael Bentley, ed., *Companion to Historiography*, London, Routledge, 1997, p. 559.

15 K. D. Bracher, *Die Auflösung der Weimarer Republik*, Stuttgart, Ring-Verlag, 1955, and with W. Sauer and G. Schulz, *Die nationalsozialistische Machtergreifung*, Cologne, Westdeutscher Verlag, 1960. Bracher's *The German Dictatorship: The Origins, Structure, and Effects of National Socialism*, trans. Jean Steinberg, New York, Praeger, 1982, was first published in Germany in 1969.

16 Hannah Arendt, *The Origins of Totalitarianism*, 2nd edn, New York, Meridian Books, [1951] 1958, p. vii.

17 Carl J. Friedrich and Zbigniew K. Brzezinski, *Totalitarian Dictatorship and Autocracy*, Cambridge, Mass., Harvard University Press, 1956, p. vii. On the debate about totalitarianism theory (as well as other controversies of interpretation) the indispensable guide in English is Ian Kershaw, *The Nazi Dictatorship: Problems and Perspectives of Interpretation*, 3rd edn, London and New York, Edward Arnold, 1993.

18 See Stefan Berger, "The Impact of Fritz Fischer," in *The Search for Normality: National Identity and Historical Consciousness in Germany Since 1800*, Providence, R.I., Berghahn Books, 1997, pp. 56–76, and Georg G. Iggers, "Critical Theory and Social History: 'Historical Social Science' in the Federal Republic of Germany," in *Historiography in the Twentieth Century: From Scientific Objectivity to Postmodern*

Challenge, Hanover, N.H., Wesleyan University Press, 1997, pp. 65–77. All of Fritz Fischer's important works were translated into English several years after their original publication in German: *Germany's Aims in the First World War*, New York, Norton, 1967; *World Power or Decline: The Controversy over Germany's Aims in the First World War*, New York, Norton, 1974; *War of Illusions: German Policies 1911–1914*, New York, Norton, 1975; and *From Kaiserreich to Third Reich: Elements of Continuity in German History, 1871–1945*, London, Allen & Unwin, 1986.

19 See Konrad H. Jarausch, "Critical Memory and Civil Society: The Impact of the 1960s on German Debates about the Past," in *Coping with the Nazi Past: West German Debates on Nazism and Generational Conflict, 1955–1975*, eds Philipp Gassert and Alan E. Steinweis, New York, Berghahn, 2006, pp. 11–30.

20 Hans-Ulrich Wehler, *The German Empire, 1871–1918*, trans. Kim Traynor, Providence, R.I., Berg, 1985 (originally published in German in 1973). Wehler applied his Sonderweg paradigm directly to the Nazi era in Vol. 4 of his massive *Deutsche Gesellschaftsgeschichte, Vom Beginn des Ersten Weltkriegs bis zur Gründung der beiden deutschen Staaten 1914–1949*, Munich, C.H. Beck, 2003.

21 Fritz Stern, *The Politics of Cultural Despair*, Berkeley, University of California Press, 1961; George L. Mosse, *The Crisis of German Ideology: Intellectual Origins of the Third Reich*, New York, Grosset & Dunlop, 1964; Kohn, *The Mind of Germany*. For a Marxist variant of the *Sonderweg* thesis, see Georg Lukács, *The Destruction of Reason* [1954], trans. Peter Palmer, Atlantic Highlands, N.J., Humanities Press, 1980.

22 James J. Sheehan, Review of *Gesellschaft, Parlament und Regierung* by Gerhard A. Ritter and *Regierung und Reichstag im Bismarckstaat* by Michael Stürmer, *Journal of Modern History*, Vol. 48 (1976), pp. 564–7.

23 David Blackbourne and Geoff Eley, *The Peculiarities of German History: Bourgeois Society and Politics in the Nineteenth Century*, Oxford, Oxford University Press, 1984.

24 Geoff Eley, "What Produces Fascism: Preindustrial Traditions or a Crisis of the Capitalist State?", in *Radical Perspectives on the Rise of Fascism in Germany*, pp. 69–99.

25 See the "Forum" on Blackbourne and Eley's *The Peculiarities of German History* in the journal *German History*, Vol. 22 (2004), pp. 229–45.

26 Ernst Nolte, *Three Faces of Fascism: Action Française, Italian Fascism, National Socialism*, trans. Leila Vennewitz, New York, Holt, Rinehart & Winston, 1966.

27 Martin Broszat, *German National Socialism, 1919–1945*, trans. Kurt Rosenbaum and Inge Pauli Boehm, Santa Barbara, Calif., Clio Press, 1966 (first published in 1960), and *The Hitler State: The Foundation and Development of the Internal Structure of the Third Reich*, New York, Longman, 1981 (first published in 1969); Hans Mommsen, *Beamtentum im Dritten Reich*, Stuttgart, Deutsche Verlagsanstalt, 1966.

28 Nicos Poulantzas, *Political Power and the Social Classes* [1968], London, NLB, 1973, and *Fascism and Dictatorship* [1970], London, NLB, 1974. For a good review of the impact of the 1960s student revolt on the historiography of Nazism, see Michael Schmidtke, "The German New Left and National Socialism," in *Coping with the Nazi Past*, pp. 176–93.

29 Tim Mason, "The Primacy of Politics – Politics and Economics in National Socialist Germany," in *Fascism in Europe*, ed. S. J. Woolf, New York, Random House, 1969, pp. 165–95. This article first appeared in German as "Der Primat der Politik: Politik und Wirtschaft im Nationalsozialismus," *Das Argument* 41 (1966), pp. 473–94.

30 R. J. Overy, "Germany, 'Domestic Crisis' and War in 1939", *Past and Present*, no. 116 (August 1987); Mason's "Comment", and Overy's "Reply", *Past and Present*, no. 122 (February 1989).

31 Raul Hilberg, *The Politics of Memory: The Journey of a Holocaust Historian*, Chicago: Ivan R. Dee, 1996, pp. 105–19.

32 Translated into English as *Anatomy of the SS State*, eds Hans Buchheim, Hans Adolf Jacobsen, Martin Broszat, and Helmut Krausnick, New York, Walker, 1968.

33 Tim Mason, "Intention and Explanation: A Current Controversy about the Interpretation of National Socialism," *Der "Führerstaat": Mythos und Realität*, eds G. Hirschfeld and L. Kettenacker, Stuttgart, Klett, 1981. This book contains the proceedings of a symposium held in 1979.

34 The metaphor is derived from the title of a book by Karl Schleunes, *The Twisted Road to Auschwitz: Nazi Policies toward German Jews, 1933–1939*, Urbana, University of Illinois Press, 1970.

35 Götz Aly, *"Final Solution": Nazi Population Policy and the Murder of the European Jews*, London, Arnold, 1999.

36 Christopher Browning, "Beyond 'Intentionalism' and 'Functionalism': The Decision for the Final Solution Reconsidered," in *Paths to Genocide: Essays on Launching the Final Solution*, Cambridge, Cambridge University Press, 1992, pp. 86–121, and "The Decision-Making Process," in *The Historiography of the Holocaust*, ed. Dan Stone, New York, Palgrave, 2004, pp. 173–96; Ian Kershaw, "Hitler and the Holocaust," in *The Nazi Dictatorship: Problems and Perspectives of Interpretation*, 3rd edn, London, Edward Arnold, 1993, pp. 80–107, and "Working Toward the Führer," in *Hitler 1889–1936: Hubris*, New York, Norton, 1999, pp. 527–91.

37 Michael Stürmer, "History in a Land without History," in *The Nazi Germany Sourcebook: An Anthology of Texts*, eds Roderick Stackelberg and Sally A. Winkle, London and New York, Routledge, 2002, p. 411.

38 Nolte's most important scholarly work in which he propounded his thesis of communist culpability for fascist excesses has not been translated into English: *Der europäische Bürgerkrieg* [The European Civil War] *1917–1945, Nationalsozialismus und Bolschewismus*, Frankfurt, Propyläen Verlag, 1987. The best works on the *Historikerstreit* in English are Charles S. Maier, *History, the Holocaust, and German National Identity*, Cambridge, Mass., Harvard University Press, 1988, and Richard J. Evans, *In Hitler's Shadow: West German Historians and the Attempt to Escape from the Nazi Past*, New York, Pantheon, 1989.

39 The American sociologist Seymour M. Lipset described Nazism as "middle-class extremism" in *Political Man: The Social Bases of Politics*, New York, Doubleday, 1960. Another strong advocate of the middle-class thesis is Michael Kater, although his *The Nazi Party: A Social Profile of Members and Leaders, 1919–1945* (Cambridge, Mass., Harvard University Press, 1983) modifies his earlier findings. The Canadian

historian Richard F. Hamilton demonstrated wide support for the Nazis among the upper middle class in *Who Voted for Hitler*, Princeton, N.J., Princeton University Press, 1982. Other research has confirmed that the Nazis drew support from all classes. See Richard Hamilton, Thomas Childers, and Jürgen Falter, *Hitlers Wähler*, Munich, C. H. Beck, 1991; and Thomas Childers, *The Nazi Voter: The Social Foundations of Fascism in Germany, 1917–1933*, Chapel Hill, University of North Carolina Press, 1983. A brief overview of research on the background of Nazi Party members before 1933 and a good discussion of how the same statistical data can be interpreted in very different ways is provided by Detlev Mühlberger, "Who Were the Nazis? The Social Characteristics of the Support mobilised by the Nazi Movement, 1920–1933," in *Fascism: Critical Concepts in Political Science*, ed. Roger Griffin with Matthew Feldman, Vol. II, *The Social Dynamics of Fascism*, London and New York, Routledge, 2004, pp. 198–211.

40 Rainer Zitelmann, *Hitler: Selbstverständnis eines Revolutionärs*, Hamburg, Berg, 1987, and *Adolf Hitler: Eine politische Biographie*, Göttingen, Muster-Schmidt Verlag, 1989.

41 Götz Aly, *Hitlers Volksstaat: Raub, Rassenkrieg und nationaler Sozialismus*, Frankfurt, S. Fischer, 2005; trans. as *Hitler's Beneficiaries: Plunder, Racial War, and the Nazi Welfare State*, New York, Metropolitan Books, 2006.

42 Hans-Ulrich Wehler, "Engstirniger Materialismus," *Der Spiegel*, April 14, 2005, 50–4.

43 Adam Tooze, "Stramme junge Männer in braunen Uniformen," *Die Zeit*, April 28, 2005; "Economics, Ideology and Cohesion in the Third Reich: A Critique of Goetz Aly's *Volksstaat*," at <www.hist.cam.ac.uk-academic_staff/further_details/tooze. html>; and *The Wages of Destruction: An Economic History of the Third Reich*, London, Allen Lane, 2006.

44 Michael Wildt, "Vertrautes Ressentiment," *Die Zeit*, May 4, 2005; Aly interview with *Die Welt*, March 10, 2005. See also Aly's article, "Federal Republic of Welfare," *Wall Street Journal*, June 7, 2005.

45 Henry A. Turner, "Fascism and Modernization," in *Reappraisals of Fascism*, New York, New Viewpoints, 1975, pp. 117–39. See also, Mark Roseman, "National Socialism and Modernization," in Richard Bessel, ed., *Fascist Italy and Nazi Germany: Comparisons and Contrasts*, Cambridge, Cambridge University Press, 1996, pp. 197–229.

46 Jeffrey Herf, *Reactionary Modernism: Technology, Culture and Politics in Weimar and the Third Reich*, Cambridge, Cambridge University Press, 1984.

47 A. James Gregor, *The Ideology of Fascism: The Rationale of Totalitarianism*, New York, Free Press, 1969; *Interpretations of Fascism*, New Brunswick, N.J., Transaction, 1974; *Italian Fascism and Developmental Dictatorship*, Princeton, N.J., Princeton University Press, 1979.

48 Michael Prinz and Rainer Zitelmann, eds, *Nationalsozialismus und Modernisierung*, Darmstadt, Wissenschaftliche Buchgesellschaft, 1991.

49 Peter Fritzsche, "Nazi Modern" (1996), in *Fascism: Critical Concepts in Political Science*, Vol. II, *The Social Dynamics of Fascism*, pp. 315ff. See also his "Fascism and

Illiberalism," in *Fascism Past and Present, West and East: An International Debate on Concepts and Cases in the Comparative Study of the Extreme Right*, eds Roger Griffin, Werner Loh, and Andreas Umland, Stuttgart, Ibidem-Verlag, 2006, pp. 110–14.

50 Hans Mommsen, "The Nazi Regime: Revolution or Counterrevolution?," in Reinhard Rürup, ed., *The Problem of Revolution in Germany, 1789–1989*, New York, Berg, 2000, pp. 109–27. See also Thomas Saunders, "Nazism and Social Revolution," in Gordon Martel, ed., *Modern Germany Reconsidered, 1870–1945*, New York, Routledge, 1993, pp. 159–77.

51 Zygmunt Bauman, *Modernity and the Holocaust*, Ithaca, N.Y., Cornell University Press, 1989, p. 7.

52 Detlev J. K. Peukert, *Inside Nazi Germany: Conformity, Opposition and Racism in Everyday Life* (1982), trans. by Richard Deveson, New Haven, Conn., Yale University Press, 1987, p. 15.

53 Ibid., p. 16. See also Detlev J. K. Peukert, *The Weimar Republic: The Crisis of Classical Modernity*, trans. Richard Deveson, New York, Hill & Wang, 1992; and Geoff Eley, "German History and the Contradictions of Modernity: The Bourgeoisie, the State, and the Mastery of Reform," in G. Eley, ed., *Society, Culture, and the State in Germany, 1870–1930*, Ann Arbor, University of Michigan Press, 1997.

54 Martin Broszat, ed., *Bayern in der NS-Zeit*, 6 vols., Munich, Oldenbourg, 1977–1983.

55 Lutz Niethammer, ed., *"Die Jahre weiss man nicht, wo man sie heute hinsetzen soll"*: *Faschismuserfahrungen im Ruhrgebiet*, Berlin, Dietz, 1986. Alf Lüdtke, ed., *The History of Everyday Life: Reconstructing Historical Experiences and Ways of Life*, Princeton, N.J., Princeton University Press, 1995. See also, Geoff Eley, "Labor History, Social History, *Alltagsgeschichte*: Experience, Culture, and the Politics of the Everyday – A New Direction for German Social History?," *Journal of Modern History* 61 (1989), pp. 297–343.

56 Hans-Ulrich Wehler, *Politik in der Geschichte*, Munich, C. H. Beck, 1998, pp. 188–94.

57 This exchange has been translated in Peter Baldwin, ed., *Reworking the German Past: Hitler, the Holocaust, and the "Historians' Debate,"* Boston, Mass., Beacon Press, 1990, pp. 102–34.

58 Konrad R. Jarausch and Michael Geyer, *Shattered Past: Reconstructing German Histories*, Princeton, N.J., Princeton University Press, 2003, p. 18.

59 Kevin Passmore, "Poststructuralism and History," in *Writing History: Theory and Practice*, eds S. Berger, H. Feldner, and K. Passmore, London, Arnold, 2003, pp. 118–40; Geoff Eley, "Is All the World a Text? From Social History to the History of Society Two Decades Later," in *The Historic Turn in the Human Sciences*, ed. Terrence McDonald, Ann Arbor, University of Michigan Press, 1996, pp. 193–243. On Holocaust denial, see Deborah E. Lipstadt, *Denying the Holocaust: The Growing Assault on Truth and Memory*, New York, Free Press, 1993; Richard J. Evans, *Lying About Hitler: History, Holocaust, and the David Irving Trial*, New York, Basic Books, 2001.

60 See Franklin H. Littell, ed., *Hyping the Holocaust: Scholars Answer Goldhagen*, East Rockaway, N.Y., Cummings & Hathaway, 1997; Norman G. Finkelstein and Ruth

Bettina Birn, *A Nation on Trial: The Goldhagen Thesis and Historical Truth*, New York, Henry Holt, 1998; and Geoff Eley, ed., *The "Goldhagen Effect": History, Memory, Nazism – Facing the German Past*, Ann Arbor, University of Michigan Press, 2000.

61 Doris L. Bergen, "Controversies about the Holocaust: Goldhagen, Arendt, and the Historians' Conflict," in *Historikerkontroversen*, ed. Hartmut Lehmann, Göttingen, Wallstein, 2000, p. 158.

62 See Jürgen Matthäus, "Historiography and the Perpetrators of the Holocaust," in *The Historiography of the Holocaust*, pp. 197–215.

63 Daniel Jonah Goldhagen, "*Modell Bundesrepublik*: National History, Democracy, and Internationalization in Germany," in *Unwilling Germans? The Goldhagen Debate*, ed. Robert R. Shandley, Minneapolis, University of Minnesota Press, 1998, pp. 275–85.

64 Geoff Eley, "Ordinary Germans, Nazism, and Judeocide," in *The "Goldhagen Effect,"* pp. 1–31.

65 Richard Steigmann-Gall, "Was National Socialism a Political Religion or a Religious Politics?," in *Religion und Nation, Nation und Religion*, eds Michael Geyer and Hartmut Lehmann, Göttingen, Wallstein, 2004, pp. 386–408; Neil Gregor, "Nazism – A Political Religion? Rethinking the Voluntarist Turn," in *Nazism, War and Genocide: Essays in Honour of Jeremy Noakes*, ed. Neil Gregor, Exeter (UK), University of Exeter Press, 2005, pp. 1–21. For a critique of Voegelin's interpretation, see Philippe Burrin, "Political Religion: The Relevance of a Concept," in *Passing into History: Nazism and the Holocaust beyond Memory*, ed. Gulie Ne'eman Arad, special issue of *History and Memory* 9 (Fall 1997), pp. 321–49. See also the critique by Hans Mommsen, "Der Nationalsozialismus als säkulare Religion," in *Zwischen "nationaler Revolution" und militärischer Aggression: Transformationen in Kirche und Gesellschaft während der konsolidierten NS-Gewaltherrschaft (1934–1939)*, eds Gerhard Besier and Elisabeth Müller-Luckner, Munich, R. Oldenbourg, 2001, pp. 43–53. For a concise discussion of the role of the churches in Nazism and the Holocaust, see Robert P. Erickson and Susannah Heschel, "The German Churches and the Holocaust," in *The Historiography of the Holocaust*, pp. 296–318. For a good review of post-1990 literature on Nazism, see Neil Gregor, "Politics, Culture, Political Culture: Recent Work on the Third Reich and Its Aftermath," *The Journal of Modern History* 78 (September 2006), pp. 643–83.

66 See Geoff Eley, "Hitler's Silent Majority? Conformity and Resistance under the Third Reich," *Michigan Quarterly Review*, Vol. 42 (2003), pp. 389–425 and 550–83.

67 Omer Bartov, "Whose History Is It Anyway? The Wehrmacht and German Historiography," in *War of Extermination: The German Military in World War II, 1941–1944* (1995), eds Hannes Heer and Klaus Naumann, New York, Berghahn, 2000, p. 405.

68 Five volumes of an English translation of *Germany and the Second World War* have been published by Oxford University Press to date, beginning with vol. 1, *The Build-up of German Aggression*, eds Wilhelm Deist, Manfred Messerschmidt, Hans-Erich Volkmann, and Wolfram Wette, in 1991.

69 David A. Messenger, Review of *Crimes of War: Guilt and Denial in the Twentieth*

Century, eds Omer Bartov, Atina Grossmann, and Mary Nolan, New York, New Press, 2002, published at <H-Holocaust@h-net.msu.edu> (January 2004).

70 Lothar Kettenacker, ed., *Ein Volk von Opfern? Die neue Debatte um den Bombenkrieg 1940–1945*, Berlin, Rowohlt, 2003. For American perspectives, see the articles by Mary Nolan, Elizabeth Heineman, and Thomas Childers under the heading, "Germans as Victims During the Second World War," *Central European History*, Vol. 38 (2005), pp. 7–105.

71 Examples are Hans Mommsen and Manfred Grieger, *Das Volkswagenwerk und seine Arbeiter im Dritten Reich*, Düsseldorf, Econ, 1996; Neil Gregor, *Daimler-Benz in the Third Reich*, New Haven, Conn., Yale University Press, 1998; Harold James, *The Deutsche Bank and the Nazi Economic War against the Jews: The Expropriation of Jewish-owned Property*, Cambridge, Cambridge University Press, 2001; Gerald Feldman, *Allianz and the German Insurance Business*, Cambridge, Cambridge University Press, 2001; Peter Hayes, *From Cooperation to Complicity: Degussa in the Third Reich*, Cambridge, Cambridge University Press, 2005; and Henry A. Turner, *General Motors and the Nazis: The Struggle for Control of Opel, Europe's Biggest Carmaker*, New Haven, Conn., Yale University Press, 2005.

72 Winfried Schulze and Otto Gerhard Oexle, eds, *Deutsche Historiker im Nationalsozialismus*, Frankfurt, Fischer, 1999; Ingo Haar and Michael Fahlbusch, eds, *German Scholars and Ethnic Cleansing*, New York, Berghahn, 2005. A book of interviews with leading historians on the complicity of the Erdmann–Conze–Schieder generation with Nazism was edited by Rüdiger Hohls and Konrad Jarausch under the title, *Versäumte Fragen: Deutsche Historiker im Schatten des Nationalsozialismus* (Unasked Questions: German Historians in the Shadow of National Socialism), Stuttgart and Munich, Deutsche Verlagsanstalt, 2000.

73 Nicolas Berg, *Der Holocaust und die westdeutschen Historiker: Erforschung und Erinnerung*, Göttingen, Wallstein, 2003, went even further in describing the commitment of the Institut für Zeitgeschichte to detached historical objectivity and structuralism as a form of repression of memory and guilt.

74 Representative examples of these new areas of research are Rudy Koshar, *Germany's Transient Pasts: Preservation and National Memory in the Twentieth Century*, Chapel Hill, University of North Carolina Press, 1998; Mary Fulbrook, *German National Identity after the Holocaust*, Cambridge, Polity Press, 1999; Bill Niven, *Facing the Nazi Past: United Germany and the Legacy of the Third Reich*, London, Routledge, 2002; and Norbert Frei, *Adenauer's Germany: The Politics of Amnesty and Integration*, New York, Columbia University Press, 2002. See also Alf Lüdtke, "'Coming to Terms with the Past': Illusions of Remembering, Ways of Forgetting Nazism in West Germany," *Journal of Modern History* 65 (1993), pp. 542–72, and the review essay by David Crew, "Remembering German Pasts: Memory in German History, 1871–1989," *Central European History*, Vol. 33 (2000), pp. 217–34.

75 See for instance the influential collection of essays edited by Saul Friedländer, *Probing the Limits of Representation: Nazism and the "Final Solution,"* Cambridge, Mass., Harvard University Press, 1992. A polemical attack on the new cultural history by Hans-Ulrich Wehler, "A Guide to Future Research on the Kaiserreich?," was

effectively countered by Geoff Eley, "Problems with Culture: German History after the Linguistic Turn," in the pages of *Central European History*, Vol. 29 (1996), pp. 541–72, and Vol. 31 (1998), pp. 197–227, respectively. For an excellent description of the issues at stake in the "cultural turn" and for a plea to integrate the approaches of social and cultural history, see Geoff Eley, *A Crooked Line: From Cultural History to the History of Society*, Ann Arbor, University of Michigan Press, 2005.

76 Tooze, *The Wages of Destruction*, pp. 524 and 543. Tooze credits the "compromise" interpretative model to Ulrich Herbert, *Hitler's Foreign Workers: Enforced Foreign Labor in Germany During the Third Reich*, Cambridge, Cambridge University Press, 1997, and the discovery of the importance of the food supply in German plans for mass murder to Christian Gerlach, *Krieg, Ernährung, Völkermord*, Hamburg, Hamburger Ed., 1998.

4 A–Z of historians

1 David Bankier, "German Public Awareness of the Final Solution," in *The Final Solution: Origins and Implementation*, ed. David Cesarani, London, Routledge, 1994, p. 225.

2 Adelheid von Saldern, "Victims or Perpetrators? Controversies about the Role of Women in the Nazi State," *Nazism and German Society*, ed. David F. Crew, London and New York, Routledge, 1994, p. 143.

3 Karl Dietrich Bracher, "The Role of Hitler: Perspectives and Interpretations," in *Fascism: A Reader's Guide*, ed. Walter Laqueur, Berkeley, University of California Press, 1976, p. 217.

4 Joachim C. Fest, *Hitler*, trans. Richard and Clara Winston, New York, Harcourt, Brace Jovanovich, 1974, p. 377.

5 Jeffrey Herf, *The Jewish Enemy: Nazi Propaganda during World War II and the Holocaust*, Cambridge, Mass., Harvard University Press, 2006, p. 276.

6 Peter Longerich, "Policy of Destruction: Nazi Anti-Jewish Policy and the Genesis of the 'Final Solution,'" Washington, DC, Center for Advanced Holocaust Studies, United States Holocaust Memorial Museum, 2001, p. 21.

7 Friedrich Meinecke, *The German Catastrophe: Reflections and Recollections*, trans. Sidney B. Fay, Boston, Mass., Beacon Press, [1950] 1963, p. 1.

8 Detlev J. K. Peukert, *Inside Nazi Germany: Conformity, Opposition, and Racism in Everyday Life*, trans. Richard Deveson, New Haven, Conn., Yale University Press, 1987, p. 248.

5 Origins and consolidation of Nazi Germany

1 "Proclamation of the Reich Government to the German People, 1 February 1933," in *The Nazi Germany Sourcebook*, eds Roderick Stackelberg and Sally A. Winkle, New York and London, Routledge, 2002, pp. 126–7.

2 "Vice-Chancellor Franz von Papen's Speech at Marburg, 17 June 1934," in *The Nazi Germany Sourcebook*, pp. 170–2.

6 Dictatorship in action

1 Martin Broszat, *The Hitler State: The Foundation and Development of the Internal Structure of the Third Reich*, New York, Longman, 1981, pp. xi, 294ff.

2 Ernst Fraenkel, *The Dual State: A Contribution to the Theory of Dictatorship*, New York, Octagon, 1941.

3 Nikolaus Wachsmann, *Hitler's Prisons: Legal Terror in Nazi Germany*, New Haven, Conn., Yale University Press, 2004, p. 373.

4 Dietrich Orlow, *The History of the Nazi Party: 1919–1933*, Pittsburgh, Pa., University of Pittsburgh Press, 1969, p. 8.

5 Otto Dietrich, *Hitler*, Chicago, Ill., Regnery, 1955, p. 113.

6 Ian Kershaw, "Hitler as Dictator: 'Working Towards the Führer.' Reflections on the Nature of the Hitler Dictatorship," in *The Third Reich: The Essential Readings*, ed. Christian Leitz, Malden, Mass., Blackwell, 1999, p. 235.

7 Carl-Wilhelm Reibel, *Das Fundament der Diktatur: Die NSDAP-Ortsgruppen 1932–1945*, Paderborn, Ferdinand Schöningh, 2004, p. 382.

8 Hans Mommsen, "Die Realisierung des Utopischen: Die Endlösung der Judenfrage im 'Dritten Reich,'" *Geschichte und Gesellschaft* 9 (1983), p. 387.

9 Ian Kershaw, "Working Toward the Führer: Reflections on the Nature of the Hitler Dictatorship," *Central European History* 2 (1993), pp. 103–18.

10 Ian Kershaw, *The "Hitler Myth": Image and Reality in the Third Reich*, Oxford, Oxford University Press, 1987, pp. 253–69.

11 Robert Gellately, *The Gestapo and German Society: Enforcing Racial Policy 1933–1945*, Oxford, Clarendon Press, 1990, p. 7; and "Surveillance and Disobedience: Aspects of the Political Policing of Nazi Germany," in Francis R. Nicosia and Lawrence D. Stokes, eds, *Germans against Nazism: Nonconformity, Opposition and Resistance in the Third Reich (Essays in Honor of Peter Hoffmann)*, New York, Berg, 1990, p. 34.

12 Eric A. Johnson, *Nazi Terror: The Gestapo, Jews, and Ordinary Germans*, New York, Basic Books, 1999, p. 17.

13 Robert Gellately, *Backing Hitler: Consent and Coercion in Nazi Germany*, Oxford, Oxford University Press, 2001, p. 259.

14 "The Nazi Party Program, 1920," in *The Nazi Germany Sourcebook: An Anthology of Texts*, New York and London, Routledge, 2002, pp. 64–6.

15 "Hitler's Memorandum on the Four-Year Plan, August 1936," in *The Nazi Germany Sourcebook*, pp. 198, 199.

16 See Richard J. Overy, "Germany, 'Domestic Crisis' and War in 1939," *Past & Present* 116 (1987), pp. 138–68, and "Debate: Germany, 'Domestic Crisis' and War in 1939," *Past & Present* 122 (1989), pp. 200–40.

17 Götz Aly, *Hitler's Beneficiaries: Plunder, Racial War, and the Nazi Racial State*, New York, Metropolitan Books, 2006; Adam Tooze, *The Wages of Destruction: The Making and Breaking of the Nazi Economy*, New York, Penguin, 2006.

18 Benjamin Sax and Dieter Kunz, eds, *Inside Hitler's Germany: A Documentary History of Life in the Third Reich*, Lexington, Mass., D. C. Heath, 1992, p. 229.

19 Frederic Spotts, *Hitler and the Power of Aesthetics*, Woodstock and New York, Overlook Press, 2004, pp. 10, 12.

20 Jonathan Petropolous, *Art as Politics in the Third Reich*, Chapel Hill, University of North Carolina Press, 1996, p. 283.

21 Adolf Hitler, *Mein Kampf*, trans. Ralph Manheim, Boston, Mass., Houghton Mifflin, 1971, p. 303.

22 Peter Reichel, "Bildende Kunst und Architektur," *Enzyklopädie des National-sozialismus*, eds Wolfgang Benz, Hermann Graml, and Hermann Weiss, Munich, Deutscher Taschenbuch Verlag, 1997, p. 160.

23 Richard Steigmann-Gall, *The Holy Reich: Nazi Conceptions of Christianity, 1919–1945*, Cambridge, Cambridge University Press, 2003, p. 114.

24 "Proclamation of the Reich Government to the German People, 1 February 1933," in *The Nazi Germany Sourcebook*, p. 127.

25 Kurt Nowak, "Kirchen und Religion," *Enzyklopädie des Nationalsozialismus*, p. 189.

26 Letter of Martin Bormann to Alfred Rosenberg, 24 February 1940, in *The Nazi Germany Sourcebook*, p. 238.

27 John F. Morley, *Vatican Diplomacy and the Jews during the Holocaust, 1939–1943*, New York, KTAV, 1980, p. 300, n. 188.

28 Michael Phayer, *The Catholic Church and the Holocaust, 1930–1955*, Bloomington, Indiana University Press, p. 58.

7 Foreign policy, war, and the Holocaust

1 Adolf Hitler, "Mein Kampf," in *The Nazi Germany Sourcebook*, eds R. Stackelberg and S. A. Winkle, New York and London, Routledge, 2002, p. 93.

2 Koppel S. Pinson, *Modern Germany: Its History and Civilization*, 2nd edn, New York, Macmillan, 1966, p. 520.

3 "Speech by the Führer, 22 August 1939," in *The Nazi Germany Sourcebook*, p. 246.

4 See Karl Schleunes, *The Twisted Road to Auschwitz: Nazi Policy toward German Jews, 1933–1939*, Urbana, University of Illinois Press, 1970.

5 Cited in "Goering's authorization to Heydrich, 31 July 1941," in *The Nazi Germany Sourcebook*, p. 340.

6 "Karl Binding and Alfred Hoche, *Permitting the Destruction of Unworthy Lives*, 1920," in *The Nazi Germany Sourcebook*, p. 73.

7 "SS Order for the Entire SS and Police, 28 October 1939," in *The Nazi Germany Sourcebook*, p. 202.

8 "Hitler's Reichstag Speech, 30 January 1939," in *The Nazi Germany Sourcebook*, p. 229.

9 "Goering's Authorization to Heydrich, 31 July 1941," in *The Nazi Germany Sourcebook*, p. 340.

8 Opposition and legacy

1 Theodore S. Hamerow, *On the Road to the Wolf's Lair: German Resistance to Hitler*, Cambridge, Mass., Harvard University Press, 1997, p. 285.

2 "Gestapo Report on Stauffenberg's Relations with Foreign Countries, 2 August 1944," in *The Nazi Germany Sourcebook*, eds R. Stackelberg and S. A. Winkle, London and New York, Routledge, 2002, p. 312.

3 Nathan Stoltzfus, *Resistance of the Heart: Intermarriage and the Rosenstrasse Protest in Nazi Germany*, New York, Norton, 1996; Wolf Gruner, "The Factory-Action and the Events at the Berlin Rosenstrasse: Facts and Fiction about 27 Feburary 1943 – Sixty Years Later," *Central European History* 36 (2003), pp. 179–208.

4 Richard Overy, *Interrogations: The Nazi Elite in Allied Hands, 1945*, New York, Penguin, 2001, p. 22.

5 T. H. Tetens, *The New Germany and the Old Nazis*, London, Secker & Warburg, 1961, p. 37.

6 Daniel Ganser, *NATO's Secret Armies: Operation Gladio and Terrorism in Western Europe*, New York, Frank Cass, 2005.

BIBLIOGRAPHY

- *This bibliography is limited to books in English.*
- *It is organized into four parts corresponding to the four sections of Part II. Books are listed only once.*
- *The selection includes the older classic studies as well as the most important recent scholarly literature on the Third Reich.*

Origins and consolidation of Nazi Germany

Abraham, David, *The Collapse of the Weimar Republic: Political Economy and Crisis*, 2nd edn, New York, Holmes & Meier, 1986.

Allen, William Sheridan, *The Nazi Seizure of Power in a Single German Town*, rev. edn, New York, Franklin, Watts, 1984.

Baranowski, Shelley, *The Sanctity of Rural Life: Nobility, Protestantism, and Nazism in Weimar Prussia*, Oxford, Oxford University Press, 1995.

Bergerson, Andrew Stuart, *Ordinary Germans in Extraordinary Times: The Nazi Revolution in Hildesheim*, Bloomington, University of Indiana Press, 2004.

Berghahn, V. R., *Germany and the Approach of War in 1914*, London, Macmillan, 1973.

—— *Imperial Germany, 1871–1914: Economy, Society, Culture, and Politics*, Providence, R.I., Berghahn Books, 1994.

Bessel, Richard, *Germany After the First World War*, Oxford, Clarendon Press, 1993.

Blackbourne, David and Eley, Geoff, *The Peculiarities of German History: Bourgeois Society and Politics in Nineteenth-Century Germany*, Oxford, Oxford University Press, 1984.

Broszat, Martin, *Hitler and the Collapse of Weimar Germany*, trans. by V. R. Berghahn, Leamington Spa, Berg, 1987.

Brustein, William, *The Logic of Evil: The Social Origins of the Nazi Party, 1925–1933*, New Haven, Conn., Yale University Press, 1996.

Caldwell, Peter C. and Scheuerman, William E., eds, *From Liberal Democracy to Fascism: Legal and Political Thought in the Weimar Republic*, Boston, Mass., Humanities Press, 2000.

Campbell, Bruce, *The SA Generals and the Rise of Nazism*, Lexington, University Press of Kentucky, 1998.

Carsten, F. L., *The Reichswehr and Politics 1918–1933*, Berkeley, University of California Press, 1973.

—— *The Rise of Fascism*, 2nd edn, Berkeley, University of California Press, 1980.

Chickering, Roger, *We Men Who Feel Most German: A Cultural Study of the Pan-German League, 1866–1914*, Boston, Mass., George Allen & Unwin, 1984.

Childers, Thomas, *The Nazi Voter: The Social Foundations of Fascism in Germany, 1919–1933*, Chapel Hill, University of North Carolina Press, 1983.

—— ed., *The Formation of the Nazi Constituency 1919–1933*, Totowa, N.J., Barnes & Noble, 1986

Clinefelder, Joan L., *Artists for the Reich: Culture and Race from Weimar to Nazi Germany*, Oxford, Berg, 2005.

Diehl, James M., *Paramilitary Politics in Weimar Germany*, Bloomington, Indiana University Press, 1977.

Dobkowski, Michael N. and Wallimann, Isidor, eds, *Towards the Holocaust: The Social and Economic Collapse of the Weimar Republic*, Westport, Conn., Greenwood Press, 1983.

—— eds, *Radical Perspectives on the Rise of Fascism in Germany 1919–1945*, New York, Monthly Review Press, 1989.

Dorpalen, Andreas, *Hindenburg and the Weimar Republic*, Princeton, N.J., Princeton University Press, 1964.

Eley, Geoff, *Reshaping the German Right: Radical Nationalism and Political Change after Bismarck*, New Haven, Conn., Yale University Press, 1980.

—— *From Unification to Nazism: Reinterpreting the German Past*, Boston, Mass., Unwin Hyman, 1986.

Evans, Richard J., *The Coming of the Third Reich*, London, Penguin Books, 2003.

Farquharson, J. E., *The Plough and the Swastika: N.S.D.A.P. and Agriculture in Germany, 1928–1945*, Bloomington, Indiana University Press, 1976.

Feldman, Gerald D., *The Great Disorder: Politics, Economics, and Society in the German Inflation, 1914–1924*, New York, Oxford University Press, 1997.

Field, Geoffrey G., *Evangelist of Race: The Germanic Vision of Houston Stewart Chamberlain*, New York, Columbia University Press, 1981.

Fischer, Conan, *The Rise of the Nazis*, Manchester, University of Manchester Press, 1995.

Fischer, Fritz, *Germany's Aims in the First World War*, New York, Norton, 1967.

—— *World Power or Decline: The Controversy Over Germany's Aims in the First World War*, New York, Norton, 1974.

—— *War of Illusions: German Policies from 1911 to 1914*, New York, Norton, 1975.

—— *From Kaiserreich to Third Reich: Elements of Continuity in German History, 1871–1945*, trans. by Roger Fletcher, London, Allen & Unwin, 1986.

Fritzsche, Peter, *Rehearsals for Fascism: Populism and Political Mobilization in Weimar Germany*, New York, Oxford University Press, 1990.

—— *Germans into Nazis*, Cambridge, Mass., Harvard University Press, 1998.

Goodrick-Clarke, Nicholas, *The Occult Roots of Nazism: Secret Aryan Cults and Their Influence on Nazi Ideology*, New York, New York University Press, 1993.

Gordon, Harold J., *Hitler and the Beer Hall Putsch*, Princeton, N.J., Princeton University Press, 1972.

Haffner, Sebastian, *The Ailing Empire: Germany from Bismarck to Hitler*, trans. by Jean Steinberg, New York, Fromm International Publishing, 1989.

Hamann, Brigitte, *Hitler's Vienna: A*

Dictator's Apprenticeship, Oxford, Oxford University Press, 1999.

Hamilton, Richard F., *Who Voted for Hitler?*, Princeton, N.J., Princeton University Press, 1982.

Harsch, Donna, *German Social Democracy and the Rise of Nazism*, Chapel Hill, University of North Carolina Press, 1993.

Heberle, Rudolf, *From Democracy to Nazism: A Regional Case Study on Political Parties in Germany*, New York, Grosset & Dunlap, 1970.

Heilbronner, Oded, *Catholicism, Political Culture, and the Countryside: A Social History of the Nazi Party in South Germany*, Ann Arbor, University of Michigan Press, 1997.

Herf, Jeffrey, *Reactionary Modernism: Technology, Culture and Politics in Weimar and the Third Reich*, Cambridge, Cambridge University Press, 1984.

Hewitson, Mark, *Germany and the Causes of the First World War*, Oxford, Berg, 2004.

Hitler, Adolf, *Mein Kampf*, trans. by Ralph Manheim, Boston, Mass., Houghton Mifflin, 1971.

Holborn, Hajo, *Republic to Reich: The Making of the Nazi Revolution*, New York, Pantheon, 1972.

Hughes, H. Stuart, *The Sea Change: The Migration of Social Thought, 1930–1965*, New York, Harper & Row, 1975.

Jäckel, Eberhard, *Hitler's World View: A Blueprint for Power*, trans. by Herbert Arnold, Cambridge, Mass., Harvard University Press, 1981.

Jones, Larry Eugene, *German Liberalism and the Dissolution of the Weimar Party System, 1918–1933*, Chapel Hill, University of North Carolina Press, 1988.

Kaes, Anton, Jay, Martin, and Dimendberg, Edward, eds, *The Weimar Republic Sourcebook*, Berkeley, University of California Press, 1994.

Kater, Michael H., *The Nazi Party: A Social Profile of Members and Leaders, 1919–1945*, Cambridge, Mass., Harvard University Press, 1983.

Kauders, Anthony, *German Politics and the Jews: Düsseldorf and Nuremberg 1910–1933*, Oxford, Clarendon Press, 1996.

Kehr, Eckart, *Economic Interest, Militarism, and Foreign Policy: Essays on German History*, trans. by Grete Heinz, Berkeley, University of California Press, 1977.

Kellogg, Michael, *The Russian Roots of Nazism: White Émigrés and the Making of National Socialism, 1917–1945*, Cambridge, Cambridge University Press, 2005.

Kershaw, Ian, ed., *Weimar: Why Did Weimar Democracy Fail?*, New York, St Martin's, 1990.

Klemperer, Klemens von, *Germany's New Conservatism: Its History and Dilemma in the Twentieth Century*, Princeton, N.J., Princeton University Press, 1957.

Kocka, Jürgen, *Facing Total War: German Society, 1914–1918*, trans. by Barbara Weinberger, Cambridge, Mass., Harvard University Press, 1984.

Koshar, Rudy, *Social Life, Local Politics, and Nazism, 1880–1935*, Chapel Hill, University of North Carolina Press, 1986.

Lane, Barbara Miller and Rupp, Leila J., eds, *Nazi Ideology before 1933: A Documentation*, Austin, University of Texas Press, 1978.

Large, David Clay, *Where Ghosts Walked: Munich's Road to the Third Reich*, New York, Norton, 1997.

Lebovics, Herman, *Social Conservatism and the Middle Classes in Germany, 1914–1933*, Princeton, N.J., Princeton University Press, 1969.

Leopold, John A., *Alfred Hugenberg: The Radical Nationalist Campaign against the Weimar Republic*, New Haven, Conn., Yale University Press, 1977.

Levy, Richard S., *The Downfall of the Anti-Semitic Political Parties in Imperial Germany*, New Haven, Conn., Yale University Press, 1975.

McElligott, Anthony, *Contested City: Municipal Politics and the Rise of the Nazis in Altona, 1917–1937*, Ann Arbor, University of Michigan Press, 1998.

Maier, Charles S., Hoffmann, Stanley, and Gould, Andrew, eds, *The Rise of the Nazi Regime: Historical Reassessments*, Boulder, Colo., Westview, 1986.

Martel, Gordon, ed., *Modern Germany Reconsidered, 1870–1945*, London, Routledge, 1992.

Mommsen, Hans, *From Weimar to Auschwitz*, trans. by Philip O'Connor, Princeton, N.J., Princeton University Press, 1991.

—— *The Rise and Fall of Weimar Democracy*, trans. Elborg Forster and Larry Eugene Jones, Chapel Hill, University of North Carolina Press, 1996.

Mosse, George L., *The Crisis of German Ideology: Intellectual Origins of the Third Reich*, New York, Grosset & Dunlap, 1964.

—— *Germans and Jews: The Right, the Left, and the Search for a "Third Force" in Pre-Nazi Germany*, New York, Grosset & Dunlap, 1970.

—— *The Nationalization of the Masses: Political Symbolism and Mass Movements in Germany from the Napoleonic Wars Through the Third Reich*, New York, Howard Fertig, 1975.

Mühlberger, Detlev, *Hitler's Followers: Studies in the Sociology of the Nazi Movement*, London, Routledge, 1991.

Niewyk, Donald L., *Socialist, Anti-Semite, and Jew: German Social Democracy Confronts the Problem of Anti-Semitism, 1918–1933*, Baton Rouge, Louisiana State University Press, 1971.

Noakes, Jeremy, *The Nazi Party in Lower Saxony, 1921–1933*, Oxford, Oxford University Press, 1971.

—— and Pridham, Geoffrey, eds, *Nazism 1919–1945: A History in Documents and Eyewitness Accounts*: Vol. 1, *The Nazi Party, State and Society, 1919–1939*, New York, Schocken, 1983.

Orlow, Dietrich, *The History of the Nazi Party, 1919–1933*, Pittsburgh, Pa., University of Pittsburgh Press, 1969.

—— *The History of the Nazi Party, 1933–1945*, Pittsburgh, Pa., University of Pittsburgh Press, 1973.

Payne, Stanley G., Sorkin, David J., and Tortorice, John S., eds, *What History Tells: George L. Mosse and the Culture of Modern Europe*, Madison, University of Wisconsin Press, 2004.

Peukert, Detlev J. K., *The Weimar Republic: The Crisis of Classical Modernity*, trans. by Richard Deveson, New York, Hill & Wang, 1992.

Pridham, Geoffrey, *The Nazi Movement in Bavaria, 1923–1933*, New York, Harper & Row, 1973.

Pulzer, Peter, *The Rise of Political Anti-Semitism in Germany and Austria*, rev. edn, Cambridge, Mass., Harvard University Press, 1988.

Röhl, John C. G., *From Bismarck to Hitler: The Problem of Continuity in German*

History, New York, Barnes & Noble, 1970.

Schorske, Carl E., *Fin-de-siècle Vienna: Politics and Culture*, New York, Alfred A. Knopf, 1981.

Shirer, William L., *The Rise and Fall of the Third Reich: A History of Nazi Germany*, New York, Simon & Schuster, 1960.

Stachura, Peter, *The German Youth Movement, 1900–1945*, New York, St Martin's, 1981.

—— *Gregor Strasser and the Rise of Nazism*, London, Allen & Unwin, 1983.

Stackelberg, Roderick, *Idealism Debased: From Völkisch Ideology to National Socialism*, Kent, Oh., Kent State University, 1981.

—— *Hitler's Germany: Origins, Interpretations, Legacies*, London and New York, Routledge, 1999.

—— and Winkle, Sally, eds, *The Nazi Germany Sourcebook: An Anthology of Texts*, London, Routledge, 2002.

Stern, Fritz, *The Politics of Cultural Despair: A Study in the Rise of the Germanic Ideology*, Garden City, NY, Doubleday Anchor, 1965.

—— *Dreams and Delusions: The Drama of German History*, New York, Vintage Books, 1989.

—— *The Failure of Illiberalism: Essays on the Political Culture of Modern Germany*, New York, Columbia University Press, 1992.

Strong, George V., *Seedtime for Fascism: The Disintegration of Austrian Political Culture, 1867–1918*, Armonk, N.Y., M. E. Sharpe, 1998.

Struve, Walter, *Elites Against Democracy: Leadership Ideals in Bourgeois Political Thought in Germany, 1890–1933*, Princeton, N.J., Princeton University Press, 1973.

Szejnmann, Claus-Christian, *Nazism in Central Germany: The Brownshirts in "Red" Saxony*, New York, Berghahn Books, 1999.

Tal, Uriel, *Christians and Jews in Germany: Religion, Politics, and Ideology in the Second Reich, 1870–1914*, trans. by Noah Jonathan Jacobs, Ithaca, N.Y., Cornell University Press, 1975.

Taylor, A. J. P., *The Course of German History: A Survey of the Development of Germany Since 1815*, New York, Coward-McCann, 1946.

Taylor, Simon, *Prelude to Genocide: Nazi Ideology and the Struggle for Power*, New York, St Martin's, 1985.

Tilton, Timothy Alan, *Nazism, Neo-Nazism, and the Peasantry*, Bloomington, Indiana University Press, 1975.

Tobias, Fritz, *The Reichstag Fire*, New York, Putnam, 1964.

Turner, Henry Ashby, Jun., *German Big Business and the Rise of Hitler*, New York, Oxford University Press, 1985.

—— *Hitler's Thirty Days to Power: January 1933*, Reading, Mass., Addison-Wesley, 1996.

Verhey, Jeffrey, *The Spirit of 1914: Militarism, Myth, and Mobilization in Germany*, Cambridge, Cambridge University Press, 2000.

Volkov, Shulamit, *The Rise of Popular Antimodernism in Germany: The Urban Master Artisans, 1873–1896*, Princeton, N.J., Princeton University Press, 1978.

Waite, Robert G. L., *Vanguard of Nazism: The Free Corps Movement in Postwar Germany, 1918–1923*, Cambridge, Mass., Harvard University Press, 1952.

Wehler, Hans Ulrich, *The German Empire, 1871–1918*, trans. by Kim Traynor, Providence, R.I., Berg, 1985.

Wheeler-Bennett, John W., *The Nemesis of*

Power: The German Army in Politics, 1918–1945, London, Macmillan, 1953.

Woods, Roger, The Conservative Revolution in the Weimar Republic, New York, St Martin's, 1996.

Dictatorship in action

Ayçoberry, Pierre, The Nazi Question: An Essay on the Interpretations of National Socialism (1922–1975), trans. by Robert Hurley, New York, Pantheon, 1981.

—— The Social History of the Third Reich 1933–1945, trans. by Janet Lloyd, New York, New Press, 1999.

Baranowski, Shelley, Confessing Church, Conservative Elites, and Nazi State, Lewiston, N.Y., E. Mellen Press, 1986.

—— Strength Through Joy: Consumerism and Mass Tourism in the Third Reich, Cambridge, Cambridge University Press, 2004.

Barkai, Avraham, Nazi Economics: Ideology, Theory, and Policy, trans. by Ruth Hadass-Vashitz, New Haven, Conn., Yale University Press, 1990.

Baynes, Norman H., ed., The Speeches of Adolf Hitler, April 1933–August 1939, 2 vols., New York, Howard Fertig, 1969.

Bergen, Doris L., Twisted Cross: The German Christian Movement in the Third Reich, Chapel Hill, University of North Carolina Press, 1996.

Bessel, Richard, ed., Life in the Third Reich, Oxford, Oxford University Press, 1987.

—— ed., Fascist Italy and Nazi Germany: Comparisons and Contrasts, Cambridge, Cambridge University Press, 1996.

Beyerchen, Alan D., Scientists Under Hitler: Politics and the Physics Community in the Third Reich, New Haven, Conn., Yale University Press, 1977.

Bracher, Karl Dietrich, The German Dictatorship: The Origins, Structure, and Effects of National Socialism, trans. by Jean Steinberg, New York, Praeger, 1970.

Bramstead, Ernest K., Goebbels and National Socialist Propaganda, 1925–1945, East Lansing, Michigan State University Press, 1965.

Bridenthal, Renate, Grossmann, Atina, and Kaplan, Marion, eds, When Biology Became Destiny: Women in Weimar and Nazi Germany, New York, Monthly Review Press, 1984.

Broszat, Martin, German National Socialism, 1919–1945, trans. by Kurt Rosenbaum and Inge Pauli Boehm, Santa Barbara, Calif., Clio Press, 1966.

—— The Hitler State: The Foundation and Development of the Internal Structure of the Third Reich, New York, Longman, 1981.

Bullock, Alan, Hitler: A Study in Tyranny, rev. edn, New York, Harper & Row, 1964.

—— Hitler and Stalin: Parallel Lives, New York, Alfred A. Knopf, 1992.

Burleigh, Michael, The Third Reich: A New History, New York, Hill & Wang, 2000.

—— and Wippermann, Wolfgang, The Racial State: Germany 1933–1945, Cambridge, Cambridge University Press, 1991.

Carsten, F. L., The German Workers and the Nazis, Aldershot, Scolar Press, 1995.

Childers, Thomas and Caplan, Jane, eds, Revaluating the Third Reich, New York, Holmes & Meier, 1993.

Conway, John S., The Nazi Persecution of the Churches, 1933–1945, New York, Basic Books, 1968.

Cornwell, John, Hitler's Pope: The Secret

History of Pius XII, New York, Viking, 1999.

—— *Hitler's Scientists: Science, War, and the Devil's Pact*, New York, Viking, 2003.

Crew, David F., ed., *Nazism and German Society, 1933–1945*, London, Routledge, 1994.

Cuomo, Glen R., ed., *National Socialist Cultural Policy*, New York, St Martin's, 1995.

Dülffer, Jost, *Nazi Germany 1933–1945: Faith and Annihilation*, trans. by Dean Scott McMurry, London, Arnold, 1996.

Durham, Martin, *Women and Fascism*, London, Routledge, 1998.

Engelmann, Bernt, *In Hitler's Germany: Daily Life in the Third Reich*, trans. by Krishna Winston, New York, Pantheon, 1986.

Ericksen, Robert P., *Theologians Under Hitler: Gerhard Kittel, Paul Althaus, and Emanuel Hirsch*, New Haven, Conn., Yale University Press, 1985.

Etlin, Richard A., ed., *Art, Culture, and Media Under the Third Reich*, Chicago, Ill., University of Chicago Press, 2002.

Evans, Richard J., *The Third Reich in Power*, London, Penguin, 2005.

Fest, Joachim C., *The Face of the Third Reich: Portraits of the Nazi Leadership*, trans. by Michael Bullock, New York, Pantheon, 1970.

—— *Hitler*, trans. by Richard and Clara Winston, New York, Vintage Books, 1975.

Fischer, Klaus P., *Nazi Germany: A New History*, New York, Continuum, 1995.

Fraenkel, Ernst, *The Dual State: A Contribution to the Theory of Dictatorship*, New York, Octagon, 1969.

Frei, Norbert, *National Socialist Rule in Germany: The Führer State 1933–1945*, trans. by Simon B. Steyne, Oxford, Blackwell, 1993.

Friedländer, Saul, *Pius XII and the Third Reich: A Documentation*, New York, Alfred A. Knopf, 1966.

Gellately, Robert, *The Gestapo and German Society: Enforcing Racial Policy 1933–1945*, Oxford, Clarendon Press, 1990.

—— *Backing Hitler: Consent and Coercion in Nazi Germany*, Oxford, Oxford University Press, 2001.

—— and Stotzfus, Nathan, eds, *Social Outsiders in Nazi Germany*, Princeton, N.J., Princeton University Press, 2001.

Giles, Geoffrey J., *Students and National Socialism in Germany*, Princeton, N.J., Princeton University Press, 1985.

Gispen, Kees, *Poems in Steel: National Socialism and the Politics of Inventing from Weimar to Bonn*, New York, Berghahn Books, 2002.

Griech-Polelle, Beth A., *Bishop von Galen: German Catholicism and National Socialism*, New Haven, Conn., Yale University Press, 2002.

Grunberger, Richard, *The 12-Year Reich: A Social History of Nazi Germany 1933–1945*, New York, Holt, Rinehart & Winston, 1971.

Guenther, Irene, *Nazi Chic? Fashioning Women in the Third Reich*, Oxford, Berg, 2004.

Haffner, Sebastian, *The Meaning of Hitler*, trans. by Ewald Osers, Cambridge, Mass., Harvard University Press, 1983.

Hayes, Peter, *From Cooperation to Complicity: Degussa in the Third Reich*, Cambridge, Cambridge University Press, 2004.

Helmreich, Ernst Christian, *The German Churches Under Hitler: Background, Struggle, and Epilogue*, Detroit, Mich., Wayne State University Press, 1979.

Herzog, Dagmar, ed., *Sexuality and German Fascism*, New York, Berghahn Books, 2005.

Hiden, John and Farquharson, John, *Explaining Hitler's Germany: Historians and the Third Reich*, Totowa, N.J., Barnes & Noble, 1983.

Hildebrand, Klaus, *The Third Reich*, London, George Allen & Unwin, 1984.

Höhne, Heinz, *The Order of the Death's Head*, New York, Ballantine, 1977.

James, Harold, *The Nazi Dictatorship and the Deutsche Bank*, New York, Cambridge University Press, 2004.

Johnson, Eric A., *Nazi Terror: The Gestapo, Jews, and Ordinary Germans*, New York, Basic Books, 1999.

—— and Reuband, Karl-Heinz, *What We Knew: Terror, Mass Murder, and Everyday Life in Nazi Germany*, New York, Basic Books, 2005.

Kater, Michael H., *Doctors Under Hitler*, Chapel Hill, University of North Carolina Press, 1989.

—— *Composers of the Nazi Era: Eight Portraits*, New York, Oxford University Press, 2000.

—— *Hitler Youth*, Cambridge, Mass., Harvard University Press, 2004.

—— and Riethmüller, Albrecht, eds, *Music and Nazism: Art Under Tyranny, 1933–1945*, Laaber, Laaber-Verlag, 2003.

Kershaw, Ian, *Popular Opinion and Political Dissent in the Third Reich: Bavaria 1933–1945*, Oxford, Clarendon Press, 1983.

—— *The "Hitler Myth": Image and Reality in the Third Reich*, Oxford, Oxford University Press, 1987.

—— *Hitler*, London, Longman, 1991.

—— *The Nazi Dictatorship: Problems and Perspectives of Interpretation*, 3rd edn, London, Edward Arnold, 1993.

—— *Hitler, 1889–1936: Hubris*, New York, Norton, 1998.

—— *Hitler, 1936–1945: Nemesis*, New York, Norton, 2000.

—— and Lewin, Moshe, eds, *Stalinism and Nazism: Dictatorships in Comparison*, Cambridge, Cambridge University Press, 1997.

Klemperer, Victor, *I Will Bear Witness: A Diary of the Nazi Years*: Vol. 1, *1933–1941*, Vol. 2, *The Nazi Years*, trans. Martin Chalmers, New York, Random House, 1998, 1999.

—— *The Language of the Third Reich: LTI-Lingua Tertii Imperii: A Philologist's Notebook*, trans. Martin Brady, London, Athlone Press, 2000.

Koonz, Claudia, *Mothers in the Fatherland: Women, the Family and Nazi Politics*, New York, St Martin's, 1987.

—— *The Nazi Conscience*, Cambridge, Mass., Harvard University Press, 2003.

Krausnick, Helmut, *et al.*, *Anatomy of the SS State*, trans. by Richard Barry, Marian Jackson, and Dorothy Long, New York, Walker & Company, 1968.

Leitz, Christian, *The Third Reich: The Essential Readings*, Malden, Mass., Blackwell, 1999.

Lewy, Günter, *The Catholic Church and Nazi Germany*, New York, McGraw-Hill, 1964.

Lixfeld, Hannjost, *Folklore and Fascism: The Reich Institute for German Volkskunde*, ed. and trans. by James R. Dow, Bloomington, Indiana University Press, 1994.

Lochner, Louis P., ed., *The Goebbels Diaries*, New York, Doubleday, 1948.

Lüdtke, Alf, ed., *The History of Everyday Life: Reconstructing Historical Experiences and Ways of Life*, trans. by William Templer, Princeton, N.J., Princeton University Press, 1995.

Lukacs, John, *The Hitler of History*, New York, Alfred A. Knopf, 1997.

McElligott, Anthony and Kirk, Tim, eds, *Working towards the Führer: Essays in Honour of Sir Ian Kershaw*, Manchester, Manchester University Press, 2003.

McKale, Donald M., *The Nazi Party Courts: Hitler's Management of Conflict in His Movement, 1921–1945*, Lawrence, University Press of Kansas, 1974.

Macrakis, Kristie, *Surviving the Swastika: Scientific Research in Nazi Germany*, New York and Oxford, Oxford University Press, 1993.

Mason, Timothy, *Social Policy in the Third Reich: The Working Class and the "National Community", 1918–1939*, ed. by Jane Caplan, Oxford, Berg Publishers, 1993.

Meissner, Hans-Otto, *Magda Goebbels: The First Lady of the Third Reich*, trans. by Gwendolen Mary Keeble, New York, Dial Press, 1980.

Mommsen, Hans, ed., *The Third Reich Between Vision and Reality: New Perspectives on German History, 1918–1945*, Oxford, Berg, 2001.

Müller, Ingo, *Hitler's Justice: The Courts of the Third Reich*, trans. by Deborah Lucas Schneider, Cambridge, Mass., Harvard University Press, 1991.

Neumann, Franz, *Behemoth: The Structure and Practice of National Socialism 1933–1944* (1944), rpt New York, Harper & Row, 1966.

Overy, R. J., *The Nazi Economic Recovery 1932–1938*, 2nd edn, Cambridge, Cambridge University Press, 1996.

—— *The Penguin Historical Atlas of the Third Reich*, London, Penguin, 1996.

Padfield, Peter, *Dönitz: The Last Führer*, New York, Harper & Row, 1984.

Pauley, Bruce F., *Hitler, Stalin, and Mussolini: Totalitarianism in the Twentieth Century*, Wheeling, Ill., Harlan Davidson, 1997.

Peterson, Edward N., *The Limits of Hitler's Power*, Princeton, N.J., Princeton University Press, 1969.

Petropolous, Jonathan, *Art as Politics in the Third Reich*, Chapel Hill, University of North Carolina Press, 1996.

—— *The Faustian Bargain: The Art World in Nazi Germany*, Oxford, Oxford University Press, 2000.

Peukert, Detlev J. K., *Inside Nazi Germany: Conformity, Opposition and Racism in Everyday Life*, trans. by Richard Deveson, New Haven, Conn., Yale University Press, 1987.

Pine, Lisa, *Nazi Family Policy, 1933–1945*, Oxford, Berg, 1997.

Reese, Dagmar, *Growing Up Female in Nazi Germany*, trans. by William Templer, Ann Arbor, University of Michigan Press, 2006.

Renneberg, Monika and Walker, Mark, eds, *Science, Technology and National Socialism*, Cambridge, Cambridge University Press, 1994.

Sax, Benjamin and Kuntz, Dieter, *Inside Hitler's Germany: A Documentary History of Life in the Third Reich*, Lexington, Mass., D. C. Heath, 1992.

Schoenbaum, David, *Hitler's Social Revolution: Class and Status in Nazi Germany, 1933–1939* (1966), rpt New York, Norton, 1980.

Snyder, Louis L., *Hitler's Third Reich: A Documentary History*, Chicago, Nelson-Hall, 1981.

—— *Encyclopedia of the Third Reich*, New York, Paragon House, 1989.

Speer, Albert, *Inside the Third Reich: Memoirs*, trans. by Richard and Clara Winston, New York, Macmillan, 1970.

Steigmann-Gall, Richard, *The Holy Reich:*

Nazi Conceptions of Christianity, 1919–1945, Cambridge, Cambridge University Press, 2003.

Steinweis, Alan E., *Art, Ideology, and Economics in Nazi Germany: The Reich Chambers of Music, Theater, and the Visual Arts*, Chapel Hill, University of North Carolina Press, 1993.

Stephenson, Jill, *Women in Nazi Society*, New York, Barnes & Noble, 1975.

—— *The Nazi Organisation of Women*, London, Croom Helm, 1981.

Stern, J. P., *Hitler: The Führer and the People*, rev. edn, Berkeley, University of California Press, 1992.

Stibbe, Matthew, *Women in the Third Reich*, London, Arnold, 2003.

Stone, Norman, *Hitler*, Boston, Mass., Little, Brown, 1980.

Sydnor, Charles W. Jun., *Soldiers of Destruction: The SS Death's Head Division, 1933–1945*, Princeton, N.J., Princeton University Press, 1977.

Von Lang, Jochen, *The Secretary Martin Bormann: The Man Who Manipulated Hitler*, trans. by Christa Armstrong and Peter White, New York, Random House, 1979.

Von Maltitz, Horst, *The Evolution of Hitler's Germany: The Ideology, the Personality, the Moment*, New York, McGraw-Hill, 1961.

Wachsmann, Nikolaus, *Hitler's Prisons: Legal Terror in Nazi Germany*, New Haven, Conn., Yale University Press, 2004.

Welch, David, ed., *Nazi Propaganda: The Power and the Limitations*, London, Croom Helm, 1983.

—— *The Third Reich: Politics and Propaganda*, London, Routledge, 1993.

Wistrich, Robert S., *Who's Who in Nazi Germany*, London, Routledge, 1995.

Zentner, Christian and Bedürftig, Friedemann, eds, *The Encyclopedia of the Third Reich*, trans. by Amy Hackett, New York, Da Capo Press, 1997.

Ziegler, Herbert F., *Nazi Germany's New Aristocracy: The SS Leadership, 1925–1939*, Princeton, N.J., Princeton University Press, 1989.

Foreign policy, war, and the Holocaust

Allen, Michael Thad, *The Business of Genocide: The SS, Slave Labor, and the Concentration Camps*, Chapel Hill, University of North Carolina Press, 2002.

Anderson, Mark M., ed., *Hitler's Exiles: Personal Stories of the Flight from Nazi Germany to America*, New York, New Press, 1998.

Aronson, Shlomo, *Hitler, the Allies, and the Jews*, Cambridge, Cambridge University Press, 2004.

Aschheim, Steven E., *Culture and Catastrophe: German and Jewish Confrontations with National Socialism and Other Crises*, New York, New York University Press, 1996.

Baer, Elizabeth R. and Goldenberg, Myrna, eds, *Experience and Expression: Women, the Nazis, and the Holocaust*, Detroit, Mich., Wayne State University Press, 2003.

Baird, Jay W., *To Die For Germany: Heroes in the Nazi Pantheon*, Bloomington, Indiana University Press, 1992.

Bankier, David, *The Germans and the Final Solution: Public Opinion under Nazism*, Oxford, Blackwell, 1992.

—— ed., *Probing the Depths of German Antisemitism: German Society and the Persecution of the Jews, 1933–1941*, New York, Berghahn Books, 2000.

Bard, Mitchell G., *Forgotten Victims: The Abandonment of Americans in Hitler's Camps*, Boulder, Colo., Westview, 1994.

Barnett, Victoria J., *Bystanders: Conscience and Complicity During the Holocaust*, Westport, Conn., Greenwood, 1999.

Bartov, Omer, *Hitler's Army: Soldiers, Nazis, and War in the Third Reich*, New York, Oxford University Press, 1992.

—— *Murder in Our Midst: The Holocaust, Industrial Killing, and Representation*, New York, Oxford University Press, 1996.

—— ed., *The Holocaust: Origins, Implementation, Aftermath*, London, Routledge, 2000.

—— *Germany's War and the Holocaust: Disputed Histories*, Ithaca, N.Y., Cornell University Press, 2003.

—— Grossmann, Atina, and Nolan, Mary, eds, *Crimes of War: Guilt and Denial in the Twentieth Century*, New York, New Press, 2002.

Bauer, Jehuda, *A History of the Holocaust*, New York, Franklin, Watts, 1982.

—— *Rethinking the Holocaust*, New Haven, Conn., Yale University Press, 2001.

Bauman, Zygmunt, *Modernity and the Holocaust*, Ithaca, N.Y., Cornell University Press, 1989.

Beevor, Antony, *The Fall of Berlin, 1945*, New York, Penguin, 2002.

Bell, P. M. H., *The Origins of the Second World War in Europe*, London and New York, Longman, 1986.

Berkhoff, Karel C., *Harvest of Despair: Life and Death in Ukraine under Nazi Rule*, Cambridge, Mass., Harvard University Press, 2004.

Boyce, Robert and Maiolo, Joseph A., eds,

The Origins of World War Two: The Debate Continues, New York, Palgrave Macmillan, 2003.

Braham, Randolph I, with Miller, Scott, eds, *Last Victims: The Holocaust in Hungary*, Detroit, Mich., Wayne State University Press, 1997.

Breitman, Richard, *The Architect of Genocide: Himmler and the Final Solution*, Hanover, N.H., University Press of New England, 1992.

—— *et al.*, *US. Intelligence and the Nazis*, Washington, DC, National Archives Trust Fund Board, 2004.

Browning, Christopher, *Ordinary Men: Reserve Police Battalion 101 and the Final Solution in Poland*, New York, HarperCollins, 1992.

—— *Paths to Genocide: Essays on Launching the Final Solution*, Cambridge, Cambridge University Press, 1992.

—— *The Origins of the Final Solution: The Evolution of Nazi Jewish Policy, September 1939–March 1942*, Lincoln, University of Nebraska Press, 2004.

Bukey, Evan Burr, *Hitler's Austria: Popular Sentiment in the Nazi Era, 1938–1945*, Chapel Hill, University of North Carolina Press, 1999.

Burleigh, Michael, *Germany Turns Eastwards: A Study of Ostforschung in the Third Reich*, Cambridge, Cambridge University Press, 1988.

—— *Death and Deliverance: Euthanasia in Germany 1900–1945*, Cambridge, Cambridge University Press, 1994.

—— *Ethics and Extermination: Reflections on Nazi Genocide*, New York, Cambridge University Press, 1997.

Burrin, Philippe, *Hitler and the Jews: The Genesis of the Holocaust*, trans. by Patsy Southgate, London, Edward Arnold, 1994.

Cesarani, David, ed., *The Final Solution:*

Origins and Implementation, London, Routledge, 1994.

Churchill, Winston, *The Second World War*, 6 vols., Boston, Mass., Houghton Mifflin, 1948–1953.

Crowe, David M., *Oskar Schindler: The Untold Account of his Life, Wartime Activities, and the True Story Behind the List*, Cambridge, Mass., Westview, 2004.

Dawidowicz, L. S., *The War Against the Jews 1933–1945*, New York, Holt, Rinehart & Winston, 1975.

—— *A Holocaust Reader*, West Orange, N.J., Berman House, 1976.

Dear, I. C. B. and Foot, M. R. D., *The Oxford Companion to World War II*, Oxford, Oxford University Press, 1995.

Ericksen, Robert P. and Heschel, Susannah, eds, *Betrayal: German Churches and the Holocaust*, Minneapolis, Minn., Fortress Press, 1999.

Eubank, Keith, *The Origins of World War II*, 2nd edn, Arlington Heights, Ill., Harlan Davidson, 1990.

Finkelstein, Norman G. and Birn, Ruth Bettina, eds, *A Nation on Trial: The Goldhagen Thesis and Historical Truth*, New York, Henry Holt, 1998.

Finney, Patrick, ed., *The Origins of the Second World War*, London, Arnold, 1997.

Fleming, Gerald, *Hitler and the Final Solution*, Berkeley, University of California Press, 1984.

Friedländer, Saul, *Prelude to Downfall: Hitler and the United States 1929–1941*, New York, Alfred A. Knopf, 1967.

—— ed., *Probing the Limits of Representation: Nazism and the "Final Solution"*, Cambridge, Mass., Harvard University Press, 1992.

—— *Nazi Germany and the Jews*: Vol. 1, *The Years of Persecution, 1933–1939*, New York, HarperCollins, 1997.

Friedlander, Henry, *The Origins of Nazi Genocide: From Euthanasia to the Final Solution*, Chapel Hill, University of North Carolina Press, 1995.

Fritz, Stephen G., *Endkampf: Soldiers, Civilians, and the Death of the Third Reich*, Lexington, University Press of Kentucky, 2004.

Garrett, Stephen A., *Ethics and Airpower in World War II: The British Bombing of German Cities*, New York, St Martin's, 1993.

Gigliotti, Simone and Lang, Berel, eds, *The Holocaust: A Reader*, Malden, Mass., Blackwell, 2005.

Gilbert, Martin, *Holocaust Journey: Travelling in Search of the Past*, New York, Columbia University Press, 1997.

Glantz, David and House, Jonathan, *When Titans Clashed: How the Red Army Stopped Hitler*, Lawrence, University of Kansas Press, 1995.

Goldhagen, Daniel Jonah, *Hitler's Willing Executioners: Ordinary Germans and the Holocaust*, New York, Alfred A. Knopf, 1996.

Gregor, Neil, ed., *Nazism, War and Genocide: Essays in Honour of Jeremy Noakes*, Exeter, University of Exeter Press, 2005.

Haar, Ingo and Fahlbusch, Michael, eds, *German Scholars and Ethnic Cleansing, 1919–1945*, New York, Berghahn Books, 2005.

Hancock, Eleanor, *National Socialist Leadership and Total War, 1941–1945*, New York, St Martin's, 1991.

Harvey, Elizabeth, *Women and the Nazi East: Agents and Witnesses of Germanization*, New Haven, Conn., Yale University Press, 2003.

Hayes, Peter, ed., *Lessons and Legacies:*

The Meaning of the Holocaust in a Changing World, Evanston, Ill., Northwestern University Press, 1991.

Heiber, Helmut and Glantz, David M., eds, *Hitler and his Generals: Military Conferences 1942–1945*, New York, Enigma Books, 2003.

Hilberg, Raul, *The Destruction of the European Jews* (1961), rev. edn, New York, Holmes & Meier, 1985.

—— *Perpetrators, Victims, Bystanders: The Jewish Catastrophe 1933–1945*, New York, HarperCollins, 1992.

Hildebrand, Klaus, *The Foreign Policy of the Third Reich*, trans. by Anthony Fothergill, London, Batsford, 1973.

Hillgruber, Andreas, *Germany and the Two World Wars*, trans. by William C. Kirby, Cambridge, Mass., Harvard University Press, 1981.

Independent International Commission of Experts, *Switzerland, National Socialism, and the Second World War*, Zurich, Pendo, 2002.

Kaplan, Marion A., *Between Dignity and Despair: Jewish Life in Nazi Germany*, New York, Oxford University Press, 1998.

Katz, Jacob, *From Prejudice to Destruction: Anti-Semitism, 1700–1933*, Cambridge, Mass., Harvard University Press, 1980.

Keegan, John, *The Second World War*, New York, Viking, 1989.

Kitchen, Martin, *A World in Flames: A Short History of the Second World War in Europe and Asia 1939–1945*, London, Longman, 1990.

—— *Nazi Germany at War*, London, Longman, 1995.

Klee, Ernst, Dressen, Willi, and Riess, Volker, eds, *"The Good Old Days": The Holocaust as Seen by Its Perpetrators and Bystanders*, trans. by Deborah Burnstone, New York, Konecky & Konecky, 1991.

Kochavi, Arieh J., *Confronting Captivity: Britain and the United States and their POWs in Nazi Germany*, Chapel Hill, University of North Carolina Press, 2005.

Kreis, Georg, ed., *Switzerland and the Second World War*, London, Frank Cass, 2000.

Kühl, Stefan, *The Nazi Connection: Eugenics, American Racism, and German National Socialism*, New York, Oxford University Press, 1994.

Laqueur, Walter, *The Terrible Secret: Suppression of the Truth about Hitler's "Final Solution"*, New York, Penguin, 1980.

—— *Generation Exodus: The Fate of Young Jewish Refugees from Nazi Germany*, Hanover, N.H., Brandeis University Press, 2001.

—— and Baumel, Judith Tydor, eds, *The Holocaust Encyclopedia*, New Haven, Conn., Yale University Press, 2001.

Large, David Clay, *Between Two Fires: Europe's Path in the 1930s*, New York, Norton, 1991.

Leckie, Robert, *Delivered from Evil: The Saga of World War II*, New York, Harper & Row, 1987.

Lee, Marshall M. and Michalka, Wolfgang, *German Foreign Policy 1917–1933: Continuity or Break?*, Leamington Spa, Berg, 1987.

Levin, Nora, *The Holocaust: The Destruction of European Jewry 1933–1945*, New York, Schocken, 1973.

Levy, Richard S., *Antisemitism in the Modern World: An Anthology of Texts*, Lexington, Mass., D. C. Heath, 1991.

Lewy, Guenter, *The Nazi Persecution of the Gypsies*, Oxford, Oxford University Press, 2000.

Lifton, Robert J., *The Nazi Doctors: Medical Killing and the Psychology of Genocide*, New York, Basic Books, 1986.

Lindemann, Albert S., *Esau's Tears: Modern Anti-Semitism and the Rise of the Jews*, Cambridge, Cambridge University Press, 1997.

Littell, Franklin H. and Locke, Hubert G., *The German Church Struggle and the Holocaust*, Detroit, Mich., Wayne State University Press, 1974.

Longerich, Peter, *The Unwritten Order: Hitler's Role in the Final Solution*, Stroud, UK, Tempus, 2001.

Lower, Wendy, *Nazi Empire-Building and the Holocaust in Ukraine*, Chapel Hill, University of North Carolina Press, 2005.

McFarland-Icke, Bronwyn Rebekah, *Nurses in Nazi Germany: Moral Choice in History*, Princeton, N.J., Princeton University Press, 1999.

Mann, Michael, *Fascists*, Cambridge, Cambridge University Press, 2004.

—— *The Dark Side of Democracy: Explaining Ethnic Cleansing*, Cambridge, Cambridge University Press, 2005.

Marrus, Michael, *The Holocaust in History*, New York, Meridian, 1987.

Mayer, Arno J., *Why Did the Heavens Not Darken? The "Final Solution" in History*, New York, Pantheon, 1990.

Meehan, Patricia, *The Unnecessary War: Whitehall and the German Resistance to Hitler*, London, Sinclair-Stevenson, 1992.

Militärgeschichtliches Forschungsamt, *Germany and the Second World War*, 7 vols., New York, Oxford University Press, 1990–2006.

Morley, John F., *Vatican Diplomacy and the Jews During the Holocaust 1939–1943*, New York, KTAV Publishing House, 1980.

Mosse, George L., *Toward the Final Solution: A History of European Racism*, New York, Howard Fertig, 1977.

Müller-Hill, Benno, *Murderous Science: Elimination by Scientific Selection of Jews, Gypsies, and Others, Germany 1933–1945*, Oxford, Oxford University Press, 1988.

Nicosia, Francis R., *The Third Reich and the Palestine Question*, Austin, University of Texas Press, 1985.

Noakes, Jeremy and Pridham, Geoffrey, eds, *Nazism 1919–1945: A History in Documents and Eyewitness Accounts*: Vol. 2, *Foreign Policy, War and Racial Extermination*, New York, Schocken, 1988.

Overy, R. J., *The Air War 1939–1945*, Chelsea, Mich., Scarborough House, 1980.

—— *War and Economy in the Third Reich*, Oxford, Clarendon Press, 1994.

—— *Why the Allies Won*, New York, W. W. Norton, 1995.

Overy, Richard and Wheatcroft, Andrew, *The Road to War*, London, Macmillan, 1989.

Pauley, Bruce F., *Hitler and the Forgotten Nazis: A History of Austrian National Socialism*, Chapel Hill, University of North Carolina Press, 1981.

Paxton, Robert O., *Vichy France: Old Guard and New Order, 1940–1944*, New York, Columbia University Press, 1982.

Phayer, Michael, *The Catholic Church and the Holocaust, 1930–1965*, Bloomington, Indiana University Press, 2000.

Postone, Moishe and Santner, Eric, eds, *Catastrophe and Meaning: The Holocaust and the Twentieth Century*,

Chicago, University of Chicago Press, 2003.

Potter, Pamela M., *Most German of the Arts: Musicology and Society from the Weimar Republic to the End of Hitler's Reich*, New Haven, Conn., Yale University Press, 1998.

Powers, Thomas, *Heisenberg's War: The Secret History of the German Bomb*, New York, Alfred A. Knopf, 1993.

Pringle, Heather, *The Master Plan: Himmler's Scholars and the Holocaust*, New York, Hyperion, 2006.

Proctor, Robert N., *Racial Hygiene: Medicine Under the Nazis*, Cambridge, Mass., Harvard University Press, 1988.

—— *The Nazi War on Cancer*, Princeton, N.J., Princeton University Press, 1999.

Reinhardt, Klaus, *Moscow – The Turning Point: The Failure of Hitler's Strategy in the Winter of 1941–1942*, trans. by Karl B. Keenan, Oxford, Berg, 1992.

Rich, Norman, *Hitler's War Aims*: Vol. 1, *Ideology, the Nazi State, and the Course of Expansion*; Vol. 2, *The Establishment of the New Order*, New York, Norton, 1973–1974.

—— *Great Power Diplomacy Since 1914*, New York, McGraw-Hill, 2003.

Robertson, E. M., *Hitler's Pre-War Policy and Military Plans, 1933–1939*, New York, Citadel Press, 1967.

Rose, Paul Lawrence, *German Question/ Jewish Question: Revolutionary Antisemitism from Kant to Wagner*, Princeton, N.J., Princeton University Press, 1990.

—— *Heisenberg and the Nazi Atomic Bomb Project: A Study in German Culture*, Berkeley, University of California Press, 1998.

Roseman, Mark, *A Past in Hiding: Memory and Survival in Nazi Germany*, New York, Metropolitan Books, 2000.

—— *The Villa, the Lake, the Meeting: Wannsee and the Final Solution*, London, Allen Lane, 2002.

Rosenbaum, Alan S., ed., *Is the Holocaust Unique? Perspectives on Comparative Genocide*, Boulder, Colo., Westview, 1996.

Rossino, Alexander B., *Hitler Strikes Poland: Blitzkrieg, Ideology, and Atrocity*, Lawrence, University Press of Kansas, 2003.

Rubinstein, William D., *The Myth of Rescue: Why the Democracies Could Not Have Saved More Jews from the Nazis*, London and New York, Routledge, 1997.

Schleunes, Karl, *The Twisted Road to Auschwitz: Nazi Policy toward German Jews 1933–1939*, Urbana, University of Illinois Press, 1970.

Shepherd, Ben, *War in the Wild East: The German Army and Soviet Partisans*, Cambridge, Mass., Harvard University Press, 2004.

Smith, Arthur L, Jun., *Hitler's Gold: The Story of the Nazi War Loot*, Oxford, Berg, 1996.

Sofsky, Wolfgang, *The Order of Terror: The Concentration Camp*, trans. by William Templer, Princeton, N.J., Princeton University Press, 1997.

Stark, Tamás, *Hungarian Jews During the Holocaust and After the Second World War, 1939–1949: A Statistical Review*, Boulder, Colo., East European Monographs, 2000.

Steinert, Marlis G., *Hitler's War and the Germans: Public Mood and Attitude During the Second World War*, trans. by Thomas E. J. De Witt, Athens, Ohio University Press, 1977.

Stone, Dan, *Responses to Nazism in Britain, 1933–1939: Before War and Holocaust*, New York, Palgrave Macmillan, 2003.

—— ed., *The Historiography of the Holocaust*, New York, Palgrave Macmillan, 2004.

Taylor, A. J. P., *The Origins of the Second World War*, Greenwich, Conn., Fawcett Publications, 1961.

Taylor, Telford, *Munich: The Price of Peace*, Garden City, N.Y., Doubleday, 1979.

Tooze, Adam, *The Wages of Destruction: The Making and Breaking of the Nazi Economy*, London, Allen Lane, 2006.

Watt, Donald Cameron, *How War Came: The Immediate Origins of the Second World War, 1938–1939*, New York, Pantheon Books, 1989.

Watt, Richard, M., *The Kings Depart: The Tragedy of Germany, Versailles and the German Revolution*, New York, Simon & Schuster, 1968.

Weinberg, Gerhard L., *The Foreign Policy of Hitler's Germany: Diplomatic Revolution in Europe, 1933–36*, Chicago, Ill., University of Chicago Press, 1970.

—— *The Foreign Policy of Hitler's Germany: Starting World War II, 1937–1939*, Chicago, Ill., University of Chicago Press, 1980.

—— *A World at Arms: A Global History of World War II*, Cambridge, Cambridge University Press, 1994.

—— *Germany, Hitler, and World War II: Essays in Modern German and World History*, New York, Cambridge University Press, 1995.

—— *Visions of Victory: The Hopes of Eight World War II Leaders*, Cambridge, Cambridge University Press, 2005.

Weiss, John, *The Ideology of Death: Why the Holocaust Happened in Germany*, Chicago, Ill., Ivan R. Dee, 1996.

—— *The Politics of Hate: Anti-Semitism, History, and the Holocaust in Modern Europe*, Chicago, Ill., Ivan R. Dee, 2003.

Weitz, John, *Hitler's Banker: Hjalmar Horace Greeley Schacht*, Boston, Mass., Little, Brown, 1997.

Westermann, Edward B., *Hitler's Police Battalions: Enforcing Racial War in the East*, Lawrence, University Press of Kansas, 2005.

Wildenthal, Lora, *German Women for Empire, 1884–1945*, Durham, N.C., Duke University Press, 2001.

Wright, Gordon, *The Ordeal of Total War 1939–1945*, New York, Harper & Row, 1968.

Wyman, David, *The Abandonment of the Jews: America and the Holocaust, 1941–1945*, New York, Pantheon Books, 1984.

Yahil, Leni, *The Holocaust: The Fate of European Jewry*, trans. by Ina Friedman and Haya Galai, New York, Oxford University Press, 1990.

Opposition and legacy

Alter, Reinhard and Monteath, Peter, eds, *Rewriting the German Past: History and Identity in the New Germany*, Atlantic Highlands, N.J., Humanities International Press, 1997.

Annas, George J. and Grodin, Michael A., eds, *The Nazi Doctors and the Nuremberg Code: Human Rights in Human Experimentation*, New York, Oxford University Press, 1992.

Arad, Gulie Ne'eman, ed., *Passing into History: Nazism and the Holocaust beyond Memory*, Special issue of *History & Memory*, Vol. 9 (Fall 1997).

Baldwin, Peter, ed., *Reworking the Past: Hitler, The Holocaust, and the Historians' Debate*, Boston, Mass., Beacon Press, 1990.

Barnouw, Dagmar, *Germany 1945: Views of War and Violence*, Bloomington, Indiana University Press, 1996.

Berger, Stefan, *The Search for Normality: National Identity and Historical Consciousness in Germany since 1800*, Providence, R.I., Berghahn, 1997.

Bergmann, Werner and Erb, Rainer, *Anti-Semitism in Germany: The Post-Nazi Epoch Since 1945*, New Brunswick, N.J., Transaction Publishers, 1997.

Bessel, Richard and Schumann, Dirk, eds, *Life After Death: Approaches to a Social and Cultural History of Europe During the 1940s and 1950s*, Cambridge, Cambridge University Press, 2003.

Bloxham, Donald, *Genocide on Trial: War Crimes Trials and the Formation of Holocaust History and Memory*, Oxford, Oxford University Press, 2001.

Boehling, Rebecca L., *A Question of Priorities: Democratic Reforms and Economic Recovery in Postwar Germany*, Providence, R.I., Berghahn Books, 1996.

Bower, Tom, *The Pledge Betrayed: America and Britain and the Denazification of Postwar Germany*, Garden City, N.Y., Doubleday, 1982.

Bredthauer, Karl D. and Heinrich, Arthur, *Aus der Geschichte lernen/How to Learn from History*, Bonn, edition Blätter 2, 1997.

Burleigh, Michael, ed., *Confronting the Nazi Past: New Debates on Modern German History*, New York, St Martin's, 1996.

Buruma, Ian, *The Wages of Guilt: Memories of War in Germany and Japan*, New York, Farrar, Straus Giroux, 1994.

Chandler, Andrew, ed., *The Moral Imperative: New Essays on the Ethics of Resistance in National Socialist Germany, 1933–1945*, Boulder, Colo., Westview, 1998.

Cheles, L., Ferguson, R., and Vaughan, M., eds, *The Far Right in Western and Eastern Europe*, 2nd edn, London, Longman, 1995.

Cole, Tim, *Selling the Holocaust: From Auschwitz to Schindler, How History is Bought, Packaged, and Sold*, New York, Routledge, 1999.

Confino, Alon and Fritzsche, Peter, eds, *The Work of Memory: New Directions in the Study of German Society and Culture*, Urbana, University of Illinois Press, 2002.

Conot, Robert E., *Justice at Nuremberg*, New York, Harper & Row, 1983.

Dahrendorf, Ralf, *The Unresolved Past: A Debate in German History*, New York, St Martin's, 1990.

Davidson, Eugene, *The Death and Life of Germany: An Account of the American Occupation*, New York, Alfred A. Knopf, 1961.

Davies, Peter, *Dangerous Liaisons: Collaboration and World War Two*, Harlow, Pearson, 2004.

De Mildt, Dick, *In the Name of the People: Perpetrators of Genocide in the Reflection of Their Post-War Prosecution in West Germany: The "Euthanasia" and "Aktion Reinhard" Trial Cases*, The Hague, Martinus Nijhoff, 1996.

Diefendorf, Jeffry M., Frohn, Axel, and Rupieper, Hermann-Josef, eds, *American Policy and the Reconstruction of West Germany, 1945–1955*, Cambridge, Cambridge University Press, 1993.

The Dilemmas of Commemoration: German Debates on the Holocaust in the 1990s, Special Issue of *German Politics and Society*, Vol. 17 (Fall 1999).

Diner, Dan, *Beyond the Conceivable:*

Studies on Germany, Nazism, and the Holocaust, Berkeley, University of California Press, 2000.

Eley, Geoff, ed., *The "Goldhagen Effect": History, Memory, Nazism – Facing the German Past*, Ann Arbor, University of Michigan Press, 2000.

—— *A Crooked Line: From Cultural History to the History of Society*, Ann Arbor, University of Michigan Press, 2005.

Evans, Richard J., *In Hitler's Shadow: West German Historians and the Attempt to Escape from the Nazi Past*, New York, Pantheon Books, 1989.

Frei, Norbert, *Adenauer's Germany and the Nazi Past: The Politics of Amnesty and Integration*, trans. by Joel Golb, New York, Columbia University Press, 2002.

Friedländer, Saul, *Reflections of Nazism: An Essay on Kitsch and Death*, New York, Harper & Row, 1984.

—— *Memory, History, and the Extermination of the Jews in Europe*, Bloomington, Indiana University Press, 1993.

Frommer, Benjamin, *National Cleansing: Retribution Against Nazi Collaborators in Postwar Czechoslovakia*, Cambridge, Cambridge University Press, 2005.

Fulbrooke, Mary, *German National Identity after the Holocaust*, Cambridge, Polity Press, 1999.

Garton Ash, Timothy, *In Europe's Name: Germany and the Divided Continent*, New York, Random House, 1993.

Geyer, Michael and Boyer, John W., eds, *Resistance Against the Third Reich, 1933–1990*, Chicago, Ill., University of Chicago Press, 1994.

Gimble, John, *The American Occupation of Germany: Politics and the Military, 1945–1949*, Stanford, Calif, Stanford University Press, 1968.

Goldensohn, Leon, *Nuremberg Interviews: An American Psychiatrist's Conversations with the Defendants and Witnesses*, ed. by Robert Gellately, New York, Vintage Books, 2005.

Gollancz, Victor, *In Darkest Germany*, Hinsdale, Ill., Henry Regnery, 1947.

Golsan, Richard J., ed., *Fascism's Return: Scandal, Revision, and Ideology since 1980*, Lincoln, University of Nebraska Press, 1998.

Graml, Hermann, *et al.*, *The German Resistance to Hitler*, Berkeley, University of California Press, 1970.

Habermas, Jürgen, *The New Conservatism: Cultural Criticism and the Historians' Debate*, trans. by Sherry Weber Nicholsen, Cambridge, Mass., MIT Press, 1989.

—— *A Berlin Republic: Writings on Germany*, trans. by Steven Rendall, Lincoln, University of Nebraska Press, 1997.

Harms, Kathy, Reuter, Lutz R., and Dürr, Volker, *Coping with the Past: Germany and Austria after 1945*, Madison, University of Wisconsin Press, 1990.

Harris, Geoffrey, *The Dark Side of Europe: The Extreme Right Today*, Edinburgh, Edinburgh University Press, 1994.

Hartman, Geoffrey H., ed., *Bitburg in Moral and Political Perspective*, Bloomington, Indiana University Press, 1986.

Heineman, Elizabeth D., *What Difference Does a Husband Make? Women and Marital Status in Nazi and Postwar Germany*, Berkeley, University of California Press, 1999.

Herf, Jeffrey, *Divided Memory: The Nazi Past in the Two Germanys*, Cambridge, Mass., Harvard University Press, 1997.

Herzog, Dagmar, *Sex After Fascism: Memory and Morality in Twentieth-*

Century Germany, Princeton, N.J., Princeton University Press, 2005.

Hilberg, Raul, *The Politics of Memory: The Journey of a Holocaust Historian*, Chicago, Ill., Ivan Dee, 1996.

Hockenos, Matthew D., *A Church Divided: German Protestants Confront the Nazi Past*, Bloomington, Indiana University Press, 2004.

Hoffmann, Peter, *German Resistance to Hitler*, Cambridge, Mass., Harvard University Press, 1988.

—— *Stauffenberg: A Family History, 1905–1944*, Cambridge, Cambridge University Press, 1995.

Hunt, Linda, *Secret Agenda: The United States Government, Nazi Scientists, and Project Paperclip, 1945–1990*, New York, St Martin's, 1991.

Iggers, Georg, ed., *The Social History of Politics: Critical Perspectives in West German Historical Writing Since 1945*, New York, St Martin's, 1986.

Kansteiner, Wulf, *In Pursuit of German Memory: History, Television, and Politics after Auschwitz*, Athens, Ohio University Press, 2006.

Kattago, Siobhan, *Ambiguous Memory: The Nazi Past and German National Identity*, Westport, Conn., Praeger, 2001.

Kettenacker, Lothar, *Germany Since 1945*, Oxford, Oxford University Press, 1997.

Koshar, Rudy, *Germany's Transient Pasts: Preservation and National Memory in the Twentieth Century*, Chapel Hill, University of North Carolina Press, 1998.

—— *Monuments to Traces: Artifacts of German Memory, 1870–1990*, Berkeley, University of California Press, 2000.

Kurthen, Hermann, Bergmann, Werner, and Erb, Rainer, eds, *Antisemitism and Xenophobia in Germany After*

Unification, New York and Oxford, Oxford University Press, 1997.

Landau, Ronnie S., *Studying the Holocaust: Issues, Readings, and Documents*, London, Routledge, 1998.

Large, David Clay, ed., *Contending with Hitler: Varieties of German Resistance in the Third Reich*, Cambridge, Cambridge University Press, 1991.

Levy, Daniel and Sznaider, Natan, *The Holocaust and Memory in the Global Age*, trans. by Assenka Oksiloff, Philadelphia, Pa., Temple University Press, 2005.

Low, Alfred D., *The Third Reich and the Holocaust in German Historiography: Toward the* Historikerstreit *of the Mid-1980s*, Boulder, Colo., East European Monographs, 1994.

Maier, Charles S., *The Unmasterable Past: History, the Holocaust, and German National Identity*, Cambridge, Mass., Harvard University Press, 1988.

Marcuse, Harold, *Legacies of Dachau: The Uses and Abuses of a Concentration Camp, 1933–2001*, Cambridge, Cambridge University Press, 2001.

Meinecke, Friedrich, *The German Catastrophe: Reflections and Recollections*, trans. by Sidney B. Fay, Cambridge, Mass., Harvard University Press, 1950.

Merritt, Richard L., *Democracy Imposed: U.S. Occupation Policy and the German Public, 1945–1949*, New Haven, Conn., Yale University Press, 1995.

Moeller, Robert G., *War Stories: The Search for a Usable Past in the Federal Republic of Germany*, Berkeley, University of California Press, 2001.

Moltke, Freya von, *Memories of Kreisau and the German Resistance*, trans. by Julie M. Winter, Lincoln, University of Nebraska Press, 2003.

Monod, David, *Settling Scores: German*

Music, Denazification, and the Americans, 1945–1953, Chapel Hill, University of North Carolina Press, 2005.

Naimark, Norman M., *The Russians in Germany: A History of the Soviet Zone of Occupation, 1945–1949*, Cambridge, Mass., Harvard University Press, 1995.

Neaman, Elliot Y., *A Dubious Past: Ernst Jünger and the Politics of Literature after Nazism*, Berkeley, University of California Press, 1999.

Niven, Bill, *Facing the Nazi Past: United Germany and the Legacy of the Third Reich*, London, Routledge, 2002.

Nolte, Ernst, *Marxism, Fascism, Cold War*, Atlantic Highlands, N.J., Humanities Press, 1982.

Novick, Peter, *The Holocaust in American Life*, Boston, Mass., Houghton Mifflin, 1999.

Overy, Richard, *Interrogations: The Nazi Elite in Allied Hands, 1945*, London, Penguin Books, 2001.

Paret, Peter, *An Artist against the Third Reich: Ernst Barlach, 1933–1938*, Cambridge, Cambridge University Press, 2003.

Pick, Hella, *Guilty Victim: Austria from the Holocaust to Haider*, London, I.B. Tauris, 2000.

Posner, Gerald L., *Hitler's Children: Sons and Daughters of Leaders of the Third Reich Talk About Their Fathers and Themselves*, New York, Random House, 1991.

Rapaport, Lynn, *Jews in Germany after the Holocaust: Memory, Identity, and German–Jewish Relations*, Cambridge, Cambridge University Press, 1997.

Remy, Steven P., *The Heidelberg Myth: The Nazification and Denazification of a German University*, Cambridge, Mass., Harvard University Press, 2002.

Rosenbaum, Ron, *Explaining Hitler: The Search for the Origins of his Evil*, New York, Random House, 1998.

Rosenfeld, Alvin H., *Thinking about the Holocaust: After Half a Century*, Bloomington, University of Indiana Press, 1997.

Rosenfeld, Gavriel D., *Munich and Memory: Architecture, Monuments, and the Legacy of the Third Reich*, Berkeley, University of California Press, 2000.

—— *The World Hitler Never Made*, Cambridge, Cambridge University Press, 2005.

Rothfels, Hans, *The German Opposition to Hitler: An Appraisal*, trans. by Lawrence Wilson, Chicago, Ill., Henry Regnery, 1962.

Rousso, Henry, *The Vichy Syndrome: History and Memory in France since 1944*, trans. by Arthur Goldhammer, Cambridge, Mass., Harvard University Press, 1991.

Sa'adah, Anne, *Germany's Second Chance: Trust, Justice and Democratization*, Cambridge, Mass., Harvard University Press, 1998.

Sichrovsky, Peter, *Born Guilty: Children of Nazi Families*, trans. by Jean Steinberg, New York, Basic Books, 1988.

Simpson, Christopher, *Blowback: America's Recruitment of Nazis and Its Effects on the Cold War*, New York, Weidenfeld & Nicolson, 1988.

Smith, Arthur L., Jun., *The War for the German Mind: Re-Educating Hitler's Soldiers*, Providence, R.I., Berghahn Books, 1996.

Smith, Bradley F., *Reaching Judgment at Nuremberg*, New York, Basic Books, 1977.

Smyser, W. R., *From Yalta to Berlin: The Cold War Struggle Over Germany*, New York, St Martin's, 2000.

Spicer, Kevin, *Resisting the Third Reich: The Catholic Clergy in Hitler's Berlin*, DeKalb, Northern Illinois University Press, 2004.

Steinweis, Alan E. and Rogers, Daniel E., eds, *The Impact of Nazism: New Perspectives on the Third Reich and its Legacy*, Lincoln, University of Nebraska Press, 2003.

Stolzfus, Nathan, *Resistance of the Heart: Intermarriage and the Rosenstrasse Protest in Nazi Germany*, New York, Norton, 1996.

Teschke, John P., *Hitler's Legacy: West Germany Confronts the Aftermath of the Third Reich*, New York, Peter Lang, 1999.

Tetens, T. H., *The New Germany and the Old Nazis*, London, Secker & Warburg, 1961.

Trachtenberg, Marc, *A Constructed Peace: The Making of the European Settlement, 1945–1963*, Princeton, N.J., Princeton University Press, 1999.

Vogt, Timothy R., *Denazification in Soviet-Occupied Germany: Brandenburg, 1945–1948*, Cambridge, Mass., Harvard University Press, 2000.

Watson, Alan, *The Germans: Who Are They Now?*, Chicago, Ill., Edition Q, 1992.

Wittmann, Rebecca, *Beyond Justice: The Auschwitz Trial*, Cambridge, Mass., Harvard University Press, 2005.

Wrench, John and Solomos, John, eds, *Racism and Migration in Western Europe*, Oxford, Berg, 1993.

INDEX